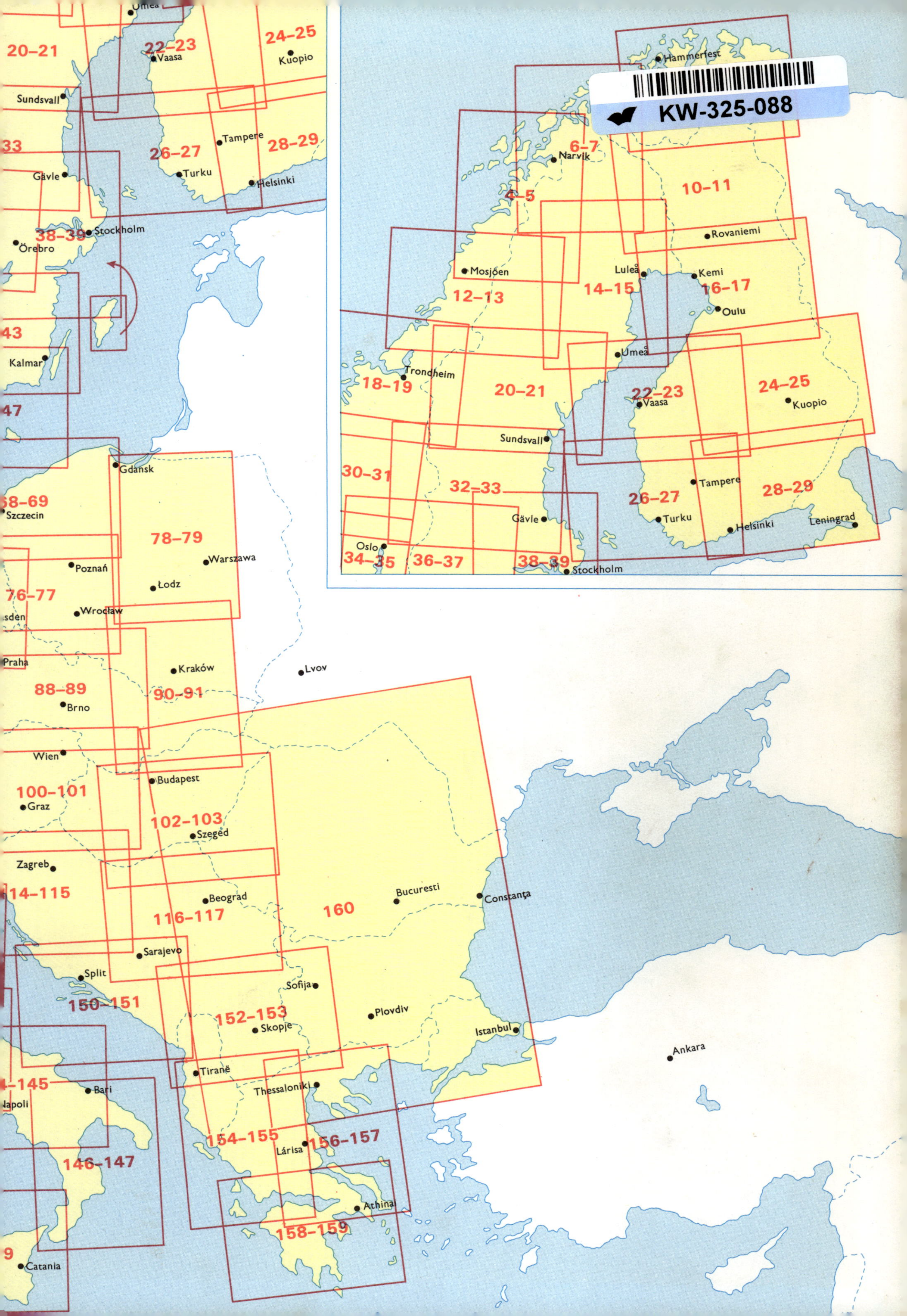

Main map (left):

20–21 · Umeå
22–23 · Vaasa
24–25 · Kuopio
Sundsvall
33
Gävle
Tampere
26–27 · Turku
28–29 · Helsinki
38–39 · Stockholm
Örebro
43
Kalmar
47
Gdańsk
68–69 · Szczecin
78–79 · Warszawa
Poznań
Łodz
76–77
Wrocław
sden
Praha
Kraków · Lvov
88–89 · Brno
90–91
Wien
100–101 · Budapest
Graz
102–103 · Szeged
Zagreb
14–115
116–117
160 · Bucureşti · Constanţa
Sarajevo
Split
150–151
152–153 · Sofija
Skopje · Plovdiv
Istanbul
Tiranë
Ankara
4–145 · Bari
Thessaloniki
Napoli
154–155 · 156–157
146–147 · Lárisa
158–159 · Athína
9 · Catania

Hammerfest
6–7 · Narvik
4–5
10–11 · Rovaniemi
Mosjöen
12–13
14–15 · Luleå · Kemi
16–17 · Oulu
18–19 · Trondheim
20–21 · Sundsvall
Umeå
22–23 · Vaasa
24–25 · Kuopio
30–31
32–33 · Gävle
26–27 · Tampere · Turku
28–29 · Helsinki · Leningrad
34–35 · Oslo
36–37
38–39 · Stockholm

Philips'
Road Atlas
EUROPE

George Philip & Son Limited, London.

First Edition – November 1972

Route Planning Map

Carte de preparation d'itinéraires

Distances in Kilometres
Distances en Kilomètres
Entfernungen in Kilometern
Distanze in Chilometri

Vaasa
Kuopio
Sundsvall
393
416
215
333
Gävle
Turku
165
Helsinki
188
Stockholm
199
Örebro
424
Kalmar
Hammerfest
412
Nordkjosbotn
212
Narvik
557
913
156
Tornio
Luleå
134
Oulu
279
Umeå
285
320
Kuopio
Trondheim
457
279
Vaasa
631
Sundsvall
564
393
333
416
215
399
Turku
Gävle
165
Helsinki
Leningrad
Oslo
188
Stockholm
Gdansk
370
361
Szczecin
289
Poznań
303
Warszawa
348
369
Wroclaw
291
254
273
Kraków
312
226
Brno
302
362
Wien
344
204
255
Budapest
257
Oradea
457
171
Graz
348
204
Szeged
509
Braşov
Zagreb
218
170
Constanţa
264
386
Beograd
Bucuresti
446
387
399
Split
225
667
Sofiya
Dubrovnik
562
Istanbul
319
636
305
Bari
Thessaloniki
264
Napoli
114
185
Brindisi
Lárisa
Igoumenitsa
503
364
Athínai
573
Réggio Calábria
97
Catania

* By Ferry
Distances in these tables are based upon Main Routes as far as possible and are not necessarily the shortest distances between any two towns.

* Par ferry
Les distances sur ces tableaux se basent autant que possible sur les itinéraires principaux, mais ne sont pas nécessairement les plus courtes distances entre deux villes données.

Kilometres

	Amsterdam	Athínai	Barcelona	Basel	Beograd	Berlin	Bordeaux	Brindisi	Bruxelles	Bucuresti	Budapest	Calais	Cherbourg	Dover	Edinburgh	Frankfurt	Genève	Genova	Gibraltar	Hamburg	Helsinki	Istanbul	København
Amsterdam		1842	946	455	1115	416	659	1289	125	1385	874	225	383	225*	685*	268	549	805	1539	271	1005*	1709	465*
Athínai	2964		1976	1542	727	1526	2017	356*	1819	787	969	1982	2052	1982*	2504*	1575	1573	1432	2717	1811	2214*	736	1727*
Barcelona	1523	3180		628	1249	1150	373	1227	821	1706	1222	818	776	818*	1278*	808	473	551	741	1109	1842*	1855	1299*
Basel	732	2481	1011		815	547	572	844	336	1186	674	441	519	441*	900*	205	155	322	1369	506	1241*	1404	696*
Beograd	1795	1170	2010	1311		799	1296	414*	1099	441	242	1230	1325	1230*	1690*	848	849	705	1996	1084	1487*	590	1000*
Berlin	670	2456	1850	880	1286		1009	1198	470	1069	557	594	833	594*	1054*	342	670	735	1889	181	688*	1389	201*
Bordeaux	1060	3246	601	921	2086	1624		1263	534	1731	1259	506	403	506*	966*	708	446	634	880	890	1626*	1654	1079*
Brindisi	2074	573*	1974	1359	666*	1928	2032		887	821*	983	1285	1340	1285*	1807*	1074	817	676	1967	1310	2039*	709*	1499*
Bruxelles	201	2928	1322	541	1769	756	859	1428		1363	858	124	360	124*	584*	245	424	665	1414	356	1091*	1689	550*
Bucuresti	2229	1267	2746	1908	710	1720	2786	1322*	2193		511	1487	1660	1487*	1885*	1117	1296	1156	2447	1353	1757*	429	1270*
Budapest	1406	1559	1966	1085	389	897	2026	1582	1380	823		982	1149	982*	1442*	606	821	671	1962	842	1245*	831	759*
Calais	362	3190	1316	709	1980	956	815	2068	200	2393	1580		283	*	460*	370	483	744	1386	455	1190*	1808	644*
Cherbourg	617	3303	1249	836	2133	1340	648	2156	579	2672	1849	456		142*	426*	574	529	775	1283	716	1445*	1915	905*
Dover	362*	3190*	1316*	709*	1980*	956*	815*	2068*	200*	2393*	1580*	*	228*		460	370*	483*	744*	1386*	455*	1190*	1808*	644*
Edinburgh	1102*	4030*	2056*	1449*	2720*	1696*	1555*	2908*	940*	3033*	2320*	740*	685*	740		830*	943*	1204*	1846*	915*	906*	2274*	1104*
Frankfurt	431	2534	1300	330	1364	550	1140	1729	395	1798	975	595	924	595*	1335*		360	526	1548	301	1031*	1437	490*
Genève	883	2532	761	250	1367	1079	718	1314	682	2086	1322	778	852	778*	1518*	580		252	1214	662	1396*	1438	862*
Genova	1295	2304	886	518	1134	1183	1021	1088	1070	1860	1080	1198	1247	1198*	1938*	847	405		1291	828	1560*	1304	1017*
Gibraltar	2476	4372	1192	2203	3212	3040	1416	3166	2275	3938	3158	2231	2064	2231*	2971*	2492	1953	2078		1770	2499*	2596	1952*
Hamburg	436	2914	1785	815	1744	291	1432	2109	573	2178	1355	733	1152	733*	1473	485	1065	1332	2848		734*	1673	194*
Helsinki	1618*	3563*	2960*	1997*	2393*	1107*	2616*	3281*	1755*	2827*	2004*	1915*	2326*	1915*	1458*	1660*	2247*	2510*	4022*	1182*		2077*	541*
Istanbul	2751	1185	2985*	2260	949	2235	2648	1141*	2718	690	1338	2909	3082	2909*	3659*	2313	2314	2099	4177	2693	3342*		1590*
København	748*	2780*	2090*	1120*	1610*	324*	1736*	2413*	885*	2044*	1221*	1037*	1456*	1037*	1777*	790*	1387*	1636*	3142*	312*	870*	2559*	
Köln	258	2714	1340	519	1544	545	1100	1869	214	1978	1155	414	784*	414*	1154*	180	769	1028	2516	427	1618*	2493	730*
Lisboa	2287	4451	1271	2144	3291	2851	1227	3145	2086	4017	3137	2042	1875	2042*	2782*	2443	1945	2157	664	2659	3841*	4292	2963*
London	480*	3308*	1434*	827*	2098*	1074*	933*	2286*	318*	2411*	1698*	118*	127*	118	622	713*	896*	1316*	2349*	851*	2033*	3037*	1155*
Luxembourg	390	2717	1150	325	1547	735	910	1684	216	2038	1215	416	684	416*	1156*	240	495	843	2342	617	1791*	2496	921*
Madrid	1759	3802	622	1620	2642	2323	699	2596	1558	2746	1966	1514	1347	1514*	2254*	1915	1383	1508	717	2131	3313*	2985	2435*
Marseille	1198	3296	522	673	1526	1522	657	1480	1024	2252	1472	1064	1113	1064*	1804*	972	423	392	1714	1424	2636*	2491	1728*
Milano	1087	2205	1032	372	1049	1033	1045	987	913	1759	979	1081	1169	1081*	1821*	702	327	146	2224	1187	2140*	1998	1499*
München	826	2139	1351	400	969	594	1271	1319	790	1508	685	1011	1164	1011*	1751*	395	590	589	2543	775	1948*	1918	1078*
Napoli	1898	946*	1619	1166	814*	1720	1802	373	1697	1470*	1467	1875	1963	1875*	2615*	1496	1121	733	2811	1901	2827*	1514*	2204*
Narvik	2802*	4857*	4144*	3178*	1474	2401*	3798*	4470*	2939*	4121*	3298*	3091*	3518*	3091*	1825*	2861*	3444*	3700*	5206*	2366*	1640	4636*	2064*
Nürnberg	661	2304	1461	450	1134	429	1347	1484	625	1568	745	825	1143	825*	1565*	230	700	754	2653	610	1783*	2083	913*
Oslo	1328*	3383*	2670*	1704*	2213*	927*	2324*	2996*	1465*	2647*	1824*	1617*	2044*	1617*	669*	1387*	1970*	2226*	3732*	892*	789*	3162*	590*
Paris	496	2965	1027	498	1795	1051	564	1818	295	2334	1511	289	338	289*	1029*	586	504	909	1980	868	2050*	2744	1180*
Porto	2088	4384	1204	1949	3052	2652	1028	3006	1887	3778	2998	1843	1676	1843*	2783*	2244	1746	1918	960	2460	3642*	3017	2764*
Praha	919	2116	1740	730	946	340	1627	1708	905	1380	557	1105	1423	1105*	1845*	510	979	978	2932	631	1447*	1895	664*
Roma	1681	1145*	1402	949	1010*	1503	1585	572	1480	1666*	1250	1658	1746	1658*	2398*	1279	904	516	1594	1684	2610*	1713*	1987*
Sevilla	2309	4211	1031	2042	3051	2873	1249	3005	2108	3777	2997	2064	1897	2064*	2804*	2465	1792	1917	251	2681	3863*	4016	2985*
Sofiya	2189	868	2423	1698	387	1673	2465	923*	2156	391	776	2367	2520	2367*	3107*	1751	1754	1537	3615	2131	2780*	562	1997*
Stockholm	1384*	3429*	2726*	1746*	2259*	973*	2380*	2886*	1521*	2693*	1870*	1673*	2092*	1673*	1224*	1433*	2023*	2156*	3788*	948*	234*	3208*	636*
Strasbourg	625	2509	1082	134	1339	768	998	1493	425	1878	1055	641	794	641*	1381*	215	384	652	2174	700	1874*	2288	1003*
Thessaloniki	2469	549	2703	1978	667	1953	2753	505*	2436	718	1056	2647	2880	2647*	3387*	2031	2027	1817	3895	2311	3060*	636	2277*
Valencia	1877	3534	354	1365	2374	2204	818	2328	1676	3100	2320	1633	1466	1633*	2373*	1654	1115	1240	838	2139	3314*	3339	2444*
Venezia	1309	1948	1258	643	778	1070	1316	874	1184	1488	724	1376	1429	1376*	2116*	871	598	372	2450	1251	2177*	1727	1554*
Warszawa	1250	2212	2361	1351	1042	592	2318	2127	1335	1476	653	1535	1932	1535*	2277*	1129	1600	1599	3874	870	1505*	1991	649*
Wien	1151	1814	1847	830	644	642	1738	1455	1115	1078	255	1315	1594	1315*	2055*	720	1020	961	3031	1100	1749*	1593	966*

*Fähren
Die in diesen Tabellen angegebenen Entfernungen beziehen sich so weit wie möglich auf die Hauptrouten. Es handelt sich dabei nicht unbedingt um die kürzeste Entfernung zwischen zwei Städten.

*Servizi di Traghetto
Le distanze indicate su queste tavole per quanto possibile si basano sulle strade principali e non nécessariamente sono quelle più brevi fra due date città.

Miles

	London	Luxembourg	Madrid	Marseille	Milano	München	Napoli	Narvik	Nürnberg	Oslo	Paris	Porto	Praha	Roma	Sevilla	Sofiya	Stockholm	Strasbourg	Thessaloniki	Valencia	Venezia	Warszawa	Wien
Amsterdam	298*	242	1093	744	675	513	1179	1741*	411	825*	308	1297	571	1045	1435	1360	860*	388	1534	1166	813	777	715
Athínai	2056*	1688	2362	2048	1370	1329	588	3018*	1432	2102*	1842	2724	1315	712*	2617	539	2131*	1559	341	2196	1210	1375	1127
Barcelona	891*	715	387	324	641	840	1006	2575*	908	1659*	638	748	1081	871	641	1506	1694*	672	1680	220	782	1467	1148
Basel	514*	202	1007	418	231	249	725	1975*	280	1059*	309	1211	454	590	1269	1055	1085*	83	1229	848	400	840	516
Beograd	1304*	961	1642	948	652	602	506	916*	705	1375*	1115	1896	588	628*	1896	240	1404*	832	414	1475	483	647	400
Berlin	667*	457	1443	946	642	369	1069	1492*	267	576*	653	1648	211	934	1785	1040	605*	477	1214	1370	665	368	399
Bordeaux	580*	565	434	408	649	790	1120	2360*	837	1444*	350	639	1011	985	776	1532	1479*	620	1711	508	818	1440	1080
Brindisi	1420*	1046	1613	920	612	820	232	2778*	922	1862*	1130	1868	1061	355	1867	574	1793*	928	314*	1447	543	1322	904
Bruxelles	198*	134	968	636	567	491	1055	1826*	388	910*	183	1173	562	920	1310	1340	945*	264	1514	1041	736	830	693
Bucuresti	1498*	1266	1706	1399	1093	937	913	2561*	974	1645*	1450	2348	858	1035*	2347	243	1673*	1167	446	1926	925	917	670
Budapest	1055*	755	1222	917	608	426	916	2049*	463	1133*	939	1863	346	777	1862	482	1162*	656	656	1442	450	406	158
Calais	73*	259	941	661	672	628	1165	1921*	513	1005*	180	1145	687	1030	1283	1471	1040*	398	1645	1015	855	954	817
Cherbourg	79*	425	837	692	726	723	1220	2186*	710	1270*	210	1041	884	1085	1179	1566	1300*	493	1790	911	888	1200	990
Dover	73	259*	941*	661*	672*	628*	1165*	1921*	513*	1005*	180*	1145*	687*	1030*	1283*	1471*	1040*	398*	1645*	1015*	855*	954*	817*
Edinburgh	387	718*	1401*	1121*	1132*	1088*	1625*	1134*	972*	416*	639*	1729*	1146*	1490*	1742*	1931*	761*	858*	2105*	1475*	1315*	1415*	1277*
Frankfurt	443*	149	1190	604	436	245	930	1778*	143	862*	364	1394	317	795	1532	1088	890*	134	1262	1028	541	702	447
Genève	557*	308	859	263	203	367	697	2140*	435	1224*	313	1085	608	562	1114	1090	1257*	239	1260	693	372	994	634
Genova	818*	524	937	244	91	366	455	2299*	469	1383*	565	1192	608	321	1191	955	1340*	405	1129	771	231	994	597
Gibraltar	1460*	1455	446	1065	1382	1580	1747	3235*	1649	2319*	1230	597	1822	991	156	2246	2354*	1351	2420	521	1522	2407	1883
Hamburg	529*	383	1324	885	738	482	1181	1470*	379	554*	539	1529	392	1046	1666	1324	589*	435	1436	1329	777	541	684
Helsinki	1263*	1113*	2057*	1638*	1330*	1210*	1757*	1019	1108*	490*	1274*	2263*	899*	1622*	2400*	1727*	145*	1165*	1901*	2059*	1353*	935*	1087*
Istanbul	1887*	1551	1855	1548	1242	1192	941	2881*	1294	1965*	1705	1875	1178	1064*	2495	349	1993*	1422	395	2075	1073	1237	990
København	718*	572*	1513*	1074*	931*	670*	1370*	1283*	567*	367*	733*	1717*	413*	1235*	1855*	1241*	395*	623*	1415*	1519*	966*	403*	600*
Köln	331*	118	1118	620	554	357	1047	1741*	255	825*	333	1322	429	912	1460	1200	848*	239	1374	1053	653	700	552
Lisboa	1342*	1328	403	1114	1431	1575	1796	3122*	1599	2207*	1113	199	1823	1661	257	2318	2241*	1383	2492	621	1528	2139	1888
London		332*	1014*	734*	745*	702*	1238*	1307*	586*	588*	253*	1219*	760*	1104*	1356*	1544*	1113*	472*	1718*	1088*	928*	1028*	890*
Luxembourg	534*		1000	502	433	359	926	1849*	294	933*	215	1204	468	792	1342	1202	968*	129	1358	935	601	825	626
Madrid	1632*	1609		937	1028	1226	1393	2794*	1294	1874*	785	376	1468	1258	342	1506	1913*	1059	1680	218	782	1811	1534
Marseille	1182*	808	1508		334	610	699	2356*	908	1440*	482	965	851	564	965	1199	1469*	469	1373	544	475	1237	841
Milano	1199*	697	1654	538		275	493	2208*	378	1292*	516	1283	523	364	1303	907	1327*	314	1066	861	168	903	506
München	1129*	578	1973	981	443		700	1958*	103	1042*	513	1452	242	565	1480	843	974*	230	1017	1059	296	628	267
Napoli	1993*	1491	2241	1125	794	1126		2652*	802	1736*	1010	1647	941	135	1647	744	1765*	808	546	1226	472	1327	833
Narvik	2103*	2975*	4497*	3792*	3554*	3151*	4268*		1855*	916	2008*	2998*	1703*	2517*	2513*	2531*	1013	1906*	2705*	2795*	2248*	1677*	1891*
Nürnberg	943*	473	2083	1461	608	165	1291	2986*		940	500	1520	174	667	1549	945	871*	219	1119	1128	398	560	304
Oslo	947*	1501*	3023*	2318*	2080*	1677*	2794*	1474	1512*		1092*	2082*	787*	1601*	2219*	1616*	345*	990*	1790*	1879*	1332*	761*	975*
Paris	407*	346	1263	775	831	826	1625	3232*	805	1758*		989	674	875	1127	1356	1128*	283	1530	858	678	1040	780
Porto	1961*	1938	605	1553	2064	2336	2651	4824*	2446	3350*	1592		1693	1512	447	1525	2118*	1259	2321	594	1423	2016	1719
Praha	1223*	753	2363	1370	832	389	1515	2741*	280	1267*	1085	2725		807	1722	828	816*	391	1002	1301	497	386	188
Roma	1776*	1274	2024	908	577	909	217	4051*	1074	2577*	1408	2434	1298		1518	787	1630*	673	669	1091	337	1192	698
Sevilla	2182*	2159	550	1553	2063	2382	2650	4045*	2492	3571*	1813	719	2771	2433		2146	2255*	1313	2320	421	1422	2108	1783
Sofiya	2485*	1934	2423	1929	1436	1356	1197*	4074*	1521	2600*	2182	2455	1333	1267*	3454		1644*	1073	198	1726	724	888	641
Stockholm	791*	1557*	3079*	2364*	2135*	1567*	2840*	1630	1402*	555	1816*	3408*	1313*	2623*	3629*	2646*		1018*	1818*	1914*	1269*	777*	1004*
Strasbourg	759*	208	1704	754	506	370	1300	3068*	349	1594*	456	2026	629	1083	2113	1726	1639*		1246	880	483	777	497
Thessaloniki	2765*	2186	2703	2209	1716	1636	878*	4354*	1801	2880*	2462	3735	1613	1077	3734	319	2926*	2006		1900	898	1062	815
Valencia	751*	1504	351	876	1386	1705	1973	4498*	1815	3024*	1381	956	2094	1756	677	2777	3080*	1416	3057		1002	1687	1368
Venezia	494*	968	1258	764	271	476	759	3618*	641	2144*	1091	2290	800	542	2289	1165	2043*	777	1445	1612		789	371
Warszawa	655*	1327	2915	1991	1453	1010	2136	2699*	901	1225*	1675	3244	621	1919	3392	1429	1250	1250	1709	2715	1269		418
Wien	433*	1008	2469	1353	815	430	1340	3043*	490	1569*	1256	2766	302	1123	2870	1031	1615*	800	1311	2201	597	672	

Pass/Country Col/Pays Paß/Staat Passo/Paese	Route Number Numéro d'itinéraire Route Nummer Strada Numero	Height Altitude Höhe Altezza	Months when Closed Mois de fermeture Monate, in des Gesperrt Periodi di Chiusura	Pass/Country Col/Pays Paß/Staat Passo/Paese	Route Number Numéro d'itinéraire Route Nummer Strada Numero	Height Altitude Höhe Altezza	Months when Closed Mois de fermeture Monate, in des Gesperrt Periodi di Chiusura
Achen Österreich	181 Tegernsee-Jenbach	885	*	Mauria Italia	52 Forni di sotto-Lozzo di Cadore	1298	
Aprica Italia	39 Edolo-Tresenda	1176	*	Mendola Italia	42 Revo-Appiano	1363	
Arlberg Österreich	1 Bludenz-Landeck	1802	*	Mt Cenis France/Italia	E13 Molaretto-Lanslebourg	2084	XI-V
Azpiroz España	240 Iruzun-Betelu	616		Montgenevre France/Italia	94/24 Briancon-Cesana Tor	1854	
Bayard France	85 Gap-Chauffayer	1246	*	Mosses Suisse	77 Aigle-Château-d'Oex	1445	
Braus France	204 Sospel-L'Escarène	995		Navacerrada España	601 Segovia-Collado-Mediano	1849	*
Brenner Öst./Italia	182/12 Vipiteno-Steinach	1374	*	Oberalp Suisse	19 Andermatt-Disentis/Muster	2044	X-VI
Brunig Suisse	4 Lungern-Brienz	1007	*	Piccolo S. Bernard Italy/France	26/90 Aosta-Bourge St. Maurice	2188	X-VI
Cabrejas España	400 Cuenca-Tarancon	1150		Pordoi Italia	48 Arraba-Canazei	2239	*
Carrales España	623 Escalada-Cilleruelo	1020		Potschenhöhe Österreich	158 Bad Aussee-Bad Goisern	992	
Contreras España	III Villargordo-Motilla del Palanca	890		Puymorens France	20 Ur-Ax-les-Thermes	1915	*
Croix Haute France	75 Serres-Monestier-de-Clermont	1179	*	Pyhrn Österreich	138 Liezen-Windischgarsten	945	
Envalira Andorra	20b Andorra-Cilleruelo	2407	*	Radstadter-Tauern Österreich	112 Liezen-Radstadt	1739	*
Escudo España	623 Mestas-Entrambas	1011	*	Resia Öst./Italia	187/40 Nauders-Resia	1508	
Fluela Suisse	28 Dorf-Susch	2381	XI-V	Restefond France	64 Jausiers-St Etienne-de-Tinée	2678	X-VI
Forclaz Suisse/France	115/506 Martigny-Chamonix	1527	XII-V	San Bernardino Suisse	21 Splügen-Mesocco	2065	XI-V
Furka Suisse	19 Gletsch-Hospenthal	2431	XI-VI	Semmering Österreich	17 Spital-Gloggnitz	985	
Grd. S. Bernard Italy/Suisse	27/114 Aosta-Martigny	2469	XI-VI	Simplon Suisse	9 Brig-Simplon	2005	
Grimsel Suisse	6 Gletsch-Innertkirchen	2165	XI-VI	Somport España	330 Urdos-Canfranc	1631	
Guadarrama España	VI Madrid-Villacastín	1516	*	Splügen Suisse/Italia	64/36 Splügen-Campodoicino	2113	XI-V
Hardangervidda Norge	7 Eidfjord-Fagerheim	1250	XI-V	S. Gottardo Suisse	2 Airolo-Hospenthal	2108	X-V
Höchtor Österreich	107 Ferleiten-Heiligenblut	2759	XII-IV	Stelvio Italia	38 Bormio-Gomagol	2757	X-VI
Höhentauern Österreich	114 Trieben-St Johann	1265		Susten Suisse	20 Gadmen-Wassen	2224	X-VI
Iseran France	202 Lanslebourg Bourge-St.Maurice	2769	X-VI	Tenda France/Italia	204/20 Tende-Vernante	1279	*
Julier Suisse	3 Mulegns-Silvaplana	2284	*	Thurn Österreich	159 Jochberg-Mittersill	1274	
Katschberghöhe Österreich	99 Gmund-St Michael	1641	*	Tonale Italia	42 Pellizano-Ponte di Legno	1883	
Klausen Suisse	17 Altdorf-Linthal	1948	XI-VI	Tosas España	152 Puigcerdá-Ribas de Freser	1800	
Larche France/Italy	100/21 Larch-Argentera	1992	XII-IV	Turracher Höhe Österreich	95 Predlitz-Reichenau	1783	XI-IV
Loibl Öst./Jugo.	91/1 Klagenfurt-Kranj	1370	XI-V	Videster Norge	15 Grotli-Videseter	1.139	XI-VI
Maloja Suisse	3 Silvaplana-Vicosoprano	1815		Vikafjell Norge	13 Vinje-Viksøyri	1281	X-V

* Closed occasionally * Fermée de temps à autre * Gelegentlich gesperrt * Chius occasionalment

Leggenda   Legend   Legénde   Zeichenerklärung

Scala Scale Echelle Maßstab 1:1,000,000

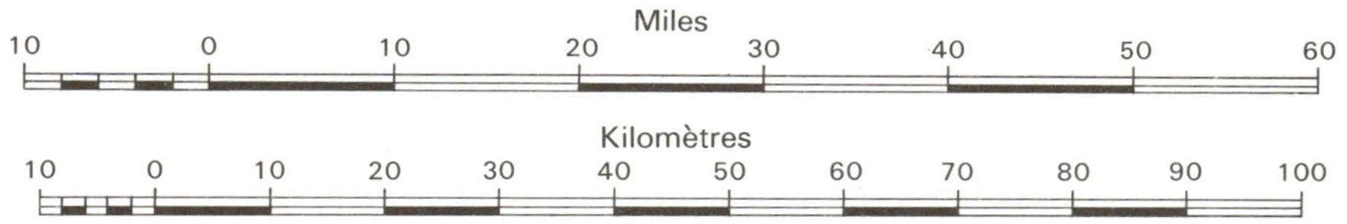

Italiano	English		Français	Deutsch
Autostrade	Motorways		Autoroutes	Autobahnen
Strade di grande comunicazione	Principal trunk highways		Routes de grand Transit	Wichtige Durchgangsstraßen
Altre strade principali	Other main highways		Autres routes principales	Sonstige Durchgangsstraßen
Altre strade importanti	Other important roads		Autres routes importantes	Sonstige wichtige Straßen
Altre strade	Other roads		Autres routes	Sonstige Straßen
Strade non asfaltate	Unsurfaced roads		Routes non revêtues	Nicht staubfreie Straßen
Autostrade in costruzione	Motorways under construction		Autoroutes en construction	Autobahnen im Bau
Strade in costruzione	Roads under construction		Routes en construction	Straßen im Bau
Ferrovie	Railways		Chemins de fer	Eisenbahnen
Funicolari	Funiculars		Funiculaires	Bergbahnen
Strade a pedaggio	Toll roads		Routes à péage	Gebührenpflichtige Straßen
Forti pendenze	Steep hills		Fortes déclivités	Starke Steigungen
Passi	Passes		Cols	Pässe
Frontiere internazionali	International boundaries		Frontières internationales	Staatsgrenzen
Numeri distintivi di strade europee	European road numbers	E14	Numéros des routes européennes	Nummern der Europastraßen
Altri numeri di strade	Other road numbers	54	Autres numéros des routes	Sonstige Straßennummern
Distanze: totali	Distances: Major	56	Distances: totalisées	Entfernungen: Grosse
parziali (Distanze in chilometri)	Minor (Distances in Kilometres)	20	partielles (Distances en Kilomètres)	Kleine (Entfernungen in Kilometern)
Trasporto auto: In aereo	Car ferries: Air		Transport d'autos: Avion	Autotransport: Flugzeuge
Traghetti	River	F	Bacs	Fähren
Piroscafi	Sea		Bateaux	Schiffe
Ferrovia	Rail		Voie ferrée	Eisenbahn
Aeroporti internazionali	International airports		Aéroports internationaux	Internationale Verkehrsflughäfen
Castelli	Castles		Châteaux	Burgen
Monasterie cattedrali	Monasteries and cathedrals		Monastères et cathédrales	Klöster und Kathedralen
Antichità	Ancient monuments		Monuments anciens	Alte Ruinen
Grotte	Caves		Grottes	Höhlen
Altri punti de interesse	Other points of interest		Autres curiosités	Sonstige Sehenswürdigkeiten

Warning Signs   Signaux de danger

Danger
Danger
Gefahrstelle
Pericolo generico

Bend to right
Virage à droite
Kurve (rechts)
Curva a destra

Double bend
Virage double
Doppelkurve
Doppia curva

Cross roads
Intersection
Kreuzung
Incrocio

Intersection with minor road
Intersection avec route sans priorité
Kreuzung mit Strasse ohne Vortrittsrecht
Incrocio con una strada senza diritto di precedenza

Road narrows
Chaussée rétrécie
Verengte Fahrbahn
Strettoia

Slippery road
Chaussée glissante
Schleudergefahr
Strada sdrucciolevole

Falling rock
Chute de pierres
Steinschlag
Caduta di massi

Two-way traffic
Circulation à double sens
Gegenverkehr
Doppio senso

Traffic signals
Signaux lumineux
Lichtzeichenanlage
Semaforo

Pedestrian crossing
Passage pour piétons
Fussgängerüberweg
Passaggio per pedoni

Children
Enfants
Kinder
Bambini

Prohibitive and Compulsory Signs   Signaux comportant une prescription absolue

Stop and give way
Arrêt à l'intersection
Halt! Vorfahrt gewähren
Stop e precedenza

Closed to all vehicles
Circulation interdite à tous véhicules
Verbot für Fahrzeuge aller Art
Divieto di transito nei due sensi

No entry
Sens interdit
Verbot der Einfahrt
Divieto di accesso

Entry of motorcars prohibited
Accès interdit aux autos
Verbot für Kraftwagen
Divieto di transito a tutti gli autoveicoli

Entry of motorcycles prohibited
Accès interdit aux motocyclettes
Verbot für Krafträder
Divieto di transito ai motocicli

Entry of lorries prohibited
Accès interdit aux poids lourds
Verbot für Lastkraftwagen
Divieto di transito agli autocarri

No overtaking
Interdiction de dépasser
Überholen verboten
Divieto di sorpasso

No overtaking by lorries
Interdiction de dépasser pour les poids lourds
Überholen für Lastwagen verboten
Divieto di sorpasso tra autocarri

Maximum speed limit
Limitation de vitesse
Höchstgeschwindigkeit
Limite di velocità

End of traffic limitations
Fin de prescriptions
Ende sämtlicher Streckenverbote
Fine della limitazione

Do not sound horn
Signaux sonores interdits
Hupverbot
Divieto di segnalazioni acustiche

Give priority to vehicles from opposite direction
Croisement interdit
Dem Gegenverkehr Vorrang gewähren
Dare precedenza, nei sensi unici alternati

Informative Signs   Signaux comportant une simple indication

Priority over vehicles from opposite direction
Priorité devant circulation en contre-voie
Vorrang vor dem Gegenverkehr
Diritto di precedenza nei sensi unici alternati

One-way street
Voie à sens unique
Einbahnstrasse
Senso unico

No through road
Chemin sans issue
Sackgasse
Vicalo cieco
(Strada sensa uscite)

Motorway
Entrée d'autoroute
Autobahn
Inizio autostrada

End of motorway
Fin d'autoroute
Ende der Autobahn
Fine dell' Autostrada

Motor vehicles only
Route pour automobiles seulement
Kraftfahrstrasse
Riservato alle autovetture

First aid station
Poste de secours
Erste Hilfe
Posto di pronto soccorso

Repairs
Poste de dépannage
Pannenhilfe
Assistenza meccanica

Telephone
Poste d'appel téléphonique
Fernsprecher
Posto telefonico

Filling station
Poste de ravitaillement en carburant
Tankstelle
Rifornimento carburante

Camp site
Terrain réservé au camping
Campingplatz
Campeggio

Caravan site
Terrain pour caravanes
Wohnwagenplatz
Terreno per rimorchi abitabili

Gefahrzeichen   Segnali di pericolo

Uneven road
Cassis ou dos d'âne
Unebene Fahrbahn
Cunetta o dosso

Opening bridge
Pont mobile
Bewegliche Brücke
Ponte mobile

Level crossing with barrier
Passage à niveau avec barrières
Bahnübergang mit Schranken
Passaggio a livello con barriere

Level crossing without barrier
Passage à niveau sans barrières
Unbeschrankter Bahnübergang
Passaggio a livello senza barriere

Road works
Travaux
Baustelle
Lavori in corso

Steep hill downwards
Descente dangereuse
Gefälle
Discesa pericolosa

Cattle
Animaux domestiques
Tiere
Animali

Wild animals
Animaux sauvages
Wildwechsel
Attenzione agli animali

Major road ahead
Respecter la priorité
Vorfahrt gewähren
Dare precedenza

'Count-down' markers approaching level crossing
Indicateur de distance avant un passage à niveau
Baken vor Bahnübergang
Pannelli con righe di distanza

Location of level crossing
Passage à niveau
Warnkreuz am Bahnübergang
Passaggio a livello

Traffic merges from right
Route débouchant de droite
Strasseneinmündung
Confluenza da destra

Verbots—und Gebotszeichen   Segnali Obbligatori e di Divieto

Width limit
Largeur maximum
Höchstbreite
Larghezza massima

Height limit
Hauteur maximum
Höchsthöhe
Altezza massima

Total weight limit
Poids maximum
Höchstgewicht
Peso lordo massimo

Axle weight limit
Charge maximum par essieu
Höchste Achslast
Circolazione vietata a mezzi con carico per asse

No left turn
Interdiction de tourner à gauche
Links abbiegen verboten
Divieto di svolta a sinistra

No U turns
Interdiction de faire demi-tour
Wenden verboten
Divieto di inversione ad U

Stop: Customs
Arrêt: poste de douane
Halt: Zoll
Alt-Dogana

No waiting
Stationnement interdit
Eingeschränktes Halteverbot
Sosta vietata

Direction to be followed
Sens obligatoire
Vorgeschriebene Fahrtrichtung
Direzione obbligatoria

Roundabout
Sens giratoire obligatoire
Kreisverkehr
Rotatoria

Route for cyclists
Piste obligatoire pour cyclistes
Gebot für Radfahrer
Pista per ciclisti

Minimum speed limit
Minimum de vitesse imposé
Mindestgeschwindigkeit
Limitazione di velocita

Hinweiszeichen   Segnali indicatori

One-way traffic
Circulation à sens unique
Richtzeichen für Einbahnstrasse
Fine del doppio senso di circolazione

Two lanes of traffic
Double voie
Einordnung in zwei Kolonnen
Disporsi su 2 file

Priority road
Route avec priorité
Vorfahrtstrasse
Strada con diritto di precedenza

End of priority road
Fin de la route prioritaire
Ende der Vorfahrtstrasse
Fine diritto di precedenza

Parking place
Parc de stationnement
Parkplatz
Parcheggio

Hospital
Hôpital
Hospital
Ospedale

Youth hostel
Auberge de jeunesse
Jugendherberge
Ostello della gioventu

Cafeteria
Café-restaurant
Autobahnkiosk
Bar

Restaurant
Restaurant
Autobahngasthaus
Ristorante

Hotel
Hôtel
Autobahnhotel
Motel

Diversion for lorries
Déviation du trafic lourd
Umleitung für Schwerverkehr
Deviazione autocarri in transito

Danger of forest fire
Forêt facilement inflammable
Feuergefahr
Pericolo d'Incendio

VESTERÅLEN
LOFOTEN
Vestfjorden
Andøya
Andenes
Bleik
Haugnes
Dverberg
Nordmjele
Nøss
Risøyhamn
Åknes
Dragnes
Fornes
Maurnes
Andfjorden
Senja
Svanfjell
901
Grunnfarnes
Kaldfarnes
Silsand
Finnsnes
Stormoen
Sørreisa
Vangsvik
Rødsand
Solbergfjorden
Skrolsvik
Stonglandet
Dyrøy
Dyrøya
Stangnes
Brøstadbotn
Kastneshamn
Salangsverket
Sjøvegan
Bjarkøya
Grøtavær
Grytøya
1003
Grytøya Nona
Andørja
Andørja
Anstad
Kasfjord
Harstad
Rolla
Ibestad
Vågsfjorden
Borkenes
Kilbotn
Straumen
Refsnes
Lavangen
Tennevoll
Fossbakken
Setermoen
Djupdal
Bardufoss
Målselv
Moen
Heia
Rundhaug
Bjør
Snøhetta
1505
Bonnes
Sørgard
Innset
Foldvik
Grovfjord
Tovik
Gratangen
Bjerkvik
Narvik
Ankenes
Katterat
Riksgrensen
Kopparåsen
Björkliden
Abisko
Grindjord
Skjærvik
Bjørkåsen
Ballangen
Kjeldebotn
Ofotfjorden
Forra
Liland
Bogen
Evenes
Skånland
Gausvik
Ramsund
Tjeldøya
Tjeldnes
Lødingen
Kongsvik
Hinnøya
Flesnes
Sigerfjord
Strand
Sortland
Møysalen
1266
Kanstadbotn
Rinøyvåg
Vestbygd
Tengelfjord
Digermulen
Hanøy
Hennes
Kvitnes
Langenes
Strengelvåg
Myre
Alsvåg
Skjoldehamn
Holm
Gavlfjorden
Sandset
Hovden
Nykvåg
Kråkberget
Langøya
Straumsjøen
Eidsfjord
Straumsnes
Skagen
Grytting
Sandnes
Stokmarknes
Hadsel
Hadseløya
Melbu
Vesterålsfjorden
Hadselfjorden
Fiskebøl
Laupstad
Austvågøy
Sydalen
Gimsøy
Svolvær
Kabelvåg
Skrova
Lyngvær
Henningsvær
Kvalnes
Eggum
Borge
Smorten
Vestvågøy
Valberg
Stamsund
Leknes
Buksnes
Ballstad
Lilleeidet
Napp
Gravdal
Ramberg
Fredvang
Flakstadøya
Moskenesøya
Reine
Sørvågen
Å
Tind
Moskenstraumen
Værøy
Værøy
Hamarøy
Hamnsund
Hamarøy
Skutvik
Engeløya
Steigen
Alstad
Bogen
Holkstad
Nordskot
Nordfold
Leiranger
Nordfolda
Sagfjorden
Tranøy
Ulvsvåg
Drag
Helland
Innhavet
Kråkmoen
Mørsvikbotn
Kjøpsvik
Bognes
Skarberget
Korsnes
Tysfjorden
Sætran
Forså
Frostisen
1744
Skjomen
Skjombotn
Bokholm
Sitasjaure
Sielmatjåkka
2005
Nikkaluokta
Akkajaure
Kårsatjåkka
Vaisa
83
E6
19
82
820
850
83
848
84
86
87
815
81
A
B
1
2
3
4
5
6
7
8
13°
14°
15°
16°
17°
18°
19°
69°
68°

5
Bodø
Fauske
Sandhornøya
Helligvær
Landegode
Fugløya
Meløya
Åmøya
Rødøya
Gjerøya
Lurøya
Svartisen
Polarsirkelen
Saltfjellet
Polcirkeln
Mo i Rana
Sommarset
Sørfold
Sørfolda
Megården
Djupvik
Straumsnes
Finneid
Leivset
Skjerstad
Hunstad
Hopen
Vågan
Geitvågen
Festvåg
Kjerringøy
Os
Bliksvær
Saltfjorden
Straumen
Alsvik
Sørarnøy
Mårnes
Sund
Inndyr
Børvasstindan
1180
Misvær
Beiarn
Storjord
Storvik
Fore
Ørnes
Glomfjord
Bjærangfjord
Halsa
Ågskaret
Vågaholmen
Tjongsfjord
Rødøy
Skjelåtinden
1640
Leiråmoen
Storglomvatnet
Kilboghamn
Konsvik
Sørfjorden
Høgtuvbreen
1291
Brattland
Onøy
Stokkvåg
Sjona
Sørsjona
Hemnesberget
Nesna
Lurøy
Husby
Rana
Leland
Sandnessjøen
Søttaren
Søfting
Drevja
Elsfjord
Korgen
Bjerka
Finneidfjord
Lejrvik
Låvong
Nordrana
Båsmoen
Storforshei
Ranelva
Dunderland
Bjøllånes
Stødi
Lønsdal
1754
Ølfjellet
Øvre Saltdal
Graddis fjellstue
Rognan
Kjøvihytta
Balvatnet
Nordsaulo
1776
Jakobsbakken
Sulitjelma
Suliskongen
1913
Blåmannsisen
1571
Umbukta fjellstue
Kåtaviken
Leirskar
Oksskolten
1915
Bleikvassli
Rossåga
Överuman
Artfjället
Båmåive
1554
Umfors
Norra Storfjället
Tärnasjön
Ammarnäs
Ammarfjället
1609
Vindelälven
Björkfjället
Svaipa
1426
Adolfsström
1609
Fierras
Vuoggatjålme
Tjidtjak
1579
Sädvaluspen
Jäckvik
Laisvall
Arjeplog
Uddjaur
Hornavan
Riebnesjaure
Stenudden
Tjeggelvas
Tåråktjåkkå
1386
Seper
878
Övernäs
N. Bergnäs
Forsnäs
Piteälven
Stuor Stäkke
796
Laisälven
Staika
1799
Peskehaure
Tarrekaise
Kvikkjokk
Saggat
Skalka
Karatj
Seitevare
Tjåmotis
Tjaktjajaure
1090
Ultevis
Sarek
2090
Stora Sjöfallet
Vietas
Pårtefjällen
2021
Rapaälven
Padjelanta
Virihaure
Vastenjaure
Staloluokta
NORRBOTTENS LÄN
VÄSTERBOTTENS LÄN
67°
66°
13°
14°
15°
16°
17°
18°
C
D
E
1
2
3
4
5
6
7
12
13
14
E6
80
826
812
805
77
361
17
93
181

6
Nord-Kvaløy
Grøtøy
Rebbenesøy
Torsvåg
Helgøy
Vanna
Vannsundet
Vannvåg
Fugløya
Fugløysund
Arviksand
Slettfjellet 1053
Arnøy
Laukøy
Lauksletta
Akkarvik
Karlsøy
Skjervøy
Kågen
Loppa
Silda
Stjernøy
Andsnes
Olderfjord
Bergsfjord
Øksfjord
Øksfjord-jøkelen 1166
Spildra
Kvænangen
Langfjord
Burfjord
Badderen
Kjækan
Kvænangsbotn
Sørstraumen
Sandbukt
Rieppe 1337
Hamneidet
Uløya
Sørkjosen
Nordreisa
Djupvik
Lyngen
Kåfjord
Kåfjordbotn
Bilto
Skogsfjord
Skattøra
Ringvassøy
Reinøy
Finnkroken
Grøtsundet
Snarby
Ullsfjorden
Nord-Lenangen
Lenangsøra
Jægervatn
1596 Store Lenangstind
Koppangen
Svensby
Breivik
Lyngseidet
Samuelsberg
Vengsøy
Futrikelv
Skulgam
Tønsvik
Kvaløysletta
Ersfjordbotn
Kvaløy
Tromsø
Tromsdalen
Tromsdalstind 1238
Tulleng
Hillesøy
Mjelde
Sandvik
Fagernes
Skarmunken
Ullsfjord
Skognes
Pollen
Jiekkevarre 1833
Lakselvbukt
Furuflaten
Skibotn
Agjet 1405
Andersdal
Balsfjorden
Malangen
Ansnes
Botnhamn
Mefjordvær
Senjehopen
Skaland
Lysnes
Jøvik
Malangen
Rossfjord
Oldervik
Straumsnes
Gryllefjord
Torsken
Senja
Svanfjell 901
Gibostad
Bjorelvnes
Målsnes
Grunnfarnes
Kaldfarnes
Silsand
Finnsnes
Stormoen
Vangsvik
Sørreisa
Skjæret
Ytre Laksvatn
Slettmo
Seljelvnes
Storsteinnes
Nordkjosbotn
Stubbeng
Storfjord
Skibotnelva
Helligskogen
Kilpisjärvi
Paltsa 1448
Paras
Målselv
Heia
Moen
Solbergfjorden
Rødsand
Skrolsvik
Stonglandet
Dyrøy
Dyrøya
Brøstadbotn
Bardufoss
Rundhaug
Målselva
Skjold
Tverrelvmo
Rostaelva
Reisaelva
Konkämäeno
Stangnes
Kastneshamn
Bjarkøya
Grøtavær
Grytøya 1003
Grytøya Nona
Andørja
Salangsverket
Sjøvegan
Setermoen
Barduelva
Bjørkås
Høgskarhus
Andørja
Anstad
Kasfjord
Harstad
Andenes
Haugnes
Bleik
Andøya
Dverberg
Andfjorden
E6
E78
6
91
86
87
84
82
88
21
8
4
16°
17°
18°
19°
20°
21°
22°
70°
69°

Hinnøya
Tjeldøya
Narvik
Ankenes
Kiruna
Gällivare
Malmberget
Ofotfjorden
Tysfjorden
Torne Träsk
Altevatnet
Akkajaure
Stora Lulevatten
Vastenjaure
Virihaure
Sitasjaure
Vaisa
Padjelanta
Sjaunjaape
Ultevis
Snøhetta 1505
Tsåktso 1120
Tjiuru 687
Sielmatjåkka 2005
Frostisen 1744
Kårsatjåkka 1730
Akkavare 2013
Sarek 2090
Pårtefjällen 2021
Blåmannsisen 1571
Suliskongen 1913
Dundret 820
Riksgränsen
Björkliden
Abisko
Kaisepakte
Bergfors
Rautas
Kurravaara
Tuolluvaara
Jukkasjärvi
Kalixfors
Svappavaara
Vittangi
Övre Soppero
Karesuando
Markkina
Kelottijärvi
Idivuoma
Masugnsbyn
Parakka
Kaitum
Linaälv
Koskullskulle
Dokkas
Leipojärvi
Nilivaara
Markitta
Saittarova
Skaulo
Nikkaluokta
Pirttivuopio
Vietas
Stora Sjöfallet
Allouokta kapell
Staloluokta
Sulitjelma
Lødingen
Kongsvik
Gausvik
Skånland
Evenes
Bogen
Liland
Forra
Bjerkvik
Gratangen
Grovfjord
Fossbakken
Sørgard
Innset
Bonnes
Kopparåsen
Katterat
Grindjord
Skjærvik
Bjørkåsen
Ballangen
Kjeldebotn
Sætran
Forså
Skarberget
Korsnes
Bognes
Ulvsvåg
Kjøpsvik
Drag
Helland
Innhavet
Skjomen
Skjombotn
Bokholm
Ramsund
Tjeldnes
E6
19
83
205
395
396
98
97
850
5
10
14
7

Hjelmsøya
Ingøy
Ingøya
Gjesvær
Skarsvåg
Magerøya
Kamøyvær
Tufjord
Gunnarnes
Havøysund
Måsøy
Rolvsøya
Honningsvåg
Rolvsøysundet
Revsbotn
Steingammen
Akkarfjord
Snøfjord
Porsanger-
halvøya
Repvåg
Sværholthalvøya
Forsøl
Hammerfest
Sørvær
Dønnesfjord
Breivikbotn
Sørøya
Kvaløya
Kokelv
Store
Tamsøya
Karhamn
Hasvik
Sørøysundet
Kvalsund
Russenes
1075
Seiland
Nordmanns-
fjordjøkelen
Seilandsjøkelen
981
Skaidi
Kistrand
Silda
Porsangen
Indre Leirpollen
Stjernøya
Indre Billefjord
Børselv
Storfjordbotn
Bergsfjord
Nuvsvåg
Øksfjord
Komagfjord
Kolvik
Øksfjord-
jøkelen
1166
Storekorsnes
Reinøya
Leirbotn
Langfjord
Altafjorden
Talvik
Alteidet
Hambukt
Gaissene
Lakselv
Rafsbotn
Burfjord
Kåfjord
Alta
Elvebakken
1139
Čuokkarašša
Rastigaissa
1067
Sørstraumen
Badderen
Lakselva
Lævvajok
Kjækan
Gargia
Skoganvarre
Kvænangsbotn
Altaelva
Luostejokka
Tana
Lodiken
641
Valjok
Paistunturit
646
Vesterelva
Jiesjavrre
Nattvatnstua
Suolovuobme
FINNMARKSVIDDA
Karasjok
Assebakte
Jiesjokka
Masi
Karigasniemi
Biggeluobbal
Kaamasmukka
Kautokeinoelva
Lappoluobbal
Bæivašgiedde
Karasjokka
Anarjokka
Ranttila
Kautokeino
Koarvikod
590
Storfosen
Angeli
Suolojavrre
Vaskojoki
Aiddejavrre
Pöyrisjärvi
Lemmenjoki
71°
70°
69°
22°
23°
24°
25°
26°
1
2
3
4
5
6
A
B
C
D
6
10
93
94
95
96
92
4
6

7
8
9
10
11
A
B
C
D
27°
28°
29°
30°
31°
71°
70°
69°
Varnesodden
Gamvik
Mehamn
Kjøllefjord
Oksevåg
Nordkinnhalvøya
Skjånes
Tanahorn
269
Berlevåg
Store Molvik
Kongsfjord
890
63
Makkaur
Gulgofjorden
Båtsfjord
31
891
Syltefjorden
Hammingberg
Lebesby
Tanafjorden
Ifjord
6
88
Torhop
Tana
Leirpollen
74
Rustefjelbma
Varangerhalvøya
Vardø
Svartnes
Kiberg
98
Falkefjellet
548
Komagvær
73
Skallelv
Seida
Nyborg
Skipagurra
Varangerbotn
Nesseby
68
Jacobselv
Krampenes
Vadsø
Ekkerøy
Karlebotn
Varangerfjorden
92
Nuorgam
Alleknjarg
Tana
Laksjokka
100
Sirma
Gandvik
142
Bugøynes
Laksnes
Laiti
Utsjoki
Bugøyfjord
Skogerøya
Grense-Jakobselv
Patoniva
503
Linakhamari
Neiden
Kirkenes
Tårnet
Bjørnevatn
Kuorboaivi
448
Hammerfjella
12
885
Pechenga
C
25
45
Sevettijärvi
Svanvik
Nikel'
Zapolyarnyy
94
Ijjärvi
Pavdijärvi
106
Skogfoss
11
Supru
O
M
I
Kaamajoki
Skogly
528
885
Partakko
Nyrud
100
Kaamanen
577
S.
S.
S.
R.
Inarinjärvi
32
Inari
4
Virtaniemi
Niskakoski
40
Nellimö
11
401
Konnostunturi
Koppelo

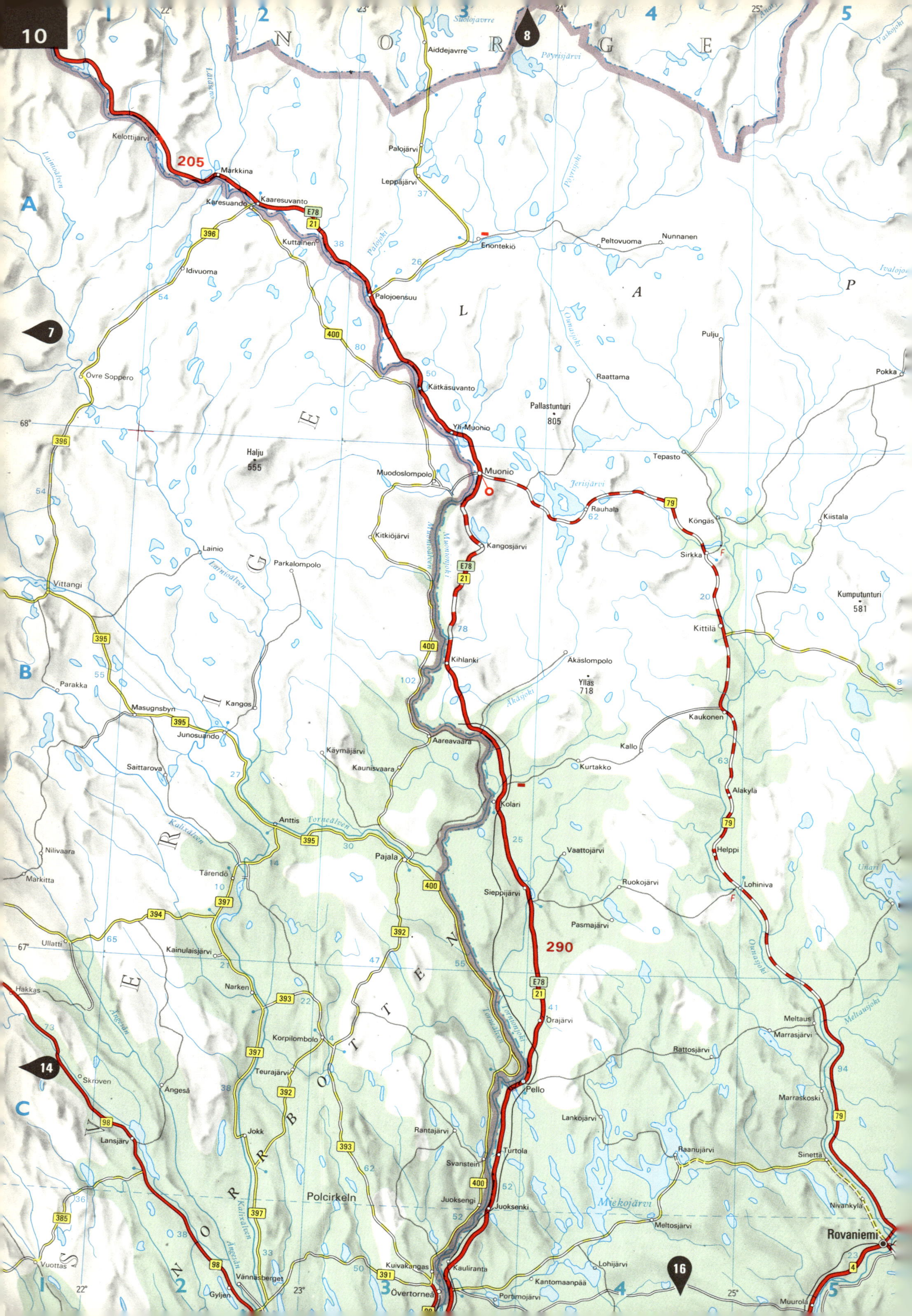
NORGE
Suolojavrre
Aiddejavrre
Pöyrisjärvi
Lätäseno
Kelottijärvi
205
Markkina
Karesuando
Kaaresuvanto
E78
21
396
Kuttainen
Idivuoma
Palojärvi
Leppäjärvi
Enontekiö
Peltovuoma
Nunnanen
Pöyrisjoki
Palojoki
Palojoensuu
Ivalojoki
LAPP
Ounasjoki
Pulju
400
Övre Soppero
Kätkäsuvanto
Raattama
Pokka
Pallastunturi
805
Yli-Muonio
Halju
555
Muodoslompolo
Muonio
Tepasto
Jerisjärvi
Rauhala
79
Köngäs
Kiistala
Kitkiöjärvi
Kangosjärvi
Sirkka
Lainio
Parkalompolo
Lainioälven
Muonioälven
Muoniojoki
Vittangi
Kumputunturi
581
Kittilä
395
Kihlanki
Äkäslompolo
Parakka
Ylläs
718
Äkäsjoki
Masugnsbyn
Kangos
Kaukonen
Junosuando
Aareavaara
Kallo
Käymäjärvi
Kaunisvaara
Kurtakko
Saittarova
Alakylä
Kolari
Anttis
Torneälven
Kalixälven
Helppi
Vaattojärvi
Nilivaara
Pajala
Tärendö
Markitta
Sieppijärvi
Ruokojärvi
Lohiniva
Unari
397
394
Pasmajärvi
Ullatti
392
Kainulaisjärvi
290
Hakkas
Narken
393
Orajärvi
Meltaus
Meltausjoki
Marrasjärvi
Korpilombolo
Torniojoki
Rattosjärvi
Teurajärvi
Skröven
Angesån
Angesä
Pello
Marraskoski
Lankojärvi
Jokk
Lansjärvi
Rantajärvi
Turtola
Raanujärvi
Sinetta
Svanstein
Polcirkeln
Juoksengi
Juoksenki
Miekojärvi
Nivankylä
385
Meltosjärvi
Rovaniemi
Kalixälven
Vuottas
Kuivakangas
Kauliranta
Lohijärvi
Vännäsberget
391
Kantomaanpää
Gyljen
Övertorneå
Portimojärvi
Muurola
NORRBOTTEN
SVERIGE
98
4
22°
23°
24°
25°
68°
67°
1
2
3
4
5
A
B
C
7
8
14
16

Menesjärvi
Koppelo
Ivalo
Törmänen
Ivalojoki
Nellimö
9
401
Konnostunturi
Lotta
Raja-
Jooseppi
Laanila
73
Saariselkä
Tankapirtti
4
544
Nattastunturit
Talkkunapää
633
Vuotso
Porttipahta
Korvatunturi
483
Lokan
tekojärvi
Madetkoski
Lokka
91
Petkula
Kersilö
Sattanen
Jeesiöjoki
Kelujärvi
Tanhau
Luiro
Kemijoki
Martti
Koukkutunturi
442
Värriöjoki
Kovdor
Sorsatunturi
626
Sodankylä
Vaalajärvi
53
Savukoski
Kuosku
Aska
Aapajärvi
39
Torvinen
Luosto
510
Kairala
Karhutunturi
518
Nousu
Pelkosenniemi
Saunavaara
Saija
Vuojärvi
103
Kotala
Raudanjoki
Ahvenselkä
Kelloselkä
82
20
Pahkakumpu
657
Tapionniemi
56
Vallovaara
Korvala
Salla
Pyhätunturi
477
Salmivaara
Kursu
40
Kemijärvi
Ala-
Nampa
60
5
26
Isokylä
Joutsijärvi
Kallunki
Selkälä
80
Misi
Kemijärvi
Tonkopuro
Napapiiri
409
Soumutunturi
41
Hautajärvi
Luusua
Ailanganselkä
Maaninkavaara
17
Oikarainen
63
Vanttauskoski
35
Tumcha
Alakurtti
6
7
8
9
10
A
B
C
27°
28°
29°
30°
67°
68°

NORSKEHAVET
Træna
Husøy
Trænfjorden
Nordesøy
Nesøya
Hestmona
Lurøya
Lurøy
Onøy
Lovunden
Lovund
Stokkvåg
Tomma
Husby
Dønnes
Glein
Nordvik
Bjørn
Dønna
Seløy
Herøy
Sandnessjøen
Alsten
Alstahaug
Tjøtta
Vefsnfjorden
Mindlandet
Vevelstad
Vega
Gladstad
Rørøy
Horn
Anndalsvåg
Velfjorden
Toft
Brønnøysund
Torget
Sømna
Hommelstø
Tosbotn
Saus
Tosen
Vennesund
Bindalsfjorden
Holm
Austra
Leka
Solsem
Møllebogen
Terråk
Arsandøy
Gravvik
Sjølstad
Foldereid
Teplingan
Bjøranes
Kongsmoen
Vikna
Rørvik
Ottersøy
Kolvereid
Nærøy
Salsbruket
Abelvær
Folda
Foldfjorden
Salen
Jøa
Grønningsfjell. 758
Høylandet
Utvorda
Otterøya
Otterøy
Namsfjorden
Lauvsnes
Nord-Statland
Namsos
Overhalla
Tøttdal
Klinga
Bangsund
Grong
Geitfjellet 869
Formofoss
Harran
Namdalen
Heimdalshaugan 1160
Skorovatn
Portfjellet 823
Kvelia
Nordli
Sanddøla
Tunnsjøen
Tunnsjø
Namsskogan
Brekkvasselv
Røyrvik
Lim
Bláfjellet 907
277
Majavatn
Svenningdal
Trofors
Kvitfjellet 1245
Grane
Laksfors
Reinfjellet
Vefsna
Mosjøen
Finnkneet 1158
Søfting
Drevja
Brekken
Søttaren
Elsfjord
Leland
Lavong
Nesna
Rana
Sjona
Hemnesberget
Lejrvik
Sørsjona
Brattland
Konsvik
Kilboghamn
Sørfjorden
Høgtuvbreen 1291
Gjerøya
Melfjorden
Osen
Hofstad
Roan
Solum
Namdalseid
Snåsa
Jørstad
Snåsavatn
Kvam
Finnvollheia
Borgefjell
805
17
771
802
770
769
768
767
766
724
760
74
763
765
764
803
76
E6
19
20
9
10°
11°
12°
13°
65°
66°
1
2
3
4
5
A
B
C

Polarsirkelen
Polcirkeln
Stødi
E6
Bjøllånes
Dunderland
Storforshei
Ranelva
Mo i Rana
Umbukta fjellstue
Kåtaviken
Överuman
Leirskar
Oksskolten
1915
Artfjället
Bäimåive
1554
Hjartfjellet
1453
Umfors
Norra Storfjället
1792
Hemavan
Joesjö
Røssvatnet
Krutå fjellstue
Tärnaby
1263
Södra Storfjället
Ryfjället
Våjtjajaure kapell
Ajaure
Skalmodalen
Kroken
Harvasstua
Gardfjället
Umnäs
Fättjaur
Dikanäs
Ransaren
Fjällfjällen
1408
Marsfjället
1589
Klimpfjäll
Fatmomakke
Kultsjön
Burgfjällen
Saxnäs
1455
Borgafjäll
Ankarvattnet
Ankarede
Stora Blåsjön
Mellanskogsfjället
1249
Sjoutnäs
Storsjouten
Gäddede
Fågelberget
Lidsjöberg
Hotagsfjällen
Risbäck
Strömnäs
Malgomaj
Skansholm
Laxbäcken
Långsele
724
Norråker
V. Ormsjö
Tåsjön
Tåsjö
Flåsjön
Alanäs
Dorotea
Vuoggatjålme
1609
Fierras
Sädvaluspen
Jäckvik
Svaipa
1426
Adolfsström
Björkfjället
Vindelälven
Ammarfjället
1609
Tärnasjön
Ammarnäs
Gillisnuole
Guvertsfjälls kapell
Grannäs
Storvindeln
Sorsele
Storjuktan
Blattnicksele
Gargnäs
Strömsund
Storuman
Stensele
Barsele
Gunnarn
Juktån
Vojmsjön
Skarvsjö
Pautträsk
Nästansjö
Vilhelmina
Latikberg
Järvsjö
Vinliden
Torvsjö
Ångermanälven
Almsele
Ålgsjö
Lomsjö
Åsele
Västermyr
Tjeggelvas
Stenudden
Riebnesjaure
Övernäs
N. Bergnäs
Hornavan
Laisvall
Arjeplog
Uddjaur
Laisälven
Kasker
LAPPLAND
VÄSTERBOTTEN
A
B
C
14
15
21
5
6
7
8
9
10
15°
16°
17°
18°
65°
66°

Malmberget
Gällivare
Koskullskulle
Dundret
820
Stora Lulevatten
Alloluokta kapell
Luspebryggan
Porjus
Ligga
Jokkmokk
Polcirkeln
Messaure
Stora Luleälven
L. Luleälven
Letsi
Murjek
Vuollerim
Kopponis
Puottaure
Holmträsk
Kåbdalis
Bodträskfors
Harads
Luleälven
Lakaträsk
Sandträsk
Gunnarsbyn
Långsund
Nattavaara
Nattavaara by
Polcirkeln
Råneälven
Pålkem
Vuottas
Nilivaara
Markitta
Dokkas
Leipojärvi
Ullatti
Hakkas
Skröven
Ängesån
Ängeså
Lansjärv
Tärendö
Kainulaisjärvi
Narken
Korpilombolo
Teurajärvi
Jokk
Vännäsberget
Gyljen
Överkalix
Grelsbyn
Svartbyn
Morjärv
Vitvattnet
Korpika
Töre
Kalix
Börjelsbyn
Rolfs
Påläng
Ytterbyn
Storön
Jämtön
Siknäs
Råneå
Bergön
Rånön
Niemisel
Årbyn
Boden
Svartbyn
Smedsbyn
Sävast
Gammelstad
Södra Sunderbyn
Notviken
Luleå
Vittjärv
Avaheden
Brännberg
Övre Tväråselet
Piteälven
Älvsbyn
Korsträsk
Vistheden
Bredsel
Vidsel
Lauker
Auktsjaur
Moskosel
Varjisträsk
Varjisån
Abraure
Allejaur
Kasker
Arjeplog
Uddjaur
Laisvall
Laisälven
Grannäs
Storvindeln
Södra Bergnäs kapell
Storavan
Hornavan
Forsnäs
Piteälven
Stuor Stäkke
796
N Bergnäs
Övernäs
Stenudden
Riebnesjaure
Seper
878
Tjeggelvas
Tåråktjåkkå
1386
Staika
1799
Pårtefjällen
2021
Tarreätno
Kvikkjokk
Saggat
1090
Tjaktjajaure
Seitevare
Tjåmotis
Skalka
Kaptensgården
Karatj
Randijour
Karatj
kvik
LAPPLAND
NORRBOTTEN
A
B
1
2
3
4
5
6
7
5
7
10
16
17°
18°
20°
21°
22°
23°
66°
67°
97
98
343
374
375
380
383
384
385
390
392
393
394
395
397
356
371
90
E4

BOTTENVIKEN
Jacobstad
Vastra Kvarken
Holmön
Junkon
Germandön
Vargön
Mellerstön
Piteholms yttre fjärd
Rosvik
Kopparnäs
Norrfjärden
Piteå
Bergsviken
Munksund
Öjebyn
Boleby
Lillpite
Roknäs
Svensbyn
Hortlax
Blåsmark
Hemmingsmark
Jävre
Åbyn
Byske
Byskeälven
Fällfors
Norrlångträsk
Drängsmark
Östvik
Kåge
Ersmark
Kusmark
Skellefteå
Skelleftehamn
Klemensnäs
Bergsbyn
Örviken
Myckle
Medle
Bureå
Bjuröklubbfiskeläge
Vallen
Lövånger
Ånäset
Sikeå
Bygdeå
Robertsfors
Rickleån
Bygdsiljum
Burträsk
Täfteå
Sävar
Tavelsjö
Talsmark
Sävarån
Ersmark
Umeå
Sörfors
Botsmark
Bygdeträsket
Sikån
Vindeln
Vännäs
Vännäsby
Tvärålund
Hällnäs
Granön
Umeälven
Vindelälven
Skivsjön
Bjurholm
Strömfors
Boliden
Bastuträsk
Kalvträsk
Åsträsk
Jörn
Kusfors
Långträsk
Myrheden
Glommersträsk
Abborrträsk
Norsjö
Risliden
Malån
Amsele
Orträsk
Mälaträsk
Adakgruvan
Adak
Skellefteälven
Kristineberg
Björksele
Rusksele
Lycksele
Vänjaurbäck
Karlsbäck
Fredrika
Lögdeälven
Vindelgransele
Norrby
Kattisavan
Rusele
Gargnäs
Blattnicksele
Juktån
Storjuktan
Barsele
Gunnarn
Pautrask
Vinliden
Västermyrriset
Tallsjö
Gideälven
Algsjö
Järvsjö
Torvsjö
Halla
E4
139
140
21
22
373
370
363
343
94
95
90
93
92
91
351
352
353
355
364
365
366
369
360
D
E
1
2
3
4
5
6
65°
64°
18°
19°
20°
21°
22°

NORRBOTTEN
SVERIGE
BOTTENVIKEN
Rovaniemi
Övertorneå
Ylitornio
Kainuunkylä
Hedenäset
Risudden
Korpikylä
Karunki
Kukkola
Kojakkala
Haparanda
Tornio
Liedakkala
Kemi
Lautiosaari
Veitsiluoto
Ajos
Viantie
Simo as
Kuivaniemi
Olhava
Ii
Jakkukylä
Martinniemi
Haukipudas
Kello
Kiiminki
Pateniemi
Oulu
Oulujoki
Oulunsalo
Kempele
Sanginjoki
Hailuoto
Liminka
Lumijoki
Karinkanta
Siikajoki
Keskikylä
Tyrnävä
Muhos
Raahe
Pattijoki
Revonlahti
Saloinen
Ruukki
Temmes
Tuomioja
Kopsa
Paavola
Piehinki
Rantsila
Vihanti
Pyhäjoki
Yppäri
Alpua
Lampinsaari
Pyhänkoski
Karhukangas
Metsäkylä
Merijärvi
Oulainen
Kalajoki
Pulkkila
Tynkä
Alavieska
Mieluskylä
Haapavesi
Piippola
Luleå
Kalix
Råneå
Töre
Morjärv
Korpika
Börjelsbyn
Rolfs
Påläng
Ytterbyn
Karlsborg
Båtskärsnäs
Sangis
Säivis
Nikkala
Seskarö
Bergön
Rånön
Storön
Haraljärden
Junkön
Germandon
Jämtön
Siknäs
Arbyn
Vitvattnet
Lappträsk
Karungi
Överkalix
Gyljen
Vännäsberget
Kuivakangas
Juoksengi
Juoksenki
Kauliranta
Kantomaanpää
Portimojärvi
Lohijärvi
Meltosjärvi
Nivankylä
Muurola
Petäjäskoski
Vammavaara 224
Koivu
Loue
Varejoki
Tervola
Arpela
Yli-Paakkola
Ilmola
Puukkokumpu
Alaniemi
Yli-Kärppä
Rovastinaho
Narkaus
Oijärvi
Tannila
Yli-Ii
Kemijoki
Simojoki
Kuivajoki
Pyhäjoki
Kalajoki
Siikajoki
Luodonselkä
E4
E78
4
8
21
77
78
81
86
98
99
356
384
390
391
397
28
106
116
128
198
10
14
15
23
A
B
C
1
2
3
4
65°
66°
23°
24°
25°
26°

Napapiiri
Kemijärvi
Luusua
Tonkopuro
409
Soumetunturi
Maaninkavaara
Hautajärvi
Ailangan selkä
Vanttauskoski
Kemijoki
Pirttikoski
Pekkala
Autti
Palotunturi
391
Pera-Posio
Käylä
Kitka
Oulankajoki
Tolva
Yli-Kitka
Posio
Vasaraperä
Rukajärvi
Määttälänvaara
578
Simojärvi
Mäntyjärvi
Impiö
Kuusamo
Muojärvi
Kärpänkylä
Petäjäjärvi
Sirniö
Kostonjärvi
Iivaare
470
Sarajärvi
Kelankylä
Inkee
Murtovaara
Kokkokylä
Iso Kero
Iivojoki
Pärjänjoki
Iso-Syöte
432
Metsala
Irnijärvi
Taivalkoski
Livo
Jokijärvi
Jurmu
Ikosenniemi
Kurtti
Tyräjärvi
Hossa
Pintamo
Aittojärvi
Pudasjärvi
Peranka
Hirvaskoski
Kurenalus
Jonku
Puhosjärvi
Puhos
Yli-Näljänka
Juntusranta
Voynitsa
Jaalanka
Kiannanniemi
Jaurakka
Vaaranniva
Kiantajärvi
Joukokylä
Suomussalmi
Juorkuna
Ämmänsaari
Palovaara
Raate
Puolanka
Leipivaara
Emäjoki
Sanginkylä
Puokio
Vuokkijärvi
Saarivaara
Hyrynsalmi
Moisiovaara
Nuojua
Vaala
Jaalanka
Törmänmäki
Ristijärvi
Rimmi
Keräsenvaara
294
Kivesjärvi
Iivantiira
Änättijärvi
Ozero Kamennoye
Veneheitto
Säräisniemi
Paltamo
Lentiira
Manamansalo
Kontiomäki
Paltaniemi
Sumsa
Oulujärvi
Kajaani
Lentua
Hietaperä
Vuolijoki
Nuasjärvi
Vuokatti
Sotkamo
Soidinvaara
Ontojärvi
Kuhma
Kotajärvi
Otanmäki
Maimua
A
B
C
S
S
S
R
66°
65°
27°
28°
29°
30°
5
6
7
8
9

1
2
3
4
A
B
C
6°
7°
8°
9°
64°
63°
Sula
Mausund
Sveliingen
Sistranda
Frøya
Flatval
Titran
Kjerringvåg
Hitra
Ansnes
Fillan
Hestvika
Kvenvær
Veidholmen
Hummelvik
Hopen
Dyrnesvågen
Smøla
Forsnes
Trondheimsleia
Skarsøy
Straumen
Stemshaug
Storodden
Ånes
Aure
Vinsternes
Golstein
Ertvågøy
Vågos
Tustna
Tommervåg
Stauraset
Vinjeøra
Engdal
Kristiansund
Bremsnes
Hendset
Engjan
Frei
Kvalvåg
Kvisvik
Halsa
Brattset
Asskard
Mo
Øye
Hustadvika
Vevang
Averøya
Tovik
Kornstad
Kvitnes
Kvernes
Hustad
Orjavik
Eide
Høgset
Torvikbukt
Gyl
Tingvoll
Halsafjorden
Surnadalsøra
Stangvik
Kvanne
Rokkum
Troll-
heimen
Bud
Bjørnsund
Ona
Sandøy
Gossen
Indre Fræna
Batnfjordsøra
Angvik
Tingvollfjorden
Ytre Fræna
Steinshamn
Harøya
Hollingsholm
Aukra
Sundsbø
Molde
Løvset
Gujord
Kleive
Eidsvåg
Toven
Ålvundfoss
Todal
Trollheimen
Ålvundeid
Nordøyane
Harøyfjorden
Sør-Aukra
Otrøy
Moldefjorden
Grønnes
Langfjorden
Vistdal
Øksendal
Sunndalsøra
Storli
Austnes
Sekken
Sølsnes
Eresfjord
Kjerstad
Skjeltene
Brattvåg
Fiksdal
Romsdalsfjorden
Afarnes
Måsvassbu
Brandstad
SUNNDALEN
Romfo
Vigra
Søvik
Helland
Vikebukt
Vågstranda
Redven
Isfjorden
Eikesdalsvatnet
Vatne
Tomra
Eidsbygda
Veblungsnes
Åndalsnes
Giske
Godøy
Ålesund
Nørvasund
Skodje
Ørskog
E69
Tresfjord
Vold
Innfjorden
220
Kors
Bøymoen
Spjelkavik
Langevåg
Magerholm
Trollstig 850
Mongefossen
Eikesdal
Finnset
Kvalsvik
Hareid
Brandal
Festøy
Storfjorden
Aure
Stordal
ROMSDALEN
Ulsteinvik
Landet
Vartdal
Verma
Aursjøen
Stranda
Gurskøy
Overåsneset
Sylte
Eidsdal
Norddal
Kolås
Sæbø
Leknes
Ørstavik
Lesjaskog
Tungaseter
Pyttegga 1999
Tafjord
Sjungseter
Volda
Kopparnes
Folkestad
Viddal
Storfjorden
Geiranger
Eagle's Road 624
30
Lesjaverk
Lora
Tverrfjellet
Syvde
16
61
62
63
64
65
66
67
71
14
58
60

Otterøya
Namsos
Overhalla
Grong
Geitfjellet 869
Formofoss
Bangsund
Klinga
Sølum
Osen
Namdalseid
Snåsa
Jørstad
Hofstad
Roan
Finnvollheia 676
Vellamelen
Kvam
Sunnan
Stod
Malm
Steinkjer
Skjækerhatten 1137
Harsvik
Stokksund
Stjern
Follafoss
Bodom
Henning
Beitstadfjorden
Åfjord
Flenstad
Skjækerfjella
Torröjen
Tiltrem
Verran
Inderøy
Mære
Sparbu
Straumen
Røra
Leksdalsvatnet
Skäcker-fjällen 1220
Fosna
Mosvik
Fines
Ytterøy
Levanger
Verdalsøra
Stiklestad
Vuku
Veren
Nes
Bjugn
Stjørna
Råkvåg
Alset
Alstadhaug
Okkenhaug
Anjan
Austrått
Brekstad
Beian
Ekne
Markabygd
Sandvika
Storrensjön
Selva
Trondheimsfjorden
Frosta
Åsen
Skalstugan
Feren
Leira
Vannviken
Medstugan
Lensvik
Skatval
Okkelberg
Stadsbygd
Trondheim
Stjørdalshalsen
Hegra
Flora
Gudå
Meråker
Kopperå
Tännforsen
Duved
Krokstadøra
Ranheim
Malvik
Hommelvik
Elvran
Stjørdalen
Lian
Storlien
Enafors
Geitastrand
Heimdal
Klæbu
Stordal
Handöl
Ånn
Orkanger
Børsøra
Buvik
Melhus
Fannrem
Skaun
Brøttem
Selbusjøen
Selbustrand
Selbu
Fongen 1459
Blåhammaren
Vålådalen
Orkladalen
Svorkmo
Flå
Løkken Verk
Hølonda
Hovin
Horg
Nea
Tydal
Sylarna 1766
Meldal
Støren
Seter
Nedalshytta
Sverige
Soknedal
Singsås
Gauldalen
Gaula
Haltdalen
Helagsfjället 1796
Ljungdalen
Rennebu
Stugudal
Budal
Ålen
Orkla
Berkåk
Storbudal
Reitan
Hessdalen
Ulsberg
Innset
Morkvoll
Klinken
Aursunden
Masslingen
Forelshogna 1332
Glåmos
Brekken
Bruksvallarna
Anåfjället 1347
Sålåhaugvoll
Hitterdal
Fjällnäs
Oppdal
Kvikne
Røros
Funäsdalen
Tänndalen
Ljusnedal
Feragen
Os
Lossnen
Drivstua
Tännäs
Vingelen
Tolga
Glåma
Sørvika
Skedbrokåtan
Borkhusseter
Høgstegia 1633
Hodal
Narbuvollen
Rogen
Savalen
Tufsingdalen
Kongsvoll
Tynset
Svukuriset
Dovrefjell 1026
Holøydal
Hjerkinn
Brydal
Elgepiggen 1604
Elgå
Dalen
Folldals verk
Tylldal
Spekedalssetra
Femunden
Valdalen
Långfjället
1204
Utvorda
Harran
Namsfjorden
Nord Statland
Lauvsnes
Tøttdal
Sanddøla
Namsen
E6
E75
17
21
724
715
720
767
766
760
74
763
72
336
322
65
71
700
701
30
31
312
3
29
26
35
68
90
203
12
20
31
32
5
6
7
8
9
A
B
C
10°
11°
12°
13°
63°
64°

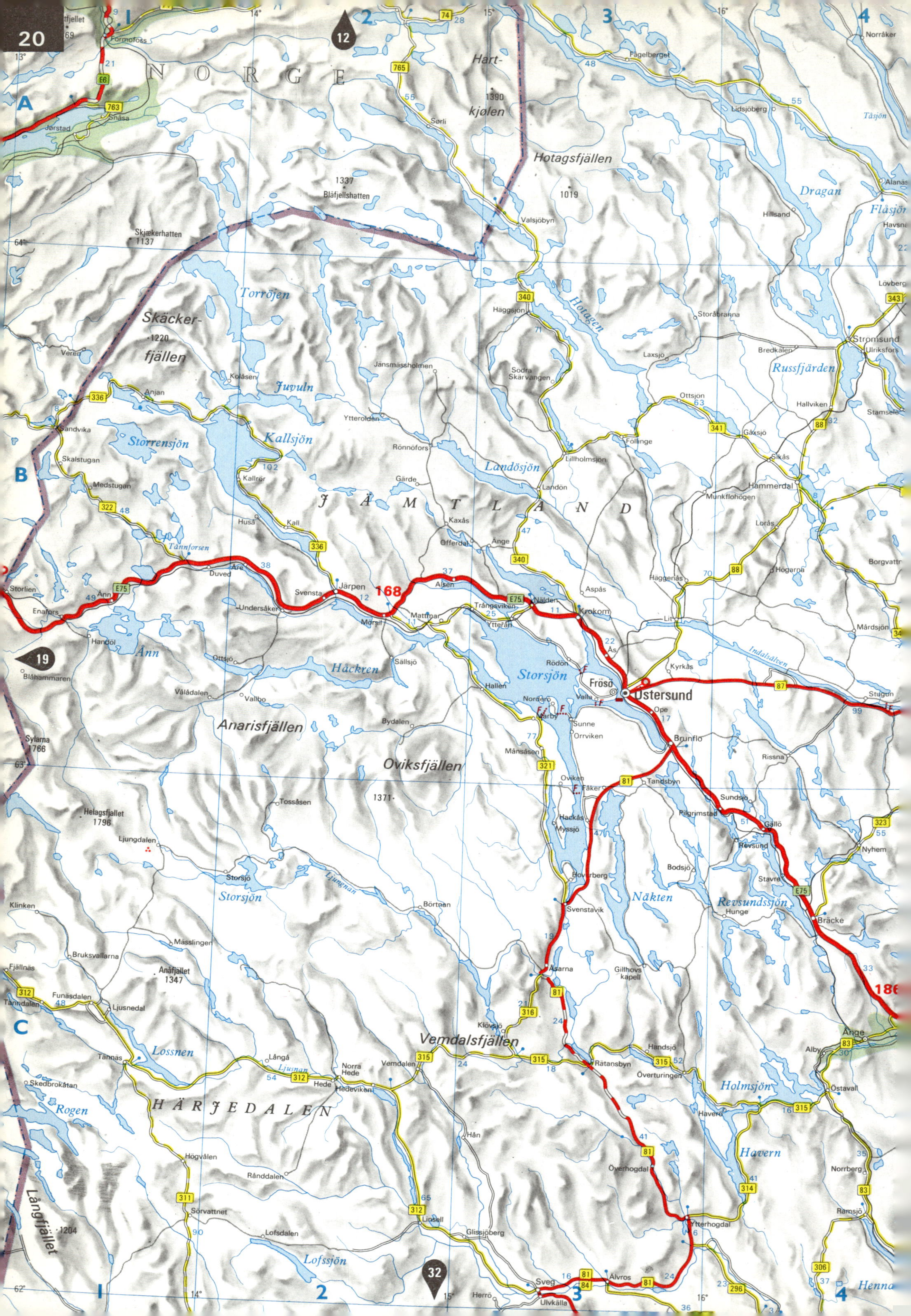
NORGE
JÄMTLAND
HÄRJEDALEN
Formofoss
Snåsa
Jørstad
Hartkjølen
1390
Hotagsfjällen
1019
1337
Blåfjellshatten
Skjækerhatten
1137
Sørli
Valsjöbyn
Fågelberget
Lidsjöberg
Tåsjön
Dragan
Hillsand
Alanäs
Flåsjön
Havsnäs
Lövberga
Torröjen
Skäcker-
1220
fjällen
Hotagen
Häggsjön
Storåbrännа
Strömsund
Ulriksfors
Bredkälen
Laxsjö
Russfjärden
Veren
Kolåsen
Juvuln
Jänsmässholmen
Södra Skärvången
Ottsjön
Hallviken
Stamsele
Anjan
Sandvika
Storrensjön
Kallsjön
Ytteråden
Föllinge
Gåxsjö
Skalstugan
Rönnöfors
Landösjön
Lillholmsjön
Sikås
Hammerdal
Medstugan
Kallrör
Gärde
Landön
Munkflohögen
Huså
Kall
Kaxås
Lorås
Tännforsen
Offerdal
Ånge
Borgvattnet
Duved
Åre
Järpen
Svensta
168
Ålsen
Högarna
Häggenås
Aspås
Storlien
Ånn
Undersåker
Mörsil
Mattmar
Trångsviken
Nälden
Krokom
Lit
Enafors
Ytterån
Mårdsjön
Handöl
Ånn
Ottsjö
Sällsjö
Häckren
Rödön
Ås
Kyrkås
Indalsälven
Frösö
Östersund
Stugun
Blåhammaren
Vålådalen
Vallbo
Anarisfjällen
Hallen
Storsjön
Norderö
Marby
Vallsta
Ope
Sunne
Orrviken
Brunflo
Sylarna
1766
Bydalen
Månsåsen
Oviksfjällen
Rissna
1371
Oviken
Fåker
Tandsbyn
Sundsjö
Tossåsen
Pilgrimstad
Gällö
Helagsfjället
1796
Hackås
Myssjö
Revsund
Nyhem
Ljungdalen
Bodsjö
Storsjö
Ljungan
Hoverberg
Stavre
Storsjön
Näkten
Revsundssjön
Hunge
Bräcke
Klinken
Börtnan
Svenstavik
Mässlingen
Bruksvallarna
Anafjället
1347
Åsarna
Gillhovs kapell
Fjällnäs
Funäsdalen
Tänndalen
Ljusnedal
186
Klövsjö
Vemdalsfjällen
Ånge
Alby
Tännäs
Lossnen
Långå
Ljusnan
Norra Hede
Vemdalen
Rätansbyn
Handsjö
Överturingen
Skedbrokåtan
Hede
Hedeviken
Holmsjön
Östavall
Rogen
Havern
Hån
Havern
Norrberg
Högvålen
Rånddalen
Överhogdal
Långfjället
1204
Sörvattnet
Linsell
Ytterhogdal
Ramsjö
Glissjöberg
Lofsdalen
Lofssjön
Sveg
Älvros
Herrö
Ulvkälla
Henna
E6
E75
12
19
32

5
6
7
8
13
15
15
A
B
C
22
33
Ormsjö
Torvsjö
Västermyrriset
Vanjaurback
Hällnäs
Granön
Vindeln
Umeälven
Vindelälven
Ångermanälven
Almsele
Dorotea
Hoting
Lomsjö
Åsele
Älgsjö
Tallsjö
Gideälven
Lögdeälven
Örträsk
Skivsjön
Tvärålund
Svanavattnet
Fredrika
Bjurholm
Vännäs
Vänn
Rossön
Bodum
Övra
Björksele
Halla
Bredträsk
Karlsbäck
Fjällsjö
Backe
Gulsele
Vallen
Solberg
Studsviken
Norrfors
Nyåker
Betarsjön
Junsele
Nyliden
Treböringssjö
Hemling
Långviksmon
Lever
Nordmaling
Lögdeå
Rundvik
Järnäs
Finfors
Myckelgensjö
Ramsele
Betåsen
Storsjön
Björna
Kubbe
Gideå
Å N G E R M A N L A N D
Bredbyn
Anundsjö
Mellansel
Moliden
Lungsjön
Ådalsliden
Näsåker
Edsele
Skorped
Grundsunda
Husum
Lövåsen
Reselse
Billsta
Västerhus
Gullänget
Arnäsvall
Sjalevad
Örnsköldsvik
Överhörnäs
Sidensjö
Domsjö
Stensjö
Forsmo
Skagsudde
Vaasa
Österås
Bjästa
Köpmanholmen
Trysunda
Helgum
Långsele
Sånga
Boteå
Solleftea
Multrä
Överlännäs
Helgum
Österforse
Ragunda
Hammarstrand
Styrnäs
Prästmon
Sandviken
Docksta
Vibyggerå
Ulvöhamn
Bispgården
Graninge
Sandslån
Bollstabruk
Sundbron
Ullånger
Mjällom
Håsjö
Kälarne
Bispfors
Graningesjön
Nyland
Väja
Lugnvik
Kramfors
Nordingrå
Frånö
Herrskog
Bönhamn
Klockestrand
Barsta
Hällesjö
Lunde
Sprängsviken
Boda
Ramvik
Berghamn
Järkvissle
Nyadal
Högsjö
Utansjö
Sörbygden
Viksjö
Ljungå
Hemsö
Hemsön
Holmsjön
Liden
Ålandsbro
Sundhamn
Norrstig
Holm
Lagfors
Härnösand
Ljustorp
Leringen
Östanbäck
Indalsälven
Härnön
BOTTENHAVET
Indal
Stavreviken
M E D E L P A D
Bergeforsen
Häggdånger
Söråker
Sörberge
Fränsta
Vivsta
Torpshammar
Hovid
Åvikebukten
Kovland
Alnö
Tunadal
Ljungan
Stöde
Selånger
Sundsvall
Ankarsvik
Stödesjön
Matfors
Stockvik
Sundsvallsbukten
Svartvik
Essvik
Attmar
Lucksta
Skottsund
Kvissleby
Njurundabommen
Njurunda
Brämön
Pori
Kölsjön
Malungen
Galtström
Hassela
Byn
Gnarp
Brännås
Algered
18°
19°
20°
62°
63°
64°
E4
E75
111
168

SVERIGE
BOTTENVIKEN
BOTTENHAVET
Umeå
Holmön
Ängesön
Västra Kvarken
Östra Kvarken
Norra Gloppet
Östra Gloppet
Södra Gloppet
Valsörarna
Mickelsörarna
Björkö
Replot
Raippaluoto
Vaasa
Vasa
Jakobstad
Pietarsaari
Nykarleby
Uusikaarlepyy
Kurikka
Kaskö
Kaskinen
Kristinestad
Kristiinankaupunki
Närpes
Närpiö
Teuva
Kauhajoki
Kankaanpää
Merikarvia
Bjurholm
Vännäs
Holmsund
Obbola
Hörnefors
Nordmaling
Rundvik
Sävar
Ersmark
Täfteå
Tavelsjö
Tvärålund
Bygdeå
Sikeå
Ornsköldsvik
Sundsvall
Skelleftehamn
Korsholm
Mustasaari
Laihia
Ilmajoki
Seinäjoki
Oravais
Oravainen
Vörå
Vöyri
Malax
Maalahti
Solf
Sulva
Bergö
Korsnäs
Petalax
Petolahti
Övermark
Ylimarkku
Pörtom
Pirttikylä
Lappfjärd
Lappväärtti
Tjöck
Tiukka
Ömossa
Metsälä
Sideby
Siipyy
Lauhavuori 231
Isojoki
Jalasjärvi
Kauhajärvi
Pohjankangas
Hämeenkangas
Niinisalo
Köörtilä
E4
E79
8
67
68
16
3
192
155
122
22
15
21
26
20°
21°
22°
63°
62°
64°
A
B
C
D
1
2
3
4

Ylivieska
Himanka
Lohtaja
Pahkala
Rautio
Alavieska
Haapavesi
Pyhäntä
Raudaskylä
Kärsämäki
Ahokylä
Nissilä
Marinkainen
Kannus
Eskola
Sievi
Järvikylä
Nivala
Maliskylä
Kalvia
Kokkola
Karleby
Välikylä
Toholampi
Kiiskilä
Parkkila
Oksava
Haapajärvi
Jokikylä
Remeskylä
Luupuvesi
Pyhäsalmi
Aittojärvi
Kiuruvesi
Nedervetil
Alaveteli
Ullava
Määttälä
Sykäräinen
Reisjärvi
Köyhänperä
Pyhäjärvi
Perhonjoki
Lestijoki
Köyhäjoki
Kaustinen
Hästbacka
Terjärv
Teerijärvi
Lestijärvi
Yli-Lesti
Muurasjärvi
Elämäjärvi
Haapamäki
Rytky
Koivujärvi
Veteli
Halsua
Evijärvi
Räyrinki
Alvajärvi
Pihtipudas
Laukkala
Vaaraslahti
Sulkavanjärvi
Kinnula
Seläntaus
Kolimajärvi
Pielavesi
Purmojärvi
Muhola
Itäkylä
Sääksjärvi
Oksakoski
Perho
Keitelepohja
Keitele
Säviä
Nilakka
Lappajärvi
Kivijärvi
Kymönkoski
Karvala
Vimpeli
Leppäselkä
Savonkylä
Viitasaari
Hoisko
Möksy
Kyyjärvi
Niinivesi
Tervo
Alajärvi
Levijoki
Kannonkoski
Vesanto
Tiistenjoki
Vastinki
Ahveniskylä
Suokonmäki
Soini
Karstula
Pääjärvi
Kuortane
Lehtimäki
Kukko
Kangasaho
Konginkangas
Kerkonkoski
Mäyry
Saarijärvi
Istunmäki
Töhninmäki
Ähtärinjärvi
Sumiainen
Rautalampi
Sydänmaa
Töysä
Pylkönmäki
Mahlu
Lannevesi
Äänekoski
Konnevesi
Suolahti
Alavus
Ähtäri
Inha
Vaetaiskylä
Hirvaskangas
Äijälä
Sapeli
Myllymäki
Uurainen
Hankavesi
Sahrajärvi
Hoytiä
Laukaa
Hankasalmi
Killinkoski
Multia
Tikkakoski
Liedenpohja
Vihtavuori
Toisvesi
Pihlajavesi
Leppävesi
Hankasalmi as.
Kotala
Keuruu
Kuoho
Vaajakoski
Lievestuore
Virrat
Haapamäki
Asunta
Petäjävesi
Jyväskylä
Pohjaslahti
Säynätsalo
Kutemajärvi
Keuruunselkä
Vaskivesi
Kolho
Tikkala
Muurame
Toivakka
Tarjannevesi
Visuvesi
Koskenpää
Mänttä
Korpilahti
Kangasniemi
Vilppula
Rutalahti
Ruovesi
Aurekoski
Kuorevesi
Jämsänkoski
Jyväskylä
Leivonmäki
Jäminkipohja
Lyly
Jämsä
Putkilahti
Kala
Kuru
Halli
Kaipola
Vankavesi
Luhanka
Murole
Korkeakoski
Juupajoki
Puulavesi
Luhalahti
Länsi-Teisko
Lankipohja
Joutsa
Tuukkala
Puukkonen
Viljakkala
Orivesi
Längelmäki
Suonne

Alavieska
Ylivieska
Mieluskylä
Haapavesi
Vuolijoki
Otanmäki
Mainua
Pyhäntä
Kärsämäki
Ahokylä
Nissilä
Eskola
Sievi
Järvikylä
Nivala
Maliskylä
Parkkila
Oksava
Haapajärvi
Kiiskilä
Tohólampi
Määttälä
Remeskylä
Salahmi
Sukeva
Vieremä
Jokikylä
Pyhäsalmi
Luupuvesi
Aittojärvi
Kiuruvesi
Sonkajärvi
Runni
Iisalmi
Paisua
Sykäräinen
Reisjärvi
Köyhänperä
Lestijärvi
Muurasjärvi
Pyhäjärvi
Haapamäki
Rytky
Koivujärvi
Elämäjärvi
Halsua
Yli-lesti
Alvajärvi
Kinnula
Pihtipudas
Laukkala
Vaaraslahti
Lapinlahti
Varpaisjärvi
Seläntaus
Sulkavanjärvi
Pielavesi
Onkivesi
Oksakoski
Muhola
Kolimajärvi
Perho
Keitelepohja
Keitele
Savia
Kivijärvi
Kymönkoski
Nilakka
Alapitkä
Maaninka
Pulkonkoski
Leppäselkä
Kurolanlahti
Viitasaari
Siilinjärvi
Möksy
Kyyjärvi
Talluskylä
Niinivesi
Tervo
Kallavesi
Lamperila
Vastinki
Kannonkoski
341
Vesanto
Itä-Karttula
Karstula
Soini
Pääjärvi
Ahvenisalmi
Keitele
Karttula
Syvänniemi
Kuo
Kangasaho
Virmavesi
Konginkangas
Saarijärvi
Pyhäjärvi
Kerkonkoski
Vaajasalmi
Airaksela
Istunmäki
Vehmasmäki
Pylkönmäki
Sumiainen
Iisvesi
Mahlu
Äänekoski
Konnevesi
Rautalampi
Suonenjoki
Lannevesi
Konnevesi
Vaajaskylä
Suolahti
Myllymäki
Hirvaskangas
Uurainen
Sapeli
Oravikoski
Saharjärvi
Hankavesi
Hoytia
Multia
Laukaa
Suonsaari
Haapakoski
Tikkakoski
Hankasalmi
Jäppilä
Pihlajavesi
Vihtavuori
Leppävesi
Varka
Haapamäki
Keuruu
Hankasalmi as.
Pieksämäki
Kuoho
Vaajakoski
Lievestuore
Asunta
Petäjävesi
Jyväskylä
Keruunselkä
Joroinen
Korpilahti
Säynätsalo
Virtasalmi
Kolho
Tikkala
Muurame
Kutemajärvi
Kantala
Toivakka
Mänttä
Vilppula
Koskenpää
Kaitainen
Haukivuori
Rutalahti
Kuorevesi
Jämsänkoski
Juokslahti
Kangasniemi
Lyly
Jämsä
Putkilahti
Leivonmäki
Kyyvesi
Halli
Läsäkoski
Kaipola
Kala
Korkeakoski
Luhanka
Lankipohja
Puulavesi
Puukkonen
Joutsa
Tuukkala

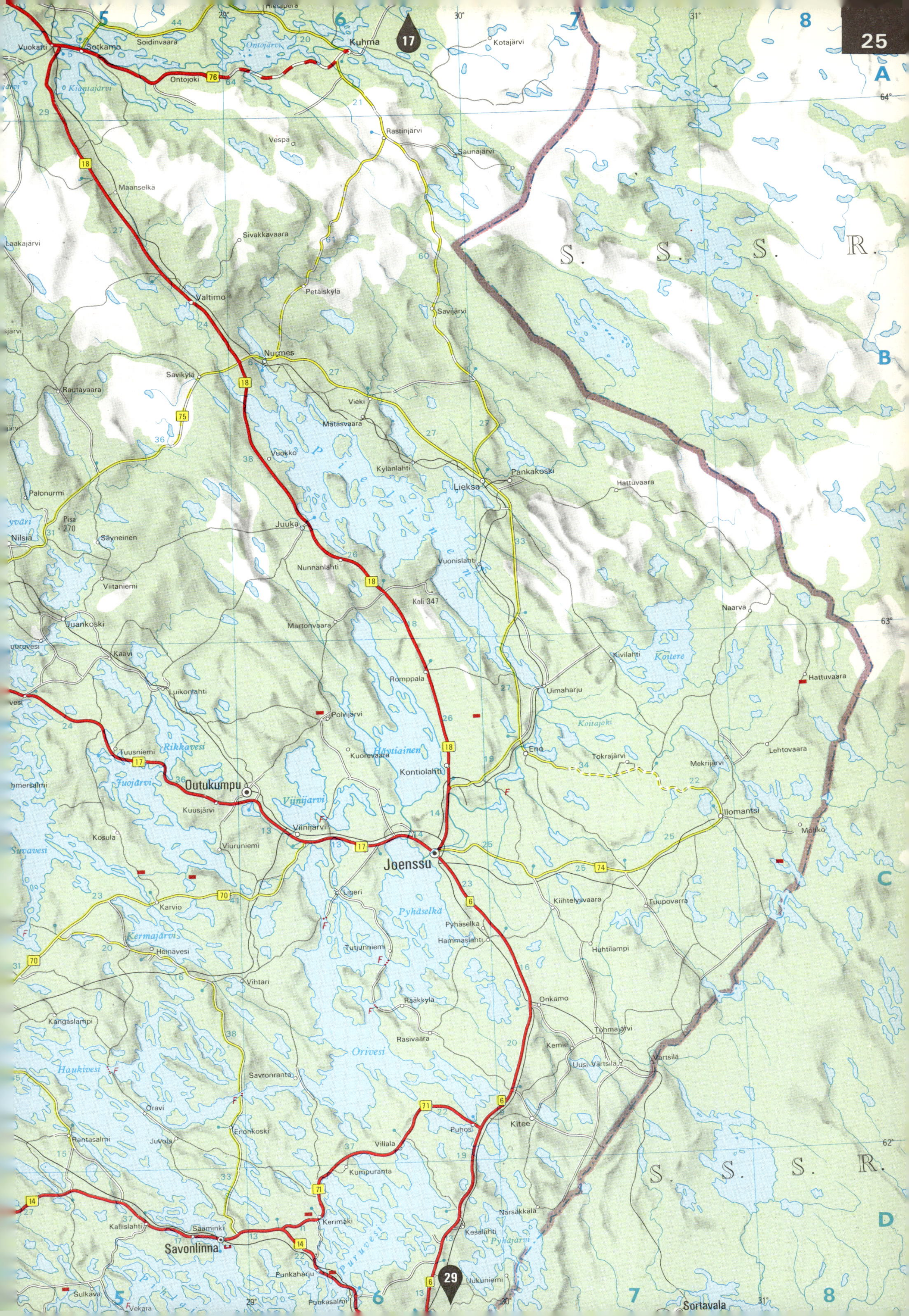

A
B
C
D
5
6
7
8
Vuokatti
Sotkamo
Soidinvaara
Ontojärvi
Kuhma
Kotajärvi
Kiantajärvi
Ontojoki
Rastinjärvi
Saunajärvi
Vespa
Maanselka
Laakajärvi
Sivakkavaara
Petäiskylä
Savijärvi
Valtimo
Nurmes
Savikylä
Rautavaara
Vieki
Mätäsvaara
Kylanlahti
Lieksa
Pankakoski
Hattuvaara
Vuokko
Pielinen
Palonurmi
Pisa 270
Nilsiä
Säyneinen
Juuka
Nunnanlahti
Vuonislahti
Koli 347
Viitaniemi
Juankoski
Martonvaara
Naarva
Kaavi
Luikonlahti
Romppala
Kivilahti
Koitere
Uimaharju
Hattuvaara
Polvijärvi
Koitajoki
Tuusniemi
Rikkavesi
Höytiainen
Kuorevaara
Eno
Tokrajärvi
Mekrijärvi
Lehtovaara
Outokumpu
Juojärvi
Kontiolahti
Viinijärvi
Kuusjärvi
Ilomantsi
Möhkö
Kosula
Viinijärvi
Viuruniemi
Joensuu
Suvavesi
Liperi
Kiihtelysvaara
Tuupovaara
Karvio
Pyhäselkä
Kermajärvi
Heinävesi
Pyhäselkä
Hammaslahti
Tutjunniemi
Huhtilampi
Vihtari
Onkamo
Kangaslampi
Rääkkylä
Rasivaara
Tohmajärvi
Kemie
Orivesi
Uusi-Vartsila
Värtsilä
Haukivesi
Savonranta
Oravi
Enonkoski
Puhos
Kitee
Rantasalmi
Juvola
Villala
Kumpuranta
Kerimäki
Närsäkkälä
Kallislahti
Sääminki
Savonlinna
Kesälahti
Pyhäjärvi
Puruvesi
Punkaharju
Uukuniemi
Sulkava
Punkasalmi
Vekara
Sortavala
S. S. S. R.
S. S. S. R.
17
29
64°
63°
62°
29°
30°
31°

POHJANLAHTI
BOTTISKA VIKEN
Åland
Ahvenanmaa
Kristiinankaupunki
Lappfjärd
Lappväärtti
Vanhakylä
Härkmeri
Isojoki
Lauhavuori
231
Ömossa
Metsälä
Jyllinkoski
Kodesjärvi
Sideby
Siipyy
Honkajoki
Riispyy
192
Merikarvia
Siikainen
Veneskoski
Köörtilä
Isojärvi
Ahlainen
Pomarkku
Reposaari
Noormarkku
Mäntyluoto
Pihlava
Ruosniemi
Saapi
Palus
Viasvesi
Pori
Ulvila
Friitala
Kokemäenjoki
Luvia
Nakkila
62
Olkiluoto
Irjanne
Eurajoki
Panelia
Kiukainen
Nurmisaari
Rauma
Lappi
Kauttua
Unaja
Kodisjoki
Nihtiö
Ihode
Hinnerjoki
Pyhämaa
Pyhäranta
Untamala
Laitila
Kalanti
Uusikaupunki
Karjala
Lokalahti
Vinkkilä
Mynämäki
Vehmaa
Mietoinen
Askainen
Kustavi
Taivassalo
Osnäs
Iniön aukko
Velkua
Naantali
Raisio
Brändö
Iniö
Rymättylä
TURKU
ÅBO
Geta
Orrdalsklint
129
Odkarby
Saltvik
Finström
Sund
Storby
Hammarland
Godby
Vårdö
Eckerö
Bomarsund
Delet
Teili
Lappvesi
Kumlinge
Skiftet
Kihti
Houtskär
Houtskari
Nagu
Nauvo
Lumparen
Jomala
Sottunga
Korpo
Korppoo
Mariehamn
Maarianhamina
Lemland
Lumparland
Degerby
Gullkrona
Kökar
Björkö
Arholma
Väto
Stockholm
19°
20°
21°
22°
62°
61°
60°
A
B
C
D
1
2
3
4
22
33
38

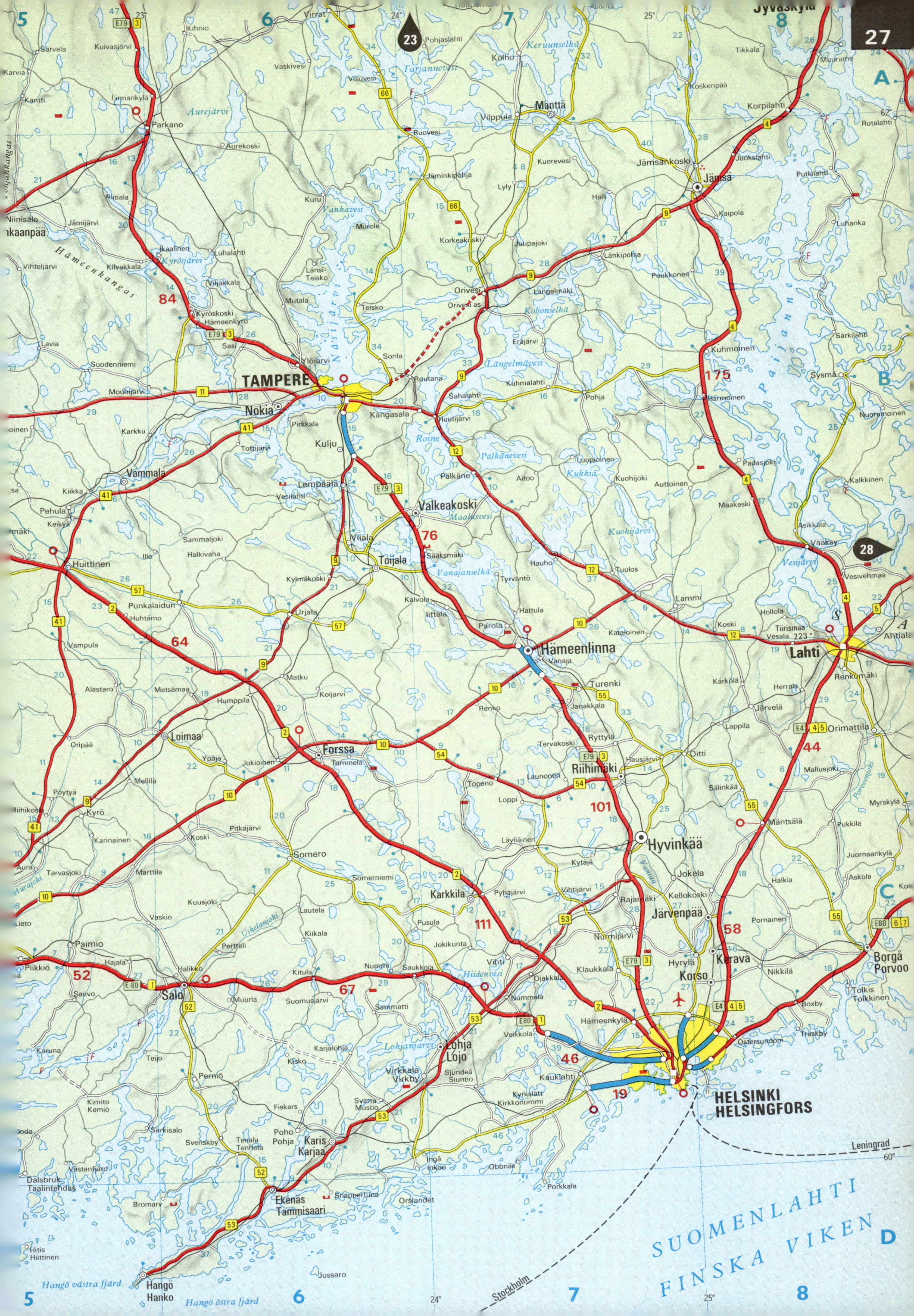
Jyväskylä
Virrat
Pohjaslahti
Keruunselkä
Kolho
Tarjannevesi
Vilppula
Mänttä
Ruovesi
Kihnio
Kuivasjärvi
Sarvela
Karvia
Kantti
Parkano
Aurejärvi
Aurekoski
Vaskivesi
Visuvesi
Jäminkipohja
Kuorevesi
Jämsänkoski
Jämsä
Koskenpää
Tikkala
Muurame
Korpilahti
Rutalahti
Jokelahti
Putkilahti
Kaipola
Luhanka
Halli
Lyly
Juupajoki
Korkeakoski
Länkipohja
Puukkonen
Orivesi
Orivesi as.
Längelmäki
Koljonselkä
Eräjärvi
Längelmävesi
Kuhmalahti
Pohja
Kuhmoinen
Harmoinen
Päijänne
Särkilahti
Sysmä
Nuoramoinen
Padasjoki
Kalkkinen
Maakeski
Asikkala
Vääksy
Vesijärvi
Vesivehmaa
Tuulos
Lammi
Hollola
Tiirismaa
Vesala
Lahti
Ahtiala
Renkomäki
Herrala
Järvelä
Orimattila
Mallusjoki
Myrskylä
Porvoonjoki
Pukkila
Mäntsälä
Juornaankylä
Askola
Halkia
Pornainen
Borgå
Porvoo
Tolkis
Tolkkinen
Boxby
Träskby
Östersundom
Kerava
Nikkilä
Korso
Hyrylä
Järvenpää
Kellokoski
Jokela
Hyvinkää
Vantaa
Kytäjä
Rajamäki
Nurmijärvi
Klaukkala
Hämeenkylä
HELSINKI
HELSINGFORS
Leningrad
SUOMENLAHTI
FINSKA VIKEN
Stockholm
Kauklahti
Kyrkslatt
Kirkkonummi
Porkkala
Obbnäs
Ingå
Inkoo
Orslandet
Jussarö
Hangö
Hanko
Hangö västra fjärd
Hangö östra fjärd
Ekenäs
Tammisaari
Snappertuna
Bromarv
Dalsbruk
Taalintehdas
Västanfjärd
Hitis
Hiittinen
Karis
Karjaa
Poho
Pohja
Tenala
Tenhola
Svensby
Särkisalo
Fiskars
Kimito
Kemiö
Svarta
Mustio
Virkkala
Vikkby
Sjundeå
Siuntio
Lohja
Lojo
Lohjanjärvi
Karjalohja
Kisko
Perniö
Teijo
Karuna
Salo
Halikko
Paimio
Piikkiö
Hajala
Sauvo
Muurla
Suomusjärvi
Kitula
Nummi
Saukkola
Sammatti
Hiidenvesi
Vihti
Ojakkala
Nummela
Veikkola
Pusula
Jokikunta
Karkkila
Pyhäjärvi
Vihtijärvi
Kiikala
Lautela
Pertteli
Uskelanjoki
Kuusjoki
Somerniemi
Somero
Pitkäjärvi
Koski
Marttila
Vaskio
Tarvasjoki
Aura
Karinainen
Kyrö
Pöytyä
Riihikoski
Oripää
Mellilä
Ypäjä
Jokioinen
Loimaa
Tammela
Forssa
Topeno
Loppi
Läyliäinen
Launonen
Riihimäki
Hausjärvi
Oitti
Sälinkää
Tervakoski
Ryttylä
Janakkala
Turenki
Renko
Vanaja
Hämeenlinna
Katalointen
Hattula
Parola
Iittala
Kalvola
Tyrväntö
Hauho
Vanajanselkä
Sääksmäki
Toijala
Viiala
Valkeakoski
Mallasvesi
Lempäälä
Vesilahti
Kylmäkoski
Urjala
Matku
Koijärvi
Humppila
Metsämaa
Alastaro
Vampula
Punkalaidun
Huhtamo
Huittinen
Ille
Halkivaha
Sammaljoki
Keikya
Pehula
Kiikka
Vammala
Tottijärvi
Karkku
Nokia
Pirkkala
Kulju
Kangasala
Huutijärvi
Roine
Pälkäne
Pälkänevesi
Aitoo
Luopioinen
Kukkia
Kuohijoki
Auttoinen
Kuohijärvi
Sahalahti
Rautana
Sorila
Teisko
TAMPERE
Ylöjärvi
Mouhijärvi
Suodenniemi
Lavia
Sasi
Kyröskoski
Hämeenkyrö
Viljakkala
Kyröjärvi
Ikaalinen
Kilvakkala
Vihteljärvi
Hämeenkangas
Jämijärvi
Niinisalo
Kankaanpää
Riitiala
Luhalahti
Länsi-Teisko
Mutala
Näsijärvi
Kuru
Vankavesi
Murole
Kärkölä
Lappila
Hämeenkangas

Jyväskylä
Vaajakoski
Pieksämäki
Keuruu
Haapamäki
Petäjävesi
Mänttä
Vilppula
Jämsä
Jämsänkoski
Orivesi
Kangasala
Kuhmoinen
Padasjoki
Sysmä
Hartola
Kangasniemi
Mikkeli
Heinola
Mäntyharju
Valkeakoski
Toijala
Hämeenlinna
Lahti
Kuusankoski
Kouvola
Riihimäki
Hyvinkää
Mäntsälä
Orimattila
Järvenpää
Kerava
Korso
Karkkila
Lohja
Lojo
Borgå
Porvoo
Loviisa
Lovisa
Kotka
Karhula
Hamina
HELSINKI
HELSINGFORS
Päijänne
Puulavesi
SALPAUS
SUOMENLAHTI
FINSKA VIKEN
Stockholm

Varkaus
Kangaslampi
Haukivesi
Joroinen
Oravi
Juvola
Enonkoski
Savonranta
Orivesi
Raakkyla
Rasivaara
Onkamo
Tohmajärvi
Kemie
Uusi-Värtsilä
Värtsilä
Kitee
Puhos
Villala
Kumpuranta
Kerimäki
Rantasalmi
Juva
Kallislahti
Sääminki
Savonlinna
Punkaharju
Puruvesi
Punkasalmi
Putikko
Akonpohja
Saari
Särkisalmi
Parikkala
Simpelejärvi
Simpele
Kesälahti
Närsäkkälä
Pyhäjärvi
Uukuniemi
Sortavala
Sulkava
Vekara
Ryhälä
Lohikoski
Vuoriniemi
Luonteri
Puumala
Lietvesi
Pohjalankila
Virmutjoki
Ruokolahti
Saimaa
Vuoksenniska
Imatra
Rauha
Savitaipale
Taipalsaari
Joutseno
Lappeenranta
Lemi
Luumäki
Simola
Haapajärvi
Nuijamaa
Vainikkala
Ylämaa
Kammenogorsk
Priozersk
S. S. S. R.
Vyborg
Vaalimaa
Sestroretsk
Kronshtadt
LENINGRAD
106
145
A
B
C
D
6
7
8
9
25
28°
29°
30°
31°
60°
61°
62°

Søreøyane
Spjelkavik
Langevåg
Storfjorden
Brandal
Hareid
Landet
Festøy
Aure
Kvalsvik
Ulsteinvik
Vartdal
Fosnavåg
Eggesbønes
Gurskøy
Stordal
Stranda
Sylte
Trollstig
850
Mongefossen
ROMS
Sande
Gursken
Leikong
Ørstavik
Kolås
Sæbø
Leknes
Overå
Eidsdal
Norddal
Tafjord
Pyttegga
1999
Stadhavet
Åram
Åtvik
Koparnes
Volda
Voldafjorden
Stadlandet
Leikanger
Folkestad
Viddal
Eagle's Road
624
Sildegapet
Vanylven
Syvde
Storfjorden
Hellesylt
Geiranger
Selje
Aheim
Austefjord
Djupvasshytta
62°
Vågsøy
Raudeberg
Djupvass
1037
Måløy
Totland
Kjølsdal
Stårheim
Hornindal
Hornindalsvatn
Strynsvatn
Videseter
Grotli
Videseter
1139
Bremangerlandet
Rugsund
Nordfjord
Nordfjordeid
Randabygd
Stryn
Loen
Hjelle
Bremanger
Oldeide
Ålfoten
Gloppen
Innvikfjorden
Innvik
Frøya
Blånibba
1672
Sandane
Utvik
Olden
Lodalskåpa
2083
Kalvåg
Frøysjøen
Svelgen
Midtgulen
Gjemmestad
Utvikfjelsl
649
Sotaseter
Hyen
Breim
Jostedalsbreen
Hovden
Norddalsfjord kpl.
Sunndal
Fåberg
Nordstedalsseter
Florø
Eikefjord
Nes
Broksdal
Åmot
Skei
Aksala
Ålhus
Jostedal
JOSTEDALEN
B
Bru
Naustdal
Jølstravatnet
Lunde
Svanøy
Vevring
Stongfjorden
Selvik
Førde
Moskog
Huldrefossen
Nes
Fortun
Skolden
Skagastølstindane
2405
Haukedal
Luster
Gaupne
Lustrafjorden
Askvoll
Holmedal
Vallestadfossen
Atløy
Dale
Bygstad
Vik
Værlandet
Hæstad
Sande
Gaular
745
Hafslo
Solvorn
Urnes
Øvre Årdal
Vettisfoss
Guddal
Øn
Vadheim
Høyanger
Hella
Dragsvik
Balholm
Leikanger
Songdalsfjøra
Hermansverk
Kaupanger
Årdalstan
Hersvik
Hyllestad
Kyrkjebø
Vangsnes
Revsnes
Sula
Leirvik
Lavik
Sognefjorden
Svartemyr
Ortnevik
Rinde (Feios)
Kvamsøy
Lærdalsøyri
Solund
Rutledal
Bjordal
Viksøyri
Fresvik
Aurlandsfjorden
Husøy
Borgund
Sognesjøen
Brekke
Arnafjord
Tønjum
LÆRDAL
61°
Eivindvik
Vikafjell
1281
Mjømna
Solheim
Skjelingsvatn
986
Nærøy
Undredal
Aurlandsvangen
Frøyset
Matre
Gudvangen
Gullbrå
Stalheim
Flåm
Stonndalen
Jungsdalsh
Fedje
Fensfjorden
Vinje
Masfjorden
Austrheim
Eksingedal
Lindås
Myrdal
Mjølfjell
Geiteryggshytta
Hordabø
Radøy
Myking
Vike
Raundal
Hjelme
Lindås-Halvøya
Stamnes
Evanger
Raggsteinhytta
Alvøy
Manger
Seim
Tysse
Bulken
Voss
Hallingskeid
Holsnøy
Alversund
Hosanger
Dale
Mønshaug
Finse
Hallingskar
Blomvåg
Osterøya
Granvin
Ulvik
Hardanger-
1862
jøkulen
C
Salhus
Lonevåg
Vaksdal
Eide
Ytre Arna
Kvanndal
Haugastøl
Solsvik
Herdla
Haus
Eidsvåg
Arna
Trengereid
Eidfjord
BERGEN
Espeland
Norheimsund
Øystese
Indre Ålvik
Utne
Haukeland
Tysse
129
Kinsarvik
Hardangervidda
1250
Fagernes
Askøy
Vikøy
Viveli
Dyranut
Store Sotra
Nesttun
Herand
Lofthus
Hardangervid
Telavåg
Strandebarm
Ullensvang
Fana
Sørfjorden
Fyllestøen
Eikelandsosen
Jondal
Hallaskar
Rauhellern
Holdhus
Osøyra
Fusa
Hårteigen
1691
Sandhaug
Krossfjorden
Strandvik
Sævareid
Folgefonn
Austevoll
Bjørnafjorden
Varaldsøy
Tyssedal
Bjornesfjorden
Hardangerfjorden
Litlos
Huftarøy
Gjermundshamn
Hatlestrand
Tysnes
Odda
Møkster
Tysnesøy
Løfallstrand
Moger
Selbjørn
Kvinnherad
Ølve
Tynemouth
60°
5°
6°
7°
1
2
3
4
A
B
C
D
18
34

Dovrefjell
Dovrefjell 1026
Snøhetta 2286
Høgstegia 1633
Drivstua
Kongsvoll
Hjerkinn
Borkhusseter
Finnset
Aursjøen
Lesjaskog
Lesjaverk
Lora
Lesja
Sjungseter
Vålåsjø
Fokstua
Dombås
Kjølen
Nyseter
Dovre
Rondane
Rondeslottet 2183
Grimsdalshytta
Dalen
Folldals verk
Krokhaug
Savalen
Vingelen
Tolga
Hodal
Narbuvollen
Tynset
Brydal
Tylldal
Alvdal
Holøydal
Elgepiggen 1604
Spekedalssetra
Hoggsetvollen
Isteren
Barkald
Unset
Fiskevollen
Øvre Rendal
Sølnsjøen
Misterdalseter
Søln 1755
Østerdalen
Hanestad
Atna
Ytre Rendal
Asheim
Elvåseter
Koppang
Stor-Elvdal
Storsjøen
Sjøli
Evenstad
Deset
Strand
Steinvik
Rena
Åsta
Øksna
Glåma
Elverum
Nordberg
Skjåk
Ottadalen
Lom
Garmo
Otta
Vågåmo
Brennhaug
Nord-Sel
Lalm
Sel
Heidal
Mysuseter
Rondablikk
Nesset
Enden
Sollia
Storfjellseter
Randsverk
Bøverdalen
Glittertind 2470
Galdhøpiggen 2469
Jotunheimen
Leirvassbu
Sjoa
Kvam
Vinstra
Kvikne
Venabygd
Hundorp
Ringebu
Store Kvien 1350
Gudbrandsdalen
Skåbu
Golå
Fåvang
Gjendesheim
Sikilsdalseter
Dalseter
Storhøliseter
Fagerhøi
Knutsholstind 2340
Valdresflyene 1640
Bygdin
Vinstervatn
Vassenden
Svatsum
Tretten
Øyer
Hornsjø
Segalstad bru
Follebu
Fåberg
Vestre Gausdal
Gausdal
Liomseter
Dokka
Beitostølen
Lidar
Hugostua
Hensås
Hurum
Øye
Vang
Heggenes
Vestre Slidre
Rogne
Lillehammer
Mesnalien
Vingnes
Stavseng
Synnfjell 1414
Brøttum
Åsmark
Biri
Hemsedal 1137
Ulnes
Fagernes
Leira
Valdres
Flatøydegard
Åmot
Kinn
Moelv
Ringsaker
Brumunddal
Redalen
Bjøberg
Hemsil
Hemsedal
Lykkja
Hovda
Aurdal
Bruflat
Reinli
Tonsåsen
Sanderstølen
Nykirke
Dokka
Nordsinni
Segård
Hamar
Vangsås
Løten
Ådalsbruk
Stavsjø
Nes
Sandvika
Gjøvik
Hunndalen
Fredheim
Raufoss
Bagn
Fluberg
Stange
Vallset
Leveld
Herad
Gol
Hallingdal
Hov
Holmen
Skute
Reinsvoll
Lena
Kolbu
Skreia
Mjøsa
Tangen
Espa
Hovet
Ål
Torpo
Begndalen
Hedal
Eina
Toten
Hol
Nesbyen
Nes
Enger
Strandlykkja
Geilo 1010
Myking
Bøvertnes
Storrustefjell 1216
Sørum
Feiring
Flatåker
Tunnhovd
Viker (Ådal)
Røykenvik
Brandbu
Jaren
Hurdalssjøen
Hurdal
Langset
1063
Dagali
Flå
Gulsvik
Sperillen
Randsfjorden
Gran
Eidsvoll
Sundet
Styri
Tunnhovdfjorden
Grymyr
Hadeland
Lunner
Råholt
Nygard
Brøstrud
Krøderen
Ørgenvika
Roa
Dal
Solheimsstøl
Uvdal
Veikåker
Sokna
Hval
Grua
Rud
Romerike
Bjørkeflåta
Rødberg
Eggedal
Veme
Hen
Jevnaker
Gardermoen
Vormsund
Numedal
Hønefoss
Viul
Harestua
Jessheim
Mårvatn
Nore
Krødsherad
Norderhov
Ringerike
Nordmarka
Krøderen
Tyristrand
Åneby
Nittedal
Kløfta
Glomma
Kalhovd
Sigdal
Bønsnes
Lørenfallet
Rånåsfoss
Austbygda
Veggli
Rollag
Snarum
Rud
Tyrifjorden
Sollihøgda
Skedsmokorset
Sørumsand
Lillestrøm
Fetsund
Oslo
Grorud
Vikersund
Vatnås
Atrå
Otta
Lågen
Begna
Dokka
Savalen
Hemsil
Glåma
Vorma
Soln
226
104
182
28
19
32
35
5
6
7
8
A
B
C
D
62°
61°
60°
9°
10°
11°

HÄRJEDALEN
ØSTERDALEN
NORGE
SOLØR
ROMERIKE
TOTEN
DALARNA
ÄLVDALEN
Tiomilaskogen
Långfjället
1204
Fulufjället
1040
Transtrandsfjällen
Femunden
Rogen
Lossnen
Isteren
Sølnsjøen
Storsjøen
Ossjøen
Höljessjön
Tisjön
Venjansjön
Trängsletsjön
Lofssjön
Mjøsa
Hurdalssjøen
Övre Fryken
Glåma
Østerdalälven
Västerdalälven
Rotälven
Tolga
Vingelen
Hodal
Narbuvollen
Tufsingdalen
Sørvika
Skedbrokåtan
Tännäs
Långå
Hede
Hedeviken
Norra Hede
Vemdalen
Ljusnan
Tynset
Savalen
Brydal
Tylldal
Holøydal
Elgepiggen
1604
Spekedalssetra
Svukuriset
Elgå
Sømådal
Valdalen
Högvålen
Rånddalen
Sörvattnet
Lofsdalen
Linsell
Hoggsetvollen
Barkald
Unset
Fiskevollen
Øvre Rendal
Misterdalseter
Søln
1755
Drevsjø
Flötningen
Idre
Lillhärdal
Hanestad
Ytre Rendal
Atna
Engerdal
Herjehogna
1172
Elvdal
Särnaheden
Särna
Åsheim
Elvåseter
Koppang
Stor-Elvdal
Sjøli
Storvarden
821
Krackelbäcken
Evenstad
Jordet
Nornäs
Sörsjön
Ljørdal
Deset
Trysil
Trängslet
Strand
Nordre Osen
Nybergsund
Grundforsen
Åsen
Brunnsberg
Steinvik
Østby
Rot
Kåtilla
Älvdalen
Västermyckeläng
Rena
Søndre Osen
Sälen
Mesnalien
Tørberget
Plassen
Rörbäcksnäs
Evertsberg
Åsta
Transtrand
Mångsbodarna
Nedreberg
Långflon
Moelv
Bingsaker
Brumunddal
Øksna
Hernes
Lima
Venjan
Elverum
Gravberget
Norra Finnskoga
Höljes
Limedsforsen
Vangsås
Løten
Hamar
Stavsjø
Gjøvik
Heradsbygd
Sandvika
Nes
Adalsbruk
Kapp
Stange
Vallset
Braskereidfoss
Finnskog
Sysslebäck
Öje
Lena
Kolbu
Skreia
Våler
Gjesås
Sønsterud
Södra Finnskoga
Malungsfors
Vallerås
Gårdås
Malung
Gävunda
Tangen
Espa
Flisa
Dalby
Långav
Likenäs
Arneberg
Dulpetorpet
Yttermalung
Strandlykkja
Feiring
Namnå
Ambjörby
Appelbo
Bruvoll
Kirkenær
Nyskoga
Hurdal
Langset
Mo
Grue
Svulrya
Stöllet
Norra Ny
Opsahedan
Nord-Odal
Eidsvoll
Sundet
Styri
Råholt
Nygård
Oppstad
Brandval
Lunderseter
Vitsand
Tyngsjö kapell
Rud
Dal
Roverud
Östmark
Gardermoen
Skarnes
Kongsvinger
Vormsund
Jessheim
Lekvattnet
Kyrkheden
Ekshärad
Årnes
Klofta
Austmarka
Oleby
Torsby
Gustav Adolf
Skedsmokorset
Lørenfallet
Rånåsfoss
Eidskog
Bogen
Sørumsand
Lillestrøm
Mengen
Skotterud
Lysvik
Edebäck
Hagfors
Uddeholm
Råda
Rämmen
62°
12°
13°
14°
11°
104

Rätansbyn
Överturingen
Holmsjön
Östavall
Ljungaverk
Ljungan
Stöde
Stödesjön
Sundsvall
Tunadal
Alvik
Selånger
Ankarsvik
Sundsvallsbukten
Vaasa
Pori
Matfors
Attmar
Stockvik
Svartvik
Essvik
Kvissleby
Skottsund
Lucksta
Njurundabommen
Njurunda
Havern
Norrberg
Naggen
Överhogdal
Brämön
Galtström
Kölsjön
Malungen
Ytterhogdal
Ramsjö
Hassela
Byn
Gnarp
Älvros
Hennan
Brännås
Storsjön
Älgered
Bergsjö
Jättendal
Ängersjö
Kårböle
Ljusnan
Strömbacka
Norra Dellen
Harmånger
Stocka
Friggesund
Ilsbo
Strömsbruk
Tallåsen
Ljusdal
Norrbo
Bjuråker
Fågelsjö
Korskrogen
Färila
Hybo
Delsbo
Rogsta
Södra Dellen
Näsviken
Forsa
Sörforsa
Sanne
Hudiksvall
Hornslandet
Los
Järvsö
Tandsjöborg
Hamra
H Ä L S I N G L A N D
Iggesund
Undersvik
Nianfors
Njutånger
Nordsjö
Agön
Vallsta
Enånger
Arbrå
Mattsmyra
BOTTENHAVET
Kvarnberg
Lottefors
Trönö
Edsbyn
Roteberg
Rengsjö
Norrala
Ovanåker
Bollnäs
Voxna
Runemo
Söderhamn
Viksjöfors
Alfta
Mo
Söderala
R I G E
Emådalen
Segersta
Marmaverken
Sandarne
Vannsätter
Bergvik
Annefors
Kilafors
Ljusne
Vallvik
Sibo
Bergviken
Dalfors
Skog
Hälsingskogen
Skattungbyn
Furudal
Kallmora
Östanvik
Amungen
Holmsveden
Hansjö
Stackmora
Orsa
Slättberg
Ore
Orsasjön
Arvet
Gruvberget
Digerberget
Katrineberg
Axmarsbruk
Gulleråsen
Svabensverk
Lingbo
Östnor
Bingsjö
Mora
Färnäs
Boda
Ljugaren
Axmarby
Vinäs
Åmot
Nusnäs
Röjeråsen
Bergby
Norrsundet
Vikarbyn
Backa
Hagsta
Hamrångefjärden
Gärdsjö
Ockelbo
Garsås
Rättvik
Svartnäs
Ryssa
Sollerön
Söderås
Gesunda
Siljan
Övertänger
Jädraås
Trödje
Tällberg
Vintjärn
Hjortnäs
Enviken
G Ä S T R I K L A N D
Björke
Siljansnäs
Linghed
Svärdsjö
Åbyggeby
Bjursås
Lumsheden
Jarbo
Gävlebukten
Alvik
Leksand
Ullvi
Västanvik
Bengtsheden
Jäderfors
Högbo
Gävle
Skutskär
Sågmyra
Grycksbo
Åshammar
Sandviken
Valbo
Gårdskär
Djura
Insjön
Kungsgården
Forsbacka
Sundborn
Storvik
Älvkarleby
Hedby
Gagnef
Bäckehagen
Falun
Stensätra
Älvkarleö bruk
Karlholm
Korsnäs
Robertsholm
Storsjön
Djurås
Djurmo
Hofors
Årsunda
Marma
Storfjärden
Ornäs
Runn
Bäsna
Vika
Torsåker
Mehedeby
Dala-Floda
Brötjärna
Mockfjärd
Borlänge
Åkerby
Björbo
Långshyttan
Hedesunda
Strömsberg
Romme
St. Skedvi
Stjärnsund
Söderfors
Tolfta
Halvarsgårdarna
Nagiarby
Solvarbo
Dala-Husby
Tierp
Idkerberget
Moraby
Hedesundafjärdarna
Säter
Bispberg
Garpenberg
Österfärnebo
Gysinge
Tuna Hästberg
Västerby
Horndal
Nyhammar
Vikmanshyttan
Hedemora
Hede
Färnebofjärden
Örbyhus
Grangärde
Månkarbo
Östervåla
Sunnansjö
Fors
Dalälven
Brunnsvik
Håksberg
Tärnsjö
Tämnaren
Vendel
Väsman
Säfsnäs
Saxdalen
Gonäs
Smedjebacken
Avesta
Folkärna
Harbo
Viksta
Blötberget
Ludvika
Krylbo
Möklinta
Huddunge
Björklinge
Grängesberg
Söderbärke
Norberg
Yxsjöberg
Hörken
Vad
Fagersta
Karbenning
Runhällen
Broddbo

Hardangervidda
30
Folgefonn
Sørfjorden
Hardangerfjorden
Bjørnafjorden
Boknafjorden
Rjuven
NJARDARHEIM VEIDEMARK
SETESDAL
Haukelifjell
JÆREN
DALANE
Lysefjorden
Høgsfjorden
Lundevatn
Sirdalsvatn
Listafjorden
Byglandsfjorden
Totak
Songavatn
Møsvatn
Fyresvatn
Bjornesfjorden
Krossfjorden
Bømlafjorden
Nesttun
Fana
Sygteland
Osøyra
Fusa
Strandvik
Strandebarm
Eikelandsosen
Holdhus
Sævareid
Varaldsøy
Jondal
Herand
Ullensvang
Tyssedal
Odda
Skare
Røldal
Hårteigen 1691
Litlos
Hallaskar
Sandhaug
Rauhellern
Mogen
Austevoll
Huftarøy
Møkster
Selbjørn
Tysnesøy
Tysnes
Gjermundshamn
Hatlestrand
Løfallstrand
Kvinnherad
Ølve
Onarheim
Uskedal
Fitjar
Jektevik
Stord
Husnes
Rubbestadneset
Bremnes
Bømlo
Litlabø
Leirvik
Sunde
Sæbøvik
Halsnøy
Lukker
Skånevik
Åkra
Fjæra
Lykling
Mosterhamn
Valevåg
Valestrand
Utbjoa
Etne
Saudasjøen
Sauda
Nesflaten
Bømlo
Espevær
Førde
Buavag
Austre Vikebygd
Ølen
Sandeid
Sveio
Skjold
Vikedal
Imsland
Sand
Suldal
Solheimsvik
Snønuten 1605
Haugesund
Førde
Vårenes
Visnes
Utvik
Fiskå
Tysvær
Nedstrand
Stranda
Jelsa
Erfjord
Ullatun
Vedavågen
Kopervik
Åkrehamn
Karmøy
Vestre Bokn
Ombo
Hjelmelandsvågen
Vindsvik
Vadla
Tøtlandsvik
Blåfjellhytta
Skudeneshavn
Finnøy
Hesby
Rennesøy
Utstein kloster
Vikevåg
Talgje
Fiskå
Årdal
Nilsebu
Ystebøhamn
Mosterøy
Tau
Jørpeland
Lysebotn
Randaberg
Hundvåg
Stavanger
Vaulen
Sola
Hommersåk
Oanes
Forsand
Espedal
Adneram
Fidjeland
Øyuvsbu
Sandnes
Ganddal
Lauvvik
Helle
Dirdal
Oltedal
Sinnes
Figgjo
Klepp
Ålgård
Bryne
Orre
Øvre Sirdal
Øvrebygd
Nærbø
Bue
Varhaug
Vigrestad
Bjerkreim
Tonstad
Haughom
Knaben
Netlandsnes
Ogna
Sirevåg
Hellvik
Egersund
Eigerøya
Helleland
Heskestad
Moi
Gyland
Sira
Kvinlog
Eiken
Grindheim
Hauge
Sokndal
Åna-Sira
Flekkefjord
Loga
Kvinesdal
Øye
Kirkehamn
Lista
Herad
Vanse
Vestbygd
Farsund
Spind
Lyngdal
Rom
Spangereid
Lindesnes
Vigeland
Mandal
Holum
Øyslebø
Vigmostad
Laudal
Konsmo
Kvås
Hægebostad
Bjelland
Finsland
Åseral
Ljosland
Åkernes
Evje
Hornnes
Grendi
Byglandsfjord
Bygland
Sandnes
Austad
Hylestad
Valle
Flateland
Bykle
Hovden
Bjåen
Haukeligrend
Edland
Grungedal
Rauland
Vinje
Åmot
Børte
Nesland
Mo
Dalen
Skafså
Vrålio
Veum
Sundsb
Hægeland
Vikeland
Kvarstein
Venne
Mosby
Greipstad
Søgne
Høllen
Mebø
Kristi
Vegu
Mårb
Mårv
Tynemouth
Harwich
E76
E18
59
120
16
240
17
11
5
6
7
8
60°
59°
58°
A
B
C
D
1
2
3

HADELAND
Krøderen
Tunnhovdfjorden
NUMEDAL
Hønefoss
RINGERIKE
NORDMARKA
ROMERIKE
Tyrifjorden
Lillestrøm
Strømmen
Lørenskog
OSLO
Grorud
Jessheim
Gardermoen
Øyeren
Rjukan
Tinnsjø
Gausta 1883
Blefjell
Kongsberg
Drammen
Mjøndalen
Hokksund
Vestfossen
Asker
Eikeren
Notodden
Skrimfjella
Lifjell
Holmestrand
Horten
Moss
Askim
Mysen
Ski
Drøbak
Sarpsborg
Fredrikstad
Halden
Tønsberg
Sandefjord
Larvik
Stavern
Skien
Porsgrunn
Brevik
Norsjø
Nisser
Kragerø
Risør
Tvedestrand
Arendal
Grimstad
Lillesand
Strömstad
Tanumshede
Lysekil
Smögen
Kungshamn
Skagerak
Hirtshals
Frederikshavn
København
Kiel

TOTEN
SOLØR
HADELAND
ROMERIKE
RINGERIKE
NORDMARKA
EDASKOG
DALSLAND
BOHUSLÄN
Krøderen
Sperillen
Randsfjorden
Hurdalssjøen
Storsjøen
Tyrifjorden
Øyeren
Glåfsfjorden
Stora Gla
Foxen
V. Silen
Ö. Silen
Lelång
Stora Le
Eikeren
Skrimfjella
Kynnefjäll
Kroppefjäll
Storrustefjell 1216
Hønefoss
Kongsvinger
Lillestrøm
Strømmen
Lørenskog
OSLO
Drammen
Kongsberg
Holmestrand
Horten
Moss
Tønsberg
Sandefjord
Larvik
Skien
Porsgrunn
Sarpsborg
Fredrikstad
Halden
Askim
Arvika
Strömstad
Uddevalla
Vänersborg
Trollhättan
Orust
Lysekil
Eidsvoll
Jessheim
Gran
Roa
Grua
Asker
Sandvika
Ski
Mysen
Ørje
Rakkestad
Årjäng
Charlottenberg
Eda glasbruk
Bengtsfors
Billingsfors
Ed
Tanumshede
Munkedal
Mellerud
Kungshamn
Smögen
Stavern
Brevik
Langesund
Frederikshavn
København
Kiel
E6
E18
E68
E76
104
182
223
28
25
114
21
72
76
26
103
117
153
31
35
41
A
B
C
1
2
3
4
10°
11°
12°
59°
60°

32
33
38
39
42
43
ÄLVDALEN
Tiomilaskogen
BERGSLAGEN
VÄRMLAND
VÄSTMANLAND
KÄGLAN
REKARNE
NÄRKE
Kilsbergen
Tiveden
ÖSTERGÖTLAND
Hålaveden
Järnlunden
Vänern
Vättern
Hjälmaren
Väsman
Yngen
Skagern
Unden
Viken
Boren
Roxen
Glan
Täkern
Tisnaren
Runn
Mellan-Fryken
Övre Fryken
Kinneviken
Dala-Järna
Vansbro
Borlänge
Säter
Hedemora
Avesta
Ludvika
Smedjebacken
Grängesberg
Norberg
Fagersta
Hagfors
Torsby
Sunne
Munkfors
Filipstad
Hällefors
Grythyttan
Lindesberg
Nora
Hallstahammar
Köping
Arboga
Kungsör
Karlstad
Kristinehamn
Karlskoga
Degerfors
Örebro
Kumla
Hallsberg
Laxå
Askersund
Grums
Skoghall
Forshaga
Kil
Mariestad
Lidköping
Skövde
Skara
Falköping
Tidaholm
Tibro
Hjo
Karlsborg
Motala
Vadstena
Mjölby
Linköping
Norrköping
Finspång
Atvidaberg
Katrineholm
Kållandsö
Torsö
Hova
Töreboda
Gullspång
Storfors
Säffle
Åmål
Ödeshög
Skänninge
Boxholm

Gävle
Uppsala
Västerås
Sandviken
Falun
Borlänge
Enköping
Sala
Norrtälje
Hofors
Avesta
Hedemora
Ludvika
Fagersta
Norberg
Smedjebacken
Grängesberg
Säter
Östhammar
Tierp
Skutskär
Sigtuna
Märsta
Hallstahammar
Surahammar
Lindesberg
Storvik
Valbo
Leksand
Rättvik
Gräsö
Singö
Storfjärden
Runn
Siljan
Dalälven
Gävlebukten
Lövstabukten
Öregrundsgrepen
Södra Kvarken
Ålands hav
GÄSTRIKLAND
UPPLAND
VÄSTMANLAND
FJÄRDHUNDRA
E4
E18
33
26

STOCKHOLM
GOTLAND
SÖDERMANLAND
ÖSTERGÖTLAND
SÖDERTÖRN
VIKBOLANDET
KINDA
REKARNE
KÅGLAN
NÄRKE
Hjälmaren
Roxen
Glan
Yxningen
Sommen
Bråviken
Krabbfjärden
Södertälje
Nyköping
Norrköping
Linköping
Eskilstuna
Örebro
Arboga
Strängnäs
Katrineholm
Flen
Finspång
Motala
Mjölby
Åtvidaberg
Tranås
Söderköping
Nynäshamn
Oxelösund
Trosa
Gnesta
Kumla
Hallsberg
Askersund
Vadstena
Visby
Slite
Hemse
Klintehamn
Ljugarn
Fårö
Fårösund
Västervik
Oskarshamn
Kappelshamn
Helsinki
Lübeck
Kilsbergen
Tumba
Tullinge
Saltsjöbaden
Runmarö
Nämdö
Utö
Ornö
Torö
Gamleby
Valdemarsvik
Kisa
Ödeshög
Vingåker
Malmköping
Mariefred
Kungsör
Hallstahammar
Gustavsberg
St. Möja

N O R G E
Vegusdal
Herefoss
Froland
Austre Moland
Stokken
Eydehamn
Kongshamn
Arendal
Tromøy
Blakstad
Rygene
Fevik
Spedalen
Grimstad
Hægeland
Finsland
Birkeland
Vennesla
Vikeland
Kvarstein
Eide
Lillesand
Mosby
Brekkestø
Høvåg
Greipstad
Søgne
Kristiansand
Høllen
Mebø
Skålevik
Tynemouth
Harwich
Leith
Immingham
Tilbury
Larvik
Oslo
S k a g e r a k
Gammel Skagen
Grenen
Skagen
Hulsig
Tannis Bugt
Ålbæk
Ålbæk Bugt
Hirtshals
Tversted
Nr. Bindslev
Tornby
Jerup
Strandby
Lønstrup
Hjørring
Sindal
Kvissel
Frederikshavn
Lendum
Tårs
Løkken
Børglum
Vrå
Vrejlev
Hørby Stby
Sæby
V E N D S Y S S E L
Jerslev
Læsø Rende
Brønderslev
Blokhus
Dybvad
Jammerbugt
Pandrup
Hellevad
Kås
Åbybro
Tylstrup
Hjallerup
Vorså
Dronninglund
Biersted
Vadum
Aså
Hanstholm
Vigsø Bugt
Torup
Fjerritslev
Halvrimmen
Brovst
Nørresundby
Vodskov
Frøstrup
Torslev
Ulsted
Klitmøller
Nors
Østerild
Gøl
Ålborg
Gandrup
Aggersund
Vorupør
Sjørring
Thisted
Løgstør
Nibe
Svenstrup
Gistrup
Mov
Hals
Limfjorden
T H Y
Sejerslev
Ranum
Ør Hornum
Snedsted
Sundby
Støvring
Sønder Kongerslev
Overlade
Hornum
Bested
Mors
Nykøbing
Ertebølle
Suldrup
Bælum
Ålborg Bugt
Agger
Karby
Glyngøre
Farsø
Års
Skørping
Terndrup
Vestervig
Hurup
Vils
Durup
Rold
Arden Stby
Ør. Hurup
Thyborøn
Ydby
Roslev
Hvalpsund
H I M M E R L A N D
Ålestrup
St. Rørbæk
Skelund
Hadsund
Nissum Bredning
Harboør
Hvidbjerg
Rødding
Jebjerg
Gedsted
Lovns Bredning
Ove
Mariager Fjord
Havndal
Assens
Hobro
Odby
Møldrup
Mariager
Randers Fjord
Lem
Gjerlev
Lemvig
Nørre Nissum
Humlum Stby
Venø Bugt
Skive
Ranbjerg
Højslev Stby
Skals
Klejtrup
Øster Tørslev
Holbæk
Ramme
Struer
Fårup
Hammershøj
Ørsted
Vinderup
Sevel
Stoholm
Sparkær
Ørum
Fjellerup
Bøvlingbjerg
Bækmarksbro
Hjerm
Viborg
Hornbæk
Randers
DJURSL
Torsminde
Nissum Fjord
Vemb
Holstebro
Skave
Hald
Bjerringbro
Langå
Allingåbro
Auning
Nimtofte
H A R S Y S S E L
Storå
Fredeniks
Rødkærsbro
Ulstrup
Ryomgård
Kolind
Husby
Ulfborg
Karup
D A N M A R K
Hadsten
Hornslet
Mørke
Rønde
Avlum
Kølvrå
Kjellerup
Ans
Hammel
Hinnerup
Kalø Vig
Tirstrup
Ørnhøj
J Y L L A N D
Vildbjerg
Sunds
Lystrup
Tim Stby
Bording
Ebeltoft Vig
Herning
Ikast
Silkeborg
Engesvang
Brabrand
ÅRHUS
Ebeltoft
Spjald
Snejbjerg
Hammerum
Virklund
Svejbæk
Galten
Videbæk
Ringkøbing
57°
58°
8°
9°
10°

Kattegat
Læsø
Østerbyhavn
Anholt
BOHUSLÄN
VÄSTERGÖTLAND
SJUHÄRADSBYGDEN
FINNVEDEN
SUNNERBO
GÖINGE
Hallandsås
Laholmsbukten
Skälderviken
Kungsbackafjord
Lygnern
Mjörn
Dalbosjön
Vidöstern
Bolmen
Nissan
Lagan
Hökensås
GÖTEBORG
Mölndal
Kungälv
Uddevalla
Trollhättan
Vänersborg
Lidköping
Skara
Skövde
Falköping
Tidaholm
Alingsås
Borås
Ulricehamn
Jönköping
Kungsbacka
Varberg
Falkenberg
Halmstad
Laholm
Båstad
Ängelholm
Höganäs
Klippan
Hässleholm
Ljungby
Värnamo
Gislaved
Markaryd
Orust
Tjörn
Stenungsund
Lysekil
Munkedal
Smögen
Kungshamn
Marstrand
Lerum
Vårgårda
Herrljunga
Svenljunga
Tranemo
Kinna
Skene
Hyltebruk
Oskarström
Smålandsstenar
Mullsjö
Götene
Hunnebostrand
Ljungskile
Lilla Edet
Surte
Landvetter
Härryda
Bollebygd
Kållered
Lindome
Åsa
Frillesås
Väröbacka
Getinge
Torekov
Munka-Ljungby
Örkelljunga
Åstorp
Perstorp
Gilleleje
Hundested
København
Rörö
Öckerö
Hönö
Torslanda
Styrsö
Vrångö
Särö
Onsala
Tvååker
Glommen
Mjöback
Anderstorp
Vaggeryd
Bottnaryd
Norrahammar
Taberg
Dalstorp
Hillerstorp
Reftele
Bredaryd
Skillingaryd
Hamneda
Strömsnäsbruk
Vittsjö
Bjärnum
Tyringe
Ekeby
Vinninge
Varnhem
Skultorp
Stenstorp
Vara
Grästorp
Nossebro
Floby
Vartofta
Kinnarp
Tibro
Blikstorp
Fristad
Sandared
Viskafors
Fritsla
Horred
Veddige
Ullared
Fegen
Kinnared
Torup
Rydöbruk
Sennan
Simlångsdalen
Knäred
Veinge
Skottorp
Vejbystrand
Förslövsholm
Grevie
Jonstorp
Mölle
Kvidinge
Tånga
Odåkra
Tormestorp
E6
E3
E4
20
26
40
41
42
44
45
153
154
155
156
157
158
160
162
163
167
172
173
180
182
183
185
186
187
193
194
200
235
69
75
19
27
67
14
178
86
119
5
6
7
8
36
37
42
45
A
B
C

36
37
41
43
46
A
B
C
1
2
3
BOHUSLÄN
VÄSTERGÖTLAND
SJUHÄRADS BYGDEN
FINNVEDEN
SUNNERBO
GÖINGE
Kattegat
Hake fjord
Mjörn
Lygnern
Kungsbackafjord
Nissan
Bolmen
Vidöstern
Lagan
Laholmsbukten
Skälderviken
Hallandsås
Munkedal
Smögen
Kungshamn
Lysekil
Uddevalla
Vänersborg
Vargon
Trollhättan
Orust
Tjörn
Stenungsund
Ljungskile
Lilla Edet
Marstrand
Kungälv
Ytterby
Surte
Alingsås
Lerum
Floda
GÖTEBORG
Mölndal
Kållered
Lindome
Kungsbacka
Öckerö
Torslanda
Hönö
Styrsö
Vrångö
Åsa
Frillesås
Väröbacka
Varberg
Träslövsläge
Falkenberg
Halmstad
Laholm
Båstad
Ängelholm
Höganäs
Helsingborg
Helsingør
Hälsingborg
Borås
Fristad
Ulricehamn
Jönköping
Falköping
Skövde
Skara
Tidaholm
Vårgårda
Herrljunga
Sjömarken
Sandared
Kinna
Skene
Svenljunga
Tranemo
Gislaved
Anderstorp
Värnamo
Ljungby
Markaryd
Hässleholm
Klippan
Åstorp
Perstorp
Osby
Kristianstad
Skånes-Fagerhult
Hyltebruk
Smålandsstenar
Oskarström
Getinge
Simlångsdalen
Torup
Knäred
Veinge
Örkelljunga
Munka-Ljungby
Læsø
Østerbyhavn
Anholt
Frederikshavn
Leith
Oslo
Kiel
Grenå
Hundested
København
Gilleleje
Hornbæk
Tisvildeleje
Græsted
E6
E3
E4
69
75
19
27
14
67
86
178
119
9
58°
57°
56°
11°
12°
13°
14°

Linköping
Söderköping
Vadstena
Skänninge
Mjölby
Boxholm
Tranås
ÖSTERGÖTLAND
Åtvidaberg
Valdemarsvik
KINDA
Kisa
Överum
Gamleby
Västervik
Vimmerby
Eksjö
Nässjö
Hultsfred
Vetlanda
NJUDUNG
SMÅLAND
Oskarshamn
Högsby
Mönsterås
Lenhovda
Växjö
Alvesta
VÄREND
Nybro
Kalmar
Färjestaden
ÖLAND
Borgholm
Böda
Emmaboda
MÖRE
Tingsryd
Ronneby
Karlskrona
Karlshamn
Olofström
Sölvesborg
Lyckeby
Kalmar sund
Sommen
Åsunden
Yxningen
Roxen
Tåkern
Hålaveden
Visby
Klintehamn
Nynäshamn
Lübeck
Helsinki

JYLLAND
DANMARK
FYN
SØNDERJYLLAND
HARSYSSEL
DJURSLAND
Struer
Viborg
Randers
Holstebro
Herning
Ikast
Silkeborg
Skanderborg
ÅRHUS
Brabrand
Odder
Ebeltoft
Samsø
Ringkøbing
Ringkøbing Fjord
Nissum Fjord
Skjern
Tarm
Grindsted
Horsens
Horsens Fjord
Vejle
Vejle Fjord
Billund
Varde
Esbjerg
Fanø
Fanø Bugt
Newcastle
Harwich
Blåvands Huk
Ribe
Kolding
Fredericia
Middelfart
Lille Bælt
ODENSE
Nyborg
Fåborg
Svendborg
Tåsinge
Langeland
Ærø
Marstal
Rudkøbing
Haderslev
Vojens
Christiansfeld
Åbenrå
Åbenrå Fjord
Als
Sønderborg
Tønder
Rømø
Mandø
Sylt
Westerland
Föhr
Amrum
Nordfriesische Inseln
Niebüll
Leck
Flensburg
Glücksburg
Flensburg Fd.
Geltinger Bucht
Kappeln
Husum
Nordstrand
Schleswig
Eckernförde
Kieler Bucht
Rendsburg
KIEL
Heikendorf
Preetz
Plön
Eutin
Neumünster
Heide
Tönning
St. Peter
Büsum
Meldorf
Hohenwestedt
Bordesholm
Kronshagen
Friedrichstadt
Langeness
Hooge
Endelave
Juelsminde
Bogense
Kerteminde
Hindsholm

Kattegat
Laholmsbukten
Skälderviken
Hallandsås
Båstad
Torekov
Ängelholm
Höganäs
Markaryd
Örkelljunga
Hässleholm
Klippan
Åstorp
Perstorp
Tyringe
Osby
Helsingborg
Helsingør
Hillerød
Landskrona
Øresund
Eslöv
Hörby
Lund
Malmö
Saltholm
Amager
KØBENHAVN
Roskilde
Tåstrup
Ballerup
Frederiksværk
Frederikssund
Isefjord
Holbæk
Kalundborg
Sjællands Odde
Nykøbing
Sejerø
Sejerø Bugt
SJÆLLAND
Ringsted
Sorø
Slagelse
Køge
Køge Bugt
Næstved
Stevns
Store Heddinge
Fakse
Fakse Bugt
Præstø
Vordingborg
Storstrømmen
Smålandsfarvandet
Møn
Stege
Hjelm Bugt
Falster
Nykøbing
Gedser
Guldborgsund
LOLLAND
Nakskov
Maribo
Rødby
Rødby Havn
Fehmarnbelt
Fehmarn
Puttgarden
Mecklenburger Bucht
Trelleborg
Skanör
Falsterbo
Ystad
Sjöbo
Skurup
Svedala
Anderslöv
Smygehamn
RÜGEN
Sassnitz
Bergen
Binz
Sellin
Göhren
Putbus
Greifswalder Bodden
Stralsund
Greifswald
Barth
Zingst
Prerow
Ribnitz-Damgarten
Warnemünde
ROSTOCK
Ostseebad Kühlungsborn
Bad Sülze
Tribsees
Grimmen
Wolgast
Stockholm
Helsinki
Rønne
Travemünde
Göteborg
Oslo

Kattegat
Anholt
Varberg
Halmstad
Laholmsbukten
Hallandsås
Skälderviken
Ängelholm
Höganäs
Klippan
Hälsingborg
Helsingør
Gilleleje
Hillerød
Landskrona
Eslöv
Lund
Øresund
KØBENHAVN
Amager
Saltholm
MALMÖ
Trelleborg
Skanør
Falsterbo
DJURSLAND
Grenå
Ebeltoft
Ebeltoft Vig
Århus
Samsø
Samsø Bælt
Sejerø
Sejerø Bugt
Sjællands Odde
Isefjord
Nykøbing
Holbæk
Kalundborg
Roskilde
Tåstrup
Frederikssund
Frederiksværk
Hundested
DANMARK
SJÆLLAND
Køge
Køge Bugt
Ringsted
Sorø
Slagelse
Korsør
Næstved
Skælskør
Store Bælt
Hindsholm
Kerteminde
Nyborg
Stevns
Faxe
Fakse Bugt
Smålandsfarvandet
Storstrømmen
Vordingborg
Møn
Hjelm Bugt
Langeland
Langelands Bælt
LOLLAND
Nakskov
Maribo
Rødby
Falster
Nykøbing
Gedser
Guldborgsund
Femer Bælt
Fehmarnbelt
Fehmarn
Puttgarden
Heiligenhafen
Oldenburg
RÜGEN
Bergen
Barth
Stralsund
Travemünde
Warnemünde
Oslo
Göteborg
Kiel

42
45
67

Vislanda
Hovmantorp
Lessebo
Nybro
Kalmar
Färjestaden
ÖLAND
Kalmarsund
Möckeln
Åsnen
Mien
MÖRE
Almhult
Tingsryd
Ryd
Osby
GÖINGE
Olofström
Kallinge
Ronneby
Karlshamn
Karlskrona
Lyckeby
Torhamn
Hässleholm
Kristianstad
Sölvesborg
Bromölla
Åhus
Hanöbukten
Simrishamn
Tomelilla
Ystad
Bornholmsgattet
Hammeren
Ertholmene
BORNHOLM
Allinge
Gudhjem
Svaneke
Hasle
Rønne
Nexø
Åkirkeby
Dueodde
Snogebæk
Ø S T E R S Ø E N
Nynäshamn
Helsinki
Darlowo
Jarosławiec
Świnoujście
Göhren
Skillinge
Degerhamn
Mörbylånga
Torsås
Bergkvara
Emmaboda
Vissefjärda
Tving
Sandvig
Klemensker
Nyker
Arsdale
Pedersker
Ør Marie

C

1 2 3 4

Cape Wrath
Kyle of Durness
Durness
Whit
Head
Loch Inchard
Rhiconich
Laid
Polla
Heilam
Loch
Hope
Ben Ho
927
Loch Erchill
Loch Laxford
Foinavon
908
Laxford Bridge
Scourie
Achfary
Loch More
Kylestrome
Kinloch
Merkland
Lodge
Altn
Eddrachillis
Bay
Drumbeg
Unapool
Little
Assynt
Loch Assynt
Inchnadamph
Overscaig
Hotel
Point of Stoer
Clachtoll
Lochinver
Canisp
847
Ben More Assynt
998
Loch
Shinl
Butt of Lewis
Port of Ness

Outer Hebrides

South
Dell
Five Penny
Borve
Barvas
North
Tolsta
Tolsta Head
Rhu Coigach
Enard
Bay
Elphin
Ledmore
Shawbost
Gress
Back
Tiumpan Head
Gallan Head
Great
Bernera
Beinn Mholach
291
Portnaguiran
Garrabost
Ben More
Coigach
744
Strathkanaird
Lubcroy
Auchness
Aird Uig
Carloway
Newmarket
Garynahine Stornoway
Broad Bay
Loch
Lurgainn
Oykel
Bridge
Uig
Gisla
Lewis
Crossbost
Chicken Head
Ullapool
Oyke
Balallan
Ardcharnich
19
58°
Scarp
Kintaravay
Lemreway
Kebock Head
Loch Broom
835
Bein Dearg
1081
Braemore
Strathpeffer
Tirga More
679
Ardvourlie
Castle
Clisham
799
Beinn Mhor
571
North Minch
Melvaig
Cove
Loch Ewe
Tuirnaig
Little
Grinard
An Teallach
1062
32
Husinish
West Loch Tarbert
Ardhasig
Tarbert
Scalpay
Loch Seaforth
Shiant
Islands
Longa
Island
Londubh
Loch na
Sealga Fionn
Loch
Sgurr Mor
1109
Ben Wy
1045
835
Taransay
Harris
Loch Gairloch
Gairloch
Port Henderson
Kerrysdale
Loch Maree
Gorstan
Toe Head
Scarastavore
Scalpay
Talladale
Loch Fannich
Strathpeffer
21
Pabbay
Leverburgh
Rodel
Renish Point
Rubha Hunish
Red Point
Kinlochewe
Achnasheen
Contin
Berneray
Sound of Harris
Duntulm
Loch Torridon
Liathach
1053
Muir
Be
Balmartin
Newton
Clachan
The Little Minch
Vaternish
Point
Clachan
Torridon
Achnashellach
Lodge
North Uist
Loch Maddy
Lochmaddy
Trumpan
Loch
Snizort
Uig
Rona
Shieldaig
Coulags
Loch
Monar
Farrat
Struy

D

Carinish
Dunvegan
Head
Stein
Applecross
Loch
Kishorn
Lochcarron
Carron
Loch
Mullardoch
Cannich
Drumnadr
Gramisdale
Ronay
Milovaig
Lephin
Dunvegan
Skeabost
Borve
Portree
Roskhill
Bracadale
Coillore
Skye
Raasay
Crowlin
Islands
Stromeferry
Stromemore
Glen Affric
Loch
Affric
Wiay
Benbecula
Fernilea
Drynoch
Peinchorran
Scalpay
Kyle of
Lochalsh
Auchtertyre
Dornie
82
Invermoriston
Creagorry
Sligachan
Broadford
Corry
Kyleakin
Loch Alsh
Kylerhea
87
Torgyle
Bridge
887
82
South
Uist
Loch Bracadale
Cuillin Hills
Sgurr Alasdair
1009
Kinloch
Glenelg
F
Invershiel
19
Cluanie Inn
39
Fort Aug
Caledonian
Canal
Lochboisdale
Loch Boisdale
Elgol
Soay
Loch Eishort
Teangue
Loch Hourn
Kinloch
Hourn
Tomdoun
Loch
Quoich
Invergarry
Sound of Barra
Eriskay
Canna
Sanday
Armadale
Castle
Ardvasar
Sound of Sleat
Inverie
Loch
Garry
Laggan
Lochlag
Eoligarry
Culer
57
Barra
Castlebay
Vatersay
Sandray
Rhum
Sound of Rhum
Eigg
Mallaig
Loch Morar
Arisaig
Tarbet
Murlaggan
Loch Arkaig
Clunes
Loch
Lochy
Gairlochy
Spean
Bridge Roybridge
Creag Meagai
1128
Moy
Glen Spean

E

Coll
Muck
Loch Nevis
830
Glenfinnan
Kinlochiel
Loch
Treig
Lochailort
Corpach
6
Sorisdale
Clabhach
Arinagour
Arileod
Treshnish
Isles
Ardnamurchan
Achosnich
Kilchoan
Salen
Strontian
Inversanda
Kinlochmoidart
45
Loch Shiel
Loch
Eil
Fort William
Ben Nevis
1343
82
North
Ballachulish
Kinlochleven
Blackwater
Reservoir
Tiree
Middleton
Scarinish
Hynish
Gometra
Ulva
Staffa
Inner Hebrides
Calgary
Dervaig
Kilninian
Tobermory
Drimnin
Morvern
Keil
Portnacroish
Ardtornish
Lochaline
Sound of Mull
Salen
Mull
Derryguaig
Craignure
Kerrera
Oban
Kinloch Hotel
Ciamalieu
Lismore
Island
Appin Ho
Ballachulish
House
Laroch
Glencoe
Glen Coe
Kingshouse
Hotel
Bidean nam Bian
1148
37
Victoria
Bridge
82
Connel
Taynuilt
Ben Cruachan
1124
828
Dallachoilish
Loch
Etive
Glen Orchy
Loch Linnhe
Corran
Duror
82
Loch Etive
Brea
Bridge of
Orchy
50
Dalmally
Tyndrum
Crianlarich

SHETLAND ISLANDS
ORKNEY IS.
Scale 1:1 250 000
Scale 1:1 250 000
Pentland Firth
Moray Firth
Dornoch Firth
Dunnet Bay
Spey Bay
Burghead Bay
Firth of Tay
Lunan Bay
Stronsay Firth
Westray Firth
North Ronaldsay Firth
The North Sound
Sanday Sound
Scapa Flow
St. Magnus Bay
Yell Sound
Strath of Kildonan
Strathspey
Strathmore
Sidlaw Hills
Braes of Angus
Ladder Hills
Cairngorm Mountains
Mountains
Forest of Atholl
HIGHLAND
Strathy Point
Holborn Head
Dunnet Head
Duncansby Head
Noss Head
Thurso
Wick
Castletown
John o' Groats House Hotel
Scrabster
Melvich
Bettyhill
Forsinard Station
Kinbrace
Morven 705
Helmsdale
Brora
Golspie
Dornoch
Tarbat Ness
Portmahomack
Tain
Invergordon
Cromarty
Rosemarkie
Fortrose
Dalcross
Campbelltown (Ardersier)
Nairn
Forres
Burghead
Hopeman
Lossiemouth
Elgin
Fochabers
Findochty
Portknockie
Cullen
Buckie
Portsoy
Banff
Macduff
Troup Head
Rosehearty
Kinnairds Head
Fraserburgh
Inverallochy
St. Combs
Rattray Head
Strichen
Mintlaw
Peterhead
Boddam
Buchan Ness
Port Erroll
Ellon
Oldmeldrum
Inverurie
Newburgh
Balmedie
Dyce
Bridge of Don
ABERDEEN
Girdle Ness
Bucksburn
Cults
Peterculter
Banchory
Aboyne
Ballater
Braemar
Lochnagar 1154
Stonehaven
Inverbervie
Johnshaven
Montrose
Brechin
Forfar
Arbroath
Carnoustie
DUNDEE
Monifieth
Buddon Ness
Inchcape or Bell Rock
Tayport
Newport on Tay
Leuchars
St Andrews
Perth
Blairgowrie
Alyth
Kirriemuir
Pitlochry
Blair Atholl
Pass of Killiecrankie 141
Aberfeldy
Dunkeld
Kingussie
Aviemore
Carrbridge
Grantown-on-Spey
Tomintoul
Cairn Gorm 1245
Braeriach 1295
Ben Macdui 1311
Devil's Elbow 671
Glas Maol 1067
Beinn Dearg 1008
Beinn a'Ghlo 1121
Schiehallion 1081
Dalwhinnie
Keith
Huntly
Dufftown
Rothes
Turriff
Alford
Kemnay
Lerwick
Bressay
Sumburgh Head
Fair Isle
Unst
Yell
Fetlar
Whalsay
Mainland
Kirkwall
Stromness
Hoy
South Ronaldsay
Sanday
Stronsay
Westray
Rousay
Eday
Shapinsay
North Ronaldsay
Papa Westray
Flotta
South Walls
Swona
Stroma
Pentland Skerries
Brough Ness
51

Ardnamurchan
Salen
Strontian
Corran
North Ballachulish
Kinlochleven
Blackwater Reservoir
Rannoch Station
Grampians
Kinloch Rannoch
Loch Tummel
Pitlochry
Tobermory
Loch Sunart
Liddesdale
Morvern
Glencoe
Glen Coe
Kingshouse Hotel
Loch Rannoch
Schiehallion 1081
Tummel Bridge
Sound of Mull
Drimnin
Ballachulish House
Bidean nam Bian 1148
Glen Lyon
Aberfeldy
Calgary
Dervaig
Kilninian
Ardtornish
Loch Linnhe
Keil
Appin Ho
Portnacroish
Victoria Bridge
Fearnan
Kenmore
Treshnish Isles
Gometra
Ulva
Lochaline
Salen
Lismore Island
Dallachoilish
Loch Etive
Bridge of Orchy
Breadalbane
Ben Lawers 1214
Lawers
Amulree
Staffa
Mull
Craignure
Derryguaig
Connel
Ben Cruachan 1124
Glen Orchy
Tyndrum
Killin
Loch Tay
Newton Bridge
Oban
Kerrera
Taynuilt
Ardchyle
Loch Earn
St. Fillans
Methven
Kinloch Hotel
Pennyghael
Fionnphort
Iona
Bunessan
Kilninver
Dalmally
Crianlarich
Lochearnhead
Ben More 1174
Ben Vorlich 983
Comrie
Crieff
Taychreggan (North Port)
Cladich
Port Sonachan
Loch Voil
Strathyre
Muthill
Firth of Lorne
Seil
Balvicar
Loch Awe
Luing
Kilmelford
Clachan
Portinnisherrich
Inveraray
Beinn Ime 1011
Loch Katrine
Stronachlachar
The Trossachs
Callander
Braco
Blackford
Ochil
Auchterarder
Ardbane
Arrochar
Tarbet
Drumvaich
Doune
Dunblane
Ben Clach 720
Dollar
Scarba
Kintraw
Lochgoilhead
Strachur
Ben Lomond 974
Aberfoyle
Loch Venachar
Teith
Thornhill
Bridge of Allan
Tillicoultry
Alva
Alloa
Clackmannan
Aird
Ford
Crarae
Loch Goil
Loch Long
Craggan
Loch Lomond
Kippen
Stirling
Kiloran
Colonsay
Scalasaig
Kilmartin
Leanach
Luss
Buchlyvie
Balfron
Bannockburn
Dunfermline
Crinan
Lochgilphead
Loch Fyne
Dunans
Loch Eck
Garelochhead
Drymen
Campsie Fells
Fintry
Cairnoch
Larbert
Kincardine
Grangemouth
Inverlussa
Jura
Sound of Jura
Ardentinny
Coulport
Rosneath
Helensburgh
Alexandria
Dumbarton
Baptiston
Lennox Hills
Lennoxtown
Kilsyth
Denny
Falkirk
Laurieston
Cumbernauld
Otter Ferry
Sandbank
Dunoon
Strone
Gourock
Milngavie
Kirkintilloch
Slamannan
Armadale
Bathgate
Ardrishaig
Keillmore
Knapdale
Lagg
Beinn an Oir 784
Feolin Ferry
Craighouse
Ardentraive
Rhubodach
Tighnabruaich
Kames
Innellan
Greenock
Port Glasgow
Kilmacolm
Clydebank
Glasgow
Renfrew
Coatbridge
Airdrie
Sanaigmore
Port Askaig
Tarbert
Kilberry
Port Bannatyne
Rothesay
Wemyss Bay
Skelmorlie
Bridge of Weir
Ranfurly
Johnstone
Paisley
Rutherglen
Harthill
Shotts
Whitburn
Islay
Bridgend
Bowmore
Beinn Bheigeir 490
Kennacraig
Claonaig
Skipness
Largs
Lochwinnoch
Barrhead
Neilston
Hamilton
Motherwell
Wishaw
Fauldhouse
Kintyre
Kingarth
Millport
Fairlie
Kilburnie
Newton Mearns
East Kilbride
Larkhall
Carluke
Forth
Portnahaven
Crossaig
Kilbrannan Sound
Lochranza
Firth of Clyde
West Kilbride
Dalry
Beith
Dunlop
Stewarton
Stonehouse
Blackwood
Carstairs
Port Ellen
Ardbeg
Killean
Goat Fell 874
Corrie
Ardrossan
Saltcoats
Auchentiber
Kilwinning
Fenwick
Strathaven
Lanark
Mull of Oa
Glenbarr
Dippen
Imachar
Arran
Brodick
Stevenston
Irvine
Dreghorn
Kilmaurs
Kilmarnock
Darvel
Newmilns
Lesmahagow
Dungavel
Hyndford Bridge
Saddell
Lamlash
Holy Island
Troon
Hurlford
Galston
Douglas
Rigside
Westport
South Feorline
Lagg
Monkton
Prestwick
Ayr
Loans
Mauchline
Muirkirk
Sorn
Tarbolton
Catrine
Auchinleck
Abington
Machrihanish
Campbeltown
Ochiltree
Coylton
Cumnock
New Cumnock
Southern Uplands
Leadhills
Green Lowther 733
Fisherton
Littlemill
Connel Park
Kirkconnel
Sanquhar
Rathlin Island
Southend
Dalrymple
Dalmellington
Maybole
Kirkoswald
Crosshill
Patna
Nithsdale
Lowther Hills
Daer Reservoir
Queensberry 697
Mull of Kintyre
Sanda Island
Turnberry
Dailly
Girvan
Loch Doon
Drumjohn
Carronbridge
Thornhill
Ballycastle
Fair Head
Ballyvoy
Torr Head
Barr
Carsphairn
Moniaive
Closeburn
Knocklayd 517
Armoy
Cushendun
Lendalfoot
Merrick 843
Corserine 813
Castlefairn
Blackwood
Mountains of Antrim
Cushendall
Red Bay
Garron Point
Ballantrae
Pinwherry
Barrhill
Colmonell
Dunscore
Dalry
Balmaclellan
Corsock
New Bridge
Dumfries
Ballymoney
Trostan 554
Glenkens
Parkmore
Cloughmills
Carnlough
Glenarm
North Channel
Milleur Point
Loch Ryan
716
Lamachan Hill
New Galloway
Crocketford
Rasharkin
Cairnryan
Kirkcolm
Newton Stewart
Cairnsmore of Fleet 710
Haugh of Urr
Dalbeattie
Ballymena
Broughshane
Agnew's Hill 476
Larne
Stranraer
Innermessan
Laurieston
Castle Douglas
Criffel 569
Ahogill
Portslogan
Glenluce
Kirkcowan
Wigtown
Creetown
Gatehouse of Fleet
Ringford
Caulkerbush
Kilwaughter
Island Magee
Kildrochat
Portpatrick
Auchenmalg
Whauphill
Wigtown Bay
Minto Cott
Kirkcudbright
Auchencairn
Ballynure
Kells
Randalstown
Ballyclare
Antrim
Doagh
Greenisland
Whitehead
Eden
Carrickfergus
Sandhead
Luce Bay
Ardwell
Sorbie
Garlieston
Dundrennan
Kirkcudbright Bay
Solway Firth
Port William
Newtownabbey
Belfast Lough
Bangor
Copeland Island
Donaghadee
Millisle
Port Logan
Whithorn
Isle of Whithorn
Lough Neagh
Crumlin
Belfast
Holywood
Dundonald
Newtownards
Drummore
Mull of Galloway
Burrow Head
Maryport
Workington
Glenavy
Upper Ballinderry
Aghalee
Lisburn
Comber
Ballywalter
Greyabbey
Ballyhalbert
Whitehaven
Distington
Cleator
St. Bees Head
Lurgan
Moira
Hillsborough
Saintfield
Strangford Lough
Kircubbin
Ardkeen
Egremont
Ireland
Dromore
Ballynahinch
Killyleagh
Crossgar
Portaferry
Strangford
Point of Ayre
Laurencetown
Banbridge
Dromara
Isle of Man
Downpatrick
Ballyquintin Point
Ramsey
Sulby
Ballaugh
Kirk Michael
Maughold Head
Katesbridge
Clough
Dundrum
Ballyroney
Rathfriland
Liverpool
Douglas
Heysham
Preston
Lancaster

NORTH SEA
Montrose
Lunan Bay
Arbroath
Forfar
Kirriemuir
Braes of Angus
Sidlaw Hills
DUNDEE
Carnoustie
Monifieth
Buddon Ness
Tayport
Newport on Tay
Firth of Tay
Inchcape or Bell Rock
Perth
Newburgh
Cupar
Leuchars
St. Andrews
Kingsbarns
Fife Ness
Crail
Anstruther Wester
Pittenweem
St. Monance
Isle of May
Glenrothes
Leven
Methil
Buckhaven
East Wemyss
Lochgelly
Kirkcaldy
Burntisland
Kinghorn
Aberdour
Inverkeithing
North Queensferry
Inchkeith
Firth of Forth
Bass Rock
North Berwick
Gullane
Dunbar
EDINBURGH
Prestonpans
Musselburgh
Tranent
Haddington
Dalkeith
Newtongrange
Bonnyrigg & Lasswade
Loanhead
Penicuik
Lammermuir Hills
Moorfoot Hills
Peebles
Innerleithen
Galashiels
Melrose
Newtown St. Boswells
Selkirk
Kelso
Coldstream
Lauder
Earlston
Greenlaw
Duns
Chirnside
Eyemouth
St. Abb's Head
Coldingham
Cockburnspath
Berwick-upon-Tweed
Holy Island
Farne Islands
Bamburgh
Seahouses
Belford
Wooler
Jedburgh
Hawick
Teviotdale
Cheviot Hills
The Cheviot 816
Embleton
Alnwick
Alnmouth
Warkworth
Amble
Rothbury
Morpeth
Ashington
Newbiggin-by-the-Sea
Bedlington
Blyth
Whitley Bay
Tynemouth
SOUTH SHIELDS
NEWCASTLE UPON TYNE
GATESHEAD
SUNDERLAND
Jarrow
Hexham
Haltwhistle
Langholm
Lockerbie
Annan
Gretna
Longtown
Brampton
Carlisle
Wigton
Aspatria
Cockermouth
Keswick
Penrith
Appleby
Kirkby Stephen
Windermere
Ambleside
Kendal
Sedbergh
Lake District
Scafell Pikes 978
Helvellyn 950
Skiddaw 931
Cross Fell 893
Mickle Fell 790
Consett
Stanley
Chester le Street
Durham
Houghton le Spring
Seaham
Easington Colliery
Peterlee
Hartlepool
TEESSIDE
Redcar
Marske by the Sea
Saltburn by the Sea
Middlesbrough
Guisborough
Billingham
Stockton on Tees
Darlington
Bishop Auckland
Spennymoor
Crook
Barnard Castle
Richmond
Northallerton
Teesdale
Weardale
Wensleydale
Pennines
North York Moors
Cleveland Hills
ENGLAND
Whitby
49
58

1
2
3
10°
9°
8°
A
B
C
55°
54°
Tory Island
Horn Head
Sheep Haven
Inishbofin
Dunfanaghy
Bloody Foreland
Falcarragh
Creeslo
Inishfree Bay
Bunbeg
Gweedore
Errigal 752
Crolly
Aran Island
Burtonport
Slieve Snaght 683
Derryveagh Mts.
Dunglow
Crohy Head
Kingarrow
Gweebarra Bay
Lettermacaward
Fintown
Dawros Head
Loughros More Bay
Maas
Glenties
Ardara
Blue Stack Mts.
674
Slievetooey 517
Rossan Point
Glencolumbkille
Malin More
Rathlin O'Birne Island
Slieve League 601
Carrick
Killybegs
Inver
Donegal
Carrigan Head
Dunkineely
Mountcharles
Laghy
Muckros Head
McSwyne's Bay
Inver Bay
St. John's Point
Ballintra
Pettigo
Donegal Bay
Bundoran
Ballyshannon
Lough
Belleek
Lough Melvin
Inishmurray
Cliffony
Kinlough
Glenade
Grange
Truskmore 644
Roskeeragh Point
Drumcliff
Lough Macnean
Downpatrick Head
Lenadoon Point
Sligo Bay
Benwee Head
Erris Head
Broad Haven
Belderg
Easky
Sligo
Manorhamilton
Glenfarne
Mullet Peninsula
Glenamoy
Ballycastle
Killala Bay
Dromore West
Dromard
Belmullet
Carrowmore Lough
Killala
Inishcrone
Beltra
Ballysadare
Lough Gill
Shannon
Inishkea North
Inishkea South
Bangor
The Ox Mountains
545
Collooney
Lough Allen
Bellacorick
Crossmolina
Ballina
Blacksod Bay
Slieve Car 721
Lough Arrow
Ballymote
Saddle Head
Slieve More 672
Nephin Beg Range
Nephin 806
Lough Conn
Tubbercurry
Lough Key
Drumshanbo
Ballycroy
Dooagh
Keel
Moy
Achill Head
Foxford
Callow
Leitrim
Achill Island
Dooega Head
Achill
Beltra Lough
Beltra
Lough Cullin
Charlestown
Carracastle
Boyle
Carrick on Shannon
Mullaranny
Lough Gara
Drumsna
Swinford
Newport
Castlebar
Bellavary
Tawnyinah
Ballaghaderreen
Clare Island
Clew Bay
Frenchpark
Bellanagare
Balla
Rooskey
Westport
Louisburgh
Castlerea
Strokestown
Ballyhaunis
Tulsk
Inishturk
Claremorris
Ballinlough
Scramoge
Cregganbaun
Partry Mountains
C O N N A U G H T
Longford
Ballymoe
Mweelrea 819
Cloonfad
Pollremon
Ballydooley
Ballyclare
Inishbofin
Ballindine
Williamstown
Lanesborough
Inishark
Lough Mask
Ballinrobe
Roscommon
Milltown
Dunmore
Ballymurray
Letterfrack
Leenaun
Lough Ree
Moyard
Maumturk Mts.
Kilmaine
Athleague
The Twelve Pins 730
Maum
Clonbur
Cong
Shrule
I R E
Clifden
Tuam
Ballygar
Mount Talbot
Newbridge
Mannin Bay
Recess
Moylough
Thomas Street
Kiltoom
Connemara
Maam Cross
Lough Corrib
Headford
Barnaderg
Clare
Mount Bellew Bridge
Ballyforan
Brideswell
Slyne Head
Derryrush
Oughterard
Screeb
Rosscahill
Athlone
Bertraghboy Bay
Glinsk
Suck
Ballynahown
Kilkieran
Moycullen
Claregalway
Ballinasloe
Kilconnell
Ballydangan
Kilkieran Bay
Costelloe
Galway
Athenry
Aughrim
Gorumna Island
Spiddle
Oranmore
Kiltullagh
Ferbane
Barna
Craughwell
Kilreekill
Cashla Bay
Inveran
Clarinbridge
Laurencetown
North Sound
Galway Bay
Kilcolgan
Loughrea
Ballydavid
Clogham
Black Head
Burren
Ardrahan
Killimor
Shannon
54

Arran
Brodick
Lamlash
Holy Island
South Feorline
Lagg
Kilbrannan Sound
Dippen
Saddell
Glenbarr
Westport
Machrihanish
Campbeltown
Southend
Mull of Kintyre
Sanda Island
Port Ellen
Mull of Oa
Rathlin Island
Malin Head
Ballygorman
Glengad Head
Trawbreaga Bay
Malin
Culdaff
Dunaff Head
Clonmany
Carndonagh
Slieve Snaght 615
Gleneely
Moville
Inishowen Head
Portstewart
Portrush
Benbane Head
Bushmills
Ballycastle
Fair Head
Ballyvoy
Torr Head
Knocklayd 517
Armoy
Derrykeighan
Cushendun
Cushendall
Red Bay
Garron Point
Trostan 554
Parkmore
Carnlough
Glenarm
Mountains of Antrim
Buncrana
Lough Swilly
Lough Foyle
Downhill
Coleraine
Macosquin
Ballybogey
Ballymoney
Limavady
Muff
Burnfoot
Rathmelton
Londonderry
Eglinton
Newtown Cunningham
St. Johnston
New Buildings
Garvagh
Kilrea
Rasharkin
Cloughmills
Dungiven
Claudy
Feeny
Swatragh
Portglenone
Ballymena
Broughshane
Agnew's Hill 476
Larne
Larne Lough
Kilwaughter
Island Magee
Whitehead
Dunamanagh
Maghera
Ahogill
Kells
Ballyclare
Ballynure
Strabane
Sion Mills
Sperrin Mts.
Sawel 683
Draperstown
Tobermore
Lough Beg
Toome
Randalstown
Doagh
Greenisland
Carrickfergus
Eden
Plumbridge
Gortin
Desertmartin
Magherafelt
Moneymore
Antrim
Newtownabbey
Belfast Lough
Bangor
Copeland Island
Donaghadee
Millisle
Newtownstewart
Cookstown
Coagh
Lough Neagh
Crumlin
Glenavy
BELFAST
Holywood
Dundonald
Newtownards
Mountfield
Pomeroy
Tullyhogue
Stewartstown
Omagh
Sixmilecross
Beragh
Coalisland
Upper Ballinderry
Aghalee
Lisburn
Comber
Carryduff
Ballywalter
Greyabbey
Ballyhalbert
Kircubbin
Strangford Lough
Dungannon
Seskinore
Garvaghey
Dromore
Fintona
Ballygawley
Aughnacloy
Moy
Craigavon
Lurgan
Moira
Hillsborough
Saintfield
Ballynahinch
Killyleagh
Ardkeen
Portaferry
Strangford
Crossgar
Ballyquintin Point
Irvinestown
Trillick
Ballinamallard
Augher
Clogher
Portadown
Dromore
Laurencetown
Gilford
Banbridge
Dromara
Downpatrick
Enniskillen
Tempo
Fivemiletown
Caledon
Emyvale
Armagh
Tandragee
Loughbrickland
Katesbridge
Clough
Dundrum
Dundrum Bay
Ardglass
Killough
St. John's Point
Lisbellaw
Brookeborough
Maguiresbridge
Lisnaskea
Monaghan
Middletown
Markethill
Poyntzpass
Rathfriland
Ballyroney
Castlewellan
Kilcoo
Newcastle
Slieve Donard 852
Smithborough
Keady
Newtownbutler
Derrylin
Clones
Newbliss
Newtownhamilton
Newry
Mourne Mountains
Glasdrummond
Annalong
Lough Erne
Ballyconnell
Belturbet
Drum
Ballybay
Castleblayney
Cootehill
Culloville
Warrenpoint
Rostrevor
Lisnacree
Kilkeel
Carlingford
Carlingford Lough
Greenore
Kilcurry
Dundalk
Dundalk Bay
Cavan
Stradone
Shercock
Carrickmacross
Carrigallen
Lough Oughter
Crossdoney
Bellananagh
Bailieborough
Kingscourt
Castlebellingham
Annagassan
Dunany Point
Ballyjamesduff
Lough Gowna
Kilnaleck
Virginia
Ardee
Dunleer
Lough Ramor
Nobber
Finnea
Granard
Lough Sheelin
Oldcastle
Collon
Newtown Monasterboice
Clogherhead
Clogher Head
Termonfeckin
Ceanannus Mór
Slane
Drogheda
Boyne
Julianstown
Mostrim
Rathowen
Lough Derravaragh
Castlepollard
Crossakeel
Blackwater
Clonmellon
An Uaimh (Navan)
Athboy
Balbriggan
Skerries
Ballinalack
Delvin
Naul
Rush
Lambay Island
Mullingar
Clogan
Trim
Bellivor
Dunshaughlin
Ballyboghil
Ashbourne
Summerhill
Killucan
Rathmolyon
The Downs
Lough Ennell
Kinnegad
Ballynadrumny
Clonard
Dunboyne
Swords
Malahide
Cloghran
Ireland's Eye
Howth Head
Ballynagore
Rochfortbridge
Innfield
Kilcock
Clonee
Maynooth
Johnstown Bridge
Carbury
Tyrellspass
Kilbeggan
Edenderry
Celbridge
Lucan
DUBLIN
(Baile Atha Cliath)
Dun Laoghaire
(Dunleary)
Durrow
Kilnane
Clondalkin
Rathcoole
Tullamore
Allenwood
Clane
Liffey
Tallaght
Daingean
Ballinagar
Kill
Brittas
Enniskerry
Bray
Killeigh
Cushina
Rathangan
Naas
Kippure 754
Poulaphouca Reservoir
Droichead Nua
Kildare
Portarlington
Greystones
Girvan
Ailsa Craig
Turnberry
Kirkoswald
Fisherton
Lendalfoot
Ballantrae
Colmonell
Pinwherry
Milleur Point
Kirkcolm
Loch Ryan
Stranraer
Cairnryan
Innermessan
Portslogan
Portpatrick
Kildrochat
Ardwell
Sandhead
Luce Bay
Port Logan
Mull of Galloway
Drummore
North Channel
IRISH SEA
NORTHERN IRELAND
IRELAND
Ardrossan
Douglas
Heysham
Preston
Douglas Liverpool
Liverpool
Holyhead
Calf of Man
50
55
56
4
5
6
7
B
C
54°
55°
5°
6°
7°

Clare Island
Clew Bay
Westport
Louisburgh
Inishturk
Cregganbaun
Mweelrea 819
Inishbofin
Inishark
Partry Mountains
Lough Mask
Letterfrack
Leenaun
Moyard
The Twelve Pins 730
Maumturk Mts.
Clifden
Mannin Bay
Maum
Recess
Maam Cross
Connemara
Slyne Head
Derryrush
Screeb
Oughterard
Lough Corrib
Rosscahill
Bertraghboy Bay
Glinsk
Kilkieran
Kilkieran Bay
Moycullen
Costelloe
Gorumna Island
Spiddle
Galway
Cashla Bay
Inveran
Barna
North Sound
Galway Bay
Inishmore
Aran Islands
Inishmaan
Inisheer
South Sound
Black Head
Burren
Ballyvaghan
Kinvarra
Lisdoonvarna
Hags Head
Liscannor Bay
Ennistimon
Mal Bay
Milltown Malbay
Spanish Point
Inagh
391 Slievecallan
Ennis
Quilty
Doonbeg
Kilkee
Kilrush
Carrigaholt
Shannon
Loop Head
Mouth of The Shannon
Tarbert
Glin
Foynes
Askeaton
Shanagolden
Ballybunnion
Kerry Head
Listowel
Newcastle West
Ardagh
Rathkeale
Adare
Brandon Bay
Rough Point
Brandon Point
Tralee Bay
Tralee
Ballydavid Head
Brandon Mountain 953
Stradbally Mountain 826
853
Slieve Mish Mountains
Sybil Point
Murreagh
Anascaul
Dingle
Milltown
Castlemaine Harbour
Castlemaine
Great Blasket Island
Slea Head
Dingle Bay
Inishvickillane
Killorglin
Glenbeigh
Killarney
Lough Leane
Carrauntoohil 1041
Macgillycuddy's Reeks
Doulus Head
Valencia Island
Cahersiveen
Bray Head
New Chapel Cross
Lough Currane
St. Finan's Bay
Waterville
Ballinskelligs Bay
The Skelligs
Bolus Head
Hog's Head
Scariff Island
Kenmare River
Lamb's Head
Coulagh Bay
Cod's Head
Castletown Bearhaven
Dursey Island
Dursey Head
Crow Head
Bear Island
Bantry Bay
Muntervary or Sheeps Head
Dunmanus Bay
Mizen Head
Cape Clear
Clear Island
Sherkin Island
Toe Head
Skibbereen
Schull
Goleen
Roaringwater Bay
Glandore Harbour
Rosscarbery Bay
Galley Head
Clonakilty Bay
Seven Heads
Courtmacsherry Bay
Old Head of Kinsale
Kinsale Harbour
Kinsale
Frower Point
Caha Mountains
Hungry Hill 686
Knockowen 661
Glengarriff
Adrigole
Kenmare
Sneem
Parknasilla
Templenoe
Upper Lough
Mangerton Mountain 840
Muckross
The Paps 696
Derrynasaggart Mts
Ballyvourney
Macroom
Shehy Mts.
Shehy Mountain 547
Knockboy 707
Carran 606
Bantry
Nowen Hill 537
Dunmanway
Drimoleague
Bandon
Crookstown
Boggeragh Mts
Millstreet
Ballynamona
Mallow
Kanturk
Mullaghareirk Mountains
Abbeyfeale
Castleisland
Farranfore
Rathmore
Nagles Mts. 429
Fermoy
Blarney
CORK
Ballincollig
Passage West
Cobh
Carrigaline
Midleton
Crosshaven
Cork Harbour
Mitchelstown
Galty Mountain 920
Galtymore
Kilmallock
Rath Luirc (Charleville)
Newtown
Milford
Buttevant
Croom
Bruff
Hospital
Tipperary
Herbertstown
Pallas Green (New)
Limerick
Patrickswell
Caherconlish
Newport
Keeper Hill 694
Nenagh
Killaloe
Slieve Bernagh 533
Sixmilebridge
Cratloe
Newmarket on Fergus
Clarecastle
Tulla
Scarriff
Lough Derg
Whitegate
Slieve Aughty Mts.
Peterswell 367
Gort
Crusheen
Ardrahan
Kilcolgan
Loughrea
Craughwell
Athenry
Oranmore
Clarinbridge
Claregalway
Ballinasloe
Kilconnell
Aughrim
Portumna
Borrisokane
Tuam
Headford
Shrule
Kilmaine
Cong
Clonbur
Ballinrobe
Claremorris
Ballyhaunis
Castlerea
Roscommon
Dunmore
Milltown
Ballindine
Balla
CONNACHT
MUNSTER
I
2
3
A
B
C
53°
52°
10°
9°

4
5
6
53
A
B
57
60
4
5
6
6°
7°
53°
52°
DUBLIN
(Baile Atha Cliath)
Dun Laoghaire
(Dunleary)
Liverpool
Holyhead
Fishguard
Swansea
St. George's Channel
Longford
Newtown Forbes
Ballinalee
Granard
Finnea
Lough Sheelin
Lough Ramor
Virginia
Oldcastle
Nobber
Collon
Dunleer
Clogherhead
Clogher Head
Newtown Monasterboice
Termonfeckin
Drogheda
Julianstown
Balbriggan
Skerries
Rush
Lambay Island
Malahide
Swords
Ireland's Eye
Howth Head
Ceanannus Mór
Slane
Boyne
Blackwater
An Uaimh (Navan)
Crossakeel
Clonmellon
Athboy
Castlepollard
Mostrim
Rathowen
Lough Derravaragh
Killashee
Ballymahon
Lough Ree
Tang
Carrickboy
Ballinalack
Delvin
Mullingar
Trim
Ballivor
Dunshaughlin
Ashbourne
Ballyboghil
Naul
Ward
Cloghran
Summerhill
Dunboyne
The Downs
Killucan
Ballymore
Killare
Lough Ennell
Kinnegad
Clonard
Rathmolyon
Ballynadrumny
Innfield
Enfield
Kilcock
Clonee
Johnstown Bridge
Maynooth
Celbridge
Lucan
Clondalkin
Athlone
Moate
Horseleap
Ballynagore
Rochfortbridge
Tyrellspass
Kilbeggan
Brosna
Ballynahown
Clara
Durrow
Tullamore
Edenderry
Killane
Carbury
Allenwood
Clane
Liffey
Rathcoole
Tallaght
Ferbane
Screggan
Daingean
Ballinagar
Bathangan
Kill
Naas
Brittas
Kippure 754
Enniskerry
Bray
Greystones
Poulaphouca Reservoir
Killeigh
Kilcormac (Frankford)
Cushina
Droichead Nua
Kildare
Portarlington
Kilcullen
Monasterevin
Mountmellick
Cadamstown
Kinnitty
Slieve Bloom Mts.
Arderin 529
Clareen
Mountrath
Port Laoise
New Inn
Stradbally
Fontstown
Ballitore
Timolin
Moone
Athy
Hollywood
Roundwood
Laragh
Wicklow Mountains
Lugnaquillia Mountain 926
Newtown Mount Kennedy
Ballinalea
Rathnew
Wicklow
Wicklow Head
Glenealy
Rathdrum
Avoca
Woodenbridge
Mizen Head
Arklow
Aughrim
Croghan Mountain 607
L E I N S T E R
Roscrea
Castletown
Borris in Ossory
Dunkerrin
Abbeyleix
Ballinakill
Ballylynan
Arles
Baltinglass
Kiltegan
Castledermot
Rathvilly
Hacketstown
Tullow
Tinahely
Shillelagh
Carnew
Craanford
Gorey
Kilmichael Point
Ballycanew
Ballickmoyler
Graigue
Carlow
Ballycolla
Rathdowney
Durrow
Castlecomer
Ballyragget
Johnstown
Freshford
Leighlinbridge
Urlingford
Thurles
Whitehall
Muine Bheag (Bagenalstown)
Ballon
Kildavin
Bunclody
Slaney
Blackstairs Mountains
Mount Leinster 796
Borris
Ballycarney
Ferns
Camolin
Cahore Point
Littleton
Kilkenny
Bennettsbridge
Graiguenamanagh
Barrow
Ballingarry
Laffansbridge
Ballinure
Killenaule
Callan
Thomastown
Inistioge
Nore
Enniscorthy
Cashel
Rosegreen
Fethard
Ninemilehouse
Clonroche
Oilgate
Castlebridge
Ballyclerahan
Rosbercon
New Ross
Ballynabola
Wexford
Wexford Harbour
Rosslare
Rosslare Harbour
Greenore Point
Carnsore Point
Cahir
Clonmel
Suir
Kilsheelan
Carrick-on-Suir
Carrickbeg
Mullinavat
Comeragh Mts.
755
Monavullagh Mts.
Seefin 727
792
Waterford
Passage East
Ramsgrange
Arthurstown
Wellingtonbridge
Killinick
Kilmore
Kilmore Quay
Crossfarnoge Point
Saltee Islands
Kilmacthomas
Tramore
Tramore Bay
Annestown
Dunmore East
Brownstown Head
Hook Head
Bunmahon
Millstreet
Lismore
Abbeyside
Dungarvan
Dungarvan Harbour
Helvick Head
Clashmore
Youghal
Youghal Bay
Ram Head
Knockadoon Head
St. David's Head
St. David's
Ramsey Island
St. Bride's Bay
Skomer Island
Skokholm Island

NEWCASTLE UPON TYNE
GATESHEAD
SUNDERLAND
SOUTH SHIELDS
Tynemouth
Whitley Bay
Blyth
Durham
Hexham
Consett
Bishop Auckland
Darlington
Stockton on Tees
Hartlepool
Middlesbrough
Thornaby on Tees
Northallerton
Richmond
Ripon
Harrogate
Knaresborough
Wetherby
LEEDS
BRADFORD
Halifax
HUDDERSFIELD
Wakefield
Barnsley
Dewsbury
Keighley
Skipton
Ilkley
Burnley
Nelson
Colne
Accrington
BLACKBURN
Darwen
Rochdale
OLDHAM
Bury
BOLTON
Wigan
Chorley
PRESTON
Leyland
Southport
Ormskirk
Crosby
BLACKPOOL
Lytham St. Annes
Fleetwood
Thornton Cleveleys
Lancaster
Morecambe
Heysham
Morecambe Bay
Kendal
Windermere
Penrith
Keswick
Carlisle
Cockermouth
Workington
Whitehaven
Maryport
Egremont
St. Bees Head
Barrow-in-Furness
Isle of Walney
Ulverston
Millom
Lake District
Wensleydale
Wharfedale
Forest of Bowland
Teesdale
Weardale
Annan
Dumfries
Castle Douglas
Kirkcudbright
Newton Stewart
Wigtown Bay
Stranraer
Loch Ryan
Luce Bay
Mull of Galloway
Burrow Head
Solway Firth
ISLE OF MAN
Ramsey
Douglas
Peel
Castletown
Port Erin
Calf of Man
Point of Ayre
Maughold Head
North Channel
IRISH SEA
Liverpool Bay
Belfast
Larne

Holyhead
Holy Island
Anglesey
Bangor
Caernarvon
Caernarvon Bay
Conwy
Colwyn Bay
Rhyl
Abergele
Flint
Ellesmere Port
Runcorn
Chester
Wrexham
Llangollen
Oswestry
Shrewsbury
Wellington
Telford
Dawley
Crewe
Nantwich
Whitchurch
Newcastle under Lyme
STOKE-ON-TRENT
Stafford
Burton upon Trent
DERBY
Chesterfield
Macclesfield
Knutsford
Buxton
Mansfield
Coalville
Cannock
Lichfield
Tamworth
WALSALL
WOLVERHAMPTON
WEST BROMWICH
DUDLEY
WARLEY
BIRMINGHAM
SOLIHULL
COVENTRY
Halesowen
Stourbridge
Kidderminster
Bromsgrove
Redditch
Warwick
Leamington
Stratford-upon-Avon
Banbury
Worcester
Great Malvern
Evesham
Tewkesbury
Cheltenham
Gloucester
Stroud
Cirencester
Hereford
Leominster
Ludlow
Ross-on-Wye
Monmouth
Abergavenny
Newtown
Welshpool
Machynlleth
Dolgellau
Aberystwyth
Cardigan Bay
Llandrindod Wells
Builth Wells
Brecon
Black Mountains
Brecon Beacons
Merthyr Tydfil
Carmarthen
Haverfordwest
Milford Haven
Pembroke Dock
Fishguard
Cardigan
Aberayron
Lleyn Peninsula
Pwllheli
Portmadoc
Cambrian Mountains
Berwyn Mts
Mynydd Eppynt
Mynydd Prescelly
WALES

NORTH SEA
A
B
1
2
3
4
5
Consett
Stanley
Birtley
Leadgate
Chester le Street
Houghton le Spring
Seaham
Murton
Hetton le Hole
Easington Colliery
Peterlee
Durham
Brandon
Tow Law
Stanhope
Weardale
Wolsingham
Crook
Willington
Spennymoor
Ferryhill
Trimdon
Wheatley Hill
Hartlepool
TEESSIDE
Redcar
Bishop Auckland
Teesdale
Middleton in Teesdale
West Auckland
Shildon
Coundon
Sedgefield
Newton Aycliffe
Stockton on Tees
Billingham
Marske by the Sea
Saltburn by the Sea
Middlesbrough
Loftus
Guisborough
Hinderwell
Barnard Castle
Staindrop
Gainford
Darlington
Thornaby on Tees
Yarm
Great Ayton
Whitby
High Hawsker
Robin Hood's Bay
Stokesley
Cleveland Hills
North York Moors
Richmond
Catterick
Catterick Camp
Scotch Corner
Northallerton
Keld
Reeth
Swale
Nensleydale
Hawes
Aysgarth
Middleham
Leyburn
Bedale
Leeming Bar
Laskill
Eller Beck Bridge
Saltergate
Cloughton
Kirkby Moorside
Scalby
Scarborough
Thirsk
Sowerby
Helmsley
Pickering
Thornton le Dale
Snainton
Filey
Reighton
Hunmanby
Flamborough
Flamborough Head
Bridlington
Bridlington Bay
Kidstones
Masham
Great Whernside 704
Kettlewell
Grassington
Wharfedale
Ripon
Pateley Bridge
Summer Bridge
Boroughbridge
Easingwold
Malton
Norton
Stillington
Hovingham
Rillington
Sherburn
Foxholes
Rudston
Sledmere
Wolds
Yorkshire
Strensall
Haxby
Huntington
Fridaythorpe
Driffield
Burton Agnes
Nafferton
Lissett
Skipsea
Hornsea
Skipton
Hellifield
Harrogate
Knaresborough
Addingham
Ilkley
Burley in Wharfedale
Silsden
Otley
Wetherby
Spofforth
YORK
Stamford Bridge
Barmby Moor
Pocklington
Middleton on the Wolds
Leven
Beverley
Keighley
Bingley
Shipley
Colne
Nelson
Burnley
BRADFORD
Pudsey
LEEDS
Collingham
Harewood
Tadcaster
Cawood
Sherburn in Elmet
Riccall
Market Weighton
Holme upon Spalding Moor
South Cave
Cottingham
KINGSTON UPON HULL
Hessle
Holderness
Aldbrough
Preston
Hedon
Roos
Withernsea
Hebden Bridge
Halifax
Brighouse
Dewsbury
Rothwell
Castleford
Selby
Howden
Elloughton
North Ferriby
Humber
New Holland
Keyingham
Patrington
Easington
Spurn Head
Bacup
Littleborough
Wakefield
Pontefract
Rawcliffe
Snaith
Goole
Barton upon Humber
Barrow upon Humber
Immingham Dock
Immingham
Healing
Grimsby
Cleethorpes
Humberston
OLDHAM
HUDDERSFIELD
Holmfirth
Darton
Barnsley
Hemsworth
South Kirkby
Adwick le Street
Bentley
Thorne
Hatfield
Crowle
Winterton
Scunthorpe
Broughton
Brigg
Barnetby le Wold
Laceby
Waltham
Ashton under Lyne
Penistone
Goldthorpe
Mexborough
Conisbrough
Doncaster
Belton
Epworth
Messingham
Hibaldstow
Caistor
Trent
Don
MANCHESTER
Stocksbridge
Grenoside
STOCKPORT
New Mills
SHEFFIELD
Rotherham
Maltby
New Rossington
Bawtry
Tickhill
Misterton
Kirton in Lindsey
Gainsborough
Beckingham
Lea
Caenby Corner
Market Rasen
Binbrook
Ludford Magna
Ludborough
North Somercotes
Grainthorpe
Saltfleet
Saltfleetby St. Clement
Louth
Mablethorpe
Sutton-on-Sea
Withern
Tothill
Scamblesby
Whaley Bridge
Hazel Grove
Chapel en le Frith
Macclesfield
Hathersage
Dronfield
Eckington
Blyth
Worksop
East Retford
Staveley
Whitwell
Saxilby
Nettleham
Wragby
Faldingworth
Göteborg
1°
0°
2°
54°
51
56
80
68
31
84
19
37
71
63
64
18
24

Great Yarmouth
Lowestoft
NORWICH
IPSWICH
Felixstowe
Harwich
Clacton-on-Sea
Colchester
Chelmsford
SOUTHEND-ON-SEA
LONDON
CAMBRIDGE
Bury St. Edmunds
Newmarket
King's Lynn
Peterborough
Boston
Spalding
Grantham
Stamford
NOTTINGHAM
LEICESTER
DERBY
NORTHAMPTON
Kettering
Bedford
Luton
Stevenage
Watford
High Wycombe
OXFORD
READING
Swindon
Cheltenham
BIRMINGHAM
COVENTRY
Rugby
Banbury
Stoke-on-Trent
Stafford
Wash
The Broads
Rotterdam
Oostende
Hoek van Holland
Esbjerg
Göteborg
Kristiansand
Antwerpen

St. George's Channel
Rosslare
Cork
Roscoff
55
80
Strumble Head
Goodwick
Fishguard
Dinas Head
Cemaes Head
Cardigan
Aberporth
New Quay
Aberayron
Lampeter
Cambrian Mts.
Llandovery
Mynydd Prescelly
Mynydd Eppynt
Builth Wells
Llandrindod Wells
St. David's Head
St. David's
Ramsey Island
Solva
Newgale
St. Bride's Bay
Haverfordwest
Skomer Island
Skokholm Island
Milford Haven
Pembroke Dock
Pembroke
Narberth
Whitland
St. Clears
Carmarthen
Saundersfoot
Tenby
Caldy Island
Carmarthen Bay
St. Govan's Head
St. Ann's Head
Kidwelly
Burry Port
Llanelli
Llandeilo
Ammanford
Pontardawe
Gorseinon
Gower
Rhossili
Port Eynon
Mumbles Head
SWANSEA
Swansea Bay
Neath
Port Talbot
Maesteg
Bridgend
Porthcawl
Llantwit-Major
Brecon Beacons
Fforest Fawr
Merthyr Tydfil
Aberdare
WALES
Bristol Channel
Lundy
Ilfracombe
Lynton
Foreland Point
Porlock
Exmoor
Dunkery Beacon 520
Barnstaple
Barnstaple or Bideford Bay
Bideford
Hartland Point
Clovelly
South Molton
Tiverton
Great Torrington
Bude
Bude Bay
Holsworthy
Okehampton
Crediton
Exeter
Boscastle
Tintagel
Launceston
Camelford
Port Isaac
Padstow
Trevose Head
Bodmin Moor
Brown Willy 419
Wadebridge
Bodmin
Newquay
Liskeard
Tavistock
Dartmoor
High Willhays 621
Newton Abbot
Torquay
Paignton
Brixham
PLYMOUTH
Saltash
Torpoint
Looe
Whitsand Bay
Rame Head
Totnes
Dartmouth
Kingsbridge
Start Bay
Start Point
Bolt Tail
Salcombe
Bigbury Bay
St. Austell
St. Austell Bay
Fowey
Lostwithiel
Mevagissey
Perranporth
St. Agnes Head
Truro
Redruth
Camborne
St. Ives
St. Ives Bay
Hayle
Penryn
Falmouth
Falmouth Bay
St. Mawes
Dodman Point
Veryan Bay
Helston
Penzance
Mount's Bay
St. Just
Land's End
Lizard
Lizard Point
Coverack
St. Keverne
ENGLISH
Isles of Scilly
Tresco
St. Martin's
St. Mary's
St. Agnes

Worcester
Redditch
Droitwich
Leamington
Warwick
Daventry
Stratford-upon-Avon
Leominster
Great Malvern
Evesham
Banbury
Towcester
Wolverton
Kempston
Hereford
Ledbury
Tewkesbury
Bletchley
Leighton Buzzard
Ross-on-Wye
Gloucester
Cheltenham
Stow-on-the-Wold
Bicester
Aylesbury
Dunstable
Hemel Hempstead
Monmouth
Abergavenny
Cinderford
Stroud
Cirencester
Witney
OXFORD
Thame
Berkhamsted
Chesham
Watford
Pontypool
Chepstow
Abingdon
Didcot
Wallingford
High Wycombe
Amersham
Beaconsfield
Cwmbran
NEWPORT
Swindon
Henley on Thames
Marlow
Slough
CARDIFF
BRISTOL
Portishead
Chippenham
Calne
Marlborough
Newbury
READING
Maidenhead
Windsor
Staines
Egham
Clevedon
Weston-super-Mare
Bath
Keynsham
Melksham
Devizes
Hungerford
Wokingham
Bracknell
Ascot
Chertsey
Camberley
Farnborough
Woking
Trowbridge
Basingstoke
Fleet
Aldershot
Guildford
Burnham-on-Sea
Frome
Warminster
Salisbury Plain
Andover
Farnham
Godalming
Wells
Shepton Mallet
Glastonbury
Amesbury
Alton
Bridgwater
Street
Salisbury
Winchester
Haslemere
Taunton
Wincanton
Shaftesbury
Romsey
Eastleigh
Petersfield
Yeovil
Sherborne
SOUTHAMPTON
Havant
Chard
Crewkerne
Fordingbridge
Ringwood
Totton
Fareham
PORTSMOUTH
Chichester
Bognor Regis
Axminster
Bridport
Dorchester
Christchurch
POOLE
BOURNEMOUTH
New Milton
Lymington
Gosport
Cowes
Ryde
Isle of Wight
Newport
Sandown
Shanklin
Ventnor
Lyme Regis
Lyme Bay
Weymouth
Swanage
The Needles
St. Catherine's Point
Bill of Portland
Mendip Hills
New Forest
Cotswolds
CHANNEL
Lisbon
Cherbourg
Le Havre
57
59
62
81
4
5
6
A
B
C
D

NORTHAMPTON
CAMBRIDGE
Bedford
Newmarket
Bury St. Edmunds
IPSWICH
Felixstowe
Harwich
Colchester
Clacton-on-Sea
Chelmsford
Maldon
Cheltenham
OXFORD
Banbury
Bletchley
Luton
Stevenage
Hatfield
Harlow
Aylesbury
High Wycombe
Watford
Swindon
READING
Newbury
Basingstoke
Guildford
Woking
LONDON
CROYDON
Crawley
Reigate
Tonbridge
Tunbridge Wells
Maidstone
Chatham
Gillingham
Rochester
Gravesend
SOUTHEND-ON-SEA
Basildon
Canterbury
Margate
Ramsgate
Deal
Dover
Folkestone
Ashford
Hastings
Bexhill
Eastbourne
BRIGHTON
Worthing
Chichester
PORTSMOUTH
SOUTHAMPTON
Winchester
Salisbury
BOURNEMOUTH
Christchurch
Isle of Wight
Newport
Calais
Boulogne-sur-Mer
Strait of Dover
The Weald
North Downs
South Downs
Salisbury Plain
Rotterdam
Oostende
Dieppe
Le Havre
Le Touquet
Zeebrugge
Dunkerque
Hoek van Holland
Bremerhaven
Hamburg
Antwerpen
Esbjerg
Göteborg
Kristiansand
59
61
63

ENGLISH CHANNEL
Strait of Dover
BELGIQUE
PICARDIE
The Weald
South Downs
London
Gravesend
Rochester
Chatham
Gillingham
Sheerness
Maidstone
Canterbury
Margate
Ramsgate
Deal
Dover
Folkestone
Hythe
Ashford
Tonbridge
Tunbridge Wells
Crawley
Horsham
Guildford
Worthing
Brighton
Hove
Lewes
Eastbourne
Hastings
Bexhill
Tenterden
Dungeness
Calais
Dunkerque
Boulogne-sur-Mer
Étaples
Montreuil
Berck-Plage
Abbeville
Dieppe
Le Tréport
Amiens
Arras
Lille
Roubaix
Tourcoing
Lens
Béthune
St. Omer
Oostende
Brugge
Kortrijk
Roeselare
Ieper
Douai
Doullens
Hesdin
Southend

NORDSEE
NEDERLAND
Terschelling
Ameland
Schiermon
Vlieland
Texel
Den Burg
Den Helder
Hippolytushoef
Harlingen
Franeker
Leeuwarden
Bolsward
Sneek
Joure
Heerenveen
Wolvega
Lemmer
Ijsselmeer
Medemblik
Enkhuizen
Schagen
Alkmaar
Bergen
Egmond aan Zee
Heiloo
Castricum
Hoorn
Purmerend
Edam
Volendam
Beverwijk
Ijmuiden
Velsen
HAARLEM
Zandvoort
Heemstede
Zaandam
AMSTERDAM
Hillegom
Amstelveen
Aalsmeer
Naarden
Bussum
Huizen
Muiden
Weesp
HILVERSUM
Lisse
Noordwijk aan Zee
Katwijk aan Zee
LEIDEN
Wassenaar
Voorburg
'S GRAVENHAGE
Rijswijk
Delft
Monster
'S Gravenzande
Hoek van Holland
Europoort
Maassluis
Schiedam
Vlaardingen
ROTTERDAM
Gouda
Alphen a/d Rijn
Woerden
UTRECHT
Zeist
De Bilt
Amersfoort
Barneveld
Lelystad
Urk
Emmeloord
NOORDOOST-POLDER
OOSTELIJK-FLEVOLAND
Kampen
Zwolle
Harderwijk
Nunspeet
Ermelo
Putten
Nijkerk
Apeldoorn
Ede
ARNHEM
Oosterbeek
Wageningen
Rhenen
Veenendaal
Culemborg
Tiel
NIJMEGEN
Wijchen
Oss
Dordrecht
Gorinchem
Zaltbommel
Spijkenisse
Brielle
Goeree
Schouwen
Zierikzee
Walcheren
Middelburg
Vlissingen
Goes
Tholen
Bergen op Zoom
Roosendaal
BREDA
Oosterhout
Waalwijk
's-Hertogenbosch
TILBURG
Boxtel
Helmond
EINDHOVEN
Geldrop
Venraij
Boxmeer
Cuijk
Groesbeek
Hollandsch Diep
Oosterschelde
Westerschelde
Breskens

4
5
6
A
B
C
Wangerooge
Spiekeroog
Baltrum
Langeoog
Norderney
Juist
Memmert
Borkum
Alte Mellum
Norden
Esens
Wittmund
Jever
WILHELMSHAVEN
Schortens
Sande
Aurich
Emden
Leer
Papenburg
Westerstede
Bad Zwischenahn
OLDENBURG
Edewecht
Varel
Nordenham
BREMERHAVEN
Langen
Brake
Rastede
Osterholz-Scharmbeck
Ritterhude
Lilienthal
BREMEN
Delmenhorst
Ganderkesee
Achim
Kirchweyhe
Hude
Wardenburg
Hatten
Großenkneten
Wildeshausen
Syke
Bassum
Twistringen
Sulingen
Vechta
Cloppenburg
Emstek
Friesoythe
Löningen
Quakenbrück
Dinklage
Lohne
Diepholz
Steinfeld
Damme
Fürstenau
Lingen
Meppen
Haselünne
Nordhorn
Rheine
Bramsche
OSNABRÜCK
Ibbenbüren
Mettingen
Recke
Hopsten
Emsdetten
Greven
Lengerich
Melle
Lübbecke
Espelkamp
Bad Oeynhausen
Bünde
Herford
Bad Salzuflen
Lemgo
Lage
BIELEFELD
Halle
Steinhagen
Brackwede
Gütersloh
Rheda
Wiedenbrück
Verl
Harsewinkel
Warendorf
Ahlen
Beckum
Oelde
Lippstadt
Paderborn
Salzkotten
Geseke
Erwitte
Soest
Werl
Unna
Hamm
MÜNSTER
Dülmen
Coesfeld
Borken
Bocholt
Rhede
Gescher
Ahaus
Gronau
Ochtrup
Burgsteinfurt
Borghorst
Nordwalde
Lüdinghausen
Selm
Werne
Bergkamen
Lünen
Haltern
Marl
Dorsten
RECKLINGHAUSEN
Herten
Gladbeck
HERNE
WANNE EICKEL
GELSENK.
BOTTROP
OBERHSN.
ESSEN
BOCHUM
Witten
DORTMUND
Kamen
Schwerte
Menden
Neheim
Hüsten
Arnsberg
Wesel
Xanten
Voerde
Dinslaken
Moers
Rheinberg
Kamp-Lintfort
Schermbeck
Hengelo
ENSCHEDE
Almelo
Oldenzaal
Borne
Winterswijk
Aalten
Lichtenvoorde
Groenlo
Eibergen
Haaksbergen
Neede
Vriezenveen
Coevorden
Hoogeveen
Emmen
Assen
Veendam
Hoogezand
Delfzijl
Appingedam
Winschoten
Stadskanaal
Musselkanaal
Ter Apel
Klazienaveen
Dedemsvaart
Ommen
Rijssen
Wierden
Nijverdal
GRONINGEN
DEUTSCHLAND
Teutoburger Wald
Wiehen geb.
Münsterland
Emsland
Hümmling
Dollart
66
71
72

Langeness
Hooge
Pellworm
Nordstrand
Bredstedt
Husum
Schleswig
Eckernförde
Kieler Bucht
Friedrichstadt
Tönning
St. Peter
Rendsburg
Kronshagen
KIEL
Heikendf.
Schönberg
Heiligenhafen
Oldenburg
Preetz
Plön
Malente
Eutin
Neustadt
Heide
Wesselburen
Büsum
Meldorf
Neumünster
Einfeld
Bordesholm
Hanerau-Hademarschen
Hohenwestedt
Harwich
Scharhörn
Neuwerk
Marne
Brunsbüttelkoog
Itzehoe
Kellinghusen
Bad Bramstedt
Bad Segeberg
Bad Schwartau
Timmendorfer Strand
Travemünde
LÜBECK
Bad Oldesloe
Reinfeld
Cuxhaven
Otterndorf
Glückstadt
Elmshorn
Quickborn
Kaltenkchn.
Henstedt
Norderstedt
Ahrensburg
Großhansdorf
Ratzeburg
Mölln
Uetersen
Pinneberg
Wedel
HAMBURG
Stade
Buxtehude
Harburg
Bergedorf
Glinde
Reinbek
Schwarzenbek
Geesthacht
Lauenburg
Boizenburg
Winsen
Buchholz
Lüneburg
Alte Mellum
Dorum
Langen
BREMERHAVEN
Nordenham
Bremervörde
Brake
Hagen
Zeven
Tostedt
Osterholz-Scharmbeck
Ritterhude
Lilienthal
BREMEN
Delmenhorst
Ganderkesee
Achim
Rotenburg
Schneverdingen
LÜNEBURGER HEIDE
Soltau
Munster
Uelzen
Bevensen
Wildeshausen
Großenkneten
Syke
Verden
Walsrode
Fallingbostel
Bergen
Visbek
Twistringen
Bassum
Vechta
Diepholz
Sulingen
Nienburg
Hoya
Celle
Wittingen
Gifhorn
Neustadt am Rübenberge
Langenhagen
Burgdorf
Fallersleben
Wolfsburg
Wunstorf
HANNOVER
Lehrte
Peine
BRAUNSCHWEIG
Minden
Bückeburg
Lübbecke
Bad Oeynhausen
Rinteln
Barsinghausen
Springe
Sarstedt
Wolfenbüttel
Helmstedt
Espelkamp
Rahden
Steinhuder Meer
Dümmer See
Mittellandkanal
Wiehen-geb.

Fehmarn
Mecklenburger
Bucht
RÜGEN
Sassnitz
Bergen
Putbus
Binz
Sellin
Göhren
Greifswalder
Bodden
Zingst
Prerow
Barth
Stralsund
Ribnitz-Damgarten
Grimmen
Greifswald
Wolgast
Ostseebad Kühlungsborn
Warnemünde
Bad Doberan
ROSTOCK
Kröpelin
Schwaan
Tessin
Gnoien
Tribsees
Loitz
Demmin
Jarmen
Anklam
Usedom
Wismar
Neukloster
Bützow
Güstrow
Teterow
Malchin
Stavenhagen
Altentreptow
Friedland
Schwerin
Crivitz
Sternberg
Goldberg
Krakow a. See
Waren
Malchow
Neubrandenburg
Burg Stargard
Strasburg
Pasewalk
Parchim
Lübz
Plau
Röbel
Neustrelitz
Woldegk
Prenzlau
Ludwigslust
Neustadt-Glewe
Grabow
Mirow
Wesenberg
Fürstenberg
Templin
Dömitz
Perleberg
PRIGNITZ
Pritzwalk
Wittstock
Rheinsberg
Wittenberge
Kyritz
Neuruppin
Gransee
Zehdenick
Havelberg
Osterburg
Seehausen
Oranienburg
Bernau
Eberswalde
HAVELLÄNDISCHES LUCH
Rathenow
Stendal
Tangermünde
Nauen
Falkensee
Velten
Hennigsdorf
BERLIN
POTSDAM
Teltow
Erkner
Brandenburg
Werder
Premnitz
Ketzin
Genthin
Tangerhütte
Burg
Wolmirstedt
Ziesar
ZAUCHE
Beelitz
Königs Wusterhausen
Zossen
Blankenfelde
Ludwigsfelde
Rüdersdorf

1
2
3
Bornholm
Dueodde
47
Trelleborg
Ystad
Dranske
Altenkirchen
Wiek
Kloster
Neuendorf
Trent
Sagard
Sassnitz
RÜGEN
Gingst
Bergen
Binz
Sellin
Göhren
Samtens
Putbus
Garz
Thießow
Stralsund
Brandshagen
Zudar
Greifswalder Bodden
Reinberg
Grimmen
Greifswald
Lubmin
Peenemünde
Kemnitz
Zinnowitz
Koserow
Wolgast
Rakow
Poggendorf
Loitz
Görmin
Achterwasser
Lassan
Bansin
Heringsdorf
Ahlbeck
Świnoujście
Międzyzdroje
Oderbucht
Jarmen
Gützkow
Tutow
Demmin
Murchin
Usedom
Anklam
Lubin
Wolin
Kołczewo
Międzywodzie
Dziwnów
Pobierowo
Kamień Pomorski
Niechorze
Rewal
Mrzeżyno
Kołobrzeg
Ustronie Morskie
Dygowo
Wrzosow
Trzebiatów
Gołańcz-Pomorska
Gościno
Cerkwica
Gorawino
Ryman
Świerzno
Gryfice
Gołczewo
Moracz
Przybiernów
Płoty
Resko
Starogard
Świdwin
Oderhaff
Leopoldshagen
Mönkebude
Ueckermünde
Ducherow
Rothebur
Burow
Sarnow
Altentreptow
Friedland
Ferdinandshof
Wilhelmsburg
Eggesin
Ahlbeck
Hintersee
Nw. Warpno
Trzebież
Stepnica
Babigoszcz
Nowogard
Wierzbięcin
Łobez
Rossow
Rothemühl
Torgelow
Schönbeck
Jatznick
Neubrandenburg
Rosenow
Penzlin
Burg Stargard
Woldegk
Strasburg
Pasewalk
Rothenklempenow
Police
Tanowo
Dobra
Goleniów
Miękowo
Mosty
Dobra
Kania
Węgorzyno
Drawsko Pomorskie
Lubczyna
Maszewo
Przemocze
Chociwel
Ińsko
Ciemnik
Löcknitz
Wolfshagen
Bredenfelde
Möllenbeck
Fürstenwerder
Göritz
Grambow
Brüssow
SZCZECIN (STETTIN)
Neustrelitz
Dedelow
Kleptow
Krackow
Oleszna
Kobylanka
Stargard Szczeciński
Dobrzany
Sulibórz
Schönermark
Feldberg
Prenzlau
Schmölln
Penkun
Storkow
Sommersdorf
Kolbacz
J. Miedwie
Kluczewo
Wierzbno
Suchań
Wapnica
Recz
Triepkendorf
Hardenbeck
Boitzenburg
Bietikow
Gartz
Gryfino
DEUTSCHLAND
Lychen
Mittenwalde
Haßleben
Gerswalde
Gramzow
Kasekow
Linie
Pyrzyce
Lubiatowo
Dolice
Choszczno
Suliszewo
Fürstenberg
Densow
Stolpsee
Templin
Milmersdorf
Stegelitz
Polßen
Passow
Widuchowo
Banie
Zieleniewo
Gransee
Hammelspring
Gollin
Greiffenberg
Vierraden
Schwedt
Felchow
Mielęcin
Krępcin
Pełczyce
Bierzwnik
Friedrichswalde
Groß-Dölln
Zehdenick
Joachimsthal
Werbellinsee
Ziethen
Angermünde
Krajnik Dolny
Swobnica
Grzybno
Lipiany
Barlinek
Jarosławsko
Krewelin
Piasek
Chojna
Trzcińsko-Zdrój
Rów
Dobiegniew
Falkenthal
Groß Schönebeck
Parstein
Myślibórz
Bobrówko
Strzelce Krajeńskie
Przyłęg
Liebenwalde
Zerpenschleuse
Oderberg
Hohenwutzen
Cedynia
Moryń
Str. Rudnica
Siekierki
Różańsko
Ściechów
Kłodawa
Drezdenko
Nassenheide
Kloster Felde
Finow
Eberswalde
Falkenberg
Bad Freienwalde
Mieszkowice
Barnówko
Gorzów Wielkopolski (Landsberg)
Santok
Noteć
Oranienburg
Germendorf
Biesenthal
Birkenwerder
Heckelberg
Wriezen
Boleszkowice
Dębno
Goszczanowo
Velten
Hohen Neuendorf
Bernau
Steinbeck
Tiefensee
Altlewin
Mühlenbeck
Neutrebbin
Letschin
Witnica
Bogdaniec
Hennigsdorf
MÄRKISCHE SCHWEIZ
Werneuchen
Prötzel
Sarbinowo
Warta
Murzynowo
BERLIN
Seefeld
Altlandsberg
Strausberg
Marxwalde
Kostrzyn
Kietz
Krzeszyce
Skwierzyna
Falkensee
Buckow
Słońsk
Lubniewice
Przytoczna
Petershagen
Müncheberg
Seelow
Oder
Odra
Hohensaaten-Friedrichsthaler Wasserstraße
Oder-Havel-Kanal
Vosskanal
Ruppiner Kanal
67
76
E6
E14
E74
T81
A
B
C

4
5
6
17°
18°
A
B
C
Jastrzębia-Góra
Rozewie
Władysławowo
Chałupy
Mierzeja Helska
Jastarnia
Jurata
Hel
Krokowa
Zarnowiec
J. Żarnowieckie
Puck
Łeba
J. Sarbsko
Sasino
Choczewo
J. Łebsko
Żelazno
Piaśnica Wielka
Wicko
Kostkowo
Rowy
J. Gardno
Główczyce
Cecenowo
Wejherowo
Reda
Rumia
Rewa
Gościcino
GDYNIA
Sopot (Zoppot)
GDAŃSK (DANZIG)
Ustka
Żelkowo
Lębork
Bożepole Wielkie
Luzino
Szemud
Chwaszczyno
Jarosławiec
Duninowo
J. Wicko
Lubuczewo
Pogorzelice
Potęgowo
Postomino
J. Kopań
Słupsk (Stolp)
Mianowice
Łupawa
Linia
Strzepcz
Kokoszki
Darłowo
Wieprza
Stary Jarosław
Sycewice
Kwakowo
Czarna-Dąbrówka
Budowo
Sierakowice
Kartuzy
Borkowo
Sławno
Bukowo Morskie
Korzybie
Unichowo
Brodnica Graniczna
Kiełpino
Pruszcz Gd.
Malechowo
Barcino
Suchorze
Kołczygłowy
Egiertowo
Ostrowiec
J. Jamno
Jamno
Sianów
Kępice
Krąg
Borzytuchom
Stężyca
Przywidz
Sobowidz
Pszczółki
Koszalin (Köslin)
Trzebielino
Bytów
Nakło
Korne
Kościerzyna
Kaliska
Nowa Karczma
Godziszewo
Tczew
Manowo
Nacław
Polanów
Niezabyszewo
Półczno
Tuchomie
Studzienice
Lipusz
Skarszewy
Liniewo
Czarlin
Niedalino
Mostowo
Dretyń
Kawcze
Borzyszkowy
Sominy
Dziemiany
Białogard
Świetlino
Miastko
J. Bobięcińskie
Drzewiany
Płaszczyca
Lipnica
J. Wdzydze
Kiszewa Stara
Starogard Gd.
Pelplin
Bobolice
Wiele
Tychowo
Biały Bór
Koczała
Brusy
Karsin
Kaliska
Lubichowo
Morzeszczyn
Gniew
Tychówko
Parsęta
Grzmiąca
Wierzchowo
Brzezie
Konarzyny
Macikał
Czarna Woda
Czersk
Skórcz
Połczyn-Zdrój
Przechlewo
J. Charzykowskie
Rytel
Osiek
Smętowo
Barwice
Rzeczenica
Charzykowy
Chojnice
Legbąd
Śliwice
Ostropole
Szczecinek (Neustettin)
Gwda Wielka
Czarne
Człuchów
Silno
Bory Tucholskie
Nowe
Gawroniec
Kluczewo
Jeleniono
Poźna
Lotyń
Barkowo
Zamarte
Tuchola
Osie
Warlubie
J. Siecino
J. Pile
Łubowo
Cierznie
Debrzno
Kamień Kraj.
Pamiętowo
Byslaw
Grudziądz
J. Drawsko
Czaplinek
Broczyno
Okonek
Ledyczek
Jeżewo
Grupa Graniczna
Złocieniec
Pojezierze
Wierzchowo
Sypniewo
Podgaje
Lipka
Sępólno-Krajeńskie
Gostycyn
J. Koronowskie
Świecie
Iłowiec
Jastrowie
Złotów
Makowarsko
Przechowo
Chełmno
Piecnik
Szwecja
Sypniewo
Więcbork
Koronowo
Kotomierz
Zbrachlin
Stolno
Płytnica
Wałcz
J. Bytyńskie
Marcinkowice
Krępsko
Łobżenica
Mrocza
Tryszczyn
Trzeciewiec
Świętosław
Dobrzyca
Wysoka
Osielsko
Unisław
Chełmża
Tuczno
Gostomia
Fordon
Grzywna
Rusinowo
Szydłowo
Piła (Schneidemühl)
Śmiłowo
Wyrzysk
Sadki
Nakło n. N.
Kanał Bydgoski
BYDGOSZCZ
Czarnowo
Pędzewo
Łysomice
Stobno
Osiek
Białe Błota
TORUŃ
Człopa
Białośliwie
Miasteczko Krajeńskie
Noteć
Rynarzewo
Solec Kujawski
Puszcza Bydgoska
Szczuczarz
Trzcianka
Ujście
Szamocin
Smogulec
Szubin
Nowa-Wieś Wielka
Cierpice
Siedlisko
Chodzież
Margonin
Kcynia
Łabiszyn
Kuźnica Czarnkowska
Gołańcz
Złotniki Kujawskie
Gniewkowo
Otłoczyn
Wieleń
Czarnków
Huta
Czeszewo
Wapno
Barcin
Aleksandrów Kujawski
Budzyń
Żnin
Piechcin
Pakość
Lubasz
Ryczywół
Wągrowiec
Domasławek
Inowrocław
Puszcza Notecka
Wenecja
Tupadły
Klempicz
Dąbrowa
Janikowo
Pieranie
Ludomy
Rogoźno
Mieścisko
Janowiec Wielkopolski
Rogowo
Kruszwica
Kanał Bachorze
Dobre
Chojno
Wronki
Obrzycko
Popowo Kościelne
Mogilno
Radziejów
Biezdrowo
Warta
Skoki
Modliszewko
Strzelno
Szamotuły
Oborniki
Kłecko
Sierakowo
Gopło
Piotrków Kujawski
Nojewo
Murowana Goślina
Kiszkowo
Trzemeszno
Ostrowo
Kaźmierz
Chludowo
Owińska
Gniezno
Jankowo Dolne
Orchowo
Rokietnica
Pniewy
78
77

BREDA TILBURG EINDHOVEN

OOSTENDE Brugge GENT ANTWERPEN Mechelen BRUXELLES Leuven

Roeselare Kortrijk LILLE Tournai ROUBAIX Mons Charleroi Namur

Valenciennes Maubeuge Dinant

Cambrai St. Quentin Charleville-Mézières Sedan

Laon Soissons REIMS

Wesel
Xanten
Goch
Kevelaer
Venlo
Venraij
Roermond
Weert
Sittard
Heerlen
Maastricht
Aachen
Eupen
Verviers
Spa
Malmedy
St. Vith
Bastogne
Luxembourg
Esch-s.-Alzette
Dudelange
Thionville
Hayange
Longwy
Arlon
Trier
Bitburg
Wittlich
Bernkastel-Kues
Traben-Trarbach
Cochem
Mayen
Koblenz
Neuwied
Andernach
Boppard
Bingen
Bad Kreuznach
Idar-Oberstein
Kaiserslautern
Zweibrücken
Homburg
Neunkirchen
Saarbrücken
Saarlouis
Merzig
Völklingen
St. Ingbert
St. Wendel
Bonn
Bad Godesberg
Köln
Leverkusen
Düsseldorf
Neuß
Mönchengladbach
Rheydt
Krefeld
Duisburg
Mülheim
Essen
Oberhsn.
Bottrop
Gelsenk.
Bochum
Herne
Wanne-Eickel
Recklinghausen
Dortmund
Hagen
Wuppertal
Solingen
Remscheid
Lüdenscheid
Iserlohn
Unna
Soest
Siegen
Siegburg
Düren
Jülich
Zulpich
Euskirchen
Bergisch Gladbach
Gummersbach
Limburg
Bad Ems
Montabaur
Rüdesheim
Simmern
Deutschland
Luxembourg
Eifel
Westerwald
Sauerland
Hunsrück
Pfälzer Bergland
Nürburg Ring

Celle
Gifhorn
Wolfsburg
Braunschweig
Helmstedt
Wolfenbüttel
Salzgitter
Peine
Hannover
Hildesheim
Goslar
Halberstadt
Wernigerode
Nordhausen
Sondershausen
Mühlhausen
Göttingen
Northeim
Einbeck
Holzminden
Höxter
Hameln
Bad Pyrmont
Detmold
Paderborn
Herford
Bielefeld
Gütersloh
Minden
Nienburg
Diepholz
Osnabrück
Rheine
Lingen
Nordhorn
Münster
Hamm
Soest
Lippstadt
Unna
Dortmund
Bochum
Hagen
Iserlohn
Lüdenscheid
Remscheid
Kassel
Korbach
Bad Wildungen
Arolsen
Eschwege
Heiligenstadt
Witzenhausen
Hessisch Lichtenau
Melsungen
Fritzlar
Warburg
Brilon
Meschede
Arnsberg
Frankenberg
Bad Langensalza
Duderstadt
Osterode
Herzberg

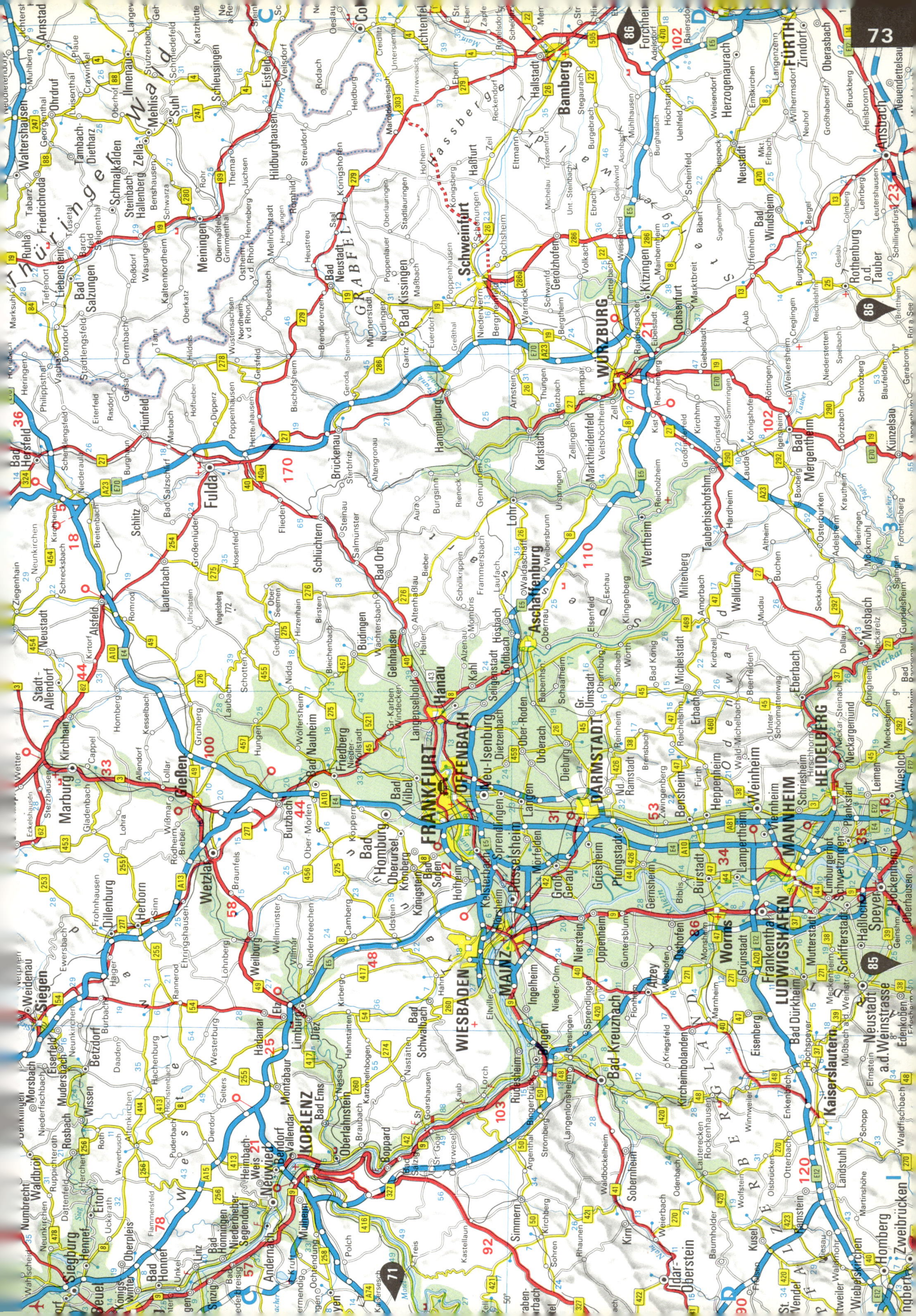
FRANKFURT
OFFENBACH
WIESBADEN
MAINZ
DARMSTADT
MANNHEIM
LUDWIGSHAFEN
HEIDELBERG
KOBLENZ
WÜRZBURG
Schweinfurt
Bamberg
FÜRTH
Fulda
Gießen
Marburg
Wetzlar
Siegen
Limburg
Worms
Speyer
Kaiserslautern
Bad Kreuznach
Aschaffenburg
Hanau
Neuwied
Bad Hersfeld
Meiningen
Suhl
Ansbach
Kitzingen
Bad Kissingen
Bad Mergentheim
Weinheim
Bingen
Idar-Oberstein
Zweibrücken
Siegburg
Thüringer Wald
Haßberge
Steigerwald

HANNOVER
Langenhagen
Burgdorf
Lehrte
Sehnde
Peine
Gifhorn
Fallersleben
Wolfsburg
BRAUNSCHWEIG
Wolfenbüttel
Helmstedt
Schöningen
Gardelegen
Haldensleben
Stendal
Tangermünde
Tangerhütte
Burg
MAGDEBURG
Schönebeck
Hildesheim
SALZGITTER
Salzgitter-Bad
Goslar
Bad Harzburg
Wernigerode
Halberstadt
Oschersleben
Quedlinburg
Thale
Aschersleben
Bernburg
Staßfurt
Calbe
Dessau
Köthen
Alfeld
Einbeck
Seesen
Northeim
Osterode
Herzberg
Bad Lauterberg
Braunlage
Harz
Hettstedt
Eisleben
Mansfeld
Sangerhausen
HALLE
Merseburg
GÖTTINGEN
Duderstadt
Nordhausen
Sondershausen
Bad Frankenhausen
Münden
Heiligenstadt
Dingelstädt
Mühlhausen
Eschwege
Bad Langensalza
Sömmerda
Weissenfels
Naumburg
Zeitz
Apolda
Weimar
ERFURT
Gotha
Eisenach
Jena
GERA
Bad Hersfeld
Arnstadt
Ilmenau
Suhl
Zella-Mehlis
Schmalkalden
Meiningen
Thüringer Wald
Saalfeld
Rudolstadt
Pößneck
Greiz
Plauen
Fulda
Hildburghausen
Sonneberg
Coburg
Kronach
Frankenwald
Hof
Münchberg
Bad Kissingen
Lichtenfels
Grabfeld

BERLIN
POTSDAM
Brandenburg
Falkensee
Nauen
Teltow
Werder
Erkner
Strausberg
Woltersdorf
Rüdersdorf
Petershagen
Altlandsberg
Müncheberg
Fürstenwalde
Frankfurt
Słubice
Rzepin
Königs Wusterhausen
Storkow
Blankenfelde
Ludwigsfelde
Rangsdorf
Zossen
Beelitz
Michendorf
Lehnin
Belzig
Treuenbrietzen
Luckenwalde
Jüterbog
Baruth
Eisenhüttenstadt
Beeskow
Neuzelle
Wilhelm-Pieck-Stadt (Guben)
Gubin
Lübben
Lübbenau
Luckau
Dahme
Golßen
SPREEWALD
FLÄMING
ZAUCHE
Wittenberg
Coswig
Wörlitz
Oranienbaum
Gräfenhainichen
Bad Schmiedeberg
Bad Düben
Jessen
Herzberg
Schlieben
Finsterwalde
Calau
Cottbus
Forst
Spremberg
Welzow
Großräschen
Senftenberg
Lauchhammer
Schwarzheide
Lauta
Hoyerswerda
Weißwasser
Bad Muskau
Niesky
Rothenburg
LAUSITZ
Torgau
Falkenberg
Bad Liebenwerda
Elsterwerda
Doberlug-Kirchhain
Eilenburg
Taucha
LEIPZIG
Wurzen
Brandis
Naunhof
Grimma
Oschatz
Riesa
Strehla
Gröditz
Großenhain
Kamenz
Königsbrück
Ottendorf-Okrilla
Pulsnitz
Bautzen
Görlitz
Löbau
Bischofswerda
Radeberg
Großröhrsdorf
Meißen
Radebeul
Coswig
Lommatzsch
Döbeln
Leisnig
Colditz
Roßwein
Nossen
Waldheim
Hartha
Geringswalde
Rochlitz
Geithain
Frohburg
Bad Lausick
Regis Breitingen
Altenburg
Mittweida
Penig
Burgstädt
Hainichen
Frankenberg
Freiberg
Brand-Erbisdorf
DRESDEN
Freital
Tharandt
Heidenau
Pirna
Dippoldiswalde
Glashütte
Schmiedeberg
Bad Gottleuba
Königstein
Sebnitz
Bad Schandau
Neustadt
Stolpen
Arnsdorf
Zittau
Ostritz
Ebersbach
Neugersdorf
Seifhennersdorf
Großschönau
Oppach
Bernstadt
KARL-MARX-STADT (CHEMNITZ)
Flöha
Oederan
Eppendorf
Großhartmannsdorf
Zschopau
Lengefeld
Pockau
Sayda
Olbernhau
Marienberg
Zöblitz
Wolkenstein
Ehrenfriedersdorf
Annaberg-Buchholz
Geyer
Thalheim
Stollberg
Burkhardtsdorf
Hohenstein-Ernstthal
Glauchau
Meerane
Limbach-Oberfrohna
Lugau
Oelsnitz
Lichtenstein
ZWICKAU
Aue
Schneeberg
Lößnitz
Schwarzenberg
Eibenstock
Johanngeorgenstadt
Zwönitz
Crottendorf
Oberwiesenthal
Fichtel Bg. 1214
Klínovec 1244
Klášterec n. Ohří
Kadaň
Chomutov
Jirkov
Most
Litvínov
Bílina
Teplice
Duchcov
Krupka
Dubí
Ústí n. Labem
Děčín
Česká Kamenice
Česká Lípa
Nový Bor
Mimoň
Litoměřice
Lovosice
Třebenice
Roudnice n. Labem
Mělník
Louny
Žatec
Postoloprty
Karlovy Vary
Ostrov
Chodov
Stará Role
Nejdek
Kraslice
Klingenthal
Sokolov
Slaný
Kladno
Kralupy n. Vltavou
PRAHA
Neratovice
Brandýs n. Labem-Stará Boleslav
Čelákovice
Liberec
Hrádek n. Nisou
Jablonné v Podještědí
Varnsdorf
Rumburk
Krásná Lípa
Šluknov
Jílové
ČESKOSLOVENSKO
Krušné Hory
Erzgebirge
Lužické Hory
Sulęcin
Ośno
Cybinka
Lubsko
Tuplice
Łęknica
Przewóz
Bogatynia
Sieniawka
Zgorzelec
Boczów
Lubin
Maszewo
Wężyska
Dychów
Brody
Jasień
Zasieki
Kostrzyn
Słońsk
Górzyca
Lisów
68
76
87
88

BERLIN
POTSDAM
Oranienburg
Eberswalde
Bad Freienwalde
Bernau
Strausberg
Müncheberg
Frankfurt
Slubice
Kostrzyn
Gorzów Wielkopolski (Landsberg)
Dębno
Witnica
Skwierzyna
Międzyrzecz
Sulęcin
Rzepin
Świebodzin
Sulechów
Krosno Odrzańskie
Zielona Góra (Grünberg)
Fürstenwalde
Königs Wusterhausen
Storkow
Beeskow
Eisenhüttenstadt
Ludwigsfelde
Zossen
Luckenwalde
Jüterbog
Dahme
Lübben
Lübbenau
Luckau
Wilhelm-Pieck-Stadt (Guben)
Gubin
Lubsko
Cottbus
Forst
Żary (Sorau)
Żagań
Herzberg
Finsterwalde
Torgau
Falkenberg
Doberlug-Kirchhain
Großräschen
Senftenberg
Spremberg
Bad Muskau
Weißwasser
Lauchhammer
Schwarzheide
Lauta
Hoyerswerda
Bad Liebenwerda
Elsterwerda
Gröditz
Riesa
Oschatz
Strehla
Großenhain
Kamenz
Niesky
Bolesławiec
Görlitz
Zgorzelec
Lubań
Bautzen
Bischofswerda
Löbau
Meißen
Radebeul
Coswig
Radeberg
DRESDEN
Freital
Pirna
Heidenau
Döbeln
Nossen
Mittweida
Hainichen
Freiberg
Frankenberg
KARL-MARX-STADT (CHEMNITZ)
Dippoldiswalde
Neustadt
Sebnitz
Neugersdorf
Ebersbach
Zittau
Bogatynia
Děčín
Česká Kamenice
Česká Lípa
Nový Bor
Liberec
Jablonec n. Nisou
Ústí n. Labem
Teplice
Most
Chomutov
Bílina
Litoměřice
Lovosice
Mladá Boleslav
Turnov
Jičín
Annaberg-Buchholz
Marienberg
Olbernhau
DEUTSCHLAND
SPREEWALD
LAUSITZ
MÄRKISCHE SCHWEIZ
ČESKOSLOVENSKO
Lužické Hory
Jizerské Hory
75
68
87
88
1
2
3
4
A
B
C

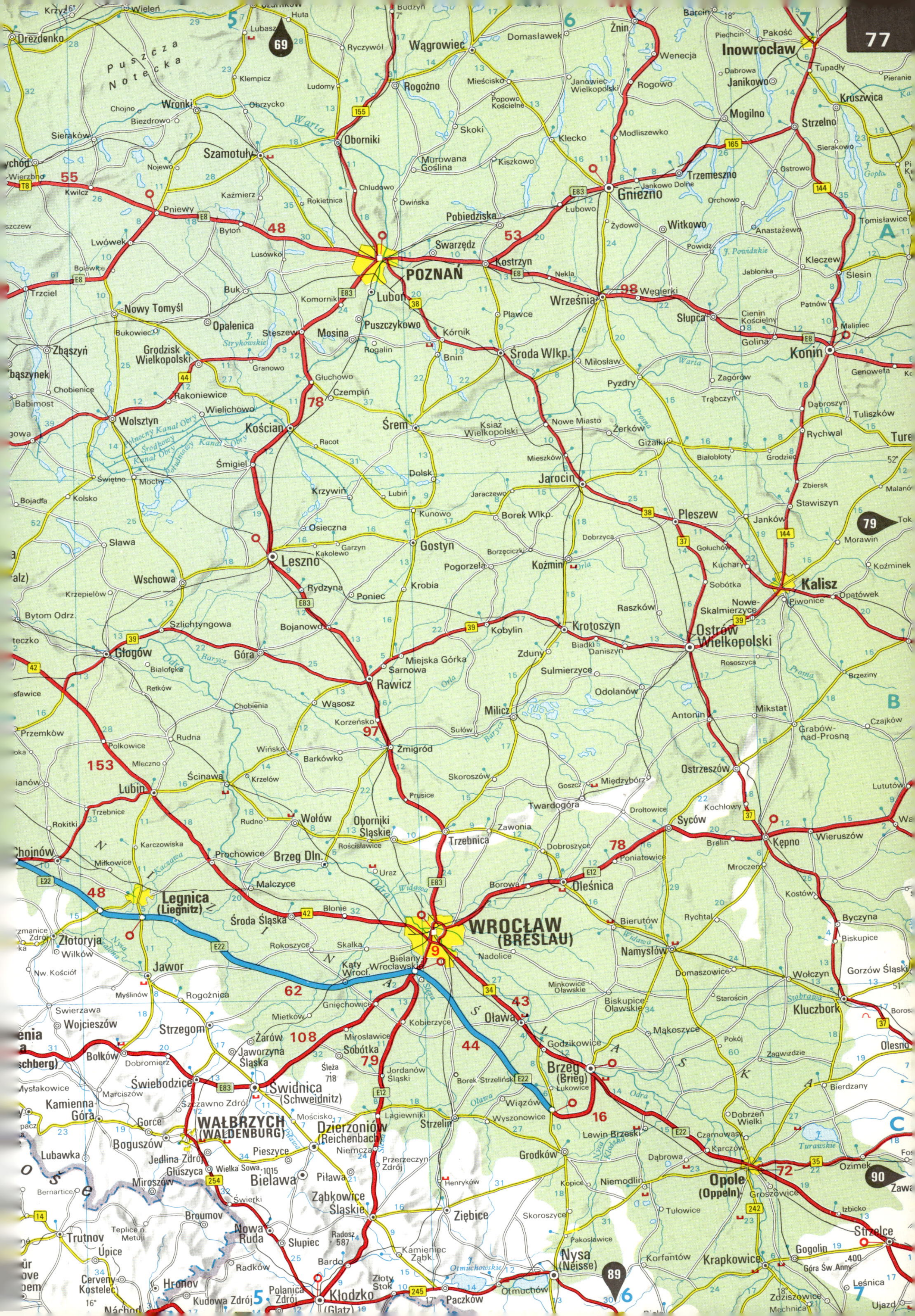
Poznań
Wrocław
(Breslau)
Kalisz
Leszno
Gniezno
Konin
Inowrocław
Legnica
(Liegnitz)
Wałbrzych
(Wałdenburg)
Opole
(Oppeln)
Głogów
Lubin
Września
Jarocin
Pleszew
Ostrów Wielkopolski
Krotoszyn
Rawicz
Gostyń
Kościan
Śrem
Środa Wlkp.
Kórnik
Oborniki
Szamotuły
Wągrowiec
Rogoźno
Mogilno
Strzelno
Kruszwica
Trzemeszno
Witkowo
Słupca
Kleczew
Nowy Tomyśl
Grodzisk Wielkopolski
Opalenica
Wolsztyn
Zbąszyń
Międzychód
Sieraków
Wronki
Pniewy
Lwówek
Trzciel
Buk
Stęszew
Mosina
Puszczykowo
Luboń
Swarzędz
Kostrzyn
Pobiedziska
Murowana Goślina
Skoki
Kłecko
Żnin
Janikowo
Pakość
Czempiń
Śmigiel
Krzywiń
Osieczna
Wschowa
Sława
Rydzyna
Poniec
Krobia
Pogorzela
Borek Wlkp.
Koźmin
Kobylin
Zduny
Sulmierzyce
Odolanów
Milicz
Żmigród
Trzebnica
Oborniki Śląskie
Wołów
Ścinawa
Prusice
Oleśnica
Syców
Kępno
Wieruszów
Ostrzeszów
Grabów nad Prosną
Mikstat
Międzybórz
Twardogóra
Bierutów
Namysłów
Byczyna
Kluczbork
Wołczyn
Olesno
Oława
Brzeg
(Brieg)
Grodków
Niemodlin
Krapkowice
Gogolin
Strzelce
Nysa
(Neisse)
Otmuchów
Paczków
Ziębice
Ząbkowice Śląskie
Kłodzko
(Glatz)
Polanica Zdrój
Kudowa Zdrój
Nowa Ruda
Bielawa
Dzierżoniów
(Reichenbach)
Świdnica
(Schweidnitz)
Strzegom
Jawor
Złotoryja
Chojnów
Bolków
Świebodzice
Kamienna Góra
Boguszów
Strzelin
Sobótka
Kąty Wrocławskie
Środa Śląska
Prochowice
Brzeg Dln.
Chocianów
Polkowice
Sulmierzyce
Szlichtyngowa
Góra
Bojanowo
Trutnov
Úpice
Náchod
Puszcza Notecka
Poznań
Ślęża
718
E8
E83
E12
E22
E14
E261
42
38
39
37
35
34
44
144
155
165
242
245
254
55
48
53
98
78
97
108
153
62
43
44
79
72
16
9
69
79
89
90
A
B
C
5
6
7

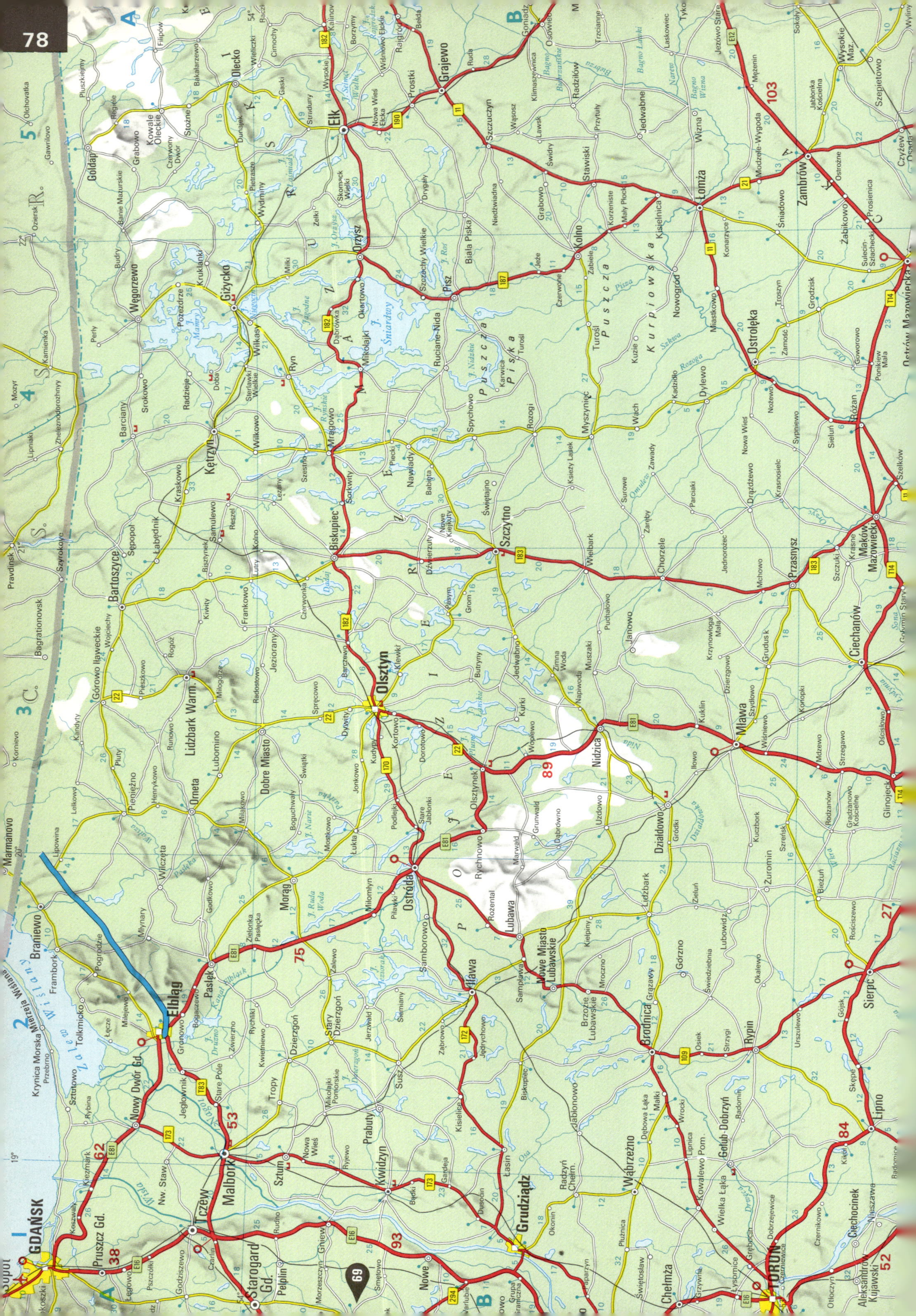
GDAŃSK
Sopot
Pruszcz Gd.
Tczew
Malbork
Starogard Gd.
Pelplin
Gniew
Nowe
Kwidzyn
Sztum
Prabuty
Grudziądz
Chełmno
Wąbrzeźno
Brodnica
Golub-Dobrzyń
Rypin
Lipno
Ciechocinek
Aleksandrów Kujawski
Nowy Dwór Gd.
Elbląg
Braniewo
Frombork
Tolkmicko
Krynica Morska
Pasłęk
Morąg
Ostróda
Iława
Susz
Lubawa
Nowe Miasto Lubawskie
Działdowo
Nidzica
Mława
Olsztynek
Olsztyn
Dobre Miasto
Orneta
Lidzbark Warm.
Górowo Iławeckie
Bartoszyce
Biskupiec
Kętrzyn
Mrągowo
Ryn
Giżycko
Węgorzewo
Gołdap
Olecko
Ełk
Orzysz
Pisz
Mikołajki
Grajewo
Goniądz
Kolno
Szczytno
Wielbark
Myszyniec
Łomża
Zambrów
Ostrołęka
Różan
Przasnysz
Maków Mazowiecki
Ciechanów
Glinojeck
Sierpc
Żuromin
Bieżuń
Lidzbark
Bagrationovsk
Pravdinsk
Mamonovo
Ozersk
Zheleznodorozhnyy
Kornevo
Krasnoye
Wizna
Jedwabne
Stawiski
Szczuczyn
Raigród
Puszcza Piska
Puszcza Kurpiowska
Zalew Wiślany
Mierzeja Wiślana
Wisła
Narew
Ostrów Mazowiecka
62
38
53
93
75
89
103
84
52
27
69

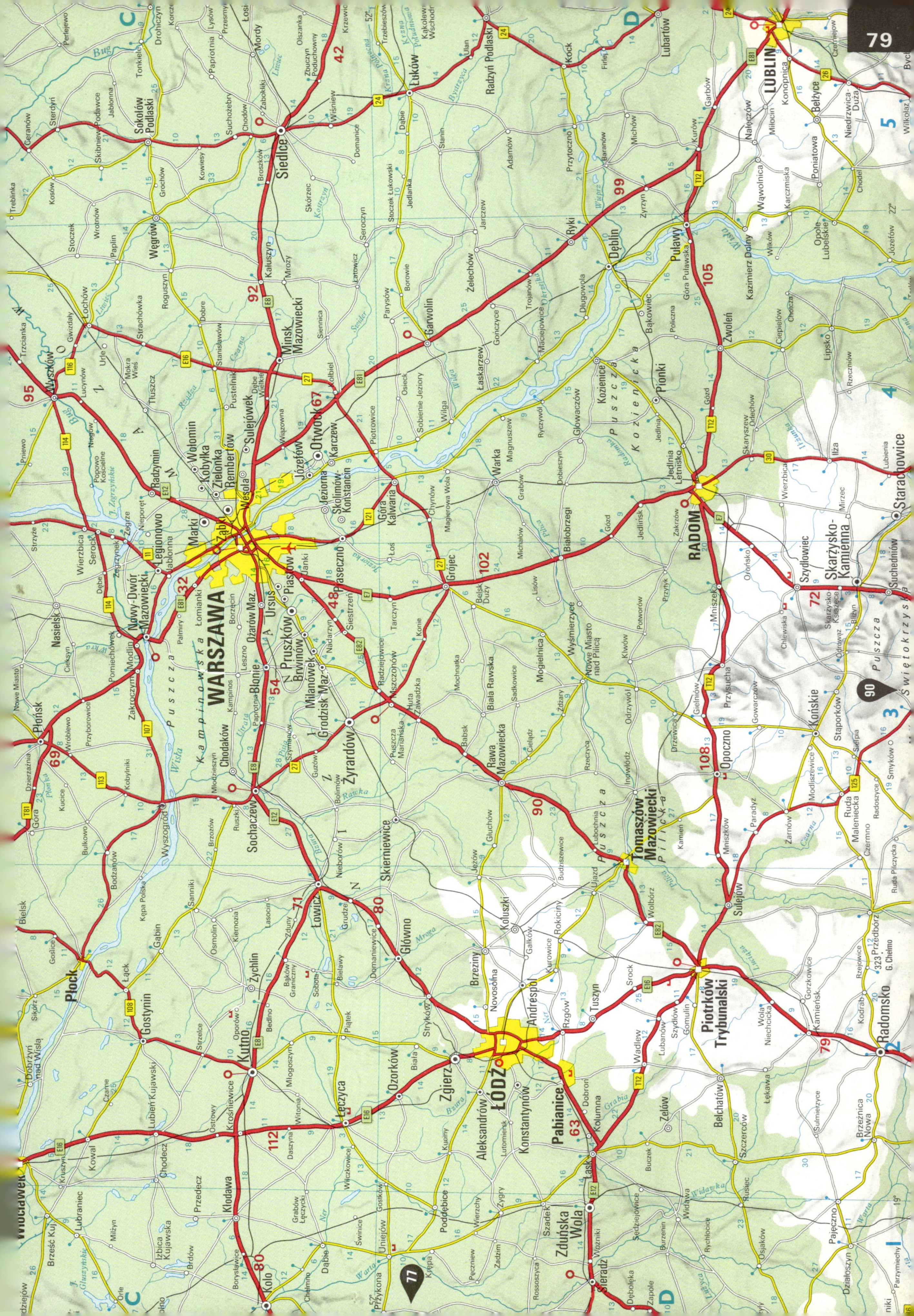

WARSZAWA
ŁÓDŹ
RADOM
LUBLIN
Płock
Siedlce
Włocławek
Kutno
Łowicz
Skierniewice
Żyrardów
Sochaczew
Grodzisk Maz.
Pruszków
Piaseczno
Otwock
Mińsk Mazowiecki
Węgrów
Sokołów Podlaski
Łuków
Radzyń Podlaski
Garwolin
Dęblin
Puławy
Ryki
Kozienice
Grójec
Rawa Mazowiecka
Tomaszów Mazowiecki
Piotrków Trybunalski
Bełchatów
Pabianice
Zgierz
Zduńska Wola
Sieradz
Łask
Radomsko
Opoczno
Końskie
Skarżysko-Kamienna
Starachowice
Zwoleń
Wyszków
Legionowo
Nowy Dwór Mazowiecki
Płońsk
Gostynin
Łęczyca
Koło
Kłodawa
Wołomin
Marki
Ząbki
Kobyłka
Zielonka
Sulejówek
Józefów
Brwinów
Milanówek
Błonie
Ożarów Maz.
Ursus
Piastów
Koluszki
Brzeziny
Głowno
Ozorków
Aleksandrów
Konstantynów
Tuszyn
Sulejów
Puszcza Kampinoska
Puszcza Kozienicka
Puszcza Pilicka
Puszcza Świętokrzyska
Wisła
Bug
Pilica
Narew
Wieprz
Bzura
Warta
C
D
1
2
3
4
5

Plymouth
60
Guernsey
St. Peter P
Ile de Bréhat
Perros-Guirec
Plougrescant
Ploumanac'h
Trégastel
Pleubian
Lézardrieux
Ploubazlanec
Paimpol
Tréguier
Lannion
Trébeurden
Ilde de Batz
Roscoff
St. Pol-de-Léon
Primel-Trégastel
Plougasnou
Locquirec
St. Michel en-Grève
Pontrieux
Plouézec
Plouha
St. Quay-Portrieux
Etables-sur-Mer
Binic
Baie de St. Brieuc
Lanvollon
Bégard
Plestin-les-Grèves
Plouaret
Lanmeur
Carantec
Taulé
Cléder
Plouescat
Brignogan
Kerlouan
Plouguerneau
Lannilis
Le Folgoët
Lesneven
Plouzévédé
Portsall
Porspoder
Ploudalmézeau
Landivisiau
Morlaix
Pleyber Christ
St. Thégonnec
Guingamp
Châtelaudren
Plouagat
St. Brieuc
Plérin
Yffiniac
Ile d' Ouessant
Lampaul
Lanildut
Plabennec
Gouesnou
St. Renan
BREST
Guipavas
Landerneau
Ploudiry
Ile Molène
Le Conquet
Pte. de St. Mathieu
Plougastel-Daoulas
Daoulas
Sizun
Huelgoat
Belle-Isle en-Terre
Plougonver
Louargat
Mousteru
Bourbriac
Callac
Quintin
Kérien
Camaret
Landévennec
Le Faou
Brasparts
Poullaouen
Carhaix Plouguer
Crozon
Morgat
Pont-de-Buis
Pleyben
Châteaulin
Châteauneuf-du-Faou
Spézet
Baie de Douarnenez
Douarnenez
Locronan
Briec
Roudouallec
Gourin
Rostrenen
Glomel
Gouarec
Mur-de-Bretagne
St. Nicolas-du-Pélem
Mael-Carhaix
Plouguernevel
Corlay
Uzel
Plœuc-sur-Lie
Loudéac
Plémet-la-Pierre
La Chèze
Ile de Sein
Pte. du Raz
Plogoff
Pont-Croix
Audierne
Plouhinec
Landudec
Plozévet
Quimper
Plogastel St. Germain
Coray
Guiscriff
Scaër
Bannalec
Rosporden
Le Faouët
Guéméné-sur-Scorff
Kernascléden
Plouray
Cléguérec
Noyal-Pontivy
Pontivy
Rohan
Canal de Nantes
Pluméliau
Moréac
Locminé
Baud
Bubry
Plouay
Arzano
Quimperlé
Pont-Scorff
Pont-Aven
Riec-s.-Belon
Moëlan
Clohars Carnoët
Le Pouldu
Névez
Port-Manech
Trégunc
Concarneau
Beg-Meil
Fouesnant
Bénodet
Loctudy
Pont-l'Abbé
Plonéour-Lanvern
St. Guénolé
Penmarch
Pte. de Penmarch
Guilvinec
Lesconil
Iles de Glénans
Hennebont
Lanester
Lorient
Ploemeur
Larmor-Plage
Port-Louis
Groix
Ile de Groix
Languidic
Camors
Landévant
Pluvigner
Ste Anne d'Auray
Grand-Champ
St. Jean-Brévelay
Auray
Vannes
Elven
Belz
Carnac
La Trinité
Locmariaquer
Port Navalo
Sarzeau
Noyalo
St. Pierre-Quiberon
Baie de Quiberon
Quiberon
St. Gildas-de-Rhuys
Ile de Houat
Ile de Hœdic
Sauzon
Le Palais
Bangor
Locmaria
Belle Île
Piriac-su

Alderney
Auderville
Cherbourg
Equeurdreville
Octeville
Tourlaville
St. Pierre-Eglise
Barfleur
Beaumont Hague
Dielette
Les Pieux
Valognes
Quettehou
St. Vaast-la-Hougue
Quinéville
Montebourg
Utah Beach
Bricquebec
Sark
Carteret
Barneville
Portbail
St. Sauveur-le-Vicomte
Ste. Mère Eglise
Ste. Marie-du-Mont
Grandcamp-les-Bains
Omaha Beach
Vierville
St. Laurent
Port-en-Bessin
Baie de la Seine
Southampton
Heuqueville
Montivillie
Ste. Adresse
LE HAVRE
Honfleur
Villerville
Trouville
Deauville
Villers-sur-Mer
Houlgate
Dives
Cabourg
Luc-sur-Mer
Riva-Bella
Lion-s.-M.
Ouistreham
St. Aubin-sur-Mer
Courseulles-sur-Mer
Arromanches
Langrune-s.-M.
Blainville-sur-Orne
Creully
Bayeux
Isigny
Carentan
La Haye-du-Puits
Jersey
St. Helier
Lessay
Périers
Sainteny
St. Jean-de-Daye
Littry-la-Mine
Balleroy
Tilly-sur-Seulles
Caen
Mondeville
Fleury-sur-Orne
Evrecy
Moult
Mézidon
Caumont-l'Eventé
St. Lô
Marigny
St. Sauveur-Lendelin
Canisy
Coutainville
Coutances
Torigni-sur-Vire
Villers-Bocage
Aunay-sur-Odon
St. Laurent-de-Condel
Bretteville-sur-Laize
St. Pierre-sur-Dives
Potigny
Thury-Harcourt
St. Martin-de-Besaces
Plateau des Minquiers
Tessy-s.-Vire
Percy
Pont Farcy
Falaise
Bréhal
Gavray
Condé-sur-Noireau
Pont d'Ouilly
Trun
Iles Chausey
Donville-les-Bains
Granville
St. Pair-sur-Mer
Villedieu-les-Poêles
Vire
Vassy
St. Sever-Calvados
Golfe de St. Malo
Jullouville
Carolles
La Haye-Pesnel
Sartilly
Brécey
Sourdeval
Tinchebray
Flers
Putanges
Ecouché
Argentan
Messei
Briouze
Rânes
Pte. du Grouin
Rothéneuf
Cancale
Baie de Mont St. Michel
Mont St. Michel
Avranches
Pontaubault
Juvigny
Mortain
Cap Fréhel
St. Malo
Dinard
Paramé
St. Servan
St. Cast
St. Lunaire
St. Briac
Lancieux
Le Vivier-sur-Mer
St. Broladre
Pontorson
Ducey
St. Hilaire-du-Harcouët
Barenton
Domfront
Bagnoles-de-l'Orne
La Ferté-Macé
Carrouges
Matignon
St. Jacut
Ploubalay
Châteauneuf-d'Ille-et-V.
Dol-de-Bretagne
Pleine-Fougères
St. James
Le Teilleul
Juvigny
Couterne
Plancoët
Le Vieux-Bourg
Antrain
Louvigné-du-Désert
Landivy
Passais
Ceaucé
Couptrain
Pré-en-Pail
Alençon
Dinan
Jugon
Combourg
St. Brice-en-Coglès
Gorron
Lassay
Javron
Evran
Tinténiac
Bécherel
Sens-de-Bretagne
Hédé
Romagné
Fougères
Ambrières-le-Grand
Villaines-la-Juhel
Yvignac
Broons
Caulnes
St. Georges Buttavent
Mayenne
Fresnay-sur-Sarthe
St. Aubin-d'Aubigné
Dompierre-du-Chemin
Ernée
Bais
Montauban
St. Aubin-du-Cormier
Liffré
Taillis
St. M'Hervé
Chailland
St. Méen-le-Grand
Bédée
St. Gilles
Le Bourgneuf-la-Forêt
Evron
Sillé-le-Guillaume
Gaël
Montfort
RENNES
Vitré
Montsûrs
Conlie
Domfront
Mordelles
Châteubourg
La Gravelle
Louverné
Ste. Suzanne
Parennes
Mauron
St. Jacques-de-la-Lande
Châteaugiron
Argentré-du-Plessis
Loiron
Laval
Argentré
Vaiges
St. Denis-d'Orques
Paimpont
Bruz
Piré-sur-Seiche
Plélan-le-Grand
St. Poix
Meslay-du-Maine
Brûlon
Loué
Maxent
Corps-Nuds
Janzé
Cossé-le-Vivien
Ploërmel
Guer
Guichen
La Guerche-de-Bretagne
Retiers
Grez-en-Bouère
Noyen
Sablé-sur-Sarthe
Monteneuf
Maure-de-Bretagne
Poligné
Le Sel
Bain-de-Bretagne
Craon
St. Aignan-sur-Roë
Malestroit
Carentoir
Pipriac
Messac
Teillay
Martigné-Ferchaud
Rougé
Renazé
Château-Gontier
Bierné
Malicorne-sur-Sarthe
La Gacilly
Grand-Fougeray
Châteaubriant
Pouancé
Miré
Rochefort-en-Terre
Redon
Beslé
Segré
Châteauneuf-sur-Sarthe
Durtal
La Flèche
Allaire
St. Nicholas-de-Redon
Derval
Moisdon-la-Rivière
St. Julien
La Chapelle-Glain
Vern-d'Anjou
Champtocé-sur-Loire
Le Lion-d'Angers
Tiercé
Feneu
Seiches-sur-le-Loir
Jarzé
Baugé
Guémené-Penfao
Candé
La Meilleraye-de-Bretagne
Nozay
Plessé
St. Gildas-des-Bois
Missillac
Blain
St. Mars-la-Jaille
Riaillé
Le Louroux-Béconnais
Bécon-les-Granits
Avrillé
ANGERS
Trélaze
Beaufort-en-Vallée
Nort-sur-Erdre
Joué-sur-Erdre
Pontchâteau
Bouvron
Héric
Couffé
Ancenis
Varades
Ingrandes
Montjean-s.-L.
St. Georges-sur-Loire
Les Ponts-de-Cé
Brissac-Quincé
La Ménitré
Les Rosiers
Longué
Vivy
St. Joachim
Montoir
Trignac
Savenay
Le Temple-de-Bretagne
Donges
La Chapelle-sur-Erdre
Oudon
Liré
Champtoceaux
St. Pierre-Montlimart
St. Florent-le-Vieil
Chalonnes-sur-Loire
Gennes
St. Lambert-des-Levées
Saumur
La Baule
St. Nazaire
Paimboeuf
Orvault
Carquefou
St. Julien-de-Concelles
St. Laurent-des-Autels
Montrevault
Thouarcé
Martigné-Briand

Southampton
Newhaven
Baie de la Seine
LE HAVRE
Ste. Adresse
Harfleur
Montivilliers
Étretat
Cap d'Antifer
Fécamp
Yport
Bolbec
Lillebonne
Yvetot
Dieppe
Neuville
Envermeu
Arques-la-Bataille
Offranville
St. Valéry-en-Caux
Barentin
Mt.-St. Aignan
Bois - Guillaume
ROUEN
Darnétal
Sotteville
Elbeuf
Louviers
Les Andelys
Gaillon
Vernon
Évreux
Mantes-la-Jolie
Mantes-la-Ville
Limay
Neufchâtel-en-Bray
Forges-les-Eaux
Gournay-en-Bray
Aumale
Abbeville
Eu
Le Tréport
Mers-les-Bains
Cayeux-s.-Mer
St. Valery-sur-Somme
Le Crotoy
Honfleur
Trouville
Deauville
Pont l'Évêque
Pont Audemer
Lisieux
Caen
Mondeville
Ouistreham
Cabourg
Dives
Houlgate
Bernay
Brionne
Le Neubourg
Orbec
Vimoutiers
Falaise
Argentan
Flers
Gacé
L'Aigle
Verneuil-sur-Avre
Dreux
Nonancourt
Rambouillet
Chartres
Maintenon
Sées
Alençon
Mortagne-au-Perche
Nogent-le-Rotrou
La Ferté-Bernard
Mamers
Bellême
Illiers
Bonneval
Châteaudun
Brou
LE MANS
Sablé-sur-Sarthe
Orléans
Vendôme
Mayenne
Lassay
La Ferté-Macé
Bagnoles-de-l'Orne
MAINE
NORMANDIE
Circuit automobile
50°
48°
0°
1°
1
2
3
A
B
C
D
63
81
93

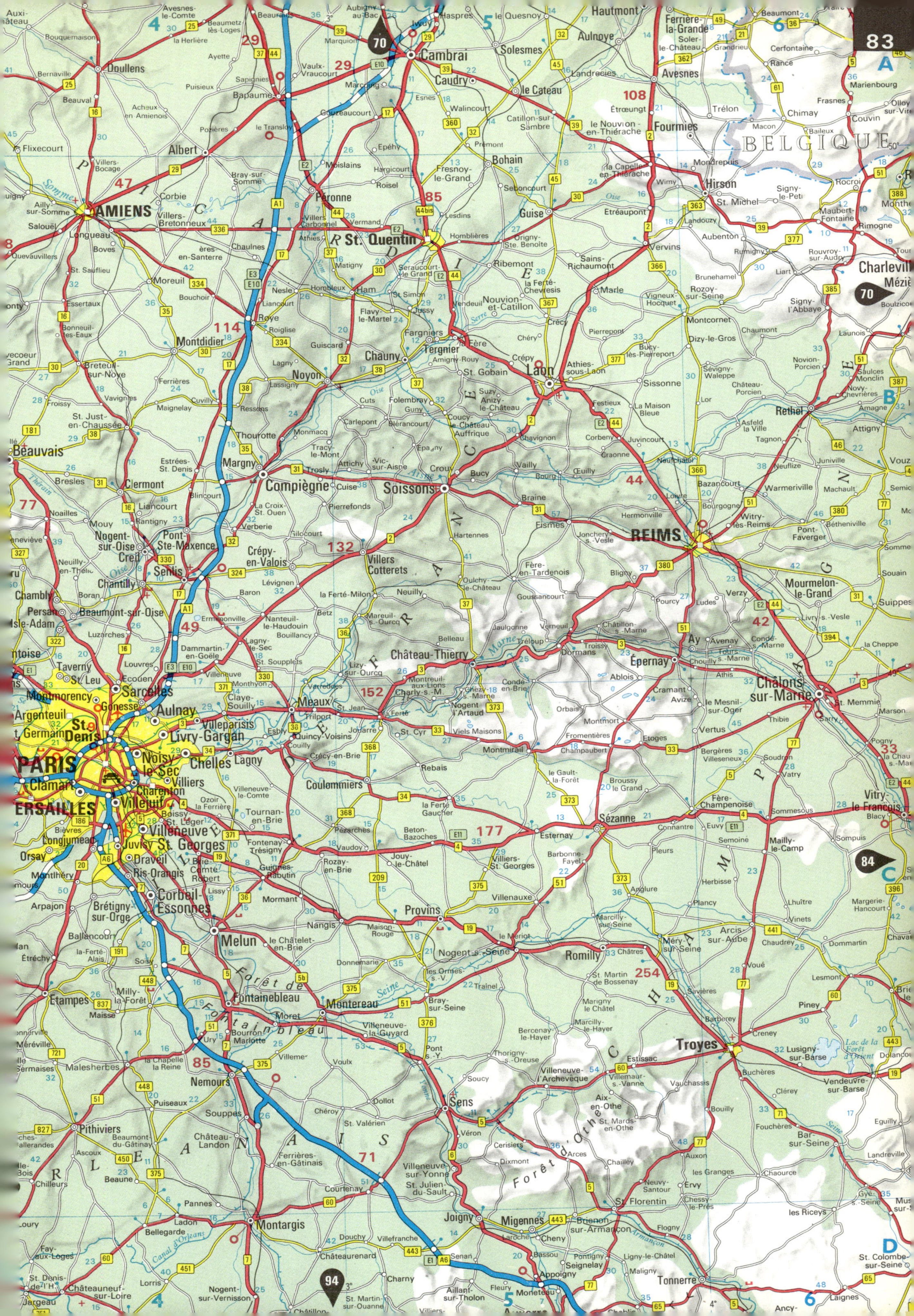
Doullens
Cambrai
Solesmes
Hautmont
Aulnoye
Ferrière-la-Grande
Caudry
le Cateau
Avesnes
Landrecies
Bapaume
Albert
Fourmies
Trélon
Chimay
BELGIQUE
Péronne
AMIENS
St. Quentin
Bohain
Guise
Hirson
St. Michel
Vervins
Charleville
Mézières
Rocroi
Montdidier
Ham
Chauny
Tergnier
Noyon
Laon
Marle
Rethel
Breteuil-sur-Noye
Beauvais
Clermont
Compiègne
Soissons
REIMS
Nogent-sur-Oise
Creil
Senlis
Chantilly
Crépy-en-Valois
Villers Cotterets
Fismes
Château-Thierry
Épernay
Châlons sur-Marne
Meaux
Aulnay
Livry-Gargan
Montmorency
Argenteuil
Sarcelles
St. Denis
PARIS
VERSAILLES
Noisy le Sec
Chelles
Lagny
Villejuif
Charenton
Villeneuve St. Georges
Corbeil-Essonnes
Coulommiers
Sézanne
Vitry-le-François
Provins
Romilly
Melun
Fontainebleau
Forêt de Fontainebleau
Montereau
Nogent-s.-Seine
Troyes
Étampes
Nemours
Sens
Pithiviers
Montargis
Joigny
Migennes
St. Florentin
Tonnerre
Bar-sur-Seine
Forêt d'Othe
Villeneuve-sur-Yonne
Courtenay
Étrépagny
Sissonne
Arcis-sur-Aube
Méry-sur-Seine
Mailly-le-Camp
Nangis
Lizy-sur-Ourcq
Dammartin-en-Goële
Pont-Ste-Maxence
Ay
Seine
Marne
Oise
Somme
Aisne
Yonne

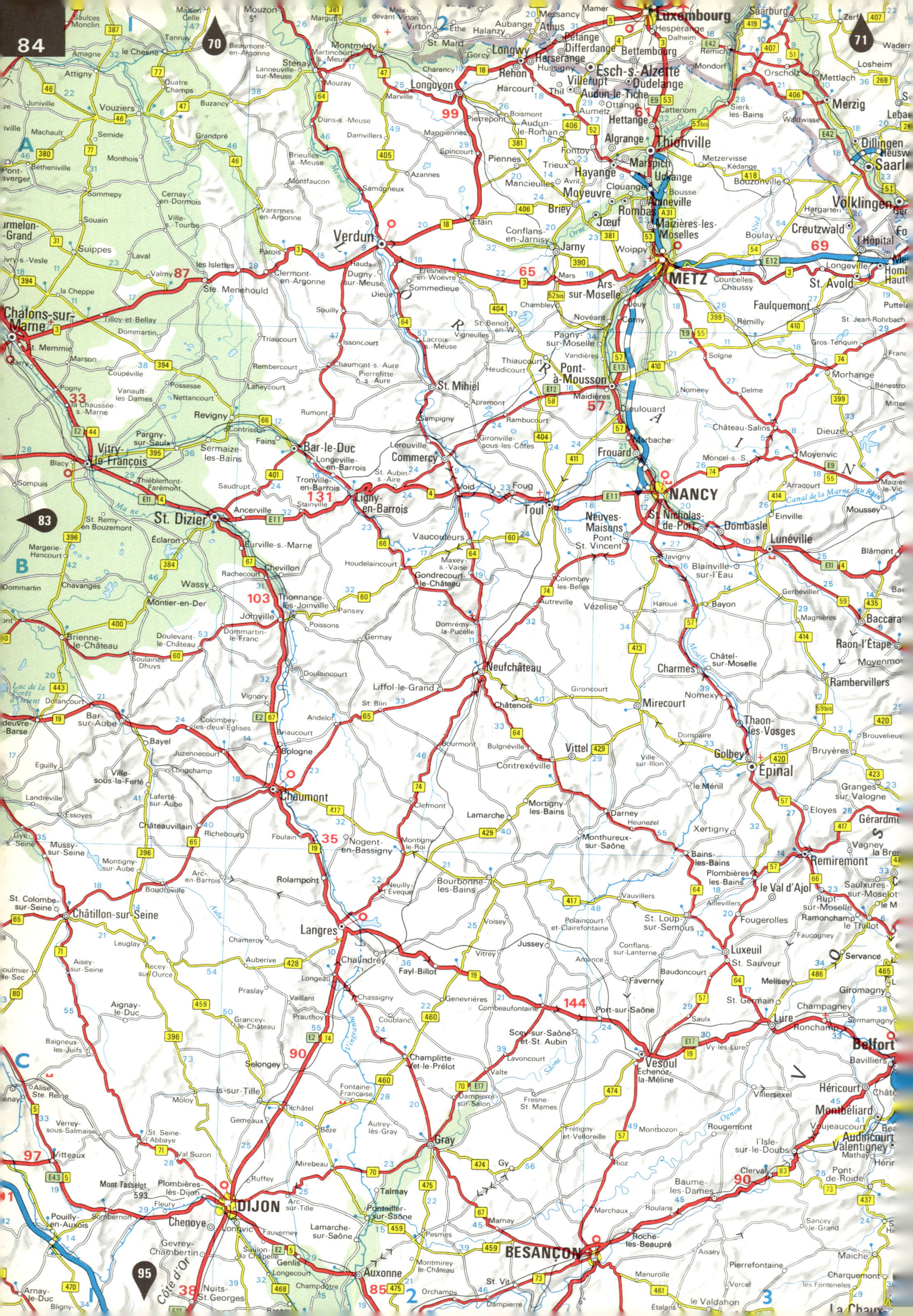
70
71
83
95
Luxembourg
Esch-s.-Alzette
Dudelange
Thionville
Longwy
Longuyon
Montmédy
Mouzon
Stenay
Vouziers
Attigny
Sedan
Verdun
Étain
Briey
Hayange
Moyeuvre
Metz
Saarlouis
Völklingen
Creutzwald
St. Avold
Faulquemont
Merzig
Ste. Menehould
Clermont-en-Argonne
Suippes
Châlons-sur-Marne
Pont-à-Mousson
St. Mihiel
Commercy
Bar-le-Duc
Ligny-en-Barrois
Toul
Nancy
Lunéville
Vitry-le-François
St. Dizier
Joinville
Wassy
Montier-en-Der
Brienne-le-Château
Bar-sur-Aube
Neufchâteau
Mirecourt
Charmes
Épinal
Rambervillers
Baccarat
Raon-l'Étape
Vittel
Contrexéville
Chaumont
Langres
Bourbonne-les-Bains
Remiremont
Plombières-les-Bains
Luxeuil
Lure
Belfort
Héricourt
Montbéliard
Vesoul
Gray
Châtillon-sur-Seine
Dijon
Auxonne
Besançon
Nuits-St. Georges
Baume-les-Dames
Pontarlier

Worms
Weinheim
LUDWIGSHAFEN
MANNHEIM
HEIDELBERG
Frankenthal
Bad Dürkheim
Kaiserslautern
Neustadt a.d.Weinstrasse
Speyer
Hockenheim
Schwetzingen
Wiesloch
Sinsheim
Mosbach
Eberbach
Neckarsulm
Heilbronn
Homberg
Zweibrücken
SAARBRÜCKEN
St. Ingbert
St. Wendel
Pirmasens
Landau
Sarreguemines
Bitche
Bad Bergzabern
Wissembourg
Bruchsal
Bretten
KARLSRUHE
Ettlingen
Pforzheim
Mühlacker
Vaihingen
Bietigheim
Ludwigsburg
Kornwestheim
Waiblingen
STUTTGART
Eßlingen
Böblingen
Sindelfingen
Leonberg
Haguenau
Rastatt
Baden-Baden
Gaggenau
Gernsbach
Bühl
Achern
Kehl
STRASBOURG
Saverne
Molsheim
Sélestat
Offenburg
Oberkirch
Baiersbronn
Freudenstadt
Nagold
Herrenberg
Tübingen
Reutlingen
Rottenburg
Hechingen
Balingen
Lahr
Haslach
Schramberg
Rottweil
Emmendingen
Waldkirch
Triberg
St. Georgen
Villingen
Schwenningen
Tuttlingen
Sigmaringen
Colmar
Breisach
FREIBURG
Donaueschingen
Neustadt
Singen
Konstanz
Überlingen
Friedrichshafen
Radolfzell
Schaffhausen
MULHOUSE
Müllheim
Lörrach
Rheinfelden
BASEL
Waldshut
Säckingen
Frauenfeld
Winterthur
St. Gallen
Wil
Baden
ZÜRICH
Aarau
Olten
Solothurn
Grenchen
Biel
Delémont
Porrentruy
Rapperswil
Bodensee
DEUTSCHLAND
SCHWARZWALD
SCHWÄBISCHE ALB
HEGAU

Aschaffenburg
Lohr
Hammelburg
Bad Kissingen
Schweinfurt
Lichtenfels
Kulmbach
Bayreuth
Bamberg
Hallstadt
Karlstadt
Marktheidenfeld
WÜRZBURG
Wertheim
Miltenberg
Kitzingen
Ochsenfurt
Dettelbach
Gerolzhofen
Forchheim
Erlangen
Herzogenaurach
FÜRTH
Zirndorf
NÜRNBERG
Lauf
Hersbruck
Tauberbischofshm.
Walldürn
Bad Mergentheim
Neustadt
Bad Windsheim
Uffenheim
Rothenburg o.d. Tauber
Ansbach
Schwabach
Roth
Mosbach
Bad Friedrichshall
Neckarsulm
Heilbronn
Öhringen
Künzelsau
Schwäbisch Hall
Crailsheim
Feuchtwangen
Dinkelsbühl
Gunzenhausen
Weißenburg
Ellwangen
Aalen
Nördlingen
Oettingen
Treuchtlingen
Eichstätt
Ingolstadt
Neuburg
Donauwörth
Backnang
Murrhardt
Ludwigsburg
Waiblingen
Schwäbisch Gmünd
STUTTGART
Eßlingen
Göppingen
Kirchheim
Geislingen
Heidenheim
Giengen
Lauingen
Dillingen
Günzburg
Ulm
Neu-Ulm
Reutlingen
Metzingen
Nürtingen
Ehingen
Laupheim
Biberach
AUGSBURG
Friedberg
Gersthofen
Aichach
Schrobenhausen
Pfaffenhofen
Dachau
MÜNCHEN
Fürstenfeldbruck
Landsberg
Buchloe
Mindelheim
Memmingen
Krumbach
Schwabmünchen
Kaufbeuren
Marktoberdorf
Schongau
Weilheim
Starnberg
Sigmaringen
Saulgau
Bad Waldsee
Weingarten
Ravensburg
Leutkirch
Kempten
Überlingen
Fränkische Schweiz
Steigerwald
Frankenhöhe
Schwäbische Alb
Fränkische Alb
Hassberge
Main
Donau
Neckar
Lech
Ammersee
Starnberger See
74
73
85
97

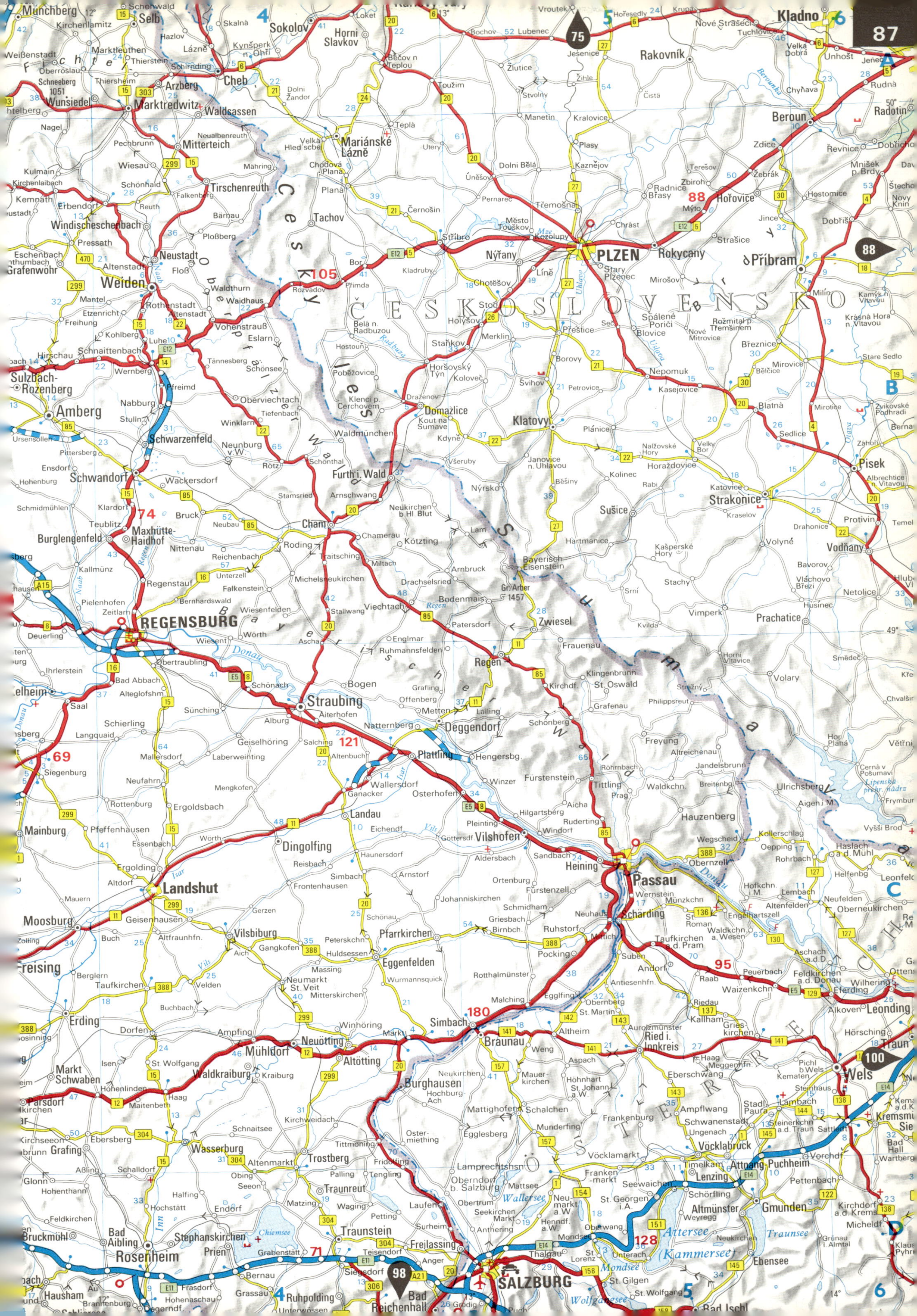
Münchberg
Selb
Sokolov
Horní Slavkov
Loket
Kladno
Nové Strašecí
Tuchlovice
Velká Dobrá
Unhošť
Rakovník
Jesenice
Lubenec
Žlutice
Bochov
Bečov n. Teplou
Toužim
Cheb
Arzberg
Marktredwitz
Wunsiedel
Waldsassen
Mariánské Lázně
Teplá
Mitterteich
Tirschenreuth
Tachov
Planá
Stříbro
Nýřany
PLZEŇ
Rokycany
Beroun
Zdice
Hořovice
Příbram
Radotín
Dobřichovice
Řevnice
Mníšek p. Brdy
Dobříš
Kralovice
Plasy
Manětín
Kaznějov
Kozolupy
Město Touškov
Třemošná
Chrást
Hostomice
Jince
Strašice
Mýto
Radnice
Březnice
Zbiroh
Weiden
Neustadt
Windischeschenbach
Pressath
Eschenbach
Grafenwöhr
Floß
Waidhaus
Vohenstrauß
Rozvadov
Bor
Přimda
Kladruby
Holýšov
Stod
Chotěšov
Staňkov
Horšovský Týn
Domažlice
Klatovy
Přeštice
Nepomuk
Blatná
Spálené Poříčí
Blovice
Rožmitál p. Třemšínem
Mirovice
Písek
Strakonice
Horažďovice
Sušice
Vodňany
Protivín
Volyně
Vimperk
Prachatice
Netolice
Kašperské Hory
Nýrsko
Kdyně
Kout na Šumavě
Furth i. Wald
Waldmünchen
Cham
Roding
Kötzting
Lam
Bayerisch Eisenstein
Gr. Arber 1457
Zwiesel
Bodenmais
Viechtach
Regen
Frauenau
Grafenau
Freyung
Volary
Horní Planá
Český Krumlov
Amberg
Sulzbach-Rozenberg
Schwandorf
Schwarzenfeld
Nabburg
Pfreimd
Burglengenfeld
Maxhütte-Haidhof
Regenstauf
REGENSBURG
Wörth
Straubing
Bogen
Deggendorf
Plattling
Osterhofen
Vilshofen
Hengersbg.
Hauzenberg
Passau
Schärding
Wegscheid
Obernzell
Ulrichsberg
Kelheim
Saal
Bad Abbach
Schierling
Langquaid
Siegenburg
Mainburg
Pfeffenhausen
Rottenburg
Ergoldsbach
Dingolfing
Landau
Landshut
Moosburg
Freising
Vilsbiburg
Eggenfelden
Pfarrkirchen
Pocking
Rotthalmünster
Simbach
Braunau
Ried i. Innkreis
Peuerbach
Eferding
Leonding
Wels
Grieskirchen
Altötting
Neuötting
Mühldorf
Burghausen
Waldkraiburg
Erding
Dorfen
Markt Schwaben
Wasserburg
Trostberg
Traunreut
Traunstein
Freilassing
Bad Reichenhall
SALZBURG
Mondsee
St. Gilgen
Wolfgangsee
Bad Ischl
Attersee (Kammersee)
Vöcklabruck
Attnang-Puchheim
Gmunden
Traunsee
Ebensee
Lambach
Schwanenstadt
Rosenheim
Prien
Chiemsee
Bad Aibling
Bruckmühl
Grafing
Ebersberg
Ruhpolding
Bernau
Grassau
Hausham
ČESKOSLOVENSKO
ÖSTERREICH
Český les
Šumava
Oberpfälzer Wald
Bayerischer Wald
Donau
Isar
Inn
Vils
Regen
Naab
Lipenská přehr. nádrž
Wallersee

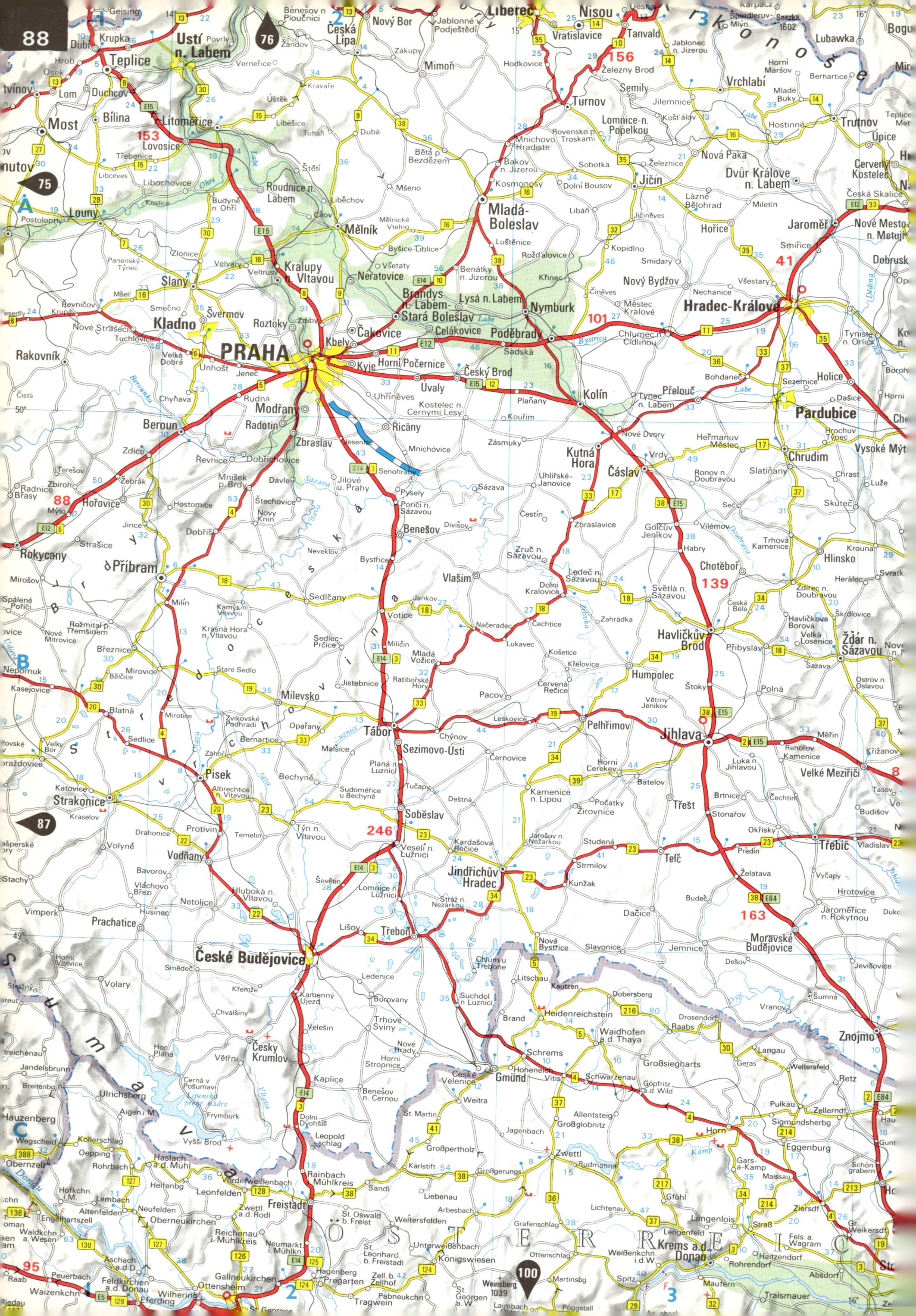
PRAHA
Liberec
Ústí n. Labem
Teplice
Most
Litoměřice
Louny
Kladno
Slaný
Kralupy n. Vltavou
Mělník
Mladá Boleslav
Jičín
Turnov
Hradec-Králové
Pardubice
Jaroměř
Trutnov
Nymburk
Poděbrady
Kolín
Kutná Hora
Čáslav
Chrudim
Beroun
Rakovník
Příbram
Rokycany
Beneşov
Tábor
Písek
Strakonice
Vodňany
České Budějovice
Český Krumlov
Jindřichův Hradec
Třeboň
Soběslav
Pelhřimov
Jihlava
Havlíčkův Brod
Humpolec
Chotěboř
Hlinsko
Žďár n. Sázavou
Třebíč
Telč
Velké Meziříčí
Moravské Budějovice
Znojmo
Freistadt
Gmünd
Zwettl
Horn
Krems a.d. Donau
Krkonoše
Šumava
Brdy
ÖSTERREICH

P O L S K A
Wałbrzych (Waldenburg)
Dzierżoniów
Bielawa
Ząbkowice Śląskie
Ziębice
Strzelin
Grodków
Nysa
Otmuchów
Paczków
Kłodzko
Nowa Ruda
Polanica Zdrój
Duszniki Zdrój
Lądek Zdrój
Bystrzyca Kłodzka
Międzylesie
Opole (Oppeln)
Krapkowice
Gogolin
Strzelce Opolskie
Lubliniec
Tarnowskie Góry
Bytom
Chorzów
Ruda Śl.
Gliwice
Zabrze
Katowice
Mikołów
Kędzierzyn
Koźle
Głogówek
Prudnik
Głuchołazy
Zlaté Hory
Jeseník
Głubczyce
Krnov
Racibórz
Rybnik
Rydułtowy
Wodzisław Śl.
Jastrzębie-Zdrój
Żory
Bruntál
Šumperk
Rýmařov
Opava
Hlučín
Nový Bohumín
Karviná
Orlová
Havířov
Ostrava
Český Těšín
Cieszyn
Třinec
Frýdek Místek
Příbor
Nový Jičín
Kopřivnice
Frenštát p. Radhoštěm
Valašské Meziříčí
Rožnov p. Radhoštěm
Vsetín
Hranice
Lipník
Přerov
Olomouc
Šternberk
Litovel
Uničov
Mohelnice
Zábřeh
Lanškroun
Česká Třebova
Svitavy
Moravská Třebová
Boskovice
Blansko
Prostějov
Vyškov
Kroměříž
Holešov
Bystřice p. Hostýnem
Gottwaldov
Otrokovice-Kvitkovice
Uherské Hradiště
Staré Město
Kunovice
Uherský Brod
Veselí
Kyjov
Hodonín
Břeclav
Mikulov
Brno
Tišnov
Kuřim
Slavkov u. Brna
Hustopeče
Valtice
Skalica
Holíč
Senica
Myjava
Stará Turá
Nové Mesto
Trenčín
Piešťany
Hlohovec
Trnava
Malacky
Modra
Topoľčany
Bánovce
Prievidza
Partizánske
Považská Bystrica
Púchov
Žilina
Bytča
Čadca
Dubnica
Nová Baňa
Zlaté Moravce
Mistelbach a.d.Z.
Laa a.d. Thaya
Korneuburg
Wolkersdorf
Beskydy
Moravskoslezské
Javorníky
Bílé Karpaty
Orlické Hory
Malá Fatra
E7
E12
E14
E15
E16
E22
E22a
E85
77
90
91
101

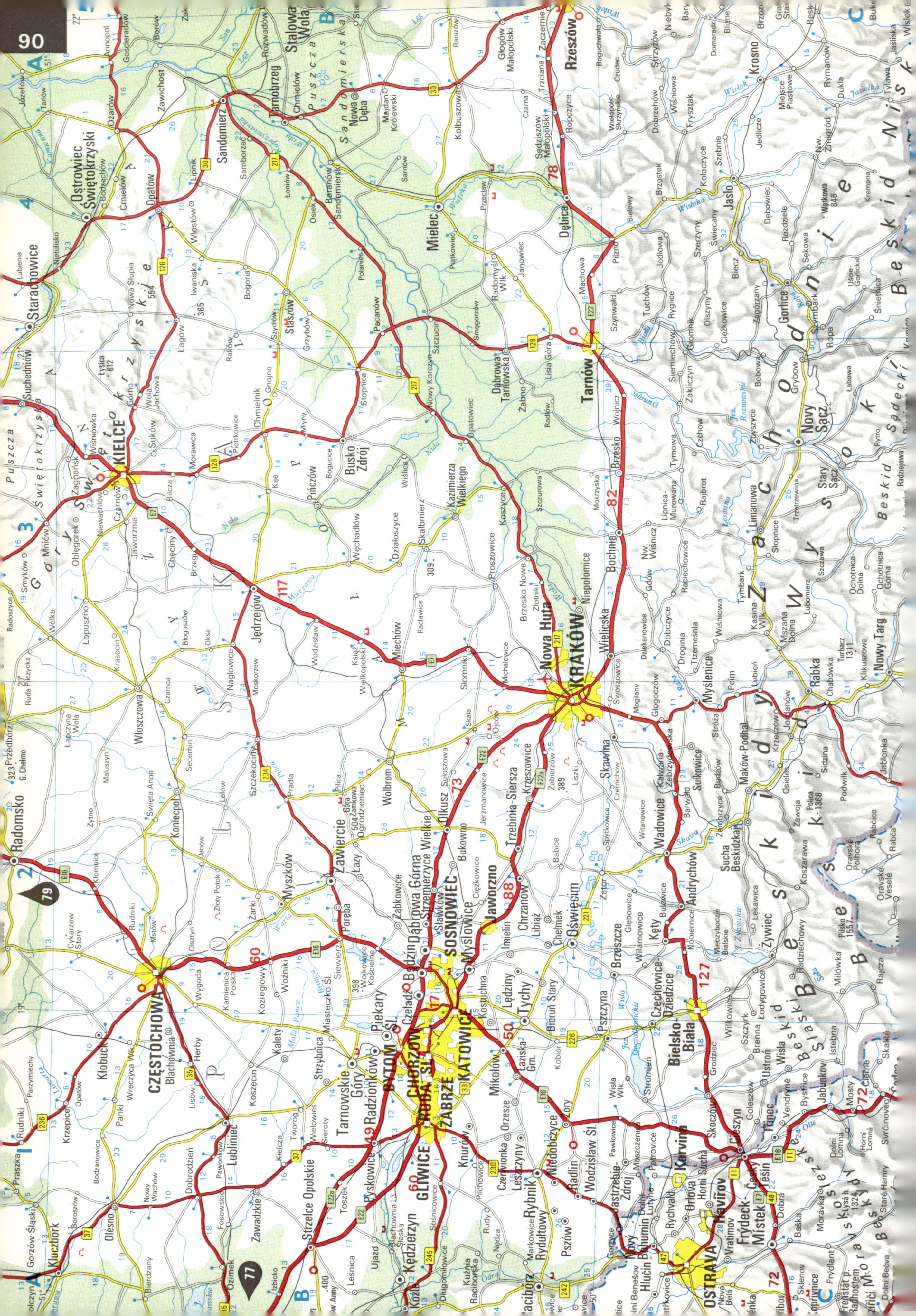

Kraków
Nowa Huta
Katowice
Sosnowiec
Chorzów
Bytom Śl.
Zabrze
Gliwice
Ruda Śl.
Dąbrowa Górnicza
Częstochowa
Kielce
Radomsko
Ostrowiec Świętokrzyski
Starachowice
Sandomierz
Tarnobrzeg
Stalowa Wola
Rzeszów
Mielec
Dębica
Tarnów
Nowy Sącz
Gorlice
Jasło
Krosno
Bochnia
Wieliczka
Myślenice
Limanowa
Rabka
Nowy Targ
Bielsko-Biała
Cieszyn
Oświęcim
Wadowice
Andrychów
Żywiec
Tychy
Rybnik
Jastrzębie-Zdrój
Wodzisław Śl.
Racibórz
Kędzierzyn
Strzelce Opolskie
Lubliniec
Tarnowskie Góry
Zawiercie
Myszków
Olkusz
Jaworzno
Chrzanów
Jędrzejów
Miechów
Busko Zdrój
Pińczów
Staszów
Opatów
Kluczbork
Olesno
Ostrava
Karviná
Frýdek-Místek
Třinec
Český Těšín
G ó r y   Ś w i ę t o k r z y s k i e
B e s k i d   N i s k i
B e s k i d   S ą d e c k i
B e s k i d   W y s p o w y
B e s k i d   Ś l ą s k i
P u s z c z a   S a n d o m i e r s k a
Wisła
Nida
Dunajec

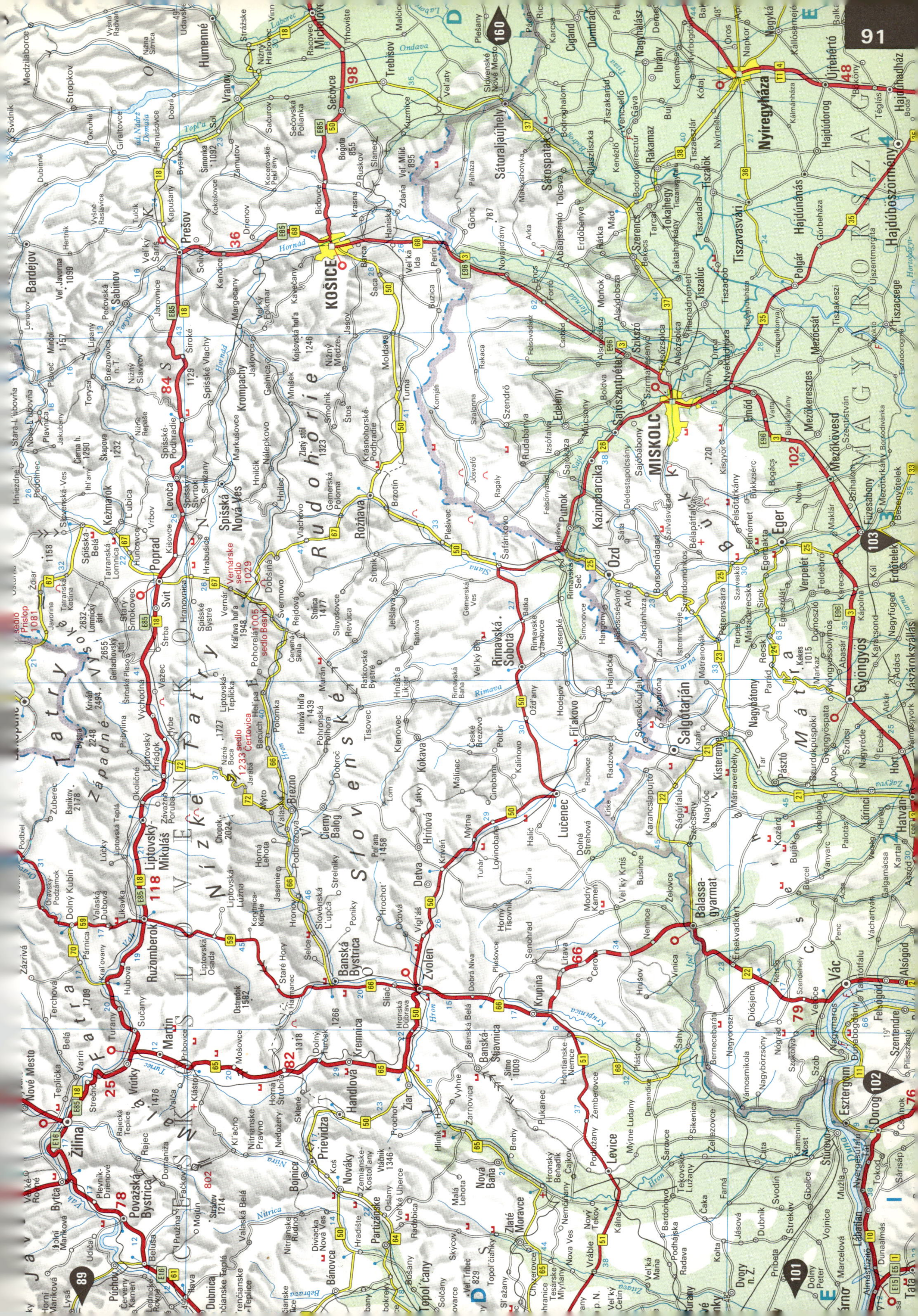

Žilina
Martin
Ružomberok
Liptovský Mikuláš
Poprad
Prešov
Košice
Humenné
Michalovce
Trebišov
Sátoraljaújhely
Sárospatak
Nyíregyháza
Miskolc
Eger
Gyöngyös
Salgótarján
Lučenec
Zvolen
Banská Bystrica
Prievidza
Levice
Vác
Esztergom
Balassagyarmat
Rimavská Sobota
Rožňava
Spišská Nová Ves
Bardejov
Vranov
Ózd
Kazincbarcika
Hatvan
Tokaj
Mezőkövesd
Považská Bystrica
Tatry
Západné
Nízke
Tatry
Slovenské
Rudohorie
Mátra
Bükk
Magyarország

Rennes
St. Jacques-de-la-Lande
Vitré
Châteaubourg
Châteaugiron
Laval
Montauban
St. Méen-le-Grand
Montfort
Mordelles
Bédée
Liffré
du-Cormier
Chailland
Louverné
Evron
Sillé-le-Guillaume
Montsûrs
Ste. Suzanne
Argentré
Vaiges
St. Denis d'Orques
Brûlon
Meslay-du-Maine
Sablé-sur-Sarthe
Grez-en-Bouère
Bierné
Château-Gontier
Miré
Châteauneuf-sur-Sarthe
Champigné
Tiercé
Seiches-sur-le-Loir
Le Lion-d'Angers
Feneu
Avrillé
Angers
Trélazé
Les Ponts-de-Cé
Brissac-Quincé
Gennes
Bécon-les-Granits
Segré
Craon
Cossé-le-Vivien
Loiron
La Gravelle
Le Bourgneuf-la-Forêt
Argentré-du-Plessis
La Guerche-de-Bretagne
St. Aignan-sur-Roë
Renazé
Pouancé
Martigné-Ferchaud
Rougé
Châteaubriant
Janzé
Retiers
Corps-Nuds
Bain-de-Bretagne
Le Sel
Teillay
Messac
Pipriac
Guichen
Bruz
Poligné
Maure-de-Bretagne
Guer
Plélan-le-Grand
Paimpont
Mauron
Ménéac
Merdrignac
Gaël
La Trinité-Porhoët
Josselin
Ploërmel
Maxent
Monteneuf
Sérent
Malestroit
Carentoir
Elven
Questembert
Rochefort-en-Terre
Allaire
Redon
St. Nicholas-de-Redon
La Gacilly
Grand-Fougeray
Derval
Moisdon-la-Rivière
St. Julien
La Chapelle-Glain
Vern-d'Anjou
Candé
Le Louroux-Béconnais
Guémené-Penfao
Plessé
Nozay
La Meilleraye-de-Bretagne
Riaillé
St. Mars-la-Jaille
Muzillac
La Roche-Bernard
Herbignac
Missillac
St. Gildas-des-Bois
Blain
Nort-sur-Erdre
Joué-sur-Erdre
Pontchâteau
Bouvron
Héric
Couffé
Oudon
Ancenis
Varades
Ingrandes
Champtocé-sur-Loire
St. Georges-sur-Loire
Montjean
Chalonnes-sur-Loire
Thouarcé
Martigné-Briand
Doué-la-Fontaine
Guérande
La Turballe
Le Croisic
La Baule
Le Pouliguen
Pornichet
St. Nazaire
St. Joachim
Montoir
Trignac
Donges
Savenay
Le Temple-de-Bretagne
La Chapelle-sur-Erdre
Carquefou
Orvault
Paimbœuf
Mindin
St. Brévin-les-Pins
St. Michel-Chef-Chef
St. Etienne-de-Montluc
Le Pellerin
St. Père-en-Retz
Bouguenais
Nantes
Bouaye
Pont St. Martin
Vertou
St. Julien-de-Concelles
Le Loroux-Bottereau
Liré
Champtoceaux
St. Laurent-des-Autels
Montrevault
St. Florent-le-Vieil
St. Pierre-Montlimart
Beaupréau
Jallais
Chemillé
Vihiers
Montreuil-Bellay
Gesté
Vallet
Clisson
Aigrefeuille-s-Maine
Montfaucon
Le May-sur-Evre
Cholet
Nuaillé
Torfou
Préfailles
Pornic
La Bernerie-en-Retz
Arthon
Lac de Grand-Lieu
St. Philbert-de-Grand-Lieu
Baie de Bourgneuf
Bourgneuf-en-Retz
Machecoul
Île de Noirmoutier
Noirmoutier-en-l'Île
La Guérinière
Barbâtre
Bouin
Beauvoir-sur-Mer
La Garnache
Touvois
Vieillevigne
Rocheservière
La Bruffière
Montaigu
La Gaubretière
Mortagne-sur-Sèvre
St. Laurent-sur-Sèvre
Maulévrier
Argenton-Château
Les Aubiers
Mauléon
Les Herbiers
St. Fulgent
Chavagnes-en-Pailliers
Les Lucs-sur-Boulogne
Legé
Challans
La Barre-de-Monts
St. Jean-de-Monts
St. Christophe-du-Ligneron
Palluau
Le Poiré-sur-Vie
Belleville-sur-Vie
Les Essarts
Aizenay
St. Hilaire-de-Riez
St. Gilles-sur-Vie
Croix-de-Vie
Sion-sur-l'Océan
Ile d'Yeu
Port-Joinville
Beaulieu-s/s la Roche
La Roche-sur-Yon
La Ferrière
La Chaize-le-Vicomte
St. Michel-Mont-Mercure
Pouzauges
Cerizay
Bressuire
St. Varent
Chiché
Chantonnay
Mouilleron-en-Pareds
Montcoutant
La Châtaigneraie
L'Absie
Secondigny
Mazières-en-Gâtine
Bourg-la-Roche
Aubigny
La Mothe-Achard
Bournezeau
La Caillère
Ste. Hermine
St. Martin-de-Brem
Olonne-s-Mer
Les Sables-d'Olonne
Talmont
Jard-s-Mer
Mareuil-sur-Lay
Moutiers-les-Mauxfaits
Longeville
Angles
Luçon
Triaize
Ste. Gemme-la-Plaine
Nalliers
Fontenay-le-Comte
St. Hilaire-des-Loges
Coulonges-sur-l'Autize
Champdeniers
St. Maixent-l'Ecole
Oulmes
Maillezais
Benet
Echiré
La Crèche
Niort
Chaillé-les-Marais
L'Aiguillon-sur-Mer
La Tranche-sur-Mer
St. Michel-en-l'Herm
Marans
Pertuis Breton
Île de Ré
Ars-en-Ré
St. Martin-de-Ré
La Flotte
Rivedoux-Plage
Nieul-sur-Mer
Nuaillé-d'Aunis
Courçon
Epannes
Frontenay-Rohan-Rohan
Beauvoir-sur-Niort
Mauzé-sur-le-Mignon
Dompierre-s.-M.
La Rochelle
La Pallice
Aytré
Aigrefeuille-d'Aunis
Surgères
Brioux-sur-Boutonne
Pertuis d'Antioche
Chatelaillon Plage
Ile d'Aix
St. Denis-d'Oléron
Ciré-d'Aunis
Muron
Puyrolland
Loulay
Aulnay
La Villedieu
Tonnay-Boutonne
St. Jean-d'Angély
St. Georges
St. Pierre
La Cotinière
Île d'Oléron
Fouras
Port-des-Barques
Le Château
Rochefort
Tonnay-Charente
St. Savinien
St. Hilaire-de-Villefranche
Matha
St. Trojan
Marennes
Bourcefranc
St. Agnant
St. Porchaire
Ronce-les-Bains
La Tremblade
Saintes
Burie
Loire
Vilaine
Sèvre
Charente
Mayenne
Sarthe
B R E T A G N E
M A I N E
A N J O U
P O I T O U
A U N I S

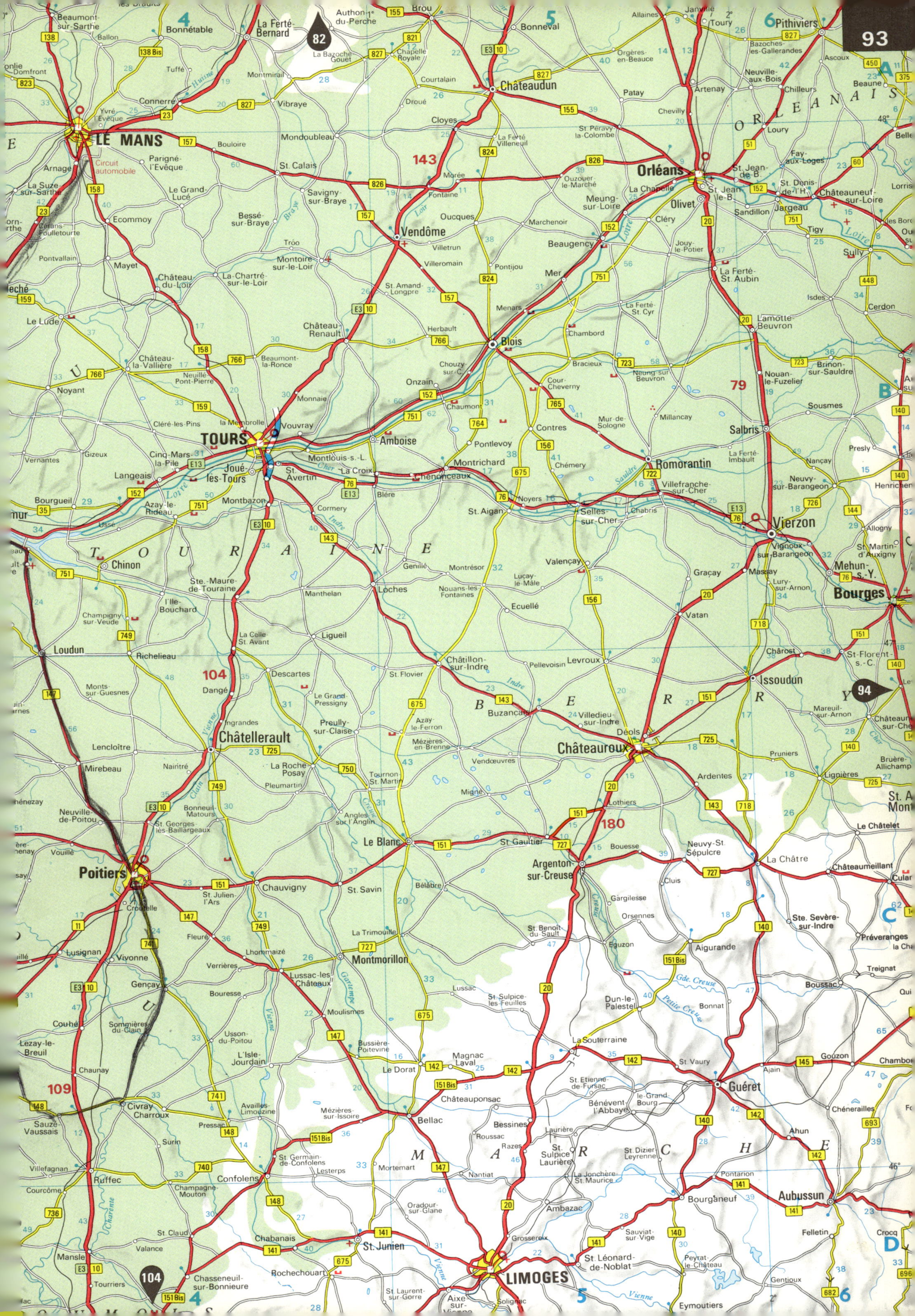
LE MANS
TOURS
Orléans
Blois
Vendôme
Châteaudun
Romorantin
Vierzon
Bourges
Issoudun
Châteauroux
Châtellerault
Poitiers
Le Blanc
Montmorillon
Argenton-sur-Creuse
Guéret
Aubusson
LIMOGES
St. Junien
Bellac
Confolens
Ruffec
Civray
Loudun
Chinon
Loches
Amboise
Montrichard
Salbris
Pithiviers
Jargeau
Châteauneuf-sur-Loire
Sully
Beaugency
Meung-sur-Loire
Olivet
St. Calais
Mondoubleau
La Ferté-Bernard
Bonnétable
Beaumont-sur-Sarthe
Château-du-Loir
Château-Renault
Château-la-Vallière
Langeais
Joué-lès-Tours
Azay-le-Rideau
Ste. Maure-de-Touraine
Richelieu
Descartes
La Châtre
Levroux
Vatan
Valençay
Buzançais
Châtillon-sur-Indre
St. Gaultier
Chauvigny
Lussac-les-Châteaux
La Souterraine
Bourganeuf
Dun-le-Palestel
Montmorillon
Lusignan
Mirebeau
Chambord
Chenonceaux
Selles-sur-Cher
Lamotte-Beuvron
La Ferté-St. Aubin
Mehun-s.-Y.
St. Florent-s.-C.
Lignières
Ardentes
Neuvy-St. Sépulcre
St. Léonard-de-Noblat
Rochechouart
Chabanais
Le Dorat
Magnac Laval
Bessines
Ambazac
Felletin
T O U R A I N E
B E R R Y
M A R C H E
O R L É A N A I S
143
79
104
180
109
82
94
104
4
5
6
A
B
C
D

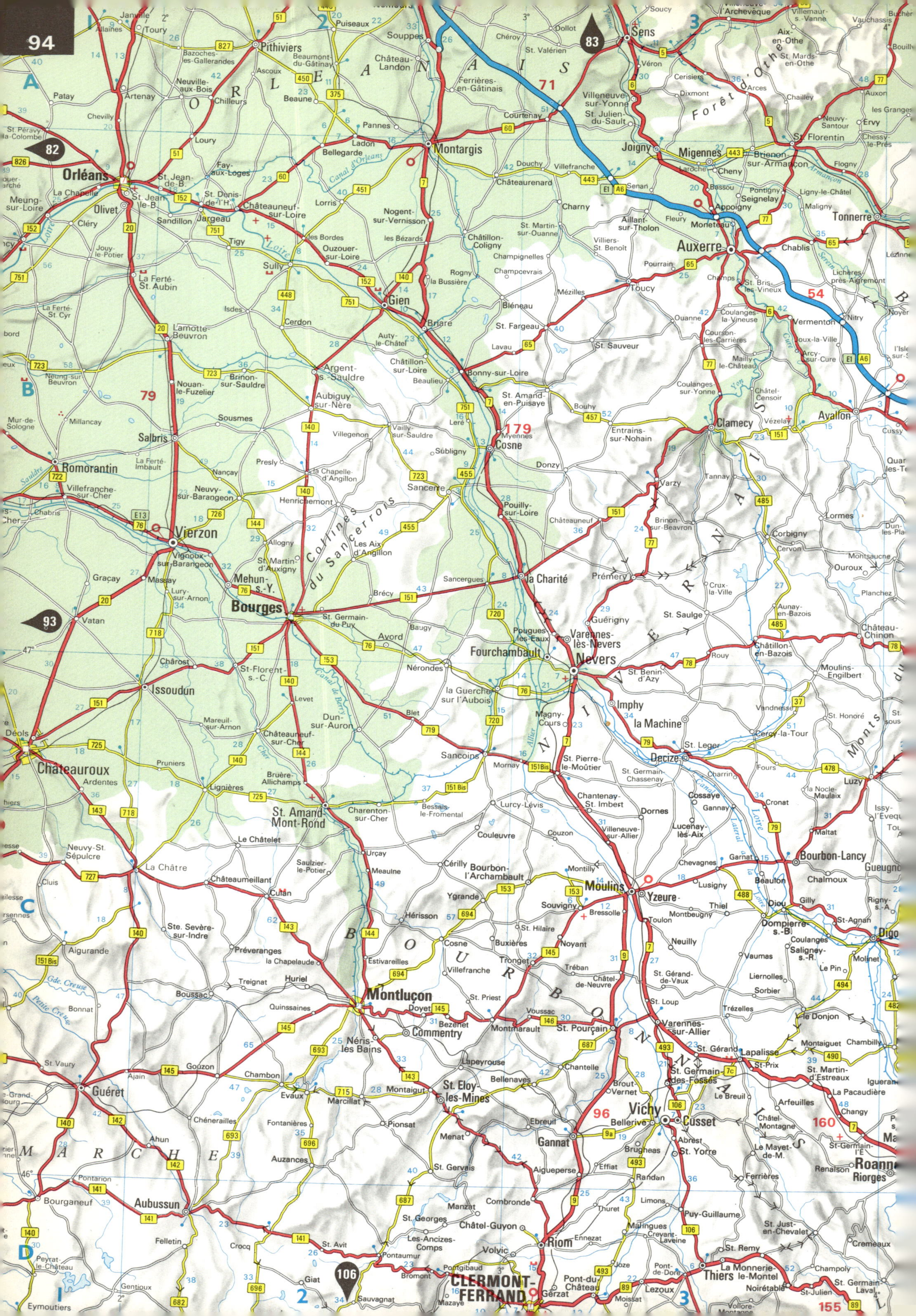
Orléans
Pithiviers
Montargis
Sens
Joigny
Migennes
Auxerre
Tonnerre
St. Florentin
Courtenay
Gien
Briare
Sully
Châteauneuf-sur-Loire
Jargeau
Olivet
Meung-sur-Loire
Lamotte-Beuvron
Salbris
Romorantin
Vierzon
Bourges
Mehun-s.-Y.
Issoudun
Châteauroux
Déols
La Châtre
St. Amand-Mont-Rond
Montluçon
Commentry
Néris-les Bains
St. Eloy-les-Mines
Guéret
Aubusson
Bourganeuf
Felletin
Riom
Volvic
CLERMONT-FERRAND
Thiers
Vichy
Cusset
Gannat
Moulins
Yzeure
Decize
Nevers
Fourchambault
La Charité
Cosne
Sancerre
Pouilly-sur-Loire
Clamecy
Avallon
Corbigny
Varzy
Bourbon-Lancy
Digoin
Lapalisse
Roanne
Riorges
Le Donjon
Dompierre-s.-B.
Bourbon-l'Archambault
Souvigny
St. Pourçain
Varennes-sur-Allier
Aigueperse
Châtel-Guyon
Pont-du-Château
Lezoux
Sancoins
Dun-sur-Auron
Châteauneuf-sur-Cher
Lignières
Vatan
Graçay
Aubigny-sur-Nère
Argent-s.-Sauldre
Bonny-sur-Loire
St. Fargeau
Toucy
Chablis
Vermenton
Nogent-sur-Vernisson
Châtillon-Coligny
Châteaurenard
Ferrières-en-Gâtinais
Château-Landon
Puiseaux
Beaune
Artenay
Patay
Janville
Toury
ORLEANAIS
GATINAIS
NIVERNAIS
BOURBONNAIS
MARCHE
Collines du Sancerrois
Forêt d'Othe
Monts
Canal d'Orléans
Canal de Berry
Loire
Allier
Cher
Yonne
E1 A6
E13
71
79
54
96
160
179
155
82
83
93
106
A
B
C
D
1
2
3

Chaumont
Langres
Épinal
Vittel
Contrexéville
Remiremont
Luxeuil
Vesoul
Lure
Bourbonne-les-Bains
Châtillon-sur-Seine
Dijon
Gray
Besançon
Dôle
Auxonne
Beaune
Pontarlier
Chalon-sur-Saône
Le Creusot
Montceau-les-Mines
Lons-le-Saunier
Champagnole
Poligny
Arbois
Tournus
Macon
Bourg
Oyonnax
St. Claude
Genève
Lausanne
Lac Léman
Annemasse
Annecy
Nyon
Thonon
Villefranche
Lyon
Ambérieu-en-Bugey
Bellegarde
Morez
Salins-les-Bains
Montbéliard
Baume-les-Dames
Tarare
Cluny
Charolles
Louhans
Seurre
Nuits-St. Georges
Mâcon
Côte d'Or
Lac de Vouglans
Lac d'Annecy

FREIBURG
MULHOUSE
Belfort
BASEL
Lörrach
Rheinfelden
Säckingen
Waldshut
Liestal
Aarau
Olten
Zofingen
Delémont
Porrentruy
Montbéliard
Héricourt
Vesoul
Lure
Luxeuil
BESANÇON
Pontarlier
La Chaux-de-Fonds
Le Locle
Neuchâtel
Biel (Bienne)
Solothurn
Grenchen
BERN
Burgdorf
Langenthal
Sursee
Luzern
Fribourg
Thun
Steffisburg
Interlaken
Spiez
Yverdon
Payerne
Lac de Neuchâtel
Murten
Bulle
LAUSANNE
Morges
Vevey
Montreux
Lac Léman
Evian
Thonon
Nyon
GENÈVE
Annemasse
St. Claude
Champagnole
Morez
Aigle
Monthey
Martigny
Sion
Sierre
Brig
Zermatt
Chamonix
Cluses
Annecy
Rumilly
Aix-le-Bains
Chambery
Albertville
Ugine
Megève
Aosta
Biella
Domodóssola
Villadóssola
Col des Mosses 1445
Col du Pillon 1546
Jaunpass 1509
Col de Gets 1163
C. des Aravis 1498
Tunnel du Grd St. Bernard
Tunnel du Mt. Blanc
Simplon Pass 2005
Simplon Tunnel
Lötschberg Tunnel
Colle d. Piccolo St. Bernardo
Matterhorn 4482
Monte Rosa 4638
Mont Blanc 4810
Jungfrau 4159
Wildhorn 3247
Dents du Midi 3180
Niesen 2366
Alpi Pennine
Dora Baltea
Berner Alpen

DEUTSCHLAND
ÖSTERREICH
Tuttlingen
Singen
Konstanz
Stockach
Überlingen
Radolfzell
Ravensburg
Weingarten
Friedrichshafen
Lindau
Bregenz
Memmingen
Kaufbeuren
Kempten
Leutkirch
Wangen
Isny
Marktoberdorf
Füssen
Schongau
Immenstadt
Sonthofen
Oberstdorf
Bodensee
Schaffhausen
Winterthur
ZÜRICH
St. Gallen
Wil
Herisau
Appenzell
Frauenfeld
Kreuzlingen
Romanshorn
Rorschach
Dornbirn
Hohenems
Götzis
Rankweil
Feldkirch
Bludenz
Vaduz
LIECH.
Buchs
Rapperswil
Wädenswil
Horgen
Zug
Einsiedeln
Schwyz
Glarus
Walensee
Sargans
Bad Ragaz
Chur
Davos-Platz
Klosters
Landeck
Imst
Reutte
Lechtaler Alpen
Ötztaler Alpen
Arlberg Tunnel
Arlberg Pass 1802
Silvrettahorn 3248
Wildspitze 3774
Passo di Resia 1508
Scuol-Schuls
Zernez
St. Moritz
Samedan
Pontresina
Albula Tunnel
Julier-Pass 2284
Piz. Bernina 4055
Maloja
Splügenpass 2113
Chiavenna
Andermatt
St. Gotthard Tunnel
Pso. del S. Gottardo 2108
Airolo
Disentis-Muster
Thusis
Tunnel Pso. del S. Bernardino
Bellinzona
Locarno
Lugano
Monte Ceneri 554
Lepontine
Poschiavo
Tirano
Sondrio
Morbegno
Alpi Orobie
Bormio
Pso. dello Stelvio 2757
Ortles 3899
Pso. del Tonale 1883
Pso. dell' Aprica 1176
Edolo
Breno
Lovere
Lecco
Como
Varese
Chiasso
Mendrisio
Gallarate
Busto Arsizio
Legnano
Saronno
Monza
BERGAMO
BRESCIA
Salò
Desenzano
Lago Maggiore
Lago di Como
Lago d'Iseo
Lago di Garda
86
98
99
111

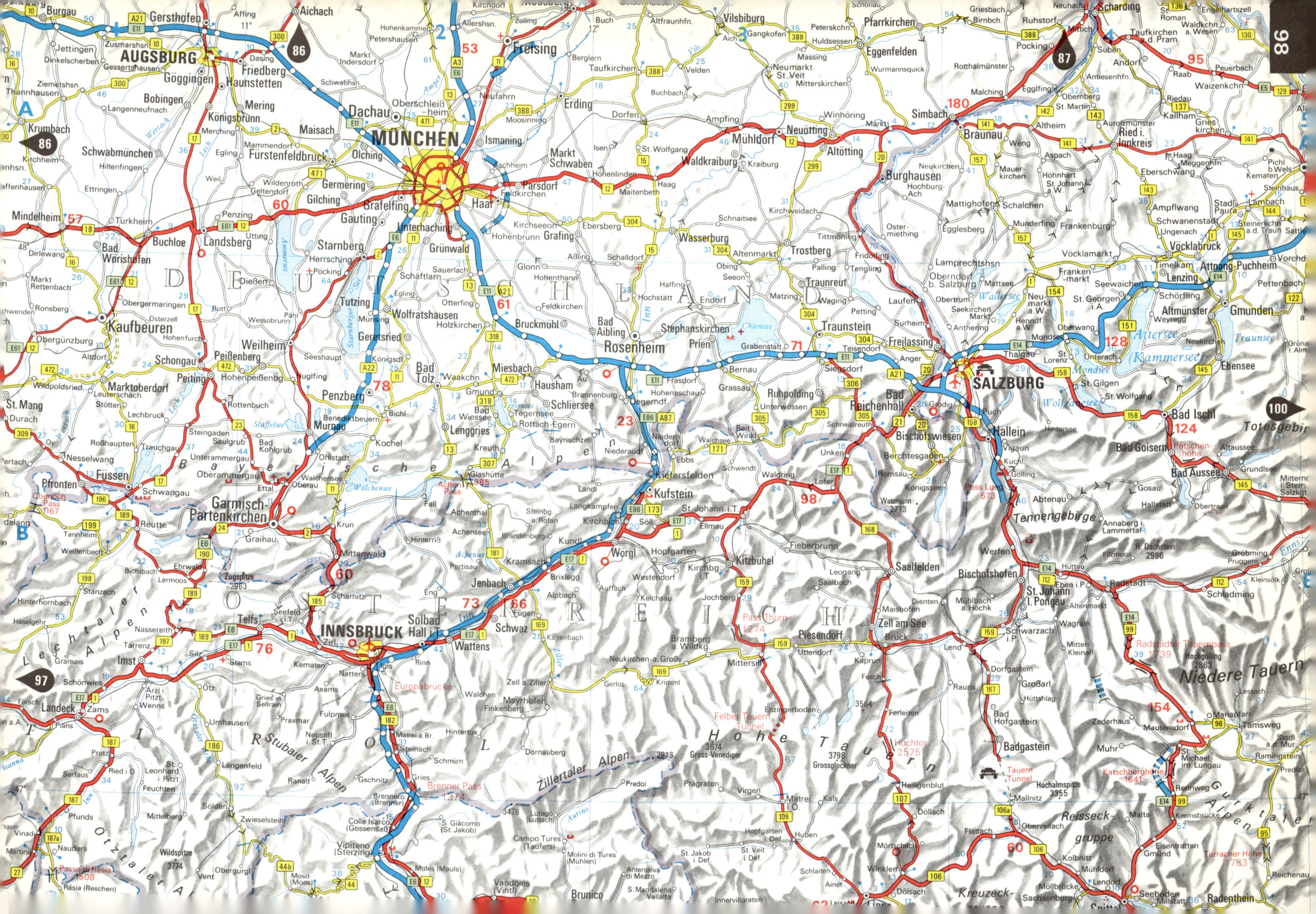

AUGSBURG
MÜNCHEN
SALZBURG
INNSBRUCK
Rosenheim
Kufstein
Garmisch-Partenkirchen
Kaufbeuren
Landsberg
Dachau
Freising
Erding
Simbach
Braunau
Burghausen
Altötting
Mühldorf
Wasserburg
Traunstein
Bad Reichenhall
Bischofswiesen
Hallein
Bad Ischl
Bad Aussee
Bad Goisern
Gmunden
Vöcklabruck
Attnang-Puchheim
Schärding
Kitzbühel
Wörgl
Schwaz
Zell am See
Saalfelden
Bischofshofen
Badgastein
Landeck
Imst
Telfs
Füssen
Schongau
Weilheim
Starnberg
Tutzing
Penzberg
Murnau
Bad Tölz
Miesbach
Mindelheim
Memmingen
Buchloe
Germering
Fürstenfeldbruck
Ammersee
Starnberger See
Chiemsee
Attersee
Traunsee
Mondsee
Wolfgangsee
Wallersee
Walchensee
Achensee
D E U T S C H L A N D
Ö S T E R R E I C H
Bayerische Alpen
Lechtaler Alpen
Stubaier Alpen
Zillertaler Alpen
Ötztaler Alpen
Hohe Tauern
Niedere Tauern
Tennengebirge
Totesgebirge
Reisseck-gruppe
Gurktaler Alpen
Kreuzeck-
Großglockner 3798
Gross-Venediger 3674
Hochtor 2575
Felber Tauern Tunnel
Tauern Tunnel
Brenner Pass 1374
Europabrücke
Pass Lueg 573
Pass Thurn 1274
Achen Pass
Oberjoch Pass 1167
Radstädter Tauernpass 1739
Katschberghöhe 1641
Turracher Höhe 1783
Passo di Resia 1508
Zugspitze 2963
H. Dachstein 2996
Watzmann 2713
Hochalmspitze 3355
Wildspitze 3774
Brenner (Brennero)
Vipiteno (Sterzing)
Brunico
A
B
86
87
97
100

TRIESTE
VENEZIA
PADOVA
VERONA
Vicenza
Treviso
Udine
Pordenone
Belluno
Trento
Bolzano (Bozen)
Gorizia
Monfalcone
Mantova
Rovigo
Chióggia
Mestre
Villach
Koper
Piran
Izola
Rovinj
Poreč
Umag
Grado
Caorle
Bibione
Lido
Jesolo
Montebelluna
Bassano d. Grappa
Castelfranco Veneto
Cittadella
Conegliano
Vittorio Veneto
Feltre
Cortina d'Ampezzo
Tolmezzo
Gemona d. Friuli
Cividale d. Friuli
Palmanova
Latisana
Portogruaro
S. Donà di Piave
Oderzo
Schio
Thiene
Valdagno
Arzignano
Legnago
Este
Monsélice
Abano Terme
Rovereto
Riva
Arco
Desenzano d. Garda
Peschiera
Villafranca di Verona
Castiglione d. Stiviere
Golfo di Venézia
Laguna Veneta
Lago di Garda
Alpi Carniche
Dolomiti
Pátrai
Ancona

Passau
Schärding
Ried i. Innkreis
LINZ
Leonding
Traun
Wels
Enns
Steyr
St. Valentin
Amstetten
Ybbs a.d. Donau
Melk
St. Pölten
Krems a.d. Donau
Herzogenburg
Freistadt
Zwettl
Vöcklabruck
Attnang-Puchheim
Lenzing
Gmunden
Kremsmünster
Waidhofen a.d. Ybbs
Lilienfeld
Mariazell
Bad Ischl
Bad Aussee
Bad Goisern
Liezen
Schladming
Eisenerz
Leoben
Bruck a.d. Mur
Kapfenberg
Mürzzuschlag
Kindberg
Knittelfeld
Judenburg
Fohnsdorf
Murau
Köflach
Voitsberg
GRAZ
Gleisdorf
Frohnleiten
Leibnitz
Deutschlandsberg
Wolfsberg
St. Veit
Klagenfurt
Villach
Spittal
Radenthein
Maribor
Celje
Velenje
Kranj
Jesenice
Totesgebirge
Sengsengebirge
Göstlinger Alpen
Hochschwab
Eisenerzer Alpen
Rottenmanner Tauern
Wölzer Tauern
Niedere Tauern
Gurktaler Alpen
Gleinalpe
Karawanken
Savinjske Alpe
Julijske Alpe
Pohorje
Ö S T E R R E I C H
J U G O S L A V
Donau
Drau
Enns
Mur
Attersee
Traunsee
Wörther See
Millstätter See
Ossiacher See
88
98
99
114

WIEN
BRATISLAVA
Schwechat
Mödling
Baden
Bad Vöslau
Wiener Neustadt
Eisenstadt
Neusiedler See
Stockerau
Korneuburg
Klosterneuburg
Mistelbach a.d.Z.
Hainburg
Bruck a.d. Leitha
Malacky
Stupava
Pezinok
Modra
Senec
Trnava
Hlohovec
Piešťany
Topoľčany
Nitra
Šaľa
Sereď
Galanta
Sládkovičovo
Dunajská Streda
Nové Zámky
Komárno
Komárom
Kolárovo
Šamorín
Partizánske
Mosonmagyaróvár
Győr
Sopron
Kapuvár
Csorna
Pápa
Tata
Tatabánya
Oroszlány
Mór
Zirc
Várpalota
Székesfehérvár
Veszprém
Ajka
Devecser
Sümeg
Tapolca
Keszthely
Balatonfüred
Siófok
Balaton
Fonyód
Celldömölk
Sárvár
Szombathely
Kőszeg
Körmend
Szentgotthárd
Zalaegerszeg
Nagykanizsa
Letenye
Čakovec
Varaždin
Marcali
Kaposvár
Dombóvár
Tamási
Enying
Nagyatád
Csurgó
Komló
Bakony
MAGYARORSZÁG
ČESKOSLOVENSKO
89
91
102
115

BUDAPEST
Komárno
Komárom
Esztergom
Vác
Gyöngyös
Tata
Tatabánya
Dorog
Szentendre
Gödöllő
Hatvan
Jászárokszállás
Heves
Oroszlány
Bicske
Biatorbágy
Budaörs
Törökbálint
Vecsés
Monor
Jászberény
Nagykáta
Érd
Szigetszentmiklós
Dunaharaszti
Vértes
Mór
Zirc
Várpalota
Székesfehérvár
Velencei-tó
Albertirsa
Ceglédbercel
Cegléd
Abony
Szolnok
Siófok
Balatonfüred
Enying
Ráckeve
Dömsöd
Kunszentmiklós
Dunaújváros
Kecskemét
Nagykőrös
Lajosmizse
Tiszaföldvár
Tiszakécske
Sárbogárd
Dunaföldvár
Solt
Szabadszállás
Izsák
Kiskunfélegyháza
Csongrád
Szentes
Tamási
Simontornya
Paks
Kalocsa
Kiskőrös
Soltvadkert
Kecel
Dombóvár
Tolna
Szekszárd
Bonyhád
Kiskunhalas
Kiskunmajsa
Hódmezővásárhely
Komló
Pécs
Mecsek
Baja
Jánoshalma
Mélykút
Mohács
Siklós
Szeged
Subotica
Palić
Horgoš
Kanjiža
Senta
Bajmok
Sombor
Apatin
Osijek
Donji Miholjac
Beli Manastir
Valpovo
Đakovo
Vukovar
Bačka Topola
Mali Iđoš
Feketić
Kula
Vrbas
Srbobran
Bečej
Temerin
Crvenka
Sivac
Odžaci
Bač
Čantavir
Ada
Mol
Kisač
JUGOSLAVIJA
Duna
Dunav
Tisza
Drava
Balaton

Mezőkövesd
Szihalom
Szentistván
Tiszakeszi
Újszentmargita
Hajdúdorog
Újfehértó
Balkány
Szakoly
Piricse
Vállaj
Berveni
Doba
Mădăras
Ardud
Carei
Moftinu Mic
Crasna
Nyírbéltek
Nyírlugos
Nyíradony
Encsencs
Bököny
Téglás
Hajdúhadház
Hajdúböszörmény
Balmazújváros
Hortobágy
Tiszacsege
Tiszafüred
Egyek
Poroszló
Sarud
Kömlő
Tiszanána
Tiszaszőlős
Tiszaigar
Tiszaörs
Tiszaderzs
Tiszaszentimre
Nagyiván
Abádszalók
Kunmadaras
Nádudvar
Hajdúszoboszló
DEBRECEN
Józsa
Hajdusamson
Nyírmártonfalva
Vámospércs
Nyíracsád
Nyírábrány
Penészlek
Pişcolt
Căuaş
Acîş
Santău
Tăşnad
Valea lui Mihai
Sălacea
Supuru de Sus
Bogdand
Bobota
Bagamér
Tarcea
Mikepércs
Hajdúszovát
Sáránd
Monostorpályi
Almosd
Létavértes
Hosszúpályi
Săcueni
Marghita
Pâtal
Zalnoc
Măieriște
Kaba
Kunhegyes
Püspökladány
Karcag
Báránd
Derecske
Konyár
Diosig
Camăr
Şimlăul Silvaniei
Fegyvernek
Kenderes
Sárrétudvari
Földes
Esztár
Pocsaj
Kismarja
Voivozi
Nuşfalău
Crasna
Boghiş
Bucsa
Szerep
Berettyóújfalu
Váncsod
Nagykereki
Sálard
Halmăşd
Kisújszállás
Biharnagybajom
Nagyrábé
Biharkeresztes
Biharea
Brusturi
Törökszentmiklós
Ecsegfalva
Zsáka
Munții Plopișului
Alesd
Cizer
Túrkeve
Füzesgyarmat
Berekböszörmény
ORADEA
Tileagd
Borod
Negreni
Ciucea
Mezőtúr
Dévaványa
Szeghalom
Csökmő
Magyarhomorog
Körösszegapáti
Sebes-Körös
Komádi
Vadu Crişului
Bratca
Nojorid
Les
Vîrciorog
Drăgești
Körösladány
Zsadány
Endrőd
Gyoma
Vésztő
Okány
Mezőgyán
Miersig
Sititelec
Ceica
Damiș
Remeti
Vişagu
Békésszentandrás
Szarvas
Körösttarcsa
Mezőberény
Sarkadkeresztúr
Salonta
Ripa
Holod
Simbăta
Roşia
Câbeşti
Vf. Vladeasa 1836
Kondoros
Békés
Doboz
Ménkerék
Kötegyán
Tulca
Tinca
Belfir
Petig
Remetea
Răchițele
Sarkad
Ciumeghiu
Batăr
Olcea
Budureasa
Stina de Vale
Nagyszénás
Békéscsaba
Gádoros
Csorvás
Gyula
Gyulavári
Crişul Negru
Berechiu
Beiuș
Munții Codru Moma
Munții Bihorului
Újkígyós
Vărşand
Zerind
Nagymágocs
Gerendás
Szabadkígyós
Şepreus
Drăgănești
Orosháza
Csanádapáca
Kétegyháza
Elek
Grăniceri
Chişineu-Criş
Sintea Mare
Vf. Pleșu 1112
Nucet
Pusztaföldvár
Medgyesbodzás
Medgyesegyháza
Socodor
Nădab
Beliu
Vaşcău
Scărişoara
Magyarbánhegyes
Nagykamarás
Şiclău
Cintei
Moneasa
Vf. Curcubăta 1848
Kaszaper
Lőkösháza
Şicula
Ineu
Cărpinet
Békéssámson
Kunágota
Dombiratos
Zărand
Bocsig
Dezna
Tótkomlós
Mezőkovácsháza
Kevermes
Şimand
Végegyháza
Macea
Seleuş
Bîrsa
Sebiş
Földeák
Pitvaros
Mezőhegyes
Dombegyház
Curtici
Sintana
Pincota
Tîrnova
Cuied
Buteni
Crişul Alb
Vîrfurile
Bulzeşti
Királyhegyes
Battonya
Zimandu Nou
Taut
Almaş
Gurahonț
Hălmagiu
Csanádpalota
Turnu
Şiria
Agrișu Mare
Nădaș
Vf. Drocea 836
Vața
Makó
Apátfalva
Nădlac
Pecica
ARAD
Covăsînt
Munții Zarandului
Baia de Criș
Szőreg
Magyarcsanád
Cenad
Felnac
Mureşul
Simbăteni
Păulis
Odvoş
Bîrzava
Groşii Noi
Căzănești
Brad
Căpruta
Visca
P. Valisoara 463
Valisoara
Sînnicolau Mare
Frumușeni
Zăbrani
Lipova
Neudorf
Periam
Şagu
Alioș
Bata
Săvîrşin
Zam
Beșenova Veche
Lovrin
Vinga
Fibiș
Zăbalt
Birchiș
Pojoga
Burjuc
Ilia
Sîrbi
Oriţişoara
Cuveşdia
Teremia Mare
Satchinez
Sandra
Hodoni
Dobra
Vețel
Comloşu Mare
Biled
Pişchia
Brestovăț
Roşcani
Nakovo
Lenauheim
Banatsko Veliko Selo
Iecea
Iecea Mică
Becicherecu Mic
Giarmata
Mârgina
Făget
Curtea
Kikinda
Jimbolia
Căpiniș
Remetea Mare
Recaş
Balinț
Clicova
Traian Vuia
Cerbăl
Rusko Selo
Novi Kozarc
Radojevo
Beregsăul
TIMIŞOARA
Topolovățu Mare
Belinț
Costeiu
Firdea
Luncani
Munții Poiana Ruscăi
Ghelar
Srpska Crnja
Vojvoda Stepa
Cenei
Cheveruşu Mare
Hitiaş
Lugoj
Vf. Padeş 1378
Lunca Cernii de Jos
Nova Crnja
Şag
Sacoşu Turcesc
Buziaș
Sinersig
Rushița
Timişul
Demsus
Otelec
Parța
Peciu Nou
Berini
Pogănişul
Sacu
Rusca Montană
Torda
Srpski Itebej
Giulvăz
Jebel
Liebling
Visag
Zgribești
P. Poarta de Fier
Valea Bistrei
Sarmizegetusa
Bucova
Begejski Kanal
Iohanisfeld
Foeni
Ciacova
Tormac
Cadăr
Vermeş
Măru
Begejci
Žitište
Krajišnik
Voiteg
Firliug
Valea Boului
Obreja
Poiana Mărului
Jaša Tomić
Birda
Gătaia
Berzovia
Brebu
Caransebeş
Vf. Pietrii 2190
Râul Mare
Gura Zlata
Zrenjanin
Sutjeska
Sečanj
Giera
Deta
Măureni
Bocşa Vasiovei
Ezeriş
Rugi
Buchin
Borlova
Banatski Despotovac
Banloc
Denta
Semlacu
Fizeş
Bocşa Română
Clinic
Boka
Tamiš
Munții

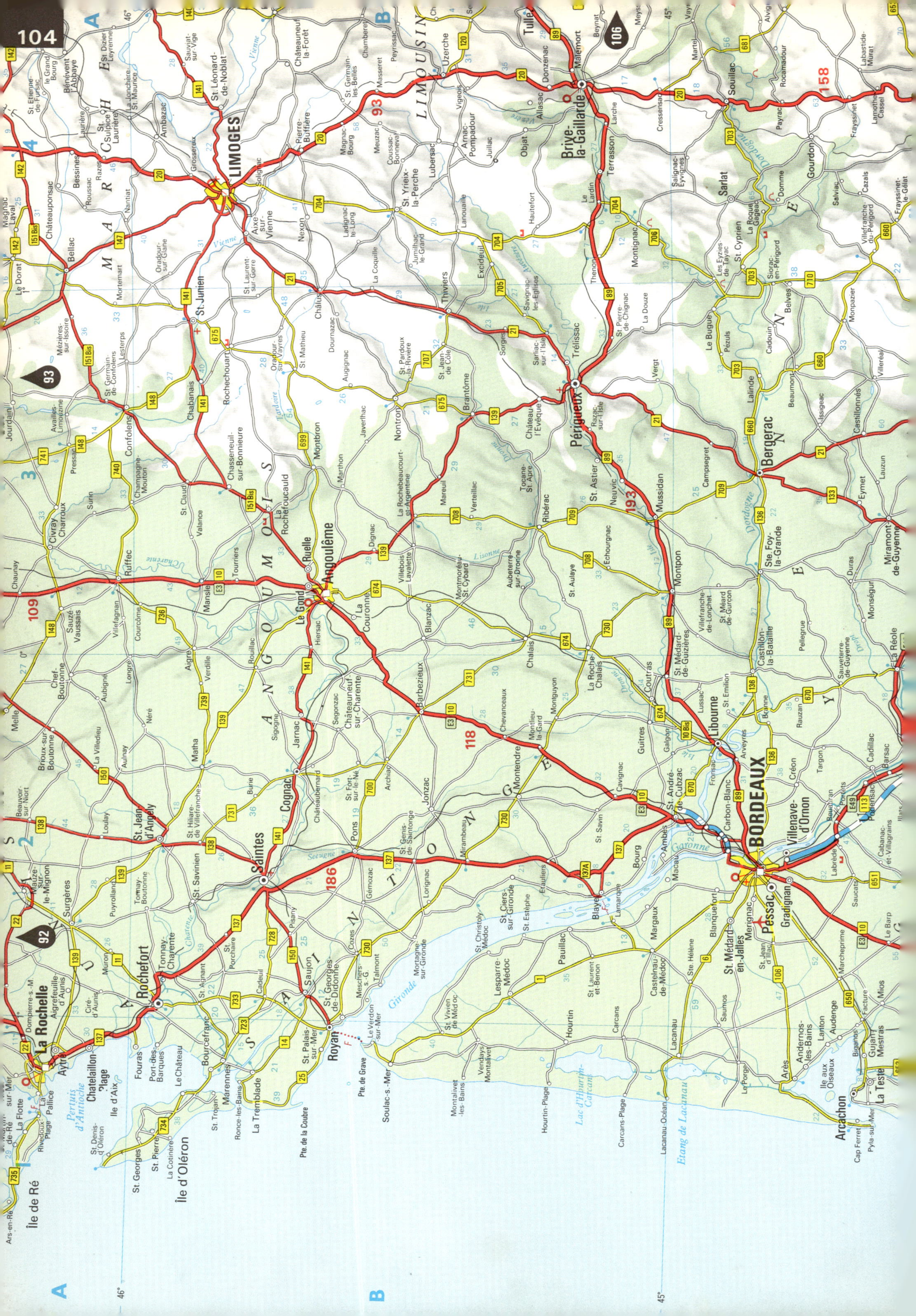
LIMOGES
Brive-la-Gaillarde
Tulle
Périgueux
Bergerac
Angoulême
Cognac
Saintes
Rochefort
La Rochelle
Royan
BORDEAUX
Libourne
Arcachon
Pessac
Mérignac
Ste. Foy-la-Grande
Sarlat
Souillac
Gourdon
Uzerche
St. Junien
Bellac
Confolens
Ruffec
Barbezieux
Jonzac
Blaye
Pauillac
Lesparre-Médoc
Soulac-s.-Mer
Le Verdon-sur-Mer
St. Jean-d'Angély
Surgères
Marennes
Ile d'Oléron
Ile de Ré
Ile d'Aix
Pertuis d'Antioche
Gironde
Garonne
Dordogne
Charente
Vienne
Lac d'Hourtin-Carcans
Etang de Lacanau
Ribérac
Mussidan
Montpon
Coutras
Castillon-la-Bataille
Nontron
Brantôme
Thiviers
Excideuil
Terrasson
Montignac
Le Bugue
Lalinde
Beaumont
Eymet
Miramont-de-Guyenne
Duras
La Réole
Cadillac
Langon
Villenave-d'Ornon
Gradignan
St. Médard-en-Jalles
Castelnau-de-Médoc
Lacanau
Hourtin
Andernos-les-Bains
Audenge
La Teste
Gujan-Mestras
Biganos
Chalais
Aubeterre-sur-Dronne
Montmoreau-St. Cybard
Châteauneuf-sur-Charente
Jarnac
Pons
Mirambeau
Montendre
Montguyon
St. André-de-Cubzac
Bourg
St. Savin
Matha
Aulnay
Melle
Civray
Chasseneuil-sur-Bonnieure
La Rochefoucauld
Rochechouart
Chalus
Nexon
St. Yrieix-la-Perche
Pierre-Buffière
Lubersac
Donzenac
Malemort
Allassac
Objat
Hautefort
Salignac-Eyvignes
Domme
Belvès
Le Dorat
Magnac-Laval
Châteauponsac
Bessines
Ambazac
Aixe-sur-Vienne
Oradour-sur-Glane
Mortemart
Mézières-sur-Issoire
Availles-Limouzine
Champagne-Mouton
Tonnay-Charente
Châtelaillon-Plage
Aytré
La Tremblade
Saujon
Cozes
Talmont
Meschers-s.-G.
St. Georges-de-Didonne
St. Palais-sur-Mer
Pte. de la Coubre
Pte. de Grave
Montalivet-les-Bains
Carcans-Plage
Lacanau-Océan
Hourtin-Plage
Margaux
Blanquefort
Cap Ferret
LIMOUSIN
MARCHE
ANGOUMOIS
SAINTONGE
AUNIS
GUYENNE
93
106
92
109
118
186
158
193
A
B
1
2
3
4
45°
46°
0°

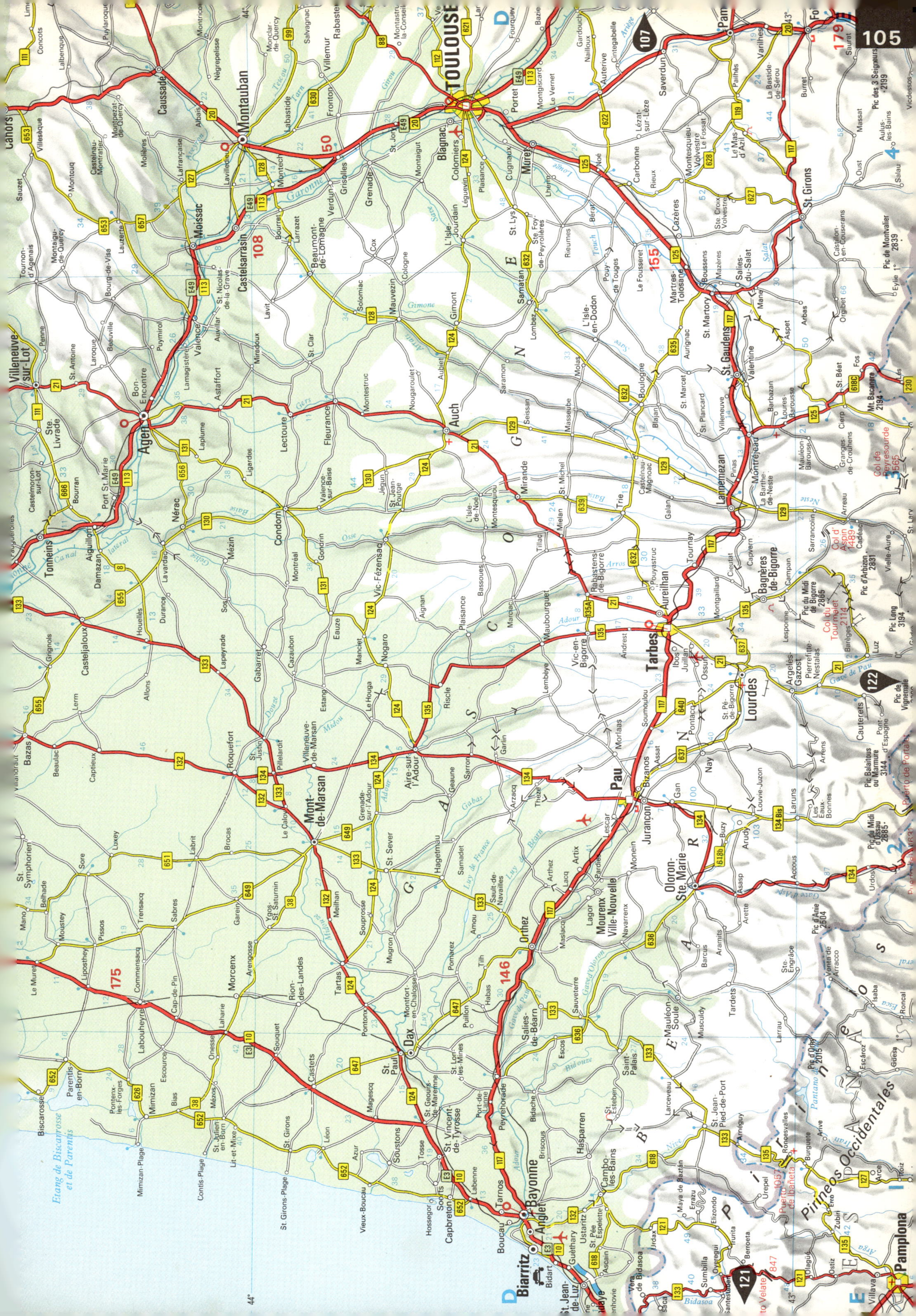
TOULOUSE
Montauban
Caussade
Moissac
Castelsarrasin
Agen
Villeneuve-sur-Lot
Tonneins
Aiguillon
Nérac
Condom
Lectoure
Fleurance
Auch
Mirande
Vic-Fézensac
Eauze
Nogaro
Aire-sur-l'Adour
Mont-de-Marsan
Roquefort
Bazas
Casteljaloux
Tartas
Dax
Morcenx
Labouheyre
Biscarrosse
Mimizan
Parentis-en-Born
Étang de Biscarrosse et de Parentis
St. Sever
Hagetmau
Orthez
Peyrehorade
Bayonne
Anglet
Biarritz
St. Jean-de-Luz
Capbreton
Hossegor
Soustons
Salies-de-Béarn
Sauveterre
Mauléon-Soule
St. Jean-Pied-de-Port
Oloron-Ste. Marie
Pau
Jurançon
Lescar
Nay
Lourdes
Tarbes
Bagnères-de-Bigorre
Lannemezan
Montréjeau
St. Gaudens
St. Girons
Muret
Samatan
L'Isle-Jourdain
Colomiers
Blagnac
Grenade
Beaumont-de-Lomagne
Cazères
Saverdun
Pamplona
Roncesvalles
Pirineos Occidentales
Pic du Midi de Bigorre 2865
Pic Long 3194
Pic d'Anie 2504
Pic du Midi d'Ossau 2885
Col du Tourmalet 2114
Col d'Aspin 1489
Col de Peyresourde 1565
Gave de Pau
Adour
Garonne
Tarn
Gers
Baïse
Midou
Douze
Gimone
Save
Bidouze
Bidasoa
Pic de Montvalier 2839
Pic des 3 Seigneurs 2199
Aulus-les-Bains
Luz
Cauterets
Argelès-Gazost
Arudy
Laruns

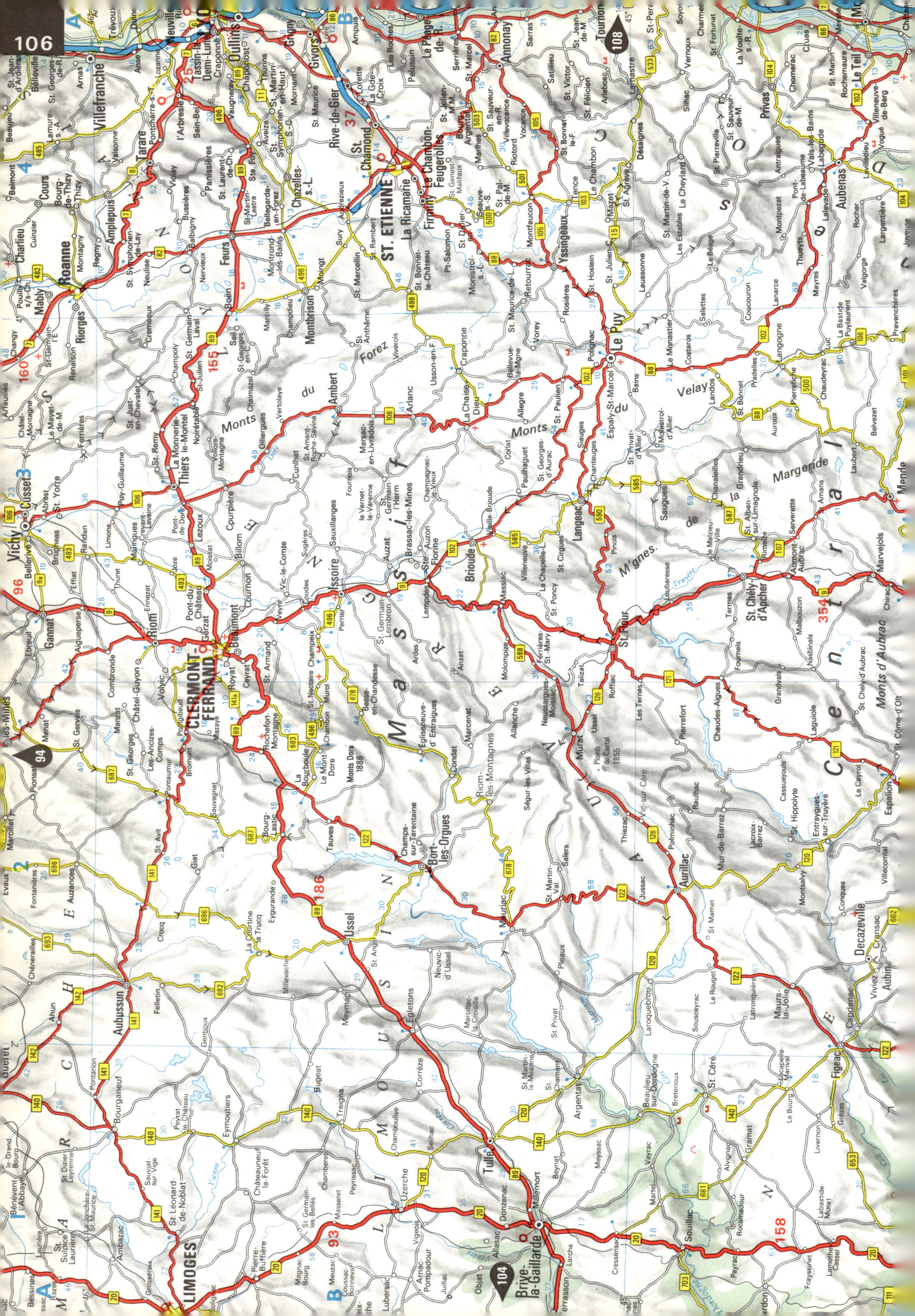

Villefranche
Roanne
Tarare
Feurs
Montbrison
ST. ETIENNE
Rive-de-Gier
Givors
Annonay
Yssingeaux
Le Puy
Vichy
Thiers
Ambert
Riom
CLERMONT-FERRAND
Issoire
Brioude
Langeac
St. Flour
Mende
Aubenas
Privas
Le Teil
Monts du Forez
Monts du Velay
Monts Dore
Margeride
Monts d'Aubrac
Murat
Aurillac
Mauriac
Ussel
Bort-les-Orgues
Aubusson
Bourganeuf
LIMOGES
Tulle
Brive-la-Gaillarde
Figeac
Decazeville
Souillac
Gramat
Massif Central

Avignon
Villeneuve-lès-Avignon
Tarascon
Arles
Beaucaire
Bagnols-s-Cèze
Pont-St-Esprit
Uzès
Nîmes
Alès
Besseges
La Grand Combe
St Gilles
Aigues-Mortes
Lunel
Les Stes-Maries
Montpellier
Sète
Frontignan
Agde
Pézenas
Béziers
Narbonne
Lodève
Ganges
Millau
St Affrique
Rodez
Villefranche-de-Rouergue
Carmaux
Albi
Gaillac
Castres
Mazamet
Carcassonne
Castelnaudary
Limoux
Quillan
Lézignan-Corbières
Rivesaltes
Toulouse
Montauban
Caussade
Pamiers
Foix
Lavelanet
Mirepoix
Revel
Graulhet
Lavaur
St Pons
Bédarieux
Causse du Larzac
Causse Méjean
Col de la Bassine 885
Col des Usclats 575
Col de Serrières 681
Col Notre Dame 667
Pic de St Barthelemy 2348
Pic des 3 Seigneurs 2199
Canal du Midi
Tarn
Aveyron
Ariège
Montagne Noire
Garonne
Hérault
Orb
Aude
Vidourle
Gard
Rhône

GENÈVE
Annemasse
Thonon
Bonneville
Cluses
Sallanches
Chamonix
Martigny
Aosta
Courmayeur
TORINO
Moncalieri
Nichelino
Carignano
Carmagnola
Racconigi
Savigliano
Saluzzo
Pinerolo
Rivoli
Avigliana
Susa
Bardonecchia
Briançon
Modane
St-Jean-de-M.
Albertville
Annecy
Rumilly
Aix-les-Bains
Chambéry
Montmélian
Ugine
Megève
Moûtiers
Bourg-St. Maurice
Val-d'Isère
Lanslebourg
Grenoble
Voiron
Vizille
La Mure
St. Marcellin
Romans-sur-Isère
Bourg-de-Péage
Valence
Crest
Die
Livron
Privas
Montélimar
Le Teil
Tournon
Tain-l'H.
Annonay
St. Étienne
St. Chamond
Rive-de-Gier
Givors
Vienne
Roussillon
Bourgoin
Jallieu
LYON
Villeurbanne
Oullins
Villefranche
Tarare
Bourg
Ambérieu-en-Bugey
Belley
Nantua
Oyonnax
Bellegarde
Seyssel
Massif du Pelvoux
Alpi Pennine
Gran Paradiso 4061
Monte Viso 3841
Col du Mont Cenis 2084
Col du Galibier 2556
Col de l'Iseran 2769
Col d'Izoard 2360
Col de Rousset
Col de la Croix Haute 1179
Chaîne de Belledonne
L. du Bourget
Rhône

MARSEILLE
TOULON
NICE
Cannes
Antibes
Grasse
Fréjus
St. Raphaël
St.-Tropez
Hyères
Îles d'Hyères
La Seyne
La Ciotat
Cassis
Aubagne
Aix-en-Provence
Avignon
Arles
Nîmes
Orange
Carpentras
Cavaillon
Apt
Manosque
Digne
Sisteron
Château-Arnoux
Castellane
Draguignan
Brignoles
Salon
Martigues
Marignane
Istres
Port-de-Bouc
Port-St.-Louis
Tarascon
Beaucaire
St.-Rémy-de-Provence
Bagnols-s.-Cèze
Pont-St.-Esprit
Bollène
Valréas
Nyons
Vaison-la-Romaine
Forcalquier
Pertuis
Gardanne
Menton
MONACO
Monte Carlo
Ventimiglia
Cuneo
Vence
Villefranche
Cap Camarat
Cap Croisette
Cap d'Antibes
Maures
Durance
Étang de Berre

TORINO
GÉNOVA
Golfo di Génova
Chamonix
Aosta
Mauvoisin
Matterhorn 4482
Monte Rosa 4638
Breuil-Cervinia
Valtournanche
Courmayeur
Tunnel du Mt. Blanc
Tunnel du Grd. St. Bernard
Étroubles
Morgex
La Thuile
Colle di Piccolo S. Bernardo
Ste-Foy-Tarentaise
Val-d'Isère
C. de l'Iseran 2769
Gran Paradiso 4061
Graie
Alpi Pennine
Châtillon
St. Vincent
Verrès
Pont-S.-Martin
Ivrea
Biella
Cossato
Borgosésia
Varallo Sésia
Omegna
Verbania-Intra
Pallanza
Stresa
Arona
Gravellona Toce
Lago Maggiore
Lugano
Varese
Como
Chiasso
Mendrisio
Gallarate
Busto Arsizio
Legnano
Saronno
Rho
Magenta
Novara
Vercelli
Santhià
Trecate
Vigévano
Abbiategrasso
Mortara
Pavia
Casale Monferrato
Valenza
Alessándria
Tortona
Voghera
Asti
Chieri
Moncalieri
Nichelino
Collegno
Rivoli
Chivasso
Settimo Torinese
Volpiano
Ciriè
Cuorgnè
Caselle Torinese
Venaria Reale
Alpignano
Avigliana
Giaveno
Susa
Col du Mont Cenis 2084
Bussoleno
Pinerolo
Luserna S. Giovanni
Carmagnola
Carignano
Racconigi
Saluzzo
Savigliano
Fossano
Bra
Alba
Cúneo
Mondovì
Borgo S. Dalmazzo
Monte Viso 3841
Colle di Tenda
Limone
Nizza Monferrato
Canelli
Acqui Terme
Ovada
Novi Ligure
Serravalle Scrivia
Arenzano
Pegli
Bolzaneto
Pontedécimo
Nervi
Recco
Camogli
S. Margherita Ligure
Varazze
Celle Ligure
Albissola Marina
Savona
Vado Ligure
Spotorno
Finale Ligure
Pietra Ligure
Loano
Albenga
Alássio
Laiguéglia
Diano Marina
Impéria
Porto Maurízio
Tággia
Arma di Tággia
Sanremo
Bordighera
Ventimiglia
Menton
MONACO
Monte Carlo
Beaulieu
Villefranche
NICE
Antibes
Cannes
Vallauris
Grasse
Mougins
Vence
St.-Laurent
Cap d'Antibes
Sospel
Breil
Tende
St. Martin-Vésubie
C. de Braus 995
C. de Brouis 875
Col St. Martin 1500
C. de Valberg 1669
Alpi Marittime
FRANCE
SCHWEIZ
Appennino Ligure
Bastia
Calvi
Ajaccio
Porto Torres

Lecco
Bérgamo
Brescia
Verona
Vicenza
Rovereto
Riva
Arco
Mori
Lodi
Crema
Cremona
Piacenza
Mántova
Parma
Reggio nell' Emilia
Modena
Bologna
Ferrara
La Spézia
Carrara
Massa
Viaréggio
Lucca
Pisa
Livorno
Pistóia
Prato
Firenze
Empoli
Cáscina
Pontedera
Legnago
Este
Thiene
Schio
Valdagno
Arzignano
Asiago
Piovene
Marostica
Desenzano d. Garda
Peschiera d. Garda
Bussolengo
Villafranca di Verona
Castiglione d. Stiviere
Ghedi
Chiari
Treviglio
Caravággio
Soresina
Casalpusterlengo
Codogno
Fiorenzuola d'Arda
Fidenza
Salsomaggiore Terme
Busseto
Casalmaggiore
Guastalla
Viadana
Suzzara
Reggiolo
Novellara
Corréggio
Carpi
Mirándola
Finale Emília
Cento
Sassuolo
Scandiano
Vignola
Pontrémoli
Sarzana
Lérici
Forte dei Marmi
Camaiore
Montecatini Terme
Péscia
Fucécchio
Sesto Fiorentino
Fiésole
Borgo S. Lorenzo
Lago di Garda
Po
F R I G N A N O
A p p e n n i n o T o s c o - E m i l i a n o
Pso. della Cisa
Pso. d. Futa 903
Pso. d. Raticosa 968
Pso. d. Porretta 932
Monte Cimone 2165
M. Giovo 1991
97
99
112

Crema
Soncino
Quinzano d'Oglio
Leno
Manèrbio
Verolanuova
Carpenèdolo
97
Villafranca di Verona
Valéggio s. Mincio
Volta Mantovana
Guidizzolo
Gòito
S. Bonifácio
Lonigo
Zévio
Albaredo d'Adige
Cologna Véneta
Noventa Vicentina
Abano Terme
PADOVA
Monsélice
Este
Montagnana
Bovolone
Isola d. Scala
Cerea
Legnago
Nogara
Castel d'Ario
Castelleone
Soresina
Castiglione d'Adda
Casalbuttano
Pontevico
Pizzighettone
Casalpusterlengo
Codogno
Cremona
Monticelli d'Ongina
Asola
Acquanegra s. Chiese
Canneto s. Oglio
Piádena
Castellucchio
Mántova
Marcaria
Bozzolo
Piacenza
Caorso
Cortemaggiore
Busseto
Scandolara Ravara
Roccabianca
Casalmaggiore
Rivarolo Mantovano
Sabbioneta
Suzzara
Borgoforte
Gonzaga
Ostiglia
Revere
S. Benedetto Po
Quistello
Badia Polésine
Lendinara
Castelmassa
Sérmide
Trecenta
Fiesso Umbertiano
Ficarolo
Occhiobello
Fiorenzuola d'Arda
Pontenure
Podenzano
Carpaneto Piacentino
Soragna
Fidenza
Salsomaggiore Terme
S. Secondo Parmense
Colorno
Guastalla
Viadana
Gualtieri
Brescello
Reggiolo
Fábbrico
Novellara
Concordia s. Sécchia
Mirándola
Novi di Módena
S. Felice s. Panaro
Finale Emilia
Bondeno
FERRARA
Copparo
Poggio Renatico
Cento
Pieve di Cento
PARMA
Noceto
Collécchio
Sala Baganza
Montécchio Emilia
S. Ilário d'Enza
REGGIO NELL' EMILIA
Corréggio
Carpi
MODENA
Campogalliano
Castelfranco Emilia
S. Giovanni in Persiceto
Crevalcore
Nonántola
Portomaggiore
Argenta
Molinella
Medicina
Búdrio
Consélice
Lugo
BOLOGNA
S. Lazzaro di Sávena
Castel S. Pietro Terme
Imola
Castel Bolognese
Faenza
Brisighella
Fornovo di Taro
Langhirano
Varano de Melegari
Scandiano
Sassuolo
Maranello
Vignola
Spilamberto
Bazzano
Casalecchio
Sasso Marconi
Marzabotto
Borgo Val di Taro
Bedónia
Bardi
Pso. della Cisa
Pontrémoli
Villafranca in Lunigiana
Aulla
Fivizzano
Castelnovo ne' Monti
Carpineti
Baiso
Pavullo nel Frignano
Montefiorino
Lama Mocogno
FRIGNANO
Appennino Tosco Emiliano
Monte Cimone 2165
Fanano
Porretta Terme
Castiglione dei Pépoli
Vérnio
Firenzuola
Pso. d. Raticosa 968
Pso. d. Futa 903
Marradi
Modigliana
LA SPEZIA
Lérici
Portovénere
Sarzana
Carrara
Massa
Marina di Carrara
Marina di Massa
Forte dei Marmi
Pietrasanta
Camaiore
Castelnuovo di Garfagnana
Barga
Gallicano
Bagni di Lucca
Borgo a Mozzano
Viaréggio
Torre d. Lago Puccini
Massarosa
Lucca
Capánnori
Péscia
Montecatini Terme
Monsummano Terme
Pistóia
PRATO
Sesto Fiorentino
Fiésole
FIRENZE
Pontassieve
Borgo S. Lorenzo
Scarperia
Vicchio
Dicomano
Rufina
Stia
Poppi
Bibbiena
Pratomagno 1592
Pisa
Cascina
Marina di Pisa
Tirrénia
Pontedera
Ponsacco
Castelfiorentino
Empoli
Fucécchio
Montelupo Fiorentino
Lastra a Signa
Impruneta
S. Casciano in V. di Pesa
Greve
Figline Valdarno
S. Giovanni Valdarno
Montevarchi
LIVORNO
Collesalvetti
Péccioli
Gambassi
Certaldo
Poggibonsi
S. Gimignano
Colle di Val d'Elsa
Siena
Radda in Chianti
Castellina in Chianti
CHIANTI
Castelnuovo Berardenga
Gorgona
Quercianella Sonnino
Rosignano Marittimo
Castiglioncello
Rosignano Solvay
Volterra
Saline
Cécina
Vada
Marina di Cécina
Colline Metallifere
Pomarance
Radicóndoli
Bibbona
Castagneto Carducci
Castelnuovo di V. di Cécina
Donorático
S. Vincenzo
Capraia
Campiglia Marittima
Venturina
Massa Marittima
Roccastrada
Piombino
Follónica
Gavorrano
Asciano
Buonconvento
Montalcino
Montepulciano
Sinalunga
Torrita d. Siena
Pienza
Rapolano Terme
Monte S. Savino
Chianciano Terme
Abbadia
111
142
44°
43°
10°
11°

Golfo di Venézia
JADRANSKO MORE
MARE ADRIATICO
ISTRA
Kvarner
Laguna Véneta
Chióggia
Sottomarina
Pellestrina
Alberoni
S. Pietro in Volta
Pontelongo
Cavárzere
Loreo
Adria
Contarina
Táglio di Po
Porto Tolle
Scardovari
Mésola
Pomposa
Codigoro
Volano
Massa Fiscáglia
Lagosanto
Comácchio
Porto Garibaldi
Valli di Comácchio
S. Alberto
Mezzano
Marina di Ravenna
RAVENNA
Savio
Cérvia
Cesenático
Gatteo a Mare
Bellária
Igea Marina
Forlimpopoli
Bertinoro
Méldola
Cesena
Savignano sul Rubicone
Borello
Rimini
Riccione
Cattólica
S. Arcángelo di Romagna
Sogliano al Rubicone
Mercato Saraceno
Serravalle
SAN MARINO
Pésaro
Fano
Marotta
Senigállia
Marzocca
Falconara Marittima
ANCONA
Morciano di Romagna
Saludécio
Mercatino Conca
Macerata Féltria
Montécchio
Mombaróccio
S. Costanzo
Calcinelli
Mondolfo
Monte Pórzio
Urbino
Fossombrone
Urbánia
S. Angelo in Vado
Sestino
Lunano
Carpegna
Sassocorvaro
Pennabilli
S. Leo
Novafeltria
Talamello
Sársina
S. Piero in Bagno
S. Agata Féltria
Badia Tedalda
Pieve S. Stéfano
Borgo Pace
Sansepolcro
S. Giustino
Città di Castello
Apécchio
Piobbico
Cagli
Acqualagna
Pérgola
S. Lorenzo in Campo
Mondavio
Corinaldo
Ostra
Chiaravalle
Rocca Priora
S. Marcello
Iesi
Móie
Montecarotto
Arcévia
Serra S. Quirico
Cupramontana
Filottrano
Ósimo
Castelfidardo
Camerano
Sirolo
Numana
Porto Recanati
Loreto
Recanati
Montefano
Cíngoli
Montecassiano
Potenza Picena
Porto Potenza Picena
Civitanova Alta
Civitanova Marche
Tréia
Passo di Tréia
Macerata
Sforzacosta
Corridónia
Montegranaro
Porto S. Elpídio
S. Elpídio a Mare
Porto S. Giórgio
Fermo
Pedaso
Tolentino
Mogliano
Montegiórgio
Caldarola
S. Ginésio
Monterubbiano
Serviglianо
S. Vittoria in Matenano
Montalto d. Marche
Ripatransone
Cupra Marittima
Grottammare
S. Benedetto del Tronto
Porto d'Ascoli
Acquaviva Picena
Offida
Comunanza
Rotella
Montefortino
Amándola
Sarnano
Bolognola
Pieve Torina
Visso
Serravalle di Chienti
Muccia
Camerino
Pióraco
Serrapetrona
Castelraimondo
Matélica
S. Severino Marche
Cerreto d'Esi
Fabriano
Apiro
Sassoferrato
Cantiano
Schéggia
Gúbbio
Sigillo
Fossato di Vico
Gualdo Tadino
Nocera Umbra
Valtopina
Colfiorito
Casenove
Foligno
Spello
Assisi
Bastia
S. Maria d'Angeli
Bettona
Cannara
Deruta
Bevagna
Ponte S. Giovanni
PERUGIA
Valfábbrica
Casa Castalda
Piccione
Branca
Scritto
Umbértide
Camporeggiano
Niccone
Pietralunga
S. Lucia
Tréstina
Cortona
Mercatale
Tuoro sul Trasimeno
Passignano sul Trasimeno
Magione
Ponte Felcino
Castiglione d. Lago
Trasimeno
Mugnano
Tavernelle
Piegaro
Città d. Pieve
Cerqueto
Marsciano
Casalina
Appennino
Monte Catria
APPENNINO
Marche
Novigrad Podravski
Grožnjan
Vižinada
Motovun
Poreč
Vrsar
Rovinj
Bale
Barbariga
Vodnjan
Brijuni
Pula
Medulin
Marčana
Svetvinčenat
Kanfanar
Žminj
Pazin
Baderna
Kršan
Plomin
Labin
Rabac
Barban
Mošćenička Draga
Vranja
Sušnjevica
Cres
Foce del Po
Lamone
Ronco
Metauro
Cesano
Esino
Potenza
Chienti
Tenna
Aso
Marecchia
Foglia
Tévere
99
114
138
99
234
76
124
143
221
309
516
495
253
67
254
310
16
71
E7
E2
A14
3bis
258
72
423
73bis
73
298
3
256
77
78
210
485
220
75bis
75
209
E45
2

Tarvisio
Jesenice
Karawanken Tunnel
Loibl Pass 1370
Loibl Tunnel
Eisenkappel
Slovenjgradec
Maribor
Kranjska Gora
Julijske alpe
Triglav 2864
Bled
Lesce
Radovljica
Tržič
Vellach
Seeberg Sattel
Savinjske alpe
Grintavec 2558
Gornji Grad
Črna
Šoštanj
Velenje
Mislinja
Mozirje
Bovec
Zaga
Kobarid
Bohinjsko Jezero
Bohinjska Bistrica
Železniki
Kranj
Šenčur
Kamnik
Menges
Vransko
Šempeter
Žalec
Celje
Vojnik
Slovenske Konjice
Šmarje
Tarcento
Nimis
Tricésimo
Faédis
Púlfero
Tolmin
Cerkno
Škofja Loka
Medvode
Gorenja Vas
Šentvid
LJUBLJANA
Domžale
Trzin
Zagorje
Trbovlje
Hrastnik
Laško
Litija
Radeče
Sevnica
Bohor
Brestanica
Cividale d. Friuli
Udine
Kanal
Anhovo
Čepovan
Idrija
Žiri
Vrhnika
Borovnica
Ig
Škofljica
Grosuplje
Višnja Gora
Trebnje
Mirna
Mokronog
Videm-Krško
Cormons
Gorízia
Nova Gorica
Palmanova
Črni Vrh
Ajdovščina
Logatec
Kalce
Gradisca d'Isonzo
Ronchi d. Legionari
Monfalcone
Aquiléia
Grado
Duino
Sistiana
Vipava
Planina
Ratek
Cerknica
Velike Lašče
Žužemberk
Novo Mesto
Kostanjevica
Gorjanci
Postojna
Dutovlje
Sežana
Senožeče
Opicina
TRIESTE
Basovizza
Múggia
Kozina
Pivka
Iga Vas
Dolenja Vas
Ribnica
Kočevje
Sošice
Uršna Sela
Metlika
Jastrebarsko
Krašić
Ozalj
Črnomelj
Knežak
Ilirska Bistrica
Snežnik 1796
Čabar
Izola
Piran
Portoroz
Koper
Podgrad
Rupa
Klana
Gerovo
Risnjak 1528
Umag
Buje
Buzet
Novigrad
Motovun
Delnice
Skrad
Kupjak
Kupa
Vrbovsko
Bosanci
Zdihovo
Karlovac
Duga Resa
Opatija
Matulji
Lovran
RIJEKA
Cavle
Bakar
Lovke
Ravna Gora
Mrkopalj
Fužine
Generalski Stol
Krnjak
I S T R A
Poreč
Pazin
Mošćenička Draga
Omišalj
Kraljevica
Viševica 1428
Bjelolasica 1533
Jasenak
Ogulin
Oštarije
Veleka Kapela
Zminj
Crikvenica
Josipdol
Primišlje
Labin
Rabac
Plomin
Krk
Vrbnik
Novi Vinodolski
Plaški
Slunj
Rovinj
Barban
Bale
Punat
Baska
Brinje
Saborsko
Vodnjan
Marčana
Cres
Senj
Jurjevo
Konačišta 1494
Otočac
Pula
Medulin
Kvarner
Kvarnerić
Sv. Grgur
Prvič
Lopar
Goli
Rab
Velebit
Vrhovine
Lešće
Krasno
M. Rajinac 1699
Mala Kapela
Jablanac
Gornji Kosinj
Perušić
Nerezine
Stara Novalja
Novalja
Cesarica
Lički Osik
Gospić
Mali Lošinj
Veli Lošinj
Susak
Pag
Karlobag
Kanal
Ilovik
Skarda
Lukovo Šugarje
Medak
Maun
Baric Draga
Silba
Kruščica
Premuda
Olib
Vir
Virsko more
Ist
Molat
Privlaka
Ražanac
Starigrad Paklenice
Nin
Poljica
Posedarje
Sestrunj
Zadarski kanal
Poličnik
Novigrad
Ugljan
Zadar
Ancona
Preko
D. Zemunik
Dugi Otok
Iž
Bibinje
Sukošan
Benkovac
Kozje
Kostanjevica
Pragersko
99
100
113

Nagykanizsa
Ptuj
Čakovec
Varaždin
Letenye
Kaposvár
Dombóvár
Csurgó
Nagyatád
MAGYARORSZÁG
PÉCS
Koprivnica
Ivanščica
Kalnik
Đurđevac
Barcs
Szigetvár
Križevci
Bjelovar
Pitomača
Virovitica
Medvednica
ZAGREB
Velika Gorica
Dugo Selo
Sesvete
Zabok
Zelina
Vrbovec
Ivanić Grad
Moslavačka gora
Podravska Slatina
Daruvar
Papuk
Sisak
Petrinja
Kutina
Glina
Pakrac
Lipik
Novska
Nova Gradiška
Slavonska Požega
Slavonski Brod
Zrinska gora
Kostajnica
Bosanska Dubica
Bosanska Gradiška
Prosara
Kozara
Bosanski Novi
Prijedor
Bosanska Krupa
Bihać
Sanski Most
Banja Luka
Derventa
Prnjavor
Doboj
Kotor Varoš
Teslić
Borja planina
Manjača
Bosanski Petrovac
Mrkonjić Grad
Jajce
Drvar
Travnik
Zenica
Donji Vakuf
Bugojno
Knin
Gračac
Donji Lapac
Drava
Sava
Una
Vrbas
Bosna
Glamoč
Vitorog 1907
Šator 1872
Klekovača 1961
E94
E96
68
124
101
102
116
150

Donji Miholjac
Petlovac
Beli Manastir
Kneževi Vinogradi
102
Sombor
Kljajićevo
Bačka Topola
Njegoševo
Bajša
Ada
Jagodnjak
Belišće
Valpovo
Apatin
Prigrevica
Sivac
Crvenka
Mali Iđoš
Feketić
Lipar
Kula
Bačko Petrovo
Bečej
Darda
Bilje
Osijek
Petrijevci
Bizovac
Koška
Josipovac
Beničanci
Čačinci
Zdenci
Đurđenovac
Feričanci
Našice
Breznica Našička
Čepinski Martinci
Čepin
Tenja
Sonta
Stapar
Bački Brestovac
Srpski Miletić
Ruski Krstur
Vrbas
Srbobran
Kucura
Savino Selo
Odžaci
Pivnice
Erdut
Dalj
Bačko Gradište
Čurug
Kutjevo
Podgorač
Ernestinovo
Trpinja
Borovo
Deronje
Ratkovo
Despotovo
Zmajevo
Ravno Selo
Sirig
Temerin
Bač
Bođani
Selenča
Silbaš
Bački Petrovac
Satnica Đakovačka
Markušica
Semeljci
Vukovar
Plavna
Gajdobra
Maglić
Kisač
Zabalj
Levanjska Varoš
Đakovo
Vinkovci
Tovariševo
Mladenovo
Obrovac
Rumenka
Mošorin
Ruševo
Stari Mikanovci
Ivankovo
Sotin
Bačko Novo Selo
Bačka Palanka
Gložan
NOVI SAD
Šajkaš
Trnava
Stari Jankovci
Orolik
Šarengrad
Ilok
Petrovaradin
Kovilj
Sibinj
Andrijevci
Strizivojna
Vrpolje
Cerna
Privlaka
Beočin
Stremski Karlovci
Slavonski Brod
Velika Kopanica
Gundinci
Gradište
Komletinci
Nijemci
Tovarnik
Fruška gora
Kaniža
Svilaj
Babina Greda
Otok
Šid
Ležimir
Crveni Čot 539
Novo Selo
Donja Bebrina
Donja Dubica
Županja
Vašica
Erdevik
Grgurevci
Irig
Bosanski Šamac
Domaljevac
Adaševci
Čalma
Kukujevci
Polje
Odžak
Orašje
Bošnjaci
Lipovac
Radinci
Ruma
Inđija
Kulina
Botajica
Podnovlje
Obudovac
Vrbanja
Morović
Kuzmin
Lаćarak
Stremska Mitrovica
Putinci
Golubinci
Nova Pazova
Modran
Modriča
Gornji Žabar
Drenovci
Zasavica
Vojka
Mišinci
Gradačac
Brčko
Račinovci
Jamena
Stremska Rača
Ravnje
Glušci
Jarak
Pećinci
Kožuhe
Osinja
Kotorsko
Brezovo Polje
Donje Crnjelovo
Crna Bara
Hrtkovci
Brestač
Nikinci
Šimanovci
Brka
Velika Obarska
Bogatić
Klenje
Belotić
Platičevo
Karlovčić
Lukavica
Srnice
Dubrave
Klenak
Donji Tovarnik
Dobanovci
Doboj
Soko
Maoča
Bijeljina
Badovinci
Grabovci
Ašanja
Majevica
Šabac
Srebrnik
Tutnjevac
Obrež
Kuninovo
Boljevci
115
Gračanica
Celic
Suhopolje
Petlovača
Tešanj
V. Ostravica 917
Miričina
Janja
Prnjavor
Varna
Sava
Uglejevik
Lopare
Lešnica
Obrenovac
Vrućica
Donja Dobošnica
Priboj
Vladimirci
Jalovik
Debrc
Grabovac
Maglaj
Tuzla
Gornja Tuzla
Glavičice
Šor
Stubline
Lukavac
Bistarac
Husina
Rastošnica
Loznica
Draginja
Banjani
Ozimica
Zavidovići
Poljice
Tojšići
Kozluk
Banja Koviljača
Korenita
Zavlaka
Žepče
Živinice
Spreča
Kostajnik
Koceljevo
Tamnava
Ub
Manjača 1360
Banovići Selo
Banovići
Đurđevik
Capardi
Zvornik
Radalj
Jadar
Osečina
Lajkovac
Ribnica
Jagodnja 940
Krupanj
Brankovina
Tvrtkovac 1304
Ravan
1328
Konjuh
Javornik
Kamenica
Valjevo
Popučke
Crnča
Peka
Zenica
Kladanj
Tupanari
Nova Kasaba
Gračanica
Kolubara
Mionica
Lipnica 1458
1087
Vlasenica
Bratunac
Ljubovija
Kakanj
Zgošća
Vareš
Očevlja
Vrhpolje
Povljen
Busovača
Olovo
Drlače
Brijezde
Srebrenica
Breza
Han Pijesak
Rogačica
Kostojevići
Visoko
Gromiljak
Kiseljak
Ilijaš
Devetak 1417
Devetak
Romanija
Skelani
Bajina Bašta
Dub
1022
Kosjeric
Družetići
Vogošća
Sokolac
Kobila Glava 625
SARAJEVO
Podromanija
Perućac
Zaglavak
Čestobrodica
Kreševo
Ilidža
Hadžići
Hrasnica
Tarčin
Pale
Bioska
Karan
Titovo Užice
Servojno
Požega
Kremna
Lisin 1744
Bradina
Rogatica
Mokra Gora
Đetinja
Bjelašnica 2067
Sjenište 1913
Osječani
Višegrad
Cajetina
Arilje
Jahorina
Zlatibor
Rožanstvo
Trnovo
Goražde
Ustiprača
Crni Rzav
Vranići
Rudo
Uvac
Treskavica
Ustikolina
Drina
Čajniče
Priboj
Ustibar
Banja
Kom 1779
Foča
Goleša
Negbina
Jasenovo
1534
Glavatičevo
Kalinovik
Bistrica
Rutoši
Crvanj
Obalj
Lelija 2032
Bistrica
Nova Varoš
Ćehotina
Ulog
Brasina 1897
151
Šuplja stijena 1469
Gradac
Pljevlja
Prijepolje
Kladnica
Jabuka
Milošev
Neretva
Tara
Dunav
Drava
Bosna
Sava
Lim
Vuka
Bosut
Veliki Kanal
Mali Kanal
E94
E5
54
85
74
55
78
100
122
16

TIMIŞOARA
Lugoj
Caransebeş
Reşiţa
Zrenjanin
BEOGRAD
Pančevo
Vršac
Bela Crkva
Smederevo
Požarevac
Kragujevac
Kraljevo
Kruševac
Niš
Zaječar
Knjaževac
Negotin
Bor
Orşova
Turnu Severin
Kladovo
Mladenovac
Smederevska Palanka
Svetozarevo
Ćuprija
Paraćin
Aleksinac
Majdanpek
Kula
Anina
Oraviţa
Buziaş
Deta
Jebel
Sag
Sacu
Băile Herculane
Mehadia
Topleţ
Moldova Nouă
Moldova Veche
Golubac
Kovin
Kostolac
Vrčin
Ripanj
Topola
Aranđelovac
Lapovo
Batočina
Jagodina
Velika Plana
Svilajnac
Despotovac
Žagubica
Boljevac
Sokobanja
Trstenik
Vrnjačka Banja
Stalać
Ražanj
Ćićevac
Svrljig
Belgrade
Negotin
Kučevo
Veliko Gradište
Bačka
Jabuka
Opovo
Kovačica
Padina
Alibunar
Banatsko Novo Selo
Banatski Karlovac
Deliblatska Peščara
Homoljske planine
Kučaj
Deli Jovan
Severni Kučaj
Munţii Locvei
Munţii Semenicului
Munţii Almăjului
Munţii Mehedinţului
Munţii Ţarcului
Munţii Poiana Ruscai
Miroč
Bukovik
Svrljiške pl.
Veliki Jastrebac
ROMÂNIA
BULGARIJA
Dunav
Timiş
Morava
Velika Morava
Zapadna Morava
Juzna Morava
Pek
Mlava
Nera
Timok
Crni Timok
Beli Timok
Porţile de Fier
E94
E5
E70
103
104
118
157
60
41
34
66
69
160
152
153
6
4
5
A
B
C

1
2
3
A
B
C
9°
8°
43°
42°
Cabo Ortegal
Ría de Sta. Marta
Ría del Barquero
Ría de Vivero
Cabo Morás
Cedeira
Ortigueira
Vivero
Jove
Cervo
Burella de Cabo
Foz
Barreiros
Valdoviño
Cabo Prior
S. Martín de Covas
El Ferrol del Caudillo
Neda
Mugardos
Ría de Betanzos
Ares
Cabañas
Puentes de García Rodríguez
Sierra de la Carba
Mondoñedo
Lorenzana
Trabada
Islas Sisargas
LA CORUÑA
Torre de Hércules
Puentedeume
Sada
Malpica
Ría de Lage
Lage
Puente-Ceso
Carballo
Laracha
Cambre
Betanzos
Bergondo
Montero
Villalba
Pastoriza
Riotorto
Cabo Villano
Camariñas
Ría de Camariñas
Mugía
Cabo Toriñana
Vimianzo
Zas
Carral
Cesuras
Guitiriz
Castro de Rey
Meira
Ordenes
Sobrado
Otero de Rey
Fonsa
Friol
Lugo
Castroverde
Cée
Corcubión
Finisterre
Cabo de Finisterre
Mazaricos
Negreira
Sigüeiro
Arzúa
Mellid
Palas de Rey
Guntín
Corgo
Becerreá
Carnota
Outes
Brión
Santiago de Compostela
Touro
Boqueijón
Villa de Cruces
Monterroso
Sarria
Los Nogales
Muros
Noya
Ría de Muros y Noya
Puerto del Son
Padrón
Teo
Vedra
Golada
Taboada
Embalse de Belesar
Samos
Triacastela
La Estrada
Silleda
Lalín
Rodeiro
Chantada
Puebla del Caramiñal
Rianjo
Catoira
Caldas de Reyes
Cuntis
Forcarey
Dozón
Sierra del Faro
Bóveda
Folgoso de Caurel
Ribeira (Sta. Eugenia)
Isla de Arosa
Villanueva de Arosa
Villagarcía
Ría de Arosa
Isla Sálvora
Cambados
Grove
Cerdedo
Carballeda
Piñor
Puebla del Brollón
Pantón
Monforte de Lemos
Quiroga
Sanjenjo
Marín
Pontevedra
Puente Caldelas
Sierra del Suido
Carballino
Maside
Boboras
Cea
La Peroja
Sober
Isla de Ons
Ría de Pontevedra
Bueu
Moaña
Redondela
Fornelos de Montes
Orense
Nogueira de Ramuín
Pereiro de Aguiar
Embalse de S. Esteban
Castro-Caldelas
Puebla de Trives
Islas Cíes
Cangas
VIGO
Ría de Vigo
Bouzas
Ribadavia
Melón
Toén
Barbadanes
Maceda
Baños de Molgas
Montederramo
Manzaneda
Chandreja de Queija
Sierra de Queija
Porriño
Mondariz
La Cañiza
Puenteáreas
Crecente
Ramiranes
Celanova
Allariz
Villar de Barrio
Junquera de Ambía
Milagros del Monte
Viana del Bollo
Bayona
Cabo Silleiro
Gondomar
Monterreal
Nieves
Melgaço
Sandianes
Tuy
Valença do Minho
Monção
Rairiz de Veiga
Ginzo de Limia
Laza
Castrelo del Valle
Bande
Trasmiras
Cualedro
Monterrey
Verín
Villardevós
Ríos
La Guardia
Vilz Nova da Cerveira
Caminha
Muiños
Blancos
Baltar
Oimbra
Serra da Peneda
Soajo
Lindoso
Ponte da Barca
Arcos de Valdevez
Serra do Gerez
Vila Praia de Ancora
Ancora
Ponte de Lima
Viana do Castelo
Darque
Chaves
Barragem do Alto Cávado
Barragem do Alto Rabagão
Barragem de Venda Nova
Serra do Barroso
Castelo do Neiva
Forjães
Vila Verde
Prado
Barcelos
Braga
Vila Pouca de Aguiar
Póvoa de Lanhoso
Carrazedo de Montenegro
Valpaços
Esposende
Guimarães
Fafe
Vila Nova de Famalicão
Póvoa de Varzim
Vila do Conde
Sto Tirso
Felgueiras
Celorico de Basto
Mondim de Basto
Serra do Alvão
Murça
124
168
150
137
249
68

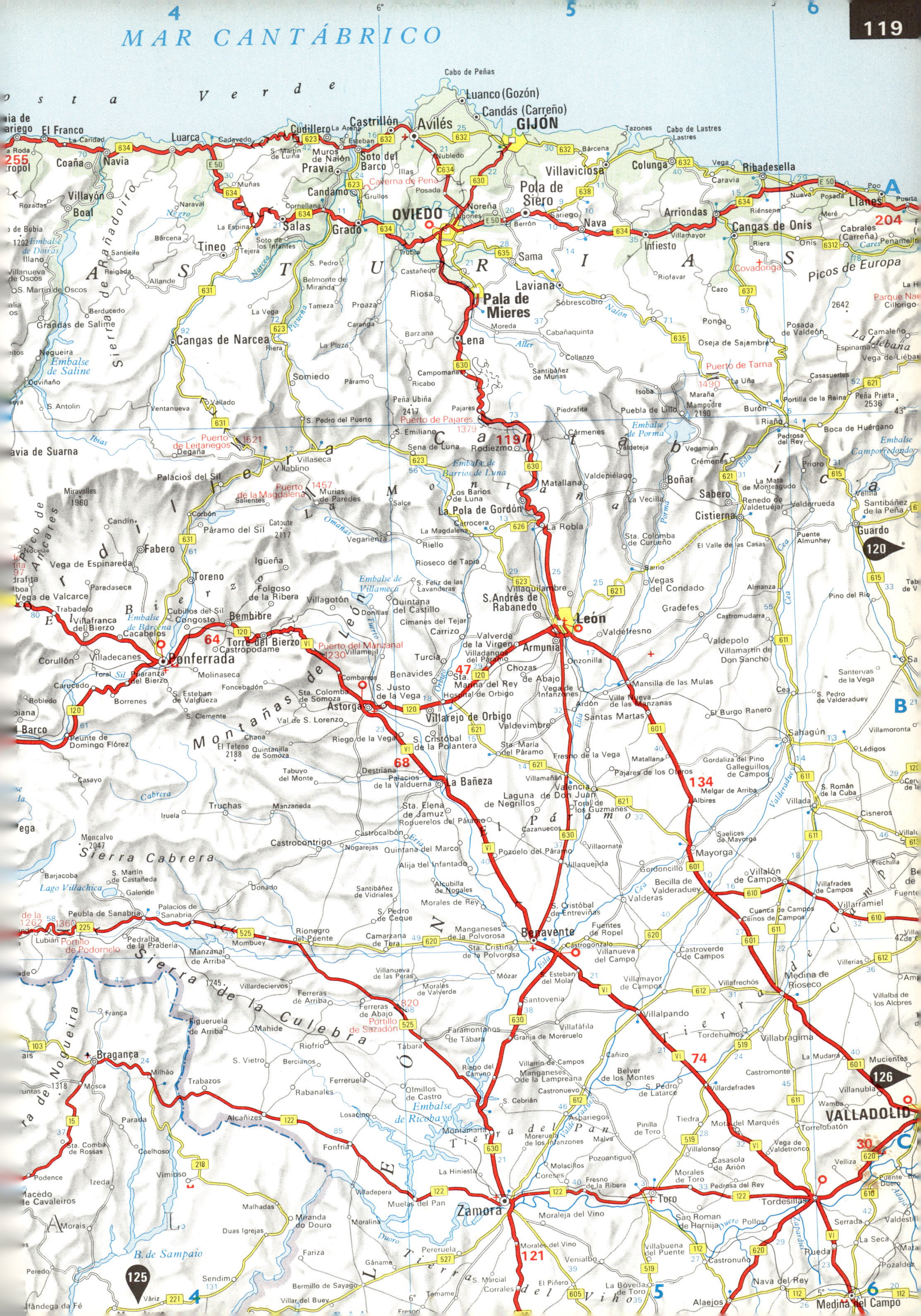

MAR CANTÁBRICO

Costa Verde

Cabo de Peñas

Luanco (Gozón)
Candás (Carreño)
GIJÓN
Cabo de Lastres
Tazones
Vega
Ribadesella
Colunga
Caravia
Nueva Posada
Poo
A
Llanes
Puerta
Cabrales (Carreña)
Penamellera
204
Cares
Picos de Europa

El Franco
La Caridad
Cudillero La Arena
Castrillón
AVILÉS
Luarca
Cadavedo
S. Esteban
Soto del Barco
Nubledo
Colunga
255
Coaña
Navia
Muros de Nalón
Pravia
Illas
Posada
Pola de Siero
Villaviciosa
Arriondas
Cangas de Onís
Onís
Covadonga
La Llera
Vega de Ribadeo

Villayón
Boal
Naraval
Candámo
Grullos
Cornellana
OVIEDO
Noreña
Sariego
Nava
Villamayor
Riera
Parque Nac.
Cilloigo
Posada de Valdeón
La Liébana

Rozadas
Salas
Grado
Trubia
El Berrón
Sama
Infiesto
Espinama
Vega de Liébana

S. Martín de Oscos
Tineo
La Espina
S. Pedro
Castañedo
Laviana
Sobrescobio
Riofavar
Cazo
Posada de Valdeón
Camaleño

ASTURIAS

Cangas de Narcea
La Vega
Proaza
Riosa
Pola de MIERES
Moreda
Cabañaquinta
Ponga
Oseja de Sajambre
Maraña
2642

Somiedo
Páramo
Barzana
Caranga
Lena
Aller
Collanzo
Isoba
Puerto de Tarna
La Uña
Burón
Peña Prieta 2536
43°

Ventanueva
S. Pedro del Puerto
Peña Ubiña 2417
Campomanes
Santibáñez de Murias
Puebla de Lillo
Maraña
Mampodre 2190
Portilla de la Reina
Pedrosa del Rey

Puerto de Leitariegos 1521
Degaña
Pajares
Puerto de Pajares 1379
119
Rodiezmo
Piedrafita
Embalse de Porma
Vegamián
Crémenes
Prioro
Boca de Huérgano
Embalse Camporredondo

S. Emiliano
Sena de Luna
Cármenes
Valdeteja
Riaño
Cantábrica

Cordillera
Villaseca
Villablino
623
Los Barrios de Luna
Embalse de Barrios de Luna
Matallana
Valdepiélago
Boñar
Sabero
Cistierna
Santibáñez de la Peña
615
Guardo **120**

Palacios del Sil
Corbón
Puerto de la Magdalena 1457
Murias de Paredes
La Magdalena
La Pola de Gordón
La Vecilla
Sta. Colomba de Curueño
Renedo de Valdetuéjar
Valderrueda

Miravalles 1960
Candín
Salientes
Catoute 2117
S'alce
Carrocera
La Robla
626
El Valle de las Casas
Puente Almuhey

Pico de Ancares
Fabero
Páramo del Sil
Vegarienza
Riello
Rioseco de Tapia
Barrio
Vegas del Condado
Almanza
Pino del Rio

Nogueira
Vega de Espinareda
Toreno
Igüeña
Folgoso de la Ribera
Villagatón
S. Feliz de las Lavanderas
Villaquilambre
S. Andrés de Rabanedo
Gradefes
Castromudarra
B

Trabadelo
Vilafranca del Bierzo
Cubillos del Sil
Congosto
Bembibre
Quintana del Castillo
Cimanes del Tejar
Carrizo
León
Valdefresno
Villamartín de Don Sancho
Santervás de la Vega

Corullón
Villadecanes
64
Torre del Bierzo
Castropodame
Puerto del Manzanal 1230
Villamejil
Benavides
Sta. Marina del Rey
Armunia
Onzonilla
Mansilla de las Mulas
S. Pedro de Valderaduey
Ledigos
Villamoronta
Villada

Cacabelos
120
Ponferrada
Molinaseca
Sta. Colomba de Somoza
S. Justo de la Vega
47
Sta. 120
Chozas de Abajo
Villanueva de las Manzanas
El Burgo Ranero
Sahagún
Cea
Cisneros

Barco
Toral del Bierzo
Priaranza del Bierzo
S. Esteban de Valdueza
S. Clemente
Foncebadón
Astorga
Villarejo de Órbigo
Valdevimbre
Sta. María del Páramo
Matallana
Santas Martas
Gordaliza del Pino
Galleguillos de Campos
S. Román de la Cuba
Villalón de Campos
Villarramiel

120
Peñute de Domingo Flórez
Chana
Quintanilla de Somoza
Riego de la Vega
S. Cristóbal de la Polantera
68
Destriana
Palacios de la Valduerna
La Bañeza
Villamañán
Valencia de Don Juan
Fresno de la Vega
Pajares de los Oteros
134
Melgar de Arriba
Cuenca de Campos
Ceinos de Campos
Cisneros

Casayo
Tabuyo del Monte
El Teleno 2188
Sta. Elena de Jamuz
Ropuelos del Páramo
Laguna de Negrillos
Toral de los Guzmanes
Cazanuecos
Albires
Valderas
Gordoncillo
Villalón de Campos

Iruela
Truchas
Manzaneda
Castrocalbón
Quintana del Marco
Alija del Infantado
Pozuelo del Páramo
Villaornate
Villaquejida
Mayorga
Becilla de Valderaduey
611
Villafrades de Campos

Sierra Cabrera
Moncalvo 2047
Barjacoba
S. Martín de Castañeda
Donado
Santibáñez de Vidriales
Morales de Rey
Alcubilla de Nogales
S. Cristóbal de Entreviñas
Fuentes de Ropel
Castroverde de Campos
Villafrechós
Medina de Rioseco

Lago Villachica
Galende
Palacios de Sanabria
Rionegro del Puente
Manganeses de la Polvorosa
Sta. Cristina de la Polvorosa
Benavente
Castrogonzalo
Villanueva del Campo
Villalpando
Tordehumos
Villabrágima

Puebla de Sanabria **1262**
Lubián
Portillo de Padornelo
Pedralba de la Pradería
Mombuey
Camarzana de Tera
Villanueva de las Peras
Mózar
S. Esteban del Molar
Villamayor de Campos
612
Villardefrancos
Villalba de los Alcores
126

Sierra de la Culebra
Manzanal de Arriba
Villardeciervos
1245
Ferreras de Arriba
Morales de Valverde
Santovenia
Villalpando
74
Castromonte
Villanubla
Mucientes
VALLADOLID

Bragança
Milhão
Trabazos
Figueruela de Arriba
Mahide
Riofrío
Ferreras de Abajo 820
Portillo de Sazadón **525**
Faramontanos de Tábara
Granja de Moreruela
Villarrín de Campos
Manganeses de la Lampreana
Belver de los Montes
Pinilla de Toro
Tiedra
Mota del Marqués
Torrelobatón
Wamba
30
C

Mosca
Parada
Alcañices
122
Losacio
Olmillos de Castro
Castronuevo
Asbariegos
Castronuevo
Tiedra
Vega de Valdetronco
Velliza
Puente Duero

Coelhoso
Fornillas
Fonfría
Embalse de Ricobayo
Moreruela de los Infanzones
Malva
Pozoantiguo
Villalonso
Casasola de Arión
Morales de Toro
Serrada
La Seca
Valdest.

Macedo de Cavaleiros
Izeda
Vimioso
Aldeadávila
Villadepera
122
Zamora
Toro
San Román de Hornija
Pollos
Tordesillas
610
Rueda

Morais
Vários
Muelas del Pan
Moraleja del Vino
La Bóveda de Toro
Pedrosa del Rey
Nava del Rey
Pozaldez

Duas Igrejas
Fariza
Pereruela
Bermillo de Sayago
121
Morales del Vino
Venialbo
Castronuño
Medina del Campo

Fermoselle
125
Variz
221
Villar del Buey
Fresno
Tamame
Corrales del Vino
El Piñero
La Bóveda de Toro
605
Alaejos
Medina del Campo
6

MAR CANTÁ

Costa Montañesa

SANTANDER

ASTURIAS

Picos de Europa

Parque Nacional

CANTABRIA

Reinosa

Burgos

VALLADOLID

Palencia

Aranda de Duero

Peñafiel

Tordesillas

CASTILLA

R I C O
Cabo Machichaco
Bermeo
Mundaca
Algorta
Sestao
BILBAO
Munguía
Guernica y Luno
Lequeitio
Ondárroa
Motrico
Deva
Zumaya
Guetaria
Zarauz
SAN SEBASTIÁN
Fuenterrabía
Irun
Hendaye
St. Jean-de-Luz
Biarritz
Bayonne
Anglet
Renteria
Oyarzun
Hernani
Andoain
Tolosa
Villabona
Azpeitia
Azcoitia
Eibar
Elgóibar
Placencia
Amorebieta
Durango
Vergara
Mondragón
Oñate
Villafranca de Oria
Beasain
Ataun
Alsasua
Olazagutía
Vitoria
Embalse de Ullívarri
Sierra de Urbasa
Sierra de Andía
Pamplona
Puerto Velate
Puerto de Azpiroz
Pirineos Occidentales
Roncesvalles
Puerto de Ibañeta
St. Jean-Pied-de-Port
Mauléon-Soule
Dax
St. Paul
Soustons
Capbreton
Hossegor
Tarnos
Boucau
Peyrehorade
Salies-de-Béarn
Hasparren
Cambo-les-Bains
Saint-Palais
F R A N C E
B É A R N
Miranda de Ebro
Sierra de Cantabria
Haro
Sto. Domingo de la Calzada
Logroño
Viana
Estella
Puente la Reina
Tafalla
Olite
Sangüesa
Embalse de Yesa
Monasterio de Leyre
Lumbier
Aoiz
Calahorra
Arnedo
Alfaro
Corella
Tudela
Cintruénigo
Cervera del Río Alhama
Tarazona
Borja
Sierra del Moncayo
Las Bardenas
Ejea de los Caballeros
Tauste
Alagón
ZARAGOZA
Épila
La Almunia de Doña Godina
Soria
Almazán
Puerto Piqueras
Puerto de Oncala
Sierra de la Demanda
San Lorenzo 2262
Urbión 2228
Embalse de la Cuerda del Pozo
Cameros
Ibérica
Llano de Plasencia
El Castellar
105
122
127
4
5
6
A
B
C

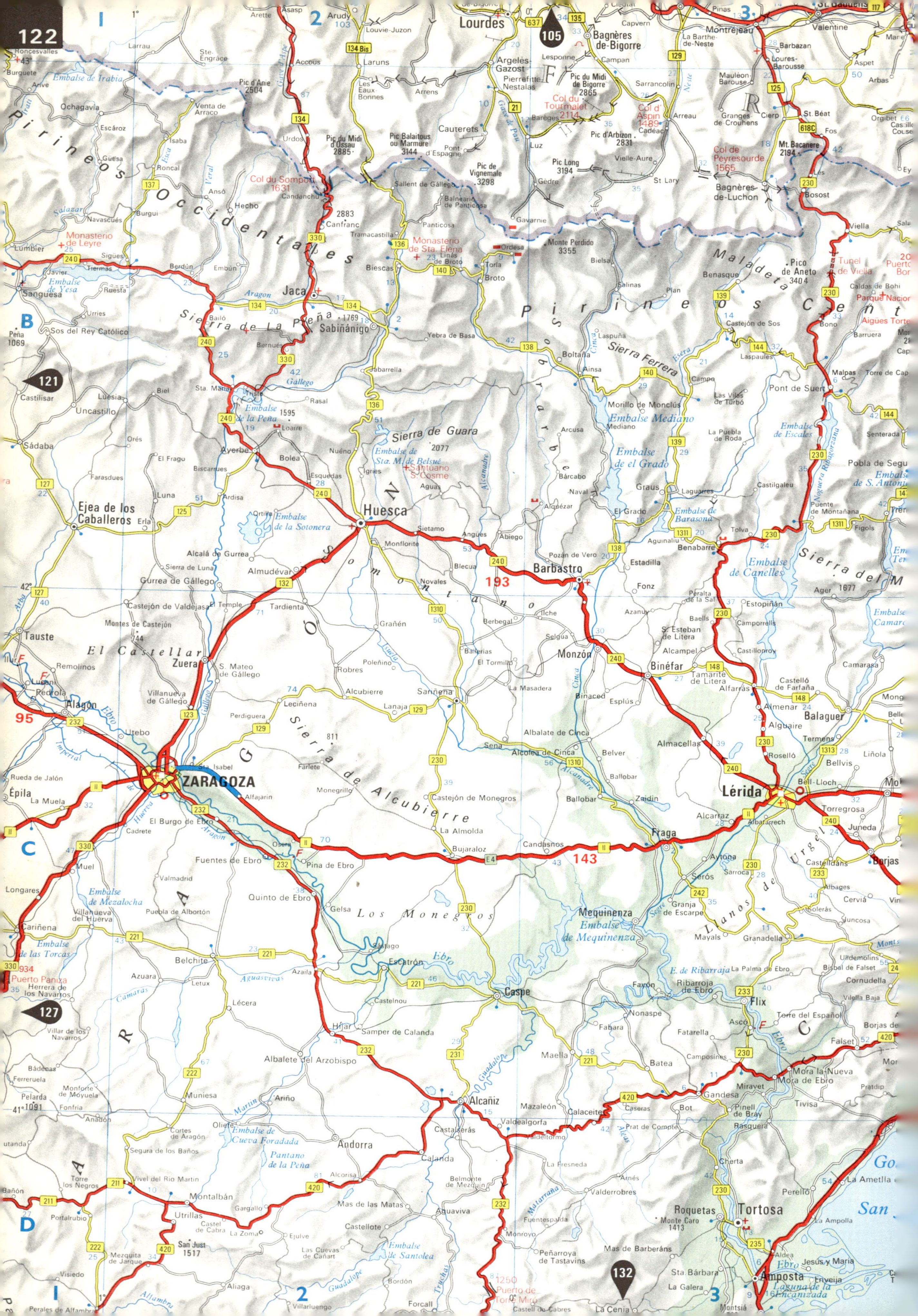

Roncesvalles
Burguete
Embalse de Irabia
Arive
Ochagavía
Escároz
Pirineos Occidentales
Larrau
Ste. Engrâce
Arette
Asasp
Arudy
Louvie-Juzon
Lourdes
Bagnères de-Bigorre
Capvern
Montréjeau
La Barthe-de-Neste
Valentine
St. Gaudens
Barbazan
Loures-Barousse
Mauléon-Barousse
Aspet
Arbas
Pic d'Anie 2504
Venta de Arraco
Accous
Laruns
Les Eaux Bonnes
Arrens
Argelès-Gazost
Pierrefitte-Nestalas
Lesponne
Campan
Pic du Midi de Bigorre 2865
Col du Tourmalet 2114
Sarrancolin
Col d'Aspin 1489
Cadéac
Arreau
Granges-de-Crouhens
Cierp
St. Béat
Fos
Orgibet
Urdos
Pic du Midi d'Ossau 2885
Pic Balaïtous ou Marmure 3144
Cauterets
Pont-d'Espagne
Barèges
Luz
Pic d'Arbizon 2831
Vielle-Aure
Mt. Bacanère 2194
Col de Peyresourde 1565
Isaba
Güesa
Roncal
Col du Somport 1631
Candanchú
Pic de Vignemale 3298
Pic Long 3194
Gèdre
St Lary
Bagnères-de-Luchon
Les
Bosost
Ansó
Hecho
Burgui
Salazar
Navascués
Canfranc
2883
Sallent de Gállego
Balneario de Panticosa
Panticosa
Gavarnie
Viella
Monasterio de Leyre
Lumbier
Tramacastilla
Monasterio de Sta. Elena
Ordesa
Monte Perdido 3355
Sigüés
Tiermas
Berdún
Embún
Biescas
Linás de Broto
Torla
Broto
Bielsa
Maladeta
Pico de Aneto 3404
Túnel de Viella
Caldas de Bohi
Parque Nacional
Aigües Tortes
Benasque
Salinas
Plan
Javier
Embalse de Yesa
Sangüesa
Ruesta
Aragón
Jaca
Urriés
Sos del Rey Católico
Peña 1069
Bailo
Sierra de La Peña
1769
Sabiñánigo
Yebra de Basa
Pirineos Centrales
Sobrarbe
Boltaña
Laspuña
Sierra Ferrera
Castejón de Sos
Bono
Barruera
Ainsa
Esera
Laspaúles
Campo
Las Vilas de Turbó
Pont de Suert
Malpas
Torre de Capdella
Castilisar
Luesia
Uncastillo
Biel
Sta. María
Embalse de la Peña
1595
Loarre
Rasal
Gállego
Jabarrella
Sierra de Guara
2077
Embalse de Sta. M. de Belsué
Santuario S. Cosme
Morillo de Monclús
Embalse Mediano
Mediano
Arcusa
La Puebla de Roda
Embalse de Escales
Senterada
Pobla de Segur
Embalse de S. Antonio
Sádaba
Orés
El Frago
Biscarrues
Ayerbe
Bolea
Nueno
Igriés
Esquedas
Aguas
Alcanadre
Bárcabo
Naval
Embalse de el Grado
Graus
Laguarres
Castigaleu
Noguera Ribagorzana
Puente de Montañana
Tremp
Farasdues
Luna
Ardisa
Ejea de los Caballeros
Erla
Ortilla
Embalse de la Sotonera
Huesca
Sietamo
Angüés
Abiego
Alquézar
El Grado
Embalse de Barasona
Aguinaliu
Benabarre
Tolva
Figols
Sierra del Montsec
Alcalá de Gurrea
Sierra de Luna
Almudévar
Monflorite
Blecua
Barbastro
Pozán de Vero
Estadilla
Embalse de Canelles
Ager 1677
Gurrea de Gállego
Castejón de Valdejasa
El Temple
Tardienta
Somontano
Novales
Fonz
Peralta de la Sal
Azanuy
Estopiñán
Montes de Castejón
744
Grañén
Berbegal
Ilche
Selgua
Baells
Camporrells
Tauste
El Castellar
Zuera
Isuela
Monzón
S. Esteban de Litera
Alcampel
Castillonroy
Embalse de Camarasa
Remolinos
S. Mateo de Gállego
Robres
Poleñino
Ballerías
El Tormillo
Binéfar
Tamarite de Litera
Castelló de Farfaña
Camarasa
Luceni
Pedrola
Villanueva de Gállego
Alcubierre
Sariñena
La Masadera
Binaced
Alfarràs
Almenar
Esplús
Balaguer
Alagón
Leciñena
Lanaja
Alguaire
Ebro
Perdiguera
Sierra de Alcubierre
811
Albalate de Cinca
Almacellas
Termens
Bellvís
Liñola
Imperial
Utebo
Farlete
Sena
Alcolea de Cinca
Belver
Rosellò
Rueda de Jalón
Sta. Isabel
Zaragoza
Alfajarín
Monegrillo
Castejón de Monegros
Ballobar
Zaidín
Lérida
Bell-Lloch
Épila
La Muela
Huerva
Cadrete
El Burgo de Ebro
La Almolda
Fraga
Alcarraz
Albatàrrech
Torregrosa
Juneda
Borjas Blancas
Osera
Candasnos
Aytona
Castelldans
Muel
Fuentes de Ebro
Pina de Ebro
Bujaraloz
Serós
Sarroca
Llanos de Urgel
Albages
Cervià
Longares
Embalse de Mezalocha
Valmadrid
Monegros
Quinto de Ebro
Gelsa
Los Monegros
Mequinenza
Embalse de Mequinenza
Granja de Escarpe
Mayals
Granadella
Juncosa
Cariñena
Villanueva de Huerva
Puebla de Albortón
Embalse de las Torcas
Puerto Paniza 934
Herrera de los Navarros
Belchite
Azuara
Letux
Aguasvivas
Cámaras
Azaila
Escatrón
Sástago
Castelnou
Caspe
E. de Ribarroja
Ribarroja de Ebro
Fayón
La Palma de Ebro
Ulldemolins
Bisbal de Falset
Cornudella
Vilella Baja
Lécera
Nonasque
Flix
Torre del Español
Borjas del Campo
Villar de los Navarros
Híjar
Samper de Calanda
Fabara
Fatarella
Ascó
Falset
Bádenas
Ferreruela
Albalate del Arzobispo
Maella
Batea
Camposines
Mora la Nueva
Mora de Ebro
Monforte de Moyuela
Pelarda
1091
Fonfría
Muniesa
Ariño
Alcañiz
Mazaleón
Calaceite
Gandesa
Miravet
Pratdip
Tivisa
Pinell de Bray
Rasquera
Anadón
Cortes de Aragón
Oliete
Martín
Embalse de Cueva Foradada
Pantano de la Peña
Andorra
Castelserás
Valdealgorfa
Valdeltormo
Caseras
Bot
Prat de Compte
Algás
Segura de los Baños
Calanda
La Fresneda
Arnés
Cherta
Vivel del Río Martín
Torre los Negros
Alcorisa
Belmonte de Mezquín
Valderrobres
Matarraña
Perelló
La Ametlla de Mar
Bañón
Montalbán
Mas de las Matas
Aguaviva
Roquetas
Tortosa
Monte Caro 1413
San Jordi
Portalrubio
Gargallo
Utrillas
Castel de Cabra
La Zoma
Castellote
Fuentespalda
Monroyo
Peñarroya de Tastavins
La Ampolla
Ejulve
Las Cuevas de Cañart
Embalse de Santolea
Mas de Barberáns
Aldea
Jesús y María
Mezquita de Jarque
San Just 1517
Guadalope
Bordón
1250 Puerto de Torre Miró
Sta. Bárbara
Amposta
Enveija
Visiedo
Aliaga
Alfambra
Forcall
La Galera
Laguna de la Encanizada
Perales de Alfambra
Villarluengo
Castell de Cabres
La Cenia
Montsiá
Tuejar
Golfo de San Jordi
105
121
127
132

Pamiers
Mirepoix
Limoux
St. Girons
Foix
Lavelanet
Quillan
Tarascon-sur-Ariège
Ax-les-Thermes
Perpignan
Rivesaltes
Sigean
Port-la-Nouvelle
Leucate
Salses
Canet-Plage
Elne
Argelès
Port Vendres
Cap Béar
Banyuls-s-Mer
Cerbère
Port Bou
Céret
Amélie-les-Bains-Palalda
Arles
Prades
Vinca
Ille-sur-Tet
Thuir
Mt.Canigou 2785
ANDORRA
Andorra la Vella
Port d'Envalira 2407
Col de Puymorens 1915
Pic Carlit 2921
Puigcerdá
Bourg-Madame
Font Romeu
Col de la Perche
La Cerdaña
Seo de Urgel
Sierra del Cadí
Pirineos Orientales
Ripoll
S. Juan de las Abadesas
Camprodón
Olot
Figueras
El Ampurdán
Golfo de Rosas
Rosas
Cadaqués
Cabo Creus
Ampurias
La Escala
Bañolas
Gerona
La Bisbal
Palafrugell
Palamós
S.Feliu de Guixols
Lloret de Mar
Blanes
Malgrat
Calella
Arenys de Mar
Mataró
Premiá de Mar
Badalona
BARCELONA
HOSPITALET
Prat de Llobregat
Castelldefels
Sitges
Villanueva y Geltru
Vendrell
Tarragona
Cabo de Salou
Valls
Montblanch
Villafranca del Panadés
Martorell
Tarrasa
SABADELL
Granollers
Manresa
Igualada
Cervera
Tárrega
Solsona
Cardona
Berga
Vich
Manlleu
Torelló
Sierra de Montseny
Costa Brava
Costa Dorada
Costas de Garraf
Oliana
Organá
Puigreig
Sallent
Genova
Palma
Valencia

118

249

Grove Cambados Sotelo de Montes Regueiro Piñor Pantón Monforte de Lemos Quiroga Rubiana
Isla de Ons Sangenjo Puente Caldelas Carballino Villamarín La Peroja Los Peares Sober Ribas de Sil La Rua El Barco Robledo
Portonovo Marín Fornelos de Montes Maside S. Amaro Noguera de Ramuín Doade Castro-Caldelas Villamartín de Valdeorras Domingo

Pontevedra

Redondela Estacas Carballeda Beade Embalse del Muro Puebla de Trives El Bollo Casa
Moaña Cangas Faro de Avión de Avia Ribadavia Melón **Orense** Esgos Montederramo Manzaneda La Vega
VIGO Bouzas Mondariz Cortegada Barbadanes Baños de Molgas Chandreja de Queija Reigada Viana del Bollo
Bayona Porriño La Cañiza Puenteáreas Creciente S. Martiño Junquera de Ambia Villar de Barrio Laza Campo de Becerros La Gudiña Vilavieja Canda
Cabo Silleiro Gondomar Nieves Celanova Sandianes Sarreaus Albergueria Lubián de la Canda
Tuy Monçao Lamas de Mouro Bande Rairiz de Veiga Villar de Santos **Ginzo de Limia** Castelo del Valle La Mezquita
Valença do Minho Merufe Castro Laboreiro Trasmiras Estivadas Ríos Hermisende
Arrabal S. Pedro da Torre Muiños Blancos Baltar Randín Cualedro Monterrey Verín Villardevós Vinhais
Vila Nova da Cerveira Sistelo Cabreiro Lindoso Montalegre Chaves Rebordelo Penhas Juntas Sta. Comba de Rossas
La Guardia Paredes de Coura Soajo Barragem do Alto Cávado Córtico Sapiaos Podence
Caminha Moledo do Minho Arcos de Valdevez Ponte da Barca Touvedo Terras do Bouro Vila de Veiga Venda Nova Vidago Valpaços Torre de D. Chama Macedo de Cavaleiro
Vila Praia de Ancora Ponte de Lima Facha Vieira Salto Cabreira Boticas Loivos Carrazedo de Montenegro Sezulfe Bornes
Viana do Castelo Darque Balugães Prado Póvoa de Lanhoso Arco de Baúlhe Ribeira da Pena Vila Pouca de Aguiar Murça Franco Alfarela de Jales Mirandela
Castelo do Neiva Forjães **Braga** Amares Soengas Rossas Cabeceiras de Basto Cerva Mondim de Basto Jorjães Abreiro Freixeda Trindade
Esposende Marinhas Barcelos S. Torcato Fafe Celorico de Basto Vila Real Mateus Sabrosa Pinhão Carracedo de Anciães
Ofir Fão Apúlia Estela **Guimarães** Vila Nova de Famalição Felgueiras Sto. Tirso Lousada Amarante Baião Sta. Marta de Penaguião Régua S. João da Pesqueira Torre de Moncorvo Vila Nova de Foscôa
Póvoa de Varzim Vila do Conde Maceira Trofa Paços de Ferreira Padornelo Marco de Canaveses Mesão Frio Armamar Tabuaço Horta Barca de Alva
Perafita **Matosinhos** Ermezinde Águas Santas Alfena Paredes Penafiel Baião Resende Lamego Freixo de Espada a Cinta
PORTO Infesta Campo Gondomar Eja Anreade Leocadia S. João da Pesqueira Vila Nova de Foscôa
Vila Nova de Gaia Valbom Lagares Cinfães Sobrado de Paiva Tarouca Penedono Almendra
Canidelo Valadares Avintes Raiva Montemuro Moimenta da Beira Meda Congroiva
Perozinho P O R T U G A L Alvarenga Almofala Barragem de Távora Longroiva Cidadelhe
Espinho Caldas de S. Jorge Castro Daire Touro Sernancelhe Castelção Figueira de Castelo Rodrigo
Esmoriz Corga de Lobão Arouca Burgo Rossas Vila Nova de Paiva Aguiar da Beira Trancoso Pinhel
Ovar Vila da Feira S. João da Madeira Vale de Cambra Móes Figueiredo de Alva Quintela Freixeda Pereiro Almeida
Torreira Valega Oliveira de Azeméis Pinheiro S. João da Serra S. Pedro do Sul Satão Douro Calvo Souro Pires Vila Franca das Navas Aldeia do Ob.
Murtosa Estarreja Albergaria-a-Nova Sever do Vouga Bigas Cavernais Maceira Pinzio Castelo Mendo Fuent
Aveiro Angeja Albergaria-a-Velha Oliveira de Frades Vouzela **Viseu** Penalva do Castelo Celorico da Beira Bocas
Ílhavo Lamas Talhadas Cambarinho Mangualde Fornos de Algodres **Guarda** Cerdeira Nave de Haver
Vagos Oiã Palhaça Varziela Baiuca Parada Nelas Carrapichana Folgosinho Trinta Pega Alfaiates
Mira Guardão Silgueiros Gouveia Nabais Aldeia do Bispo Navasfr.
Cantanhede Agueda Tondela Canas Oliveira de Conde Mangualde Manteigas Valhelhas Belmonte
Serra de Caramulo Mortágua Sta. Comba Dão Tábua Carregal do Sal Lagares Seia Poço do Inferno Sabugal
Mealhada Luso Bucaco Candosa Oliveira do Hospital Galices Covilhã Caria Meimão
Anadia B. de Aguieira Mouronho Vide Serra da Estrela Tortosendo Pera Boa
Pampilhosa Penacova Raiva Arganil Unhais da Serra Capinha
Figueira da Foz Lavos Coimbra Poiares Góis Silvares Serra da Guardunha Pedrogao
Mondego Buarcos Ceira Portela Vale de Prazeres Fundão
Quiaios Condeixa Lousã Souto Valverde del Fresno
Maiorca Montemor Miranda do Corvo Barragem de Sta. Luzia **128** Silvares Soalheira
Soure Seca

137 133 138 57 59

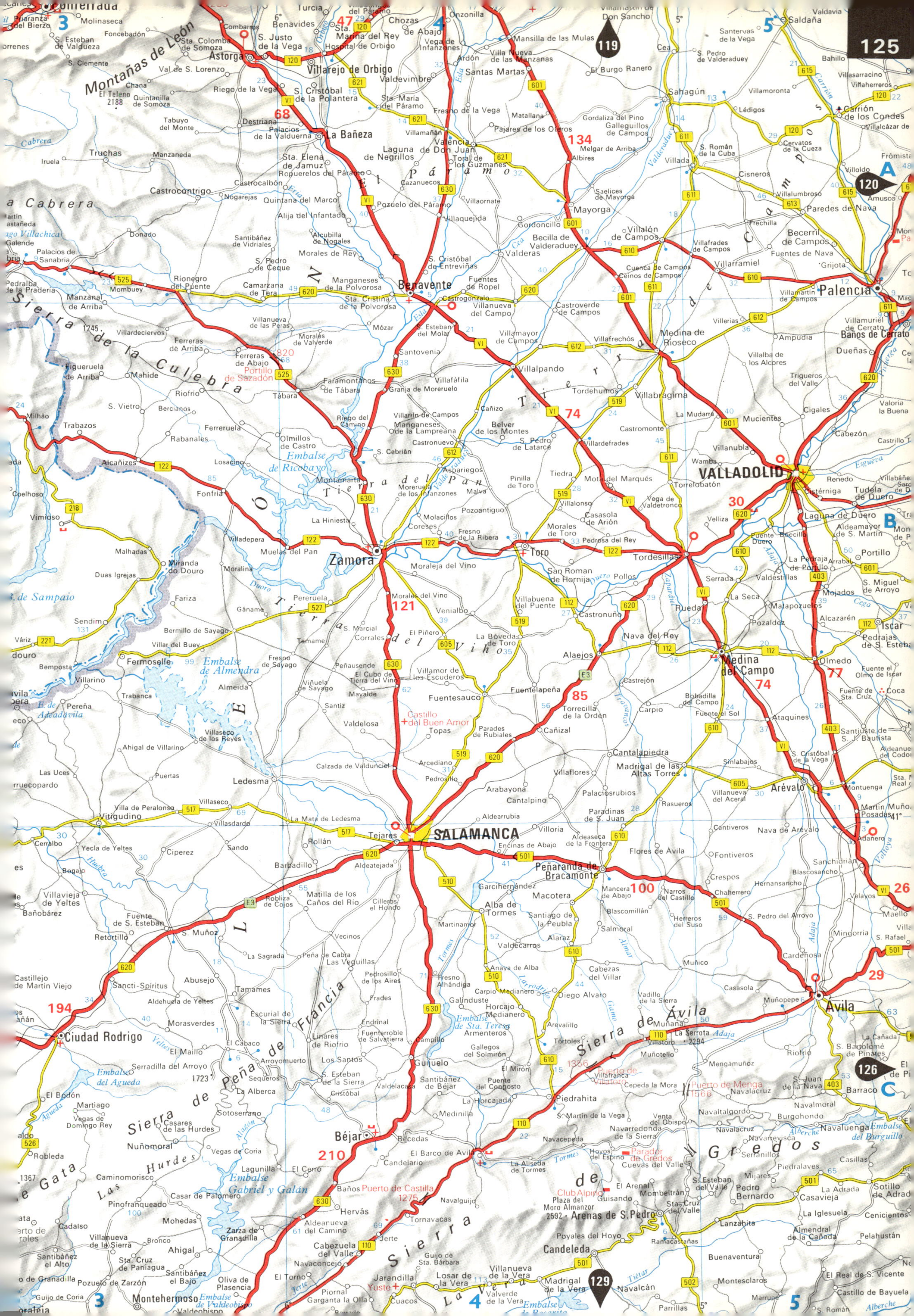
Astorga
Montañas de León
El Teleno 2188
La Bañeza
Villarejo de Órbigo
Hospital de Órbigo
Sahagún
Mansilla de las Mulas
Santas Martas
Valencia de Don Juan
El Páramo
Mayorga
Benavente
Castrocontrigo
La Cabrera
Sierra de la Culebra
Portillo de Sazadón
Medina de Rioseco
Tierra de Campos
Palencia
Carrión de los Condes
Saldaña
Paredes de Nava
Dueñas
Baños de Cerrato
Villalpando
Tordehumos
VALLADOLID
Tordesillas
Toro
Zamora
Embalse de Ricobayo
Tierra del Pan
Tierra del Vino
Miranda do Douro
Fermoselle
Embalse de Almendra
Alcañices
Medina del Campo
Rueda
Olmedo
Íscar
Portillo
Alaejos
Fuentesaúco
Castillo del Buen Amor
Madrigal de las Altas Torres
Arévalo
Cantalapiedra
Ledesma
Vitigudino
SALAMANCA
Tejares
Peñaranda de Bracamonte
Alba de Tormes
Ciudad Rodrigo
Embalse del Águeda
Sierra de Peña de Francia
Sierra de Gata
Las Hurdes
Embalse Gabriel y Galán
Béjar
Puerto de Castilla 1275
Hervás
Piedrahita
El Barco de Ávila
Sierra de Ávila
Puerto de Villatoro
Puerto de Menga 1566
Ávila
Sierra de Gredos
Parador de Gredos
Club Alpino
Arenas de S. Pedro
Candeleda
Embalse de Sta. Teresa
Embalse del Burguillo
La Vera
Jarandilla
Yuste
Montehermoso
Embalse de Valdeobispo
Navalcán
119
120
126
129
A
B
C
3
4
5

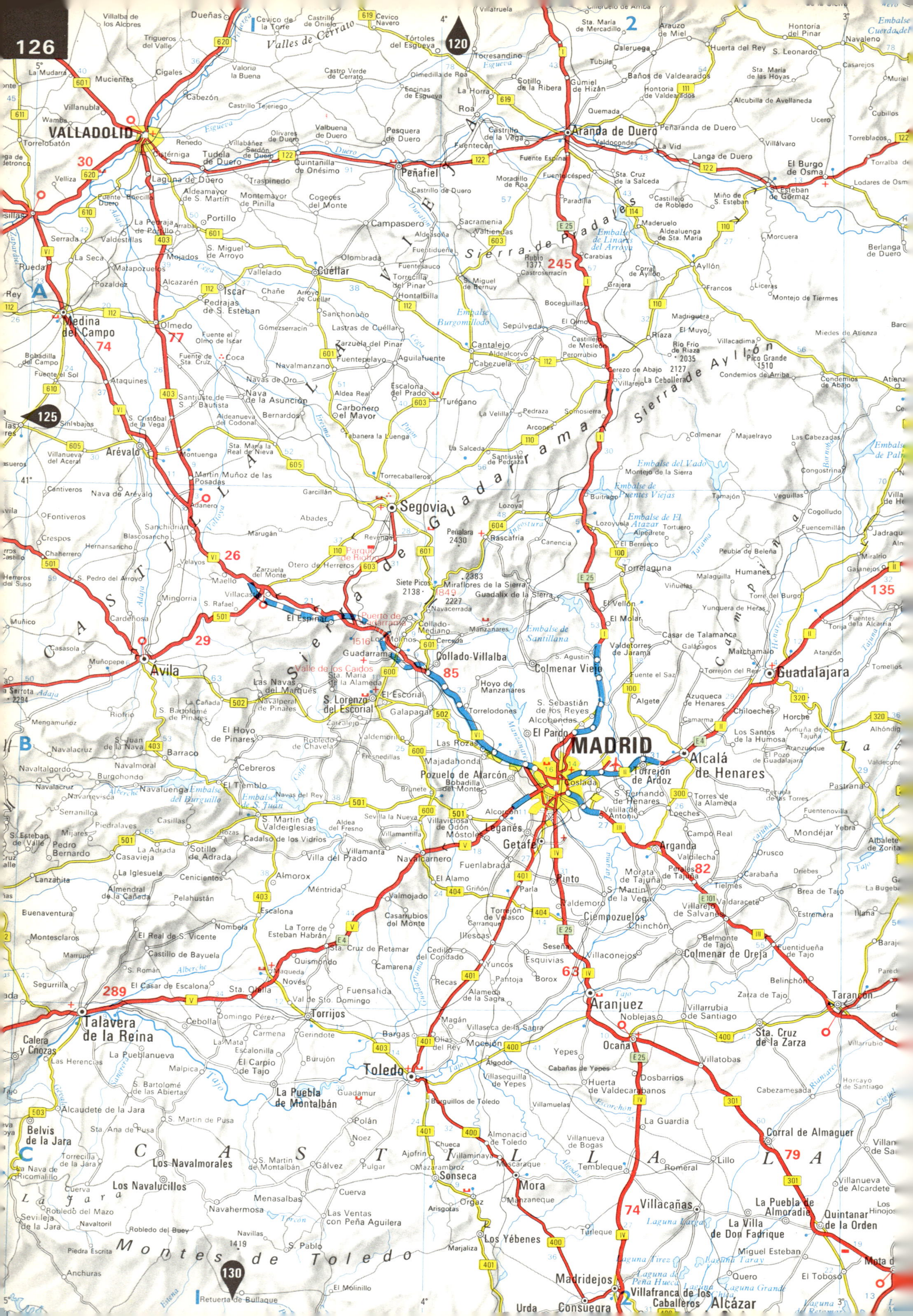
VALLADOLID
MADRID
Segovia
Avila
Toledo
Guadalajara
Aranda de Duero
Peñafiel
Cuéllar
Medina del Campo
Olmedo
Arévalo
Alcalá de Henares
Torrejón de Ardoz
Aranjuez
Talavera de la Reina
Tarancón
Ocaña
Getafe
Leganés
Móstoles
Colmenar Viejo
Collado-Villalba
El Escorial
S. Lorenzo del Escorial
Guadarrama
Navalcarnero
Torrijos
Sonseca
Mora
Madridejos
Consuegra
Villacañas
Alcázar
Quintanar de la Orden
Corral de Almaguer
Sta. Cruz de la Zarza
Colmenar de Oreja
Chinchón
Arganda
Ayllón
El Burgo de Osma
S. Esteban de Gormaz
Dueñas
Tordesillas
Iscar
Coca
Cantalejo
Riaza
Buitrago
Torrelaguna
Sepúlveda
Cebreros
Belvis de la Jara
Los Navalmorales
Los Navalucillos
La Puebla de Montalbán
Los Yébenes
Orgaz
Valles de Cerrato
Sierra de Pradales
Sierra de Ayllón
Sierra de Guadarrama
Montes de Toledo
CASTILLA
Campiña
La Jara
Sierra de Guadarrama
Puerto de Navacerrada
Valle de los Caídos
Parque de Riofrío
Embalse de Santillana
Embalse de El Atazar
Embalse del Burguillo
Duero
Tajo
Alberche
Jarama
Henares
E 25
E 4
E 101
120
125
130
A
B
C
1
2

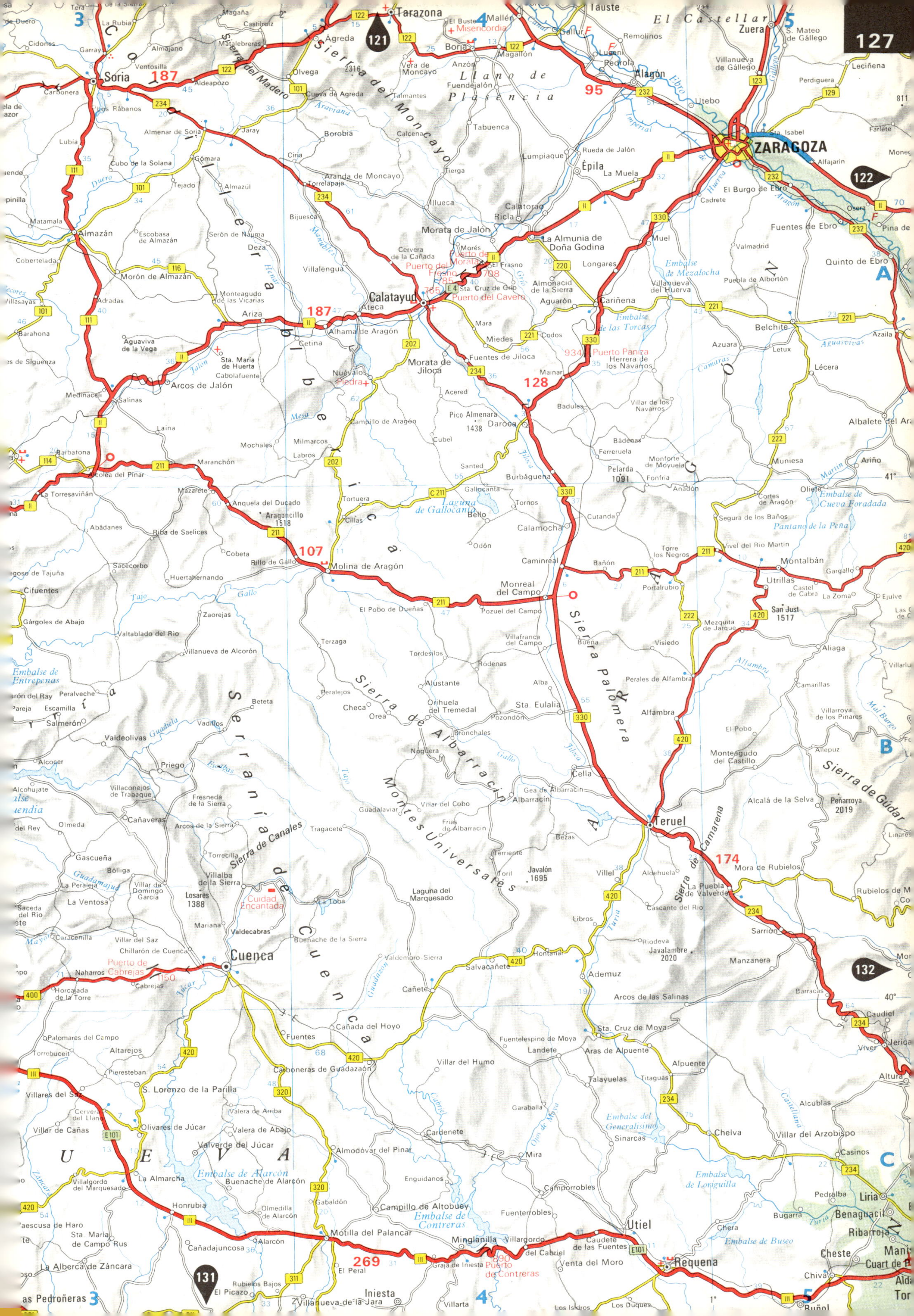

Tarazona
Tauste
El Castellar
Zuera
S. Mateo de Gállego
Mallén
El Buste
Misericordia
Magaña
Castilruiz
La Rubia
Garray
Almajano
Matalebreras
Sierra del Madero
Ágreda
Sierra del Moncayo
2316
Borja
Vera de Moncayo
Magallón
Gallur
Luceni
Pedrola
Remolinos
Alagón
Villanueva de Gállego
Leciñena
Perdiguera
Soria
187
Ventosilla
Carbonera
Aldeapozo
Olvega
Cueva de Agreda
Talmantes
Anzón
Llano de Plasencia
Fuendejalón
95
Utebo
Farlete
Sta. Isabel
ZARAGOZA
Alfajarín
Monegrillo
Los Rábanos
Almenar de Soria
Jaray
Araviana
Borobia
Calcena
Tabuenca
Imperial
Rueda de Jalón
Lumpiaque
Épila
La Muela
122
Lubia
Cubo de la Solana
Gómara
Ciria
Aranda de Moncayo
Torrelapaja
Tierga
Duero
Tejado
Almazúl
El Burgo de Ebro
Cadrete
Osera
Pina de Ebro
Matamala
Almazán
Escobasa de Almazán
Serón de Nágima
Deza
Bijuesca
Manubles
Illueca
Calatorao
Ricla
Morata de Jalón
La Almunia de Doña Godina
Muel
Fuentes de Ebro
Valmadrid
Quinto de Ebro
Cobertelada
Morón de Almazán
Henar
Villalengua
Cervera de la Cañada
Puerto de Morata
Puerto del Fresno
708
785
765
Morés
El Frasno
Sta. Cruz de Grío
Puerto del Cavero
Almonacid de la Sierra
Longares
Embalse de Mezalocha
Villanueva del Huerva
Puebla de Albortón
Villasayas
Adradas
Monteagudo de las Vicarias
Calatayud
Ateca
Aguarón
Cariñena
Barahona
Ariza
Alhama de Aragón
Cetina
Mara
Miedes
Codos
Embalse de las Torcas
Belchite
Azaila
Aguaviva de la Vega
Sta. María de Huerta
Jalón
Cabolafuente
Nuévalos
Piedra
Morata de Jiloca
Fuentes de Jiloca
934 Puerto Paniza
Herrera de los Navarros
Azuara
Letux
Aguasvivas
Lécera
es de Sigüenza
Arcos de Jalón
Medinaceli
Salinas
Mesa
Campillo de Aragón
Acered
Pico Almenara 1438
Daroca
Mainar
128
Badules
Villar de los Navarros
Cámaras
Albalate del Arzobispo
Laina
Mochales
Milmarcos
Labros
Cubel
Bádenas
Ferreruela
Muniesa
Ariño
Barbatona
Alcolea del Pinar
Maranchón
Santed
Pelarda 1091
Fonfría
Monforte de Moyuela
Martín
41°
La Torresaviñán
Mazarete
Anquela del Ducado
Aragoncillo 1518
Tortuera
Gallocanta
Laguna de Gallocanta
Burbáguena
Anadón
Cortes de Aragón
Oliete
Embalse de Cueva Foradada
Abánades
Riba de Saelices
Cillas
Bello
Tornos
Calamocha
Cutanda
Segura de los Baños
Pantano de la Peña
Cobeta
107
Odón
Caminreal
Torre los Negros
Vivel del Río Martín
Sacecorbo
Huertahernando
Rillo de Gallo
Molina de Aragón
Baños
Montalbán
Gargallo
Cifuentes
Tajo
Gallo
Monreal del Campo
Portalrubio
Utrillas
Castel de Cabra
La Zoma
Ejulve
Zaorejas
El Pobo de Dueñas
Pozuel del Campo
Sierra Palomera
San Just 1517
Mezquita de Jarque
Gárgoles de Abajo
Valtablado del Río
Terzaga
Villafranca del Campo
Visiedo
Aliaga
Villanueva de Alcorón
Tordesilos
Ródenas
Alustante
Alba
Perales de Alfambra
Alfambra
Embalse de Entrepeñas
Peralveche
Peralejos
Sierra de Albarracín
Orihuela del Tremedal
Sta. Eulalia
Camarillas
Villarroya de los Pinares
Mal Burgo
Escamilla
Checa
Orea
Beteta
Pozondón
Salmerón
Vadillos
Bronchales
El Pobo
Valdeolivas
Guadiela
Serranía de Cuenca
Noguera
Cella
Monteagudo del Castillo
Allepuz
Alcocer
Priego
Escabas
Montes Universales
Gea de Albarracín
Albarracín
Sierra de Gúdar
Villaconejos de Trabaque
Fresneda de la Sierra
Guadalaviar
Villar del Cobo
Frías de Albarracín
Alcalá de la Selva
Peñarroya 2019
Cañaveras
Arcos de la Sierra
Tragacete
Teruel
Bezas
Olmeda
Sierra de Canales
Sierra de Camarena
Gascueña
Torrecilla
Terriente
Javalón 1695
Villel
Aldehuela
174
Mora de Rubielos
Bólliga
Guadamajud
Villalba de la Sierra
Toril
La Peraleja
Villar de Domingo García
Losares 1388
Ciudad Encantada
La Puebla de Valverde
Rubielos de Mora
La Ventosa
La Toba
Laguna del Marquesado
Cascante del Río
Saceda del Río
Libros
Turia
Mariana
Valdecabras
Sarrión
Caracenilla
Villar del Saz
Buenache de la Sierra
Riodeva
Javalambre 2020
Chillarón de Cuenca
Valdemoro-Sierra
Hontanar
Manzanera
Puerto de Cabrejas
1150
Cuenca
Naharros
Cabrejas
Júcar
Salvacañete
Ademuz
Horcajada de la Torre
Cañete
Guadazaón
Arcos de las Salinas
Barracas
40°
Caudiel
Palomares del Campo
Fuentes
Cañada del Hoyo
Fuentelespino de Moya
Sta. Cruz de Moya
Landete
Aras de Alpuente
Torrebuceit
Altarejos
Viver
Jérica
Piqueras
Carboneras de Guadazaón
Villar del Humo
Alpuente
Talayuelas
Titaguas
Villares del Saz
S. Lorenzo de la Parrilla
Garaballa
Altura
Cervera del Llano
Valera de Arriba
Cabriel
Ojos de Moya
Embalse del Generalísimo
Sinarcas
Alcublas
Villar de Cañas
Olivares de Júcar
Valera de Abajo
Cardenete
Chelva
Villar del Arzobispo
Valverde del Júcar
Almodóvar del Pinar
Casinos
Castellana
UEVA
Embalse de Alarcón
Buenache de Alarcón
Mira
Záncara
La Almarcha
Villalgordo del Marquesado
Enguídanos
Camporrobles
Embalse de Loriguilla
Pedralba
Liria
Gabaldón
Campillo de Altobuey
Embalse de Contreras
Fuenterrobles
Utiel
Benaguacil
Honrubia
Olmedilla de Alarcón
Bugarra
Chera
Ribarroja
Embalse de Buseo
Motilla del Palancar
Minglanilla
Villargordo del Cabriel
Caudete de las Fuentes
Manises
Vaescusa de Haro
Sta. María de Campo Rus
Cañadajuncosa
Alarcón
890
Venta del Moro
Requena
Cheste
Cuart de Poblet
269
Graja de Iniesta
Puerto de Contreras
La Alberca de Záncara
El Peral
Chiva
Aldaya
Torrente
Rubielos Bajos
El Picazo
Las Pedroñeras
Iniesta
Villanueva de la Jara
Villarta
Los Isidros
Los Duques
Buñol
1°
2°
121
131
132
3
4
5
A
B
C

Coimbra
Figueira da Foz
Pombal
Leiria
Marinha Grande
Batalha
Fátima
Nazaré
Alcobaça
Caldas da Rainha
Óbidos
Peniche
Tomar
Torres Novas
Abrantes
Santarém
Almeirim
Rio Maior
Torres Vedras
Lourinha
Mafra
Sintra
Cascais
Estoril
Amadora
LISBOA
Sacavem
Barreiro
Almada
Seixal
Montijo
Setúbal
Sesimbra
Baía de Setúbal
Vila Franca de Xira
Benavente
Coruche
Vendas Novas
Montemor-o-Novo
Évora
Estremoz
Arraiolos
Redondo
Reguengos
Alcáçovas
Grândola
Ferreira do Alentejo
Beja
Castelo Branco
Portalegre
Alter do Chao
Ponte de Sôr
Nisa
Sertã
Proença-a-Nova
Vila de Rei
Lousã
Serra da Estrela
Ilhas Farilhões
Ilha Berlenga
Cabo Carvoeiro
Cabo da Roca
Cabo de Espichel
Tejo
Sado

125
Béjar
210
Sierra de Gata
Las Hurdes
Sierra de Gredos
Arenas de S. Pedro
Candeleda
Plasencia
Malpartida de Plasencia
Jaraiz de la Vera
La Vera
Moraleja
Coria
Torrejoncillo
Embalse de Alcántara
Ceclavin
Garrovillas
Alcántara
Brozas
Navalmoral de la Mata
Embalse de Valdecañas
Puerto de Mirabete 665
Trujillo
Cáceres
Malpartida de Cáceres
Arroyo de la Luz
Valencia de Alcántara
S. Vicente de Alcántara
Sierra de San Pedro
Alburquerque
Campo Maior
Elvas
BADAJOZ
Talavera la Real
Montijo
Mérida
Puebla de la Calzada
Miajadas
Madrigalejo
Logrosan
Sierra de Guadalupe
Guadalupe
Zorita
Villanueva de la Serena
Don Benito
Navalvillar de Pela
Orellana la Vieja
Talarrubias
Campanario
Castuera
Cabeza del Buey
Olivenza
Almendralejo
Villafranca de los Barros
Zafra
Los Santos de Maimona
Jerez de los Caballeros
Oliva de la Frontera
Fregenal de la Sierra
Higuera la Real
Encinasola
Fuentes de Leon
Fuente de Cantos
Monesterio
Montemolín
Llerena
Azuaga
Berlanga
Granja de Torrehermosa
Fuente-Obejuna
Peñarroya-Pueblonuevo
Guadalcanal
Belalcázar
Hinojosa del Duque
Sierra del Pedroso
Sierra de Tudia
Picos de Aroche
E S P A Ñ A
E X T R E M A D U R A
130
135
47
66
88
165

Béjar
Piedrahita
El Barco de Avila
Sierra de Gredos
Arenas de S. Pedro
Candeleda
Jaraiz de la Vera
Navalmoral de la Mata
Oropesa
Talavera de la Reina
Calera y Chozas
Belvis de la Jara
Los Navalmorales
Los Navalucillos
Toledo
Torrijos
La Puebla de Montalbán
Sonseca
Orgaz
Los Yébenes
Montes de Toledo
Sierra de Chorito
Embalse del Cíjara
Herrera del Duque
Guadalupe
Sierra de Guadalupe
Logrosán
Trujillo
Madroñera
Zorita
Madrigalejo
Navalvillar de Pela
Talarrubias
Villanueva de la Serena
Orellana la Vieja
Siruela
Campanario
Castuera
Cabeza del Buey
Almadén
Puebla de Don Rodrigo
Piedrabuena
Ciudad Real
Miguelturra
Almodóvar del Campo
Puertollano
Argamasilla de Calatrava
Sierra Madrona
Sierra de Alcudia
Valle de Alcudia
Sierra del Pedroso
Monterrubio de la Serena
Hinojosa del Duque
Belalcázar
El Viso
Los Pedroches
Pozoblanco
Villanueva de Córdoba
Cardeña
Peñarroya-Pueblonuevo
Fuente-Obejuna
Bélmez
Azuaga
Espiel
Villaviciosa de Córdoba
Sierra de los Santos
Andújar
Bailén
Virgen de la Cabeza
Embalse de Valdecañas
Embalse de Orellana
Embalse de Zújar
Embalse de García Sola
Getafe
Leganés
Móstoles
Navalcarnero
Illescas
Malagón
125
126
129
135
136

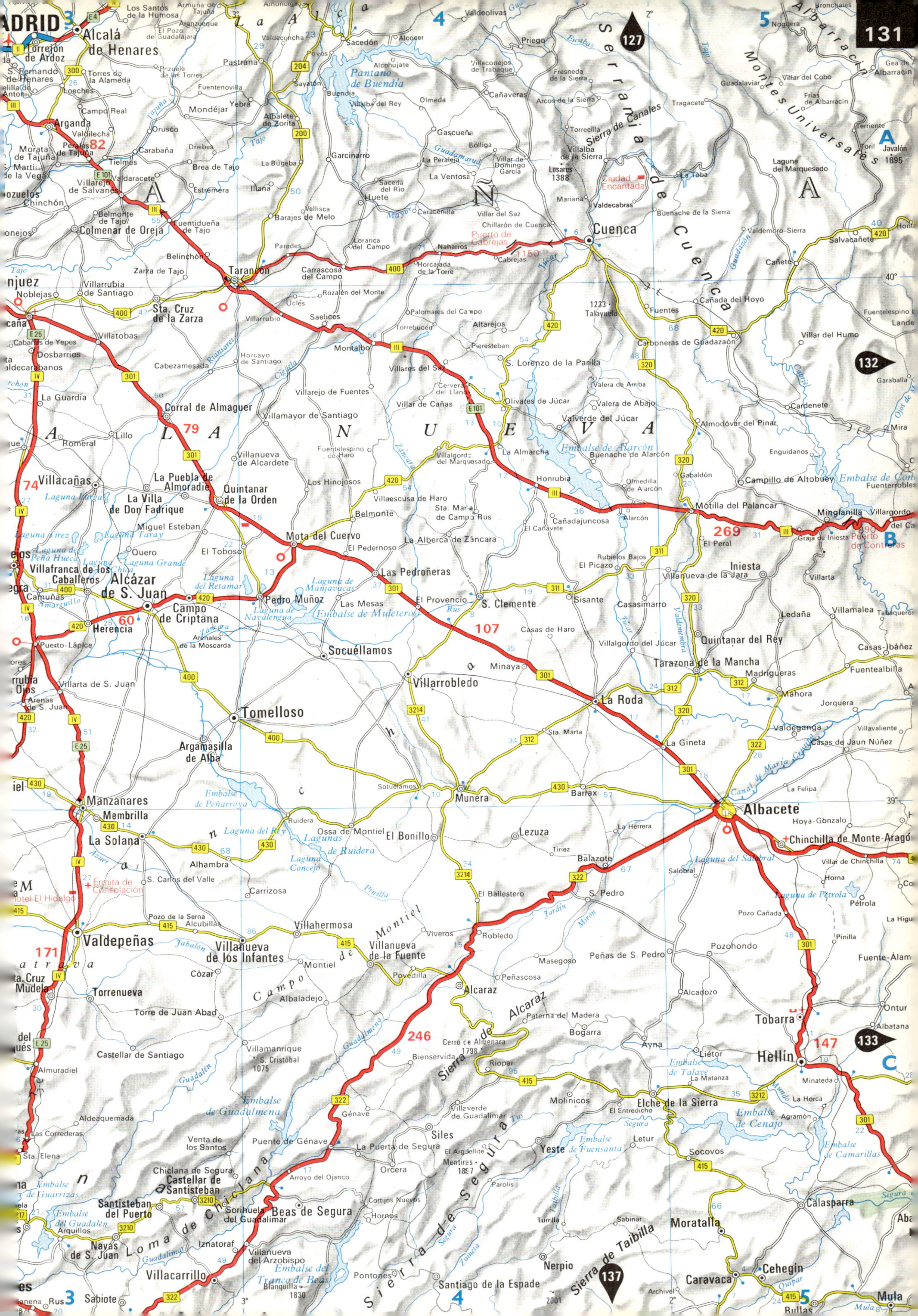

MADRID

Torrejón de Ardoz
Alcalá de Henares
Los Santos de la Humosa
Anchuelo
Valdeavero
Valdeolivas
Valdeconcha
Bronchales
Albarracín
Montes de Albarracín

Fernando de Henares
Meco
Villalbilla de Antonio
Torres de la Alameda
Loeches
Pozuelo del Rey
Pastrana
Fuentenovilla
Alcohujate
Villalba del Rey
Olmeda
Cañaveras
Arcos de la Sierra
Fresneda de la Sierra
Gea de Albarracín
Frías de Albarracín

Campo Real
Arganda
Villarejo de Salvanés
Valdaracete
Orusco
Driebes
Brea de Tajo
La Bügeba
Gascueña
Sölliga
Torrecilla
Villar de Domingo García
Losares 1388
Mariana
Valdecabras
Buenache de la Sierra
Valdemoro-Sierra
Salvacañete
Javalón 1695

Morata de Tajuña
Perales de Tajuña
Tielmes
Carabaña
Estremera
Illana
Saceda del Rio
Huete
La Ventosa
Caracenilla
Villar del Saz
Ciudad Encantada
Cuenca
Cañada del Hoyo
Cañete
Villar del Humo

Chinchón
Colmenar de Oreja
Belmonte de Tajo
Fuentidueña de Tajo
Barajas de Melo
Loranca del Campo
Puerto de Cabrejas
Naharros
Horcajada de la Torre
Cabrejas
Talayuelo
Fuentes
Carboneras de Guadazaón
Valdemoro-Sierra

Aranjuez
Noblejas
Villarrubia de Santiago
Sta. Cruz de la Zarza
Tarancón
Carrascosa del Campo
Uclés
Rozalén del Monte
Saelices
Palomares del Campo
Altarejos
Piresteban
S. Lorenzo de la Parilla
Valera de Arriba
Valera de Abajo
Almodóvar del Pinar
Cardenete
Mira

Ontígola
Cabañas de Yepes
Villatobas
Villarrubio
Montalbo
Villares del Saz
Cervera del Llano
Olivares de Júcar
Valverde del Júcar
Enguidanos

La Guardia
Dosbarrios
Villaldecarabanos
Corral de Almaguer
Cabezamesada
Horcayo de Santiago
Villarejo de Fuentes
Villar de Cañas
La Almarcha
Buenache de Alarcón
Campillo de Altobuey
Embalse de Contreras
Fuenterrobles

Lillo
Romeral
Villanueva de Alcardete
Fuentelespino de Haro
Villagordo del Marquesado
Honrubia
Olmedilla de Alarcón
Motilla del Palancar
Minglanilla
Villagordo del Cabriel

Villacañas
La Puebla de Almoradiel
Quintanar de la Orden
Los Hinojosos
Belmonte
Villaescusa de Haro
Sta. Maria de Campo Rus
Cañadajuncosa
Alarcón
Graja de Iniesta
Puerto de Contreras

La Villa de Don Fadrique
Miguel Esteban
El Toboso
Mota del Cuervo
La Alberca de Záncara
El Cañavete
Rubielos Bajos
El Peral
Villanueva de la Jara
Villalta

Quero
Villafranca de los Caballeros
Alcázar de S. Juan
Pedro Muñoz
Las Mesas
El Pedernoso
Las Pedroñeras
El Picazo
Iniesta
Villamalea
Tarazona de la Mancha

Camuñas
Herencia
Campo de Criptana
Las Pedroñeras
El Provencio
S. Clemente
Sisante
Casasimarro
Villagordo del Júcar
Quintanar del Rey
Casas-Ibáñez

Puerto Lápice
Arenales de la Moscarda
Socuéllamos
Minaya
Casas de Haro
Villarrobledo
Madrigueras
Mahora
Jorquera

Villarta de S. Juan
Tomelloso
Sta. Marta
La Roda
La Gineta
La Felipa
Valdeganga
Casas de Juan Núñez
Villavaliente

Manzanares
Argamasilla de Alba
Sotuélamos
Munera
Barrax
Albacete
Hoya-Gonzalo
Chinchilla de Monte-Aragón

Membrilla
Embalse de Peñarroya
Ruidera
Lezuza
La Herrera
Villar de Chinchilla
Horna
Pétrola

La Solana
Laguna del Rey
Ossa de Montiel
El Bonillo
Tiriez
Balazote
S. Pedro
Laguna de Pétrola
Pinilla
Fuente-Álam

Ermita de Consolación
Alhambra
Lagunas de Ruidera
Laguna Concejo
El Ballestero
Pozo Cañada
Pozohondo
La Higu

Hotel El Hidalgo
S. Carlos del Valle
Carrizosa
Villahermosa
Viveros
Robledo
Masegoso
Peñas de S. Pedro
Alcadozo

Valdepeñas
Villanueva de los Infantes
Montiel
Villanueva de la Fuente
Povedilla
Alcaraz
Peñascosa
Ayna
Liétor
Tobarra
Albatana

Sta. Cruz de Mudela
Torrenueva
Cózar
Albaladejo
Alcaraz
Paterna del Madera
Bogarra
Hellín

Torre de Juan Abad
Castellar de Santiago
Villamanrique
S. Cristóbal 1075
Cerro de Almenara 1798
Bienservida
Riópar
Molinicos
Elche de la Sierra
Minateda
La Horca

Almuradiel
Venta de los Santos
Génave
Villaverde de Guadalimar
El Entredicho
Agramón
Embalse de Cenajo

Aldeaquemada
Las Corredoras
Puente de Génave
La Puerta de Segura
El Argüellite
Mentiras 1367
Yeste de Fuensanta
Letur
Socovos
Embalse de Camarillas

Sta. Elena
Chiclana de Segura
Castellar de Santisteban
Sorihuela del Guadalimar
Beas de Segura
Siles
Orcera
Parolis
Segura
Túrrilla
Calasparra

Santisteban del Puerto
Navas de S. Juan
Iznatoraf
Villanueva del Arzobispo
Cortijos Nuevos
Hornos
Sabinar
Moratalla

Villacarrillo
Embalse del Tranco de Beas
Pontones
Santiago de la Espada
Nerpio
Cehegín
Caravaca
Mula

Embalse de Guarrizas
Embalse del Guadalén
Arquillos
Sabiote
Villanueva del Arzobispo
Blanquilla 1830
Sierra de Taibilla
Sierra de Segura
2001

127
150
400
420
320
301
269
311
312
322
430
415
3214
3212
3210
E101
E25
132
133
137
B
C

LA MANCHA
Sierra de Cuenca
Serranía de Canales
Montes Universales
Campo de Montiel
Loma de Cazorla
Sierra de Segura

Golfo de San Jorge
Cabo de Tortosa
Tortosa
Roquetas
Amposta
S. Carlos de la Rápita
Puerto de los Alfaques
Ulldecona
Alcanar
Vinaroz
Benicarló
Peñíscola
Alcalá de Chivert
Torreblanca
Oropesa
Cabo de Oropesa
Benicasim
Castellón de la Plana
Villarreal
Onda
Almazora
Burriana
Nules
Vall de Uxó
Islas Columbretes
Sagunto
Grao de Sagunto
Puzol
Masamagrell
Moncada
Paterna
Burjasot
VALENCIA
Golfo de Valencia
La Albufera
Silla
Catarroja
Torrente
Alcira
Sueca
Carlet
Alginet
Picasent
Requena
Utiel
Buñol
Chiva
Cheste
Liria
Segorbe
Jérica
Teruel
Sierra Palomera
Sierra de Albarracín
Montes Universales
Albarracín
Monreal del Campo
Mollina de Aragon
Montalbán
Utrillas
Sierra de Gúdar
El Maestrazgo
Morella
Mora de Rubielos
Rubielos de Mora
Peñagolosa 1813
Peñarroya 2019
Javalambre 2020
Javalón 1695
Ademuz
Chelva
Motilla del Palancar
Iniesta
Quintanar del Rey
Tarazona de la Mancha
Embalse de Contreras
Puerto de Contreras
Tarragona
Palma
Islas Columbretes

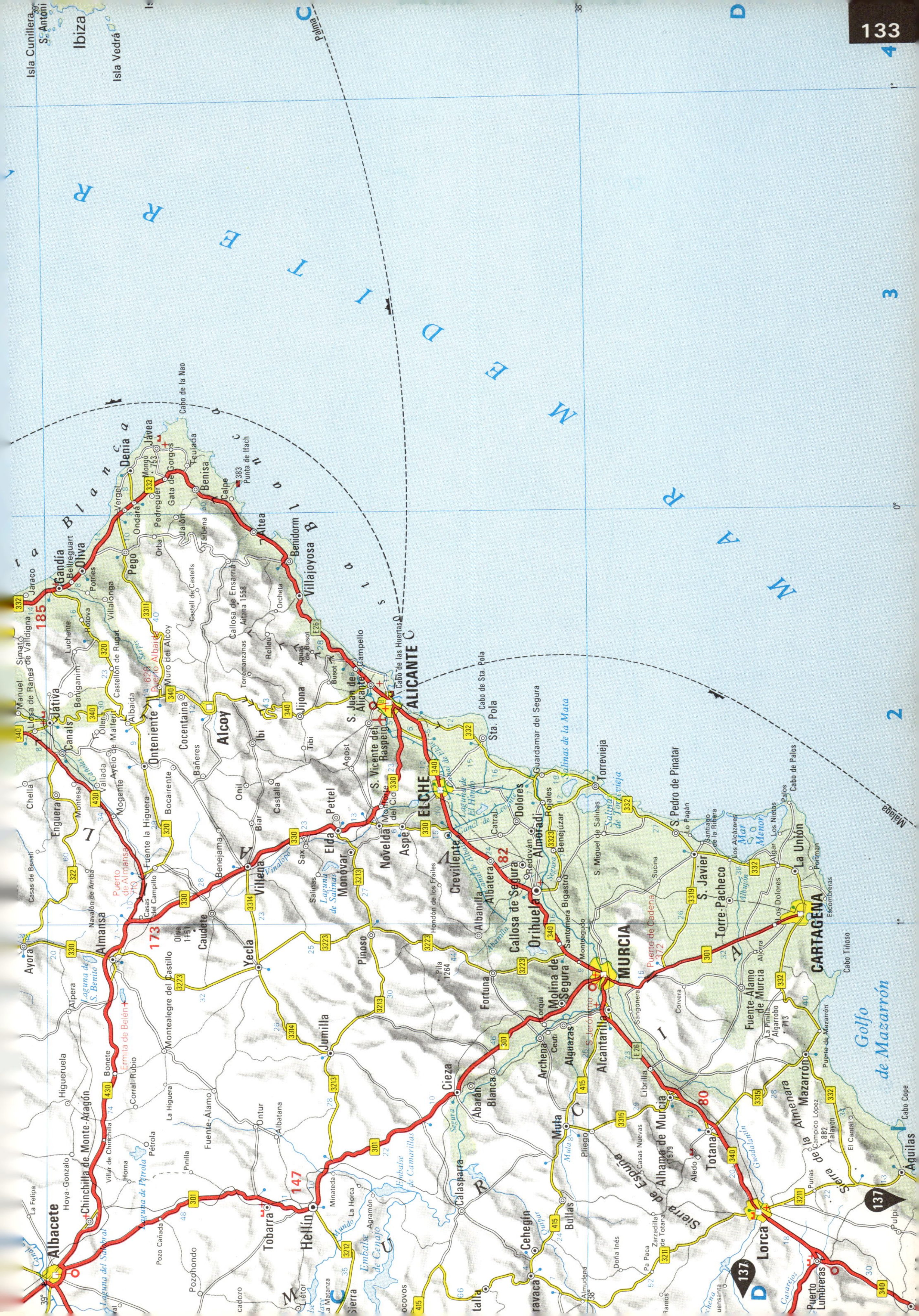
M A R M E D I T E R R
Ibiza
Isla Cunillera
S. Antoni
Isla Vedrá
Palma
Málaga
ALICANTE
ELCHE
MURCIA
CARTAGENA
Albacete
Almansa
Villena
Yecla
Jumilla
Hellín
Cieza
Alcoy
Onteniente
Játiva
Gandía
Oliva
Denia
Jávea
Benidorm
Villajoyosa
Altea
Calpe
Benisa
Teulada
Cabo de la Nao
Punta de Ifach
Pego
Cocentaina
Ibi
Jijona
Elda
Petrel
Monóvar
Novelda
Aspe
Crevillente
Orihuela
Callosa de Segura
Albatera
Dolores
Almoradí
Rojales
Guardamar del Segura
Torrevieja
S. Pedro de Pinatar
S. Javier
Torre-Pacheco
La Unión
Mar Menor
Cabo de Palos
Cabo Tiñoso
Golfo de Mazarrón
Mazarrón
Águilas
Lorca
Totana
Alhama de Murcia
Mula
Bullas
Cehegín
Calasparra
Molina de Segura
Alcantarilla
Archena
Fortuna
Pinoso
Caudete
Chinchilla de Monte-Aragón
Tobarra
Ayora
Enguera
Canals
Sta. Pola
Cabo de Sta. Pola
Salinas de la Mata
Puerto Lumbreras
Fuente-Álamo de Murcia
Puerto de Cadena
Sierra de Espuña
Embalse de Camarillas
Embalse de Cenajo
S. Vicente del Raspeig
S. Juan de Alicante
Campello
Cabo de las Huertas
185
173
147
82
80
137

Baía de Setúbal
Alcácer do Sal
Salazar
Torrão
Viana Alentejo
Oriola
128
Monte do Trigo
S. Marcos de Campo
Mourão
Villanueva del Fresno
Portel
Serra Mendro
Vidigueira
Alvito
Vila Ruiva
Vila Nova da Baronia
Cuba
Alqueva
Vera Cruz
Amieira
Estrela
Granja
Valencia de Mombuey
Almareleja
Póvoa
Moura
Sto. Amador
Safara
Sto. Aleixo
Sobral da Adica
Pedrogão
Brinches
Pias
Grândola
Serra de Grândola
Melides
Torroal
Casa Branca
107
S. Lourenço
Sta. Margarida do Sado
Odivelas
Alfundão
Figueira dos Cavaleiros
Azinheira dos Bairros
Ferreira do Alentejo
Peroguarda
S. Matias
Beja
Baleizao
Quintos
Salvada
Serpa
Vale de Vargo
Aldeia Nova
Vila Verde de Ficalho
Rosal de la Frontera
Sto. André
Santiago do Cacém
S. Bartolomé da Serra
Canhestros
Ermidas
Abela
Cabo de Sines
Sines
Cravadas
S. Domingos
Barragem de Campilhas
Morgavel
Porto Covo
Taganheira
Alvalade
Montes Velhos
Ervidel
Barragem de Roxo
Mina de Juliana
Trindade
Sta. Clara de Louredo
Aljustrel
Vale de Agua
Messejana
Cercal
Albernoa
Vale de Açor
Amendoeira
Conceição
Casével
Entradas
P O R T U G A L
Vila Nova de Milfontes
S. Luiz
Colos
Sta. Luzia
Garvão
Castro Verde
Algodor
Alcaria Ruiva
Paymoyo
Cabezas Rubias
Corte do Pinto
Mertola
Morianes
Mina de S. Domingos
Herrerias
Puebla de Guzmán
S. Martinho das Amoreiras
Ourique
S. Marcos da Ataboeira
Penilhos
Odemira
Cavaleiro
Rosário
142
Sta. Bárbara de Padrões
S. João dos Caldeireiros
Sant'Ana de Cambas
Romarão
El Granado
El Almendro
Praia da Zambugueira
Sta. Clara-a-Velha
Gomes Aires
S. Miguel do Pinheiro
S. Sebastião
Espirito Santo
S. Teotónio
Saboia
Sta. Ana de Serra
Almodôvar
Sta. Clara-a-Nova
Serra do Caldeirão
Barragem Marcelo Caetano
S. Pedro de Solis
Via Gloria
Giões
Alcoutim
Villanueva de los Castillejos
Sanlúcar de Guadiana
Odeceixe
Pereiro
Dogueno
Martim-Longo
S. Bartolomé de la Torre
Tariquejo
S. Silvestre de Guzmán
Serra de Monchique
S. Marcos da Serra
Almeixial
Aljezur
Foia 902
Alferce
Monchique
Marmelete
S. Barnabé
Mú 575
Vaqueiros
Cachopo
Odeleite
Villablanca
Lepe
Cartaya
Vale de Rosa
Peralva
S. Bartolomeu de Messines
Alfambra
Barragem de Arade
Barragem de Odeaxere
Azinhal
Castro Marim
Ayamonte
Pozo del Camino
La Redondela
El Rompido
Las Antillas
Silves
Porto de Lagos
Alte
Salir
Barranco do Velho
Isla-Cristina
Isla Canela
Monte Gordo
Bordeira
Algoz
Tunes
Paderne
S. Braz de Alportel
Vila Real de S. Antonio
Bensafrim
Odiáxere
Portimão
Boliqueime
Loulé
S. Romão
Cacela
Lagoa
Alcantarilha
Sta. Catarina
Sto. Estêvão
Tavira
Vila do Bispo
Budens
Alvor
Praia da Rocha
Pêra
Estói
Burgau
Luz
Lagos
Praia de Carvoeiro
Armação de Pêra
Albufeira
Almansil
Moncarapacho
Cabo de São Vicente
Sagres
Baía de Lagos
Ponta da Piedade
Quarteira
S. João da Venda
Pechão
Ilha da Armona
Golfo de Cá
Ponta de Sagres
Faro
Olhão
Ilha da Barreta
Ilha da Culatra
Cabo de Sta. Maria
O C E A N O A T L A N T I C
Guadiana
Ardila
Sado
Xarrama
Roxo
Campilhas
Terges
Cobres
Chança
Malagón
Vascão
Foupana
Odeleite
Mira
Arade
A
B
C
D
1
2
3
9°
8°
38°
37°
36°

Jerez de los Caballeros
Fregenal de la Sierra
Higuera la Real
Encinasola
Fuentes de Leon
Segura de León
Bodonal de la Sierra
Valencia del Ventoso
Medina de las Torres
Calzadilla de los Barros
Fuente de Cantos
Montemolín
Monesterio
Bienvenida
Usagre
Llerena
Villagarcia de las Torres
Berlanga
Granja de Torrehermosa
Azuaga
Ahillones
Valverde de Llerena
Fuente del Arco
Trasierra
Guadalcanal
Malcocinado
Fuente-Obejuna
Peñarroya-Pueblonuevo
Bélmez
Espiel
Villaviciosa de Córdoba
Sierra de los Santos
Embalse del Puente Nuevo
Aroche
Cortegana
Galaroza
Jabugo
Aracena
Sierra de Aracena
Almonaster la Real
Cumbres Mayores
Sierra de Tudia
Arroyomolinos de León
Cala
Real de la Jara
Sta. Olalla del Cala
Almadén de la Plata
Cazalla de la Sierra
Constantina
Alanis
S. Nicolás del Puerto
Las Navas de la Concepción
Embalse de Retortillo
Hornachuelos
Almodóvar del Río
Posadas
Guadalquivir
La Puebla de los Infantes
El Pedroso
Palma del Río
Fuente Palmera
La Carlota
Lora del Río
Villanueva del Río
Cantillana
Peñaflor
La Campana
La Luisiana
Ecija
Fuentes de Andalucía
Carmona
Necropolis Romana
Brenes
Tocina
Alcolea del Río
El Cerro de Andévalo
Zalamea la Real
Nerva
Minas de Riotinto
El Castillo de las Guardas
El Ronquillo
Castilblanco de los Arroyos
Valverde del Camino
Gerena
Guillena
Burguillos
Alcalá del Río
La Rinconada
La Algaba
Aznalcóllar
Ruinas de Itálica
Santiponce
Camas
SEVILLA
El Viso del Alcor
Mairena del Alcor
Alcalá de Guadaira
Dos Hermanas
San Juan de Aznalfarache
Coria del Río
La Puebla del Río
Paradas
El Arahal
Marchena
Osuna
La Puebla de Cazalla
Morón de la Frontera
El Saucejo
Puente-Genil
Herrera
Marinaleda
El Rubio
Aguadulce
Gilena
Estepa
Huelva
Trigueros
Niebla
La Palma del Condado
Bollullos par del Condado
Sanlúcar la Mayor
Manzanilla
Moguer
Palos de la Frontera
Almonte
Rociana del Condado
Hinojos
Pilas
Villamanrique de la Condesa
Mazagón
El Rocío
Playa de Castilla
Las Marismas
Los Palacios y Villafranca
Utrera
Los Morales
El Coronil
Embalse de la Torre del Águila
Las Cabezas de S. Juan
Laguna de Zarracatín
Montellano
Coripe
Pruna
Olvera
Teba
Cañete la Real
Ardales
Alcalá del Valle
Algodonales
Setenil
Puerto Serrano
Lebrija
Trebujena
El Cuervo
Espera
Villamartín
Bornos
Prado del Rey
Zahara
Grazalema
Ronda
Cueva de la Pileta
Sierra de Ronda
Sierra de Tolox
Parque Natural
Sanlúcar de Barrameda
Chipiona
Rota
JEREZ DE LA FRONTERA
Arcos de la Frontera
Embalse de Guadalcacín
Ubrique
Cortes de la Frontera
El Puerto de Sta. María
Bahía de Cádiz
CÁDIZ
Puerto Real
S. Fernando
Chiclana de la Frontera
Medina-Sidonia
Paterna de Rivera
Alcalá de los Gazules
Jimena de la Frontera
Casares
Estepona
Manilva
Marbella
Castellar de la Frontera
Conil
Vejer de la Frontera
Cabo de Trafalgar
Barbate de Franco
Zahara de los Atunes
Facinas
Los Barrios
Algeciras
S. Roque
La Línea
Gibraltar
Punta de Europa
Bahía de Algeciras
Tarifa
Punta Marroquí
Estrecho de Gibraltar
Ceuta (Esp.)
Tanger
Málaga
Casablanca
Tenerife
S I E R R A   M O R E N A
A N D A L U C Í A

Sierra de Alcudia
Valle de Alcudia
130
Sierra Mestanza
Sierra Madrona
Sta. Eufemia
Hinojosa del Duque
El Viso
Los Pedroches
Torrecampo
Villaralto
Dos-Torres
Añora
Pedroche
Villanueva del Duque
Alcaracejos
Pozoblanco
Conquista
Villanueva de Córdoba
Cardeña
Bélmez
Espiel
Sierra de los Santos
Villaviciosa de Córdoba
Obejo
Embalse del Puente Nuevo
Embalse del Guadalmellato
Cerro Muriano
Adamuz
Montoro
Marmolejo
Andújar
Villafranca de Córdoba
Pedro Abad
Villa del Río
Alcolea
Embalse de Bembézar
Sta. María de Trassierra
CÓRDOBA
El Carpio
Bujalance
Arjonilla
Lopera
Arjona
Almodóvar del Río
Posadas
Guadalquivir
Cañete de las Torres
Porcuna
Torres-Cabrera
Guadalcázar
Fuente-Palmera
La Carlota
Fernán-Núñez
Espejo
Castro del Río
Montemayor
La Rambla
Montilla
Nueva Carteya
Baena
Alcaudete
Écija
Santaella
Aguilar
Doña Mencía
Luque
Cabra
Priego de Córdoba
Alcalá la Real
Castillo de Locubín
Puente-Genil
Lucena
Carcabuey
Herrera
Rute
Iznájar
Embalse de Iznájar
Benamejí
Montefrío
Íllora
Estepa
Osuna
Gilena
Pedrera
La Roda de Andalucía
Alameda
Cuevas de S. Marcos
Loja
Huétor-Tajár
Sierra de Yeguas
Mollina
Villanueva de Algaidas
Archidona
El Saucejo
Campillos
Laguna Salada
Antequera
Teba
Cañete la Real
Alcalá del Valle
Ardales
Villanueva del Rosario
Alfarnate
Periana
Colmenar
Alhama de Granada
Sierra de Almijara
Casabermeja
Cómpeta
Ronda
Sierra de Ronda
Sierra de Tolox
Casarabonela
Alora
Pizarra
Almogía
Cártama
Coín
Alhaurín de la Torre
Alhaurín el Grande
Mijas
Vélez-Málaga
Torre del Mar
Torrox
Nerja
Almuñécar
Salobreña
Motril
MÁLAGA
Rincón de la Victoria
Torremolinos
Benalmádena
Fuengirola
Marbella
Estepona
S. Pedro de Alcántara
Tanger
Melilla
Costa del Sol
MAR
Bailén
Linares
Baños de la Encina
La Carolina
Vilches
Ubeda
Baeza
Mengíbar
Jaén
Torredonjimeno
Martos
Torre del Campo
Mancha Real
Jódar
Cambil
Huelma
Sierra de Magina
Valdepeñas de Jaén
Iznalloz
Moclín
Pinos-Puente
Atarfe
Santafé
GRANADA
Sierra Harana
Guadix
Zubía
Padul
Dúrcal
Lanjarón
Órjiva
Alpujarras
Sierra Nevada
Mulhacén 3478
Pico Veleta
El Viso del Marqués
Santisteban del Puerto
Cabra del Sto. Cristo
Peal de Becerro

Albaladejo
Villamanrique
S. Cristóbal 1075
Embalse Guadalmena
Puente de Génave
Génave
Arroyo del Ojanco
Beas de Segura
Villanueva del Arzobispo
Embalse del Tranco de Beas
Blanquilla 1830
Sierra de Segura
Siles
La Puerta de Segura
Orcera
Hornos
Cortijos Nuevos
Pontones
Santiago de la Espade
Bienservida
Cerro de Almenara 1798
Sierra de Alcaraz
Paterna del Madera
Bogarra
Riopar
Villaverde de Guadalimar
El Arguellite
Mentiras 1897
Parolis
Yeste
Embalse de Fuensanta
Molinicos
Elche de la Sierra
El Entredicho
Letur
Ayna
Liétor
La Matanza
Embalse de Talave
Tobarra
Ontur
Albatana
Hellín
Minateda
La Horca
Agramón
Embalse de Cenajo
Embalse de Camarillas
Socovos
Jumilla
Pinoso
Salinas
Laguna de Salinas
Hondón de los Frailes
Pila 1264
Cieza
Calasparra
Abarán
Blanca
Fortuna
Albanilla
Albater
Orihuela
Moratalla
Sabinar
Turrilla
Nerpio
Sierra de Taibilla
2001
Caravaca
Cehegín
Archivel
Bullas
Mula
Pliego
Archena
Ceuti
Alguazas
Lorqui
Molina de Segura
Santomera
Bigastro
Monteagudo
S. Jerónimo
Alcantarilla
MURCIA
Almudena
Doña Inés
Royos
La Sagra 2381
Puebla de Don Fradique
Sierra de Espuña
Casas Nuevas
Librilla
Sangonera
Puerto de Cadena 372
Pa Paca
Zarzadilla de Totana
Alhama de Murcia
1579
Aledo
Totana
Topares
Zarcilla de Ramos
Fuensanta
La Iruela
Cabañas 2036
Castril
Huéscar
Galera
Castillejar
Orce
Alcón
Cortes de Baza
Cuevas del Campo
María
Vélez Blanco
Vélez Rubio
Sierra de María
2043
Lorca
Corvera
Torre-Pacheco
Fuente-Álamo de Murcia
La Pinilla
Algarrobo 713
Aljorra
Los Dolores
CARTAGENA
Escombrera
Benamaurel
Cúllar de Baza
Chirivel
Puerto Lumbreras
Purias
Sierra de la Almenara
Campico López 882
Talayón
Mazarrón
Puerto de Mazarrón
El Cantal
Cabo Tiñoso
Golfo de Mazarrón
Zújar
Baza
Sierra de las Estancias
Los Cerricos
Oria
Sta. María de Nieva
Pulpí
Águilas
Cabo Cope
Caniles
Sta. Bárbara 2269
Gor
Sierra de Baza
Hijate
Lúcar
Somontín
Urracal
Albox
Huércal-Overa
Cuevas del Almanzora
Alcóntar
Serón
Tíjola
Purchena
Macael
Cantoria
Zurgena
Albánchez
Bacares
Tahal
Lubrín
Antas
Vera
Palomares
Sierra de los Filabres
2168
Senés
Velefique
Uleila del Campo
Los Gallardos
Garrucha
Mojacar
Huéneja
Fiñana
Abla
Puerto de la Ragua 2000
Gérgal
Ohanes
Canjáyer
Sorbas
Tabernas
Lucainena de las Torres
S. Cabrera
Carboneras
Sierra de Alhamilla
Laujar
Instinción
Alcolea
Sierra de Gádor
Morrón 2242
Gádor
Rioja
Alhama de Almería
Benahadux
Huércal de Almería
Níjar
Campo de Níjar
Fernán Pérez
Las Negras
Félix
El Alquián
Berja
Dalías
Almería
El Ejido
Roquetas de Mar
Mojonera
Golfo de Almería
El Cabo de Gata
Sierra de Gata
S. José
Cabo de Gata
Balerma
Guardias Viejas
Punta de las Entinas
Alicante
Melilla
MEDITERRANEO
246
147
203
80
251
322
415
3212
3213
3314
3223
301
415
3315
3211
340
342
E26
3319
332
324
4
5
6
A
B
C
131
133
37°
38°
2°

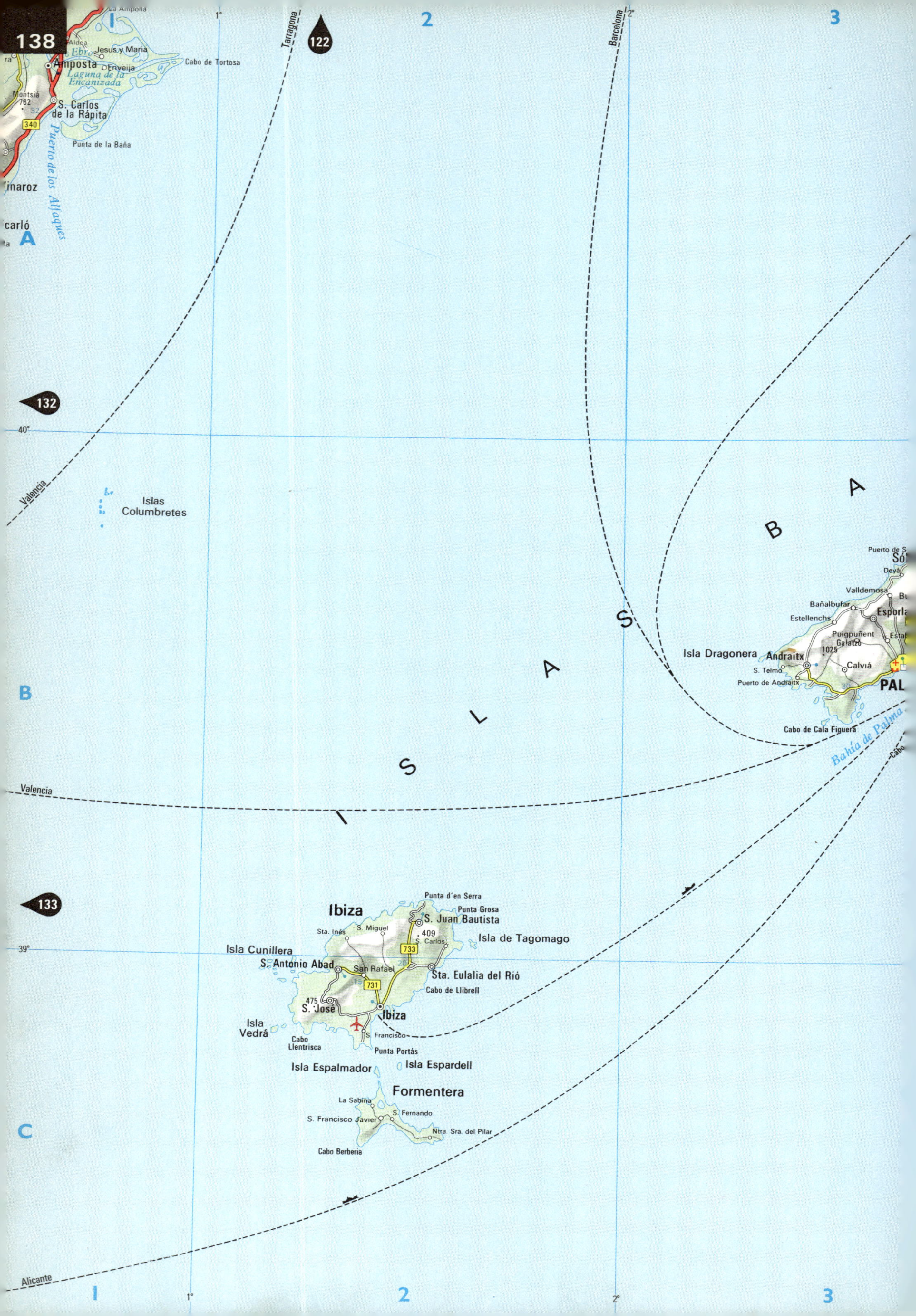
Aldea
Ebro
Jesus y Maria
Amposta
Enveija
Laguna de la Encanizada
Cabo de Tortosa
Montsiá
762
S. Carlos de la Rápita
340
Punta de la Baña
Puerto de los Alfaques
Tarragona
122
Barcelona
132
Valencia
Islas Columbretes
I S L A S B A
Puerto de S
Sóller
Deyá
Valldemosa
Bañalbufar
Estellenchs
Esporlas
Puigpuñent
Galatzó
1025
Isla Dragonera
Andraitx
S. Telmo
Puerto de Andraitx
Calviá
PAL
Cabo de Cala Figuera
Bahía de Palma
Valencia
133
Ibiza
Punta d'en Serra
Punta Grosa
S. Juan Bautista
Sta. Inés
S. Miguel
409
S. Carlos
Isla de Tagomago
Isla Cunillera
733
S. Antonio Abad
San Rafael
Sta. Eulalia del Río
731
Cabo de Llibrell
475
S. José
Ibiza
Isla Vedrá
S. Francisco
Cabo Llentrisca
Punta Portás
Isla Espalmador
Isla Espardell
Formentera
La Sabina
S. Fernando
S. Francisco Javier
Ntra. Sra. del Pilar
Cabo Berberia
Alicante
1
2
3
A
B
C
1°
2°
40°
39°

123

A

B A L E A R E S

40°

A

Cabo de Caballeria
Fornells

Punta Nati

Ciudadela   721   24   Mercadal   723
                              Ferrerias   Toro
                              Sant Cristófol   358
Cabo Dartuch   Alayor
                          Menorca   721   Mahón
                                    S. Clemente   Villacarlos
                                    S. Luis
                          Isla del Aire

Cabo de Formentor

Punta Beca
Pollensa   Puerto de Pollensa
            Alcudia   Cabo del Pinar
            Puerto de Alcudia
Selva   Bahía da Alcudía
La Puebla   C'an Picafort
Lloseta   Muro   Cabo Farruch
            712   Morey   Cabo del Freu
Inca   35   560   Cala Ratjada
I-1   Sta. Margarita   Artá   10   Capdepera
Binisalem   Cuevas de Arta
Maria   Sineu   715   Cabo des Piná
Sancellas   Petra   22   Son Severa
        S. Lorenzo
        de Descardazar   Punta de Amer
        Montuiri   Manacor
Algaida   715   48   Porto Cristo
    Monasterio   Cuevas del Drach
    de Cora   Porreras

B

hmayor   50   Felanitx
717   Porto Colom
mpos del Puerto   Porto Petro
    Lagunas   Ses Salines
    d'es Salobra   Santany
allorca   Cabo de Salinas

Conejera

uerto Cabrera

39°

M A R

C

M E D I T E R R A N E O

Gorgona
Capraia
C. Corse
Ersa
Pino
Sta.-Severa
Marine de Sisco
Nonza
Patrimonio
St. Florent
Bastia
Etang de Biguglia
L'Ile Rousse
Calvi
Belgodère
Muro
Calenzana
Santo-Pietro -di-Tenda
Casamozza
Vescovato
Venzolasca
Ponte Leccia
Moriani-Plage
Piedicroce
Cervione
Manso
M. Cinto 2710
Castirla
Calacuccia
Golfe de Porto
Porto
Piana
Evisa
Corte
C O R S E
Venaco
Vivario
Vezzani
Guagno
Cargèse
Sagone
Vizzavona
Ghi
Aleria
Golfe de Sagone
Bocognano
Bastelica
Ghisonaccia
Ajaccio
Cauro
Frasseto
Zicavo
Golfe d' Ajaccio
Solenzara
Petreto-Bicchisano
Aullène
Zonza
Olmeto
S. Lucia
Golfe de Valinco
Propriano
Sartène
Porto Vecchio
Pte. de Chiappa
Pte. d'Ovace 1339
Sotta
Figari
Bonifacio
Cavallo
Pte. S. Antoine
Bocche di Bonifácio
S. Maria
S. Teresa Gallura
Pta. Falcone
Spargi
Capo Testa
Maddalena
La Maddalena
Caprera
Palau
Capo Ferro
Bassacutena
Arzachena
Mortório
S. Francesco d'Aglientu
Luogosanto
S. Pantaleo
G A L L U R A
Asinara
Pta. Caprara o dello Scorno
la Reale
Portoferráio
Marciana Marina
Prócchio
Marina di Campo
Elba
Pianosa
Montecristo
Nice
109
110
141
142

Bocche
S. Maria
S. Teresa Gallura
Pta. Falcone
Spargi
Maddalena
La Maddalena
Caprera
Capo Testa
Palau
Capo Ferro
Bassacutena
Arzachena
S. Pantaleo
Mortório
S. Francesco d'Aglientu
Luogosanto
G A L L U R A
L. di Liscia
Golfo Aranci
Capo Figari
S. Antonio
Golfo di Olbia
Ólbia
Trinità d'Agultu
Àggius
Lúras
Calangiánus
Tempio Pausánia
Telti
Tavolara
Molara
Capo Coda Cavallo
La Variante 676
M. Limbara 1362
Berchidda
Monti
Lóiri
Padru
Straulas
Tanaunella
Posada
Torpè
Siniscóla
Capo Comino
Pta. Caprara o dello Scorno
Asinara
la Reale
Golfo dell'Asinara
Fornelli
Pta. del Falcone
Piana
Stintino
Castelsardo
Valledória
Sédini
Pérfugas
Porto Tórres
Sorso
Sennori
Ósilo
Nulvi
Mártis
L. del Coghinas
Chiaramonti
Tula
Óschiri
Argentiera
Sássari
Úsini
Ossi
Ploaghe
Árdara
Ozieri
M. Lerno 1094
Pattada
Alà dei Sardi
Buddusò
Lodè
Olmedo
Tramariglio
Capo Cáccia
Fertilia
Alghero
Íttiri
L O G U D O R O
Mores
Ittireddu
Osidda
Monte Albo
Monti Remule
Villanova Monteleone
Thiesi
Torralba
Romana
M. Rasu 1259
Foresta di Burgos
Bono
Nule
Bitti
Lula
Irgoli
Galtellì
Orune
Orosei
Pádria
Pozzomaggiore
Bonorva
Montresta
Capo Marargiu
Bosa
Bolótana
Sindia
Silánus
Macomer
Orotelli
Núoro
Dorgali
Oliena
Orani
Tresnuraghes
Suni
Cúglieri
Dualchi
Bórore
Ottana
Olzai
Mamoiada
M. Corrasi 1463
Orgósolo
Golfo di Orosei
Gavoi
Sedilo
M. Ferru 1050
Bonárcado
Santu Lussúrgiu
Ghilarza
Abbasanta
L. Omodeo
Fonni
Psd di Caravai 1235
Capo di M. Santu
Séneghe
Paulilátino
Áustis
Ovodda
Urzulei
Baunei
S A R D E G N A
Capo Mannu
Tramatza
Busachi
Sórgono
Tonara
Desulo
Monti del Gennargentu
Pta. La Marmora 1834
Villagrande Strisáili
Lotzorai
Riola Sardo
Fordongiánus
Meana Sardo
Aritzo
Tortolì
Arbatax
I. di Mal di Ventre
Cábras
Solarussa
Samugheo
Oristano
Simáxis
Villaurbana
Seúlo
Lanusei
S. Giusta
Capo S. Marco
Golfo di Oristano
A R B O R É A
Láconi
Seúi
Ussássai
Gáiro
Bari Sardo
Sénis
Arborèa
M. Arci 812
Usellus
Ales
Nurallao
Ierzu
Capo d. Frasca
Ísili
Terralba
Úras
Turri
Barúmini
Nurri
Tertenia
Mógoro
Lunamatrona
Perdasdefogu
Mándas
Sárdara
Villamar
L. Mulargia
Escalaplano
Guasila
Goni
Ballao
Árbus
Gúspini
S. Gavino Monreale
Sanluri
Suelli
Senorbì
S. Nicolò Gerrei
Serrenti
Samassi
S. Andrea Frius
S. Vito
Villaputzu
Capo Pécora
Gonnosfanádiga
M. Linas 1236
Villacidro
Serramanna
Fluminimaggiore
Dolianova
Muravera
Buggerru
Vallermosa
Villasor
Monastir
Pta. Serpeddì 1069
Burcei
S. Priamo
Masúa
Domusnóvas
Decimomannu
Sestu
Sínnai
Iglésias
Siliqua
Assémini
Selárgius
M. dei Sette Fratelli 1023
Capo Ferrato
Gonnesa
Villamassárgia
Stagno di Cagliari
CÁGLIARI
Quartu S. Élena
Castiádas
Portoscuso
Carbónia
Capoterra
Narcao
Acquacadda
Villasimíus
Carloforte
M. Caravius 1116
Golfo di Cágliari
S. Pietro
S. Giovanni Suérgiu
Capo Carbonara
Calasetta
Santadi
S. Antioco
Giba
Sarroch
S. Antíoco
Golfo di Pálmas
I G L E S I E N T E
S Ú L C I S
C A M P I D A N O
Pula
Capo Sperone
Teulada
Dómus de Maria
Capo Teulada
Capo Spartivento
Genova
Civitavecchia
Nápoli
Palermo
140
142

A
B
C
D
1
2
112
140
Donorático
S. Vincenzo
Sassetta
Suvereto
Campiglia Marittima
Venturina
Monterotondo Marittimo
Montieri
Massa Marittima
Prata
Populónia
Piombino
Follónica
Gavorrano
Ribolla
Roccastrada
Roccatederighi
Valpiana
Vetulónia
Paganico
Buonconvento
Montalcino
Torrenieri
S. Quirico d'Orcia
Montepulciano
Pienza
Chianciano Terme
Acquaviva
Torrita d. Siena
Sinalunga
Chiusi
Castiglione d. Lago
Città d. Pieve
Sarteano
Castiglione d'Orcia
Sasso d'Ombrone
Castel d. Piano
Abbadia S. Salvatore
Piancastagnaio
Radicófani
Arcidosso
Cinigiano
Campagnático
Sticciano Scalo
Montepescali
Batignano
Terme di Roselle
Istia d'Ombrone
Grosseto
Castiglione della Pescáia
Marina di Grosseto
Scansano
Magliano in Toscana
Fonteblanda
Talamone
Albinia
Orbetello
Orbetello Scalo
Porto San Stéfano
Port 'Ercole
Capalbio
Manciano
Saturnia
Samprugnano
S. Caterina
Roccalbegna
S. Fiora
Castell Azzara
Sorano
Pitigliano
Acquapendente
Onano
Grotte di Castro
S. Lorenzo Nuovo
Látera
Lago di Bolsena
Valentano
Farnese
Ischia di Castro
Canino
Arlena di Castro
Tuscania
Marta
Montefiascone
Bolsena
Bagnorégio
Orvieto
Ficulle
Monteleone d'Orvieto
S. Casciano d. Bagni
Viterbo
Vetralla
L. di Vico
Caprarola
Vignanello
Montalto di Castro
Monte Romano
Tarquinia
Blera
Allumiere
Tolfa
Civitavécchia
San Marinella
San Severa
Manziana
Bracciano
L. di Bracciano
Cerveteri
Ladispoli
Palidoro
Maccarese
Fregene
Fiumicino
Lido di Ostia
Portoferráio
Marciana Marina
Prócchio
Marina di Campo
Rio Marina
Porto Azzurro
Cavo
Elba
Pianosa
ARCIPELAGO TOSCANO
Montecristo
Gíglio
Giglio Porto
Giannutri
M A R E T I R R E
Olbia
Cagliari
43°
42°
41°
11°
12°
230
143
65
77
E1
E6
A1
1
2
74
398
439
73
146
326
71
204

Perúgia
Assisi
Spello
Foligno
Camerino
Tolentino
Mogliano
Montegiórgio
Porto S. Giórgio
Fermo
Pedaso
Cupra Maríttima
Ripatransone
Grottammare
S. Benedetto del Tronto
Porto d'Ascoli
Martinsicuro
Áscoli Piceno
Offida
Acquaviva Picena
Nereto
Tortoreto Lido
Giulianova
Roseto degli Abruzzi
Téramo
Notaresco
Pineto
Atri
Silvi
Montesilvano Marina
Pescara
Francavilla al Mare
Ortona
Chieti
San Vito Chietino
Lanciano
Fossacesia
Paglieta
Casalbordino
Vasto
Trevi
Spoleto
Nórcia
Terni
Rieti
Amatrice
Gran Sasso d'Italia
M. Corno 2914
M. Vettore 2476
Monti Sabini
Appennino Abruzzese
L'Aquila
Pagánica
Antrodoco
Cittaducale
Pópoli
Sulmona
Pratola Peligna
Guardiagrele
M. Amaro 2795
Celano
Avezzano
Tagliacozzo
Pescina
Scanno
Castel di Sangro
Agnone
Trivento
Isérnia
Venafro
Monti del Matese
Piedimonte d'Alife
Boiano
Campobasso
Tívoli
Guidónia
Mentana
Monterotondo
ROMA
Frascati
Marino
Albano Laziale
Genzano di Roma
Velletri
Palestrina
Subiaco
Fiuggi
Anagni
Colleferro
Alatri
Ferentino
Frosinone
Sora
Isola del Liri
Arpino
Ceccano
Monti Lepini
Cisterna di Latina
Aprília
Ánzio
Nettuno
Latina
Agro Pontino
Sezze
Priverno
Monti Ausoni
Fondi
Terracina
Sabáudia
S. Felice Circeo
Sperlonga
Gaeta
Fórmia
Monti Aurunci
Minturno
Pontecorvo
Cassino
Sessa Aurunca
Teano
Mondragone
Cápua
Caserta
Maddaloni
Aversa
Giugliano
Afragola
Acerra
Nola
NÁPOLI
Pozzuoli
Pórtici
Ercolano
Torre del Greco
Torre Annunziata
Castellammare di Stábia
M. Vesuvio 1277
Pompei
Ischia
Prócida
Golfo di Nápoli
Golfo di Gaeta
Isole Ponziane
Palmarola
Ponza
Zannone
Ventotene
Split
113
144
4
5
A
B
C
D

143
Rieti
Cittaducale
Antrodoco
L'Aquila
Paganica
Penne
Pescara
Francavilla al Mare
Loreto Aprutino
Pianella
Chieti
Ortona
Miglianico
San Vito Chietino
Lanciano
Fossacesia
Alanno
Capestrano
Scafa
Guardiagrele
Orsogna
Castel Frentano
Paglieta
Casalbordino
Vasto
Popoli
Caramanico
Pratola Peligna
Sulmona
Raiano
Castelvecchio Subequo
Celano
Avezzano
Magliano de Marsi
Tagliacozzo
Carsoli
Arsoli
Vicovaro
Tivoli
Orvinio
Poggio Moiano
Fara in Sabina
Monte Libretti
Palombara Sabina
Licenza
Subiaco
Palestrina
Genazzano
Frascati
Valmontone
Anagni
Fiuggi
Guarcino
Alatri
Artena
Colleferro
Ferentino
Veroli
Rocca di Papa
Velletri
Lanuvio
Cisterna di Latina
Cori
Norma
Sermoneta
Frosinone
Carpineto Romano
Supino
Ceccano
Castro dei Volsci
Sezze
Priverno
Latina
Pontinia
Nettuno
Sonnino
Fondi
Terracina
Sabaudia
S. Felice Circeo
Sperlonga
Itri
Formia
Gaeta
Minturno
Castelforte
Sessa Aurunca
Carinola
Teano
Sora
Isola del Liri
Arpino
Arce
Ceprano
Roccasecca
Aquino
Cassino
Cervaro
Pontecorvo
Pico
Esperia
Pescina
Luco dei Marsi
Trasacco
Pescasseroli
Scanno
Villetta Barrea
Castel di Sangro
Isernia
Venafro
Atina
S. Elia Fiumerapido
Agnone
Trivento
Casacalenda
Campobasso
Boiano
Piedimonte d'Alife
Alife
Cusano Mutri
Cerreto Sannita
Morcone
Pontelandolfo
Telese
Solopaca
Benevento
Montesarchio
S. Agata de Goti
Caiazzo
Pignataro Maggiore
Capua
Caserta
Maddaloni
S. Maria Capua Vetere
Marcianise
Aversa
Giugliano
Afragola
Acerra
Casoria
Marigliano
Nola
Avellino
Mondragone
Cancello ed Arnone
Castel Volturno
Casal di Principe
NÁPOLI
Pozzuoli
Bácoli
Prócida
Ischia
Forío
Portici
Resina
Torre del Greco
Torre Annunziata
Castellammare di Stábia
Vico Equense
Sorrento
Massa Lubrense
Capri
Pta. Campanella
Gragnano
Pompei
Scafati
Nocera
Pagani
Cava de' Tirreni
Vietri sul Mare
Amalfi
SALERNO
Ottaviano
Palma
Sarno
S. Anastasia
Golfo di Gaeta
Golfo di Nápoli
Golfo di Salerno
Isole Ponziane
Palmarola
Ponza
Zannone
Ventotene
MARE TIRRENO
Cagliari
Palermo
Monti Sabini
Appennino Abruzzese
Monti Lepini
Monti Ausoni
Monti Aurunci
Monti del Matese
Agro Pontino
Monti del Sannio
M. Corno 2914
M. Amaro 2795
M. Cairo 1669
M. Miletto 2050
M. Vesuvio 1277
M. S. Angelo 1443
M. Taburno 1393
M. Avella 1591
M. Petrella 1533
M. Semprevisa 1536
M. delle Fate 1090
Pso. di Diavolo 1441
Pso. di Miralago 1102
A
B
C
1
2
3
41°
40°
13°
14°

MARE ADRIATICO
Isole Trémiti
Rodi Gargánico
Peschici
Vieste
Ischitella
Vico del Gargano
Carpino
Lesina
Poggio Imperiale
Chieuti
Serracapriola
Sannicandro Gargánico
Cagnano Varano
Apricena
San Marco in Lamis
S. Paolo di Civitate
Torremaggiore
San Severo
Casalnuovo Monterotaro
Castelnuovo della Dáunia
Rignano Gargánico
San Giovanni Rotondo
Mattinata
Monte Sant'Angelo
Manfredónia
Motta Montecorvino
Lucera
Arpinova
TAVOLIERE
CAPITANATA
FÓGGIA
Zapponeta
Margherita di Savóia
Biccari
Tróia
Carapelle
Orta Nova
Castellúccio de Sauri
Giardinetto
Trinitápoli
S. Ferdinando di Púglia
Barletta
Trani
Bisceglie
Molfetta
Giovinazzo
S. Spirito
BARI
Orsara di Púglia
Bovino
Deliceto
Stornara
Cerignola
Áscoli Satriano
Canosa di Púglia
Ándria
Corato
Terlizzi
Bitonto
Palo del Colle
Modugno
Bitetto
Triggiano
Noicáttaro
Mola di Bari
Rutigliano
Capurso
Adelfia
Savignano di Púglia
Monteleone di Púglia
Accadia
Villanova d. Battista
S. Ágata di Púglia
Candela
Rocchetta S. António
Lacedónia
Vallata
Bisáccia
Aquilonia
Melfi
Lavello
Posta Piana
Minervino Murge
Montemilone
Spinazzola
Ruvo di Púglia
Grumo Áppula
Toritto
Sannicandro di Bari
Casamássima
Conversano
Acquaviva delle Fonti
Turi
Cassano delle Murge
Sammichele di Bari
Castellana Grotte
Gióia dell Colle
Putignano
Noci
Alberobello
Rapolla
M. Vúlture 1327
Rionero in Vúlture
Venosa
Ripacándida
Palazzo S. Gervásio
Genzano di Lucánia
Atella
Forenza
Acerenza
Gravina in Púglia
Altamura
Santéramo in Colle
MURGE
Guárdia
Andretta
S. Ángelo dei Lombardi
Calitri
Teora
Lioni
Sella di Conza 697
Pescopagano
Ruvo del Monte
S. Fele
Bella
Pso. d. Crocelle 1136
Muro Lucano
Avigliano
Pietragalla
Cancellara
Oppido Lucano
Vaglio Basilicata
Tolve
Irsina
Ruoti
Picerno
S. Gregório Magno
Buccino
Potenza
Laviano
Calabritto
Campagna
Contursi
Tricárico
Grassano
Gróttole
Matera
L. di S. Giuliano
Laterza
Castellaneta
Móttola
Massafra
Palagiano
Ginosa
TÁRANTO
Cheradi
Capo S. Vito
Talsano
Marina di Ginosa
Montescaglioso
Miglionico
Pomárico
Bernalda
Vietri di Potenza
Tito
Caggiano
Auletta
Serre
Pso. Croce d. Scrivano
Trivigno
Garaguso
Anzi
Salandra
Ferrandina
Accettura
Laurenzana
Calvello
S. Mauro Forte
Stigliano
M. Alburno 1742
Controne
Polla
Brienza
Corleto Monforte
S. Rufo
Roccadáspide
Sella d. Corticato 1026
Felitto
Capáccio
Sala Consilina
M. Volturino 1836
Márisco Nuovo
Corleto Perticara
Cirigliano
Craco
Pisticci
Lido di Metaponto
Montalbano Iónico
Teggiano
Padula
Viggiano
Montemurro
Missanello
Tursi
Scanzano
Golfo di Táranto
M. Cervati 1899
Laurino
Stio
Montesano sulla Marcellana
Spinoso
Vallo della Lucánia
Buonabitácolo
Casalbuono
Sella Cessuta
Moliterno
S. Arcángelo
Roccanova
S. Chirico Raparo
Colobraro
Policoro
Rotondella
Sanza
Rofrano
Ceraso
M. Sacro 1705
Montano Antilia
M. Sirino 2005
Castelsaraceno
Senise
Chiaromonte
Torre Orsáia
Lagonegro
Latrónico
Noépoli
Rocca Imperiale
Oriolo
Francavilla in Sinni
Episcopia
Montegiordano Marina
Ascea
Pisciotta
Foria
M. Bulgheria 1225
S. Giovanni a Piro
Sapri
Rivello
Lauria
Palinuro
Capo Palinuro
Camerota
Golfo
Castelluccio Inferiore
S. Severino Lucano
CILENTO
Appennino Lucano
Dubrovnik
Piraievs

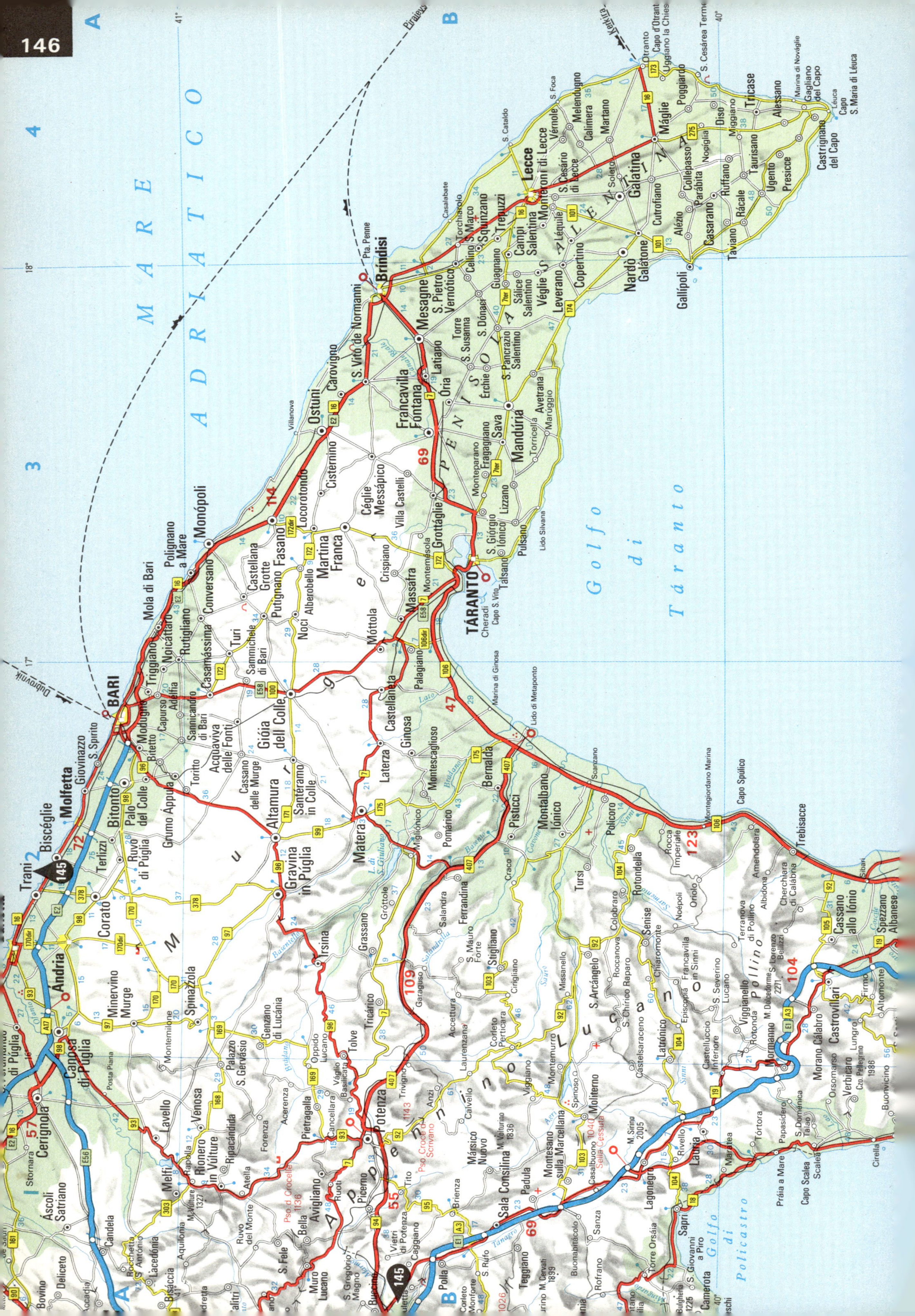
A
B
3
4
MARE ADRIATICO
Golfo di Táranto
Golfo di Policastro
BARI
Molfetta
Bisceglie
Trani
Andria
Barletta
Canosa di Puglia
Cerignola
Ascoli Satriano
Corato
Bitonto
Giovinazzo
Terlizzi
Ruvo di Puglia
Palo del Colle
Modugno
Minervino Murge
Spinazzola
Altamura
Gravina in Puglia
Santeramo in Colle
Gióia dell Colle
Acquaviva delle Fonti
Cassano delle Murge
Grumo Appula
Casamassima
Turi
Sammichele di Bari
Rutigliano
Noicáttaro
Triggiano
Mola di Bari
Conversano
Polignano a Mare
Monópoli
Castellana Grotte
Putignano
Fasano
Alberobello
Noci
Locorotondo
Martina Franca
Cisternino
Ostuni
Carovigno
Céglie Messápico
Villa Castelli
Grottáglie
Crispiano
Massafra
Móttola
Palagiano
Castellaneta
Laterza
Ginosa
Matera
Montescaglioso
Bernalda
Pisticci
Montalbano Iónico
Policoro
Tursi
TÁRANTO
Brindisi
S. Vito dei Normanni
Mesagne
Francavilla Fontana
Oria
Latiano
Manduria
Sava
Lecce
Squinzano
Trepuzzi
Campi Salentina
Copertino
Nardò
Galatone
Galatina
Maglie
Otranto
Gallipoli
Casarano
Tricase
Castrignano del Capo
Capo S. Maria di Léuca
PENISOLA SALENTINA
Potenza
Melfi
Lavello
Venosa
Rionero in Vulture
Avigliano
Irsina
Tolve
Tricárico
Grassano
Stigliano
Ferrandina
Corleto Perticara
Moliterno
Lauria
Lagonegro
Sapri
Maratea
Sala Consilina
Padula
Teggiano
Polla
Senise
Rotondella
Trebisacce
Castrovillari
Cassano allo Iónio
Morano Calabro
Scalea
Pollino
Appennino Lucano
Murge
E2
A14
A3
16
7
96
99
106
114
109
145
123
104
69
47
55
57
72

MARE IONIO

MARE TIRRENO

C D E

Crotone
Capo Colonna
Cirò Marina
Pta. Alice
Ciró
Strongoli
Cariati
Cropalati
Longobucco
Acri
Cosenza
Rende
Montalto Uffugo
Paola
Amantea
Catanzaro
Catanzaro Lido
Golfo di Squillace
Soverato
Guardavalle
Pta. Stilo
Stilo
Caulónia
Roccella Iónica
Marina di Gioiosa Iónica
Siderno
Locri
Bovalino Marina
Bianco
Capo Spartivento
Golfo di S. Eufémia
Pizzo
Vibo Valéntia
Tropea
Capo Vaticano
Nicòtera
Golfo di Gióia
Gioia Tauro
Palmi
Bagnara Cálabra
Scilla
Villa S. Giovanni
REGGIO DI CALABRIA
MESSINA
Mélito di Porto Salvo
Bova Marina
Montebello Iónico

Nicastro
Lamezia Terme
Serra S. Bruno
Polistena
Cittanova
Taurianova
Gioiosa Iónica

149

96   127

Cagliari
Nápoli
Tunis
A
B
C
1
2
3
12°
13°
38°
37°
Capo S. Vito
S. Vito lo Capo
M. Spáragio 1110
Golfo di Castellammare
Terrasini
Ísola della Fémmine
Capo Gallo
Mondello
Capaci
Carini
PALERMO
Ficarazzi
Bagheria
Casteldáccia
Golfo di Términi Imerese
Trabía
Términi Imerese
Montelepre
Balestrate
Monreale
Altofonte
Partinico
Misilmeri
Bolognetta
Marineo
Trápani
Érice
Valdérice
Castellammare del Golfo
Lévanzo
Isole Égadi
Maréttimo
Favignana
Favignana
Paceco
Fulgatore
Rilievo
Álcamo
S. Cipirello
Piana degli Albanesi
Calatafimi
Camporeale
Villafrati
Cáccamo
Cerda
Ciminna
Stagnone
Vita
Salemi
Mezzoiuso
Rca. Busambra 1613
Montemaggiore Belsito
Vicari
Roccapalumba
Caltavu
Marsala
V A L D I M A Z A R A
Gibellina
Roccamena
Corleone
Plla. Imbriaca 718
Lercara Friddi
Ália
S. Ninfa
Salaparuta
Campofiorito
Plla. di Scavo 566
Strasatti
Partanna
S. Margherita di Belice
Bisacquino
Prizzi
Vallelunga Pratameno
Villalba
Trinità
Castelvetrano
Plla. Misilbesi 295
Chiusa Sclafani
Palazzo Adriano
S. Stéfano Quisquina
Mazara del Vallo
Campobello di Mazara
Menfi
Sambuca di Sicília
S. Carlo
Bivona
Cammarata
Alessándria della Rocca
M. Cammarata 1580
Granitola
Capo Granítola
Marinella
Caltabellotta
Búrgio
Casteltérmini
Mussomeli
Sciacca
Cianciana
Capo S. Marco
Ribera
Cattólica Eraclea
S. Biágio Plátani
Campofranco
Montedoro
Raffadali
Racalmuto
Aragona
Montallegro
Siculiana
Agrigento
Favara
Castrofilippo
Porto Empédocle
Plla. di Rocca Corvo 162
Palma di Montechiaro
M A R E M E D I T E R R A N E O
Pantelleria
Pantelleria
113
186
187
188
188A
188B
188C
115
115D
119
121
118
189
285
122
E1

4
5
6
15°
16°
B
C
37°
38°
Strómboli
Panarea
Salina
Filicudi
Alicudi
Isole Eolie o Lipari
Lípari
Lípari
Vulcano
Capo di Milazzo
Milazzo
Villafranca Tirrena
Spadafora
Spartà
MESSINA
Capo Calavà
Gioiosa Marea
Capo d'Orlando
Golfo di Patti
Barcellona Pozzo di Gotto
Brolo
Patti
Falcone
Naso
S Ágata di Militello
S. Piero Patti
Mazzarrà S. Andrea
Castroreale
S. Lucia del Mela
Monti Peloritani
Pzo. Poverello 1279
Novara di Sicilia
Plla Mandrazzi 1125
Mandanici
Scaletta Zanclea
Ali Terme
Roccalumera
S. Teresa di Riva
Taormina
Giardini
Castiglione di Sicilia
Francavilla di Sicilia
Antillo
Montalbano Elicona
Floresta
Ucría
Tortorici
Longi
S. Fratello
Val Démone
Monti Nebrodi
S. Doménica Vittória
Plla d. Zoppo 1264
Randazzo
Passopisciaro
Linguaglossa
Piedimonte Etneo
Máscali
Fiumefreddo di Sicília
Riposto
Giarre
Zafferana Etnea
M. Etna 3340
S. Stéfano di Camastra
Caronía
Tusa
Castelbuono
Mistretta
Pzo. Carbonara 1979
Geraci Siculo
Plla Femmina Morta 1254
M. Soro 1847
Capizzi
Cesarò
Maletto
Bronte
Troina
Cerami
L. di Ancipa
Plla Madonnuzza 1147
Colle di Contrasto 1120
Polizzi Generosa
Gangi
Petralia Sottana
Sperlinga
Nicosia
Gagliano Castelferrato
L. di Pozzillo
Salso
Alimena
Leonforte
Agira
Regalbuto
Adrano
Biancavilla
Nicolosi
Trecastagni
Acireale
Aci Catena
Aci Castello
Centúripe
Ássoro
S. Maria di Licodia
Paternò
Belpasso
Misterbianco
Motta S. Anastásia
CATÁNIA
Golfo di Catánia
Catenanuova
Plla di Recattivo 832
Villarosa
Calascibetta
Enna
Pergusa
ITALIA
Caltanissetta
Valguarnera Caropepe
Raddusa
Castel di Iúdica
Gerbini
Simeto
Piana di Catánia
Pietraperzia
Piazza Armerina
Plla Grottacalda 742
Monti Erei
Aidone
Ramacca
Gornalunga
Sommatino
Barrafranca
Mirabella Imbáccari
Palagonía
Riesi
Mazzarino
S. Michele di Ganzaria
Mineo
Militello in Val di Catánia
Scordia
Lentini
Carlentini
Villasmundo
Francofonte
Capo S. Croce
Augusta
Golfo di Augusta
Melilli
Ravanusa
Caltagirone
Grammichele
Vizzini
Buccheri
Sortino
Priolo Gargallo
Butera
Niscemi
Licodia Eubea
Monti Iblei
M. Lauro 986
Ferla
Anapo
Solarino
Floridia
Siracusa
Val di Noto
S. Pietro
Monterosso Almo
Chiaramonte Gulfi
Giarratana
Palazzolo Acréide
Canicattini Bagni
Capo Murro di Porco
Cassibile
Gela
Acate
Golfo di Gela
Vittória
Cómiso
Ragusa
Noto
Ávola
Módica
Tellaro
Golfo di Noto
Scoglitti
S. Croce Camerina
Irminio
Scicli
Íspica
Rosolini
Marina di Ragusa
Donnalucata
Sampieri
Pozzallo
Marzamemi
Pachino
Capo Pássero
Portopalo
Pizzo
Briático
Tropea
Vibo Valéntia
Capo Vaticano
M. Poro 710
Mileto
Ióppolo
Nicótera
Golfo di Gióia
Rosarno
Gióia Táuro
Polistena
Capo Barbi
Palmi
Seminara
Cittanova
Taurianova
Óppido Mamertina
Bagnara Cálabra
Torre di Faro
Scilla
Str. di Messina
S. Eufémia d'Aspromonte
Delianuova
Aspromonte
Platì
Villa S. Giovanni
Montalto 1956
Gambàrie
Laganadi
S. Luca
Cardeto
1408 Sella Entrata
Africo
RÉGGIO DI CALABRIA
Pta. di Péllaro
Montebello Iónico
Bagaladi
Staiti
Lazzàro
Bova
Bova Marina
Mélito di Porto Salvo
Capo
147
E1
E59
A3
A18
A20
113
114
115
116
117
117bis
120
121
122
122bis
124
183
184
185
188
190
191
192
194
284
288
417
514
106
111
112
113dir
111dir
261
97
58
221

Zadar
Ugljan
Preko
Bibinje
Sukošan
Benkovac
Pašman
Biograd
Pakoštane
Vransko jez.
Žut
Kornat
Murter
Pirovac
Tisno
Tribunj
Vodice
Šibenik
155
Kaprije
Kakan
Kurba
Žirje
Zlarin
Primošten
Rogoznica
Marina
D. Seget
Trogir
Kaštel Stari
Čiovo
SPLIT
Solin
Klis
Mali Drvenik
Veliki Drvenik
Splitski kanal
Šolta
Grohote
Milna
Supetar
Postira
Nerežišća
Selca
Sumartin
Bol
Brac
Hvarski kanal
Brački kanal
Hvar
Starigrad
Jelsa
Sućuraj
Šćedro
Vis
Komiža
Viski kanal
Svetac
Bisevo
Korculanski kanal
Vela Luka
Blato
Smokvica
Korčula
Lumbarda
Orebić
Trpanj
Lastrovski kanal
Sušac
Lastovo
Pescara
Omiš
Dugi Rat
Krilo
Gata
Brela
Baška Voda
Makarska
Tučepi
Podgora
130
Drvenik
Knin
Drniš
Siverić
Vrlika
Kijevo
Krka
Obrovac
Novigrad
Benkovac
Kistanje
Skradin
Sinj
Trilj
Dugopolje
Muć
Imotski
Livno
Kupres
Bugojno
Glamoč
Duvno
Posušje
Vrgorac
Velebit
Dinara
Cincar
Midena
115
JADRANSKO MO
Isole Trémiti
Rodi Garganico
Peschici
Vieste
Ischitella
Vico del Gargano
Carpino
Lesina
Poggio Imperiale
Sannicandro Garganico
Cagnano Varano
Apricena
145
A
B
C
D
2

Tetovo
Zenica
Novi Travnik
Lipnica 1458
Vareš
116
Očevlja
1087
Bratunac
Ljubovija
Vrhpolje
Kakanj
Zgošća
122
Olovo
Vlasenica
Drlače
Kruščica
Busovača
Srebrenica
Han Pijesak
Jadar
Rogačica
Kostojevići
Breza
Vranica
Fojnica
Gromiljck
Visoko
Ilijaš
Devetak 1417
Devetak
Skelani
Bajina Bašta
Dub
Gornji Vakuf
Kiseljak
Kobila Glava 625
Vogošća
Sokolac
Perućac
Zaglavak
Bitovnja
Kreševo
SARAJEVO
Romanija
Podromanija
Drina
Beli Rzav
Bioska
Titovo Užice
Makljen 1132
Ilidža
Pale
Kremna
Prozor
Hadžići
Hrasnica
Rogatica
Mokra Gora
Zlatibor
Tarčin
Lisin 1744
Prača
Višegrad
Cajetina
Jablaničko Jezero
Bradina
Sjenište 1913
Bjelašnica 2067
Jahorina
Osječani
Crni Rzav
Ustiprača
Goražde
Jablanica
Ostrožac
Konjic
Trnovo
Vranići
Lim
Rudo
Uvac
Prenj
Neretva
Treskavica
Ustikolina
Ustibar
Priboj
Banja
115
Kom 1779
Čajniče
Goleša
Negbina
Rutoši
V. Vlajno 1780
Glavatičevo
Kalinovik
Foča
Bistrica
Bistrica
Nova Varos
Obalj
Ćehotina
Lelija 2032
Šuplja stijena 1469
Gradac
Prijepolje
Potoci
Ulog
Crvanj
Lištica
Vrapčići
Brasina 1897
Pljevlja
Jabuka
Miloše Dol
Mostar
Mataruge
2238
Jadovnik
Ozren
Tara
Kifino Selo
Piva
Blagaj
1119
Nevesinje
Čitluk
Buna
Glibaći 1838
Kosanica
Brodarevo
Grubuški
Bjelašnica
Snijeznica 1262
Zovi Do
Kovren
Gacko
Avtovac
Žabljak
Čapljina
Rečice
Baba 1737
Golija
Pluzine
Pivski Monastir
1945
Pasina Voda
Sinjajevina
Tasovčići
Stolac
Bregava
Deransko Jezero
Potkrajci
Bijelo Polje
Gabela
Metković
Vidruša
Komarnica
2041
Mojkovac
953
Hutovo
Kobilja glava 1419
Ljubinje
Šavnik
Neum
Njegoš
1721
Crna glava 2137
Bileća
2253
Bjelasica
Ravno
Bjelašnica
Gornje Polje
Moračka Kapa 2227
Kolašin
Ston
Bilećko Jezero
Nikšić
Maganik
Trešnjevik 1598
Ljet
Trebišnjica
Andrijevica
Trebinje
Vilusi
Trsteno
152
Korita
Šipan
166
Lastva
Broćanac
Prekornica
Staza P. 490
Morača
Dubrovnik
Zeta
Gus
Snježnica 1234
Orjen 1895
Cavtat
Čilipi
Cevo
Danilov Grad
Spuž
Selcë
Gruda
Risan
Perast
Lepetani
Dobrota
Titograd
Herceg-novi
Tivat
Kotor
Cetinje
Bogë
Ndrejaj
Oštri rt
Rijeka Crnojev
Lovćen
Cijevna
Mahala
Golubovci
Bajzë
Budva
102
Koder Shengjergj
Sveti Stefan
Virpazar
SHQIPËRIJA
Petrovac
Koplik
Sutorman 844
Skadarsko Jezero
Ur'e Shtrenjt
Sutomore
Rumija
Kiri
Mes
Drin
Bar
Kostanica
Stari Bar
Shkodër
Pečurice
Krute
Sukobin
Muriqan
Bushat
Ulcinj
Dajç
Velipojë
Sveti Nikola
Drin
Kallme
Pellg i Drinit
Shëngjin
Lezhë
A
B
C
D
4
5
18°
19°
42°
43°
44°

Golesa
Rutoši
Bistrica
Nova Varoš
116
Lupoglav 1201
Vrmbaje
Studenica
Ušće
Rataje
Mrmoš
Alexandrovac
Šuplja stijena 1469
Gradac
Pljevlja
Jabuka
Prijepolje
Kladnica
Gledića
Baljevac
Jelakci
Jošanička Banja
Brus
Lepenac
Mataruge
Miloševo Dol
Gradac
2238
Jadovnik
Sjenica
Štavalj
1796
Raška
Brzeće
Glibaći 1838
Kosanica
1734
Trijebine
Duga Poljana
Kopaonik
Brodarevo
Ozren
Osaonica
Žabljak
Kovren
Giljevo
1499
1362
Novi Pazar
Lešak
Čardak 1590
Lukovo
Toplica
Kuršu
Pasina Voda
Sebecevo
Sočanica
Polatna
Sinjajevina
Potkrajci
Bijelo Polje
Vidrenjak
Jošanica
Komarnica
Šavnik
2041
Tutin
Ribariće
Ibar
Banje
Banjska
Mojkovac
Poda
Vuča
Trepča
Gornje Polje
2253
Crna glava 2137
Trpezi
Zubin Potok
Zvečan
Kosovska Mitrovica
Kačandolska
Moračka Kapa 2227
Kalače
Rožaj
Glavnik
Nikšic
Bjelasica
Ivangrad
Mokra gora
Kolašin
Vinicka
Rudnik
Vučitrn
Donje Ljupče
Trešnjevik 1598
Hajla 2400
Istok
Gornja Klina
Maganik
JUGOSLAVIJA
Andrijevica
Novo Selo
Srbica
Đurakovac
Prekornica
Kučište
Peć
Vitomirica
Obilić
Priština
Murino
Velika
Bistrica
Ljesane
Trstenik
Brezojevice
Marijaš 2530
Stari Raušić
Plav
Klina
Laplje Selo
Danilov Grad
Dečanska
Streoci
Iglarevo
Komoran
Spuž
Gusinje
Dečani
Orlate
Magura
Sitnica
Lipljan
Selcë
Prokletije
Junik
Miruša
Banja
Skivjani
Crnoljevo
B
151
Titograd
Jezerce 2694
Ratkovac
Orahovac
Blace
Štimlje
Cetinje
Bogë
Theth
Tropojë
Đakovica
Studenčane
Suva Reka
Rijeka Crnojev
Mahala
Cijevna
Bajram-Curr
Zrze
Uroševac
Golubovci
Bajzë
Velika Kruša
Nicaj-Shale
Kušnin
Zjum
Pirane
Mašutište
Stari Kačan
E27
Virpazar
Doganovic
Koplik
Prizren
Štrpce
Ljuboten 2499
Sutorman 844
Skadarsko Jezero
Beli Drim
Zur
Sredska
Stomore
Rumija
Ur'e Shtrenjtë
Vrbica
Vratnica
Kostanica
Mes
Bar
Stari Bar
Kiri
Drin
Shkodër
Shëmeri
Kukës
Šar planina
Dobroste Tearce
Dragaš
Pečurice
Sukobin
Murigan
Pukë
Fushë-Arrez
Tetovo
42°
Krute
Bushat
Korthpulë
Bicaj
Zelino
Grupčin
Vardar
Ulcinj
Dajç
Kashnjet
Kamenjane
Sveti Nikola
Velipojë
Kallmet
Blinisht
Suva Gora
Shëngjin
Fushë-Lurë
Vrapčište
Cegrane
Zdunje
Lezhë
Rëshen
Forino
Kodra Taurli 1853
Rubik
Kurbnesh
Vrutok
Gostivar
Pellg i Drinit
Mat
Suhodoll
Peshkopi
Žirovnica
Simnica
Mavrovi Hanovi
Milot
Laç
Murrë
Mavrovo
Rostuša
Bistra Pl.
Kep i Rodonit
Burrel
Lunar
Maqellarë
Zajas
Mamurras
Galicnik
Ishm
Debar
C
Gji i Lalzës
Krujë
Bulqizë
Kičevo
Klos
Čelopeci
Kep i Palit
Vorë
Peshk
Ostren i math
Shijak
TIRANË
Klenjë
Lukovo
Ilinska Pl.
Durrës
Vrrië
Jablanica
Labuništa
Belčište
Gji i Durrësit
Vaqarr
Ndroq
Petrelë
Zgozdh
Botun
Lešani
Vevčani
Veleštа
Mešeišta
Crni Drim
Kavajë
Mesqetë
Trebenište
Plaćenska Pl.
Murgasev
Librazhd
Struga
Labinot-Mal
Gracen
Kališta
Kosel
Ohrid
154
Kryevidh
Elbasan
Rrogozhinë
Radožda
Resen
Pegin

Niš
Prokuplje
Leskovac
Vlasotince
Surdulica
Vranje
Vranjska Banja
Bujanovac
Gnjilane
Preševo
Kumanovo
SKOPJE
Titov Veles
Štip
Kočani
Radoviš
Strumica
Kavadarci
Prilep
Gevgelija
Bela Palanka
Pirot
Dimitrovgrad
Dragoman
Slivnitsa
Kostinbrod
SOFIYA
Dimitrovo (Pernik)
Radomir
Kyustendil
Stanke Dimitrov
Blagoevgrad
Simitli
Razlog
Bansko
Sandanski
Petrich
Kulata
Sidhirókastron
Serrai
Dolni Lom
Mikhaylovgrad
Berkovitsa
Vratsa
Vŭrshets
Svoge
Kurilo
Samokov
Kriva Palanka
Kratovo
Delčevo
Berovo
Novo Selo
Dojransko Jezero
Demir Kapija
Babička gora
Kukavica
Vardenik
Osogovska planina
Plačkovica
Pirin Planina
Rila
Belasica Pl.
Kerkini Óros
Mavrovoúni
Kožuf
Selečka Planina
Babuna
Goljak
Svrljiške pl.
Stara planina
BULGARIJA
Petrokhanski prokhod
Klisurski prokhod
Morava
Vardar
Struma
Nišava
Vlasina
Vlasinsko Jezero
Yazovir Studena
Crna
Bregalnica
Kriva
Pčinja
E5N
E5S
E20
E27
117
156
160
3
4
5
A
B
C
22°
23°
43°
42°

JUGOSLAVIJA
SHQIPËRI
TIRANË
Durrës
Elbasan
Berat
Fier
Vlorë
Lushnje
Korçë
Pogradec
Gjirokastër
Kavajë
Krujë
Shijak
Stalin
Patos
Tepelenë
Përmet
Ohrid
Struga
Debar
Kičevo
Resen
Bitola
Prilep
Kavadarci
Ohridsko Jezero
Liqen i Ohrit
Prespansko Jezero
L. Megáli Préspa
L. Mikri Préspa
Flórina
Kastoriá
Ptolemaïs
Kozáni
Véroia
Édhessa
Náousa
Yiannitsá
Sérvia
Grevená
Vérmion Óros
Vérnon Óros
Voúrinos
Vória Píndos
Baba
Babuna
Selečka Planina
Jablanica
Mali i Tomorrit
Gramos
Nëmërçkë
Sazan
Kep i Gjuhëzës
Ancona
Brindisi
152
153
156

Lárisa
Tirnavos
Trikkala
Kardhitsa
Kalabáka
Métsovon
Ioánnina
Árta
Préveza
Párga
Igoumenitsa
Kérkira
KÉRKIRA
Paxoí
Andípaxoi
Levkás
LEVKÁS
Itháki
KEFALLINÍA
Sámi
Amfilokhía
Agrínion
Mesolóngion
Návpaktos
Pátrai
Aíyion
Amfissa
Karpenísion
Nótia Píndhos
Panaitolikón Óros
Vardhoúsia Óri
Óros Timfristós
Amvrakikós Kólpos
Patraïkós Kólpos
Ekhinádhes
Ákra Doukáton
Ákra Dhafnoúdhi
Ákra Asprókavos
Samothráki
Nótion Stenón Kérkiros
L. Trikhonís
Mégdhova
Akhelóos
Árakhthos
Pinios
E87
E19
E106
E88
E89
104
78
87
84
114
157
158
39°
20°
21°
22°
C
D
1
2
3
4

THESSALONIKI
Kavála
Xánthi
Dráma
Sérrai
Kilkís
Véroia
Kateríni
Édhessa
Náousa
Yiannitsá
Kozáni
Ptolemaïs
Elassón
Tírnavos
Nigríta
Langadhás
Stavroúpolis
Sidhirókastron
Gevgelija
Petrich
Khrisoúpolis
Elevtheroúpolis
Néa Moudhaniá
Polikastron
Thásos
THÁSOS
Thrakikón Pélagos
Strimonikós Kólpos (Kólpos Orfanoú)
Singitikós Kólpos (Kólpos Ayíou Órous)
Toronaíos Kólpos (Kólpos Kassándras)
Thermaïkós Kólpos
Kólpos Ierissoú
Kólpos Kavállas
Aktí (Áyion Óros)
Sithonía
Kassándra
Áthos 2033
Ákra Pínnes
Ákra Ámbelos
Ákra Kanastraíon
Ákra Posidhion
Ákra Epanomí
Ákra Salonikiós
Pangaíon Óros
Óros Vertískos
Menoíkon Óros
Falakrón
Óros Órvilos
Kerkíni Óros
Mavrovoúni
Paikon Óros
Vérmion Óros
Ólimbos 2917
Piéria Óri
Kamvoúnia Óri
Vóras Óros
L. Vólvi
L. Korónia
L. Doïránis
Dojransko Jezero
Néstos
Strimón
Axiós
Aliákmon
JUGOSLAVIJA
Kožuf
Belasica Pl.
Belasitsa Pl.
E55
E20
E90
E92
153
154
160
41°
40°
22°
23°
24°

C
D
Skíros
Ákra Lithári
Pipéri
Yioúra
Pélagos
Peristéra
Alónnisos
Skópelos
Skíathos
VORÍAI SPORÁDHES
Dhíavlos Alonnísou
Dhíavlos Skopélou
Dhíavlos Skiáthou
EVVOIA
Ákra Kimis
Ákra Sarakinikon
Dhírfis
Ákra Kafirévs
Kárìstos
Megálo Petali
ATHÍNAI
PIRAIEVS
Elevsís
Khalkís
Thívai
Levádhia
Amfissa
Lamía
Vólos
Lárisa
Fársala
Trikkala
Kardhítsa
Palamás
Almirós
Pagasitikós Kólpos
Dhíavlos Trikeri
Dhíavlos Oreon
Vórios Evvoïkós Kólpos
Nótios Evvoïkós Kólpos
Korinthiakós Kólpos
Pílion
Óros Óthris
Parnassós
Gióna
Vardhoúsia Óri
Óros Timfristós
Kallídhromon
Thermopílai
Ákra Pángalos
Yeránia Óri
Mégara
Pátrai
Návpaktos
Aiyion
Itéa
Dhelfoi
Thermopílai
Ákra Melangávi
Kiáton
Izmir
Istanbul

LEVKÁS
ITHÁKI
KEFALLINÍA
ZÁKINTHOS
Panaitolikón Óros
Vardhoúsia Óri
Gióna
Ekhinádhes
Patraïkós Kólpos
Dhiavlos Zakinthou
Erímanthos
Aroánia Óri
Maínalon Óros
PELOPONNISOS
Taíyetos Óros
Kiparissiakós Kólpos
Messiniakós Kólpos
Agrínion
Mesolóngion
Návpaktos
Pátrai
Aíyion
Amfissa
Argostólion
Lixoúrion
Sámi
Itháki
Zákinthos
Amaliás
Pírgos
Kiparissía
Filiatrá
Gargaliánoi
Messíni
Kalamáta
Megalópolis
Pílos (Navarino)
Methóni
Koróni
Sapiéntza
Skhíza
Ákra Doukáton
Ákra Dhafnoúdhi
Ákra Skinári
Ákra Killíni
Ákra Marathiás
Ákra Katákolon
Ákra Skrófa
Ákra Pápas
Ákra Moúnda
Ákra Akrítas
Ákra Kitriés
Ainos Óros
1628
1158
1924
2510
1545
1926
2224
2341
966
1421
1229
2407
E19
E89
E92
84
155
Brindisi
21°
22°
38°
37°
A
B
C
1
2

EVVOIA
157
Ákra Sarakinikon
Mandoúdhion
Rovia
Límni
Prokópion
1343
Dhírfis
1743
Ákra Kimis
Kími
Oxílithos
Psakhná
Steni Dhírfios
Kathenoi
Politiká
Néa Artáki
Monódhri
Oktoniá
Khália
Khalkis
Afráti
Vasilikón
Yimnón
Áyios Ioánnis
Alivérion
Néa Psará
Amárinthos
Vathí
Zárka
Vórios Evvoïkós Kólpos
Mólos
Kámmena Voúrla
Ákra Lithádha
Áyios Konstandínos
Arkitsa
Thermopilai
Ákra Kérata
Livanátais
Zélion
Atalándi
Malesína
Tragána
220
Lárimna
Martínon
Éxarkhos
Amfíklia
Elátia
Tithoréa
Parórí
2457
Dhávlia
Parnassós
Kharónia
Petromagoúla
Pávlon
Topólia
Akraifníon
Kókkinon
Arákhova
Áyios Vlásios
Kopaïs
Áyios Dhimítrios
Paralímni
Ilíki Límni
Levádhia
Dhístomon
Kiriáki
Áyios Yeóryios
Aliartos
1748
Palaiopanayiá
Váyia
Thívai
Thespiai
Dhrítsa
Tanágra
Skhimatárion
E92
Neokhórion
Áyios Thomás
Avlón
Khóstia
Lévktra
Domvraína
Kaparéli
Plataiaí
Erithraí
612
1409
Áyios Ioánnis
Ákra Pángalos
Korinthiakós Kólpos
Vília
Píli
1413
Dhekélia
Mándra
Fili
Skála Oropoú
Apóstoli
Kálamos
Nótios Evvoïkós Kólpos
Kapandhríti
Grammatikón
Marathón
Stíra
Ákra Kafirévs
Ekáli
Néa Mákri
Kifisiá
Akharnai
Aspropírgos
Amaroúsion
Elevsís
Áno Liósia
Khalandri
Rafína
Pallíni
Marmári
1390
Kárístos
Megálo Petalí
Kamári
Xilókastron
Melissi
Ákra Melangávi
Káto Dhimínion
Kiáton
Véllon
Perakhóra
Káto Alepokhóri
1351
Yeránia Óri
Loutráki
Mégara
Pérama
Paiania
Spáta
Loútsa
Sóuli
Ássos
Zevgolatión
E19
Kórinthos
Salamís
Ambeláki
Salamis
PIRAIÉVS
ATHÍNAI
Koropí
Stimánga
Examília
Áyios Theódhoroi
Saronikós Kólpos
Ákra Kókhi
Ellinikó
Glifádha
Voúla
Markópoulon
Kólpos Petalión
Izmir
Neméa
Athíkia
Khiliomódhion
Sofikón
Várkiza
Kalívia
Vouliagméni
Ayía Marína
Keratéa
Makronísi
Áyios Vasílios
Mesagrós
Aíyina
Angístrion
Pérdhika
Aíyina
Anávissos
Lávrion
Legrainá
Fikhtia
Prosimni
Límnes
Arakhnaíon Óros
Néa Epídhavros
Arakhnaíon
Koutsopódhi
Árgos
Áyios Adhrianós
1196
Ligoúrion
Palaia Epídhavros
Korisía
Kéa
Dhiékplous Kéas
Néa Kíos
Kefalári
Návplion
Dhrépanon
Adhámi
Méthana
Póros
Ákra Tamélos
Míloi
Tolón
E92
Akhókambos
Íria
Galatás
Ákra Skillaion
Áyios Yeóryios
Dhídhimoi
Kíthnos
Dhriopís
Argolikós Kólpos
Koilás
Ermióni
Kranídhion
Ástros
Parálion Astrous
Áyios Andréas
Áyios Ioánnis
1935
Porto-Khéli
Dhokós
Ídhra
Spétsai
KIKLÁDHES (CYCLADES)
Sérifos
Tirós
Leonídhion
Párnon Óros
Poulíthra
Ákra Tourkovíglia
Mirtóön Pélagos
Kós
Zoúpaina
Yeráki
Vrondamás
Áyios Dhimítrios
Parapóla
Skála
Vlakhióti
Andímilos
Kímolos
Moláoi
Katavóthra
Pákia
Sikéa
Elaia
Papadhiánika
Monemvasía
Mílos
Adhámas
751
Ákra Psális
Mílos
Dhaimoniá
Elika
Lakonikós Kólpos
Neápolis
Elafónisos
Lákhi
Stenón Elafonísou
Ákra Spathí
Ákra Maléa
Khaniá
Iráklion
23°
24°
38°
37°
4
5
A
B
C

Legend   Légende   Zeichenerklärung   Leggenda

Scale   Echelle   Maßstab   Scala   1:4 000 000

50   0   50   100   150 Kms

Motorways	Autoroutes		Autobahnen	Autostrade
Other important roads	Autres routes importantes		Sonstige wichtige Straßen	Altre strade importante
Other roads	Autres routes		Sonstige Straßen	Altre strade
European road numbers	Numéros des routes européenes	20	Nummern der Europastraßen	Numeri distintivi di strade europee
Other road numbers	Autres numéros des routes	94 170	Sonstige Straßennummern	Altri numeri di strade
Main through routes (Distances in kilometres)	Routes de grand Transit (Distances en kilometres)	52 79	Wichtige Durchgangsstraßen (Entfurnungen in kilometern)	Strade di grande comunicazione (Distanze in chilometri)

Abbreviazioni	Abbreviations		Abréviations	Abkürzungen
Austria	Austria	**A**	Autriche	Österreich
Albania	Albania	**AL**	Albanie	Albanien
Andorra	Andorra	**AND**	Andorre	Andorra
Belgio	Belgium	**B**	Belgique	Belgien
Bulgaria	Bulgaria	**BG**	Bulgarie	Bulgarien
Svizzera	Switzerland	**CH**	Suisse	Schweiz
Cecoslovacchia	Czechoslovakia	**CS**	Tchécoslovaquie	Tschechoslowakei
Germania-Occidente	West Germany	**D†**	Allemagne-Ouest	Bundesrepublik Deutschland
Germania-Oriente	East Germany	**D***	Allemagne-Est	Deutsche Demokratische Republik
Danimarca	Denmark	**DK**	Danemark	Dänemark
Spagna	Spain	**E**	Espagne	Spanien
Francia	France	**F**	France	Frankreich
Regno Unito	United Kingdom	**GB**	Royaume Uni	Großbritannien und Nordirland
Grecia	Greece	**GR**	Grèce	Griechenland
Ungheria	Hungary	**H**	Hongrie	Ungarn
Italia	Italy	**I**	Italie	Italien
Irlanda	Ireland	**IRL**	Irlande	Irland
Lussemburgo	Luxembourg	**L**	Luxembourg	Luxemburg
Norvegia	Norway	**N**	Norvège	Norwegen
Paesi Bassi	Netherlands	**NL**	Pays-Bas	Niederlande
Portogallo	Portugal	**P**	Portugal	Portugal
Polonia	Poland	**PL**	Polgne	Polen
Romania	Rumania	**R**	Roumanie	Rumänien
Svezia	Sweden	**S**	Suède	Schweden
Finlandia	Finland	**SF**	Finlande	Finnland
Unione Sovietica	Soviet Union	**SU**	Union Soviétique	Sowjetunion
Turchia	Turkey	**TR**	Turquie	Türkei
Jugoslavia	Yugoslavia	**YU**	Yougoslavie	Jugoslawien

128 Alcains B 3
132 Alcalá de Chivert A 3
135 Alcalá de Guadaira B 5
122 Alcalá de Gurrea B 2
126 Alcalá de Henares B 2
132 Alcalá de la Selva A 2
135 Alcalá de los Gazules C 5
132 Alcalá del Júcar B 1
135 Alcalá del Rio B 5
135 Alcalá del Valle C 5
136 Alcalá la Real B 3
148 Alcamo B 2
122 Alcampel C 3
121 Alcanadre B 4
132 Alcanar A 3
128 Alcanede B 2
122 Alcañiz C 2
119 Alcañizes C 4
129 Alcántara B 4
134 Alcantarilha B 2
133 Alcantarilla D 1
130 Alcaracejos C 2
134 Alcaria Ruiva B 3
122 Alcarraz C 3
136 Alcaucin C 2
136 Alcaudete B 2
130 Alcaudete de la Jara B 2
131 Alcázar de San Juan B 3
126 Alcazarén A 1
59 Alcester C 2
132 Alcira B 2
130 Alcoba B 2
128 Alcobaça B 1
126 Alcobendas B 2
127 Alcocer B 3
128 Alcochete C 2
128 Alcoentre B 2
127 Alcohujate B 3
137 Alcolea, Almeria, E C 4
136 Alcolea, Córdoba, E B 2
130 Alcolea de Calatra C 2
122 Alcolea de Cinca C 3
130 Alcolea de Tajo B 1
127 Alcolea del Pinar A 3
135 Alcolea del Rio B 5
129 Alcollarin B 5
59 Alconbury Hill C 3
129 Alconchel C 3
129 Alconera C 4
137 Alcóntar B 4
132 Alcora A 2
126 Alcorcón B 2
122 Alcorisa D 2
134 Alcoutim B 3
123 Alcover C 4
133 Alcoy C 2
120 Alcsútdoboz A 2
122 Alcubierre C 2
126 Alcubilla de Avellaneda A 2
119 Alcubilla de Nogales B 5
131 Alcubillas C 3
132 Alcublas B 2
139 Alcudia B 4
132 Alcudia de Carlet B 2
137 Alcudia de Guadix B 3
129 Alcuéscar B 4
132 Aldaya B 2
62 Aldbourne B 2
58 Aldbrough B 3
132 Aldea A 3
129 Aldea de Trujillo B 5
129 Aldea del Cano B 4
126 Aldea del Fresno B 1
124 Aldea del Obispo C 3
130 Aldea del Rey C 3
126 Aldea Real A 1
129 Aldeacentenera B 5
125 Aldeadávila de la Ribera B 3
126 Aldealcorvo A 2
126 Aldeamayor de S. Martin A 1
130 Aldeanueva de Barbarroya B 1
130 Aldeanueva de S. Bartolomé B 1
125 Aldeanueva del Camino C 4
126 Aldeanueva del Codonal A 1
121 Aldeapozo C 4
136 Aldeaquemada A 3
125 Aldearrubia B 4
125 Aldeaseca de la Frontera C 4
126 Aldeasoña A 1
125 Aldeatejada C 4
59 Aldeburgh C 5
132 Aldehuela A 1
127 Aldehuela de Calatañazor A 3
125 Aldehuela de Yeltes C 3
124 Aldeia do Bispo C 3
128 Aldeia do Mato B 2
128 Aldeia Gavinha B 1
134 Aldeia Nova B 3
137 Aldeire B 3
71 Aldekerk A 5
71 Aldenhoven B 5
62 Alderbury B 2
62 Aldermaston B 2
87 Aldersbach C 5
62 Aldershot B 3
153 Aldince C 3
59 Aldridge C 2
126 Alealuenga de Sta. María A 2
42 Åled C 2
133 Aledo D 1
121 Alegria B 4
128 Aleia da Serra C 3
102 Aleksa Šantic C 3
79 Aleksandrów D 2
78 Aleksandrów Kujawski C 1
117 Aleksinac C 5
43 Ålem C 6
19 Ålen C 7
82 Alençon C 2
128 Alenquer B 1
123 Alenya B 5
140 Aleria B 2
107 Alès,F C 4
141 Ales,I C 2
103 Aleşd A 6
110 Alessándria C 3
148 Alessándria della Roca B 3
146 Alessano C 4
40 Ålestrup C 3
18 Ålesund C 2
107 Alet-les-Bains E 2
156 Alexándria B 2
50 Alexandria, GB B 3
160 Alexandria, R C 4
160 Alexandroupolis E 4
117 Alexandrovac, Srbija, YU B 5
117 Alexandrovac, Srbija, YU C 5
109 Aleyrac C 1
146 Alézio B 4
136 Alfacar B 3
124 Alfaiates C 3
122 Alfajarin C 2
134 Alfambia B 2
132 Alfambra A 1
124 Alfândega da Fé B 3
124 Alfarela de Jales B 2
128 Alfarelos A 2
128 Alfarim C 1
136 Alfarnate C 2
121 Alfaro B 5
122 Alfarrás C 3
143 Alfedena C 5
128 Alfeizarão B 1
86 Alfeld, Bayern, D† B 3
72 Alfeld, Niedersachen, D† B 3
124 Alfena B 1
134 Alferca B 2
65 Alfhausen B 5
113 Alfonsine B 4
49 Alford, Aberdeen, GB D 6
58 Alford, Lincs., GB B 4
122 Alforja C 3
30 Alfoten B 2
59 Alfreton B 2
33 Alfta B 7
134 Alfundão A 2
139 Algaida B 3
135 Algar, Cadiz, E C 5
133 Algar, Murcia, E D 2
37 Ålgarås C 6
34 Ålgård C 1
136 Algarinejo B 2
136 Algarrobo C 2
135 Algatocin C 5
135 Algeciras C 5
132 Algemesi B 2
33 Ålgered A 7
128 Alges C 1
126 Algete B 2
141 Alghero B 2
43 Älghult B 5
132 Alginet B 2
135 Algodonales C 5
126 Algodor, E C 2
134 Algodor, P B 3
127 Algora B 3
121 Algorta A 4
134 Algoz B 2
84 Algrange A 3
21 Älgsjö A 6
122 Alguaire C 3
122 Alguaviva D 2
133 Alguazas C 1
99 Algund C 2
102 Algyo B 4
137 Alhama de Almeíra C 4
127 Alhama de Aragón A 4
136 Alhama de Granada C 3
133 Alhama de Murcia D 1
131 Alhambra C 3
136 Alhaurin de la Torre C 2
136 Alhaurin el Grande C 2
136 Alhendin B 3
126 Alhóndiga B 3
128 Alhos Vedros C 1
30 Ålhus B 3
149 Ali Terme B 5
130 Alía,E B 1
148 Ália,I B 3
127 Aliaga B 5
159 Alíartos A 4
117 Alibunar A 4
133 Alicante C 2
136 Alicún de Ortega B 3
144 Alife B 3
119 Alija del Infantado B 5
124 Alijó B 2
149 Alimena B 4
123 Aliña B 4
42 Alingsås B 2
103 Alios B 5
95 Alise-Ste. Reine B 4
129 Aliseda B 4
158 Alissós A 2
156 Alistráti A 3
159 Alivérion A 5
108 Alixan C 2
134 Aljaraque B 3
134 Aljezur B 2
133 Aljorra D 1
129 Aljucan B 4
134 Aljustrel B 2
70 Alken B 4
64 Alkmaar B 2
100 Alkoven A 2
72 Allagen B 2
82 Allaines C 3
81 Allaire C 4
106 Allanche B 2
101 Alland A 4
119 Allande A 4
118 Allariz B 3
104 Allasac B 4
109 Allauch D 2
106 Allegre B 3
14 Allejaur C 2
9 Alleknjarg B 8
109 Allemagne-en-Provence D 3
108 Allemont B 3
51 Allendale Town C 5
73 Allendorf C 2
88 Allentsteig C 3
55 Allenwood A 5
132 Allepuz A 2
86 Allersberg B 3
86 Allershausen C 3
108 Allevard B 3
108 Allex C 1
44 Allingåbro A 3
47 Allinge B 5
86 Allmendingen C 1
121 Allo B 4
50 Alloa A 4
94 Allogny B 2
14 Ålloluokta kapell A 3
56 Allonby B 3
82 Allones C 3
105 Allons C 2
109 Allos C 3
74 Allstedt B 3
142 Allumiere B 2
128 Almaceda B 3
122 Almacellas C 3
136 Almachar C 2
128 Almada C 1
130 Almadén C 2
135 Almadén de la Plata B 4
130 Almadenejos C 2
126 Almadrones B 3
130 Almagro C 3
121 Almajano C 4
133 Almansa C 1
134 Almansil B 2
120 Almanza B 1
129 Almaraz B 5
129 Almareleja C 3
128 Almargem C 1
136 Almargen C 1
121 Almarza C 4
103 Almaş B 6
91 Almásfüzito E 1
127 Almazán A 3
132 Almazora B 2
127 Almazúl A 3
72 Alme B 2
136 Almedinilla B 2
125 Almeida, E B 3
124 Almeida, P C 3
137 Almeíra C 4
128 Almeirim B 2
65 Almelo B 4
122 Almenar C 3
127 Almenar de Soria A 3
132 Almenara B 2
124 Almendra C 2
129 Almendral C 4
126 Almendral de la Cañada B 1
129 Almendralejo C 4
111 Almenno San Bart B 4
110 Almese B 2
134 Almexial B 3
42 Älmhult C 4
157 Almirós C 2
134 Almodôvar B 2
130 Almodóvar del Campo C 2
132 Almodóvar del Pinar B 1
136 Almodóvar del Rio B 1
124 Almofala C 2
136 Almogia C 2
129 Almoharin B 4
127 Almonacid de la Sierra A 4
126 Almonacid de Toledo C 2
135 Almonaster la Real B 4
61 Almondsbury B 4
135 Almonte B 4
133 Almoradi C 2
135 Almoraima C 5
126 Almorox B 1
103 Almosd A 5
128 Almoster B 2
13 Almsele C 9
38 Ålmsta C 5
137 Almudena A 5
122 Almudévar B 2
136 Almuñecar C 3
38 Almunge C 5
131 Almuradiel C 3
132 Almusafes B 2
49 Alness D 4
51 Alnmouth B 6
51 Alnwick B 6
154 Álonas B 3
156 Alónia B 2
157 Alónisos C 3
123 Alos de Isil B 4
134 Alosno B 3
136 Alozaina B 2
102 Alpár B 3
98 Alpbach B 2
126 Alpedrete B 2
71 Alpen A 5
133 Alpera C 1
64 Alphen C 2
64 Alphen a/d Rijn B 2
60 Alphington C 3
128 Alpiarca B 2
110 Alpignano B 2
85 Alpirsbach B 5
16 Alpua C 4
132 Alpuente B 1
128 Alqueva C 3
122 Alquézar B 3
57 Alsager C 4
121 Alsasua B 4
71 Alsdorf B 5
44 Alselv B 1
20 Alsen B 2
19 Alset B 6
73 Alsfeld C 3
38 Alsike C 4
74 Alsleben B 3
91 Alsódobsza D 4
102 Alsógöd A 3
102 Alsónémedi A 3
91 Alsóvadász D 3
91 Alsózsolca D 3
4 Ålstad C 4
19 Alstadhaug B 7
12 Alstahaug B 4
65 Alstätte B 4
43 Alsterbro C 5
56 Alston B 4
4 Alsvåg B 4
5 Alsvik C 3
8 Alta C 3
145 Altamura C 5
127 Altarejos C 3
98 Altaussee B 4
144 Altavilla Irpina B 3
145 Altavilla Silentina C 4
75 Altdöbern B 6
97 Altdorf, CH B 4
87 Altdorf, Bayern, D† C 4
86 Altdorf, Bayern, D† B 3
97 Altdorf, Bayern, D† A 6
134 Alte B 2
133 Altea C 2
112 Altedo B 3
87 Alteglofsheim C 4
71 Altena A 6
72 Altenau B 4
75 Altenberg C 5
65 Altenberge B 5
71 Altenbogge-Bönen A 6
66 Altenbruch B 1
87 Altenbuch C 4
75 Altenburg C 4
66 Altenesch B 1
100 Altenfelden A 1
73 Altengronau C 3
73 Altenhaßlau C 3
85 Altenheim B 4
72 Altenhundem B 2
71 Altenkirchen, D† B 6
67 Altenkirchen, D* A 6
66 Altenkrempe A 3
86 Altenkunstadt A 3
100 Altenmark B 2
98 Altenmarkt,A B 4
87 Altenmarkt,D† C 4
65 Altenoythe A 5
87 Altenstadt B 4
85 Altensteig B 5
67 Altentreptow B 6
66 Altenwalde B 1
74 Altenweddingen A 3
128 Alter do Chao B 3
65 Alterlünne B 5
87 Altfraunhofen C 4
98 Altheim, A A 4
86 Altheim, Baden-Württemberg, D† C 2
73 Altheim, Baden-Württemberg, D† D 3
100 Althofen C 2
85 Altkirch C 4
67 Altlandsberg C 6
100 Altlengbach A 3
76 Altlewin A 3
89 Altlich-tenwarth C 4
86 Altmannstein C 3
72 Altmorschen B 3
98 Altmünster B 4
48 Altnaharra C 4
120 Alto Campoó A 2
148 Altofonte A 3
146 Altomonte C 2
62 Alton B 2
112 Altopáscio C 2
87 Altötting C 4
87 Altreichenau C 5
67 Altruppin C 5
86 Altshausen D 1
97 Altstätten A 5
132 Altura B 2
97 Altusried A 6
38 Alunda B 5
127 Alustante B 4
50 Alva A 4
128 Alvaiázere B 2
23 Alvajärvi B 7
134 Alvalade B 2
42 Älvängen B 2
124 Alvarenga C 1
128 Alvares A 2
31 Alvdal A 7
32 Älvdalen B 5
59 Alvechurch C 2
128 Alverca C 1
30 Alversund C 2
43 Alvesta C 4
61 Alveston B 4
106 Alvignac C 1
144 Alvignano B 3
33 Alvik, Kopparbergs Län, S C 5
14 Alvik, Norrbottens Län, S C 5
21 Alvik, Västernorrlands Län, S C 6
82 Alvimare B 2
128 Alviobeira B 2
128 Alvito C 2
38 Älvkarleby B 4
38 Älvkarleö bruk B 4
134 Alvor B 2

156 Aréthousa B 3
105 Arette D 2
125 Arevalillo C 4
126 Arévalo A 1
112 Arezzo C 3
158 Arfará B 3
94 Arfeuilles C 3
157 Argalastí C 3
135 Argallón A 5
131 Argamasilla de Alba B 3
130 Argamasilla de Calatrava C 2
126 Arganda B 2
128 Arganil A 2
110 Argegno B 4
123 Argelès B 6
105 Argelès-Gazost D 2
94 Argent-sur-Sauldre B 2
112 Argenta B 3
82 Argentan C 1
106 Argentat B 1
110 Argentera C 1
83 Argenteuil C 4
71 Argenthal C 6
141 Argentiera B 2
92 Argenton-Château C 3
93 Argenton-sur-Creuse C 5
123 Argentona C 5
81 Argentré B 6
81 Argentré-du-Plessis B 5
159 Árgos B 3
154 Árgos Orestikón B 3
158 Argostólion A 1
121 Arguedas B 5
82 Argueil B 3
38 Arholma C 6
44 Århus A 3
145 Ariano Irpino B 4
113 Ariano nel Polésine B 4
108 Ariebosc B 1
142 Ariena di Castro B 2
144 Arienzo B 3
48 Arileod E 2
116 Arilje C 4
48 Arinagour E 2
95 Arinthod C 5
48 Arisaig E 3
126 Arisgotas C 2
158 Aristoménis B 2
141 Aritzo C 3
121 Arive B 5
127 Ariza A 3
36 Arjäng B 4
14 Arjeplog B 1
136 Arjona B 2
136 Arjonilla B 2
91 Arka D 4
47 Arkelstorp A 5
156 Arkhángelos A 2
159 Arkhnaion B 3
155 Arkhondokhóri D 3
157 Arkítsa D 3
55 Arklow B 5
39 Arkösund D 3
39 Ärla C 3
106 Arlanc B 3
120 Arlanzón B 3
123 Arles, Aude, F B 5
109 Arles, Bouches-du-Rhône, F D 1
55 Arless B 4
91 Arló D 3
71 Arlon C 4
110 Arma di Tággia D 2
50 Armadale B 4
48 Armadale Castle D 3
53 Armagh B 5
124 Armamar B 2
117 Armeniş A 6
110 Armeno B 3
154 Armenokhóri B 3
125 Armenteros C 4
63 Armentières B 4
154 Armídaion B 3
136 Armilla B 3
121 Armiñón B 4
53 Armoy A 5
126 Armuña de Tajuña B 2
119 Armunia B 5
30 Arna C 2
104 Arnac-Pompadour B 4
30 Arnafjord B 3
82 Arnage D 2
156 Arnaía B 3
108 Arnas, F A 1
37 Årnäs, S C 5
21 Arnäsvall B 7
95 Arnay-le-Duc B 4
44 Arnborg A 2
87 Arnbruck B 4
32 Arneberg C 3
67 Arneburg C 4
121 Arnedillo B 4
121 Arnedo B 4
64 Arnemuiden C 1
122 Arnés, E D 3
36 Årnes, N A 3
64 Arnhem B 3
156 Árnissa B 1
59 Arnold B 2
99 Arnoldstein C 4
71 Arnsberg A 7
87 Arnschwang B 4
75 Arnsdorf B 5
56 Arnside B 4
74 Arnstadt C 2
73 Arnstein D 3
87 Arnstorf C 4
44 Arnum B 1
135 Aroche B 4
91 Árokto E 3
96 Arolla B 3
72 Arolsen B 3
110 Arona B 3
35 Åros B 6
97 Arosa, CH B 5
124 Arosa, P B 1
44 Arøsund B 2
124 Arouca C 1
35 Åroysund B 6
83 Arpajon C 4
16 Arpela A 3
143 Arpino C 4
145 Arpinova B 4
143 Arquata del Tronto B 4
63 Arques B 4
82 Arques-la-Bataille B 3
136 Arquillos A 3
124 Arrabaes B 2
118 Arrabal, Pontevedra, E B 2
126 Arrabal, Valladolid, E A 1
128 Arraiolos C 2
63 Arras B 4
105 Arreau E 3
120 Arredondo A 3
105 Arrens E 2
135 Arriate C 5
121 Arrigorriaga A 4
120 Arriondas A 1
130 Arroba B 2
50 Arrochar A 3
81 Arromanches A 6
129 Arronches B 3
121 Arroniz B 4
120 Arroyo B 2
126 Arroyo de Cuéllar A 1
129 Arroyo de la Luz B 4
136 Arroyo de la Miel C 2
129 Arroyo de San Servan C 4
137 Arroyo del Ojanco A 4
129 Arroyomolinos B 4
135 Arroyomolinos de León A 4
125 Arroyomuert C 3
128 Arruda dos Vinhos C 1
40 Års C 3
92 Ars-en-Ré C 2
84 Ars-sur-Moselle A 3
12 Årsandøy B 4
47 Arsdale B 6
99 Arsiè D 2
99 Arsiero D 2
44 Årslev B 3
143 Arsoli B 4
38 Årsunda B 3
139 Artá, E B 4
155 Árta, GR C 2
121 Artajona B 5
99 Artegna C 4
108 Artemare B 2
158 Artemisia B 3
99 Arten C 2
143 Artena C 3
82 Artenay C 3
74 Artern B 3
123 Artés C 4
123 Artesa de Segro C 4
155 Artesianón C 3
97 Arth A 4
105 Arthez D 2
92 Arthon B 2
55 Arthurstown B 5
123 Artigas B 5
105 Artiz D 2
28 Artjärvi C 4
66 Artlenburg B 3
157 Artotína D 2
105 Arudy D 2
62 Arundel C 3
44 Årup B 3
33 Arvet B 6
104 Arveyres C 2
14 Arvidsjaur C 3
108 Arvieux C 3
30 Arvik A 2
36 Arvika B 4
6 Årviksand A 6
43 Åryd C 5
155 Aryiradhes C 1
156 Aryiropoúlion C 2
141 Arzachena A 3
105 Arzacq D 2
80 Arzano, F C 3
150 Aržano, YU B 2
87 Arzberg A 4
99 Arzignano D 2
128 Arzila A 2
98 Arzl im Pitztal B 1
118 Arzúa B 2
74 Aš, CS C 4
35 Ås, N B 6
20 Ås, S B 3
40 Aså B 4
116 Ašanja B 4
20 Åsarna C 3
42 Åsarp A 3
43 Asarum C 4
105 Asasp D 2
39 Åsbro C 2
43 Asby B 5
105 Ascain D 1
145 Ascea C 4
87 Ascha B 4
100 Aschach a. d. Donau A 2
73 Aschaffenburg D 3
73 Aschbach D 4
100 Aschbach Markt A 2
65 Ascheberg, Nordrhein Westfalen, D† C 5
66 Ascheberg, Schleswig-Holstein, D† A 3
65 Aschendorf A 5
74 Aschersleben B 3
87 Aschheim C 3
112 Asciano C 3
122 Asco C 3
143 Áscoli Piceno B 4
145 Áscoli Satriano B 4
97 Ascona B 4
62 Ascot B 3
83 Ascoux C 4
43 Åseda B 5
21 Åsele A 6
19 Åsen, N B 7
32 Åsen, S B 4
66 Asendorf C 2
160 Asenovgrad D 4
34 Åseral C 3
83 Asfeld la Ville B 6
35 Åsgårdstrand B 6
62 Ash, Kent, GB B 5
62 Ash, Surrey, GB B 3
38 Åshammar B 3
59 Ashbourne, GB B 2
55 Ashbourne, IRL A 5
60 Ashburton C 3
62 Ashbury B 2
59 Ashby de la Zouch C 2
32 Asheim B 2
62 Ashford B 4
51 Ashington B 6
51 Ashkirk B 5
56 Ashton in Makerfield C 4
56 Ashton under Lyne C 4
99 Asiago D 2
28 Asikkala B 3
11 Aska B 6
26 Askainen C 4
54 Askeaton B 3
39 Askeby D 2
35 Asker B 6
39 Askersund D 1
36 Askim, N B 3
42 Askim, S B 1
28 Askola C 3
39 Äsköping C 3
156 Askós B 3
44 Askov B 2
30 Askvoll B 2
46 Åslunga A 4
31 Asmark B 7
45 Asnæs B 4
111 Asola B 5
99 Asolo D 2
102 Asotthalom B 3
98 Aspach A 4
101 Aspang B 4
125 Aspariegos B 4
101 Asparn a. d. Zaya A 4
20 Aspås B 3
56 Aspatria B 3
133 Aspe C 2
47 Asperöd B 4
44 Asperup B 2
105 Aspet D 3
155 Asprángeloi C 2
155 Asprokklisia C 3
159 Asprópirgos A 4
156 Áspros B 2
156 Asproválta B 3
42 Assa B 2
105 Assat D 2
70 Asse B 3
8 Assebakte C 5
128 Asseiceira B 2
66 Assel B 2
71 Asselborn B 4
141 Assémini C 2
65 Assen A 4
64 Assendelft B 2
70 Assenede A 2
70 Assenois C 4
44 Assens, Fyn, DK B 2
40 Assens, Randers Amt, DK C 4
70 Assent B 4
70 Assesse B 4
156 Ássiros B 3
143 Assisi A 3
18 Åsskard B 4
87 Aßling D 3
110 Asso B 4
149 Ássoro B 4
159 Ássos B 3
128 Assumar B 3
32 Åsta B 2
105 Astaffort C 3
155 Astakós D 3
71 Asten A 4
110 Asti C 3
119 Astorga B 4
46 Åstorp A 3
15 Asträsk D 3
159 Ástros B 3
120 Astudillo B 2
23 Asunta C 6
101 Asvanyráró B 5
156 Asvestokhórion B 3
154 Asvestópetra B 3
101 Aszár B 5
102 Aszód A 3
101 Aszófö C 5
128 Atalaia B 3
157 Atalándi D 3
128 Atalho C 2
102 Átány A 4
126 Atanzón B 2
126 Ataquines A 1
136 Atarfe B 3
121 Ataun A 4
127 Ateca A 4
145 Atella C 4
143 Atessa B 5
70 Ath B 2
55 Athboy A 5
54 Athenry A 3
59 Atherstone C 2
83 Athies B 4
83 Athies-sous-Laon B 5
159 Athikia B 3
159 Athínai B 4
156 Athiras B 2
83 Athis B 6
156 Áthitos B 3
54 Athleague A 3
55 Athlone A 4
71 Athus C 4
55 Athy B 5
126 Atienza A 3
143 Atina C 4
91 Atkar E 2
32 Atna B 1
35 Atra B 4
42 Ätran B 2
143 Atri B 4
144 Atripalda C 3
71 Attendorn A 6
83 Attichy B 5
142 Attigliano B 3
95 Attignat C 5
84 Attigny A 1
59 Attleborough C 5
21 Attmar C 6
98 Attnang-Puchheim A 4
43 Atvidaberg A 5
74 Atzendorf B 3
97 Au, A A 5
87 Au, D† C 3
98 Au, D* B 2
73 Aub D 4
109 Aubagne D 2
71 Aubange C 4
71 Aubel B 4
106 Aubenas C 4
83 Aubenton B 6
95 Auberive B 5
104 Aubeterre-sur-Dronne B 3
105 Aubiet D 3
109 Aubignan C 2
104 Aubigné A 2
63 Aubigny, Pas de Calais, F B 4
92 Aubigny, Vendée, F C 2
70 Aubigny-au-Bac B 2
94 Aubiguy-sur-Nère B 2
106 Aubin C 2
96 Aubonne B 2
106 Aubusson B 2
105 Auch D 3
50 Auchencairn C 4
50 Auchenmalg C 3
50 Auchentiber B 3
50 Auchinleck B 3
48 Auchness D 4
50 Auchterarder A 4
51 Auchterderran A 4
51 Auchtermuchty A 4
48 Auchtertyre D 3
104 Audenge C 1
70 Auderghem B 3
81 Auderville A 5
80 Audierne B 2
84 Audincourt C 3
57 Audlem D 4
63 Audruicq B 4
84 Audun-le-Roman A 2
84 Audun-le-Tiche A 2
72 Aue, D† B 2
75 Aue, D* C 4
99 Auer C 2
86 Auerbach, D† B 3
75 Auerbach, D* C 4
101 Auersthal A 4
98 Auffach B 3
53 Augher B 4
53 Aughnacloy B 5
54 Aughrim, Galway, IRL A 3
55 Aughrim, Wicklow, IRL B 5
56 Aughton C 4
104 Augignac B 3
86 Augsburg C 2
149 Augusta B 5
44 Augustenborg C 2
65 Augustfehn I. A 5
18 Aukra C 2
14 Auktsjaur C 3
49 Auldearn D 5
86 Aulendorf D 1
145 Auletta C 4
112 Aulla B 1
140 Aullène C 2
104 Aulnay, Charente-Maritime, F A 2
83 Aulnay, Val d'Oise, F C 4
70 Aulnoye B 2
82 Ault A 3
105 Aulus-les-Bains E 4
74 Auma C 3
82 Aumale B 3
84 Aumetz A 2
106 Aumont-Aubrac C 3
94 Aunay-en-Bazois B 3
81 Aunay-sur-Odon A 6
82 Auneau C 3
83 Auneuil B 4
44 Auning A 3
109 Aups D 3
73 Aura, D† C 3
27 Aura, SF C 5
80 Auray C 4
31 Aurdal C 6
18 Aure, More og Romsdal, N B 4
18 Aure, More og Romsdal, N C 2
105 Aureilhan D 3
27 Aurekoski B 6
109 Aurel C 2
65 Aurich A 5
105 Aurignac D 3
106 Aurillac C 2
109 Auriol D 2
30 Aurlandsvangen C 4
98 Aurolzmünster A 4
99 Auronzo C 3
105 Auros C 2
106 Auroux C 3
36 Aurskog B 3
121 Ausejo B 4
143 Ausónia C 4

98 Außervillgraton C 3
34 Austad C 3
35 Austbygda A 4
30 Austefjord A 3
34 Austevoll A 1
141 Aústis B 3
36 Austmarka A 4
35 Austra Moland C 4
19 Austråt B 5
34 Austre Vikebygd B 1
30 Austrheim C 1
18 Austries C 2
105 Auterive D 4
82 Autheuil B 3
109 Authon C 3
82 Authon-du-Perche C 2
121 Autol B 4
84 Autreville B 2
95 Autrey-lès-Gray B 5
17 Autti A 6
27 Auttoinen B 8
95 Autun C 4
94 Auty-le-Châtel B 2
70 Auvelais B 3
105 Auvillar C 3
94 Auxerre B 3
63 Auxi-le-Château B 4
83 Auxon C 5
95 Auxonne B 5
95 Auxy C 4
106 Auzances A 2
106 Auzat B 3
106 Auzon B 3
14 Avaheden C 5
93 Availles-Limouzine C 4
94 Avallon B 3
14 Avaviken C 2
62 Avebury B 2
128 Aveiras de Cima B 2
124 Aveiro C 1
108 Aveize B 1
70 Avelgem B 2
144 Avellino C 3
83 Avenay B 6
96 Avenches B 3
65 Avenwedde C 6
144 Aversa C 3
83 Avesnes A 5
63 Avesnes-le-Comte B 4
38 Avesta B 3
146 Avetrana B 3
143 Avezzano B 4
99 Aviano C 3
49 Aviemore D 5
110 Avigliana B 2
145 Avigliano C 4
109 Avignon D 1
126 Ávila B 1
119 Avilés A 5
124 Avintes B 1
123 Avinyó C 4
99 Àvio D 1
83 Avize C 6
155 Avliótes C 1
159 Avlón A 4
44 Avlum A 1
55 Avoca B 5
149 Ávola C 5
94 Avord B 2
81 Avranches B 5
84 Avril A 2
81 Avrille C 6
151 Avtovac B 4
70 Awans B 4
98 Axams B 2
107 Axat E 2
61 Axbridge B 4
70 Axel A 2
156 Axíoupolis B 2
33 Axmarby C 8
33 Axmarsbruk B 8
61 Axminster C 4
42 Axvall A 3
83 Ay B 6
121 Aya A 4
134 Ayamonte B 3
133 Ayelo de Malferit C 2
96 Ayer B 3
122 Ayerbe B 2
63 Ayette B 4
156 Ayiá, Lárisa, GR C 2
155 Ayiá, Thesprotía, GR C 2
159 Ayia Anávissos B 4
157 Ayiá Anna D 3
157 Ayia Evthímía D 2
155 Ayia Triás D 3
155 Ayiófillos C 3
157 Áyioi Anáryiroi C 2
156 Áyios Dhimítrios, Kozani, GR B 1
156 Áyios Athanásios, Thessaloníki, GR B 2
159 Áyios Adhrianós B 3
159 Áyios Andréas B 3
154 Áyios Athanásios, Pella, GR B 3
159 Áyios Dhimitrios, Lakonia, GR C 3
159 Áyios Dhimitrios, Voiotía, GR A 3
156 Áyios Dhimítros B 2
159 Áyios Ioánnis, Ardkadía, GR B 3
159 Áyios Ioánnis, Evvoia, GR A 4
158 Áyios Ioánnis, Lakonia, GR B 3
159 Áyios Ioánnis, Voíotía, GR A 3
157 Áyios Konstandínos D 2
156 Áyios Mamas B 3
155 Áyios Matthaíos C 1
159 Áyios Nikólaos, Arkadhí, GR B 3
156 Áyios Nikólaos, Khalkidhikí, GR B 3
155 Áyios Nikólaos, Thesprotia, GR C 2
154 Áyios Pandeleïmon B 3
159 Áyios Pétros, Arkadhí, GR B 3
156 Áyios Pétros, Kilkís, GR B 2
155 Áyios Pétros, Levkás, GR D 2
156 Áyios Pródhromos B 3
159 Áyios Theódhoroi B 4
157 Áyios Theódhoros C 2
159 Áyios Thomás A 4
159 Áyios Vasilios B 3
157 Áyios Vlásios D 2
157 Áyios Yeóryios, Fthiotis, GR D 1
155 Áyios Yeóryios, Kardhitsa, GR C 3
155 Áyios Yeóryios, Préveza, GR C 2
159 Áyios Yeóryios, Voiotía, GR A 3
154 Áyios Yermanós B 3
62 Aylesbury B 3
62 Aylesham B 5
126 Ayllón A 2
157 Aylokambos D 3
59 Aylsham C 5
131 Ayna C 4
133 Ayora B 1
155 Áyos Nikólaos D 3
50 Ayr B 3
58 Aysgarth A 1
51 Ayton B 5
122 Aytona C 3
104 Aytré A 1
71 Aywaille B 4
121 Azagra B 5
122 Azaila C 2
128 Azambuja B 2
128 Azambujeira B 2
117 Azanja B 4
84 Azannes A 2
122 Azanuy C 3
93 Azay-le-Ferron C 5
93 Azay-le-Rideau B 4
121 Azcoitia B 4
95 Azé C 4
128 Azenha de Cima B 3
128 Azinhaga B 2
134 Azinhal B 3
134 Azinheira dos Bairros A 2
135 Aznalcázar B 4
135 Aznalcóllar B 4
128 Azóia B 2
121 Azpeitia A 4
129 Azuaga C 5
127 Azuara A 5
126 Azuqueca de Henares B 2
105 Azur D 1

B

97 Baad A 6
118 Baamonde A 3
97 Baar A 4
64 Baarn B 3
160 Babadag C 6
67 Babekuhl B 4
86 Babenhausen, Baden-Württemberg, D† C 2
73 Babenhausen, Hessen, D† D 2
90 Babice B 2
78 Babieta B 4
68 Babigoszcz B 2
77 Babimost A 4
116 Babina Greda A 2
115 Babócsa A 5
101 Bábolna B 5
89 Baborów A 5
101 Babot B 5
79 Babsk D 3
153 Babušnica A 4
116 Bač A 3
137 Bacares B 4
160 Bacău B 5
84 Baccarat B 3
48 Back C 2
33 Backa C 6
116 Bačka-Palanka A 3
102 Bačka Topola C 3
49 Backaland B 6
43 Backaryd C 5
21 Backe B 5
43 Bäckebo C 6
36 Bäckefors C 4
38 Bäckehagen B 2
37 Bäckhammar B 6
102 Backi Breg C 2
102 Bački Brestovac C 3
102 Bački Monoštor C 2
116 Backi Petrovac A 3
102 Bački Sokolac C 3
86 Backnang C 1
102 Bačko-Gradište C 4
116 Bačko Novo Selo A 3
102 Bačko Petrovo-Selo C 4
144 Bácoli C 3
82 Bacqueville B 3
102 Bácsalmás B 3
102 Bácsbokod B 3
59 Bacton C 5
91 Bacúch D 2
56 Bacup C 4
87 Bad Abbach C 4
98 Bad Aibling B 3
98 Bad Aussee B 4
85 Bad Bergzabern A 4
74 Bad Berka C 3
86 Bad Berneck A 3
74 Bad Bibra B 3
74 Bad Blakenburg C 3
66 Bad Bramstedt B 2
67 Bad Doberan A 4
72 Bad Driburg B 3
75 Bad Düben B 4
85 Bad Dürkheim A 5
74 Bad Dürrenberg B 4
85 Bad Dürrheim B 5
74 Bad Elster C 4
71 Bad Ems B 6
65 Bad Essen B 6
74 Bad Frankenhausen B 3
68 Bad Freienwalde C 2
85 Bad Friedrichshall A 6
72 Bad Gandersheim B 4
100 Bad Gleichenberg C 3
71 Bad Godesberg B 6
98 Bad Goisern B 4
75 Bad Gottleuba C 5
72 Bad Grund B 4
100 Bad Hall A 2
72 Bad Harzburg B 4
73 Bad Hersfeld C 3
98 Bad Hofgastein B 4
73 Bad Homburg C 2
71 Bad Honnef B 6
71 Bad Hönningen B 6
97 Bad Inner-Laterns A 5
98 Bad Ischl B 4
96 Bad Kemmeriboden B 3
73 Bad Kissingen C 4
98 Bad Kohlgrub B 2
73 Bad König D 3
74 Bad Kösen B 3
74 Bad Köstritz C 4
71 Bad Kreuznach C 6
85 Bad Krozingen C 4
74 Bad Langensalza B 2
74 Bad Lauchstädt B 3
75 Bad Lausick B 4
72 Bad Lauterberg B 4
75 Bad Liebenwerda B 5
85 Bad Liebenzell B 5
72 Bad Lippspringe B 3
72 Bad Meinberg B 2
73 Bad Mergentheim D 3
72 Bad Münder A 3
75 Bad Muskau B 6
73 Bad Nauheim C 2
72 Bad Nenndorf A 3
71 Bad Neuenahr B 6
73 Bad Neustadt C 4
71 Bad Niederbreisig B 6
65 Bad Oeynhausen B 6
66 Bad Oldesloe B 3
73 Bad Orb C 3
85 Bad Peterstal B 5
72 Bad Pyrmont B 3
97 Bad Ragaz B 5
85 Bad Rappenau A 6
98 Bad Reichenhall B 3
76 Bad Saarow-Pieskow A 3
72 Bad Sachsa B 4
72 Bad Salzdetfurth A 4
71 Bad Salzig B 6
73 Bad Salzschlirf C 3
72 Bad Salzuflen A 2
74 Bad Salzungen C 2
72 Bad Sassendorf B 2
75 Bad Schandau C 6
75 Bad Schmiedeberg B 4
73 Bad Schwalbach C 2
66 Bad Schwartau B 3
66 Bad Segeberg B 3
73 Bad Soden C 2
72 Bad Sooden-Allendorf B 3
100 Bad St. Leonhard C 2
74 Bad Steben C 3
74 Bad Sulza B 3
67 Bad Sülze A 5
74 Bad Tennstedt B 2
98 Bad Tölz B 2
73 Bad Vilbel C 2
101 Bad Vöslau B 4
86 Bad Waldsee D 1
98 Bad Wiessee B 2
72 Bad Wildungen B 3
67 Bad Wilsnack C 4
85 Bad Wimpfen A 6
86 Bad Windsheim B 2
86 Bad Wörishofen C 2
86 Bad Wurzach D 1
65 Bad Zwischenahn A 6
101 Badacsonytomaj C 5
129 Badajoz C 4
123 Badalona C 5
110 Badalucco D 2
49 Badanloch C 4
6 Badderen B 8
101 Baden, A A 4
96 Baden, CH A 4
66 Baden, D† C 2
85 Baden Baden B 5
127 Bádenas A 4
72 Badenhausen B 4
85 Badenweiler C 4
74 Badersleben B 2
98 Badgastein B 4
64 Badhoevedorp B 2
99 Badia C 2
99 Badia Calavena D 2
112 Badia Polésine A 3
112 Badia Prátaglia C 3
113 Badia Tedalda C 4
78 Badki B 1
115 Badljevina B 5
147 Badolato D 2
136 Badolatosa B 2
84 Badonviller B 3
116 Badovinci B 3
127 Badules A 4
8 Bæivašgiedde C 4
44 Bække B 2
44 Bækmarksbro A 1
122 Baells C 3
40 Bælum C 4
136 Baena B 2
71 Baesweiler B 5
136 Baeza B 3
65 Baflo A 4
123 Baga B 4
147 Bagaladi D 1
103 Bagamer A 5
44 Bagenkop C 3
39 Baggetorp C 3
148 Bagheria A 3
31 Bagn C 6
113 Bagnacavallo B 3
147 Bagnara Cálabra D 1
110 Bagnasco C 3
105 Bagnères de-Bigorre D 3
122 Bagnères-de Luchon B 3
97 Bagni del Másino B 5
112 Bagni di Lucca B 2
99 Bagni di Rabbi C 1
143 Bagni di Tivoli C 3
113 Bagno di Romagna C 3
81 Bagnoles-de-l'Orne B 6
144 Bagnoli del Trigno B 3
112 Bagnoli di Sopra A 3
145 Bagnoli Irpino C 4
111 Bagnolo Mella B 5
109 Bagnols D 3
109 Bagnols-sur-Cèze C 1
142 Bagnorégio B 3
111 Bagolino B 5
78 Bagrationovsk A 3
62 Bagshot B 3
123 Bagur C 6
120 Bahillo B 2
160 Baia Mare B 3
144 Baiano C 3
124 Baião B 1
86 Baienfurt D 1
85 Baiersbronn B 5
86 Baiersdorf B 3
95 Baigneux-les-Juifs B 4
55 Baile Atha Cliath A 5
117 Băile Herculane B 6
136 Bailén A 3
70 Baileux B 3
53 Bailieborough C 5
63 Bailleul B 4
122 Bailó B 2
81 Bain-de-Bretagne C 5
122 Bainearío de Panticosa B 2
106 Bains B 3
95 Bains-les-Bains A 6
81 Bais B 6
70 Baisieux B 2
112 Baiso B 2
124 Baiuca C 2
102 Baja B 2
101 Bajansenye C 4
116 Bajina Bašta C 3
102 Bajmok C 3
120 Bajna A 2
152 Bajram-Curr B 2
102 Bajša C 3
152 Bajzë B 1
101 Bak C 4
114 Bakar B 2
58 Bakewell B 2
101 Bakonybél B 5
101 Bakonycsernye B 6
101 Bakonyjákó B 5
101 Bakonyszentkirály B 5
101 Bakonyszentlászló B 5
101 Bakonyszombathely B 5
88 Bakov n. Jizerou A 2
79 Baków C 2
79 Bakowiec D 4
102 Baks B 4
102 Baksa C 2
65 Bakum B 6
57 Bala D 3
118 Balagonga A 3
122 Balaguer C 3
48 Balallan C 2
91 Balassa-gyarmat D 2
102 Balástya B 4
101 Balatonakali C 5
101 Balatonalmádi B 6
101 Balatonboglár C 5
101 Balatonbozsok C 6
101 Balatonederics C 5
101 Balatonendréd C 5
101 Balatonfenyves C 5
101 Balatonfokajár B 6
101 Balatonföldvár C 5
101 Balatonfüred C 5
101 Balatonfuzfo B 6
101 Balatonkenes B 6
101 Balatonkiliti C 6
101 Balatonlelle C 5
101 Balatonmáriafürdö C 5
101 Balatonszabadi C 6
101 Balatonszemes C 5
51 Balbeggie A 4
106 Balbigny B 4
119 Balboa B 4
55 Balbriggan A 5
160 Balchik D 6
59 Balderton B 3
62 Baldock B 3
56 Baldrine B 2
114 Bale B 1
134 Baleizao A 3
70 Balen A 4
137 Balerma C 4
148 Balestrate A 3
49 Balfour B 6
50 Balfron A 3
43 Bälganet C 5
30 Balholm B 3
142 Balignano B 2
39 Bälinge D 4
85 Balingen B 5
38 Balingsta C 4
49 Balintore D 5
152 Baljevac A 2
64 Balk B 3
65 Balkbrug B 4
52 Balla C 2

48 Ballachulish House E 3
52 Ballaghaderreen C 3
83 Ballancourt C 4
4 Ballangen B 5
50 Ballantrae B 3
141 Ballao C 3
56 Ballasalla B 2
49 Ballater D 5
56 Ballaugh B 2
74 Ballenstedt B 3
122 Ballerias C 2
81 Balleroy A 6
45 Ballerup B 5
130 Ballesteros de Calatrava C 3
55 Ballickmoyler B 4
52 Ballina B 2
55 Ballinagar A 4
55 Ballinakill B 4
55 Ballinalack A 4
55 Ballinalea A 5
53 Ballinamallard B 4
52 Ballinamore B 4
55 Ballinascarthy C 3
54 Ballinasloe A 3
54 Ballincollig C 3
54 Ballineen C 3
55 Ballingarry B 4
54 Ballingeary C 2
54 Ballinhassig C 3
52 Ballinlough C 3
49 Ballinluig E 5
111 Ballino B 5
54 Ballinrobe A 2
54 Ballinspittle C 3
52 Ballintra B 3
55 Ballinure B 4
55 Ballitore A 5
55 Ballivor A 5
122 Ballobar C 3
82 Ballon, F C 2
55 Ballon, IRL B 5
102 Ballószog B 3
154 Ballsh B 1
4 Ballstad B 2
44 Ballum B 1
53 Ballybay B 5
52 Ballybofey B 4
53 Ballybogey A 5
55 Ballyboghil A 5
54 Ballybunnion B 2
55 Ballycarnew B 5
55 Ballycarney B 5
53 Ballycastle, GB A 5
52 Ballycastle, IRL B 2
53 Ballyclare B 5
55 Ballyclerahan B 4
55 Ballycolla B 4
53 Ballyconnell B 4
55 Ballycotton C 3
52 Ballycroy B 2
54 Ballydangan A 3
54 Ballydavid A 3
54 Ballydehob C 2
54 Ballydesmond B 2
55 Ballyduff B 3
54 Ballyforan A 3
54 Ballygaf A 3
53 Ballygawley B 4
53 Ballyhalbert B 6
52 Ballyhaunis C 3
53 Ballyjamesduff C 4
54 Ballylanders B 3
55 Ballylooby B 4
55 Ballylynan B 4
53 Ballymagorry B 4
55 Ballymahon A 4
53 Ballymena B 5
54 Ballymoe A 3
53 Ballymoney A 5
55 Ballymore A 4
52 Ballymote B 3
54 Ballymurray A 3
55 Ballynabola B 5
54 Ballynacorra C 3
55 Ballynadrumny A 5
55 Ballynagore A 4
53 Ballynahinch B 6
55 Ballynahown A 4
54 Ballynamona B 3
53 Ballynure B 6
55 Ballyragget B 4
53 Ballyroney B 5
52 Ballysadare B 3
52 Ballyshannon B 3
54 Ballyvaghan A 2
54 Ballyvourney C 2
53 Ballyvoy A 5
53 Ballywalter B 6
50 Balmaclellan B 3
48 Balmartin D 1
103 Balmazújváros A 5
110 Balme B 2
49 Balmedie D 6
110 Balmuccia B 3
102 Balotaszállás B 3
123 Balsareny C 4
38 Bålsta C 4
96 Balsthal A 3
117 Balta B 6
120 Baltanas C 2
118 Baltar C 3
49 Baltasound A 8
55 Baltinglass B 5
124 Balugães B 1
71 Balve A 6
50 Balvicar A 2
97 Balzers A 5
143 Balzo B 4
131 Balzote C 4
73 Bamberg D 4
51 Bamburgh B 6
60 Bampton, Devon, GB C 3
62 Bampton, Oxon., GB B 2
138 Bañalbufar B 3
117 Banatska Palanka B 5
117 Banatski Brestovac B 4
117 Banatski Despotovac A 4
103 Banatski Dvor C 4
117 Banatski-Karlovac A 5
102 Banatsko-Arandelovo B 4
117 Banatsko-Novo Selo B 4
103 Banatsko Veliko Selo C 4
53 Banbridge B 5
62 Banbury A 2
49 Banchory D 6
70 Bande, B B 4
118 Bande, E B 3
45 Bandholm C 4
160 Bandirma E 5
54 Bandon C 3
133 Bañeres C 2
49 Banff D 6
80 Bangor, F C 3
57 Bangor, Caernarvon, GB C 2
53 Bangor, Ulster, GB B 6
52 Bangor, IRL B 2
12 Bangsund C 3
68 Banie B 2
78 Banie Mazurskie A 5
153 Banishte B 4
152 Banja, Kosovska Metohiska, YU B 2
153 Banja, Makedonia, YU C 3
116 Banja, Srbija, YU C 3
116 Banja Koviljača B 3
115 Banja Luka C 5
116 Banjani B 3
152 Banjska B 2
153 Banjsko C 4
101 Banka A 5
50 Bankend B 4
42 Bankeryd B 4
50 Bankfoot A 4
49 Bankhead D 6
153 Bankya B 5
117 Banloc A 5
80 Bannalec C 3
107 Banne C 4
110 Bannio B 3
50 Bannockburn A 4
125 Bañobárez C 3
123 Bañolas B 5
127 Bañón, E B 4
109 Banon, F C 2
125 Baños C 4
120 Baños de Cerrato C 2
135 Baños de Gigonza C 5
136 Baños de la Encina A 3
118 Baños de Molgas B 3
121 Baños de Rio Tobla B 4
126 Baños de Valdearados A 2
123 Baños San Vicente B 4
89 Bánov C 5
115 Banova Jaruga B 4
89 Bánovice C 6
116 Banovići B 2
116 Banovići Selo B 2
91 Bánréve D 3
68 Bansin B 2
91 Banská Belá D 1
91 Banská Bystrica D 2
91 Banská-Štiavnica D 1
153 Bansko C 5
62 Banstead B 3
54 Banteer B 3
72 Banteln A 3
54 Bantry C 2
85 Bantzenheim C 4
61 Banwell B 4
123 Banyuls-sur-Mer B 6
63 Bapaume B 4
50 Baptiston A 3
121 Baquio A 4
109 Bar, F D 3
151 Bar, YU C 5
84 Bar-le-Duc B 2
84 Bar-sur-Aube B 1
83 Bar-sur-Seine C 6
115 Baraći C 4
102 Baracs B 2
102 Baracska A 2
127 Barahona A 3
126 Barajes de Melo B 3
103 Báránd A 5
117 Baranda A 4
144 Baranello B 3
79 Baranów D 5
90 Baranów Sandomierski B 4
121 Barasoain B 5
129 Barbacena C 3
118 Barbadanes B 3
125 Barbadillo C 4
120 Barbadillo de Herreros B 3
120 Barbadillo del Mercado B 3
120 Barbadillo del Pez B 3
99 Barbarano Vicento D 2
122 Barbastro B 3
135 Barbate de Franco C 5
127 Barbatona A 3
92 Barbâtre C 1
105 Barbazan D 3
119 Barbeitos A 3
83 Barberey C 6
104 Barbezieux B 2
72 Barbis B 4
83 Barbonne-Fayel C 5
74 Barby B 3
91 Barca D 4
124 Barca d'Alva B 3
135 Barca de la Florida C 5
122 Bárcabo B 3
129 Barcarrota C 4
149 Barcellona Pozzo di Gotto A 5
123 Barcelona C 5
109 Barcelonnette C 3
124 Barcelos B 1
119 Bárcena A 5
120 Bárcena del Pie de Concha A 2
74 Barchfeld C 2
78 Barciany A 4
69 Barcin C 5
69 Barcino A 4
99 Bárcis C 3
128 Barco A 3
126 Barcones A 3
115 Barcs B 5
105 Barcus D 2
78 Barczewo B 3
91 Bardejov C 4
109 Bardentane D 1
111 Bardi C 4
58 Bardney B 3
89 Bardo A 4
99 Bardolino D 1
108 Bardonécchia B 3
101 Bardoňovo A 6
66 Bardowick B 3
6 Bardufoss B 4
105 Barèges E 3
75 Bärenstein C 5
82 Barentin B 2
81 Barénton B 6
115 Barevo C 5
120 Bareyo A 3
81 Barfleur A 5
112 Barga B 2
126 Bargas C 1
110 Barge C 2
109 Bargemon D 3
111 Barghe B 5
61 Bargoed B 3
66 Bargteheide B 3
44 Bargum C 1
145 Bari B 5
141 Bari Sardo C 3
114 Barič Draga C 3
143 Barisciane B 4
107 Barjac C 4
119 Barjacoba B 4
109 Barjols D 2
35 Barkåker B 6
32 Barkald B 1
62 Barking B 4
66 Barklelsby A 2
77 Barkówko B 5
69 Barkowo B 5
160 Bârlad B 5
74 Barleben A 3
109 Barles C 3
145 Barletta B 5
68 Barlinek C 3
154 Barmash B 2
58 Barmby Moor B 3
57 Barmouth D 2
66 Barmstedt B 2
54 Barna A 2
54 Barnaderg A 3
51 Barnard Castle C 6
42 Barnarp B 4
87 Bärnau B 4
100 Bärnbach B 3
67 Barnenitz C 5
62 Barnet B 3
58 Barnetby le Wold B 3
64 Barneveld B 3
81 Barneville A 5
56 Barnoldswick C 4
68 Barnówko C 2
58 Barnsley B 2
74 Barnstädt B 3
60 Barnstaple B 2
66 Barnstorf C 1
72 Barntrup B 3
83 Baron B 4
144 Baronissi C 3
153 Barovo C 4
128 Barqueiro B 2
128 Barquinha B 2
85 Barr, F B 4
50 Barr, GB B 3
124 Barra C 1
132 Barracas A 2
126 Barraco B 1
129 Barrado A 5
149 Barrafranca B 4
118 Barral B 2
134 Barranco do Velho B 3
135 Barrancos A 4
131 Barrax B 4
128 Barreiro C 1
118 Barreiros A 3
109 Barrême D 3
50 Barrhead B 3
50 Barrhill B 3
66 Barrien C 1
119 Barrio B 5
128 Barroco B 2
135 Barrosa C 4
56 Barrow-in-Furness B 3
58 Barrow upon Humber B 3
59 Barrow upon Soar C 2
56 Barrowford C 4
125 Barruecopardo B 3
120 Barruelo de Santullán B 2
122 Barruera B 3
51 Barry, Fife, GB A 5
61 Barry, Glamorgan, GB B 3
104 Barsac C 2
45 Bårse B 4
13 Barsele B 9
72 Barsinghausen A 3
65 Barßel A 5
21 Barsta C 7
85 Bartenheim C 4
67 Barth A 5
86 Bartholomä C 1
62 Barton in the Clay B 3
59 Barton Mills C 4
58 Barton upon Humber B 3
78 Bartoszyce A 3
141 Barúmini C 3
75 Baruth A 5
48 Barvas C 2
71 Barvaux B 4
66 Barver C 1
90 Barwald C 2
69 Barwice B 4
119 Barzana A 5
111 Bárzio B 4
123 Bas B 5
103 Bašaid C 4
110 Basaluzzo C 3
66 Basbeck B 3
142 Baschi B 3
120 Basconcillos del Tozo B 3
120 Bascones B 2
70 Basécles B 2
96 Basel A 3
144 Basélice B 3
123 Basella B 4
62 Basildon B 4
62 Basingstoke B 2
89 Baška, CS B 6
114 Baska, YU C 2
150 Baška Voda B 2
47 Baskemölla B 5
5 Båsmoen D 3
33 Bäsna C 6
99 Basovizza D 4
141 Bassacutena A 3
99 Bassano del Grappa D 2
142 Bassano di Sutri B 3
70 Bassilly B 2
94 Bassou B 3
105 Bassoues D 3
66 Bassum C 1
46 Båstad A 3
143 Bastardo B 3
140 Bastelica C 2
140 Bastia, F B 2
143 Bastia, I A 3
71 Bastogne B 4
59 Baston C 3
15 Bastuträsk D 4
102 Báta, H B 2
103 Bata, R B 6
116 Batajnica B 4
128 Batalha B 2
103 Batăr B 5
102 Bátaszék B 2
122 Batea C 3
88 Batelov B 3
61 Bath B 4
50 Bathgate B 4
60 Bath's Plot C 2
102 Batina C 2
91 Bátka D 3
152 Batlava B 3
18 Batnfjordsøra C 3
117 Batočina B 5
115 Batrina B 5
9 Båtsfjord B 9
16 Båtskärsnäs B 2
112 Battáglia Terme A 3
96 Batterkinden A 3
71 Battice B 4
144 Battipaglia C 3
62 Battle C 4
103 Battonya B 5
117 Batuša B 5
102 Bátya B 2
80 Baud C 3
95 Baudoncort B 6
70 Baudour B 2
93 Baugé B 3
94 Baugy B 2
97 Bauma A 4
95 Baume-les-Dames B 6
67 Baumgarten B 5
100 Baumgartenberg A 2
71 Baumholder C 6
141 Baunei B 3
75 Bautzen B 6
117 Bavanište B 4
70 Bavay B 2
84 Bavilliers C 3
88 Bavorov B 2
59 Bawdeswell C 5
65 Bawinkel B 5
53 Bawnboy B 4
58 Bawtry B 2
84 Bayel B 1
87 Bayerisch Eisenstein B 5
81 Bayeux A 6
62 Baynard's Green B 2
118 Bayo A 2
84 Bayon B 3
118 Bayona B 2
105 Bayonne D 1
109 Bayons C 3
86 Bayreuth B 3
98 Bayrischzell B 3
137 Baza B 4
83 Bazancourt B 6
105 Bazas C 2
107 Baziege D 1
83 Bazoches-les-Gallerandes C 4
82 Bazoches-sur-Hoene C 2
112 Bazzano B 3
61 Beachley B 4
62 Beaconsfield B 3
118 Beade B 2
61 Beaminster C 4
135 Beas B 4
137 Beas de Segura A 4
121 Beasin A 4
51 Beattock B 4
95 Beaubery C 4
109 Beaucaire D 1
84 Beaucourt C 3
108 Beaufort B 3
92 Beaufort-en-Vallée B 3
93 Beaugency B 5
109 Beaujeu, Basses-Alpes, F C 3

62 Bethersden B 4
57 Bethesda C 2
63 Béthune B 4
83 Beton-Bazoches C 5
71 Bettembourg C 5
71 Bettendorf C 5
39 Bettna D 3
111 Béttola C 4
143 Bettona A 3
49 Bettyhill C 4
57 Betws-y-coed C 3
83 Betz B 4
71 Betzdorf B 6
104 Beuatiran C 2
71 Beuel B 6
57 Beulah D 3
63 Beuvry B 4
82 Beuzeville B 2
143 Bevagna B 3
66 Bevensen B 3
70 Beveren A 3
58 Beverley B 3
70 Beverlo A 4
72 Bevern B 3
66 Beverstedt B 1
72 Beverungen B 3
64 Beverwijk B 2
88 Bevničov A 1
57 Bewdley D 4
96 Bex B 3
62 Bexhill C 4
62 Bexley B 4
106 Beynat B 1
132 Bezas A 1
97 Bezau A 5
102 Bezdan C 2
95 Bèze B 5
94 Bezenet C 2
107 Béziers D 3
109 Bezouce D 1
111 Bezzecca B 5
63 Biache-St. Waast B 4
77 Biadk B 6
79 Biala, PL D 2
89 Biala, PL A 5
78 Biala Piska B 5
79 Biala Rawska D 3
69 Biale Blota B 5
77 Bialobloty A 6
79 Bialobrzegi D 3
69 Bialogard A 3
77 Bialoleka B 5
69 Bialośliwie B 5
69 Bialy Bór B 4
91 Bialy-Dunajec C 3
149 Biancavilla B 4
147 Bianco D 2
110 Biandrate B 3
133 Biar C 2
105 Biarritz D 1
105 Bias C 1
97 Biasca B 4
102 Biatorbágy A 2
73 Bibart D 4
112 Bibbiena C 3
112 Bibbona C 2
86 Biberach, Baden-Württemberg, D† C 1
85 Biberach, Baden-Württemberg, D† B 5
150 Bibinje A 1
99 Bibione D 4
73 Biblis D 2
62 Bibury B 2
152 Bicaj B 2
145 Biccari B 4
62 Bicester B 2
98 Bichl B 2
97 Bichlbach A 6
132 Bicorp B 2
102 Bicske A 2
105 Bidache D 1
105 Bidart D 1
62 Biddenden B 4
64 Biddinghuizen B 3
57 Biddulph C 4
60 Bideford B 2
59 Bidford on Avon C 2
91 Bidovce D 4
39 Bie C 3
73 Bieber C 3
75 Biebersdorf B 5
90 Biecz C 4
73 Biedenkopf C 2
96 Biel, CH A 3
122 Biel, E B 2
77 Bielany Wroclawskie B 5
77 Bielawa C 5
79 Bielawy C 2
65 Bielefeld B 6
110 Biella B 3
90 Bielowy C 4
122 Bielsa B 3
79 Bielsk C 2
90 Bielsko-Biala C 2
66 Bienenbüttel B 3
76 Bieniów B 4
96 Bienne A 3
131 Bienservida C 4
129 Bienvenida C 4
77 Bierdzany C 7
73 Bieringen D 3
81 Bierné C 6
40 Biersted B 3
90 Bierun Stary B 2
77 Bierutów B 6
69 Bierzwina B 3
68 Bierzwnik B 3
122 Biescas B 2
67 Biesenthal C 6
85 Bietigheim, Baden-Württemberg, D† B 6
85 Bietigheim, Baden-Württemberg, D† B 5
67 Bietikow B 6
70 Bièvre C 4
83 Bièvres C 4
77 Biezdrowo A 5
78 Biezuń C 2
104 Biganos C 2
124 Bigas C 2
133 Bigastro C 2
60 Bigbury-on-Sea C 3
50 Biggar B 4
8 Biggeluobbal C 3
59 Biggleswade C 3
115 Bihac C 3
103 Biharea A 5
103 Biharkeresztes A 5
103 Biharnagybajom A 5
116 Bijeljina B 3
152 Bijelo Polje A 1
127 Bijuesca A 4
121 Bilbao A 4
90 Bilcza B 3
151 Bileča C 4
103 Biled C 4
88 Bílina A 1
154 Bilisht B 2
153 Biljača B 3
102 Bilje C 2
42 Billdal B 1
46 Billeberga B 4
65 Billerbeck C 5
62 Billericay B 4
59 Billesdon C 3
46 Billesholm A 3
46 Billinge B 4
51 Billingham C 6
59 Billinghay B 3
36 Billingsfors C 4
62 Billingshurst B 3
106 Billom B 3
21 Billsta B 7
44 Billund B 2
89 Bilovec B 5
71 Bilstein A 7
64 Bilthoven B 3
6 Bilto B 7
71 Bilzen B 4
122 Binaced C 3
110 Binasco B 4
58 Binbrook B 3
70 Binche B 3
86 Bindlach B 3
122 Binéfar C 3
71 Bingen C 6
71 Bingerbrück C 6
58 Bingley B 2
33 Bingsjö B 6
80 Binic B 4
85 Bining A 4
139 Binisalem B 3
67 Binz A 6
150 Biograd B 1
110 Bionaz B 2
116 Bioska C 3
70 Bioul B 3
103 Birchis C 6
117 Birda A 5
31 Biri C 7
35 Birkeland C 4
85 Birkenfeld, Baden-Württemberg, D† B 5
71 Birkenfeld, Rheinland-Pfalz, D† C 6
57 Birkenhead C 3
67 Birkenwerder C 6
100 Birkfeld B 3
51 Birkhill B 4
59 Birmingham C 2
87 Birnbach C 5
49 Birness D 7
55 Birr A 4
71 Birresborn B 5
103 Birşa B 6
73 Birstein C 3
51 Birtley C 6
103 Birzava B 5
100 Biš C 3
145 Bisáccia B 4
148 Bisacquino B 3
75 Bišany C 5
122 Bisbal de Falset C 3
122 Biscanues B 2
105 Biscarosse C 1
105 Biscarrosse-Plage C 1
145 Biscéglie B 5
73 Bischofsheim C 3
98 Bischofshofen B 4
75 Bischofswerda B 6
98 Bischofswiesen B 3
97 Bischofszell A 5
85 Bischwiller B 4
143 Bisenti B 4
51 Bishop Auckland C 6
57 Bishop's Castle D 3
61 Bishop's Cleve B 4
61 Bishop's Lydeard B 3
62 Bishop's Stortford B 4
62 Bishop's Waltham C 2
147 Bisignano C 2
85 Bisingen B 5
77 Biskupice B 7
77 Biskupice Olawskie C 6
78 Biskupiec, Bydgoszcz, PL B 2
78 Biskupiec, Olsztyn, PL B 3
67 Bismark C 4
38 Bispberg B 2
21 Bispfors B 5
21 Bispgarden B 5
66 Bispingen B 3
71 Bissen C 5
65 Bissendorf B 6
110 Bistagno C 3
116 Bistarac B 2
115 Bistrica, Bosna i Hercegovina, YU C 5
116 Bistrica, Srbija, YU C 3
153 Bistritsa B 5
78 Bisztynek A 3
71 Bitburg C 5
85 Bitche A 4
145 Bitetto B 5
154 Bitola A 3
145 Bitonto B 5
85 Bitschwiller C 4
74 Bitterfeld B 4
141 Bitti B 3
82 Biville B 3
148 Bivona B 3
71 Biwer C 5
49 Bixter A 7
105 Bizanos D 2
102 Bizovac C 2
34 Bjåen B 3
5 Bjærangfjord D 2
47 Bjärnum A 4
46 Bjärred B 4
21 Bjästa B 7
34 Bjelland C 3
115 Bjelovar B 4
5 Bjerka D 2
34 Bjerkreim C 2
4 Bjerkvik B 6
44 Bjerreby C 3
44 Bjerringbro A 2
31 Bjøberg C 5
31 Bjøkeflåta C 5
5 Bjøllånes D 3
12 Bjorånes C 4
33 Björbo C 5
6 Bjorelvnes B 4
6 Bjørkås C 5
4 Bjørkåsen B 5
27 Bjorkboda C 5
38 Björke B 4
36 Bjørkelangen B 3
42 Björketorp B 2
43 Björkfors A 5
4 Björkliden B 7
38 Björklinge B 4
42 Björkö B 1
38 Björkö-Arholma C 6
22 Björköby, SF B 3
43 Björköby, S B 4
21 Bjorksele, S B 6
15 Björksele, S D 2
39 Björkvik D 3
12 Bjørn A 4
21 Björna B 7
37 Björneborg B 6
36 Björnerod B 3
9 Bjørnevatn C 10
39 Bjornlunda C 4
18 Bjørnsund C 2
39 Björsäter D 3
19 Bjugn B 5
33 Bjuråker B 7
15 Bjurholm E 3
15 Bjuröklubbfiskeläge D 5
38 Bjursås B 2
37 Bjurtjam B 6
46 Bjuv A 3
59 Blaby C 2
152 Blace, Kosovska Metohiska, YU B 2
152 Blace, Srbija, YU A 3
90 Blachownia B 1
89 Blachownia Śląska A 6
56 Blackburn C 4
50 Blackford A 4
60 Blackmoor Gate B 3
56 Blackpool C 3
43 Blackstad B 6
50 Blackwood, Lanark, GB B 4
61 Blackwood, Monmouth, GB B 3
84 Blacy B 1
38 Bladåker B 5
70 Bladel A 4
57 Blaenau Ffestiniog D 3
61 Blaenavon B 3
34 Blåfjellhytta B 2
115 Blagaj B 4
61 Blagdon B 4
105 Blagnac D 4
82 Blagny B 3
153 Blagoevgrad B 5
20 Blåhammaren B 1
97 Blaichach A 6
81 Blain C 5
84 Blainville-sur-l'Eau B 3
82 Blainville-sur-Orne B 1
49 Blair Atholl E 5
51 Blairgowrie A 4
105 Blajan D 3
61 Blakeney, Gloucester, GB B 4
59 Blakeney, Norfolk, GB C 5
35 Blakstad C 4
84 Blâmont B 3
133 Blanca C 1
118 Blancos C 3
61 Blandford Forum C 4
123 Blanes C 5
63 Blangy B 4
43 Blankaholm B 6
74 Blankenberg B 2
70 Blankenberge A 2
67 Blankenfelde C 6
74 Blankenhain C 3
71 Blankenheim, D† B 5
74 Blankenheim, D* B 3
104 Blanquefort C 2
89 Blansko B 4
104 Blanzac B 3
95 Blanzy C 4
64 Blaricum B 3
54 Blarney C 3
125 Blascomillán C 4
126 Blascosancho B 1
65 Blasheim B 6
15 Blåsmark C 5
79 Blaszki D 1
88 Blatná B 1
101 Blatné A 5
89 Blatnice C 5
150 Blato, Hrvatska, YU B 2
150 Blato, Korcula, YU C 2
96 Blatten B 3
13 Blattnicksele B 9
71 Blatzheim B 5
86 Blaubeuren C 1
73 Blaufelden D 3
51 Blaydon C 6
104 Blaye, Gironde, F B 2
107 Blaye, Tarn, F C 2
130 Blázquez C 1
62 Blean B 5
66 Bleckede B 3
122 Blecua B 2
114 Bled A 2
85 Bleibach, Baden-Württemberg, D† B 5
99 Bleiberg Kreuth C 4
100 Bleiburg C 2
73 Bleichenbach C 3
74 Bleicherode B 2
4 Bleik A 4
12 Bleikvassli B 5
94 Bléneau B 2
142 Blera B 3
83 Blérancourt B 5
93 Bléré B 5
71 Blerick A 5
94 Blet C 2
62 Bletchley B 3
95 Bletterans C 5
38 Blidö C 5
42 Blidsberg B 3
83 Bligny B 5
95 Bligny-sur-Ouche B 4
42 Blikstorp A 4
5 Bliksvær C 2
83 Blincourt B 4
152 Blinisht C 1
59 Blisworth C 3
79 Blizyn D 3
59 Blofield C 5
90 Blogoszów B 3
93 Blois B 5
40 Blokhus B 3
64 Blokzijl B 3
37 Blombacka B 5
72 Blomberg B 3
36 Blomskog B 4
43 Blomstermåla C 6
30 Blomvåg C 1
79 Blonie, Warszawa, PL C 3
77 Blonie, Wroclaw, PL B 5
75 Blönsdorf B 4
37 Blotberget A 7
87 Blovice B 5
62 Bloxham A 2
97 Bludenz A 5
89 Bludov B 4
85 Blumberg C 5
32 Blyberg B 5
51 Blyth B 6
59 Blythburgh C 5
58 Blythe B 2
51 Blythe Bridge, Peebles, GB B 4
57 Blythe Bridge, Staffs., GB D 4
77 Bnin A 6
35 Bø, N B 5
39 Bo, S D 2
128 Boa Vista B 2
119 Boal A 4
47 Boalt A 5
111 Boário Terme B 5
49 Boat of Garten D 5
101 Boba B 5
121 Bobadilla, Logroño, E B 4
136 Bobadilla, Malága, E B 2
125 Bobadilla del Campo B 4
126 Bobadilla del Monte B 2
111 Bóbbio C 4
110 Bóbbio Pellice C 2
86 Bobingen C 2
85 Böblingen B 6
69 Bobolice B 4
118 Boboras B 2
153 Boboshevo B 4
153 Bobovdol B 4
90 Bobowa C 3
91 Bobrov C 2
88 Bobrová B 4
68 Bobrówko C 3
120 Boca de Huérgano B 2
133 Bocairente C 2
102 Bočar C 4
124 Bocas C 2
147 Bocchigliero C 2
126 Boceguillas A 2
90 Bochnia C 3
71 Bocholt, B A 4
65 Bocholt, D† C 4
87 Bochov A 5
71 Bochum A 6
43 Bockara B 6
72 Bockenem A 4
101 Bockfließ A 4
65 Bockhorn A 6
140 Bocognano B 2
102 Boconád A 4
117 Bocşa Romînă A 5
117 Bocşa Vasiovei A 5
103 Bocsig B 5
76 Boczów A 3
103 Boda, H A 5
33 Boda, Kopparbergs, S B 6
43 Boda, Øland, S B 7
21 Boda, Vasternorrlands, S C 5
43 Boda glasbruk C 5
43 Bodafors B 4

101 Bodajk B 6
116 Bodani A 3
49 Boddam, Aberdeen, GB D 7
49 Boddam, Shetland, GB B 7
67 Boddin B 4
72 Bödefeld B 2
64 Bodegraven B 2
14 Boden C 5
87 Bodenmais B 5
66 Bodenteich C 3
72 Bodenwerder B 3
97 Bodio B 4
60 Bodmin C 2
5 Bodø C 3
19 Bodom B 7
135 Bodonal de la Sierra A 4
91 Bodroghalom D 4
91 Bodrogkeresztúr D 4
20 Bodsjö C 3
14 Bodträskfors B 4
21 Bodum B 5
54 Bodyke B 3
79 Bodzanów C 3
90 Bodzanowice B 1
90 Bodzechów B 4
126 Boecillo A 1
96 Boege B 2
106 Boën B 4
91 Bogács E 3
125 Bogajo C 3
131 Bogarra C 4
136 Bogarre B 3
116 Bogatic B 3
76 Bogatynia, CS C 4
75 Bogatynia, PL C 6
156 Bogdanci A 2
76 Bogdaniec A 4
152 Bogë, AL B 1
39 Boge, S E 5
87 Bogen, D† C 4
4 Bogen, N B 6
4 Bogen, N C 4
36 Bogen, S A 4
44 Bogense B 3
103 Boghiş A 6
96 Bognanco Fonti B 4
4 Bognes B 5
49 Bogniebrae D 6
97 Bogno B 5
62 Bognor Regis C 3
153 Bogomila C 3
90 Bogoria B 4
39 Bogsta D 4
90 Boguchwala C 4
78 Boguchwaly B 3
90 Bogucice B 3
77 Boguszów C 5
117 Bogutovac C 4
102 Bogyiszio B 2
83 Bohain B 5
130 Bohanal del Ibor B 1
89 Bohdalice B 5
88 Bohdaneč A 3
100 Böheimkirchen A 3
114 Bohinjska Bistrica A 1
75 Böhlen B 4
86 Böhmenkirch C 1
65 Bohmte B 6
101 Böhönye C 5
85 Böhringen B 5
144 Boiano B 3
95 Bois-d'Amont C 6
82 Bois-Guillaume B 3
84 Boismont A 2
107 Boisseron D 4
83 Boissy-St. Leger C 4
67 Boitzenburg B 6
123 Boixols B 4
66 Boizenburg B 3
77 Bojadla B 4
77 Bojanowo B 5
89 Bojkovice B 5
101 Bojná A 6
89 Bojnice C 6
153 Bojnik A 3
117 Boka A 4
4 Bokholm B 6
66 Böklund A 2
101 Bokod B 6
91 Bököny E 4
43 Böksholm B 4
150 Bol B 2
130 Bolaños de Calatrava C 3
89 Bolatice B 6
82 Bolbec B 2
102 Bölcske B 2
44 Bolderslev C 2
102 Boldog A 3
51 Boldon C 6
91 Boldva D 3
122 Bolea B 2
15 Bolebyn C 5
77 Boleslawiec B 4
76 Boleszkowice A 3
77 Bolewice A 5
112 Bólgheri C 2
160 Bolgrad C 6
15 Boliden D 4
79 Bolimów C 3
134 Boliqueime B 2
117 Boljevac C 5
116 Böljevci B 4
117 Boljkovci B 4
77 Bolków C 5
42 Bollebygd B 2
109 Bollène C 1
127 Bólliga B 3
96 Bolligen B 3
33 Bollnäs B 7
21 Bollstabruk B 6
135 Bollullos B 4
135 Bollullos par del Condado B 4
85 Bollwiller C 4
112 Bologna B 3
84 Bologne B 2
148 Bolognetta B 3
143 Bolognola B 4
141 Bolótana B 2
142 Bolsena B 3
58 Bolsover B 2
64 Bolsward A 3
122 Boltaña B 3
67 Boltenhagen B 4
96 Boltigen B 3
56 Bolton C 4
57 Bolton Bridge C 4
102 Bóly C 2
110 Bolzaneto C 3
99 Bolzano C 2
26 Bomarsund C 3
143 Bomba B 5
128 Bombarral B 1
67 Bömerzien C 4
34 Bømlo B 1
105 Bon-Encontre C 3
39 Bona D 2
97 Bonaduz B 5
135 Bonanza C 4
119 Boñar B 5
49 Bonar Bridge D 4
141 Bonárcado B 2
135 Bonares B 4
33 Bonäs B 5
111 Bonassola C 4
51 Bonchester Bridge B 5
112 Bondeno B 3
85 Bondorf B 5
72 Bonenburg B 3
50 Bo'ness B 4
133 Bonete C 1
21 Bönhamn C 7
140 Bonifacio C 2
96 Bönigen B 3
71 Bonn B 6
5 Bonnåsjøen C 4
93 Bonnat C 5
85 Bonndorf C 5
4 Bonnes B 7
82 Bonnétable C 2
83 Bonneuil-les-Eaux B 4
93 Bonneuil-Matours C 4
82 Bonneval C 3
108 Bonneville A 3
82 Bonnières B 3
109 Bonnieux D 2
85 Bönnigheim A 6
94 Bonny-sur-Loire B 2
51 Bonnyrigg B 4
122 Bono, E B 3
141 Bono, I B 3
141 Bonorva B 2
96 Bons B 2
35 Bønsnes A 6
102 Bonyhád B 2
101 Bonyrétalap B 5
70 Booischot A 3
70 Boom A 3
66 Boostedt A 3
56 Bootle, Cumberland, GB B 3
56 Bootle, Lancs., GB C 4
86 Bopfingen C 2
71 Boppard B 6
118 Boqueijon B 2
87 Bor,CS B 4
42 Bor,S B 4
117 Bor,YU B 6
117 Borač C 4
83 Boran B 4
42 Borås B 2
128 Borba C 3
143 Borbona B 4
117 Borča B 4
115 Borci C 5
65 Borculo B 4
102 Bordány B 3
104 Bordeaux C 2
134 Bordeira B 2
66 Bordesholm A 3
110 Bordighera D 2
44 Bording A 2
132 Bordón A 2
111 Bore C 4
77 Boreciczki B 6
62 Boreham Wood B 3
77 Borek-Strzeliński C 6
77 Borek Wielkopolski B 6
51 Boreland B 4
113 Borello B 4
39 Borensberg D 2
28 Borgå C 3
13 Borgafjäll C 7
4 Borge B 2
72 Borgentreich B 3
65 Börger, D† B 5
65 Borger, NL B 4
39 Borggård D 2
111 Borghetta di Vara C 4
110 Borghetto d'Arróscia C 2
110 Borghetto Santo Spirito C 3
43 Borgholm C 6
65 Borgholzhausen B 6
65 Borghorst B 5
147 Bórgia D 2
70 Borgloon B 4
40 Børglum B 3
112 Borgo a Mozzano C 2
112 Borgo alla Collina C 3
113 Borgo Pace C 4
110 Borgo San Dalmazzo C 2
112 Borgo San Lorenzo C 3
112 Borgo Val di Taro B 1
99 Borgo Valsugana C 2
110 Borgo Vercelli B 3
112 Borgoforte A 2
110 Borgofranco d'Ivrea B 2
110 Borgomanero B 3
110 Borgomasino B 2
111 Borgonovo Val Tidone B 4
143 Borgorose B 4
110 Borgosésia B 3
20 Borgsjö C 4
42 Borgstena B 3
49 Borgue C 5
30 Borgund B 4
20 Borgvattnet B 4
37 Borgvik B 4
121 Borja C 5
122 Borjas Blancas C 3
122 Borjas del Campo C 4
16 Börjelsbyn B 1
71 Bork A 6
65 Borken C 4
4 Borkenes B 5
19 Borkhusseter C 6
44 Børkop B 2
69 Borkowo A 6
65 Borkum A 4
38 Borlänge B 2
117 Borlova A 6
109 Bormes D 3
97 Bormio B 6
135 Bormujos B 4
67 Born C 4
75 Borna B 4
65 Borne B 4
70 Bornem A 3
124 Bornes B 3
71 Bornheim B 5
66 Bornhöved A 3
67 Börnicke C 5
135 Bornos C 5
127 Borobia A 4
103 Borod B 6
88 Borohrádek A 4
141 Bórore B 2
90 Boroszów B 1
58 Boroughbridge A 2
88 Borovany C 2
114 Borovnica B 2
116 Borovo A 2
153 Borovtsi A 5
87 Borovy B 5
90 Borów B 4
77 Borowa B 6
79 Borowie D 4
126 Borox B 2
47 Borrby B 5
45 Borre, DK C 5
35 Borre, N B 6
123 Borredá B 4
119 Borrenes B 4
132 Borriol A 2
44 Borris, DK B 1
55 Borris, IRL B 5
55 Borris in Ossory B 4
54 Borrisokane B 3
55 Borrisoleigh B 4
56 Borrowdale B 3
75 Borsdorf B 4
8 Børselv B 5
101 Borsfa C 4
101 Borsky Mikuláš A 5
91 Borsodivánka E 3
91 Borsodnádasd D 3
19 Børsøra B 6
66 Borstel-Hohenraden B 2
66 Borstorf B 3
106 Bort-les-Orgues B 2
34 Børte B 3
57 Borth D 2
20 Börtnan C 2
31 Børtnes C 6
45 Borup B 4
48 Borve D 2
79 Boryslawice PL C 1
76 Boryszyn A 4
79 Borzecin C 3
111 Borzonasca C 4
69 Borzyszkowy A 5
69 Borzytuchom A 5
141 Bosa B 2
114 Bosanci B 3
115 Bosanka Dubica B 4
115 Bosanki Novi B 4
115 Bosanska Gradiska B 5
115 Bosanska Kostajnica B 4
115 Bosanska Krupa C 4
115 Bosanski Petrovac C 4
116 Bosanski Samac A 2
115 Bosansko Grahovo C 4
101 Bosany A 6
101 Bosárkány B 5
66 Bosau A 3
60 Boscastle C 2
99 Bosco Chiesanuova D 2
66 Bösdorf A 3
153 Bosiljgrad B 4
72 Bösingfeld A 3
64 Boskoop B 2
89 Boskovice B 4
116 Bošnjaci, Bosna i Hercegovina, YU A 2
153 Bošnjaci, Srbija, YU B 3
117 Bošnjane C 5
122 Bosost B 3
110 Bossolasco C 3
59 Boston C 3
35 Bostrak B 4
115 Boszénfa A 5
122 Bot C 3
116 Botajica B 2
21 Boteå B 6
56 Bothel B 3
124 Boticas B 2
6 Botnhamn B 3
45 Bøtø By C 4
117 Botoš A 4
160 Botosani B 5
147 Botricello D 2
15 Botsmark D 4
72 Bottendorf B 2
59 Bottesford C 3
36 Bottna C 3
42 Bottnaryd B 3
71 Bottrop A 5
152 Botun C 2
117 Botunje B 5
85 Bötzingen B 4
92 Bouaye B 2
124 Bouça B 2
105 Boucau D 1
70 Bouchain B 2
83 Bouchoir B 4
107 Boucoiran C 4
95 Boudreville B 4
96 Boudry B 2
93 Bouesse C 5
92 Bouguenais B 2
94 Bouhy B 3
83 Bouillancy B 4
70 Bouillon C 4
83 Bouilly C 6
92 Bouin C 2
55 Bouladuff B 4
84 Boulay A 3
123 Boule-d'Amont B 5
105 Boulogne D 3
63 Boulogne-sur-Mer B 3
82 Bouloire D 2
70 Boulzicourt C 3
63 Bouquemaison B 4
95 Bourbon-Lancy C 3
94 Bourbon-l'Archambault C 3
95 Bourbonne-les-Bains B 5
63 Bourbourg B 4
80 Bourbriac B 3
104 Bourcefranc B 1
108 Bourdeaux C 2
93 Bouresse C 4
95 Bourg, Ain, F C 5
83 Bourg, Aisne, F B 5
104 Bourg, Girone, F B 2
82 Bourg-Achard B 2
108 Bourg-Argental B 1
108 Bourg-de-Péage B 2
106 Bourg-de-Thizy A 4
105 Bourg-de-Visa C 3
92 Bourg-la-Roche C 2
106 Bourg-Lastic B 2
123 Bourg Madame B 4
109 Bourg-St.-Andéol C 1
108 Bourg-St. Maurice B 3
106 Bourganeuf B 1
94 Bourges B 2
92 Bourgneuf-en-Retz B 2
83 Bourgogne B 6
108 Bourgoin B 2
82 Bourgtheroulde B 2
93 Bourgueil B 4
84 Bourmont B 2
59 Bourne C 3
62 Bourne End B 3
61 Bournemouth C 5
92 Bournezeau C 2
105 Bourran C 3
105 Bourret D 4
83 Bourron-Marlotte C 4
62 Bourton-on-the-Water B 2
94 Boussac C 2
84 Bousse A 3
105 Boussens D 3
82 Bouttencourt B 3
109 Bouvières C 2
81 Bouvron C 5
85 Bouxwiller B 4
118 Bouzas B 2
84 Bouzonville A 3
44 Bov C 2
147 Bova E 1
147 Bova Marina E 1
147 Bovalino Marina D 2
36 Bovallstrand C 3
117 Bovan C 5
114 Bovec A 1
118 Boveda B 3
111 Bovegno B 5
66 Bovenau A 2
64 Bovenkarspel B 3
31 Bøverdalen B 5
83 Boves, F B 4
110 Bóves, I C 2
60 Bovey Tracey C 3
71 Bovigny B 4
145 Bovino B 4
44 Bøvlingbjerg A 1
113 Bovolenta A 3
112 Bovolone A 3
57 Bow Street D 2
51 Bowes C 5
50 Bowmore B 1
56 Bowness B 4
61 Box B 4
73 Boxberg, D† D 3
75 Boxberg, D* B 6
28 Boxby C 3
43 Boxholm A 5
64 Boxmeer C 3
64 Boxtel C 3
52 Boyle C 3
108 Bozel B 3
99 Bozen C 2
69 Bozepole Wielkie A 5
117 Boževac B 5
154 Bozhigrad B 2
153 Bozhurishte B 5
75 Boži Dar C 4
153 Bozica B 4
106 Bozouls C 2
117 Bozovici B 5
112 Bozzolo A 2
110 Bra C 2
43 Braås B 5
44 Brabrand A 3
48 Bracadale D 2
142 Bracciano B 3
58 Bracebridge Heath B 3
74 Brachstedt B 4

34 Bryne C 1
61 Brynmawr B 3
117 Brza Palanka B 6
152 Brzeće A 2
77 Brzeg C 6
77 Brzeg Dolny B 5
90 Brzegi B 3
79 Brześć Kuj. C 1
90 Brzesko C 3
90 Brzesko Nowe B 3
90 Brzeszcze C 2
69 Brzezie B 4
79 Brzeziny D 2
79 Brzeznica Nowa D 2
90 Brzostek C 4
91 Brzotín D 3
78 Brzozie Lubawskie B 2
79 Brzozów C 3
42 Bua B 2
128 Buarcos A 2
34 Buavag B 1
110 Bubbio C 3
80 Bubry C 3
101 Bučany A 5
149 Buccheri B 4
145 Buccino C 4
128 Bucelas C 1
86 Buch, Bayern, D† C 2
87 Buch, Bayern, D† C 4
86 Buchau C 1
87 Buchbach C 4
97 Buchboden A 5
73 Buchen,D† D 3
66 Büchen,D† B 3
97 Buchenberg A 6
83 Buchères C 6
66 Buchholz,D† B 2
74 Buchholz,D* B 2
117 Buchin A 6
153 Buchin Prokhod B 5
86 Buchloe C 2
89 Buchlovice B 5
50 Buchlyvie A 3
67 Bucholz B 5
97 Buchs A 5
82 Buchy B 3
154 Bučin A 3
117 Bučje C 6
59 Buckden C 3
72 Bückeburg A 3
60 Buckfastleigh C 3
51 Buckhaven A 4
49 Buckie D 6
62 Buckingham A 2
57 Buckley C 3
76 Buckow A 3
49 Bucksburn D 6
67 Bückwitz C 5
117 Bucova A 6
89 Bučovice B 5
103 Bucsa A 5
160 Bucureşti C 5
83 Bucy B 5
83 Bucy-le-Pierrepont B 5
79 Buczek D 2
18 Bud C 2
102 Budakalasz A 3
102 Budakesi A 2
19 Budal C 6
102 Budaörs A 2
102 Budapest A 2
141 Buddusò B 3
60 Bude C 2
88 Budeč B 3
71 Budel A 4
134 Budens B 2
71 Büderich A 5
126 Budia B 3
73 Büdingen C 3
115 Budinščina A 4
88 Budišov, Jihomoravský, CS B 3
89 Budišov, Severomoravsky, CS B 5
60 Budleigh Salterton C 3
101 Budmerice A 5
69 Budowo A 5
112 Búdrio B 3
78 Budry A 4
103 Budureasa B 6
151 Budva C 4
88 Budyně n. Ohři A 2
79 Budziszewice D 2
90 Budzów C 2
69 Budzyń C 4
34 Bue C 1
127 Bueña B 4
131 Buenache de Alarcón B 4
127 Buenache de la Sierra B 4
130 Buenaventura A 2
120 Buenavista de Valdavia B 2
126 Buendía B 3
65 Buer B 6
118 Bueu B 2
120 Buezo B 3
102 Bugac B 3
132 Bugarra B 2
106 Bugeat B 1
141 Buggerru C 2
60 Bugle C 2
115 Bugojno C 5
9 Bugøyfjord C 9
9 Bugøynes C 9
102 Bugyi A 3
97 Bühl,D† A 6
85 Bühl,D† B 5
85 Bühlertal B 5
86 Bühlertann B 1
99 Buia C 4
57 Builth Wells D 3
64 Buitenpost A 4
126 Buitrago B 2
91 Buj D 4
91 Buják E 2
136 Bujalance B 2
153 Bujanovac B 3
122 Bujaraloz C 2
114 Buje B 1
101 Bük,H B 4
77 Buk,PL A 5
91 Bükkábrány E 3
115 Bukkosd A 5
91 Bükkzsérc E 3
154 Bukovo B 3
77 Bukowiec A 5
91 Bukowina C 3
90 Bukowno B 2
69 Bukowo-Morskie A 4
97 Bülach A 4
65 Buldern C 5
49 Buldoo C 5
84 Bulgnéville B 2
66 Bülkau B 1
30 Bulken C 3
79 Bulkowo C 3
71 Bullange B 5
133 Bullas C 1
96 Bulle B 3
62 Bullington Cross Inn B 2
90 Bulowice C 2
152 Bulqizë C 2
151 Buna B 3
52 Bunbeg A 3
55 Bunclody B 5
53 Buncrana A 4
65 Bunde, Niedersachsen, D† A 5
65 Bunde, Nordhein Westfalen, D† B 6
72 Bündheim B 4
52 Bundoran B 3
50 Bunessan A 1
59 Bungay C 5
39 Bunge E 6
114 Bunic C 3
55 Bunmahon B 4
118 Buño A 2
132 Buñol B 2
138 Buñola B 3
70 Bunsbeek B 3
62 Buntingford B 3
121 Buñuel C 5
97 Buochs B 4
146 Buonabitácolo B 1
144 Buonalbergo B 3
112 Buonconvento C 3
146 Buonvicino C 1
99 Burano D 3
73 Burbach C 2
62 Burbage B 2
127 Burbáguena A 4
141 Burcei C 3
15 Bureå D 5
118 Burella de Cabo A 3
72 Büren B 2
96 Büren a. Aare A 3
6 Burfjord B 8
62 Burford B 2
66 Burg, D† B 2
75 Burg, Cottbus, D* B 6
74 Burg, Magdeburg,D* A 3
67 Burg Stargard B 6
160 Burgas D 5
101 Burgau,A B 4
86 Burgau,D† C 2
134 Burgau,P B 2
86 Burgbernheim B 2
96 Burgdorf,CH A 3
66 Burgdorf,D† C 3
73 Burgebrach D 4
74 Bürgel C 3
62 Burgess Hill C 3
59 Burgh le Marsh B 4
73 Burghaslach D 4
73 Burghaun C 3
87 Burghausen C 4
49 Burghead D 5
86 Burgheim C 3
148 Búrgio B 3
86 Burgkunstadt A 3
87 Burglengenfeld B 4
136 Burgo,E C 2
124 Burgo,P C 1
120 Burgo Ranero B 1
86 Burgoberbach B 2
126 Burgohondo B 1
120 Burgos B 3
73 Burgsinn C 3
75 Burgstädt C 4
67 Burgstall,D* C 4
99 Burgstall,I C 2
65 Burgsteinfurt B 5
39 Burgsvik C 5
121 Burguete B 5
122 Burgui B 2
135 Burguillos B 5
126 Burguillos de Toledo C 2
129 Burguillos del Cerro C 4
66 Burhave B 1
104 Burie B 2
132 Burjasot B 2
103 Burjuc C 6
86 Burk B 2
75 Burkau B 6
75 Burkhardtsdorf C 4
85 Burladingen B 6
65 Burlage A 5
58 Burley in Wharfedale B 2
49 Burness B 6
53 Burnfoot A 4
59 Burnham Market C 4
62 Burnham-on-Crouch B 4
61 Burnham-on-Sea B 3
56 Burnley C 4
51 Burnmouth B 5
51 Burntisland A 4
120 Burón A 1
110 Buronzo B 3
117 Burovac B 5
67 Burow B 6
49 Burrafirth A 8
49 Burravoe A 7
152 Burrel C 2
51 Burrelton A 4
54 Burren A 2
105 Burret E 4
132 Burriana B 2
60 Burry Port B 2
97 Burs A 5
42 Burseryd B 3
73 Bürstadt B 2
58 Burton Agnes A 3
61 Burton Bradstock C 4
59 Burton Latimer C 3
59 Burton upon Trent C 2
52 Burtonport B 3
15 Burträsk D 4
126 Burujón C 3
115 Bürüs B 5
62 Burwash C 4
49 Burwick C 6
56 Bury C 4
59 Bury St. Edmonds C 4
79 Burzenin D 1
153 Bŭrziya A 5
141 Busachi B 2
110 Busalla C 3
112 Busana B 2
110 Busano B 3
110 Busca C 2
67 Busch C 4
152 Bushat C 1
62 Bushey B 3
53 Bushmills A 5
91 Bušince D 2
39 Buskhyttan D 3
4 Busknes B 2
90 Busko Zdrój B 3
133 Busot C 2
115 Busovača C 5
136 Busquistar C 3
84 Bussang C 3
111 Busseto C 5
93 Bussière Poitevine C 4
106 Bussières B 4
99 Bussolengo D 1
110 Bussoleno B 2
64 Bussum B 3
96 Busten B 3
110 Busto Arsizio B 3
66 Büsum A 1
103 Buteni B 6
149 Butera B 4
71 Butgenbach B 5
78 Butryny B 3
97 Bütschwil A 5
86 Buttenwiesen C 2
56 Buttermere B 3
54 Buttevant B 3
74 Buttstädt B 3
73 Butzbach C 2
66 Bützfleth B 2
67 Bützow B 4
19 Buvik B 6
94 Buxières C 2
66 Buxtehude B 2
58 Buxton B 2
95 Buxy C 4
93 Buzancais C 5
84 Buzancy A 1
160 Buzău C 5
114 Buzet B 1
103 Buziaş C 5
91 Buzica D 4
101 Buzsák C 5
105 Buzy D 2
61 Bwlch B 3
38 By B 3
160 Byala D 4
77 Byczyna B 7
20 Bydalen B 2
69 Bydgoszcz B 5
59 Byfield C 2
15 Bygdeå D 4
31 Bygdin B 5
15 Bygdsiljum D 4
34 Bygland C 3
34 Byglandsfjord C 3
30 Bygstad B 2
34 Bykle B 3
57 Bylchau C 3
44 Bylderup C 2
89 Bylnice B 6
33 Byn A 8
41 Byrum B 5
88 Byšice-Liblice A 2
15 Byske D 5
89 Býškovice B 5
69 Byslaw B 5
89 Bystré, Východočeský, CS B 4
91 Bystré, **Vychodoslovenský**, CS C 4
89 Bystřice, Severomoravsky, CS B 6
88 Bystřice, Středočeský, CS B 2
89 Bystřice n. Pernstejnem B 4
89 Bystřice p. Hostýnem B 5
89 Bystrzyca Klodzka A 4
89 Bytča B 6
90 Bytom B 1
77 Bytom Odrzanski B 4
77 Bytoń A 5
69 Bytów A 5
43 Byxelkrok B 6
89 Bzenec C 5
89 Bzince C 5

C

128 Cabaço B 2
104 Cabanac-et-Villagrains C 2
119 Cabañaquinta A 5
118 Cabañas A 2
126 Cabañas de Yepes C 2
130 Cabañas del Castillo B 1
123 Cabanellas B 5
132 Cabanes A 3
121 Cabanillas B 5
114 Cabar B 2
109 Cabasse D 3
130 Cabaza del Buey C 1
124 Cabeceiras de Basto B 1
128 Cabeço de Vide B 3
110 Cabella Ligure C 4
125 Cabenzas del Villar C 4
103 Căbeşti B 6
135 Cabeza la Vaca A 4
126 Cabezamesada C 2
130 Cabezarados C 2
130 Cabezarrubias del Puerto C 2
134 Cabezas Rubias B 3
120 Cabezón C 2
120 Cabezón de la Sal A 2
120 Cabezón de Liébana A 2
126 Cabezuela A 2
129 Cabezuela del Valle A 5
127 Cabolafuente A 3
82 Cabourg B 1
136 Cabra,E B 2
124 Cabra,P C 2
136 Cabra del Santo Cristo B 3
49 Cabrach D 5
120 Cabrales A 2
141 Cábras C 2
124 Cabreiro, Braga, P B 1
118 Cabreiros A 3
127 Cabrejas B 3
128 Cabrela C 2
107 Cabrières D 3
119 Cacabelos B 4
117 Cacak C 4
128 Cacavem C 1
148 Cáccamo B 3
147 Caccuri C 2
134 Cacela B 3
129 Cáceres B 4
118 Cachafeiro B 2
134 Cachope B 3
89 Čachtice C 5
136 Cacin B 3
115 Čačinci B 5
117 Cacova A 5
128 Cadafais B 1
107 Cadalen D 2
129 Cadalso A 4
126 Cadalso de los Vidrios B 1
55 Cadamstown A 4
123 Cadaqués B 6
103 Cadăr C 5
128 Cadaval B 1
119 Cadavedo A 4
115 Cadavica, Bosna i Hercegovina, YU B 5
115 Cadavica, Bosna i Hercegovina, YU C 4
90 Čadca C 1
105 Cadéac E 3
97 Cadégolo B 6
112 Cadelbosco di Sopra B 2
97 Cadenazzo B 4
66 Cadenberge B 2
109 Cadenet D 2
104 Cadeuil B 2
104 Cadillac C 2
135 Cádiz C 4
62 Cadnam C 2
104 Cadouin C 3
122 Cadrete C 2
82 Caen B 1
58 Caenby Corner B 3
57 Caergwrle C 3
57 Caernarvon C 2
61 Caerphilly B 3
57 Caersws D 3
128 Cafede B 3
145 Caggiano C 4
113 Cagli C 4
141 Cágliari C 3
145 Cagnano Varano B 4
109 Cagnes D 4
55 Caher B 4
54 Cahercornish B 3
54 Cahermore C 1
54 Cahersiveen C 1
105 Cahors C 4
144 Caiazzo B 3
50 Cairnoch A 3
50 Cairnryan C 3
110 Cáiro Montenotte C 3
59 Caister-on-Sea C 5
58 Caistor B 3
144 Caivano C 3
123 Caixans B 4
106 Cajarc C 1
116 Cajetina C 3
91 Čajkov D 1
116 Čajniče C 3
101 Čaka A 6
101 Čakajovce A 6
115 Čakovec A 4
88 Čakovice A 2
154 Cakran B 1
135 Cala B 4
139 Cala Ratjada B 4
145 Calabritto C 4
122 Calaceite D 3
140 Calacuccia B 2
123 Calaf C 4
128 Calafell C 4
136 Calahonda C 3
121 Calahorra B 5

63 Calais B 3
127 Calamocha B 4
129 Calamonte C 4
135 Calañas B 4
122 Calanda D 2
141 Calangiánus B 3
160 Calarasi C 5
149 Calascibetta B 4
141 Calasetta C 2
133 Calasparra C 1
148 Calatafimi B 2
127 Calatayud A 4
127 Calatorao A 4
75 Calau B 5
74 Calbe B 3
127 Calcena A 4
113 Calcinelli C 4
111 Calco B 4
99 Caldaro C 2
113 Caldarola C 5
128 Caldas da Rainha B 1
123 Caldas de Malavella C 5
123 Caldas de Montbúy C 5
118 Caldas de Reyes B 2
124 Caldas de S. Jorge C 1
124 Caldas de Vizela B 1
56 Calder Bridge B 3
123 Calders C 4
110 Caldirola C 4
129 Caleadilla de los Barros C 4
53 Caledon B 5
123 Calella, Barcelona, E C 5
123 Calella, Gerona, E C 6
140 Calenzana B 1
135 Calera de León A 4
130 Calera y Chozas B 1
120 Caleruega C 3
130 Caleruela B 1
112 Calestano B 2
48 Calgary E 2
146 Calimera B 4
145 Calitri C 4
110 Calizzano C 3
80 Callac B 3
55 Callan B 4
50 Callander A 3
109 Callas D 3
110 Calliano, Piemonte, I B 3
99 Calliano, Trentino-Alto Adige, I D 2
60 Callington C 2
133 Callosa de Ensarriá C 2
133 Callosa de Segura C 2
52 Callow C 2
123 Callús C 4
116 Čalma A 3
85 Calmbach B 5
61 Calne B 5
133 Caloe C 3
111 Calolziocorte B 4
123 Calonge C 6
101 Čalovec B 5
101 Calovo B 5
62 Calshot C 2
148 Caltabellotta B 3
149 Caltagirone B 4
149 Caltanissetta B 4
148 Caltavuturo B 3
127 Caltojar A 3
110 Caluso B 2
118 Calvario C 2
145 Calvello C 4
140 Calvi B 1
138 Calvia B 3
107 Calvisson D 4
67 Calvörde C 4
85 Calw B 5
130 Calzada de Calatrava C 3
125 Calzada de Valdunciel B 4
120 Camaleño A 2
103 Camăr A 6
122 Camarasa C 3
126 Camarena B 1
107 Camarès D 2
80 Camaret B 2
109 Camaret-sur-A. C 1
127 Camarillas B 5
118 Camariñas A 1
126 Camarma B 2
119 Camarzana de Tera B 4
135 Camas B 4
148 Camastra B 3
49 Camb A 7
118 Cambados B 2
124 Cambarinho C 1
73 Camberg C 2
62 Camberley B 3
136 Cambil B 3
51 Cambo B 6
105 Cambo-les-Bains D 1
60 Camborne C 1
70 Cambrai B 2
118 Cambre A 2
59 Cambridge C 4
123 Cambrils C 4
67 Cambs B 4
74 Camburg B 3
60 Camelford C 2
118 Camelle A 1
113 Camerano C 5
113 Camerino C 5
145 Camerota C 4
147 Camigliatello Silano C 2
124 Caminha B 1
125 Caminomorisco C 3
127 Caminreal B 4
112 Camiore C 2
99 Camisano Vicentino D 2
49 Cammachmore D 6
148 Cammarata B 3
110 Camogli C 4
55 Camolin B 5
80 Camors C 4
145 Campagna C 4
143 Campagnano di Roma B 3
142 Campagnático B 2
105 Campan D 3
147 Campana C 2
129 Campanario C 5
136 Campanillas C 2
135 Campano C 4
126 Campaspero A 1
49 Campbelltown D 4
50 Campbeltown B 2
133 Campello C 2
128 Campelos B 1
112 Campi Bisénzio C 3
146 Campi Salentina B 4
133 Campico López D 1
142 Campiglia Marittima A 1
132 Campillo de Altobuey B 1
127 Campillo de Aragón A 4
136 Campillo de Arenas B 3
129 Campillo de Llerena C 5
136 Campillos B 2
125 Campilo C 4
160 Câmpina C 4
143 Campli B 4
122 Campo,E B 3
124 Campo,P B 1
118 Campo de Becerros B 3
131 Campo de Criptana B 3
110 Campo Ligure C 3
129 Campo Maior B 3
110 Campo Molina C 2
126 Campo Real B 2
98 Campo Tures C 2
144 Campobasso B 3
148 Campobello di Licata B 3
148 Campobello di Mazara B 2
99 Campodársego D 2
97 Campodolcino B 5
148 Campofelice di Roccella B 3
148 Campofiorito B 3
99 Campofórmido C 4
148 Campofranco B 3
135 Campofrio B 4
112 Campogalliano B 2
99 Campolongo C 3
119 Campomanes A 5
145 Campomarino B 4
148 Camporeale B 3
113 Camporeggiano C 4
122 Camporrella C 3
132 Camporrobles B 1
124 Campos B 2
139 Campos del Puerto B 4
124 Camposa B 1
99 Camposampiero D 2
112 Camposanto B 3
122 Camposines C 3
136 Campotéjar B 3
143 Campotosto B 4
123 Camprodón B 5
104 Campsegret C 3
51 Camptown B 5
160 Campulung C 4
160 Campulung Moldovenesc B 4
139 C'an Picafort B 4
142 Cana B 2
127 Cañada del Hoyo C 4
131 Cañadajuncosa B 4
135 Cañadarrosal B 5
160 Canakkale E 5
99 Canal San Bovo C 2
110 Canale C 2
132 Canales B 2
133 Canals C 2
130 Cañamero B 1
136 Cañate la Real C 1
129 Canaveral B 4
135 Cañaveral de León A 4
127 Cañaveras B 3
99 Canazei C 2
81 Cancale B 5
145 Cancellara C 4
144 Cancello ed Arnone B 3
104 Cancon C 3
119 Canda B 4
118 Candamil A 3
119 Candamo A 4
122 Candanchu B 2
119 Candás A 5
122 Candasnos C 3
81 Candé C 5
145 Candela B 4
125 Candelario C 4
130 Candeleda A 1
110 Cándia Lomellina B 3
99 Candide C 3
119 Candín B 4
124 Candosa C 2
49 Candy E 6
128 Canecas C 1
110 Canelli C 3
136 Canena A 3
126 Canencia B 2
132 Canet de Berenguer B 2
123 Canet de Mar C 5
123 Canet-Plage B 6
127 Cañete B 4
136 Cañete de las Torres B 2
122 Canfranc B 2
118 Cangas, Lugo, E A 3
118 Cangas, Pontevedra, E B 2
119 Cangas de Narcea A 4
120 Cangas de Onis A 1
128 Canha C 2
134 Canhestros A 2
148 Canicatti B 3
149 Canicattini Bagni B 5
121 Canicosa de la Sierra C 3
124 Canidelo B 1
137 Caniles B 4
136 Canillas de Aceituno C 2
136 Canillas de Albaida C 3
142 Canino B 2
81 Canisy A 5
125 Cañizal B 4
119 Cañizo C 5
137 Canjáyer B 4
143 Cannara B 3
97 Cannero Riveriera B 4
109 Cannes D 4
142 Canneto A 1
111 Canneto sull'Ólio B 5
48 Cannich D 4
61 Cannington B 4
97 Cannóbio B 4
57 Cannock D 4
51 Canonbie B 5
145 Canosa di Púglia B 5
110 Canove C 3
125 Cantalapiedra B 4
126 Cantalejo A 2
129 Cantalgallo C 4
143 Cantalice B 3
125 Cantalpino B 4
143 Cantalupo in Sabina B 3
124 Cantanhede C 1
132 Cantavieja A 2
102 Čantavir C 3
62 Canterbury B 5
113 Cantiano C 4
135 Cantillana B 5
125 Cantiveros C 5
137 Cantoria B 4
110 Cantu B 4
62 Canvey B 4
82 Cany-Barville B 2
123 Canyet C 5
99 Cáorle D 3
111 Caorso B 4
105 Cap-de-Pin C 2
104 Cap Ferret C 1
145 Capáccio C 4
148 Capaci A 3
142 Capalbio B 2
112 Capánnóri C 2
116 Capardi B 2
154 Capari A 3
121 Caparroso B 5
105 Capbreton D 1
122 Capdella B 3
106 Capdenac C 2
139 Capdepera B 4
62 Capel B 3
57 Capel Curig C 3
118 Capela A 2
129 Capelins C 3
123 Capellades C 4
143 Capena B 3
107 Capendu D 2
107 Capestang D 3
143 Capestrano B 4
136 Capileira C 3
128 Capinha A 3
103 Căpinis C 4
143 Capistrello C 4
149 Capizzi B 4
115 Caplje C 4
151 Capljina B 3
97 Capo di Ponte B 6
149 Capo d'Orlando A 4
97 Capolago C 4
99 Caposile D 3
141 Capoterra C 2
73 Cappel C 2
65 Cappeln B 6
51 Cappercleuch B 4
55 Cappoquin B 4
144 Capracotta B 3
142 Capránica B 3
142 Caprarola B 3
142 Capretta B 3
144 Capriati a Volturno B 3
99 Caprino Veronése D 1
103 Căpruta B 6
105 Captieux C 2
144 Capua B 3
145 Capurso B 5
105 Capvern D 3
126 Carabaña B 2
126 Carabias A 2
160 Caracal C 4
127 Caracenilla B 3
110 Caráglio C 2
123 Carálps B 5
107 Caraman D 1
143 Caramánico B 5
119 Caranga A 4
128 Caranguejeira B 2
117 Caransebeş A 6
80 Carantec B 3
145 Carapelle B 4
111 Carasco C 4
117 Caraşova A 5
110 Carate Brianza B 4
137 Caravaca A 5
111 Caravággio B 4
120 Caravia A 1
129 Carbajo B 3
118 Carballeda B 3
118 Carballeda de Avia B 2
118 Carballino B 2
118 Carballo A 2
130 Carbayuela B 1
60 Carbis Bay C 1
104 Carbon-Blanc C 2
121 Carbonera C 4
137 Carboneras B 5
127 Carboneras de Guadazaón C 4
126 Carbonero el Mayor A 1
136 Carboneros A 3
141 Carbónia C 2
99 Carbonin C 3
105 Carbonne D 4
117 Cărbunari B 5
55 Carbury A 5
129 Carcaboso A 4
136 Carcabuey B 2
133 Carcagente B 2
104 Carcans B 1
104 Carcans-Plage B 1
121 Carcar B 5
110 Cárcare C 3
107 Carcassonne D 2
121 Carcastillo B 5
133 Carcelén B 1
109 Carcès D 3
136 Carchelejo B 3
123 Cardedeu C 5
136 Cardeña A 2
127 Cardenete C 4
126 Cardeñosa B 1
147 Cardeto D 1
61 Cardiff B 3
60 Cardigan A 2
123 Cardona C 4
128 Cardosos B 2
81 Carentan A 5
81 Carentoir C 4
147 Careri D 2
115 Carevdar A 4
51 Carfraemill Hotel B 5
140 Cargèse B 1
80 Carhaix-Plouguer B 3
128 Caria A 3
147 Cariati C 2
145 Carife B 4
70 Carignan C 4
110 Carignano C 2
127 Cariñena A 4
148 Carini A 3
48 Carinish D 1
118 Cariño A 3
56 Cark B 4
149 Carlentini B 5
83 Carlepont B 5
132 Carlet B 2
84 Carling A 3
53 Carlingford B 5
56 Carlisle B 4
141 Carloforte C 2
147 Carlópoli C 2
51 Carlops B 4
55 Carlow B 5
48 Carloway C 2
59 Carlton C 2
50 Carluke B 4
110 Carmagnola C 2
120 Carmargo A 3
60 Carmarthen B 2
107 Carmaux C 2
126 Carmena C 1
119 Cármenes B 5
110 Cármine C 2
135 Carmona B 5
129 Carmonita B 4
80 Carnac C 3
128 Carnaxide C 1
53 Carndonagh A 4
55 Carnew B 5
56 Carnforth B 4
99 Cárnia C 4
53 Carnlough B 5
57 Carno D 3
135 Carnón B 4
107 Carnon Plage D 3
118 Carnota B 1
51 Carnoustie A 5
50 Carnwath B 4
147 Carolei C 2
144 Carolina B 2
65 Carolinensiel A 5
81 Carolles B 5
97 Carona B 5
149 Caronia A 4
146 Carovigno B 3
144 Carovilli B 3
111 Carpaneto Piacentino C 4
113 Carpegna C 4
111 Carpenedolo B 5
109 Carpentras C 2
112 Carpi B 2
110 Carpignano Sésia B 3
103 Cărpinet B 6
112 Carpineti B 2
143 Carpineto Ramano C 4
145 Carpino B 4
144 Carpinone B 3
125 Carpio B 4
125 Carpio Medianero C 4
81 Carquefou C 5
109 Carqueiranne D 3
52 Carracastle C 3
124 Carraceda de Anciães B 2
118 Carral A 2
126 Carranque B 2
124 Carrapichana C 2
112 Carrara B 2
130 Carrascalejo B 1
127 Carrascosa del Campo B 3
136 Carratraca C 2
124 Carrazedo de Montenegro B 2
49 Carrbridge D 5
124 Carregal do Sal C 1
119 Carreño A 5
52 Carrick B 3
52 Carrick on Shannon C 3
55 Carrick-on-Suir B 4
52 Carrickart A 4
55 Carrickbeg B 4
55 Carrickboy A 4
53 Carrickfergus B 6
53 Carrickmacross C 5
54 Carrigaholt B 2
54 Carrigahorig A 3
54 Carrigaline C 3
53 Carrigallen C 4
54 Carrigtwohill C 3
130 Carrión de Celatrava B 3
120 Carrión de los Condes B 2
119 Carrizo B 5
131 Carrizosa C 4

103 Cenad B 4
99 Cencenighe C 2
118 Cendoy B 3
107 Cendras C 4
103 Cenei C 4
136 Cenes B 3
112 Ceneselli A 3
126 Cenicientos B 1
117 Centa A 4
110 Centallo C 2
123 Centellas C 5
112 Cento B 3
113 Centóia C 3
149 Centúripe B 4
125 Cepeda la Mora C 4
102 Cepin C 2
102 Čepinski-Martinci C 2
114 Čepovan A 1
143 Ceprano C 4
115 Ćeralije B 5
149 Cerami B 4
110 Cerano B 3
79 Ceranów C 5
93 Cérans Foulletourte B 4
145 Ceraso C 4
112 Cerbáia C 3
123 Cerbère B 6
126 Cercadillo A 3
128 Cercal, Lisboa, P B 1
134 Cercal, Setúbal, P B 2
126 Cerceda B 2
144 Cercemaggiore B 3
94 Cercy-la-Tour C 3
148 Cerda B 3
118 Cerdedo B 2
124 Cerdeira C 2
94 Cerdon B 2
112 Cerea A 3
51 Ceres,GB A 5
110 Céres,I B 2
112 Cerese A 2
110 Ceresole-Reale B 2
109 Cereste D 2
123 Ceret B 5
126 Cerezo de Abajo A 2
120 Cerezo de Riotirón B 3
70 Cerfontaine B 3
95 Cergy C 4
145 Cerignola B 4
94 Cérilly C 2
83 Cerisiers C 5
92 Cerizay C 3
114 Cerknica B 2
114 Cerkno A 1
154 Cerme Proskë A 1
116 Cerna A 2
89 Černá Hora B 4
88 Cerná v. Pošumavi C 2
160 Cernavoda C 6
85 Cernay C 4
84 Cernay-en-Dormois A 1
61 Cerne Abbas C 4
120 Cérnegula B 3
115 Cernik B 5
110 Cernóbbio B 4
87 Černošin B 4
88 Černovice B 2
91 Cerovo D 2
142 Cerqueto B 3
125 Cerralbo C 3
113 Cerreto d'Esi C 4
144 Cerreto Sannita B 3
57 Cerrigydrudon C 3
154 Çerrik A 1
136 Cerro Muriano A 2
112 Certaldo C 3
110 Certosa di Pésio C 2
124 Cerva B 2
143 Cervaro C 4
120 Cervatos de la Cueza B 2
88 Červená Rečice B 3
91 Červená-Skala D 3
89 Červená Voda A 4
89 Červeny Kameň B 6
88 Cerveny Kostelec A 4
123 Cervera C 4
127 Cervera de la Cañada A 4
120 Cervera de Pisuerga B 2
127 Cervera del Llano C 3
121 Cervera del Rio Alhama B 5
142 Cervéteri C 3
122 Cerviá,E C 3
113 Cérvia,I B 4
99 Cervignano del Friuli D 4
144 Cervinara B 3
140 Cervione B 2
118 Cervo A 3
94 Cervon B 3
108 Cesana Tor C 3
114 Cesarica C 3
149 Cesarò B 4
99 Cesarolo D 4
113 Cesena B 4
113 Cesenático B 4
88 Česká Bělá B 3
75 Česká Kamenice C 6
88 Česká Lípa A 2
88 Česká Skalice A 4
89 Česká Třebova B 4
91 České Brezovo D 2
88 České Budějovice C 2
88 Ceské Velenice C 2
88 Český Brod A 2
88 Česky Krumlov C 2
89 Český Těšín B 6
117 Češljeva Bara B 5
99 Cessalto D 3
107 Cessenon D 3
88 Cestín B 3
116 Čestobrodica C 4
121 Cestona A 4
118 Cesuras A 2
127 Cetina A 4
115 Cetingrad B 3
151 Cetinje C 4
147 Cetraro C 1
133 Ceuti C 1
110 Ceva C 3
120 Cevico de la Torre C 2
120 Cevico Navero C 2
108 Cevins B 3
97 Cévio B 4
151 Cevo C 4
106 Ceyrat B 3
95 Ceyzériat C 5
64 Chaam C 2
104 Chabanais B 3
108 Chabeuil C 2
94 Chablis B 3
108 Châbons B 2
90 Chabówka C 2
93 Chabris B 5
60 Chacewater C 1
95 Chagny C 4
125 Chaherrero C 5
81 Chailland B 6
92 Chaillé-les-Marais C 2
83 Chailley C 5
107 Chalabre E 2
104 Chalais B 3
108 Chalamont B 2
62 Chale C 2
95 Chalindrey B 5
92 Challans C 2
108 Challes-les-Eaux B 2
106 Chalmazel B 3
94 Chalmoux C 3
95 Chalon-sur-Saône C 4
81 Chalonnes-sur-Loire C 6
83 Châlons-sur-Marne C 6
69 Chalupy A 6
104 Châlus B 3
97 Cham,CH A 4
87 Cham,D† B 4
108 Chamaloc C 2
104 Chamberet B 4
108 Chambery B 2
94 Chambilly C 4
84 Chambley A 2
83 Chambly B 4
94 Chambon, Creuse, F C 2
106 Chambon, Puy de Dôme, F B 2
93 Chambord B 5
107 Chamborigaud C 3
106 Chamboulive B 1
87 Chamerau B 4
95 Chameroy B 5
108 Chamonix B 3
108 Chamoux B 3
106 Champagnac-le-Vieux B 3
104 Champagne-Mouton A 3
84 Champagney C 3
95 Champagnole C 5
83 Champaubert C 5
94 Champcevrais B 2
92 Champdeniers C 3
106 Champdieu B 4
95 Champdôtre B 5
106 Champeix B 3
96 Champéry B 2
81 Champigné C 6
93 Champigny-sur-Veude B 4
95 Champlitte-et-le-Prélot B 5
110 Champoluc B 2
106 Champoly B 3
110 Champorcher B 2
82 Champrond-en-Gâtine C 3
94 Champs B 3
106 Champs-sur-Tarentaine B 2
81 Champtoce-sur-Loire C 6
81 Champtoceaux C 5
95 Champvans B 5
128 Chamusca B 2
119 Chana B 4
106 Chanac C 3
106 Chanaleilles C 3
96 Chancy B 2
118 Chandreja de Queija B 3
126 Chañe A 1
94 Changy C 3
118 Chantada B 3
94 Chantelle C 3
106 Chanteuges B 3
83 Chantilly B 4
92 Chantonnay C 2
128 Chão de Codes B 2
83 Chaource C 6
118 Chapa B 2
108 Chapareillart B 2
57 Chapel en le Frith C 5
82 Chapelle Royale C 3
108 Chaponost B 1
108 Charavines-les-Bains B 2
61 Chard C 4
84 Charency A 2
83 Charenton C 4
94 Charenton-sur-Cher C 2
62 Charing B 4
62 Charlbury B 2
70 Charleroi B 3
52 Charlestown C 3
49 Charlestown of Aberlour D 5
70 Charleville C 3
95 Charlieu C 4
36 Charlottenberg B 4
83 Charly-sur-Marne C 5
108 Charmes, Ardèche, F C 1
84 Charmes, Vosges, F B 3
96 Charmey B 3
61 Charmouth C 4
95 Charnay C 4
94 Charny B 3
95 Charolles C 4
93 Chârost C 6
84 Charquemont C 3
94 Charrin C 3
104 Charroux A 3
82 Chartres C 3
69 Charzykowy B 5
104 Chasseneuil-sur-Bonnieure B 3
95 Chassigny B 5
111 Chastiglione Chiavarese C 4
109 Château-Arnoux C 3
94 Château-Chinon B 3
96 Château-d'Oex B 3
93 Château-du-Loir B 4
81 Château-Gontier C 6
93 Château-la-Vallière B 4
83 Château Landon C 4
104 Château-l'Evêque B 3
83 Château Porcien B 6
93 Château-Renault B 4
84 Château-Salins B 3
83 Château-Thierry B 5
104 Châteaubernard B 2
81 Châteaubourg B 5
81 Châteaubriant C 5
82 Châteaudun C 3
81 Châteaugiron B 5
80 Châteaulaudren B 4
80 Châteaulin B 2
94 Châteaumeillant C 2
109 Châteauneuf, Bouches du Rhône, F D 2
94 Châteauneuf, Nièvre, F B 3
95 Chateauneuf, Saône-et-Loire, F C 4
109 Châteauneuf-de-C. C 2
80 Châteauneuf-de-Faou B 3
108 Châteauneuf-de-G. B 1
81 Chateauneuf-d'Ille-et-V. B 5
109 Châteauneuf-du-Rhône C 1
82 Châteauneuf-en-Thymerais C 3
104 Châteauneuf-la-Forêt B 4
104 Châteauneuf-sur-Charente B 2
94 Châteauneuf-sur-Cher C 2
94 Châteauneuf-sur-Loire B 2
81 Châteauneuf-sur-Sarthe C 6
104 Châteauponsac A 4
109 Châteauredon C 3
94 Châteaurenard, Loiret, F B 2
109 Châteaurenard, Vaucluse, F D 1
108 Châteauroux, Hautes Alpe, F C 3
93 Châteauroux, Indre, F C 5
84 Châteauvillain B 1
94 Châtel-Censoir B 3
94 Châtel-de-Neuvre C 3
106 Châtel-Guyon B 3
94 Châtel-Montagne C 3
96 Châtel-St.-Denis B 2
84 Châtel-sur-Mouselle B 3
104 Chatelaillon-Plage A 1
70 Châtelet B 3
93 Châtellerault C 4
94 Chatenay-St. Imbert C 3
84 Châtenois, Terr. de Belfört., F C 3
84 Châtenois, Vosges, F B 2
62 Chatham B 4
71 Châtillon,B C 4
108 Châtillon,F A 1
110 Chatillon,I B 2
94 Châtillon-Coligny B 2
108 Châtillon-de-Michaille A 2
94 Châtillon-en-Bazois B 3
108 Chatillon-en-Diois C 2
93 Châtillon-sur-Indre C 5
94 Châtillon-sur-Loire B 2
83 Châtillon-sur-Marne B 5
95 Châtillon-sur-Seine B 4
83 Châtres C 5
59 Chatteris C 4
136 Chauchina B 3
106 Chaudes-Aigues C 3
106 Chaudeyrac C 3
83 Chaudrey C 6
95 Chauffailles C 4
108 Chauffayer C 3
83 Chaulnes B 4
95 Chaumergy C 5
83 Chaumont, Ardennes, F B 6
84 Chaumont, Haute Marne, F B 2
93 Chaumont, Loir-et-Cher, F B 5
82 Chaumont-en-Vexin B 3
70 Chaumont-Gistoux B 3
84 Chaumont-sur-Aure B 2
93 Chaunay C 4
83 Chauny B 5
95 Chaussin C 5
93 Chauvigny C 4
92 Chavagnes-en-Paillers C 2
84 Chavanges B 1
124 Chaves B 2
83 Chavignon B 5
106 Chazelles-sur-Lyon B 4
108 Chazey-Bons B 2
57 Cheadle, Cheshire, GB C 4
57 Cheadle, Staffs., GB D 5
87 Cheb A 4
127 Checa B 4
90 Checiny B 3
61 Cheddar B 4
94 Chéerailles C 2
104 Chef-Boutonne A 2
129 Cheles C 3
133 Chella B 2
83 Chelles C 4
90 Chelmek B 2
78 Chelmno, Bydgoszcz, PL B 1
79 Chelmno, Poznań PL C 1
62 Chelmondiston B 5
62 Chelmsford B 4
78 Chelmza B 1
61 Cheltenham B 4
132 Chelva B 2
93 Chémery B 5
92 Chemillé B 3
95 Chemin C 5
75 Chemnitz C 4
93 Chenonceaux B 5
95 Chenoye B 4
94 Cheny B 3
61 Chepstow B 4
132 Chera B 2
110 Cherasco C 2
71 Cheratte B 4
81 Cherbourg A 5
146 Cherchiara di Calábria C 2
160 Chernovtsy A 4
83 Chéroy C 4
132 Chert A 3
122 Cherta D 3
62 Chertsey B 3
83 Chéry B 5
62 Chesham B 3
62 Cheshunt B 3
83 Chessy-le-Prés C 5
132 Cheste B 2
57 Chester C 4
51 Chester le Street C 6
58 Chesterfield B 2
153 Chetirtsi B 4
94 Chevagnes C 3
104 Chevanceaux B 2
96 Chevenez A 3
103 Cheveruşu Mare C 5
84 Chevillon B 2
82 Chevilly C 3
95 Chevroux C 4
61 Chew Magna B 4
95 Chezery C 5
83 Chézy-sur-Marne C 5
110 Chialamberto B 2
99 Chiampo D 2
110 Chianale C 2
142 Chianciano Terme A 2
149 Chiaramonte Gulfi B 4
141 Chiaramonti B 2
113 Chiaravalle C 5
147 Chiaravalle Centrale D 2
97 Chiaréggio B 5
111 Chiari B 4
146 Chiaromonte B 2
111 Chiávari C 4
97 Chiavenna B 5
92 Chiché C 3
62 Chichester C 3
61 Chicklade B 4
135 Chiclana de la Frontera C 4
62 Chiddingfold B 3
110 Chieri B 2
97 Chiesa in Valmalenco B 5
143 Chieti B 5
143 Chieti Scalo B 5
145 Chiéuti B 4
70 Chièvres B 2
127 Chillarón de Cuenca B 3
127 Chillarón del Rey B 3
83 Chilleurs C 4
130 Chillón C 2
137 Chilluevar B 3
126 Chiloeches B 2
70 Chimay B 3
136 Chimeneas B 3
133 Chinchilla de Monte-Aragón C 1
126 Chinchón B 2
62 Chinnor B 3
93 Chinon B 4
113 Chióggia A 4
110 Chiomonte B 1
135 Chipiona C 4
61 Chippenham B 4
62 Chipping Campden A 2
62 Chipping Norton B 2
61 Chipping Sodbury B 4
153 Chiprovtsi A 4
106 Chirac C 3
57 Chirbury D 3
108 Chirens B 2
137 Chirivel B 4
57 Chirk D 3
51 Chirnside B 5
62 Chiseldon B 2
103 Chisineu-Cris B 5
95 Chissey-en-Morvan B 4
99 Chiusa C 2
110 Chiusa di Pésio C 2
148 Chiusa Solanfani B 3
99 Chiusaforte C 4
142 Chiusi A 2
132 Chiva B 2
110 Chivasso B 2
79 Chlewiska D 3
77 Chludowo A 5
88 Chlum u. Trebone C 2
88 Chlumec n. Cidlinou A 3
90 Chmielnik B 3
90 Chmielów B 4
77 Chobienia B 5
77 Chobienice A 4
88 Choceň A 4
91 Chocholow C 2
77 Chocianów B 4
68 Chociwel B 3
69 Choczewo A 5
79 Chodaków C 3
79 Chodecz C 2
79 Chodel D 5
75 Chodov C 4
87 Chodová Planá B 4

79 Chodów C 5
69 Chodziez C 4
68 Chojna C 2
69 Chojnice B 5
77 Chojno A 5
77 Chojnów B 4
79 Cholcza D 4
92 Cholet B 3
62 Cholsey B 2
108 Chomerac C 1
75 Chomutov C 5
108 Chorges C 3
56 Chorley C 4
78 Chorzele B 3
90 Chorzów B 1
68 Choszczno B 3
88 Chotěboř B 3
87 Chotěšov B 5
83 Chouilly B 6
128 Chouto B 2
93 Chouzy-sur-C. B 5
119 Chozas de Abajo B 5
88 Chrast, Vychodočeský, CS B 3
87 Chrást, Zapadočeský, CS B 5
76 Chrastava C 4
75 Chřibská C 6
44 Christansfeld B 2
61 Christchurch C 5
89 Chropyně B 5
88 Chrudim B 3
90 Chrzanów B 2
101 Chtelnica A 5
135 Chucena B 4
60 Chudleigh C 3
126 Chueca C 2
97 Chur B 5
57 Church Stretton D 4
136 Churriana, Granada, E B 3
136 Churriana, Málaga, E C 2
97 Churwalden B 5
89 Chvalčov B 5
88 Chvalšiny C 2
69 Chwaszczyno A 6
88 Chynava A 2
88 Chýnov B 2
79 Chynów D 4
101 Chyzerovce A 6
90 Chyzne C 2
117 Ciacova A 5
120 Ciadoncha B 3
148 Cianciana B 3
112 Ciano d'Enza B 2
102 Cibakhaza B 4
128 Ciborro C 2
110 Cicagna C 4
144 Cicciano C 3
117 Ćićevac C 5
143 Ciciliano C 3
111 Cicognolo B 5
124 Cidadelhe C 2
121 Cidonas C 4
78 Ciechanów C 3
78 Ciechocinek C 1
79 Cieksyn C 3
79 Cieladz D 3
68 Ciemnik B 3
126 Ciempozuelos B 2
77 Cienin Kośielny A 7
79 Ciepielów D 4
77 Cieplice Slaskie Zdrój C 4
90 Čierne C 1
91 Čierny Balog D 2
105 Cierp E 3
69 Cierpice C 6
121 Ciervana A 3
89 Cieszyn B 6
105 Cieutat D 3
133 Cieza C 1
90 Ciežkowice, Kraków, PL C 3
90 Ciezkowice, Kraków, PL B 2
101 Cifer A 5
127 Cifuentes B 3
77 Cigacice A 4
120 Cigales C 2
91 Cigánd D 4
110 Cigliano B 3
151 Čilipi C 4
101 Čilizská Radvan B 5
127 Cillas B 4
129 Cilleros A 4
125 Cilleros el Hondo C 4
120 Cilleruelo B 3
120 Cilleruelo de Arriba C 3
120 Cillorigo-Castro A 2
48 Cilmalieu E 3
117 Cîlnik A 5
97 Cimalmotto B 4
119 Cimanes del Tejar B 5
148 Ciminna B 3
99 Cimoláis C 3
132 Cinctorres A 2
61 Cinderford B 4
88 Činěves A 3
70 Ciney B 4
124 Cinfães B 1
111 Cingia de Botti B 5
113 Cingoli C 5
142 Cinigiano B 2
91 Cinobaňa D 2
75 Cinovec C 5
93 Cinq-Mars-la-Pile B 4
147 Cinquefrondi D 2
105 Cintegabelle D 4
103 Cintei B 5
121 Cintruénigo B 5
121 Ciórroga A 4
125 Ciperez C 3
132 Cirat A 2
104 Ciré-d'Aunis A 2
146 Cirella C 1
61 Cirencester B 5
85 Cirey-sur-Vezouze B 3
127 Ciria A 4
110 Ciriè B 2
146 Cirigliano B 2
147 Cirò C 3
147 Cirò Marina C 3
95 Ciry-le-Noble C 4
66 Cismar A 3
99 Cismon del Grappa D 2
120 Cisneros B 2
87 Čistá A 5
143 Cisterna di Papa C 3
126 Cistérniga A 1
146 Cisternino B 3
120 Cistierna B 1
151 Čitluk, Bosna i Hercegovina, YU B 3
117 Čitluk, Srbija, YU C 6
88 Citov A 2
142 Città d. Pieve B 3
143 Citta d. Vaticano C 3
113 Città di Castello C 4
143 Citta Sant'Angelo B 5
99 Cittadella D 2
147 Cittanova D 2
160 Ciucea B 3
125 Ciudad Rodrigo C 3
139 Ciudadela B 4
103 Ciumeghiu B 5
123 Ciutadilla C 4
99 Cividale del Friuli C 4
143 Civita B 4
143 Civita Castellana B 3
113 Civitanova Alta C 5
113 Civitanova Marche C 5
142 Civitavécchia B 2
143 Civitella d. Tronto B 4
113 Civitella de Romagna B 3
143 Civitella Roveto C 4
104 Civray A 3
48 Clabhach E 2
50 Clachan, Argyll, GB A 3
48 Clachan, North Uist, GB D 1
48 Clachan, Skye, GB D 2
48 Clachtoll C 3
50 Clackmannan A 4
62 Clackton-on-Sea B 5
50 Cladich A 2
95 Clairvaux-les-Laes C 5
83 Clamart C 4
94 Clamecy B 3
55 Clane A 5
50 Claonaig B 2
55 Clara A 4
59 Clare C 4
54 Clarecastle B 3
55 Clareen A 4
54 Claregalway A 3
52 Claremorris C 3
54 Clarinbridge A 3
49 Clashmore,GB D 4
55 Clashmore,IRL B 4
53 Claudy B 4
56 Claughton B 4
75 Claußnitz C 4
72 Clausthal-Zellerfeld B 4
59 Clay Cross B 2
59 Clay next the Sea C 5
59 Claydon C 5
83 Claye-Souilly C 4
54 Cleady C 2
56 Cleator Moor B 3
80 Cléder B 2
57 Cleedownton D 4
58 Cleethorpes B 3
84 Clefmont B 2
80 Cléguérec B 3
108 Clelles C 2
66 Clenze C 3
57 Cleobury Mortimer D 4
108 Cléon-d'A. C 1
93 Cléré-les-Pins B 4
82 Clères B 3
83 Clérey C 6
83 Clermont B 4
84 Clermont-en-Argonne A 2
106 Clermont-Ferrand B 3
107 Clermont-l'Hérault D 3
95 Clerval B 6
71 Clervaux B 5
93 Cléry B 5
99 Cles C 2
63 Cléty B 4
58 Cleveland Tontine A 2
103 Clicova C 5
52 Clifden C 1
62 Cliffe B 4
52 Cliffony B 3
92 Clisson B 2
56 Clitheroe C 4
55 Cloghan A 4
55 Clogheen B 4
53 Clogher B 4
53 Clogherhead C 5
55 Cloghjordan B 3
55 Cloghran A 5
80 Clohars-Carnoët C 3
49 Clola D 7
54 Clonakilty C 3
55 Clonard A 4
54 Clonbur A 2
55 Clondalkin A 5
55 Clonee A 5
53 Clones B 4
53 Clonmany A 4
55 Clonmel B 4
55 Clonmellon A 4
55 Clonroche B 5
54 Cloonfad A 3
65 Cloppenburg B 6
50 Closeburn B 4
84 Clouange A 3
53 Clough B 6
53 Cloughmills A 5
58 Cloughton A 3
49 Clova E 5
60 Clovelly C 2
82 Cloyes D 3
54 Cloyne C 3
48 Cluanie Inn D 3
93 Cluis C 5
160 Cluj B 3
57 Clun D 3
48 Clunes E 4
95 Cluny C 4
108 Cluses A 3
111 Clusone B 4
60 Clydach B 3
50 Clydebank B 3
90 Cmielów B 4
54 Coachford C 3
53 Coagh B 5
53 Coalisland B 5
59 Coalville C 2
119 Coaña A 4
50 Coatbridge B 4
127 Coberta B 3
127 Cobertelada A 3
54 Cobh C 3
120 Cobreces A 2
74 Coburg C 2
126 Coca A 1
133 Cocentaina C 2
71 Cochem B 6
84 Cocheren A 3
74 Cochstedt B 3
49 Cock Bridge D 5
51 Cockburnspath B 5
56 Cockermouth B 3
113 Codigoro B 4
111 Codogno B 4
127 Codos A 4
99 Codroipo D 3
57 Coedpoeth C 3
125 Coelhoso B 3
65 Coesfeld C 5
65 Coevorden B 4
132 Cofrentes B 1
126 Cogeces del Monte A 1
62 Coggeshal B 4
104 Cognac B 2
110 Cogne B 2
108 Cognin B 2
109 Cogolin D 3
136 Cogollos de Guadix B 3
136 Cogollos-Vega B 3
126 Cogolludo B 2
48 Coillore D 2
128 Coimbra A 2
136 Coin C 2
118 Coirós A 2
102 Čoka C 4
128 Colares C 1
74 Colbitz A 3
62 Colchester B 4
51 Coldingham B 5
75 Colditz B 4
51 Coldstream B 5
61 Coleford B 4
123 Colera B 6
53 Coleraine A 5
59 Coleshill C 2
143 Colfiorito A 3
97 Cólico B 5
95 Coligny C 5
120 Colindres A 3
123 Coll de Nargó B 4
126 Collado-Mediano B 1
126 Collado-Villalba B 2
112 Collagna B 2
119 Collanzo A 5
106 Collat B 3
112 Colle di Val d'Elsa C 3
98 Colle Isarco C 2
144 Colle Sannita B 3
109 Colle-St.-Michel C 3
112 Collécchio B 2
144 Colledimezzo B 3
143 Colleferro C 4
110 Collegno B 2
143 Collelongo C 4
146 Collepasso B 4
143 Collepepe B 3
112 Collesalvetti C 2
148 Collesano B 3
107 Collet C 3
143 Colli a Volturno C 5
80 Collinée B 4
58 Collingham B 2
65 Collinghorst A 5
111 Cóllio B 5
109 Collobrières D 3
53 Collon C 5
52 Collooney B 3
85 Colmar B 4
109 Colmars C 3
86 Colmberg B 2
136 Colmenar C 2
126 Colmenar de Oreja B 2
126 Colmenar Viejo B 2
50 Colmonel B 3
56 Colne C 4
146 Colobraro B 2
99 Cologna Véneta D 2
105 Cologne D 3
111 Cologne al Serio B 4
84 Colombey-les-Belles B 2
84 Colombey-les-deux-Eglises B 1
96 Colombier B 2
123 Colomés B 5
105 Colomiers D 4
112 Colorno B 2
134 Colos B 2
49 Colpy D 6
59 Colsterworth C 3
59 Coltishall C 5
119 Colunga A 5
51 Colwell B 5
57 Colwich D 4
57 Colwyn Bay C 3
113 Comácchio B 4
121 Comago B 4
136 Comares C 2
123 Comarruga C 4
119 Combarros B 4
60 Combe Martin B 2
95 Combeaufontaine B 5
53 Comber B 6
71 Comblain-au-Pont B 4
108 Combloux B 3
81 Combourg B 5
106 Combronde B 3
99 Comeglians C 3
120 Comillas A 2
70 Comines B 2
103 Comloşu Mare C 4
105 Commensacq C 2
94 Commentry C 2
75 Commerau B 6
84 Commercy B 2
110 Como B 4
117 Comorişte A 5
136 Cómpeta C 3
83 Compiègne B 4
128 Comporta C 2
109 Comps D 3
50 Comrie A 4
143 Comunanza B 4
112 Cona, Emilia Romagna, I B 3
113 Cona, Veneto, I A 4
80 Concarneau C 3
134 Conceição B 2
82 Conches-en-Ouche C 2
99 Concórdia Sagittária D 3
112 Concordia sulla Séchia B 2
107 Concots C 1
109 Condamine Ch. C 3
106 Condat B 2
83 Condé-en-Brie B 5
70 Condé-sur-l'Escaut B 2
83 Conde-sur-Marne B 6
81 Condé-sur-Noireau B 6
95 Condeissiat C 5
128 Condeixa A 2
126 Condemios de Abajo A 2
126 Condemios de Arriba A 2
111 Condino B 5
105 Condom D 3
110 Condove B 2
83 Conflans C 4
84 Conflans-en-Jarnisy A 2
95 Conflans-sur-Lanterne B 6
104 Confolens A 3
54 Cong A 2
99 Congeliano D 3
107 Congeniès D 4
57 Congleton C 4
119 Congosto B 4
120 Congosto de Valdavia B 2
126 Congostrina A 2
61 Congresbury B 4
135 Conil C 4
59 Coningsby B 3
58 Conisbrough B 2
56 Coniston B 3
82 Conlie C 1
95 Conliège C 5
57 Connah's Quay C 3
83 Connantre C 5
109 Connaux C 1
50 Connel A 2
50 Connel Park B 3
82 Connerre C 2
54 Connonagh C 2
102 Conoplja C 3
106 Conques C 2
107 Conques-sur-Orbiel D 2
130 Conquista C 2
129 Conquista de la Sierra B 5
112 Consándolo B 3
112 Consélice B 3
112 Conselve A 3
51 Consett C 6
160 Constanta C 6
123 Constanti C 4
135 Constantina B 5
131 Consuegra B 3
112 Consuma C 3
113 Contarina A 4
96 Conthey B 3
143 Contigliano B 3
48 Contin D 4
105 Contis-Plage C 1
149 Cóntiso C 4
144 Contrada C 3
93 Contres B 5
84 Contrexéville B 2
84 Contrisson B 1
145 Controne C 4
145 Contursi C 4
83 Conty B 4
145 Conversano C 6
53 Convoy B 4
57 Conway C 3
53 Cookstown B 5
53 Cootehill B 4
146 Copertino B 4
112 Copparo B 3
72 Coppenbrügge A 3
96 Coppet B 2
60 Copplestone C 3
147 Coraci C 2
145 Corato B 5
80 Coray B 3
83 Corbeil-Essonnes C 4
83 Corbeny B 5
132 Corbera B 2
83 Corbie B 4
94 Corbigny B 3
70 Corbion C 4
119 Corbón B 4
51 Corbridge C 5
59 Corby C 3

59 Corby Glen C 3
107 Corconne D 3
120 Corconte A 3
118 Corcubión B 1
143 Corcumello B 4
107 Cordes C 1
136 Córdoba B 2
129 Cordobilla de Lácara B 4
99 Cordovado D 3
121 Corella B 5
125 Coreses B 4
61 Corfe Castle C 4
124 Corga de Lobão C 1
118 Corgo B 3
143 Cori C 3
129 Coria B 4
135 Coria del Rio B 4
146 Corigliano Cálabro C 2
113 Corinaldo C 5
110 Cório B 2
135 Coripe C 5
54 Cork C 3
68 Corkwica B 3
80 Corlay B 3
148 Corleone B 3
145 Corleto Monforte C 4
146 Corleto Perticara B 2
160 Çorlu E 5
95 Cormatin C 4
82 Cormeilles B 2
93 Cormery B 4
99 Cormons D 4
95 Cormoz C 5
72 Cornberg B 3
50 Corne B 2
117 Cornea A 6
123 Cornella C 5
119 Cornellana A 4
117 Cornereva A 6
112 Corniglio B 2
84 Cornimont C 3
112 Corniolo C 3
122 Cornudella C 3
120 Cornudilla B 3
107 Cornus D 3
84 Corny A 3
154 Corovodë B 2
48 Corpach E 3
108 Corps C 2
81 Corps-Nuds C 5
126 Corral de Almaguer C 2
126 Corral de Ayllon A 2
130 Corral de Calatrava C 2
133 Corral-Rubio C 1
125 Corrales B 4
48 Corran E 3
118 Corredoira A 2
112 Corréggio B 2
106 Corrèze B 1
113 Corridónia C 5
57 Corris D 3
118 Corrubedo B 1
48 Corry D 3
61 Corsham B 4
110 Córsic B 4
50 Corsock B 4
140 Corte B 2
129 Corte de Peleas C 4
134 Corte do Pinto B 3
135 Corteconcepción B 4
118 Cortegada B 2
135 Cortegana B 4
111 Cortemaggiore B 4
110 Cortemilia C 3
121 Cortes C 5
127 Cortes de Aragón B 5
132 Cortes de Arenoso A 2
137 Cortes de Baza B 4
135 Cortes de la Frontera C 5
132 Cortes de Pallás B 2
128 Cortiçadas C 2
124 Cortico B 2
130 Cortijo de Arriba B 2
135 Cortijo de San Enrique C 5
137 Cortijos Nuevos A 4
99 Cortina d'Ampezzo C 3
113 Cortona C 3
128 Coruche C 2
119 Corullón B 4
99 Corvara in Badia C 2
133 Corvera D 1
57 Corwen D 3
147 Cosenza C 2
126 Coslada B 2
94 Cosne, Allier, F C 2
94 Cosne, Nièvre, F B 2
110 Cossato B 3
94 Cossaye C 3
81 Cossé-le-Vivien C 6
96 Cossonay B 2
128 Costa da Caparica C 1
112 Costalpino C 3
128 Costância B 2
106 Costaros C 3
103 Coşteiu C 5
54 Costelloe A 2
110 Costigliole Saluzzo C 2
75 Coswig, Dresden, D* B 5
75 Coswig, Halle, D* B 4
147 Cotronei C 2
75 Cottbus B 6
59 Cottenham C 4
59 Cottesmore C 3
58 Cottingham B 3
95 Couches C 4
128 Couço C 2
106 Coucouron C 3
83 Coucy-le-Château-Auffrique B 5
106 Coudes B 3
81 Couffé C 5
93 Couhé C 4
70 Couillet B 3
83 Couilly C 4
107 Couiza E 2
48 Coulags D 3
94 Coulanges C 3
94 Coulanges-la-Vineuse B 3
92 Coulanges-sur-l'Autize C 3
94 Coulanges-sur-Yonne B 3
94 Couleuvre C 2
95 Coulmier-le-Sec B 4
83 Coulommiers C 5
50 Coulport A 3
51 Coundon C 6
51 Coupar Angus A 4
84 Coupéville B 1
81 Couptrain B 6
93 Cour-Cheverny B 5
124 Coura B 1
70 Courcelles B 3
84 Courcelles-Chaussy A 3
104 Courcôme B 3
92 Courçon C 3
96 Courgenay A 3
110 Courmayeur B 1
107 Courniou D 2
106 Cournon B 3
107 Cournonterral D 3
106 Courpière B 3
96 Courrendlin A 3
95 Cours C 4
107 Coursan D 3
82 Courseulles-sur-Mer B 1
94 Courson-les-Carrières B 3
70 Court-St. Etienne B 3
82 Courtalain C 3
83 Courtenay C 5
109 Courthezon C 1
82 Courtomer C 2
82 Courville C 3
104 Coussac-Bonneval B 4
81 Coutainville A 5
81 Coutances A 5
81 Couterne B 6
104 Coutras B 2
96 Couvet B 2
70 Couvin B 3
94 Couzon C 3
121 Covaleda C 4
120 Covarrubias B 3
124 Covas B 1
103 Covăsint B 5
48 Cove D 3
59 Coventry C 2
60 Coverack C 1
112 Covigliáio B 3
128 Covilhà A 3
60 Cowbridge B 3
51 Cowdenbeath A 4
62 Cowes C 2
62 Cowfold C 3
105 Cox D 4
50 Coylton B 3
49 Coylumbridge D 5
131 Cózar C 3
104 Cozes B 2
55 Craanford B 5
146 Craco B 2
50 Craggan A 3
53 Craigavon B 5
49 Craigellachie D 5
50 Craighouse B 2
50 Craignure A 2
49 Craigtown C 5
51 Crail A 5
86 Crailsheim B 2
160 Craiova C 3
83 Cramant C 5
51 Cramlington B 6
108 Cran Gevrie B 3
61 Cranborne C 5
62 Cranleigh B 3
106 Cransac C 2
51 Cranshaws B 5
81 Craon C 6
83 Craonne B 5
106 Craponne, Haute Loire, F B 3
108 Craponne, Rhône, F B 1
50 Crarae A 2
48 Crask Inn C 4
49 Crathie D 5
54 Cratloe B 3
128 Crato B 3
54 Craughwell A 3
134 Cravadas B 2
57 Craven Arms D 4
50 Crawford B 4
74 Crawinkel C 2
62 Crawley B 3
60 Cray B 3
48 Creagorry D 1
95 Crèches C 4
118 Creciente B 2
83 Crécy B 5
83 Crécy-en-Brie C 4
63 Crécy-en-Ponthieu B 3
60 Crediton C 3
52 Creeslough A 4
50 Creetown C 3
54 Cregganbaun A 2
73 Creglingen D 4
74 Creidlitz C 2
83 Creil B 4
107 Creissels C 3
111 Crema B 4
106 Cremeaux B 3
120 Crémenes B 1
108 Cremieu B 2
72 Cremlingen A 4
111 Cremona B 5
83 Creney C 6
104 Créon C 2
117 Crepaja A 4
83 Crépy B 5
83 Crépy-en-Valois B 4
114 Cres C 2
110 Crescentino B 3
112 Crespino B 3
125 Crespos C 5
104 Cressensac B 4
108 Crest C 2
97 Cresta B 5
81 Creully A 6
86 Creußen B 3
84 Creutzwald A 3
74 Creuzburg B 2
112 Crevalcore B 3
106 Crevant-Laveine B 3
83 Crèvecouer-le-Grand B 4
133 Crevillente C 2
96 Crévola d'Ossola B 4
57 Crewe C 4
61 Crewkerne C 4
120 Criales B 3
50 Crianlarich A 3
57 Criccieth D 2
59 Crich B 2
59 Crick C 2
61 Crickhowell B 3
61 Cricklade B 5
50 Crieff A 4
82 Criel-sur-Mer A 3
114 Crikvenica B 2
82 Crillon B 3
75 Crimmitschau C 4
49 Crimond D 7
50 Crinan A 2
59 Cringleford C 5
75 Crinitz B 5
121 Cripán B 4
82 Criquetot-l'Esneval B 2
146 Crispiano B 3
96 Crissier B 2
110 Crissolo C 2
125 Cristóbal C 4
67 Crivitz B 4
100 Črna C 2
102 Crna Bara, Pokragina Vojvodna, YU C 4
116 Crna Bara, Srbija, YU B 3
115 Crnac B 5
117 Crnajka B 6
116 Crnča B 3
153 Crne Trava B 4
115 Crni Lug C 4
114 Črni Vrh B 2
152 Crnoljevo B 2
114 Črnomelj B 3
110 Crocetta C 2
50 Crocketford B 4
106 Crocq B 2
96 Crodo B 4
56 Croglin B 4
92 Croix-de-Vie C 2
109 Croix-Valmer D 3
108 Crolles B 2
52 Crolly A 3
49 Cromarty D 4
59 Cromer C 5
59 Cromford B 2
94 Cronat C 3
51 Crook C 6
49 Crook of Alves D 5
56 Crooklands B 4
54 Crookstown C 3
54 Croom B 3
147 Cropalati C 2
147 Crópani D 2
56 Crosby, Cumberland, GB B 3
56 Crosby, Lancashire, GB C 3
57 Cross Foxes D 3
60 Cross Hands B 2
50 Crossaig B 2
55 Crossakeel A 4
48 Crossbost C 2
53 Crossdoney C 4
53 Crossgar B 6
57 Crossgates D 3
54 Crosshaven C 3
50 Crosshill B 3
51 Crosslee B 4
52 Crossmolina B 2
49 Crossroad Inn D 6
147 Crotone C 3
75 Crottendorf C 4
93 Croutelle C 4
83 Crouy B 5
62 Crowborough B 4
59 Crowland C 3
58 Crowle B 3
62 Croydon B 3
80 Crozon B 2
108 Cruas C 1
147 Crúcoli C 3
57 Crudgington D 4
109 Cruis C 2
53 Crumlin B 5
108 Cruseilles A 3
54 Crusheen B 3
94 Crux-la-Ville B 3
151 Crveni Grm B 3
102 Crvenka C 3
60 Crymmych B 2
101 Csabrendek B 5
101 Csákánydorozló C 4
101 Csákberény B 6
102 Csákvár A 2
103 Csanádapáca B 4
102 Csány A 3
102 Csanytelek B 4
101 Csapod B 4
101 Császár B 6
102 Császártöltés B 3
102 Csemö A 3
102 Csengöd B 3
102 Csépa B 4
101 Csepreg B 4
103 Cserebökény B 4
101 Csetény B 5
91 Csobád D 4
103 Csökmo A 5
101 Csököly C 5
115 Csokonyavisonta A 5
91 Csolnok E 1
102 Csongrád B 4
101 Csopak C 5
101 Csór B 6
101 Csorna B 5
103 Csorvás B 4
115 Csurgó A 5
129 Cuacos A 5
118 Cualedro C 3
132 Cuart de Poblet B 2
129 Cuaternos A 5
134 Cuba A 3
127 Cubel A 4
123 Cubellas C 4
118 Cubide B 2
126 Cubillos A 3
119 Cubillos del Sil B 4
127 Cubo de la Solana A 3
115 Čučerje B 4
62 Cuckfield B 3
109 Cucuron D 2
119 Cudillero A 4
126 Cuéllar A 1
127 Cuenca B 3
120 Cuenca de Campos B 1
109 Cuers D 3
126 Cuerva C 1
121 Cueva de Agreda C 5
136 Cuevas Bajas B 2
120 Cuevas de San Clemente B 3
136 Cuevas de San Marcos B 2
132 Cuevas de Vinroma A 3
137 Cuevas del Almanzora B 5
136 Cuevas del Becerro C 1
137 Cuevas del Campo B 4
125 Cuevas del Valle C 4
119 Cueya A 4
109 Cuges-Les-Pins D 2
141 Cúglieri B 2
105 Cugnaux D 4
130 Cuidad Real C 3
103 Cuied B 5
48 Cuier D 1
64 Cuijk C 3
95 Cuinzier C 4
83 Cuise B 5
95 Cuiseaux C 5
95 Cuisery C 5
94 Culan C 2
53 Culdaff A 4
49 Culdrain D 6
64 Culemborg C 3
137 Cúllar de Baza B 4
53 Cullaville B 5
49 Cullen D 6
132 Cullera B 2
49 Cullivoe A 7
60 Cullompton C 3
96 Cully B 2
108 Culoz B 2
49 Cults D 6
50 Cumbernauld B 4
135 Cumbres de San Bartolomé A 4
135 Cumbres Mayores A 4
110 Cumiana C 2
117 Ćumić B 4
49 Cuminestown D 6
51 Cummertrees C 4
50 Cumnock B 3
110 Cúneo C 2
106 Cunlhat B 3
49 Cunningsburgh A 7
118 Cuntis B 2
110 Cuorgnè B 2
51 Cupar A 4
144 Cupello A 3
113 Cupra Maríttima C 5
113 Cupramontana C 5
117 Ćuprija C 5
109 Curnier C 2
51 Currie B 4
61 Curry Rivel B 4
54 Curryglass C 2
103 Curtea C 6
103 Curtici B 5
118 Curtis A 2
118 Curtis Sta. Eulalia A 2
116 Ćurug A 4
144 Cusano Mutri B 3
53 Cushendall A 5
53 Cushendun A 5
55 Cushina A 4
94 Cusset C 3
94 Cussy B 4
124 Custóias B 1
127 Cutanda B 4
136 Cútar C 2
147 Cutro C 2
146 Cutrofiano B 4
83 Cuts B 5
103 Cuveşdia C 5
83 Cuvilly B 4
66 Cuxhaven B 1
75 Cvikov C 6
115 Cvrstec A 4
61 Cwmbran B 3
57 Cwrt D 3
76 Cybinka A 3
90 Cykarzew Stary B 2
60 Cynwyl Elfed B 2
70 Cysoing B 2
77 Czajków B 7
69 Czaplinek B 4
78 Czarlin A 1
90 Czarna B 4
69 Czarna-Dabrówka A 5
69 Czarna Woda B 6
90 Czarnca B 2
79 Czarne, Bydgoszcz, PL C 2
69 Czarne, Koszalin, PL B 5
69 Czarnków C 4
90 Czarnów B 3
77 Czarnowasy C 6

69 Czarnowo B 6
79 Czarnozyly D 1
90 Czarny-Dunajec C 2
90 Czchow C 3
90 Czechowice-Dziedzice C 1
90 Czeladz B 2
77 Czempiń A 5
79 Czermno D 3
90 Czernichow C 2
78 Czerniewice B 1
78 Czernikowo C 1
69 Czersk B 5
76 Czerwieńsk A 4
89 Czerwionka A 6
76 Czerwon Woda B 4
78 Czerwone B 4
78 Czerwonka B 3
78 Czerwony Dwór A 5
90 Czestochowa B 2
69 Czeszewo C 5
69 Czlopa B 4
69 Czluchów B 5
90 Czudec C 4
78 Czyzew Osada C 5

D

71 Daaden B 6
102 Dabas A 3
79 Dabie, Lublin, PL D 5
79 Dabie, Poznań, PL C 1
153 Dabilja C 4
85 Dabo B 4
77 Dabroszyn A 7
69 Dabrowa, Bydgoszcz, PL C 5
77 Dabrowa, Opole, PL C 6
77 Dabrowa Boleslawska B 4
90 Dabrowa Górna B 2
90 Dabrowa Tarnowska B 3
78 Dabrówka B 4
78 Dabrowno B 3
86 Dachau C 3
88 Dačice B 3
70 Dadizele B 2
31 Dagali C 5
96 Dagmersellen A 3
75 Dahlen B 4
66 Dahlenburg B 3
75 Dahme B 5
85 Dahn A 4
66 Dähre C 3
50 Dailly B 3
131 Daimiel B 3
55 Daingean A 4
152 Dajç C 1
152 Đakovica B 2
116 Đakovo A 2
36 Dal, Akershus, N A 3
35 Dal, Telemark, N B 4
33 Dala-Floda C 5
38 Dala-Husby B 2
33 Dala-Järna C 5
97 Dalaas A 6
39 Dalarö C 5
50 Dalbeattie C 4
46 Dalby B 4
32 Dalby Långav C 4
49 Dalcross D 4
60 Dale, GB B 1
30 Dale, Fjordane, N B 2
30 Dale, Hordaland, N C 2
36 Dalen, Akershus, N B 3
31 Dalen, Hedmark, N A 6
34 Dalen, Telemark, N B 4
33 Dalfors B 6
49 Dalhalvaig C 6
72 Dalhausen B 3
71 Dalheim C 5
39 Dalhem E 5
137 Dalías C 4
102 Dalj C 2
51 Dalkeith B 4
48 Dallachoilish E 3
85 Dallau A 6
50 Dalmally A 3
50 Dalmellington B 3
48 Dalmichy C 4
49 Dalnacardoch Lodge E 4
50 Dalry B 3
50 Dalrymple B 3
36 Dals Långed C 4
27 Dalsbruk C 5
31 Dalseter B 6
42 Dalsjöfor B 3
36 Dalskog C 4
42 Dalstorp B 3
51 Dalton B 4
56 Dalton-in-Furness B 3
109 Daluis C 3
65 Dalum, D† B 5
42 Dalum, S B 3
49 Dalwhinnie E 4
105 Damazan C 3
89 Damborce B 4
154 Damës B 1
103 Damiş B 6
83 Dammartin-en-Goële B 4
65 Damme B 6
95 Dampierre B 5
95 Dampierre-sur-Salon B 5
97 Damüls A 5
82 Damville C 3
84 Damvillers A 2
62 Danbury B 4
93 Dangé C 4
43 Dångebo C 5
82 Dangers C 3
82 Dangeul C 2
151 Danilov Grad C 5
66 Danischenhagen A 3
77 Daniszyn B 6
84 Danjoutin C 3
85 Dannemarie C 4
38 Dannemora B 4
66 Dannenberg B 4
102 Dány A 3
102 Dánszentmiklós A 3
80 Daoulas B 2
158 Dára B 3
102 Darda C 2
74 Dardesheim B 2
154 Dardhë B 2
65 Darfeld B 5
111 Darfo B 5
67 Dargun B 5
153 Darkovac B 4
51 Darlington C 6
69 Darlowo A 4
73 Darmstadt D 2
82 Darnétal B 3
84 Darney B 3
127 Daroca A 4
124 Darque B 1
54 Darragh B 2
62 Dartford B 4
60 Dartmouth C 3
58 Darton B 2
115 Daruvar B 5
50 Darvel B 3
56 Darwen C 4
88 Dašice A 3
86 Dasing C 3
72 Dassel B 3
66 Dassow B 3
79 Daszyna C 2
71 Datteln A 6
71 Dattenfeld B 6
44 Daugard B 2
71 Daun B 5
70 Dave B 3
59 Daventry C 2
49 Daviot D 4
88 Davle B 2
102 Dávod C 2
115 Davor B 5
97 Davos-Platz B 5
57 Dawley D 4
60 Dawlish C 3
105 Dax D 1
64 De Bilt B 3
63 De Panne A 4
65 De Wijk B 4
62 Deal B 5
82 Deauville B 2
152 Debar C 2
79 Debe C 3
79 Debe Wielkie C 4
117 Debeljača A 4
59 Debenham C 5
136 Debesas Viejas B 3
90 Debica B 4
79 Deblin D 4
68 Dębno C 2
79 Deboleka D 1
78 Debowa Laka B 2
90 Debowiec C 4
116 Debrc B 3
103 Debrecen A 5
153 Debrište C 3
69 Debrzno B 5
66 Debstedt B 1
152 Dečani B 2
106 Decazeville C 2
101 Dechtice A 5
70 Dechy B 2
143 Decima C 3
141 Decimomannu C 2
75 Děčín C 6
94 Decize C 3
85 Deckenpfronn B 5
147 Decollatura C 2
62 Deddington B 2
74 Dedeleben A 2
67 Dedelow B 6
65 Dedemsvaart B 4
91 Dédestapolcsány D 3
59 Deeping St. Nicholas C 3
102 Dég B 2
119 Degaña B 4
47 Degeberga B 5
37 Degerfors B 6
43 Degerhamn C 6
98 Degerndorf B 3
36 Degernes B 3
87 Deggendorf C 4
86 Deggingen C 1
110 Dego C 3
129 Degolados B 3
137 Dehesas de Guadix B 3
135 Dehesas Frias B 5
136 Deifontes B 3
86 Deining B 3
70 Deinze B 2
85 Deißlingen B 5
160 Dej B 3
37 Deje B 5
42 Delary C 3
72 Delbrück B 2
153 Delčevo C 4
65 Delden B 4
129 Deleitosa B 5
115 Đelekovec A 4
96 Delémont A 3
64 Delft C 2
65 Delfzijl A 4
149 Délia B 3
147 Delianuova D 1
117 Deliblato B 5
145 Deliceto B 4
75 Delitzsch B 4
99 Dellach C 4
85 Delle C 4
86 Dellmensingen C 1
84 Delme B 3
66 Delmenhorst B 1
114 Delnice B 2
33 Delsbo B 7
154 Delvinákion C 2
154 Delvinë C 2
91 Demandice D 1
95 Demigny C 4
153 Demir Kapija C 4
67 Demmin B 6
110 Demonte C 2
64 Den Burg A 2
65 Den Ham B 4
64 Den Helder B 2
70 Denain B 2
57 Denbigh C 3
70 Dendermonde A 3
70 Denderwindeke B 2
65 Denekamp B 5
133 Denia C 3
86 Denkendorf C 3
71 Denklingen B 6
50 Denny A 4
62 Densole B 5
67 Densow B 6
117 Denta A 5
59 Denton C 3
93 Déols C 5
61 Deptford B 5
59 Derby C 2
103 Derecske A 5
74 Derenberg B 2
96 Derendingen A 3
74 Dermbach C 2
99 Dermulo C 2
54 Derrybrien A 3
50 Derryguaig A 1
53 Derrykeighan A 5
53 Derrylin B 4
54 Derryrush A 2
59 Dersingham C 4
143 Deruta B 3
48 Dervaig E 2
81 Derval C 5
158 Dervéni A 3
115 Derventa C 5
155 Dervizianá C 2
108 Désaignes C 1
110 Desana B 3
59 Desborough C 3
111 Desenzano del Garda B 5
53 Desertmartin B 5
32 Deset B 2
59 Desford C 2
117 Desimirovac B 4
110 Désio B 4
76 Desná C 4
88 Dešov C 3
117 Despotovac B 5
116 Despotovo A 3
74 Dessau B 4
70 Dessel A 4
70 Destelbergen A 2
88 Deštná B 2
89 Deštné A 4
119 Destriana B 4
141 Desulo B 3
63 Desvres B 3
102 Deszk B 4
117 Deta A 5
72 Detmold B 2
89 Dětřichov B 5
73 Dettelbach D 4
85 Dettingen B 6
85 Dettwiller B 4
91 Detva D 2
87 Deuerling B 3
70 Deurne, B A 3
64 Deurne, NL C 3
101 Deutsch Kaltenbrunn B 4
101 Deutsch Wagram A 4
100 Deutschfeistritz B 3
101 Deutschkreutz B 4
100 Deutschlandsberg C 3
121 Deva, E A 4
160 Deva, R C 3
103 Dévaványa A 4
101 Devecser B 5
64 Deventer B 4
57 Devil's Bridge D 3
160 Devin E 4
101 Devinska Nova-Ves A 4
61 Devizes B 5
55 Devlin A 4
150 Devrske B 1
58 Dewsbury B 2
138 Deya B 3
127 Deza A 3
115 Dežanovac B 5
103 Dezna B 6
111 Dezzo di Scalve B 5
158 Dháfnai A 2
159 Dhafní C 3
158 Dháfni, Akhaia, GR B 3
156 Dháfni, Khalkidhikí, GR B 4
156 Dhafnón A 4
159 Dhaimoniá C 3
156 Dhamási C 2
155 Dharakótripa C 2
157 Dhávlia D 2
159 Dhekélia A 4
157 Dhelfoí D 2
154 Dhèrmi B 1
157 Dhesfína D 2
154 Dheskáti C 3
158 Dhiakoptón A 3
156 Dhiavatá B 2
158 Dhiavolitsi B 2
160 Dhidhimotikhon E 5
159 Dhídimoi B 4
158 Dhilianáta A 1
156 Dhímitra B 3
156 Dhimitrítsion B 3
158 Dhimitsána B 3
157 Dhístomon D 2
154 Dhístraton B 3
154 Dholianá C 2
156 Dhomenikon C 2
157 Dhomokós C 2
56 Dhoon B 2
158 Dhórion B 2
157 Dhoxará C 2
156 Dhoxáton A 4
156 Dhravískos B 3
159 Dhrépanon B 3
156 Dhrimós B 2
159 Dhriopis B 5
157 Dhrískoli C 2
159 Dhritsa A 4
156 Dhrosáton A 2
101 Diakovce A 5
146 Diamante C 1
45 Dianalund B 4
110 Diano d'Alba C 3
110 Diano Marina D 3
62 Dibden Purlieu C 2
112 Dicomano C 3
64 Didam C 4
62 Didcot B 2
108 Die C 2
84 Diebling A 3
73 Dieburg D 2
125 Diego Alvaro C 4
71 Diekirch C 5
81 Diélette A 5
108 Diémoz B 2
98 Dienten B 3
70 Diepenbeck B 4
66 Diepholz C 1
82 Dieppe B 3
67 Dierberg B 5
71 Dierdorf B 6
64 Dieren B 4
67 Dierhagen A 5
66 Diesdorf C 3
86 Diespeck B 2
86 Dießen D 3
70 Diest B 4
86 Dietenheim C 2
86 Dietfurt B 3
97 Dietikon A 4
73 Dietzenbach C 2
84 Dieue A 2
108 Dieulefit C 2
84 Dieulouard B 3
84 Dieuze B 3
65 Diever B 4
73 Diez C 2
136 Diezma B 3
71 Differdange C 4
33 Digerberget B 5
4 Digermulen B 4
104 Dignac B 3
99 Dignano C 3
109 Digne C 3
82 Digny C 3
94 Digoin C 3
95 Dijon B 5
13 Dikanäs B 7
70 Diksmuide A 1
136 Dilar B 3
73 Dillenburg C 2
86 Dillingen, Bayern, D† C 2
71 Dillingen, Saarland, D† C 5
121 Dima A 4
99 Dimaro C 1
153 Dimitrograd A 4
160 Dimitrovgrad D 4
153 Dimitrovo B 5
147 Dinami D 2
81 Dinan B 4
70 Dinant B 3
81 Dinard B 4
65 Dingden C 4
74 Dingelstädt B 2
54 Dingle, IRL B 1
36 Dingle, S C 3
87 Dingolfing C 4
38 Dingtuna C 3
48 Dingwall D 4
86 Dinkelsbühl B 2
86 Dinkelscherben C 2
65 Dinklage B 6
71 Dinslaken A 5
64 Dinteloord C 2
65 Dinxperlo C 4
43 Diö C 4
103 Diosig A 6
91 Diósjeno E 2
94 Diou C 3
50 Dippen B 2
73 Dipperz C 3
75 Dippoldiswalde C 5
34 Dirdal C 2
64 Dirksland C 2
86 Dirlewang D 2
86 Dischingen C 2
97 Disentis-Muster B 4
146 Diso B 4
59 Diss C 5
65 Dissen B 6
56 Distington B 3
65 Ditzum A 5
153 Diva Slatina A 4
121 Divega C 5
82 Dives B 1
89 Diviacka Nová Ves C 6
63 Divion B 4
88 Divišov B 2
154 Divjakë B 1
96 Divonne, CH B 2
95 Divonne, F C 6
83 Dixmont C 5
83 Dizy-le-Gros B 6
4 Djupdal B 7
30 Djupvasshytta A 4
5 Djupvik, Nordland, N C 4
6 Djupvik, Troms, N B 6
33 Djura C 5
33 Djurås C 6
33 Djurmo C 6
43 Djursdala B 5
89 Dlhé-Pole B 6
89 Dlouhá Loučka B 5
89 Dlugomilowice A 6
79 Dlugowola D 4
118 Doade B 3
53 Doagh B 5
78 Doba A 4

116 Dobanovici B 4
67 Dobbertin B 5
98 Dobbiaco C 3
90 Dobczyce C 3
75 Döbeln B 5
75 Doberlug-Kirchhain B 5
75 Döbern B 6
88 Dobersberg C 3
68 Dobiegniew C 3
79 Dobieszyn D 4
89 Dobodiel C 6
116 Doboj B 2
103 Doboz B 5
103 Dobra,R C 6
117 Dobra,YU B 5
89 Dobrá, B 6
Severomoravsky, CS C 4
91 Dobra, **Vychodoslovenský,** CS
79 Dobra, Poznań, PL D 1
68 Dobra, Szczecin, PL B 2
68 Dobra, Szczecin, PL B 3
91 Dobrá Niva D 2
117 Dobra Polje C 6
101 Dobra Voda A 5
153 Dobrčane B 3
79 **Dobre, Bydgoszcz** C 1
PL C 1
79 Dobre, Warszawa, PL C 4
78 Dobre Miasto B 3
153 Dobri Do B 3
117 Dobrica A 4
88 Dobřichovice B 2
88 Dobřiš B 2
120 Dobro B 3
91 Dobroč D 2
90 Dobrodzień B 1
101 Döbrököz C 6
77 Dobromierz C 5
79 Dobron D 2
152 Dobroste B 3
77 Dobroszyce B 6
151 Dobrota C 4
101 Dobrovnik C 4
154 Dobruševo A 3
88 Dobruska A 4
68 Dobrzany B 3
90 Dobrzehów C 4
78 Dobrzejewice B 1
77 Dobrzeń Wielki C 6
69 Dobrzyca, Koszalin, PL B 4
69 Dobrzyca, Koszalin, PL A 3
77 Dobrzyca, Poznań, PL B 6
79 Dobrzyń nad Wisla C 2
91 Dobšiná D 3
71 Dochamps B 4
59 Docking C 4
21 Docksta B 7
59 Doddington C 4
43 Döderhult B 6
64 Dodewaard C 3
64 Doesburg B 4
65 Doetinchen C 4
152 Doganovik B 3
26 Dogerby C 3
110 Dogliani C 2
117 Dognecea A 5
134 Dogueno B 3
128 Dois Portos B 1
89 Dojč C 5
31 Dokka C 7
14 Dokkas A 5
64 Dokkum A 3
81 Dol-de-Bretagne B 5
89 Dol. Životice B 5
84 Dolancourt B 1
57 Dolbenmaen D 2
110 Dolceácqua D 2
95 Dole B 5
35 Dølemo C 4
114 Dolenja Vas B 2
57 Dolgarrog C 3
57 Dolgellau D 3
159 Dolianá B 3
141 Dolianova C 3
68 Dolice B 3
98 Döllach C 3
50 Dollar A 4
67 Dolle C 4
75 Dollegen A 6
83 Dollot C 5
74 Döllstadt B 2
153 Dolna Dikanya B 5
91 Dolná Strehová D 2
101 Dolné Oresany A 5
89 Dolní Bečva B 6
87 Dolni Bělá B 5
89 Dolní Benešov B 6
88 Dolní Bousov A 3
89 Dolni Dobrouc B 4
88 Dolní Dvořiště C 2
89 Dolni Kounice B 4
88 Dolni Kralovice B 3
153 Dolni Lom A 4
89 Dolní Lomná B 6
89 Dolní Lutyně B 6
89 Dolní Mariková B 6
153 Dolni Pasarel B 5
89 Dolni Ujezd B 4
87 Dolni Žandor A 4
89 Dolní Životice B 5
153 Dolno Selo B 4
153 Dolno Uyno B 4
91 Dolný Kubin C 2
101 Dolný Peter B 6
91 Dolný Turček D 1
99 Dolo D 3
133 Dolores C 2
117 Dolovo B 4
51 Dolphinton B 4
98 Dölsach C 3
77 Dolsk B 6
57 Dolwyddelan C 3
116 Domaljevac A 2
79 Domanice C 5
79 Domaniewice C 2
89 Domaniža B 6
90 Domaradz C 4
69 Domaslawek C 5
117 Domaşnea A 6
89 Domašov A 5
102 Domaszék B 3
89 Domaszków A 4
77 Domaszowice B 6
97 Domat-Ems B 5
87 Domažlice B 4
31 Dombås A 6
84 Dombasle B 3
103 Dombegyház B 5
103 Dombiratos B 5
101 Dombóvár C 6
91 Dombrád D 4
64 Domburg C 1
108 Domène B 2
81 Domfront, Orne, F B 6
82 Domfront, Sartbe, F C 2
128 Domingão B 2
136 Domingo Pérez, Granada, E B 3
126 Domingo Pérez, Toledo, E C 1
67 Dömitz B 4
84 Dommartin B 1
84 Dommartin-le-Franc B 1
104 Domme C 4
75 Dommitzsch B 4
96 Domodóssola B 4
91 Domoszló E 3
84 Dompaire B 3
95 Dompierre C 5
81 Dompierre-du-Chemin B 5
94 Dompierre-sur-B. C 3
92 Dompierre-sur-M. C 2
84 Domrémy-la-Pucelle B 2
21 Domsjö B 7
102 Dömsöd A 3
95 Domsure C 5
141 Domus de Maria D 1
141 Domusnóvas C 2
159 Domvraina A 3
114 Domžale A 2
129 Don Benito C 5
133 Doña Inés D 1
136 Doña Mencia B 2
119 Donado B 4
53 Donaghadee B 6
85 Donaueschingen C 5
86 Donauwörth C 2
58 Doncaster B 2
70 Donchery C 3
52 Donegal B 3
64 Dongen C 2
92 Donges B 1
97 Dongo B 5
119 Donillas B 4
59 Donington C 3
118 Doniños A 2
116 Donja Bebrina A 2
116 Donja Dobošnica B 2
116 Donja Dubica A 2
115 Donja Konjscina A 4
115 Donja Kupčina B 3
153 Donja Ljubata B 4
117 Donja Mutnica C 5
116 Donje Crnjelovo B 3
152 Donje Ljupče B 3
153 Donji Barbeš A 3
153 Donji Dušnik A 4
115 Donji Lapac C 3
153 Donji Livoč B 3
150 Donji Malovan B 3
102 Donji Miholjac C 2
117 Donji Milanovac B 6
115 Donji Mosti A 4
150 Donji-Rujani B 2
115 Donji Srb C 4
116 Donji Tovarnik B 3
115 Donji Vakuf C 5
64 Donk C 3
149 Donnalucata C 4
83 Donnemarie C 5
100 Donnersbach B 2
100 Donnersbachwald B 2
101 Donnerskirchen B 4
12 Dønnes A 4
8 Dønnesfjord B 2
112 Donorático C 2
81 Donville-les-Bains B 5
86 Donzdorf C 1
104 Donzenac B 4
109 Donzère C 1
94 Donzy B 3
52 Dooagh C 1
54 Doonbeg B 2
64 Doorn B 3
64 Doornspijk B 3
118 Dor A 1
153 Đorče Petrov B 3
61 Dorchester, Dorset, GB C 4
62 Dorchester, Oxon., GB B 2
64 Dordrecht C 2
65 Dörenthe B 5
49 Dores D 4
97 Dorf B 5
87 Dorfen C 4
98 Dorfgastein B 4
101 Dörfl i. Burgenland B 4
66 Dorfmark C 2
141 Dorgali B 3
62 Dorking B 3
71 Dormagen A 5
83 Dormans B 5
98 Dornauberg B 2
97 Dornbirn A 5
74 Dornburg C 3
74 Dorndorf C 2
94 Dornes C 3
48 Dornie D 3
49 Dornoch D 4
86 Dornstadt C 1
91 Dorog E 1
160 Dorohoi B 5
13 Dorotea C 8
78 Dorotowo B 3
71 Dorsten A 5
95 Dortan C 5
71 Dortmund A 6
66 Dorum B 1
66 Dörverden C 2
73 Dörzbach D 3
132 Dos Aguas B 2
135 Dos Hermanas B 5
130 Dos-Torres C 2
126 Dosbarrios C 2
65 Dötlingen B 6
70 Dottignies B 2
96 Döttingen A 4
70 Douai B 2
80 Douarnenez B 2
94 Douchy, Loiret, F B 3
70 Douchy, Nord, F B 2
82 Doudeville B 2
92 Doué-la-Fontaine B 3
50 Douglas,GB B 4
56 Douglas,GBM B 2
84 Doulaincourt B 2
84 Doulevant-le-Château B 1
63 Doullens B 4
49 Dounby B 5
50 Doune A 3
158 Dounéika B 2
70 Dour B 2
83 Dourdan C 4
107 Dourgne D 2
104 Dournazac B 3
124 Douro Calvo C 2
96 Douvaine B 2
70 Douzy C 4
62 Dover B 5
100 Dovje C 1
31 Dovre B 6
59 Downham C 4
59 Downham Market C 4
53 Downhill A 5
53 Downpatrick B 6
94 Doyet C 2
118 Dozón B 2
82 Dozulé B 1
117 Drača B 4
153 Dračevo C 3
87 Drachselsried B 5
64 Drachten A 4
4 Drag B 5
103 Drăgănești B 6
152 Dragaš B 2
103 Drăgești B 6
116 Draginja B 3
4 Dragnes B 4
115 Dragolovci C 5
153 Dragoman B 4
144 Dragoni B 3
115 Dragotina B 4
153 Dragovishtitsa B 4
27 Dragsfjärd C 5
30 Dragsvik B 3
109 Draguignan D 3
75 Drahnsdorf B 5
88 Drahonice B 2
101 Drahovce A 5
156 Dráma A 4
35 Drammen B 6
35 Drangedal B 5
15 Drängsmark D 4
66 Drangstedt B 1
72 Dransfeld B 3
67 Dranske A 6
53 Draperstown B 5
101 Draškovec C 4
101 Draßburg B 4
101 Draßmarkt B 4
102 Drávaszabolcs C 2
83 Draveil C 4
100 Dravograd C 3
69 Drawno B 3
69 Drawsko Pomorskie B 3
78 Drazdzewo B 4
87 Drazenov B 4
116 Drazevac, Srbija, YU B 4
117 Draževac, Srbija, YU C 5
60 Dre-fach B 2
75 Drebkau B 6
50 Dreghorn B 3
117 Drenovac C 5
116 Drenovci B 2
65 Drensteinfurt C 5
75 Dresden B 5
69 Dretyń A 4
82 Dreux C 3
12 Drevja B 5
89 Drevohostice B 5
32 Drevsjø B 3
74 Drewitz A 4
69 Drezdenko C 3
115 Drežnik C 3
64 Driebergen B 3
126 Driebes B 2
91 Drienov D 4
89 Drietoma C 5
58 Driffield A 3
48 Drimnin E 3
54 Drimoleague C 2
72 Dringenberg B 3
150 Drinovci B 3
19 Drivstua C 5
154 Drizë B 2
116 Drlače B 3
89 Drnholec C 4
150 Drniš B 2
115 Drnje A 4
111 Dro B 5
35 Drøbak B 6
78 Drobin C 2
66 Drochtersen B 2
55 Drogheda A 5
90 Droginia C 3
55 Droichead Nua A 5
57 Droitwich D 4
77 Droltowice B 6
53 Dromara B 6
52 Dromard B 3
53 Dromore, Down, GB B 5
53 Dromore, Tyrone, GB B 4
52 Dromore West B 3
110 Dronero C 2
58 Dronfield B 2
70 Drongen A 2
40 Dronninglund B 4
64 Dronrijp A 3
64 Dronten B 3
88 Drosendorf C 3
101 Drösing A 4
82 Droué C 3
153 Drugan B 5
57 Druid D 3
85 Drulingen B 4
53 Drum B 4
48 Drumbeg C 3
53 Drumcard B 4
52 Drumcliff B 3
50 Drumjohn B 3
50 Drummore C 3
48 Drumnadrochit D 4
52 Drumod C 4
52 Drumshanbo B 3
52 Drumsna C 3
50 Drumvach A 3
64 Drunen C 3
64 Druten C 3
116 Druzetiči B 4
115 Drvar C 4
150 Drvenik B 3
78 Drygaly B 5
50 Drymen A 3
48 Drynoch D 2
69 Drzewiany B 4
79 Drzewica D 3
141 Dualchi B 2
125 Duas Igrejas B 3
116 Dub C 3
88 Dubá A 2
75 Duben B 5
97 Dübendorf A 4
88 Dubi A 1
115 Dubica B 4
91 Dubinné C 4
55 Dublin A 5
89 Dubňany C 5
89 Dubnica C 6
101 Dubnik B 6
117 Dubona B 4
117 Dubovac B 5
101 Dubrava, Hrvatska, YU C 4
115 Dubrava, Hrvatska, YU B 4
116 Dubrave B 2
151 Dubrovnik C 4
81 Ducey B 5
88 Duchcov A 1
67 Ducherow B 6
117 Ducina B 4
82 Duclair B 2
101 Dudar B 5
59 Duddington C 3
71 Dudelange C 5
72 Duderstadt B 4
57 Dudley D 4
70 Dudzele A 2
120 Dueñas C 2
99 Dueville D 2
70 Duffel A 3
49 Dufftown D 5
152 Duga Poljana A 2
114 Duga-Resa B 3
150 Dugi Rat B 2
150 Dugi Seget B 2
84 Dugny-sur-Meuse A 2
115 Dugo Selo B 4
150 Dugopolje B 2
72 Duingen A 3
99 Duino D 4
71 Duisburg A 5
154 Dukat,AL B 1
153 Dukat,YU B 4
90 Dukla C 4
89 Dukovany B 4
71 Dülken A 5
50 Dull A 4
65 Dülmen C 5
49 Dulnain Bridge D 5
32 Dulpetorpet C 3
60 Dulverton B 3
50 Dumbarton B 3
50 Dumfries B 4
55 Dun Laoghaire A 5
93 Dun-le-Palestel C 5
94 Dun-les-Places B 4
94 Dun-sur-Auron C 2
91 Dunaalmás E 1
91 Dunabogdány E 2
102 Dunafalva B 2
102 Dunaföldvar B 2
102 Dunaharaszti A 3
78 Dunajek A 5
101 Dunajská-Streda B 5
102 Dunakeszi A 3
101 Dunakiliti B 5
102 Dunakömlöd B 2
53 Dunamanagh B 4
50 Dunans A 2
102 Dunapataj B 3
102 Dunaszekcsö B 2
102 Dunaszentgyörgy B 2
102 Dunatetétlen B 3
102 Dunaújváros B 2
102 Dunavecse B 2
51 Dunbar A 5
49 Dunbeath C 5
50 Dunblane A 4
55 Dunboyne A 5

49 Duncansby C 5
59 Dunchurch C 2
53 Dundalk B 5
51 Dundee A 5
5 Dunderland D 3
53 Dundonald B 6
50 Dundrennan C 4
53 Dundrum B 6
50 Dunfermline A 4
53 Dungannon B 5
55 Dungarvan B 4
50 Dungavel B 3
53 Dungiven B 5
52 Dunglow B 3
54 Dungourney C 3
69 Duninowo A 4
153 Dunje C 3
50 Dunkeld A 4
39 Dunker C 3
63 Dunkerque A 4
55 Dunkerrin B 4
52 Dunkineely B 3
53 Dunleer C 5
50 Dunlop B 3
54 Dunmanway C 2
54 Dunmore A 3
55 Dunmore East B 5
49 Dunnet C 5
85 Dunningen B 5
50 Dunoon B 3
51 Duns B 5
50 Dunscore B 4
55 Dunshaughlin A 5
62 Dunstable B 3
60 Dunster B 3
48 Duntulm D 2
48 Dunvegan D 2
97 Durach A 6
152 Đurakovac B 2
121 Durana B 4
105 Durance C 3
121 Durango A 4
104 Duras C 3
107 Durban E 2
85 Durbheim B 5
136 Dúrcal C 3
102 Durdenovac C 2
115 Đurđevac A 5
116 Đurđevik B 2
71 Düren B 5
51 Durham C 6
117 Đurinci B 4
115 Durmanec A 3
85 Durmersheim B 5
48 Durness C 4
101 Dürnkrut A 4
97 Dürrboden B 5
97 Dürrenboden B 4
152 Durrës C 1
55 Durrow, Laoighis, IRL B 4
55 Durrow, Offaly, IRL A 4
61 Dursley B 4
92 Durtal B 3
40 Durup C 2
102 Dusnok B 2
78 Dusocin B 1
71 Düsseldorf A 5
85 Dußlingen B 6
75 Düßnitz B 4
89 Duszniki Zdrój A 4
114 Dutovlje B 1
20 Duved B 1
150 Duvno B 3
4 Dverberg A 5
115 Dvor B 4
89 Dvorce B 5
101 Dvorníky A 5
101 Dvory n. Žitavou B 6
88 Dvůr Králove n. Labem A 3
40 Dybvad B 4
49 Dyce D 6
76 Dychow B 4
68 Dygowo A 3
49 Dykehead E 6
49 Dykends E 5
78 Dylewo B 4
62 Dymchurch B 5
61 Dymock B 4
30 Dyranut C 4
18 Dyrnesvågen B 3
6 Dyrøy B 3
78 Dywity B 3
153 Džep B 4
153 Dzherman B 5
78 Działdowo B 3
90 Działoszyce B 3
79 Działoszyn D 1
90 Dziekanowice C 3
69 Dziemiany A 5
79 Dzierzaznia C 3
78 Dzierzgoń B 2
78 Dzierzgowo B 3
77 Dzierzoniów C 5
68 Dziwnów A 2
153 Džumajlija C 3
78 Dźwierzuty B 3

E

51 Eaglesfield B 4
62 Ealing B 3
59 Earith C 4
59 Earl Shilton C 2
59 Earl Soham C 5
51 Earlston B 5
51 Earsdon B 6
58 Easington B 4
51 Easington Colliery C 6
58 Easingwold A 2
52 Easky B 3
62 East Adderbury A 2
61 East Brent B 4
51 East Calder B 4
59 East Dereham C 4
62 East Grinstead B 4
59 East Harling C 4
62 East Hoathly C 4
62 East Ilsley B 2
50 East Kilbride B 3
51 East Linton B 5
58 East Markham B 3
58 East Retford B 3
59 East Rudham C 4
51 East Wemyss A 4
62 Eastbourne C 4
49 Easter Quarff A 7
49 Easter Skeld A 7
49 Eastern Fearn D 4
62 Eastleigh C 2
61 Easton C 4
62 Eastry B 5
59 Eastwood B 2
59 Eaton Socon C 3
105 Eauze D 3
44 Ebberup B 2
98 Ebbs B 3
61 Ebbw Vale B 3
74 Ebeleben B 2
44 Ebeltoft A 3
98 Eben im Pongau B 4
98 Ebensee B 4
86 Ebensfeld A 2
85 Eberbach A 5
101 Ebergassing A 4
72 Ebergötzen B 4
86 Ebermannstadt B 3
73 Ebern C 4
100 Eberndorf C 2
75 Ebersbach B 6
87 Ebersberg C 3
98 Eberschwang A 4
74 Ebersdorf, Bayern, D† C 3
66 Ebersdorf, Niedersachsen, D† B 2
100 Eberstein C 2
84 Ebersviller A 3
68 Eberswalde C 1
85 Ebingen B 6
97 Ebnat-Kappel A 5
145 Eboli C 4
73 Ebrach D 4
101 Ebreichsdorf B 4
94 Ebreuil C 3
66 Ebstorf B 3
70 Ecaussinnes-d'Enghien B 3
51 Ecclefechan B 4
57 Eccleshall D 4
160 Eceabat E 5
96 Echallens B 2
121 Echarri-Aranaz B 4
121 Echauri B 5
95 Échenoz-la-Méline B 6
92 Echire C 3
108 Echirolles B 2
104 Echourgnac B 3
49 Echt, GB D 6
71 Echt, NL A 4
72 Echte B 4
71 Echternach C 5
136 Ecija B 1
117 Ečka A 4
74 Eckartsberga B 3
73 Eckelshausen C 2
71 Eckenhagen B 6
66 Eckernförde A 2
26 Eckerö C 2
58 Eckington B 2
84 Éclaron B 1
93 Ecommoy B 4
82 Ecouché C 1
83 Ecouen B 4
101 Écs B 5
103 Ecsegfalva A 4
93 Ecuellé B 5
36 Ed C 3
36 Eda B 4
36 Eda glasbruk B 4
64 Edam B 3
36 Edane B 4
74 Edderitz B 3
51 Eddleston B 4
64 Ede B 3
37 Edebäck A 5
38 Edebo B 5
91 Edelény D 3
100 Edelschrott B 3
72 Edemissen A 4
53 Eden B 6
62 Edenbridge B 4
55 Edenderry A 4
85 Edenkoben A 5
53 Ederny B 4
85 Edesheim A 5
65 Edewecht A 5
70 Edgegem A 3
156 Édhessa B 2
51 Edinburgh B 4
160 Edirne E 5
34 Edland B 3
101 Edlitz B 4
51 Edmondbyers C 6
97 Édolo B 6
38 Edsbro C 5
43 Edsbruk A 6
33 Edsbyn B 6
21 Edsele B 5
37 Edsgatan B 5
36 Edsleskog B 4
37 Edsvalla B 5
49 Edzell E 6
64 Ee A 4
65 Eefde B 4
70 Eeklo A 2
64 Eerbeek B 4
70 Eernegem A 2
70 Eersel A 4
65 Eexta A 4
100 Eferding A 2
86 Effeltrich B 3
106 Effiat A 3
156 Efkarpia A 2
35 Efteløt B 5
157 Efxinoúpolis C 2
74 Egeln B 3
91 Eger E 3
91 Egerbakta E 3
44 Egernsund C 2
34 Egersund C 2
91 Egerszólát E 3
97 Egg, A A 5
86 Egg, D† C 2
31 Eggedal C 6
88 Eggenburg C 3
87 Eggenfelden C 4
18 Eggesbønes C 1
68 Eggesin B 2
98 Egglesberg A 3
87 Egglfing C 5
4 Eggum B 2
62 Egham B 3
70 Eghezée B 3
69 Egiertowo A 6
106 Egletons B 2
86 Egling, Bayern, D† D 3
86 Egling, Bayern, D† C 2
53 Eglinton A 4
97 Eglisau A 4
106 Egliseneuve-d'Entraigues B 2
97 Eglofs A 5
60 Eglwyswrw A 2
64 Egmond aan Zee B 2
99 Egna C 2
56 Egremont B 3
44 Egtved B 2
109 Eguilles D 2
84 Eguilly B 1
93 Eguzon C 5
103 Egyek A 4
101 Egyházasrádóc B 4
86 Ehekirchen C 3
86 Ehingen C 1
72 Ehmen A 4
66 Ehra-Lessien C 3
71 Ehrang C 5
75 Ehrenfriedersdorf C 4
75 Ehrenhain C 4
73 Ehringshausen C 2
98 Ehrwald B 1
121 Eibar A 4
75 Eibau C 6
73 Eibelstadt D 4
75 Eibenstock C 4
65 Eibergen B 4
100 Eibiswald C 3
87 Eichedorf C 4
74 Eichenbarleben A 3
86 Eichstätt C 3
72 Eickelborn B 2
35 Eide, Austagder Fylke, N C 4
30 Eide, Hordaland, N C 3
18 Eide, More og Romsdal, N C 3
30 Eidfjord C 4
36 Eidsberg B 3
31 Eidsbugarden B 5
18 Eidsbygda C 3
18 Eidsdal C 3
4 Eidsfjord B 3
35 Eidsfoss B 6
36 Eidskog A 4
30 Eidsvåg, Hordaland, N C 2
18 Eidsvåg, More og Romsdal, N C 4
36 Eidsvoll A 3
30 Eikefjord B 2
30 Eikelandsosen C 2
34 Eiken C 3
18 Eikesdal C 4
75 Eilenburg B 4
71 Eilendorf B 5
74 Eilsleben A 3
31 Eina C 7
72 Einbeck B 3
64 Eindhoven C 3
70 Eine B 2
66 Einfeld A 2
97 Einsiedeln A 4
86 Einsingen C 1
84 Einville B 3
74 Eisenach C 2
73 Eisenberg, D† D 2
74 Eisenberg, D* C 3
100 Eisenerz B 2
75 Eisenhüttenstadt A 6
100 Eisenkappel C 2
101 Eisenstadt B 4
98 Eisentratten C 4
71 Eiserfeld B 6
74 Eisfeld C 2
74 Eisleben B 3
86 Eistingen C 1
73 Eiterfeld C 3
71 Eitorf B 6
30 Eivindvik C 2
124 Eixo C 1
124 Eja B 1
44 Ejby B 2
122 Ejea de los Caballeros B 1
44 Ejstrup B 2
132 Ejulve A 2
70 Eke B 2
43 Ekeby, Östergötlands Län, S A 5
38 Ekeby, Uppsala Län, S B 5
27 Ekenäs D 6
43 Ekenässjön B 5
70 Ekeren A 3
46 Eket A 4
9 Ekkerøy B 10
19 Ekrie B 7
70 Eksel A 4
37 Ekshärad A 5
30 Eksingedal C 2
43 Eksjö B 4
39 Eksta E 5
126 El Alamo, Madrid, E B 2
135 El Alamo, Sevilla, E B 4
134 El Almendro B 3
120 El Almiñe B 3
137 El Alquián C 4
135 El Aquila B 5
135 El Arahal B 4
125 El Arenal, Avila, E C 4
139 El Arenal, Mallorca, E B 3
137 El Arguellite A 4
120 El Astillero A 3
131 El Ballestero C 4
119 El Barco B 4
125 El Barco de Avila C 4
119 El Berrón A 5
126 El Berrueco B 2
125 El Bodón C 3
118 El Bollo B 3
131 El Bonillo C 4
135 El Bosque C 5
130 El Bullaque B 2
122 El Burgo de Ebro C 2
126 El Burgo de Osma A 2
121 El Buste C 5
125 El Cabaco C 3
137 El Cabo de Gata C 4
120 El Callejo A 3
135 El Campillo B 4
130 El Campillo de la Jara B 1
129 El Campo B 5
131 El Cañavete B 4
133 El Cantal D 1
136 El Carpio B 2
126 El Carpio de Tajo C 1
126 El Casar de Escalona B 1
120 El Castaño A 3
135 El Castillo de las Guardas B 4
136 El Centenillo A 3
125 El Cerro C 4
135 El Cerro de Andévalo B 4
135 El Colmenar C 5
135 El Coronil B 5
125 El Cubo de Tierra del Vino B 4
135 El Cuervo C 4
137 El Ejido C 4
131 El Entredicho C 4
126 El Escorial B 1
126 El Espinar B 1
118 El Ferrol del Caudillo A 2
122 El Fragu B 2
119 El Franco A 4
127 El Frasno A 4
135 El Garrobo B 4
135 El Gastor C 5
130 El Gordo B 1
122 El Grado B 3
134 El Granado B 3
136 El Higuera B 2
130 El Hoyo C 3
126 El Hoyo de Pinares B 1
125 El Maillo C 3
125 El Mirón C 4
126 El Molar B 2
130 El Molinillo B 2
126 El Muyo A 2
126 El Olmo A 2
126 El Pardo B 2
125 El Payo C 3
131 El Pedernosa B 4
135 El Pedroso B 5
131 El Peral B 5
132 El Perelló B 2
131 El Picazo B 4
125 El Piñero B 4
132 El Pobo A 2
127 El Pobo de Dueñas B 4
126 El Pozo de Guadalajara B 2
131 El Provencio B 4
130 El Puente de Arzobispo B 1
135 El Puerto de Santa Maria C 4
121 El Quintanar C 4
135 El Real de la Jara B 4
126 El Real de S. Vicente B 1
135 El Rinconcillo C 5
130 El Robledo B 2
135 El Rocio B 4
134 El Rompido B 3
135 El Ronquillo B 4
121 El Royo C 4
136 El Rubio B 1
132 El Saler B 2
135 El Saucejo B 5
122 El Temple C 2
126 El Tiemblo B 1
131 El Toboso B 4
136 El Tocón B 3
122 El Tomillo C 2
129 El Torno A 5
120 El Valle de las Casas B 1
126 El Vellón B 2
130 El Viso C 2
135 El Viso del Alcor B 5
131 El Viso del Marqués C 3
156 Elaiokhóri B 4
157 Elaión D 2
23 Elämäjärvi B 7
156 Elassón C 2
157 Elátia D 2
157 Elatoú D 1
154 Elbasan A 2
82 Elbeuf B 3
74 Elbingerode B 2
78 Elblag A 2
64 Elburg B 3
133 Elche C 2

131 Elche de la Sierra C 4
86 Elchingen C 2
133 Elda C 2
72 Eldagsen A 3
67 Eldena B 4
46 Eldsberga A 3
103 Elek B 5
117 Elemir A 4
159 Elevsís A 4
157 Elevtheraí C 2
156 Elevtheroúpolis B 4
32 Elgå A 2
72 Elgershausen B 3
49 Elgin D 5
121 Elgóibar A 4
48 Elgol D 2
51 Elie A 5
159 Elika C 3
28 Elimäki C 4
153 Eliseyna A 5
51 Elishaw B 5
121 Elizondo A 5
78 Elk B 5
160 Elkhovo D 5
86 Ellenberg B 2
58 Eller Beck Bridge A 3
57 Ellesmere D 4
57 Ellesmere Port C 4
70 Ellezelles B 2
86 Ellingen B 2
51 Ellington B 6
159 Ellinikó B 4
98 Ellmau B 3
49 Ellon D 6
42 Ellös A 1
58 Elloughton B 3
74 Ellrich B 2
86 Ellwangen C 2
97 Elm,CH B 5
66 Elm,D† B 2
66 Elmshorn B 2
85 Elmstein A 4
123 Elne B 5
121 Elorrio A 4
102 Eloszallás B 2
84 Eloyes B 3
48 Elphin C 3
71 Elsdorf B 5
73 Elsenfeld D 3
12 Elsfjord A 5
66 Elsfleth B 1
72 Elspe B 2
64 Elspeet B 3
64 Elst C 3
75 Elster B 4
74 Elsterberg C 4
75 Elsterwerda B 5
75 Elstra B 6
73 Eltmann D 4
73 Eltville C 2
129 Elvas C 3
32 Elvåseter B 2
32 Elvdal B 2
8 Elvebakken C 3
59 Elveden C 4
80 Elven C 4
63 Elverdinge B 4
32 Elverum C 2
19 Elvran B 7
74 Elxleben B 2
59 Ely C 4
73 Elz C 2
85 Elzach B 5
72 Elze A 3
33 Emådalen B 5
51 Embleton B 6
108 Embrun C 3
122 Embún B 2
65 Emden A 5
65 Emlichheim B 4
54 Emly B 3
43 Emmaboda C 5
47 Emmaljunga A 4
64 Emmeloord B 3
96 Emmen,CH A 4
65 Emmen,NL B 4
85 Emmendingen B 4
65 Emmer-Compascuum B 5
65 Emmer-Erfscheidenveen B 5
65 Emmerich C 4
72 Emmern A 3
83 Emmonville B 4
91 Emod E 3
112 Empoli C 2
65 Emsbüren B 5
65 Emsdetten B 5
43 Emsfors B 6
86 Emskirchen B 2
65 Emstek B 6
62 Emsworth C 3
53 Emyvale B 5
20 Enafors B 1
28 Enäjärvi C 5
33 Enånger B 8
128 Encarnaçao C 1
125 Encinas de Abajo C 4
126 Encinas de Esgueva A 1
136 Encinas Reales B 2
135 Encinasola A 4
121 Encio B 3
121 Enciso B 4
91 Encs D 4
31 Enden B 7
85 Endingen B 4
87 Endorf D 4
125 Endrinal C 4
103 Endrod B 4
36 Enebakk B 3
43 Eneryda C 4
101 Enese B 5
160 Enez E 5
62 Enfield B 3
98 Eng B 2
18 Engdal B 4
65 Engel B 6
97 Engelberg B 4
100 Engelhartszell A 1
71 Engelskirchen B 6
85 Engen C 5
31 Enger C 7
32 Engerdal B 2
44 Engesvang A 2
70 Enghien B 3
18 Engjan B 4
87 Englmar B 4
65 Engter B 6
133 Enguera C 2
132 Enguidanos B 1
85 Eningen B 6
73 Enkenbach D 1
64 Enkhuizen B 3
38 Enköping C 4
149 Enna B 4
71 Ennepetal A 6
106 Ennezat B 3
43 Enngsboda C 5
65 Ennigerloh C 6
65 Ennigloh B 6
36 Enningdal C 3
54 Ennis B 3
55 Enniscorthy B 5
54 Enniskean C 3
55 Enniskerry A 5
53 Enniskillen B 4
54 Ennistimon B 2
100 Enns A 2
25 Eno C 7
29 Enonkoski A 6
10 Enontekiö A 3
156 Enótia A 2
64 Ens B 3
65 Enschede B 4
87 Ensdorf B 3
85 Ensisheim C 4
71 Ensival B 4
39 Enstaberga D 3
62 Enstone B 2
96 Entlebuch B 4
110 Entrácque C 2
94 Entrains-sur-Nohain B 3
120 Entrambasaguas A 3
120 Entrambasmestas A 3
106 Entraygues-sur-Truyère C 2
108 Entremont-le-Vx. B 2
121 Entrena B 4
109 Entrevaux D 3
129 Entrin Bajo C 4
128 Entroncamento B 2
85 Entzheim B 4
132 Enveija A 3
82 Envermeu B 3
38 Enviken B 2
101 Enying C 6
101 Enzesfeld B 4
98 Enzingerboden B 3
85 Enzklösterle B 5
85 Enzweihagen B 5
48 Eoligarry D 1
83 Epagny B 5
92 Epannes C 3
156 Epanomí B 2
65 Epe,D† B 5
64 Epe,NL B 3
83 Epéhy A 5
83 Épernay B 5
82 Epernon C 3
85 Epfig B 4
108 Épierre B 3
127 Épila A 4
95 Epinac-les-Mines C 4
84 Épinal B 3
146 Episcopiá B 2
156 Episkopí B 2
158 Epitálion B 2
95 Epoisses B 4
99 Eppan C 2
70 Eppegem B 3
71 Eppelborn C 5
85 Eppenbrunn A 4
75 Eppendorf C 5
62 Epping B 4
85 Eppingen A 5
62 Epsom B 3
154 Eptakhórion B 3
58 Epworth B 3
81 Equeurdreville A 5
99 Eraclea D 3
27 Eräjärvi B 7
157 Eratiní D 2
154 Eratira B 3
110 Erba B 4
86 Erbach, Baden-Württemberg, D† C 1
73 Erbach, Hessen, D† D 2
87 Erbendorf B 4
146 Erchie B 3
102 Ercsi A 2
102 Érd A 2
116 Erdevik A 3
87 Erding C 3
91 Erdobénye D 4
102 Erdötelek A 4
102 Erdut C 3
128 Ereira B 2
18 Eresfjord C 4
157 Erétria C 2
66 Erfde A 2
34 Erfjord B 2
71 Erftstadt B 5
74 Erfurt C 3
87 Ergolding C 4
87 Ergoldsbach C 4
65 Erica B 4
148 Érice A 2
128 Ericeira C 1
20 Erikslund C 4
43 Eriksmåla C 5
36 Erikstad C 4
35 Erikstrand B 5
154 Erind B 2
96 Eriswil A 3
159 Erithraí A 4
71 Erkelenz A 5
67 Erkner C 6
71 Erkrath A 5
122 Erla B 2
101 Erlach B 4
86 Erlangen B 3
110 Erli C 3
64 Ermelo B 3
124 Ermezinde B 1
134 Ermidas B 2
159 Ermióni B 4
74 Ermsleben B 3
72 Erndtebrück C 2
81 Ernée B 6
102 Ernestinovo C 2
101 Ernstbrunn A 4
86 Erolzheim C 2
70 Erquelinnes B 3
81 Erquy B 4
121 Errazu A 5
45 Errindlev C 4
121 Erro B 5
49 Errogie D 4
51 Errol A 4
140 Ersa B 2
102 Ersekcsanád B 2
154 Ersekë B 2
91 Érsekvadkert E 2
6 Ersfjordbotn B 4
15 Ershäs C 5
15 Ersmark, Västerbottens, S E 4
15 Ersmark, Västerbottens, S D 4
85 Erstein B 4
97 Erstfeld B 4
40 Ertebølle C 3
86 Ertingen C 1
128 Ervedal, Coimbra, P A 2
128 Ervedal, Portalegre, P B 3
115 Ervenik C 3
134 Ervidel B 2
18 Ervik B 4
83 Ervy C 5
72 Erwitte B 2
74 Erxleben A 3
44 Esbjerg B 1
83 Esbly C 4
135 Escacena del Campo B 4
118 Escairon B 3
120 Escalada B 3
120 Escalante A 3
141 Escalaplano C 3
126 Escalona B 1
126 Escalona del Prado A 1
126 Escalonilla C 1
128 Escalos de Baixo B 3
128 Escalos de Cima B 3
127 Escamilla B 3
136 Escañuela B 2
122 Escároz B 1
122 Escatrón C 2
71 Esch-s.-Alzette C 4
97 Eschach A 5
73 Eschau D 3
66 Eschede C 3
86 Eschenau B 3
87 Eschenbach B 3
97 Eschenz A 4
72 Escherhausen B 3
72 Eschwege B 4
71 Eschweiler B 5
127 Escobasa de Almazán A 3
63 Escoeuilles B 3
133 Escombreras D 2
105 Escos D 1
105 Escource C 1
109 Escragnolles D 3
129 Escurial B 5
125 Escurial de la Sierra C 4
65 Esens A 5
118 Esgos B 3
62 Esher B 3
51 Eskdalemuir B 4
37 Eskilsäter C 5
45 Eskilstrup C 4
39 Eskilstuna C 3
23 Eskola B 6
87 Eslarn B 4
121 Eslava B 5
132 Eslida B 2
72 Eslohe B 2
46 Eslöv B 4
124 Esmoriz C 1
83 Esnes A 5
71 Esneux B 4
32 Espa C 2
106 Espalion C 2
106 Espaly-St.-Marcel B 3
129 Esparragalejo C 4
129 Esparragosa de la Serena C 5
130 Esparragosa del Caudillo C 1
123 Esparraguera C 4
109 Esparron D 2
34 Espedal C 2
121 Espejo, Álava, E B 3
136 Espejo, Córdoba, E B 2
30 Espeland C 2
105 Espelette D 1
66 Espelkamp C 1
108 Espeluche C 1
136 Espeluy A 3
135 Espera C 5
129 Esperança B 3
107 Espéraza E 2
143 Espéria C 4
34 Espevær B 1
135 Espiel A 5
120 Espinama A 2
118 Espiñaredo A 3
123 Espinelvas C 5
124 Espinho B 1
120 Espinilla A 2
120 Espinosa de Cerrato C 3
120 Espinosa de los Monteros A 3
134 Espirito Santo B 3
123 Espluga de Francoli C 4
122 Esplús C 3
123 Espolla B 5
138 Esporlas B 3
124 Esposende B 1
123 Espot B 4
123 Espunyola B 4
122 Esquedas B 2
126 Esquivias B 2
22 Esse Ahtävä B 5
70 Essen, B A 3
65 Essen, Niedersachsen, D† B 5
71 Essen, Nordrhein-Westfalen, D† A 6
87 Essenbach C 4
83 Essertaux B 4
85 Eßlingen B 6
84 Essoyes B 1
21 Essvik C 6
138 Establiments B 3
118 Estacas B 2
122 Estadilla B 3
107 Estagel E 2
63 Estaires B 4
105 Estang D 2
123 Estany C 5
124 Estarreja C 1
123 Estartit B 6
96 Estavayer-l. Lac B 2
112 Este A 3
118 Esteiro A 2
124 Estela B 1
121 Estella B 4
138 Estellenchs B 3
136 Estepa B 2
120 Estépar B 3
135 Estepona C 5
83 Esternay C 5
123 Esterri de Aneu B 4
65 Esterwegen B 5
83 Estissac C 5
118 Estivadas B 3
94 Estivareilles C 2
132 Estivella B 2
134 Estói B 3
122 Estopiñán C 3
128 Estoril C 1
109 Estoublon D 3
134 Estradas B 2
63 Estrée-Blanche B 4
83 Estrées-St. Denis B 4
128 Estrela C 3
126 Estremera B 2
128 Estremoz C 3
38 Estuna C 5
103 Esztar A 5
91 Esztergom E 1
80 Etables-sur-Mer B 4
84 Etain A 2
95 Étalans B 6
71 Etalle C 4
83 Etampes C 4
95 Etang-sur-Arroux C 4
63 Étaples B 3
104 Etauliers B 2
71 Ethe C 4
34 Etne B 1
83 Etoges C 5
83 Étréaupont B 5
83 Étréchy C 4
82 Étrépagny B 3
82 Étretat B 2
83 Étrœungt A 5
110 Étroubles B 2
98 Ettal B 2
71 Ettelbrück C 5
64 Etten C 2
59 Ettington C 2
85 Ettlingen B 5
86 Ettringen, Bayern, D† C 2
71 Ettringen, Rheinland-Pfalz, D† B 6
120 Etyek A 2
87 Etzenricht B 4
82 Eu A 3
121 Eulate B 4
71 Eupen B 5
26 Eura B 5
26 Eurajoki B 4
64 Europoort C 2
84 Eurville-sur-Marne B 2
71 Euskirchen B 5
66 Eutin A 3
83 Euvy C 6
56 Euxton C 4
158 Éva B 2
30 Evanger C 3
94 Evaux C 2
4 Evenes B 5
32 Evenstad B 2
61 Evercreech B 4
73 Everdorf C 4
70 Evergem A 2
47 Everöd B 5
72 Eversberg B 2
65 Everswinkel C 5
32 Evertsberg B 4
57 Evesham D 5
96 Evian B 2
23 Evijärvi B 5
155 Evinokhórion D 3
140 Evisa B 1
34 Evje C 3
96 Evolène B 3
128 Evora C 3
128 Evoramonte C 3
155 Evpálion D 3
81 Evran B 5
81 Evrecy A 6
82 Évreux B 3
81 Evron B 6

156 Evropos B 2
156 Evzonoi A 2
62 Ewell B 3
73 Ewersbach C 2
62 Ewhurst B 3
159 Examillia B 3
156 Exaplátanon B 2
157 Éxarkhos D 3
104 Excideuil B 4
60 Exeter C 3
82 Exmes C 2
60 Exminster C 3
60 Exmouth C 3
72 Exter A 2
124 Extremo B 1
35 Eydehamn C 4
59 Eye C 5
51 Eyemouth B 5
109 Eyguians C 2
109 Eyguières D 2
106 Eygurande B 2
105 Eylie E 3
104 Eymet C 3
106 Eymoutiers B 1
62 Eynsham B 2
66 Eystrup C 2
118 Ezaro B 1
121 Ezcaray B 4
117 Ezeris A 5

F

122 Fabara C 3
112 Fábbrico B 2
31 Fåberg, Oppland, N B 7
30 Fåberg, Sogne og Fjordane, N B 4
119 Fabero B 4
44 Fåborg B 3
107 Fabrègues D 3
113 Fabriano C 4
147 Fabrízia D 2
124 Facha B 1
135 Facinas C 5
89 Fackov B 6
104 Facture C 2
128 Fadagosa B 3
102 Fadd B 2
99 Faédis C 4
112 Faenza B 3
124 Fafe B 1
99 Fagagna C 4
160 Făgăras C 4
13 Fågelberget C 6
43 Fågelfors B 5
43 Fågelmara C 5
33 Fagelsjö B 5
39 Fågelsta D 2
30 Fagerheim C 4
31 Fagerhøi B 6
43 Fagerhult B 5
31 Fagernes, Oppland, N C 6
6 Fagernes, Troms, N B 5
37 Fagersanna C 6
38 Fagersta B 2
103 Făget C 6
42 Fåglavik A 3
147 Fagnano Castello C 2
96 Fahrwangen A 4
97 Faido B 4
84 Fains B 2
57 Fairbourne D 2
62 Fairford B 2
50 Fairlie B 3
102 Fajsz B 2
59 Fakenham C 4
20 Fåker C 3
45 Fakse B 5
45 Fakse Ladeplads B 5
156 Fálaina C 2
82 Falaise C 1
99 Falcade C 2
52 Falcarragh A 3
121 Falces B 5
160 Fălciu B 6
113 Falconara Marittima C 5
149 Falcone A 5
43 Falerum A 6
87 Falkenberg, D† B 4
68 Falkenberg, Frankfurt, D* C 1
75 Falkenberg, Gottbus, D* B 5
42 Falkenberg, S C 2
67 Falkensee C 6
87 Falkenstein, D† B 4
75 Falkenstein, D* C 4
67 Falkenthal C 6
50 Falkirk B 4
51 Falkland A 4
42 Falköping A 3
98 Fall B 2
39 Falla D 2
66 Fallersleben C 3
15 Fällfors C 4
66 Fallingbostel C 2
60 Falmouth C 1
122 Falset C 3
46 Falsterbo B 3
160 Falticeni B 5
38 Falun B 2
30 Fana C 2
112 Fanano B 2
155 Fanárion C 3
44 Fangel B 3
107 Fanjeaux D 2
19 Fannrem B 5
113 Fano C 5
38 Fanthyttan C 2
124 Fão B 1
49 Far D 4
143 Fara in Sabina B 3
110 Fara Novarese B 3
119 Faramontanos de Tábara C 5
122 Farasdues B 1
43 Fårbo B 6
62 Fareham C 2
123 Farga Moles B 4
36 Färgelanda C 3
83 Fargniers B 5
33 Färila B 6
62 Faringdon B 2
38 Faringe C 5
111 Farini d'Olmo C 4
125 Fariza B 3
43 Farjestaden C 6
122 Farlete C 2
47 Färlöv A 5
102 Farmos A 3
91 Farná, CS E 1
38 Färna, S C 2
33 Färnäs B 5
62 Farnborough B 3
142 Farnese B 2
62 Farnham B 3
62 Farningham B 4
74 Farnroda C 2
74 Farnstädt B 3
134 Faro, P B 3
39 Fårö, S E 6
39 Fårösund E 6
99 Farra d'Alpago C 3
54 Farranfore B 2
157 Fársala C 2
40 Farsø C 3
43 Farstorp B 5
34 Farsund C 2
45 Farum B 5
40 Farup C 3
146 Fasano B 3
66 Faßberg C 3
38 Fasterna C 5
122 Fatarella C 3
128 Fátima B 2
13 Fatmomakke B 7
13 Fättjaur B 7
84 Faucogney C 3
109 Faucon-du-Caire C 3
105 Fauguerolles C 3
50 Fauldhouse B 4
67 Faulenrost B 5
84 Faulquemont A 3
63 Fauquembergues B 4
5 Fauske C 4
95 Fauverney B 5
82 Fauville-en-Caux B 3
31 Fåvang B 7
148 Favara B 3
108 Faverges B 3
95 Faverney B 6
62 Faversham B 4
148 Favignana B 2
62 Fawley C 2
94 Fay-aux-Loges B 2
109 Fayence D 3
95 Fayl-Billot B 5
122 Fayón C 3
70 Fayt B 3
49 Fearn D 5
50 Fearnan A 3
82 Fécamp B 2
30 Fedje C 1
53 Feeny B 4
42 Fegen B 3
103 Fegyverneck A 4
67 Fehrbellin C 5
32 Feiring C 2
100 Feistritz i. Rosental C 2
102 Feketic C 3
139 Felanitx B 4
85 Felbach B 6
68 Felchow B 2
98 Feld am See C 4
100 Feldbach C 3
67 Feldberg B 6
66 Felde A 2
91 Feldebro E 3
97 Feldkirch A 5
87 Feldkirchen, Bayern, D† D 3
87 Feldkirchen, Bayern, D† C 3
100 Feldkirchen a. d. Donau A 2
100 Feldkirchen i. Kärnten C 2
124 Felgueiras B 1
145 Felitto C 4
137 Félix C 4
62 Felixstowe B 5
110 Felizzano C 3
106 Felletin B 2
39 Fellingsbro C 2
103 Felnac B 5
91 Felnémet E 3
100 Fels a Wagram A 3
101 Felsobagod C 4
91 Felsögöd E 2
91 Felsonyárád D 3
101 Felsonyék C 6
102 Felsöszentiván B 3
115 Felsöszentmárton B 5
91 Felsotárkány E 3
91 Felsövadász D 3
91 Felsozsolca D 3
51 Felton B 6
99 Feltre C 2
59 Feltwell C 4
52 Fenagh B 4
110 Fenestrelle B 2
85 Fénétrange B 4
81 Feneu C 6
36 Fengersfors B 4
110 Fenis B 2
45 Fensmark B 4
50 Fenwick B 3
50 Feolin Ferry B 1
55 Ferbane A 4
67 Ferchland C 5
115 Ferdinandovac A 5
67 Ferdinandshof B 6
83 Fère-Champenoise C 6
83 Fère-en-Tardenois B 5
143 Ferentillo B 3
143 Ferentino C 4
129 Feria C 4
115 Feričanci B 5
149 Ferla B 4
100 Ferlach C 2
98 Ferleiten B 3
124 Fermil B 2
113 Fermo C 5
125 Fermoselle B 3
54 Fermoy B 3
136 Fernán-Núnez B 2
137 Fernán Pérez C 4
130 Fernancaballero B 3
128 Fernão Ferro C 1
95 Fernay-Voltaire C 6
61 Ferndown C 5
49 Ferness D 5
48 Fernilea D 2
55 Ferns B 5
96 Ferpécle B 3
160 Ferrai E 5
107 Ferrals D 2
146 Ferrandina B 2
112 Ferrára B 3
99 Ferrara di Mónte Baldo D 1
118 Ferreira A 3
134 Ferreira do Alentejo A 2
128 Ferreira do Zêzere B 2
119 Ferreras de Abajo C 4
119 Ferreras dè Arriba C 4
139 Ferrerias B 5
127 Ferreruela, Teruel, E A 4
119 Ferreruela, Zamora, E C 4
110 Ferret B 2
85 Ferrette C 4
111 Ferriere C 4
70 Ferrière-la-Grande B 2
106 Ferrières, Allier, F A 3
83 Ferrières, Oise, F B 4
83 Ferrières-en-Gâtinais C 4
106 Ferrières-St.-Mary B 3
51 Ferryhill C 6
141 Fertilia B 2
101 Fertorakas B 4
101 Fertöszentmiklós B 4
64 Ferwerd A 3
83 Festieux B 5
18 Festøy C 2
5 Festvåg C 3
160 Fetesti C 5
55 Fethard B 4
35 Fetsund B 7
49 Fettercairn E 6
86 Feucht B 3
98 Feuchten B 1
86 Feuchtwangen B 2
73 Feudingen C 2
82 Feuquières B 3
106 Feurs B 4
35 Fevik C 4
57 Ffestiniog D 3
110 Fiano B 2
103 Fibis C 5
148 Ficarazzi A 3
112 Ficarolo B 3
87 Fichtelberg A 3
86 Fichtenberg C 1
142 Ficulle B 3
111 Fidenza C 5
34 Fidjeland C 2
98 Fieberbrunn B 3
154 Fier B 1
154 Fier-Shegan B 1
99 Fiera di Primiero C 2
96 Fiesch B 4
112 Fiésole C 3
112 Fiesso Umbertiano B 3
140 Figari C 2
106 Figeac C 2
43 Figeholm B 6
34 Figgjo C 1
112 Figline Valdarno C 3
122 Figols B 3
128 Figueira da Foz A 2
124 Figueira de Castelo Rodrigo C 3
134 Figueira dos Cavaleiros A 2
128 Figueiredo B 2
124 Figueiredo de Alva C 2
128 Figueiró dos Vinhos B 2
123 Figueras B 5
119 Figueruela de Arriba C 4
159 Fikhtia B 3
155 Fíki C 3
18 Fiksdal C 2
147 Filadélfia D 2
91 Fil'akovo D 2
58 Filey A 3
159 Filí A 4
157 Filiadhón C 2
160 Filiaşi C 3
155 Filiátes C 2
158 Filiatrá B 2
156 Filippoi A 4
37 Filipstad B 6
97 Filisur B 5
18 Fillan B 4
157 Fillos C 2
97 Films B 5
154 Filótas B 3
113 Filottrano C 5
44 Filskov B 2
35 Filtvet B 6
98 Filzmoos B 4
112 Finale Emilia B 3
110 Finale Ligure C 3
137 Fiñana B 4
62 Finchingfield B 4
49 Findhorn D 5
49 Findochty D 6
62 Findon C 3
59 Finedon C 3
19 Fines B 6
21 Finfors B 5
118 Finisterre B 1
98 Finkenberg B 2
53 Finnea C 4
5 Finneid C 4
5 Finneidfjord D 2
37 Finnerödja C 6
6 Finnkroken B 5
18 Finnset C 4
32 Finnskog C 3
143 Finocchio C 3
67 Finow C 6
30 Finse C 4
43 Finsjö B 6
34 Finsland C 3
39 Finspång D 2
75 Finsterwalde B 5
65 Finsterwolde A 5
49 Finstown B 5
26 Finström C 2
53 Fintona B 4
52 Fintown B 3
50 Fintry A 3
50 Fionnphort A 1
111 Fiorenzuola d'Arda C 4
103 Firdea C 6
112 Firenze C 3
112 Firenzuola B 3
117 Firliug A 5
106 Firminy B 4
146 Firmo C 2
101 Fischamend Markt A 4
101 Fischau B 4
100 Fischbach, A B 3
85 Fischbach, D† A 4
67 Fischbeck C 5
97 Fischen A 6
62 Fishbourne C 2
50 Fisherton B 3
60 Fishguard B 2
34 Fiskå, Rogaland, N B 2
34 Fiskå, Rogaland, N B 1
158 Fiskárdho A 1
27 Fiskars C 6
42 Fiskebäckskil A 1
4 Fiskebøl B 3
32 Fiskevollen B 2
83 Fismes B 5
6 Fissnes B 4
121 Fitero B 5
34 Fitjar B 1
39 Fittja C 4
143 Fiuggi C 4
143 Fiumata B 4
147 Fiumefreddo Brúzio C 2
149 Fiumefreddo di Sicilia B 5
142 Fiumicino C 3
48 Five Penny Borve C 2
53 Fivemiletown B 4
112 Fivizzano B 2
117 Fizes A 5
34 Fjæra B 2
47 Fjälkinge A 5
20 Fjällnäs C 1
21 Fjallsjo B 5
38 Fjärdhundra C 3
36 Fjell bru B 3
44 Fjellerup A 3
40 Fjerritslev B 3
36 Fjøllbacka C 3
37 Fjugesta B 6
31 Flå, Buskerud Fylke, N C 6
19 Flå, Trøndelag Fylke, N B 6
95 Flace C 4
30 Flåm C 4
96 Flamatt B 3
58 Flamborough A 3
71 Flammersfeld B 6
123 Flassá B 5
109 Flassans D 3
31 Flatåker C 5
35 Flatdal B 4
34 Flateland B 3
31 Flatøydegard C 6
98 Flattach C 4
18 Flatval B 4
84 Flavigny B 3
107 Flavin C 2
83 Flavy-le-Martel B 5
97 Flawil A 5
109 Flayosc D 3
74 Flechtingen A 3
66 Fleckeby A 2
62 Fleet B 3
67 Fleetmark C 4
56 Fleetwood C 3
85 Flehingen A 5
34 Flekkefjord C 2
39 Flen C 3
44 Flensburg C 2
19 Flenstad B 6
39 Fleringe E 5
43 Flerohopp C 5
81 Flers B 6
35 Flesberg B 5
4 Flesnes B 4
67 Flessau C 4
105 Fleurance D 3
93 Fleuré C 4
95 Fleurie C 4
96 Fleurier B 2
70 Fleurus B 3
107 Fleury, Ande, F D 3
95 Fleury, Côte d'Or, F B 4
94 Fleury, Yonne, F B 3
82 Fleury-sur-Andelle B 3
82 Fleury-sur-Orne B 1
73 Flieden C 3
56 Flimby B 3
70 Flines-lès-Raches B 2
57 Flint C 3
66 Flintbek A 3
97 Flirsch A 6
32 Flisa C 3

78 Goworowo C 4
75 Goyatz A 6
79 Gózd D 4
76 Gozdnica B 4
70 Gozée B 3
119 Gozón A 5
67 Graal-Müritz A 5
98 Grabenstätt B 3
116 Grabova B 4
150 Grabovac B 3
116 Grabovci B 3
101 Grabovnik C 4
67 Grabow,D* B 4
79 Grabów,PL D 4
79 Grabów Leczycki C 1
77 Grabów-nad-Prosna B 7
78 Grabowo, Bialystok, PL B 5
78 Grabowo, Bialystok, PL A 5
97 Grabs A 5
115 Gračac C 3
116 Gračanica, Bosna i Hercegovina, YU B 2
152 Gračanica, Kosovska Metohiska, YU B 3
116 Gračanica, Srbija, YU B 3
93 Graçay B 5
154 Gracen A 1
101 Grad C 4
151 Gradac, Crna Gora, YU B 5
150 Gradac, Hrvatska, YU B 3
152 Gradac, Srbija, YU A 2
116 Gradačac B 2
5 Graddis fjellstue D 4
115 Gradec, Hrvatska, YU B 4
153 Gradec, Makedonia, YU C 4
120 Gradefes B 1
100 Grades C 2
153 Gradevo C 5
104 Gradignan C 2
128 Gradil C 1
115 Gradina B 5
99 Gradisca d'Isonzo D 4
100 Gradišče C 3
116 Gradište A 2
119 Grado,E A 4
99 Grado,I D 4
153 Gradsko C 3
78 Gradzanowo Kościelne C 3
45 Græsted A 5
86 Gräfelfing C 3
87 Grafenau C 5
86 Gräfenberg B 3
100 Grafendorf B 3
75 Gräfenhainichen B 4
100 Grafenschlag A 3
100 Grafenstein C 2
74 Gräfenthal C 3
74 Gräfentonna B 2
87 Grafenwöhr B 3
87 Grafing C 3
87 Grafling C 4
144 Gragnano C 3
55 Graiguenamanagh B 5
62 Grain B 4
98 Grainau B 2
58 Grainthorpe B 4
132 Graja de Iniesta B 1
126 Grajera A 2
44 Gram B 2
97 Gramais A 6
106 Gramat C 1
101 Gramatneusiedl A 4
68 Grambow B 2
48 Gramisdale D 1
159 Grammatikón A 4
149 Grammichele B 4
154 Gramsh B 2
68 Gramzow B 2
31 Gran C 7
136 Granada B 3
122 Granadella C 3
53 Granard C 4
118 Grañas A 3
130 Granátula de Calatrava C 3
95 Grancey-le-Château B 5
80 Grand-Champ C 4
82 Grand Couronne B 3
119 Grandas de Salime A 4
81 Grandcamp-les-Bains A 5
96 Grandcour B 2
134 Grândola A 2
84 Grandpré A 1
70 Grandrieu,B B 3
106 Grandrieu,F C 3
96 Grandson B 2
106 Grandvals C 3
82 Grandvilliers B 3
12 Grane B 5
122 Grañén C 2
37 Grangårde A 6
52 Grange B 3
56 Grange over Sands B 4
50 Grangemouth A 4
105 Granges-de-Crouhens E 3
84 Granges-sur-Valogne B 3
37 Grängesberg A 7
103 Grăniceri B 5
79 Graniczny C 2
21 Graninge B 5
67 Gräningen C 5
148 Granitola B 2
129 Granja C 3
122 Granja de Escarpe C 3
119 Granja de Moreruelo C 5
129 Granja de Torrehermosa C 5
43 Granna A 4
13 Grannäs B 9
123 Granollers C 5
15 Granön D 3
77 Granowo A 5
67 Gransee B 6
35 Gransherad B 5
59 Grantham C 3
49 Grantown-on-Spey D 5
51 Grantshouse B 5
81 Granville B 5
30 Granvin C 3
132 Grão Sagunto B 2
72 Grasleben A 5
56 Grasmere B 3
38 Gräsö B 5
145 Grassano C 5
98 Grassau B 3
109 Grasse D 3
58 Grassington A 2
44 Gråsten C 2
42 Grästorp A 2
4 Gratangen B 6
100 Gratkorn B 3
15 Gråträsk C 3
100 Gratwein B 3
107 Graulhet D 2
122 Graus B 3
121 Grávalos B 5
32 Gravberget C 3
4 Gravdal B 2
64 Grave C 3
97 Gravedona B 5
63 Gravelines B 4
110 Gravellona Toce B 3
62 Gravesend B 4
109 Graveson D 1
157 Graviá D 2
145 Gravina in Púglia C 5
12 Gravvik C 3
95 Gray B 5
62 Grays B 4
62 Grayshott B 3
100 Graz B 3
135 Grazalema C 5
111 Grazzano Visconti C 4
153 Grdelica B 4
35 Greåker B 7
51 Great Ayton C 6
59 Great Chesterford C 4
56 Great Clifton B 3
62 Great Cornard A 4
62 Great Dunmow B 4
56 Great Eccleston C 4
57 Great Malvern D 4
62 Great Missenden B 3
62 Great Shefford B 2
59 Great Shelford C 4
60 Great Torrington C 2
59 Great Yarmouth C 5
51 Greatham C 6
36 Grebbestad C 3
72 Grebenstein B 3
78 Grebocip B 1
78 Greding B 3
44 Gredstedbro B 1
51 Greenhead C 5
53 Greenisland B 6
51 Greenlaw B 5
50 Greenock B 3
53 Greenore B 5
62 Greenway B 2
71 Grefrath A 5
110 Gréggio B 3
98 Greifenburg C 4
68 Greiffenberg B 1
67 Greifswald A 6
100 Grein A 2
34 Greipstad C 3
74 Greiz C 4
16 Grelsbyn A 1
66 Gremersdorf A 3
44 Grenå A 3
105 Grenade D 4
105 Grenade-sur-l'Adour D 2
63 Grenay B 4
96 Grenchen A 3
34 Grendi C 3
108 Grenoble B 2
58 Grenoside B 2
9 Grense Jakobselv C 10
109 Greoux-les-Bains D 2
67 Gresenhorst A 5
48 Gress C 2
110 Gressoney-la-Trinité B 2
110 Gressoney-St.-Jean B 2
73 Greßthal C 4
35 Gressvik B 6
100 Gresten B 3
51 Gretna C 4
74 Greußen B 2
112 Greve C 3
65 Greven,D† B 5
66 Greven,D* B 3
154 Grevená B 3
71 Grevenbroick A 5
71 Grevenbrück A 7
71 Grevenmacher C 5
67 Grevesmühlen B 4
45 Grevestrand B 5
46 Grevie A 3
53 Greyabbey B 6
56 Greystoke B 4
55 Greystones A 5
70 Grez-Doiceau B 3
81 Grez-en-Bouère C 6
78 Grezawy B 2
106 Grèzes C 1
99 Grezzana D 2
116 Grgurevci A 3
98 Gries,A B 2
85 Gries,F B 4
98 Gries in Sellrain B 2
87 Griesbach C 5
73 Griesheim D 2
98 Grieskirchen A 4
73 Grießen C 2
100 Griffen C 2
109 Grignan C 1
99 Grigno C 2
105 Grignols C 2
108 Grignon B 3
108 Grigny B 1
120 Grijota B 2
65 Grijpskerk A 4
38 Grillby C 4
109 Grimaud D 3
70 Grimbergen B 3
75 Grimma B 4
67 Grimmen A 6
96 Grimmialp B 3
42 Grimsås B 3
58 Grimsby B 3
31 Grimsdalshytta A 6
43 Grimslöv C 4
35 Grimstad C 4
43 Grimstorp B 4
96 Grindelwald B 4
34 Grindheim C 3
4 Grindjord B 6
44 Grindsted B 1
126 Griñón B 2
43 Gripenberg B 4
105 Grisolles D 4
38 Grisslehamn B 5
49 Gritley C 6
156 Grivas B 2
157 Grízanon C 2
56 Grizebeck B 3
74 Gröbers B 4
98 Gröbming B 4
74 Gröbzig B 3
79 Grochów C 5
117 Grocka B 4
98 Grodig B 4
75 Gröditz B 5
78 Gródki B 3
77 Grodkow C 6
90 Grodziec, Katowice, PL C 1
77 Grodziec, Poznań, PL A 7
77 Grodziec, Wroclaw, PL B 4
78 Grodzisk C 4
79 Grodzisk Maz. C 3
77 Grodzisk Wielkopolski A 5
65 Groenlo B 4
60 Groes-goch B 1
64 Groesbeek C 3
74 Groitzsch B 4
80 Groix C 3
79 Grójec D 3
78 Grom B 3
151 Gromilick B 4
66 Grömitz A 3
90 Gromnik C 3
111 Gromo B 4
72 Gronau, Niedersachsen, D† A 3
65 Gronau, Nordrhein Westfalen, D† B 5
86 Grönenbach D 2
12 Grong C 4
43 Grönhögen C 6
86 Gröningen,D† B 2
74 Groningen,D* B 3
65 Groningen,NL A 4
18 Grønnes C 3
97 Grono Roveredo B 5
78 Gronowo A 2
43 Grönskåra B 5
64 Grootebroek B 3
65 Grootegast A 4
110 Gropello Cairoli B 3
35 Grorud B 6
84 Gros-Tenquin B 3
103 Groşii Noi B 6
97 Grosio B 6
117 Grošmoca C 4
67 Groß Beeren C 6
72 Groß Berkel A 3
72 Groß Denkte A 4
67 Groß-Dölln C 6
73 Groß Gerau D 2
66 Groß Grönau B 3
72 Groß Ilsede A 4
73 Groß-Karben Windecken C 2
67 Groß Kreutz C 5
72 Groß Lafferde A 4
66 Groß-Oesingen C 3
65 Groß Reken C 5
74 Groß Rosenburg B 3
75 Groß Särchen B 6
72 Groß Schneen D 2
67 Groß Schönebeck C 6
101 Groß Schweinbarth A 4
73 Groß Umstadt D 2
67 Groß Warnow B 4
100 Groß Weikersdorf A 3
67 Groß-Welle B 5
67 Groß Wokern B 5
72 Großalmerode B 3
98 Großarl B 4
74 Großbodungen B 2
75 Großbothen B 4
85 Großbottwar A 6
66 Großburgwedel C 2
75 Großchönau C 6
74 Großengottern B 2
75 Großenhain B 5
65 Großenkneten B 6
73 Großenlüder C 3
66 Großensee B 3
101 Großenzersdorf A 4
104 Grossereix B 4
86 Großerlach B 1
142 Grosseto B 2
100 Großgerungs A 2
88 Grossglobnitz C 3
86 Großhabersdorf B 2
66 Großhansdorf B 3
89 Grossharras C 4
75 Großhartmannsdorf C 5
96 Grosshöchstetten B 3
101 Großhöflein B 4
89 Grosskut C 4
74 Großörner B 3
100 Großpertholz A 2
101 Großpetersdorf B 4
75 Großpostwitz B 6
100 Großraming B 2
75 Großräschen B 6
73 Großrinderfeld D 3
75 Großröhrsdorf B 5
75 Großschirma C 5
88 Großsiegharts C 3
100 Großsölk B 1
101 Großwarasdorf B 4
100 Großwilfersdorf B 3
114 Grosuplje B 2
77 Groszowice C 6
4 Grøtavær B 5
30 Grotli A 4
39 Grötlingbo E 5
146 Grottáglie B 3
145 Grottaminarda B 4
143 Grottammare B 4
142 Grotte di Castro B 2
147 Grotteria D 2
145 Gróttole C 5
64 Grouw A 3
118 Grove B 2
4 Grovfjord B 6
31 Grua C 7
66 Grube A 4
115 Grubišno Polje B 5
151 Gruda C 4
150 Grude B 3
160 Grudovo D 5
78 Grudusk B 3
79 Grudze C 2
78 Grudziadz B 1
32 Grue C 3
107 Gruissan D 3
119 Grullos A 4
145 Grumo Áppula B 5
37 Grums B 5
100 Grünau i. Almtal B 1
86 Grunbach C 1
100 Grunbach a. Schneeberg B 3
73 Grünberg,D† C 2
76 Grünberg,PL B 4
100 Grünburg B 2
86 Gründelhardt B 1
32 Grundforsen B 3
98 Grundlsee B 4
42 Grundsund A 1
21 Grundsunda B 8
72 Grünenplan B 3
75 Grunewald B 5
34 Grungedal B 3
6 Grunnfarnes B 2
75 Grunow A 6
73 Grünsfeld D 3
73 Grünstadt D 2
78 Grunwald B 3
78 Grupa Graniczna B 1
152 Grupčin C 3
49 Grutness B 7
33 Gruvberget B 7
86 Grüwald C 3
96 Gruyères B 3
90 Grybow C 3
38 Grycksbo B 2
68 Gryfice B 3
68 Gryfino B 2
76 Gryfów Ślaski B 4
6 Gryllefjord B 3
31 Grymyr C 7
43 Gryt A 6
39 Grytgöl D 2
37 Grythyttan B 6
4 Grytting B 4
69 Grzmiaca B 4
68 Grzybno B 2
90 Grzybów B 4
78 Grzywna B 1
98 Gschnitz B 2
86 Gschwend C 1
96 Gstaad B 3
96 Gsteig B 3
136 Guadahortuna B 3
126 Guadalajara B 2
127 Guadalaviar B 4
135 Guadalcanal A 5
136 Guadalcázar B 2
126 Guadalix de la Sierra B 2
130 Guadálmez C 2
130 Guadalupe B 1
126 Guadamur C 1
126 Guadarrama B 1
136 Guadix B 3
146 Guagnano B 3
140 Guagno B 1
136 Guajar-Faragüit C 3
136 Gualchos C 3
113 Gualdo Tadino C 4
112 Gualtieri B 2
143 Guarcino C 4
51 Guard Bridge A 5
124 Guarda C 2
133 Guardamar del Segura C 2
124 Guardão C 1
147 Guardavalle D 2
142 Guardea B 3
145 Guárdia C 4
144 Guárdia Sanframondi B 3
143 Guardiagrele B 5
144 Guardiarégia B 3
135 Guardiaro C 5
137 Guardias Viejas C 4
123 Guardiola de Berga B 4
120 Guardo B 2
129 Guareña C 4
136 Guaro C 2
136 Guarromán A 3
141 Guasila C 3
112 Guastalla B 2
113 Gúbbio C 4

75 Guben B 6
76 Gubin B 3
144 Gublionesi B 3
116 Guča C 4
19 Gudå B 7
30 Guddal B 2
44 Guderup C 2
42 Gudheim A 3
47 Gudhjem B 5
85 Güdingen A 4
115 Gudovac B 4
30 Gudvangen C 3
85 Guebwiller C 4
136 Guéjar-Sierra B 3
81 Guéméné-Penfao C 5
80 Guémené-sur-Scorff B 3
121 Gueñes A 3
81 Guer C 4
92 Guérande B 1
93 Guéret C 5
94 Guérigny B 3
121 Guernica y Luno A 4
122 Guerrea de Gállego B 2
121 Guerricaiz A 4
122 Güesa B 1
121 Guetaria A 4
105 Guèthary D 1
94 Gueugnon C 4
67 Gühlen-Glienicke B 5
128 Guia B 2
81 Guichen C 5
111 Guidizzolo B 5
143 Guidónia C 3
112 Guiglia B 2
83 Guignes-Rabutin C 4
130 Guijo C 2
129 Guijo de Coria A 4
129 Guijo de Granadilla A 4
129 Guijo de Santa Bárbara A 5
125 Guijuelo C 4
62 Guildford B 3
109 Guillaumes C 3
135 Guillena B 4
108 Guillestre C 3
80 Guilvinec C 2
124 Guimarães B 1
128 Guincho C 1
63 Guines B 3
80 Guingamp B 3
80 Guipavas B 2
125 Guisando C 4
51 Guisborough C 6
83 Guiscard B 5
80 Guiscriff B 3
83 Guise B 5
123 Guisona C 4
59 Guist C 4
118 Guitiriz A 3
104 Guîtres B 2
104 Gujan-Mestras C 1
18 Gujord C 3
160 Gukovo D 4
45 Guldborg C 4
9 Gulgofjorden B 8
43 Gullabo C 5
51 Gullane A 5
21 Gullänget B 7
43 Gullaskruv C 5
30 Gullbrå C 3
42 Gullbrandstorp C 2
33 Gulleråsen B 6
35 Gullhaug B 6
42 Gullholmen A 1
43 Gullringen B 5
37 Gullspång C 6
18 Gullstein B 4
21 Gulsele B 6
31 Gulsvik C 6
126 Gumiel de Hizán A 2
71 Gummersbach A 6
85 Gundel-Fingen B 4
86 Gundelfingen C 2
85 Gundelsheim A 6
85 Gunderschoffen B 4
116 Gundinci A 2
13 Gunnarn B 9
8 Gunnarnes A 4
14 Gunnarsbyn B 5
36 Gunnarskog B 4
43 Gunnebo B 6
101 Günselsdorf B 4
74 Güntersberge B 2
73 Guntersblum D 2
88 Guntersdorf C 4
118 Guntin B 3
101 Guntramsdorf A 4
83 Guny B 5
86 Günzburg C 2
86 Gunzenhausen B 2
117 Gura Väii B 6
103 Gurahonț B 6
120 Guriezo A 3
100 Gurk C 2
153 Gŭrlyano B 4
30 Gursken A 2
115 Gušće B 4
67 Güsen C 4
153 Guševac A 4
152 Gusinje B 1
141 Gúspini C 2
38 Gusselby C 2
101 Güssing B 4
100 Gußwerk B 3
37 Gustav Adolf A 5
39 Gustavsberg C 5
36 Gustavsfors B 4
67 Güstrow B 5
43 Gusum A 6
49 Gutcher A 8
100 Gutenstein B 3
65 Gütersloh C 6
96 Guttannen B 4
100 Guttaring C 2
75 Guttau B 6
97 Güttingen A 5
67 Gützkow B 6
13 Guvertsfjälls kappell B 8
59 Guyhirn C 4
79 Guzów C 3
35 Gvarv B 5
57 Gwalchmai C 2
69 Gwda Wielka B 4
52 Gweedore A 3
79 Gwizdaly C 4
95 Gy B 5
102 Gyál A 3
101 Gyarmat B 5
95 Gye-sur-Seine A 4
115 Gyékényes A 5
18 Gyl C 4
34 Gyland C 2
16 Gyljen A 1
44 Gylling B 3
103 Gyoma B 4
101 Gyömöre B 5
102 Gyömro A 3
102 Gyón A 3
115 Gyóngyfa B 5
91 Gyöngyös E 2
91 Gyöngyöspata E 2
91 Gyöngyössolymòs E 2
102 Gyönk B 2
101 Gyor B 5
101 Gyorszemere B 5
101 Gyorszentiván B 5
101 Gyorvar C 4
96 Gypsera B 3
38 Gysinge B 3
37 Gyttorp B 6
153 Gyueshevo B 4
103 Gyula B 5
101 Gyulafirátót B 5
101 Gyulaj C 6
103 Gyulavari B 5

H

70 Haacht B 3
100 Haag, Niederösterreich, A A 2
98 Haag, Oberösterreich, A A 4
87 Haag, D† C 4
65 Haaksbergen B 4
64 Haamstede C 1
71 Haan A 6
29 Haapajärvi C 6
24 Haapakoski C 4
23 Haapamäki, Keski-Suomen, SF C 6
23 Haapamaki, Oulun, SF B 8
28 Haapasaari C 5
16 Haapavesi C 4
23 Haapjärvi B 7
87 Haar C 3
64 Haarlem B 2
105 Habas D 2
71 Habay-la-Neuve C 4
39 Hablingbo E 5
42 Habo B 4
88 Habry B 3
85 Habsheim C 4
91 Habura C 4
71 Hachenburg B 6
120 Haciñas C 3
20 Hackås C 3
55 Hacketstown B 5
56 Hackthorpe B 4
71 Hadamar B 7
59 Haddenham C 4
51 Haddington B 5
44 Haderslev B 2
62 Hadleigh A 4
62 Hadlow B 4
74 Hadmersleben B 3
88 Hadres C 4
4 Hadsel B 3
44 Hadsten A 3
40 Hadsund C 4
151 Hadžići B 4
34 Hægebostad C 3
34 Hægeland C 3
30 Hæstad B 2
66 Haffrug A 3
30 Hafslo B 4
115 Haganj B 4
43 Hagby C 6
65 Hage A 5
66 Hagen, Niedersachsen, D† B 1
71 Hagen, Nordrhein-Westfalen, D† A 6
85 Hagenbach A 5
100 Hagenberg A 2
66 Hagenburg C 2
67 Hagenow B 4
105 Hagetmau D 2
37 Hagfors A 5
21 Häggdånger C 6
20 Häggenas B 3
20 Häggsjon B 3
33 Hagsta C 8
85 Haguenau B 4
73 Hahn C 2
87 Hahnbach B 3
73 Hahnstätten C 2
101 Hahót C 4
73 Haiger C 2
85 Haigerloch B 5
73 Hailer C 3
62 Hailsham C 4
16 Hailuoto B 3
101 Hainburg A 4
100 Hainfeld A 3
75 Hainichen C 5
100 Haitzendorf A 3
27 Hajala C 5
103 Hajdúböszormény A 5
117 Hajdučica A 4
91 Hajdúdorog E 4
91 Hajdúhadház E 4
91 Hajdúnánás E 4
103 Hajdusamson A 5
103 Hajdúszoboszló A 5
103 Hajdúszovát A 5
101 Hajmaskér B 6
91 Hajnáčka D 2
102 Hajós B 3
42 Håkantorp A 2
14 Hakkas B 5
38 Håksberg B 2
71 Halanzy C 4
101 Halászi B 5
74 Halberstadt B 3
60 Halberton C 3
44 Hald A 2
66 Haldem C 1
36 Halden B 3
74 Haldensleben A 3
65 Haldern C 4
67 Halenbeck B 5
89 Halenkov B 6
57 Halesowen D 4
59 Halesworth C 5
87 Halfing D 4
91 Halič D 2
58 Halifax B 2
27 Halikko C 6
46 Häljarp B 3
27 Halkia C 8
49 Halkirk C 5
27 Halkivaha B 6
39 Hall E 5
21 Halla B 6
43 Hallabro C 5
39 Hällabrottet C 2
30 Hallasker C 4
39 Hällberga C 3
39 Hällbybrunn C 3
70 Halle, B B 3
65 Halle, D† B 6
74 Halle, D* B 3
37 Hällefors B 6
39 Hälleforsnäs C 3
98 Hallein B 4
37 Hällekis C 5
20 Hallen B 3
72 Hallenberg B 2
21 Hällesjö C 5
39 Hällestad D 2
36 Hällevadsholm C 3
47 Hällevik A 5
42 Hälleviksstrand A 1
27 Halli B 7
30 Hallingskeid C 4
38 Hållnäs, Uppsala Län, S B 4
15 Hällnäs, Västerbottens Län, S D 3
39 Hallsberg C 2
39 Hållsta C 3
73 Hallstadt D 4
38 Hallstahammar C 3
98 Hallstatt B 4
38 Hallstavik B 5
43 Halltorp C 6
70 Halluin B 2
20 Hallviken B 4
60 Hallworthy C 2
103 Hälmagiu B 6
103 Halmăşd A 6
42 Halmstad C 2
40 Hals C 4
18 Halsa, More og Romsdal, N B 4
5 Halsa, Nordland, N D 2
46 Halsingborg A 3
62 Halstead B 4
66 Halstenbek B 2
23 Halsua B 6
19 Haltdalen C 7
65 Haltern C 5
51 Haltwhistle C 5
25 Haluna B 5
38 Halvarsgårdarna B 2
71 Halver A 6
40 Halvrimmen B 3
60 Halwell C 3
83 Ham B 5
62 Ham Street B 4
31 Hamar C 8
4 Hamarøy B 4
85 Hambach A 4
66 Hambergen B 1
36 Hambergsund C 3
66 Hambuhren C 2
66 Hamburg B 2
66 Hamdorf A 2
27 Hämeenkylä C 7
27 Hämeenkyro B 6
27 Hämeenlinna C 7
72 Hameln A 3
74 Hamersleben A 3
50 Hamilton B 3
28 Hamina C 5
65 Hamm C 5
39 Hammar D 1
26 Hammarland C 2
37 Hammarn B 6
21 Hammarstrand B 5
25 Hammaslahti C 6
70 Hamme A 3
44 Hammel A 2
73 Hammelburg C 3
67 Hammelspring B 6
47 Hammenhög B 5
20 Hammerdäl B 4
8 Hammerfest B 3
44 Hammershøj A 2
44 Hammerum A 2
9 Hammingberg B 10
65 Hamminkeln C 4
8 Hamnbukt B 5
42 Hamneda C 3
6 Hamneidet B 6
4 Hamnsund B 4
71 Hamont A 4
33 Hamra, Gävleborgs Län, S B 5
39 Hamra, Gotlands Län, S F 5
33 Hamrångefjärden C 8
153 Hamzali C 4
20 Hån C 3
116 Han Pijesak B 2
47 Hanaskog A 5
73 Hanau C 2
44 Handewitt C 2
61 Handley C 4
91 Handlová D 1
20 Handöl B 1
66 Handorf B 3
20 Handsjö C 3
66 Hanerau-Hademarschen A 2
32 Hanestad B 1
89 Hanfthal C 4
27 Hangö D 5
91 Hangony D 3
66 Hänigsen C 3
91 Haniska D 4
23 Hankasalmi C 8
23 Hankasami as C 8
23 Hankavesi C 8
37 Hanken C 6
66 Hankensbüttel C 3
27 Hanko D 5
72 Hannover A 3
70 Hannut B 4
4 Hanøy B 4
33 Hansjö B 5
44 Hansted B 2
66 Hanstedt B 3
40 Hanstholm B 2
91 Hanušovce C 4
89 Hanušovice A 4
97 Hanz B 5
16 Haparanda B 3
14 Harads B 4
43 Häradsbäck C 4
33 Haradsbygden C 6
38 Harbo B 4
40 Harboør C 2
86 Harburg, Bayern, D† C 2
66 Harburg, Hamburg, D† B 2
44 Hårby B 3
84 Harcourt A 2
64 Hardegarip A 3
72 Hardegsen B 3
63 Hardelot-Plage B 3
67 Hardenbeck B 6
65 Hardenberg B 4
64 Harderwijk B 3
73 Hardheim D 3
85 Hardt B 5
18 Hareid C 2
70 Harelbeke B 2
65 Haren, D† B 5
65 Haren, NL A 4
31 Harestua C 7
58 Harewood C 4
82 Harfleur B 2
38 Harg B 5
84 Hargarten A 3
83 Hargicourt B 5
70 Hargnies B 3
38 Hargshamn B 5
26 Harjavalta B 5
102 Harkány C 2
65 Harkebrügge A 5
66 Harksheide B 3
57 Harlech D 2
59 Harleston C 5
45 Hårlev B 5
64 Harlingen A 3
72 Harlingrode B 4
46 Harlösa B 4
62 Harlow B 4
91 Harmanec D 2
33 Harmånger B 8
57 Harmerhill D 4
27 Harmoinen B 8
63 Harnes B 4
38 Härnevi C 4
21 Härnösand C 6
121 Haro B 4
49 Haroldswick A 8
115 Háromfa A 5
84 Haroué B 3
62 Harpenden B 3
42 Harplinge C 2
66 Harpstedt C 1
12 Harran C 4
62 Harringey B 3
58 Harrogate B 2
62 Harrow B 3
42 Härryda B 2
66 Harsefeld B 2
65 Harsewinkel C 6
74 Harsleben B 3
4 Harstad B 5
72 Harsum A 3
19 Harsvik A 6
102 Harta B 3
100 Hartberg B 3
83 Hartennes B 5
59 Hartest C 4
75 Hartha B 4
50 Harthill B 4
51 Hartlepool C 6
51 Hartley B 6
87 Hartmanice B 5
100 Hartmannsdorf, A B 3
75 Hartmannsdorf, D* C 4
86 Hartmannshof B 3
28 Hartola B 4
13 Harvasstua B 6
62 Harwell B 2
62 Harwich B 5
74 Harzgerode B 3

97 Häselgehr A 6
65 Haselünne B 5
21 Håsjö B 5
85 Haslach B 5
100 Haslach a. d. Mühl A 2
47 Hasle B 5
62 Haslemere B 3
45 Haslev B 4
70 Hasnon B 2
105 Hasparren D 1
70 Haspres B 2
66 Haßbergen C 2
21 Hassela C 5
74 Hasselfelde B 2
37 Hasselfors B 6
70 Hasselt, B B 4
64 Hasselt, NL B 4
73 Haßfurt C 4
37 Hassle C 5
67 Haßleben B 6
47 Hässleholm A 4
43 Hasslö C 5
85 Haßloch A 5
23 Hästbacka B 5
65 Hastbergen B 5
43 Hästholmen A 4
70 Hastière Lavaux B 3
49 Hastigrow C 5
62 Hastings C 4
47 Hästveda A 4
8 Hasvik B 2
62 Hatfield, Hertfordshire, GB B 3
58 Hatfield, Yorkshire, GB B 3
62 Hatfield Peverel B 4
60 Hatherleigh C 2
58 Hathersage B 2
34 Hatlestrand A 1
64 Hattem B 4
65 Hatten, D† A 6
85 Hatten, F B 4
13 Hattfjelldal B 5
44 Hatting B 2
71 Hattingen A 6
59 Hatton C 2
85 Hattstadt B 4
66 Hattstedt A 2
27 Hattula B 7
25 Hattuvaara C 8
25 Hattvaara B 7
102 Hatvan A 3
64 Hau C 4
70 Haubourdin B 1
30 Haugastøl C 4
34 Hauge C 2
34 Haugesund B 1
50 Haugh of Urr C 4
34 Haughom C 2
4 Haugnes A 5
88 Haugsdorf C 4
27 Hauho B 7
30 Haukedal B 3
30 Haukeland C 2
34 Haukeligrend B 3
16 Haukipudas B 4
28 Haukivuori A 5
65 Haulerwijk A 4
87 Haunersdorf C 4
86 Haunstetten C 2
30 Haus C 2
85 Hausach B 5
89 Hausbrunn C 4
98 Hausham B 2
27 Hausjärvi C 7
100 Hausmannstätten C 3
70 Haut-Fays B 4
11 Hautajärvi C 9
104 Hautefort B 4
108 Hauteluce B 3
108 Hauterives B 2
108 Hauteville-Lompnes B 2
70 Hautmont B 2
70 Hautrage B 2
87 Hauzenberg C 5
62 Havant C 3
39 Havdhem C 5
45 Havdrup B 5
70 Havelange B 4
67 Havelberg C 5
65 Havelte B 4
60 Haverfordwest B 2
59 Haverhill C 4
56 Haverigg B 3
62 Havering B 4
20 Haverö C 4
89 Havířov B 6
65 Havixbeck C 5
39 Hävla D 2
88 Havlíčkova Borová B 3
88 Havlíčkův Brod B 3
44 Havnbjerg B 2
40 Havndal C 4
44 Havneby B 1
8 Havøysund A 4
45 Havrebjerg B 4
20 Havsnäs A 4
36 Havstenssund C 3
78 Hawa B 2
57 Hawarden C 3
56 Hawes B 4
51 Hawick B 5
62 Hawkhurst B 4
58 Haxby A 2
61 Hay-on-Wye A 3
84 Hayange A 3
51 Haydon Bridge C 5
60 Hayle C 1
56 Hayton B 4
62 Haywards Heath C 3
63 Hazebrouck B 4
57 Hazel Grove C 4
87 Hazlov A 4
59 Heacham C 4
62 Headcorn B 4
54 Headford A 2
58 Healing B 3
59 Heanor B 2
62 Heath End B 2
62 Heathfield C 4
51 Hebburn C 6
58 Hebden Bridge B 2
42 Heberg C 2
38 Heby C 3
85 Hechingen B 5
86 Hechlingen C 2
122 Hecho B 2
70 Hechtel A 4
66 Hechthausen B 2
67 Heckelberg C 6
59 Heckington C 3
74 Hecklingen B 3
31 Hedal C 6
42 Hedared C 2
33 Hedby C 5
35 Heddal B 5
81 Hédé B 5
20 Hede, Jämtlands Län, S C 2
38 Hede, Kopparbergs Län, S B 3
36 Hedekas C 3
38 Hedemora B 2
16 Hedenäset A 2
44 Hedensted B 2
74 Hedersleben B 3
38 Hedesunda B 3
20 Hedeviken C 2
58 Hedon B 3
65 Heede B 5
70 Heeilaart B 3
65 Heek B 5
64 Heemskerk B 2
64 Heemstede B 2
65 Heepen B 6
71 Heer B 4
64 Heerde B 4
65 Heerenberg C 4
64 Heerenveen B 3
64 Heerhugowaard B 2
71 Heerlen B 4
70 Heers B 4
64 Heesch C 3
65 Heessen C 5
71 Heeze A 4
31 Heggenes B 6
19 Hegra B 7
101 Hegyeshalom B 5
6 Heia B 5
31 Heidal B 6
66 Heide, D† A 2
23 Heide, SF B 5
85 Heidelberg A 5
65 Heiden C 4
75 Heidenau C 5
86 Heidenheim C 2
88 Heidenreichstein C 3
66 Heikendorf A 3
48 Heilam C 4
85 Heilbronn A 6
85 Heiligenberg C 6
98 Heiligenblut B 3
67 Heiligendamm A 4
72 Heiligendorf A 4
67 Heiligengrabe B 5
66 Heiligenhafen A 3
71 Heiligenhaus A 5
101 Heiligenkreuz i. Lafnitztal C 4
86 Heiligenstadt, D† B 3
74 Heiligenstadt, D* B 2
66 Heiligenstedten B 2
64 Heiloo B 2
86 Heilsbron B 2
18 Heim B 5
71 Heimbach-Weis B 6
74 Heimburg B 2
19 Heimdal B 6
25 Heinävesi C 5
71 Heinerscheid B 5
76 Heinersdorf A 3
87 Heining C 5
86 Heiningen, Baden-Württemberg, D† C 1
72 Heiningen, Niedersachsen, D† A 4
26 Heinjoki C 5
65 Heino B 4
28 Heinola B 4
28 Heinolan mlk. B 4
71 Heinsberg A 5
71 Heinsch C 4
30 Heinseter C 4
65 Heisfelde A 5
70 Heist A 2
70 Heist-op-d-Berg A 3
85 Heitersheim C 4
29 Heituinlahti B 5
44 Hejls B 2
69 Hel A 6
74 Helbra B 3
70 Helchteren A 4
74 Heldburg C 2
74 Heldrungen B 3
130 Helechosa B 2
50 Helensburgh A 3
100 Helfenberg A 2
35 Helgen B 5
43 Helgenäs B 6
35 Helgeroa C 5
6 Helgøy A 5
21 Helgum B 5
19 Hell B 6
30 Hella B 3
18 Helland, More Og Romsdal Fylke, N C 3
4 Helland, Nordland Fylke, N B 5
34 Helle C 2
45 Hellebæk A 5
34 Helleland C 2
65 Hellendoorn B 4
71 Hellenthal B 5
30 Hellesylt A 3
40 Hellevad B 4
64 Hellevoetsluis C 2
56 Hellifield B 4
6 Helligskogen B 6
133 Hellín C 1
39 Hellvi E 5
34 Hellvik C 1
74 Helmbrechts C 3
64 Helmond C 3
49 Helmsdale C 5
58 Helmsley A 2
72 Helmstedt A 4
91 Hel'pa D 2
10 Helppi B 4
45 Helsinge A 5
27 Helsingfors C 7
45 Helsingør A 5
27 Helsinki C 7
60 Helston C 1
87 Hemau B 3
13 Hemavan B 7
62 Hemel Hempstead B 3
71 Hemer A 6
70 Hemiksem A 3
85 Héming B 3
21 Hemling B 7
72 Hemmendorf A 3
44 Hemmet B 1
15 Hemmingsmark C 5
66 Hemmingstedt A 2
5 Hemnesberget D 2
59 Hempnall C 5
39 Hemse C 5
31 Hemsedal C 5
66 Hemslingen B 2
21 Hemsö C 7
58 Hemsworth B 2
35 Hen A 6
42 Henan A 1
121 Hendaye A 5
18 Hendset B 4
73 Hendungen C 4
62 Henfield C 3
65 Hengelo B 4
87 Hengersberg C 5
61 Hengoed B 3
63 Hénin-Liétard B 4
59 Henley in Arden C 2
62 Henley on Thames B 3
62 Henlow A 3
33 Hennan A 6
98 Henndorf am Wallersee B 4
74 Henneberg C 2
80 Hennebont C 3
71 Hennef B 6
4 Hennes B 4
75 Hennickendorf A 5
67 Hennigsdorf C 6
19 Henning B 7
4 Henningsvær B 3
66 Hennstedt A 2
94 Henrichemont B 2
77 Henryków C 6
78 Henrykowo A 3
31 Hensås B 5
66 Henstedt B 3
73 Heppenheim D 2
31 Herad, Buskerud Fylke, N C 6
34 Herad, Vestagder Fylke, N C 2
32 Heradsbygd C 2
88 Herálec B 4
30 Herand C 3
93 Herbault B 5
65 Herbern C 5
54 Herbertstown B 3
70 Herbeumont C 4
92 Herbignac B 1
83 Herbisse C 6
85 Herbitzheim A 4
85 Herbolzheim B 4
73 Herborn C 2
86 Herbrechtingen C 2
74 Herbsleben B 2
90 Herby B 1
151 Hercegnovi C 4
115 Hercegovac B 5
71 Herchen B 6
71 Herdecke A 6
71 Herderen B 4
91 Heréd E 2
61 Hereford A 4
35 Herefoss C 4
131 Herencia B 3
70 Herent B 3
70 Herentals A 3
70 Herenthout A 3
107 Hérépian D 3
45 Herfølge B 5
65 Herford B 6
96 Hergiswil B 4
129 Herguijuela B 5
81 Héric C 5
84 Héricourt C 3
82 Héricourt-en-Caux B 2
84 Hérimoncourt C 3
73 Heringen C 4
66 Heringsdorf, D† A 4
68 Heringsdorf, D* B 2
97 Herisau A 5
94 Hérisson C 2
70 Herk-de-Stad B 4
45 Herlufmagle B 4
99 Hermagor C 4
66 Hermannsburg C 3
30 Hermansverk B 3
88 Heřmanuv Městec B 3
71 Hermeskeil C 5
119 Hermisende C 4
83 Hermonville B 5
74 Hermsdorf C 3
91 Hernádnémeti D 3
121 Hernani A 5
126 Hernansancho B 1
70 Herne, B B 3
71 Herne, D† A 6
62 Herne Bay B 5
32 Hernes C 2
44 Herning A 1
86 Heroldsberg B 3
12 Herøy B 4
35 Herøya B 5
135 Herradura B 5
28 Herrala C 3
121 Herramelluri B 3
38 Herräng B 5
35 Herre B 5
85 Herrenalb B 5
85 Herrenberg B 5
136 Herrera B 2
128 Herrera de Alcántara B 3
127 Herrera de los Navarros A 4
120 Herrera de Pisuergo B 2
130 Herrera del Duque B 1
134 Herrerias B 3
125 Herreros del Suso C 4
129 Herreruela B 4
71 Herringen A 6
86 Herrlingen C 1
85 Herrlisheim B 4
42 Herrljunga A 3
75 Herrnhut B 6
32 Herrö A 5
86 Herrsching C 3
21 Herrskog C 7
86 Hersbruck B 3
71 Herscheid A 6
70 Herseaux B 2
70 Herselt A 3
84 Herserange A 2
71 Herstal B 4
62 Herstmonceux C 4
30 Hersvik B 1
71 Herten A 6
62 Hertford B 3
91 Hertnik C 4
125 Hervás C 4
85 Herxheim A 5
72 Herzberg, D† B 4
75 Herzberg, Cottbus, D* B 5
67 Herzberg, Potsdam, D* C 5
65 Herzebrock C 6
76 Herzfelde A 2
65 Herzlake B 5
86 Herzogenaurach B 2
96 Herzogenbuchsee A 3
100 Herzogenburg A 3
67 Herzsprung B 5
34 Hesby B 1
63 Hesdin B 4
65 Hesel A 5
85 Hésingue C 4
34 Heskestad C 2
71 Hesperange C 5
72 Hess Oldendorf A 3
19 Hessdalen C 7
44 Hesselager B 3
74 Hessen A 2
72 Hessisch Lichtenau B 3
58 Hessle B 3
42 Hestra B 3
18 Hestvilka B 5
57 Heswall C 3
30 Hetlevik C 2
84 Hettange A 3
73 Hettenhausen C 3
51 Hetton le Hole C 6
74 Hettstedt B 3
71 Hetzerath C 5
63 Heuchin B 4
84 Heudicourt B 2
84 Heunezel B 3
82 Heuqueville B 2
70 Heusden, Flandre Orientals, B A 2
70 Heusden, Limburg, B A 4
64 Heusden, NL C 3
73 Heustreu C 4
71 Heusweiler C 5
70 Heverlee B 3
102 Heves A 4
101 Héviz C 5
51 Hexham C 5
108 Heyrieux B 2
56 Heysham B 4
58 Hibaldstow B 3
102 Hides B 2
100 Hieflau B 2
104 Hiersac B 3
28 Hietanen B 4
17 Hietaperä C 8
56 High Bentham B 4
58 High Hawsker A 3
56 High Hesker B 4
62 High Wycombe B 3
61 Highbridge B 4
62 Highworth B 2
136 Higuera de Arjona B 3
136 Higuera de Calatrava B 2
129 Higuera de la Serena C 5
135 Higuera de la Sierra B 4
129 Higuera de Llerena C 4
129 Higuera de Vargas C 4
135 Higuera la Real A 4
133 Higueruela C 1
122 Hijar C 2
137 Hijate B 4
59 Hilborough C 4
72 Hilchenbach B 2
74 Hildburghausen C 2
71 Hilden A 5
73 Hilders C 3
72 Hildesheim A 3
87 Hilgartsberg C 5
59 Hilgay C 4
42 Hillared B 3

65 Hille B 6
64 Hillegom B 2
72 Hillentrup A 3
45 Hillerød B 5
42 Hillerstorp B 3
71 Hillesheim B 5
6 Hillesøy B 4
35 Hillestad B 6
62 Hillingdon B 3
75 Hillmersdorf B 5
20 Hillsand A 4
53 Hillsborough B 5
49 Hillside A 7
49 Hillswick A 7
65 Hilltrup C 5
86 Hilpoltstein B 3
86 Hiltenfingen C 2
86 Hiltpoltstein B 3
64 Hilvarenbeek C 3
64 Hilversum B 3
23 Himanka A 5
154 Himarë B 1
101 Himberg A 4
102 Himesháza B 2
66 Himmelpforten B 2
101 Himód B 5
59 Hinckley C 2
42 Hindås B 2
96 Hindebank A 3
97 Hindelang A 6
67 Hindenberg C 4
51 Hinderwell C 7
59 Hingham C 4
26 Hinnerjoki C 5
44 Hinnerup A 3
129 Hinojal B 4
135 Hinojales A 4
135 Hinojos B 4
130 Hinojosa del Duque C 1
129 Hinojosa del Valle C 4
130 Hinojosas de Calatrava C 2
67 Hinrichshagen A 5
97 Hinterhornbach A 6
98 Hinterriß B 2
98 Hintersee, A B 4
68 Hintersee, D* B 2
100 Hinterstoder B 2
98 Hintertux B 2
97 Hinwil A 4
64 Hippolytushoef B 2
86 Hirschaid B 2
87 Hirschau B 3
74 Hirschberg, D* C 3
77 Hirschberg, PL C 4
75 Hirschfeld B 5
75 Hirschfelde C 6
85 Hirschhorn A 5
85 Hirsingue C 4
83 Hirson B 6
160 Hîrşova C 5
101 Hirtenberg B 4
40 Hirtshals B 3
23 Hirvaskangas C 7
17 Hirvaskoski B 6
28 Hirvensalmi B 4
73 Hirzenhain C 3
46 Hishult A 4
59 Histon C 4
62 Hitchen B 3
103 Hitias C 5
27 Hitis D 5
18 Hitra B 4
46 Hittarp A 3
19 Hitterdal C 7
66 Hittfeld B 2
27 Hittinen D 5
97 Hittisau A 5
66 Hitzacker B 4
96 Hitzkirch A 4
40 Hjallerup B 4
43 Hjältevad B 5
46 Hjärnarp A 3
35 Hjartdal B 4
30 Hjelle B 4
30 Hjelme C 1
34 Hjelmelandsvågen B 2
31 Hjerkinn A 6
44 Hjerm A 1
44 Hjerpsted B 1
44 Hjerting B 1
43 Hjo A 4
44 Hjordkær B 2
40 Hjørring B 3
43 Hjorted B 6
39 Hjortkvarn D 2
33 Hjortnäs C 5
43 Hjortsberga C 4
35 Hjuksebø B 5
39 Hjulsbro D 2
91 Hliník n. Hronom D 1
88 Hlinsko B 3
101 Hlohovec A 5
88 Hluboká n. Vltavou B 2
89 Hlučín B 6
91 Hniezdne C 3
91 Hnilčík D 3
91 Hnilec D 3
91 Hnúšťa Likier D 2
49 Hobbister C 5
70 Hoboken A 3
40 Hobro C 3
71 Hobscheid C 4
98 Hochburg Ach A 3
71 Hochdahl A 5
66 Hochdonn A 2
96 Hochdorf A 4
85 Hochfelden B 4
85 Hochspeyer A 4
86 Höchstädt, Bayern, D† C 2
86 Hochstadt, Bayern, D† B 2
87 Hochstätt D 4
71 Hochstenbach B 6
85 Hockenheim A 5
19 Hodal C 7
62 Hoddesdon B 4
91 Hodejov D 2
66 Hodenhagen C 2
88 Hodkovice A 3
102 Hódmezovásárhely B 4
57 Hodnet D 4
103 Hodoni C 5
89 Hodonín C 5
101 Hodos C 4
101 Hodosan C 4
91 Hódoscsépány D 3
89 Hodslavice B 6
70 Hoegaarden B 3
64 Hoek van Holland C 2
64 Hoenderlo B 3
71 Hoensbroek B 4
71 Hoeselt B 4
65 Hoetmar C 5
74 Hof, D† C 3
35 Hof, N B 6
101 Hof a. Leithaberge B 4
73 Hofbieber C 3
56 Hoff B 4
72 Hofgeismar B 3
73 Hofheim, Bayern, D† C 4
73 Hofheim, Hessen, D† C 2
100 Hofkirchen i. Mühlkreis A 1
38 Hofors B 3
19 Hofstad A 6
46 Höganas A 3
20 Högarna B 4
36 Högås C 3
38 Högbo B 3
43 Högbv B 7
36 Hogdal B 3
37 Hogfors B 7
32 Hoggsetvollen A 2
36 Högsäter C 4
43 Högsby B 6
18 Høgset C 3
39 Högsjö, Södermanlands Län, S C 2
21 Högsjö, Västernorrlands Län, S C 6
6 Høgskarhus C 5
58 Hogsthorpe B 4
32 Hogvålen A 3
102 Högyesz B 2
72 Hohegeiß B 4
67 Hohen Neuendorf C 6
98 Hohenaschau B 3
101 Hohenau A 4
100 Hohenberg B 3
87 Hohenbrunn C 3
75 Hohenbuck B 5
87 Hohenburg B 3
88 Hoheneich C 3
97 Hohenems A 5
86 Hohenfurch D 2
74 Hohengandern B 1
72 Hohenhameln A 4
85 Hohenhaslach A 6
72 Hohenhausen A 2
86 Hohenkammer C 3
75 Hohenleipisch B 5
74 Hohenleuben C 4
71 Hohenlimburg A 6
87 Hohenlinden C 3
66 Hohenlockstedt B 2
74 Hohenmölsen B 4
67 Hohennauen C 5
98 Hohenpeißenberg B 2
101 Hohenruppersdorf A 4
67 Hohenseeden C 5
86 Hohenstadt B 3
75 Hohenstein-Ernstthal C 4
100 Hohentauern B 2
85 Höhentengen C 5
87 Hohenthann D 3
72 Hohenwepel B 3
66 Hohenwestedt A 2
68 Hohenwutzen C 2
66 Hohn A 2
66 Hohne C 3
98 Höhnhart A 4
75 Hohnstein C 6
66 Hohnstorf B 3
43 Hohulslätt C 5
23 Hoisko B 5
44 Højer C 1
40 Højslev Stby C 3
43 Hok B 4
38 Hokåsen C 3
65 Hokenchn A 5
42 Hökerum B 3
38 Hökhuvud B 5
35 Hokksund B 5
43 Hökön C 4
31 Hol C 5
40 Holbæk, Jylland, DK C 4
45 Holbæk, Sjælland, DK B 4
59 Holbeach C 4
66 Holdenstedt C 3
30 Holdhus C 2
65 Holdorf B 6
45 Holeby C 4
35 Hølen B 6
89 Holešov B 5
129 Holguera B 4
89 Holič C 5
88 Holice A 3
101 Holice-Kračany A 5
32 Höljes C 3
4 Holkstad C 3
101 Hollabrunn A 4
65 Hollage B 5
49 Hollandstoun B 6
34 Høllen C 3
100 Hollenstein a. d. Ybbs B 2
86 Hollfeld B 3
18 Hollingsholm C 2
28 Hollola B 3
64 Hollum A 3
46 Hollviksnäs B 3
53 Hollywood, GB B 6
55 Hollywood, IRL A 5
66 Holm, D† B 2
12 Holm, Austra, N B 4
4 Holm, Langøya, N B 4
21 Holm, S C 5
58 Holme upon Spalding Moor B 3
30 Holmedal, N B 2
36 Holmedal, S B 3
36 Holmegil B 3
31 Holmen C 7
57 Holmes Chapel C 4
35 Holmestrand B 6
58 Holmfirth B 2
35 Holmsbo B 6
43 Holmsjö C 5
33 Holmsveden B 7
14 Holmträsk B 4
39 Hölö C 4
103 Holod B 6
19 Hølonda B 6
32 Holøydal A 2
43 Holsby B 5
42 Holsjunga B 2
44 Holstebro A 1
44 Holsted B 1
60 Holsworthy C 2
57 Holt, Denbighshire, GB C 4
59 Holt, Norfolk, GB C 5
35 Holt, N C 4
65 Holten B 4
66 Holtorf C 2
65 Holtwick B 5
34 Holum C 3
64 Holwerd A 3
57 Holywell C 3
57 Holyhead C 2
87 Holýšov B 5
75 Holzdorf B 5
85 Holzgerlingen B 6
65 Holzhausen B 6
98 Holzkirchen B 2
72 Holzminden B 3
74 Holzthaleben B 2
74 Holzweißig B 4
72 Homberg, Hessen, D† B 3
71 Homberg, Saarland, D† C 6
83 Hombleux B 4
83 Homblières B 5
84 Hombourg Haut A 3
71 Homburg A 5
12 Hommelstø B 4
19 Hommelvik B 6
34 Hommersåk C 1
64 Hommerts B 3
102 Homokmegy B 3
115 Homokszentgyorgy A 5
133 Hondón de los Frailes C 2
63 Hondschoote B 4
73 Hönebach C 3
35 Hønefoss A 6
82 Honfleur B 2
45 Høng B 4
59 Honington C 3
61 Honiton C 3
26 Honkajoki B 5
26 Honkilahti C 5
71 Hönningen B 5
8 Honningsvåg B 5
42 Hönö B 1
131 Honrubia B 4
126 Hontalbilla A 1
132 Hontanar A 1
91 Hontianske-Nemce D 1
120 Hontoria de la Cantera B 3
126 Hontoria de Valdearados A 2
120 Hontoria del Pinar C 3
64 Hoofddorp B 2
64 Hoogerheide C 2
65 Hoogeveen B 4
65 Hoogezand A 4
65 Hoogkerk A 4
65 Hoogstede Bathorn B 4
70 Hoogstraten A 3
65 Hooksiel A 6
46 Höör B 4
64 Hoorn B 3
57 Hope C 3
49 Hopeman D 5
18 Hopen, More og Romsdal Fylke, N B 4
5 Hopen, Nordland Fylke, N C 3
98 Hopfgarten B 3
98 Hopfgarten in Defereggen C 3
65 Hopsten B 5
44 Hoptrup B 2
75 Hora Svatého Šebestiána C 5
87 Horažd'ovice B 5
85 Horb B 5
45 Horbelev C 5
47 Hörby B 4
40 Hørby Stby B 4
127 Horcajada de la Torre B 3
130 Horcajo de los Montes B 2
125 Horcajo-Medianero C 4
126 Horcayo de Santiago C 2
126 Horche B 2
43 Horda B 4
30 Hordabø C 1
60 Horeb A 2
87 Hořesedly A 5
19 Horg B 6
97 Horgen A 4
102 Horgoš B 3
88 Hořice A 3
101 Horitschon B 4
75 Horka B 6
37 Hörken A 6
42 Hörle B 4
62 Horley B 3
88 Horn, A C 3
72 Horn, D† B 2
12 Horn, N B 4
43 Horn, S B 5
133 Horna C 1
91 Horná Lehota D 2
89 Horná Streda C 5
91 Horná Štrubňa D 1
89 Horná Súča C 5
129 Hornachos C 4
135 Hornachuelos B 5
85 Hornbach A 4
44 Hornbæk, Jylland, DK A 2
45 Hornbæk, Sjælland, DK A 5
85 Hornberg B 5
72 Hornburg A 4
58 Horncastle B 3
38 Horndal B 3
62 Horndean C 3
44 Horne, Fyn, DK B 3
44 Horne, Jylland, DK B 1
37 Hörnebo C 6
66 Horneburg B 2
74 Hornhausen A 3
89 Horní Bečva B 6
89 Horní Benešov B 5
88 Horni Cerekev B 3
88 Horni Jelení A 4
75 Horní Jiřetín C 5
89 Horní Lomná B 6
89 Horní Mariková B 6
88 Horni Maršov A 3
88 Horní Planá C 2
88 Horní Počernice A 2
87 Horni Slavkov A 4
88 Horni Stropnice C 2
89 Horni Suchá B 6
87 Horni Vltavice C 5
30 Hornindal B 3
44 Hørning A 3
34 Hornnes C 3
75 Horno B 6
137 Hornos A 4
58 Hornsea B 3
31 Hornsjø B 7
44 Hornslet A 3
101 Hornstein B 4
70 Hornu B 2
44 Hörnum, D† C 1
40 Hornum, DK C 3
91 Horný Tisovník D 2
88 Hořovice B 1
42 Horred B 2
100 Hörsching A 2
55 Horseleap A 4
44 Horsens B 2
62 Horsham B 3
45 Hørsholm B 5
74 Horsingen A 3
45 Horslunde C 4
87 Horšovský Týn B 4
66 Horst, D† B 2
64 Horst, NL C 4
72 Hörste B 2
65 Horstel B 5
65 Horsten A 5
65 Horstmar B 5
102 Hort A 3
124 Horta B 2
35 Horten B 6
126 Hortezuela A 3
120 Hortiguela B 3
15 Hortlax C 5
103 Hortobágy A 5
56 Horton in Ribblesdale B 4
45 Hørve B 4
47 Hörvik A 5
56 Horwich C 4
30 Hosanger C 2
73 Hösbach C 3
75 Hosena B 6
73 Hosenfeld C 3
71 Hosingen B 5
97 Hospenthal B 4
54 Hospital B 3
119 Hospital de Orbigo B 5
123 Hospitalet C 5
122 Hospitalet del Infante D 3
17 Hossa B 8
105 Hossegor D 1
102 Hosszúheteny B 2
103 Hosszúpályi A 5
101 Hosszúviz C 5
89 Hoštálková B 5
105 Hostens C 2
88 Hostinné A 3
88 Hostomice B 2
87 Hostoun B 4
21 Hoting A 5
70 Hotton B 4
49 Houbie A 8
63 Houdain B 4
82 Houdan C 3
84 Houdelaincourt B 2
105 Houellès C 3
71 Houffalize B 4
51 Houghton le Spring C 6
82 Houlgate B 1
62 Hounslow B 3
104 Hourtin B 1
104 Hourtin-Plage B 1
70 Houthalen A 4
26 Houtskär C 4
26 Houtskari C 4
44 Hov, DK B 3
31 Hov, N C 7
37 Hova C 6
35 Høvåg C 4

22 Isojoki C 3
11 Isokylä C 7
22 Isokyrö B 4
109 Isola C 4
143 Isola d. Gr. Sasso d'It. B 4
143 Isola del Liri C 4
148 Isola della Fémmine A 3
112 Isola della Scala A 3
147 Isola di Capo Rizzuto D 3
23 Isoniemi C 5
107 Ispagnac C 3
149 Ispica C 4
65 Isselburg C 4
65 Isselhorst C 6
104 Issigeac C 3
110 Issime B 2
110 Issogne B 2
106 Issoire B 3
84 Issoncourt B 2
93 Issoudun C 6
71 Issum A 5
94 Issy-l'Eveque C 3
136 Istán C 2
160 Istanbul E 6
90 Istebna C 1
91 Istenmezeje D 3
142 Istia d'Ombrone B 2
157 Istiaía D 3
153 Istibanja C 4
152 Istok B 2
109 Istres D 1
23 Istunmaki C 8
115 Istvándi A 5
24 Ita-Karttula C 4
23 Itäkylä B 5
157 Itéa D 2
158 Itháki A 1
121 Itoiz B 5
136 Ítrabo C 3
143 Itri C 4
141 Ittir B 2
141 Ittireddu B 2
66 Itzehoe B 2
11 Ivalo A 7
101 Iván B 4
89 Ivančice B 4
120 Iváncsa A 2
115 Ivanec A 4
152 Ivangrad B 1
115 Ivanic Grad B 4
100 Ivanjci C 3
116 Ivanjica C 4
115 Ivanjska C 5
101 Ivanka A 5
101 Ivanka p. Nitre A 6
116 Ivankovo A 2
89 Ivanovice na Hané B 5
115 Ivanska B 4
156 Ivira B 3
82 Ivray-la Bat'aille C 3
110 Ivrea B 2
95 Ivry-en-Montagne B 4
60 Ivybridge C 3
90 Iwaniska B 4
70 Iwuy B 2
59 Ixworth C 4
121 Izarra B 4
79 Izbica Kujawska C 1
79 Izbica Kujawski C 1
77 Izbicko C 7
117 Izbište A 5
125 Izeda B 3
70 Izegem B 2
95 Izernore C 5
160 Izmail C 6
136 Iznalloz B 3
137 Iznatoraf A 3
114 Izola B 1
102 Izsák B 3
91 Izsófalva D 3
153 Izvor, BG B 4
153 Izvor, Makekedonia, YU C 3
153 Izvor, Srbija, YU B 4
117 Izvor Makhala C 6

J

28 Jaala B 4
17 Jaalanka, Oulun, SF B 6
17 Jaalanka, Oulun, SF C 6
136 Jabalquinto A 3
122 Jabarrella B 2
114 Jablanac C 2
151 Jablanica B 3
88 Jablonec n. Jizerou A 3
88 Jablonec n. Nisou A 3
101 Jablonica A 5
90 Jablonka, Krakow, PL C 2
77 Jablonka, Poznań, PL A 7
78 Jablonka Kościelna C 5
79 Jablonna C 3
79 Jablonna, Warszawa, PL C 5
88 Jablonné Podještědi A 2
78 Jablonowo B 2
89 Jablůnka B 5
116 Jabučje B 4
135 Jabugo B 4
117 Jabuka, Pokragina Vojvodna, YU B 4
152 Jabuka, Srbija, YU A 1
115 Jabukovac, Hrvatska, YU B 4
117 Jabukovac, Srbija, YU B 6
89 Jabunkov B 6
122 Jaca B 2
75 Jáchymov C 4
5 Jäckvik D 6
66 Jacobidrebber C 1
9 Jacobselv B 9
101 Jacovce A 6
65 Jade A 6
38 Jäderfors B 3
38 Jädraås B 3
126 Jadraque B 3
45 Jægerspris B 4
6 Jægervatn B 5
136 Jaén B 3
115 Jagare C 5
88 Jagenbach C 3
102 Jagodnjak C 2
76 Jagodzin B 4
86 Jagsthausen B 2
86 Jagstzell B 2
101 Jahodna A 5
115 Jajce C 5
101 Ják B 4
102 Jakabszállás B 3
16 Jakkukylä B 4
91 Jaklovce D 3
5 Jakobsbakken C 4
22 Jakobstad B 4
115 Jakovlje B 3
115 Jakšic B 5
91 Jakubany C 3
132 Jalance B 1
22 Jalasjärvi C 4
92 Jallais B 3
108 Jallieu B 2
71 Jalnay B 4
133 Jalón C 2
116 Jalovik B 3
153 Jalovik Izvor A 4
70 Jambes B 3
116 Jamena B 3
27 Jämijärvi B 5
136 Jamilena B 3
27 Jäminkipohja B 7
43 Jämjö C 5
69 Jamno A 4
70 Jamoigne C 4
27 Jämsä B 8
27 Jämsänkoski B 8
43 Jämshog C 4
14 Jämton C 6
27 Janakkala C 7
87 Jandelsbrunn C 5
75 Jänickendorf A 5
69 Janikowo C 6
116 Janja B 3
152 Janjevo B 3
150 Janjina C 3
79 Janki C 3
88 Jankov B 2
77 Janków B 6
77 Jankowo Dolne A 6
102 Jánoshalma B 3
101 Jánosháza B 5
102 Jánoshide A 4
87 Janovice nad Uhlavou B 5
90 Janów B 2
90 Janowiec B 4
69 Janowiec Wielkopolski C 5
78 Janowo B 3
20 Jänsmässholmen B 2
82 Janville C 3
81 Janzé C 5
24 Jäppilä C 4
91 Jarabá D 2
133 Jaraco B 2
77 Jaraczewo B 6
132 Jarafuel B 1
129 Jaraicejo B 5
129 Jaraiz de la Vera A 5
116 Jarak B 3
129 Jarandilla A 5
127 Jaray A 3
38 Jarbo B 3
79 Jarczew D 4
92 Jard-sur-Mer C 2
91 Jardánháza D 3
31 Jaren C 7
94 Jargeau B 2
117 Jarkovac A 4
21 Järkvissle C 5
38 Jarlåsa C 4
67 Jarmen B 6
39 Järna C 4
104 Jarnac B 2
43 Järnforsen B 5
84 Jarny A 2
77 Jarocin B 6
88 Jaroměř A 3
88 Jaroměřice n. Rokytnou B 3
89 Jaroslavice C 4
69 Jaroslawiec A 4
68 Jaroslawsko B 3
88 Jarošov n. Nežarkou B 3
91 Jarovnice C 4
42 Järpås A 2
20 Järpen B 2
51 Jarrow C 6
28 Järvelä C 3
27 Järvenpää C 8
23 Järviky B 6
13 Järvsjö C 9
33 Järvsö B 7
92 Jarzé B 3
117 Jaša Tornic A 4
114 Jasenak B 3
114 Jasenice C 3
91 Jasenie D 2
117 Jasenova B 5
115 Jasenovac B 4
116 Jasenovo C 3
76 Jasień B 4
117 Jasika C 5
90 Jaśliska C 4
90 Jaslo C 4
91 Jasov D 3
101 Jásova B 6
95 Jasseron C 5
69 Jastarnia A 6
114 Jastrebarsko B 3
69 Jastrowie B 4
69 Jastrzebia-Góra A 6
89 Jastrzebie-Zdroj B 6
102 Jászalsószentgyorgy A 4
102 Jászapáti A 4
102 Jászárokszállás A 3
102 Jászberény A 3
102 Jászdózsa A 3
102 Jászfényszaru A 3
102 Jászjakóhalma A 4
102 Jászkarajenö A 4
102 Jászkisér A 4
102 Jászladány A 4
136 Játar C 3
133 Játiva C 2
101 Jatov A 6
33 Jättendal B 8
67 Jatznick B 6
70 Jauche B 3
83 Jaulgonne B 5
96 Jaun B 3
17 Jaurakka B 6
109 Jausiers C 3
133 Jávea C 3
67 Jävenitz C 4
104 Javerlhac B 3
121 Javier B 5
115 Javorani C 5
91 Javorina C 3
89 Javornik A 5
15 Jåvre C 5
81 Javron B 6
77 Jawor B 5
90 Jaworznia B 3
90 Jaworzno B 2
77 Jaworzyna Ślaska C 5
136 Jayena C 3
103 Jebel C 5
40 Jeberg C 3
51 Jedburgh B 5
79 Jedlanka D 5
90 Jedlicze C 4
77 Jedlina Zdrój C 5
79 Jedlinsk D 4
79 Jedlnia D 4
79 Jedlnia Letnisko D 4
78 Jednorozec B 4
89 Jedovnice B 4
78 Jedrychowo B 2
90 Jedrzejów B 3
78 Jedwabne B 5
78 Jedwabno B 3
11 Jeesiö B 6
78 Jeglownik A 2
105 Jégun D 3
34 Jektevik B 1
152 Jelakci A 2
153 Jelašnica A 4
101 Jelenec A 6
77 Jelenia Góra C 4
69 Jelenino B 4
101 Jelka A 5
44 Jelling B 2
44 Jels B 2
34 Jelsa, N B 2
150 Jelsa, YU B 2
91 Jelšava D 3
71 Jemeppe B 4
65 Jemgum A 5
88 Jemnice B 3
74 Jena C 3
97 Jenaz B 5
98 Jenbach B 2
88 Jeneč A 2
101 Jennersdorf C 4
43 Jenny B 6
22 Jeppo B 4
67 Jerchel C 4
136 Jeres del Marquesado B 3
135 Jerez de la Frontera C 4
129 Jerez de los Caballeros C 4
154 Jergucat C 2
132 Jerica B 2
67 Jerichow C 5
117 Jermenovci A 5
40 Jerslev B 4
129 Jerte A 5
40 Jerup B 4
72 Jerxheim A 4
77 Jerzmanice Zdrój B 4
90 Jerzmanowice B 2
78 Jerzwald B 2
87 Jesenice, Stredočeský, CS A 5
88 Jesenice, Stredočeský, CS B 2
114 Jesenice, YU A 2
89 Jesenik A 5
91 Jesenké D 3
75 Jeserig A 4
75 Jessen B 4
36 Jessheim A 3
74 Jeßnitz B 4
66 Jesteburg B 2
132 Jesus y Maria A 3
70 Jette B 3
86 Jettingen C 2
66 Jevenstedt A 2
65 Jever A 5
89 Jevicko B 4
88 Jevišovice C 3
35 Jevnaker A 6
78 Jeze B 4
115 Jezero C 5
114 Jezersko A 2
78 Jeziorany B 3
79 Jeziorna C 4
79 Jezów D 2
78 Jezowo B 1
88 Jičín A 3
88 Jičiněves A 3
133 Jijona C 2
88 Jilemnice A 3
88 Jilhlava B 3
75 Jilové C 6
88 Jilové u. Prahy B 2
103 Jimbolia C 4
136 Jimena B 3
135 Jimena de la Frontera C 5
135 Jimera de Libar C 5
89 Jimramov B 4
88 Jince B 1
75 Jindřichovice C 4
88 Jindřichův Hradec B 2
75 Jirkov C 5
88 Jistebnice B 2
67 Joachimsthal C 6
128 João da Loura C 2
91 Jobbágyi E 2
98 Jochberg B 3
85 Jockgrim A 5
136 Jódar B 3
83 Jodarre C 5
90 Jodlowa C 4
70 Jodoigne B 3
25 Joenssu C 6
13 Joesjö B 6
84 Jœuf A 2
75 Johanngeorgenstadt C 4
43 Johannishus C 5
87 Johanniskirchen C 4
43 Johansfors C 5
49 John o' Groats House Hotel C 5
49 Johnshaven E 6
50 Johnstone B 3
55 Johnstown B 4
55 Johnstown Bridge A 5
83 Joigny D 5
84 Joinville B 2
101 Jois B 4
27 Jokela C 7
17 Jokijärvi B 7
27 Jokikunta C 7
23 Jokikylä B 7
27 Jokioinen C 6
22 Jokipii C 4
10 Jokk C 2
14 Jokkmokk B 3
65 Jöllenbeck B 6
26 Jomala C 2
39 Jonåker D 3
83 Jonchery-sur-Vesle B 5
35 Jondal, Buskerud Fylke, N B 5
30 Jondal, Hordaland Fylke, N C 3
42 Jönköping B 4
78 Jonkowo B 3
17 Jonku B 6
109 Jonquières D 1
39 Jonsberg D 3
75 Jonsdorf C 6
42 Jonsered B 2
46 Jonstorp A 3
104 Jonzac B 2
123 Jorba C 4
90 Jordanów C 2
77 Jordanów Ślaski C 5
76 Jordanowo A 4
39 Jordbro C 5
67 Jördenstorf B 5
32 Jordet B 3
44 Jordløse B 3
124 Jorjaes B 2
66 Jork B 2
13 Jormlien C 5
15 Jörn C 4
24 Joroinen C 4
34 Jørpeland B 2
132 Jorquera B 1
19 Jørstad A 8
152 Jošanička Banja A 2
115 Jošavka C 5
114 Josipdol B 3
102 Josipovac C 2
36 Jössefors B 4
80 Josselin C 4
30 Jostedal B 4
91 Jósvafo D 3
103 Jósza A 5
93 Joué-les-Tours B 4
81 Joué-sur-Erdre C 5
17 Joukokylä B 7
64 Joure B 3
28 Joutsa B 4
29 Joutseno B 6
11 Joutsijärvi C 7
94 Joux-la-Ville B 3
82 Jouy, Eure et Loir, F C 3
84 Jouy, Moselle, F A 3
83 Jouy-le-Châtel C 5
93 Jouy-le-Potier B 5
118 Jove A 3
6 Jøvik B 4
106 Joyeuse C 4
106 Joze B 3
79 Józefów, Lublin, PL D 4
79 Józefów, Warszawa, PL C 4
25 Juankoski B 5
66 Jübek A 2
121 Jubera B 4
118 Jubia A 2
135 Jubrique al Genalguacil C 5
74 Jüchsen C 2
100 Judenburg B 2
44 Juelsminde B 3
81 Jugon B 4
104 Juillac B 4
105 Juillan D 3
65 Juist A 4
7 Jukkasjärvi D 6
55 Julianstown A 5
71 Jülich B 5
95 Julienas C 4
81 Jullouville B 5
70 Jumet B 3
82 Jumièges B 2
104 Jumilhac-le-Grand B 4
133 Jumilla C 1
24 Juminen B 4

122 Juncosa C 3
122 Juneda C 3
42 Jung A 3
85 Jungingen B 6
71 Junglingster C 5
30 Jungsdalshytta C 4
152 Junik B 2
83 Juniville B 6
10 Junosuando B 2
124 Junqueira B 2
118 Junquera de Ambía B 3
118 Junquera de Espadanedo B 3
21 Junsele B 5
120 Junta de la Cerca B 3
120 Junta de Oteo A 3
17 Juntusranta B 8
10 Juoksengi C 3
10 Juoksenki C 3
27 Juokslahti B 8
17 Juorkuna C 5
28 Juornaankylä C 3
101 Jur A 5
105 Jurançon D 2
69 Jurata A 6
114 Jurjevo C 2
17 Jurmu B 6
129 Juromenha C 3
22 Jurva C 3
106 Jussac C 2
95 Jussey B 5
83 Jussy B 5
22 Jutas B 4
75 Jüterbog B 5
25 Juuka B 6
27 Juupajoki B 7
29 Juva B 5
81 Juvigny, Manche, F B 5
81 Juvigny, Orn, F B 6
83 Juvincourt B 5
83 Juvisy C 4
29 Juvola A 6
84 Juzennecourt B 1
45 Jyderup B 4
22 Jyllinkoski C 4
23 Jyväskylä C 7

K

9 Kaamanen C 7
8 Kaamasmukka C 6
10 Kaaresuvanto A 2
27 Kaarina C 5
66 Kaarßen B 4
64 Kaatsheuvel C 3
25 Kaavi C 5
103 Kaba A 5
14 Kåbdalis B 3
4 Kabelvåg B 3
152 Kačanik B 3
117 Kačarevo B 4
153 Kačikol B 3
75 Kadaň C 5
115 Kadarkút A 5
78 Kadzidlo B 4
8 Kåfjord, Finnmark, N C 3
6 Kåfjord, Troms, N B 6
6 Kåfjordbotn B 6
15 Kåge D 4
46 Kågeröd B 4
73 Kahl C 3
74 Kahla C 3
100 Kaibing B 3
100 Kainach B 3
22 Kainasto C 4
100 Kaindorf B 3
100 Kaindorf a. d. Sulm C 3
155 Kainoúrion D 3
10 Kainulaisjärvi B 2
16 Kainuunkylä A 2
28 Kaipiainen C 5
27 Kaipola B 8
11 Kairala B 7
7 Kaisepakte C 5
71 Kaisersesch B 6
85 Kaiserslautern A 4
86 Kaisheim C 2
29 Kaitainen A 5
7 Kaitum D 6
17 Kajaani C 6
101 Kajárpéc B 5
102 Kajdacs B 2
116 Kakanj B 2
102 Kakasd B 2
77 Kakolewo B 5
158 Kakoúri B 3
158 Kakóvatos B 2
26 Kakskarta C 5
91 Kal E 3
155 Kalabáka C 3
156 Kalabáki A 4
152 Kalače B 2
16 Kalajoki C 2
23 Kalakoski C 5
158 Kalamáta B 3
159 Kálamos, Attikí, GR A 4
155 Kálamos, Kálamos, GR D 2
156 Kalándra C 3
26 Kalanti C 4
21 Kälarne C 5
158 Kalávrita A 3
67 Kalbe C 4
114 Kalce B 2
101 Káld B 5
71 Kaldenkirchen A 5
6 Kaldfarnes B 2
51 Kalemouth B 5
117 Kalenic C 4
155 Kalenji C 2
90 Kalety B 1
35 Kalhovd A 4
156 Kalí B 2
115 Kalinovac A 5
91 Kalinovo D 2
156 Kalirrákhi B 4
69 Kaliska, Gdansk, PL B 6
69 Kaliska, Gdańsk, PL A 6
154 Kališta A 2
77 Kalisz B 7
69 Kalisz Pomorski B 3
156 Kalives B 4
159 Kalívia B 4
16 Kalix B 2
7 Kalixfors D 6
28 Kalkkinen B 3
71 Kall,D† B 5
20 Kall,S B 2
43 Källa B 6
42 Kållered B 2
38 Källfallet C 2
39 Kallhäll C 4
98 Kallham A 4
157 Kallifóni C 1
43 Kallinge C 5
156 Kallipévki C 2
29 Kallislahti B 6
158 Kallithéa C 2
152 Kallmet C 1
33 Kallmora B 5
87 Kallmünz B 3
10 Kallo B 4
20 Kallrör B 2
39 Källunge E 5
11 Kallunki C 8
91 Kálmánháza E 4
43 Kalmar C 6
70 Kalmthout A 3
91 Kálna, CS D 1
153 Kalna, Srbija, YU B 4
153 Kalna, Srbija, YU A 4
102 Kalocsa B 2
156 Kalokastro A 3
153 Kalotina B 4
158 Kaloúsi A 2
102 Kaloz B 2
98 Kals B 3
100 Kalsdorf C 3
97 Kaltbrunn A 5
98 Kaltenbach B 2
85 Kaltenhouse B 4
66 Kaltenkirchen B 2
74 Kaltennordheim C 2
99 Kaltern C 2
45 Kalundborg B 4
79 Kaluszyn C 4
30 Kalvag B 1
45 Kalvehave B 5
23 Kälviä B 5
27 Kalvola B 7
15 Kalvträsk D 3
100 Kalwang B 2
90 Kalwaria-Zebrzydowska C 2
101 Kám B 4
159 Kamári A 3
155 Kamaroúla D 3
158 Kámbos C 3
71 Kamen A 6
153 Kamenica, Kovsovska Metohiska, YU B 3
153 Kamenica, Srbija, YU A 3
116 Kamenica, Srbija, YU B 3
88 Kamenica n. Lipou B 3
88 Kamenice B 3
75 Kamenicky Šenov C 6
101 Kameničná B 6
91 Kamenín-Most E 1
152 Kamenjane C 2
88 Kamenný Ujezd C 2
75 Kamenz B 6
50 Kames B 2
79 Kamień D 3
69 Kamień Krajenskie B 5
68 Kamień Pomorski B 2
90 Kamienica Polska B 2
89 Kamieniec Zabk A 4
91 Kamienka,CS C 3
78 Kamienka,SU A 4
77 Kamienna-Góra C 5
79 Kamieńsk D 2
157 Kámmen Voúrla D 2
29 Kammenogorsk C 7
100 Kammern i. Liesingtal B 2
114 Kamnik A 2
8 Kamøyvær A 5
71 Kamp-Lintfort A 5
44 Kampen,D† C 1
64 Kampen,NL B 3
79 Kampinos C 3
88 Kamýk n. Vltavou B 2
114 Kanal A 1
155 Kanália, Kardhitsa, GR C 3
157 Kanália, Magnisía, GR C 2
155 Kanallákion C 2
154 Kanatlarci A 3
85 Kandel A 5
85 Kandern C 4
96 Kandersteg B 3
155 Kandhíla, Aitolía Kai Aranania, GR D 2
158 Kandhila, Arkadhía, GR B 3
78 Kandyty A 3
23 Kangasaho C 6
27 Kangasala B 7
25 Kangaslampi C 5
28 Kangasniemi B 4
10 Kangos B 2
10 Kangosjärvi B 3
68 Kania B 3
154 Kaninë B 1
115 Kaniža B 5
102 Kanjiža B 4
27 Kankaanpää B 5
23 Kanmonkoski C 7
23 Kannus B 5
4 Kanstadbotn B 4
24 Kantala C 4
16 Kantomaanpää A 3
22 Kantti C 4
54 Kanturk B 3
117 Kaonik C 5
159 Kapandhriti A 4
159 Kaparéli A 4
100 Kapellen,A B 3
70 Kapellen,B A 3
100 Kapfenberg B 3
100 Kapfenstein C 3
88 Kaplice C 2
91 Kápolna E 3
120 Kapolnásnyék A 2
101 Kaposfo C 5
101 Kaposvár C 5
31 Kapp C 7
85 Kappel B 4
44 Kappeln C 2
39 Kappelshamn C 5
97 Kappl A 6
98 Kaprun B 3
14 Kaptensgården B 3
115 Kaptol B 5
91 Kapušany C 4
101 Kapuvár B 5
91 Karácsond E 3
101 Karád C 5
159 Karaí B 3
155 Karaiskákis D 3
116 Karan C 3
91 Karancslapujto D 2
8 Karasjok C 5
14 Karatj B 2
158 Karátoula B 2
159 Karavás C 3
38 Karbenning B 3
39 Kårberg D 1
33 Kårböle B 6
66 Karby,D† A 2
40 Karby,DK C 2
38 Karby,S C 5
103 Karcag A 4
91 Karcsa D 4
79 Karczew C 4
79 Karczmiska D 4
77 Karczów C 6
77 Karczowiska B 5
158 Kardamás B 2
88 Kardašova Rečice B 2
155 Kardhítsa C 3
157 Kardhitsemagoúla C 1
10 Karesuando A 2
77 Kargowa A 4
8 Karhamn B 3
28 Karhula C 4
156 Kariá, Larisa, GR C 2
155 Kariá, Levkás, GR D 2
156 Kariai B 4
8 Karigasniemi C 5
22 Karijoki C 3
27 Karinainen C 5
42 Käringon A 1
16 Karinkanta C 3
156 Kariotissa B 2
27 Karis C 6
45 Karise B 5
159 Káristos A 5
158 Karitaina B 3
156 Karitsa, Ioánnina, GR C 2
155 Karitsa, Larisa, GR C 2
156 Karítsa, Piería, GR B 2
27 Karjaa C 6
26 Karjala C 5
27 Karjalohja C 6
158 Karkaloú B 3
156 Karkára B 3
27 Karkkila C 7
27 Karkku B 6
27 Kärkölä C 8
16 Karkuhangas C 4
75 Karl-Marx-Stadt C 4
9 Karlebotn B 8
38 Karlholmsbruk B 4
69 Karlino A 3
114 Karlobag C 3
114 Karlovac B 3
116 Karlovčic B 4
89 Karlovice A 5
75 Karlovy Vary C 4
21 Karlsback B 7
16 Karlsborg, Norrbottens Län, S B 2
37 Karlsborg, Skaraborgs Län, S C 6
39 Karlsby D 2
72 Karlshafen B 3
43 Karlshamn C 4
66 Karlshöfen B 2
35 Karlshus B 6
37 Karlskoga B 6
43 Karlskrona C 5
6 Karlsøy A 5
85 Karlsruhe A 5
37 Karlstad B 5
73 Karlstadt D 3
100 Karlstetten A 3
100 Karlstift A 2
101 Karmacs C 5
160 Karnobat D 5
155 Karousádhes C 1
67 Karow B 5
77 Karpacz C 4
17 Kärpänkylä B 8
155 Karpenísion D 3
154 Karperón C 3
157 Karpokhóri C 1
45 Karrebæksminde B 4
23 Kärsämäki B 7
69 Karsin B 5
38 Kårsta, Stockholms, S C 5
38 Kärsta, Uppsala,S C 3
67 Karstädt B 4
23 Karstula C 6
102 Kartal A 3
99 Kartitsch C 3
24 Karttula C 3
69 Kartuzy A 6
27 Karuna C 5
16 Karungi A 2
16 Karunki A 3
44 Karup A 2
23 Karvala B 5
22 Karvia C 4
89 Karviná B 6
25 Karvio C 5
155 Karvounári C 2
78 Karwica B 4
40 Kås B 3
89 Kašava B 5
87 Kasejovice B 5
68 Kasekow B 2
4 Kasfjord B 5
152 Kashnjet C 1
115 Kašina B 4
90 Kasina Wielka C 3
14 Kasker C 1
22 Kaskinen C 3
22 Kaskö C 3
87 Kašperské Hory B 5
66 Kasseedorf A 3
72 Kassel B 3
155 Kassiópi C 1
156 Kastanerí B 2
156 Kastaniá B 2
150 Kastel Stari B 2
71 Kastellaun B 6
157 Kastélli D 2
70 Kasterlee A 3
87 Kasti B 3
43 Kastlösa C 6
6 Kastneshamn C 3
66 Kastorf B 3
158 Kastóri B 3
154 Kastoría B 3
155 Kastráki, Aitolía Kai Akarnanía, GR D 3
155 Kastráki, Tríkkala, GR C 3
155 Kastrítsa C 2
103 Kaszaper B 4
158 Katákolon B 2
27 Kataloinen B 7
158 Katastári B 1
13 Kåtaviken A 6
159 Katavóthra C 3
67 Katerbow C 5
156 Kateríni B 2
53 Katesbridge B 5
159 Kathenoi A 4
32 Kåtila B 5
10 Kätkäsuvanto A 3
153 Katlanovo C 3
72 Katlenburg-Duhm B 4
158 Káto Akhaia A 2
159 Káto Alepokhóri A 4
159 Káto Dhiminion A 3
158 Káto Figalia B 2
154 Káto Klinaí B 3
158 Káto Klitoría B 3
155 Káto Makrinón D 3
156 Káto Miliá B 2
156 Káto Nevrokópion A 3
156 Káto Skholárion B 3
156 Káto Vrondoú A 3
155 Katokhí D 3
155 Katoúna D 3
88 Katovice B 1
90 Katowice B 1
33 Katrineberg B 7
39 Katrineholm D 3
155 Katsiká C 2
46 Kattarp A 3
32 Kättbo C 5
65 Kattenvenne B 5
4 Katterat B 6
39 Katthammarsvik C 5
42 Kattilstorp A 3
15 Kattisavan D 2
153 Katuntsi C 5
64 Katwijk aan Zee B 2
77 Katy Wroclawskie B 5
102 Katyma B 3
101 Katzelsdorf B 4
71 Katzenelnbogen B 6
74 Katzhütte C 3
71 Kaub B 6
86 Kaufbeuren D 2
22 Kauhajarvi C 4
22 Kauhajoki C 4
22 Kauhava B 4
27 Kauklahti C 7
10 Kaukonen B 4
16 Kauliranta A 2
74 Kaulsdorf C 3
10 Kaunisvaara B 3
30 Kaupanger B 4
28 Kausala C 4
23 Kaustinen B 5
8 Kautokeino C 3
26 Kauttua B 5
88 Kautzen C 3
27 Kauvatsa B 5
153 Kavadarci C 4
154 Kavajë A 1
156 Kavála B 4
91 Kavečany D 4
46 Kavlinge B 4
69 Kawcze A 4
20 Kaxås B 2
43 Kaxholmen B 4
17 Käylä A 8
10 Käymäjärvi B 2
85 Kaysersberg B 4
160 Kazanluk D 4
91 Kazár D 2
79 Kazimierz Dolny D 4
90 Kazimierza Wielkiego B 3
91 Kazincbarcika D 3
77 Kazmierz A 5
87 Kaznějov B 5
88 Kbely A 2

69 Kcynia C 5
87 Kdyně B 5
159 Kéa B 5
53 Keady B 5
54 Kealkill C 2
91 Kecerovské-Pekľany D 4
102 Kecskemét B 3
84 Kédange A 3
157 Kédhron C 2
89 Kędzierzyn A 6
52 Keel C 1
70 Keerbergen A 3
159 Kefalári, Argolis, GR B 3
159 Kefalári, Korinthia, GR B 3
155 Kefalóvrison C 3
59 Kegworth C 2
85 Kehl B 4
75 Kehrigk A 5
58 Keighley B 2
27 Keikyä B 5
48 Keil E 3
50 Keillmore B 2
49 Keiss C 5
23 Keitele B 8
23 Keitelpohja B 7
49 Keith D 6
44 Keitum C 1
156 Kekhrókambos A 4
17 Kelankylä B 6
71 Kelberg B 5
74 Kelbra B 3
89 Kelč B 5
98 Kelchsau B 3
154 Këlcyrë B 2
102 Kelebia B 3
87 Kelheim C 3
49 Kellas D 5
154 Kélli B 3
66 Kellinghusen B 2
16 Kello B 4
27 Kellokoski C 8
11 Kelloselkä C 8
53 Kells B 5
7 Kelottijarvi C 7
51 Kelso B 5
73 Kelsterbach C 2
11 Kelujärvi B 7
62 Kelvedon B 4
98 Kematen, Tirol, A B 2
100 Kematen, Upper Austria, A A 1
100 Kematen a. d. Krems A 2
75 Kemberg B 4
85 Kembs C 4
91 Kemecse D 4
101 Kemeten B 4
16 Kemi B 3
25 Kemie C 7
11 Kemijärvi C 7
27 Kemiö C 5
87 Kemnath B 3
49 Kemnay D 6
75 Kemnitz, Potsdam, D* A 4
67 Kemnitz, Rostock, D* A 6
16 Kempele C 4
71 Kempen A 5
57 Kempsey D 4
59 Kempston C 3
97 Kempten A 6
97 Kemptthal A 4
56 Kendal B 4
103 Kenderes A 4
91 Kendice D 4
156 Kendrikó A 2
91 Kenézlo D 4
102 Kengyel A 4
59 Kenilworth C 2
54 Kenmare C 2
50 Kenmore A 4
50 Kennacraig B 2
59 Kenninghall C 5
158 Kéntron B 2
101 Kenyeri B 5
85 Kenzingen B 4
79 Kepa Polska C 2
69 Kepice A 4
77 Kepno B 7
26 Kepola B 5
56 Keppel Gate B 2
158 Keramidhiá B 2
155 Keramítsa C 2
156 Keramoti B 4
154 Kerásovon B 2
159 Keratéa B 4
27 Kerava C 8
102 Kercel B 3
91 Kerecsend E 3
102 Kerekegyháza B 3
102 Kerepes A 3
158 Keri B 1
80 Kérien B 3
29 Kerimäki B 7
101 Kerkafalva C 4
156 Kerkíni A 3
155 Kérkira C 1
24 Kerkonkoski C 3
70 Kerksken B 2
80 Kerlouan B 2
80 Kernascléden B 3
96 Kerns B 4
71 Kerpen B 5
48 Kerrysdale D 3
11 Kersilö B 6
101 Kerta B 5
44 Kerteminde B 3
158 Kérteza B 2
96 Kerzers B 3
29 Kesälahti B 7
160 Keşan E 5
53 Kesh B 4
85 Keskastel B 4
16 Keskikylä C 3
64 Kessel C 4
73 Kesselbach C 2
59 Kessingland C 5
16 Kestilä C 5
56 Keswick B 3
101 Keszthely C 5
103 Kétegháza B 5
101 Kéthely C 5
78 Kętrzyn A 4
59 Kettering C 3
58 Kettlewell A 1
59 Ketton C 3
71 Kettwig A 5
90 Kety C 2
67 Ketzin C 5
23 Keuruu C 6
71 Kevelaer A 5
103 Kevermes B 5
102 Kevi C 3
58 Keyingham B 3
62 Keymer C 3
61 Keynsham B 4
91 Kežmarok C 3
159 Khairónia A 3
159 Khalandri A 4
158 Khalandritsa A 2
156 Khalástra B 2
159 Khália A 4
157 Khálki C 2
155 Khalkiádhes C 2
159 Khalkís A 4
160 Kharmanli E 4
158 Kharokopión C 2
156 Kharopó A 3
160 Khaskovo E 4
158 Khávari B 2
158 Khavdháta A 1
156 Kherson A 2
159 Khiliomódhion B 3
156 Khímarros A 3
158 Khóra B 2
156 Khoristi A 4
156 Khortiátis B 3
159 Khóstia A 3
155 Khoúni D 3
159 Khrisafa B 3
156 Khrisi B 2
156 Khrisokhóri B 4
155 Khrisomiliá C 3
157 Khrisón D 2
156 Khrisós A 3
156 Khrisoúpolis B 4
155 Khrisovítsa C 3
160 Khurdzhali E 4
160 Khust A 3
17 Kiannanniemi B 8
159 Kiáton A 3
44 Kibæk A 1
9 Kiberg B 11
48 Kibride D 1
59 Kibworth Beachamp C 3
152 Kičevo C 2
57 Kidderminster D 4
62 Kidlington B 2
115 Kidričevo A 3
57 Kidsgrove C 4
58 Kidstones A 1
60 Kidwelly B 2
98 Kiefersfelden B 3
66 Kiel A 3
90 Kielce B 3
90 Kielcza B 1
69 Kielpino A 6
78 Kielpiny B 2
79 Kiernozia C 2
71 Kierspe A 6
89 Kietrz A 6
76 Kietz A 3
78 Kiezmark A 1
151 Kifino Selo B 4
159 Kifisiá A 4
10 Kihlanki B 3
23 Kihnio C 5
25 Kiihtelysvaara C 7
27 Kiikala C 6
27 Kiikka B 5
27 Kiikoinen B 5
16 Kiiminki B 4
23 Kiiskilä B 6
10 Kiistala B 5
90 Kije B 3
150 Kijevo B 2
103 Kikinda C 4
78 Kikol C 2
35 Kil, N C 5
39 Kil, Örebro, S C 2
37 Kil, Värmland, S B 5
33 Kilafors B 7
100 Kilb Rabenstein A 3
55 Kilbeggan A 4
54 Kilbeheny B 3
50 Kilberry B 2
5 Kilboghamn D 2
4 Kilbotn B 5
50 Kilburnie B 3
48 Kilchoan E 2
55 Kilcock A 5
54 Kilcoe C 2
54 Kilcolgan A 3
54 Kilconnell A 3
53 Kilcoo B 5
55 Kilcormac A 4
55 Kilcullen A 5
53 Kilcurry B 5
55 Kildare A 5
55 Kildavin B 5
49 Kildonan C 5
54 Kildorrery B 3
50 Kildrochat C 3
35 Kilegrend C 4
35 Kilen B 4
54 Kilgarvan C 2
54 Kilkee B 2
53 Kilkeel B 6
55 Kilkenny B 4
60 Kilkhampton C 2
54 Kilkieran A 2
54 Kilkinlea B 2
156 Kilkis B 2
54 Kilkishen B 3
55 Kill A 5
52 Killala B 2
54 Killaloe B 3
55 Killane A 4
55 Killare A 4
54 Killarney B 2
55 Killashee A 4
55 Killeagh C 3
50 Killean B 2
42 Killeberg C 4
55 Killeigh A 4
55 Killenaule B 4
53 Killeshandra B 4
54 Killimor A 3
50 Killin A 3
158 Killini B 2
55 Killinick B 5
23 Killinkoski C 5
54 Killorglin B 2
53 Killough B 6
55 Killucan A 4
52 Killybegs B 3
53 Killyleagh B 6
50 Kilmacolm B 3
52 Kilmacrenan A 4
55 Kilmacthomas B 4
54 Kilmaine A 2
54 Kilmallock B 3
50 Kilmarnock B 3
50 Kilmartin A 2
50 Kilmaurs B 3
50 Kilmelford A 2
55 Kilmore B 5
55 Kilmore Quay B 5
49 Kilmuir D 4
53 Kilnaleck C 4
48 Kilninian E 2
50 Kilninver A 2
6 Kilpisjärvi B 6
53 Kilrea B 5
54 Kilreekill A 3
54 Kilrush B 2
55 Kilsheelan B 4
39 Kilsmo C 2
50 Kilsyth B 3
55 Kiltegan B 5
54 Kiltullagh A 3
27 Kilvakkala B 5
53 Kilwaughter B 6
50 Kilwinning B 3
159 Kími A 5
156 Kímina B 2
27 Kimito C 5
22 Kimo B 4
159 Kímolos C 5
39 Kimstad D 2
49 Kinbrace C 5
50 Kincardine A 4
100 Kindberg B 3
74 Kindelbruck B 3
59 Kineton C 2
52 Kingarrow B 3
50 Kingarth B 2
51 Kinghorn A 4
59 King's Lynn C 4
62 King's Worthy B 2
51 Kingsbarns A 5
60 Kingsbridge C 3
62 Kingsclere B 2
53 Kingscourt C 5
48 Kingshouse Hotel E 4
60 Kingskerswell C 3
57 Kingsley C 4
60 Kingsteignton C 3
62 Kingston B 3
58 Kingston upon Hull B 3
60 Kingswear C 3
61 Kingswood B 4
57 Kington D 3
49 Kingussie D 4
48 Kinloch D 3
48 Kinloch, Skye, GB D 3
48 Kinloch, Sutherland, GB C 4
50 Kinloch Hourn Hotel A 2
49 Kinloch Rannoch E 4
48 Kinlocheil E 3
48 Kinlochewe D 3
48 Kinlochleven E 4
48 Kinlochmoidart E 3
52 Kinlough B 3
31 Kinn C 7
42 Kinna B 2
42 Kinnared B 3
42 Kinnarp A 3
37 Kinne-Kleva C 5
55 Kinnegad A 4
55 Kinnitty A 4
23 Kinnula B 6
71 Kinrooi A 4
51 Kinross A 4
54 Kinsale C 3
30 Kinsarvik C 3
48 Kintaravay C 2
49 Kintore D 6
50 Kintraw A 2
54 Kinvarra A 3
158 Kióni A 1
158 Kiparissia B 2
157 Kipárissos C 2
86 Kipfenberg C 3
17 Kipinä B 5
50 Kippen A 3
103 Királyhegyes B 4
73 Kirberg C 2
100 Kirchbach i. Steiermark C 3
96 Kirchberg, CH A 3
86 Kirchberg, Baden-Württemberg, D† B 1
71 Kirchberg, Rheinland-Pfalz, D† C 6
100 Kirchberg a. d. Pielach A 3
100 Kirchberg a. Wechsel B 3
98 Kirchberg in Tirol B 3
98 Kirchbichl B 3
86 Kirchdorf, Bayern, D† C 3
87 Kirchdorf, Bayern, D† C 5
66 Kirchdorf, Niedersachsen, D† C 1
67 Kirchdorf, D* B 4
100 Kirchdorf a.d. Krems B 2
73 Kircheimbolanden D 2
87 Kirchenlaibach B 3
87 Kirchenlamitz A 3
87 Kirchenthumbach B 3
73 Kirchhain C 2
86 Kirchheim, Baden-Württemberg, D† C 1
86 Kirchheim, Bayern, D† C 2
73 Kirchheim, Bayern, D† D 3
73 Kirchheim, Hessen, D† C 3
72 Kirchhundem B 2
66 Kirchlinteln C 2
101 Kirchschlag B 4
87 Kirchseeon C 3
87 Kirchweidach C 4
66 Kirchweyhe C 1
85 Kirchzarten C 4
73 Kirchzell D 3
53 Kircubbin B 6
156 Kiria A 4
159 Kiriáki A 3
56 Kirk Michael B 2
50 Kirkbean C 4
56 Kirkbride B 3
56 Kirkby C 4
56 Kirkby Lonsdale B 4
58 Kirkby Moorside A 3
56 Kirkby Stephen B 4
51 Kirkcaldy A 4
51 Kirkcambeck B 5
50 Kirkcolm C 2
50 Kirkconnel B 4
50 Kirkcowan C 3
50 Kirkcudbright C 3
34 Kirkehamn C 2
32 Kirkenær C 3
9 Kirkenes C 10
56 Kirkham C 4
50 Kirkintilloch B 3
27 Kirkkonummi C 7
160 Kirklareli E 5
51 Kirkliston B 4
49 Kirkmichael E 5
50 Kirkoswald B 3
51 Kirkstile B 5
49 Kirkton of Glenisla E 5
51 Kirkton of Largo A 5
49 Kirktown of Auchterless D 6
49 Kirkwall C 6
71 Kirn C 6
49 Kirriemuir E 6
59 Kirton C 3
58 Kirton in Lindsey B 3
73 Kirtorf C 3
7 Kiruna D 6
43 Kisa B 5
116 Kisać A 3
101 Kisbárapáti C 5
101 Kisber B 6
151 Kiseljak B 4
91 Kisgyor D 3
160 Kishinev B 6
78 Kisielice B 2
78 Kisielnica B 5
27 Kisko C 6
101 Kiskomarom C 5
103 Kisköre A 4
102 Kiskörös B 3
102 Kiskundörozsma B 4
102 Kiskunfélegyháza B 3
102 Kiskunhalas B 3
102 Kiskunlacháza A 3
102 Kiskunmajsa B 3
101 Kisláng C 6
103 Kismarja A 5
91 Kišovce C 3
36 Kissleberg C 3
97 Kißlegg A 5
157 Kissós C 3
73 Kist D 3
150 Kistanje B 1
102 Kistarcsa A 3
102 Kistelek B 3
91 Kisterenye D 2
8 Kistrand B 5
103 Kisújszállás A 4
69 Kiszewa Stara B 6
77 Kiszkowo A 6
103 Kiszombor B 4
29 Kitee A 8
159 Kíthnos B 5
22 Kitinoja C 4
17 Kitka A 7
10 Kitkiöjärvi B 3
156 Kitros B 2
67 Kittendorf B 5
10 Kittilä B 4
101 Kittsee A 5
27 Kitula C 6
98 Kitzbühel B 3
73 Kitzingen D 4
26 Kiukainen B 5
23 Kiuruvesi B 8
17 Kivesjärvi C 6
23 Kivijärvi B 7
47 Kivik B 5
25 Kivilahti C 7
154 Kivotós B 3
78 Kiwity A 3
6 Kjækan B 8
4 Kjeldebotn B 5
44 Kjellerup A 2

5 Kjerringøy C 3
18 Kjerringvåg B 4
18 Kjerstad C 2
9 Kjøllefjord B 7
30 Kjølsdal B 2
35 Kjopmannskjær B 6
4 Kjøpsvik B 5
5 Kjorvihytta D 4
89 Kl'ačno C 6
116 Kladanj B 2
67 Kläden C 4
42 Klädesholmen B 1
152 Kladnica A 2
150 Kladnice B 2
88 Kladno A 2
87 Kladorf B 4
117 Kladovo B 6
87 Kladruby B 4
19 Klæbu B 6
71 Klafeld B 6
100 Klagenfurt C 2
46 Klagstorp B 4
75 Klaistow A 4
153 Klajić B 3
28 Klamila C 5
114 Klana B 2
36 Klässbol B 4
75 Klášterec n. Ohří C 5
91 Kláštor D 1
87 Klatovy B 5
27 Klaukkala C 7
100 Klaus a. d. Pyhrnbahn B 2
99 Klausen C 2
100 Klausenleopoldsdorf A 3
43 Klavreström B 5
65 Klazienaveen B 5
77 Klecko A 6
77 Kleczew A 7
67 Klein Plasten B 5
100 Klein St. Paul C 2
74 Kleinpaschleben B 3
100 Kleinzell B 3
18 Kleive C 3
40 Klejrup C 3
117 Klek A 4
47 Klemensker B 5
15 Klemensnäs D 5
69 Klempicz C 4
87 Klenci pod Cerchovem B 4
152 Klenjë, AL C 2
116 Klenje, YU B 3
91 Klenovec D 2
115 Klenovnik A 4
34 Kleppe C 1
68 Kleptow B 2
78 Kleszewo C 4
75 Klettwitz B 5
64 Kleve C 4
78 Klewki B 3
117 Kličevac B 5
100 Kliening C 2
67 Klietz C 5
90 Klikuszowa C 2
155 Klimatiá C 2
89 Klimkovice B 6
13 Klimpfjäll B 6
152 Klina B 2
115 Klinca Selo B 3
12 Klinga C 3
101 Klingenbach B 4
73 Klingenberg D 3
87 Klingenbrunn C 5
85 Klingenmünster A 5
75 Klingenthal C 4
20 Klinken C 1
39 Klintehamn C 5
44 Kliplev C 2
46 Klippan A 4
150 Klis B 2
153 Klisura,BG B 5
153 Klisura,YU B 4
40 Klitmøller B 2
32 Klitten B 5
44 Klixbüll C 1
102 Kljajićevo C 3
150 Kljake B 2
115 Ključ C 4
89 Klobouky B 4
90 Klobuck B 1
21 Klockestrand C 6
79 Klodawa, Poznań, PL C 1
68 Klodawa, Zielona Góra, PL C 3
89 Klodzko A 4
36 Kløfta A 3
117 Klokočevac B 6
89 Klokočov B 6
90 Klomnice B 2
70 Kloosterzande A 3
152 Klos C 2
115 Klostar B 5
115 Kloštar Ivanić B 4
67 Kloster A 6
67 Klosterfelde C 6
97 Klösterle A 6
74 Klostermansfeld B 3
101 Klosterneuburg A 4
97 Klosters B 5
97 Kloten A 4
67 Klötze C 4
20 Klövsjö C 3
77 Kluczbork C 7
69 Kluczewo, Koszalin, PL B 4
68 Kluczewo, Szczecin, PL B 3
64 Klundert C 2
71 Klüppelberg A 6
67 Klütz B 4
79 Klwów D 3
34 Knaben C 3
36 Knapstad B 3
46 Knåred A 4
58 Knaresborough A 2
62 Knebworth B 3
115 Kneginec A 4
66 Knesebeck C 3
70 Knesselare A 2
114 Knezak B 2
102 Knezevi-Vinogradi C 2
102 Kneževo C 2
117 Knić C 4
154 Knídhi B 3
57 Knighton D 3
150 Knin A 2
47 Knislinge A 5
100 Knittelfeld B 2
38 Knivsta C 4
117 Knjaževac C 6
56 Knocksharry B 2
70 Knokke A 2
59 Knowle C 2
89 Knurów A 6
38 Knutby C 5
57 Knutsford C 4
114 Kobarid A 1
45 København B 5
100 Kobenz B 2
101 Kobersdorf B 4
90 Kobiernice C 2
77 Kobierzyce C 5
90 Kobiór B 1
117 Kobisnica B 6
96 Koblenz,CH A 4
71 Koblenz,D† B 6
68 Kobylanka B 2
89 Kobylí C 4
77 Kobylin B 6
79 Kobylka C 4
79 Kobylniki C 3
153 Kočane A 3
153 Kočani C 4
116 Koceljevo B 3
151 Kočerin B 3
114 Kočevje B 2
98 Kochel B 2
153 Kocherinovo B 5
77 Kochlowy B 6
101 Kocs B 6
102 Kocsér B 3
101 Kocsola C 6
69 Koczala B 5
35 Kodal B 6
75 Kodersdorf B 6
22 Kodesjärvi C 4
26 Kodisjoki B 4
79 Kodrab D 2
70 Koekelare A 1
71 Koerich C 4
70 Koersel A 4
100 Köflach B 3
45 Køge B 5
100 Koglhof B 3
87 Kohlberg B 4
71 Kohlscheid B 3
27 Koijärvi C 6
159 Koilás B 4
156 Koímisis A 3
42 Köinge B 2
16 Koivu Ä 4
89 Kojetín B 5
102 Kóka A 3
26 Kökar D 3
91 Kokava D 2
8 Kokelv B 4
27 Kokemäki B 5
159 Kókkinon A 4
17 Kokkokylä B 5
23 Kokkola B 5
89 Kokory B 5
91 Kokošovce D 4
69 Kokoszki A 6
63 Koksijde A 4
36 Köla B 4
90 Kolaczyce C 4
10 Kolari B 3
160 Kolarovgrad D 5
101 Kolárovo B 5
30 Kolås A 3
20 Kolåsen B 1
152 Kolašin B 1
38 Kolbäck C 3
68 Kolbacz B 2
79 Kolbiel C 4
98 Kolbnitz C 4
35 Kolbotn B 6
31 Kolbu C 7
90 Kolbuszowa B 4
44 Kolby Kås B 3
69 Kolczyglowy A 5
44 Kolding B 2
15 Koler C 4
102 Kölesd B 2
23 Kolho C 6
88 Kolín A 3
44 Kolind A 3
156 Kolindrós B 2
87 Kolinec B 5
158 Koliri B 2
44 Kølkær A 2
75 Kolkwitz B 6
74 Kölleda B 3
100 Kollerschlag A 1
158 Kollinai B 3
64 Kollum A 4
71 Köln B 5
78 Kolno, Bialystok, PL B 4
78 Kolno, Olsztyn, PL B 3
79 Kolo C 1
68 Kolobrzeg A 3
75 Kolochau B 5
87 Koloveč B 5
22 Kolppi B 4
67 Kolrep B 5
21 Kölsjön C 5
77 Kolsko B 4
38 Kolsva C 2
101 Kolta A 6
79 Kolumna D 2
79 Koluszki D 2
12 Kolvereid C 3
8 Kolvik B 5
44 Kølvrå A 2
103 Komádi A 5
8 Komagfjord B 3
9 Komagvær B 10
154 Kómanos B 3
101 Komárno B 6
101 Komárom B 6
101 Komárváros C 5
157 Kombotádhes D 2
155 Kombóti C 3
151 Komin B 3
150 Komiža B 2
91 Komjáti D 3
101 Komjatice A 6
116 Komletinci A 2
102 Komló, Baranya, H B 2
103 Kömlö, Heves, H A 4
157 Kómma D 2
155 Komméno C 3
71 Kommern B 5
154 Komninón B 3
101 Komoča B 6
152 Komoran B 2
77 Komorniki A 5
160 Komotini E 4
117 Konak A 4
78 Konarzyce B 5
69 Konarzyny B 5
153 Končulj B 3
103 Kondoros B 4
45 Køng B 4
43 Konga C 5
10 Köngäs B 4
23 Konginkangas C 7
35 Kongsberg B 5
9 Kongsfjord B 9
35 Kongshamn C 4
12 Kongsmoen C 4
4 Kongsvik B 5
36 Kongsvinger A 3
31 Kongsvoll A 6
89 Konice B 4
79 Konie D 3
90 Koniecpol B 2
67 Königs Wusterhausen C 6
73 Königsberg C 4
86 Königsbronn C 2
86 Königsbrunn C 2
98 Königsdorf B 2
74 Königsee C 3
73 Königshofen, Baden-Württemberg, D† D 3
73 Königshofen, Bayern, D† C 4
72 Königslutter A 4
98 Konigssee B 3
73 Königstein,D† C 2
75 Königstein,D* C 6
101 Königstetten A 4
75 Königswartha B 6
100 Königswiesen A 2
71 Königswinter B 6
77 Konin A 7
75 Königsbrück B 5
155 Konispol C 2
154 Kónitsa B 2
96 Köniz B 3
151 Konjic B 3
74 Könnern B 3
35 Konnerud B 6
23 Konnevesi C 8
22 Könni C 4
155 Konopína D 3
153 Konopište C 4
78 Konopki C 3
74 Konradsreuth C 3
79 Końskie D 3
34 Konsmo C 3
79 Konstantynów D 2
85 Konstanz C 6
5 Konsvik D 2
70 Kontich A 3
25 Kontiolahti C 6
17 Kontiomäki C 7
158 Kontovázaina B 2
101 Kóny B 5
103 Konyár A 5
153 Konyavo B 4
71 Konz C 5
64 Koog a/d Zaan B 2
26 Köörtilä B 4
158 Kopanáki B 2
155 Kopáni C 2
30 Koparnes A 2
89 Kopčany C 5
114 Koper B 1
67 Köpernitz B 5
34 Kopervik B 1
101 Kópháza B 4
77 Kopice C 6
88 Kopidlno A 3
38 Köping C 2
47 Köpinge B 5
47 Köpingebro B 4
43 Köpingsvik C 6
152 Koplik B 1
21 Köpmanholmen B 7
32 Koppang B 2
6 Koppangen B 6
4 Kopparåsen B 7
37 Kopparberg B 7
15 Koppamäs C 5
11 Koppelo A 7
19 Kopperå B 7
73 Köppern C 2
36 Koppom B 4
14 Kopponis B 4
115 Koprivnica, Hrvatska, YU A 4
117 Koprivnica, Srbija, YU B 6
89 Kopřivnice B 6
16 Kopsa C 3
71 Kopstal C 5
72 Korbach B 2
72 Körbeck B 2
70 Korbeck-Lo B 3
153 Korbevac B 4
154 Korçë B 2
150 Korčula C 3
76 Korczycόw A 3
116 Korenita B 3
153 Koretin B 3
89 Korfantów A 5
12 Korgen A 5
28 Koria C 4
156 Korinos B 2
44 Korinth B 3
159 Kórinthos B 3
159 Korisía B 5
154 Korissós B 3
151 Korita C 3
67 Köritz C 5
25 Korkea A 7
27 Korkeakoski B 7
101 Körmend B 4
69 Korne A 5
74 Körner B 2
101 Korneuburg A 4
77 Kórnik A 6
36 Kornsjø C 3
18 Kornstad C 3
85 Kornwestheim B 6
101 Környe B 6
158 Koróni C 2
69 Koronowo B 5
159 Koropí B 4
103 Körösladány B 5
103 Körösszegapáti A 5
103 Köröstarcsa B 5
25 Korpijärvi B 4
16 Korpika B 2
16 Korpikylä A 2
27 Korpilahti A 8
10 Korpilombolo C 3
26 Korpo C 4
26 Korppoo C 4
18 Kors C 3
42 Korsberga A 4
22 Korsholm B 3
33 Korskrogen B 6
38 Korsnäs,S B 2
22 Korsnäs,SF C 3
4 Korsnes B 5
27 Korso C 8
45 Korsør B 4
14 Korsträsk C 4
70 Kortemark A 2
23 Kortesjärvi B 5
152 Korthpulë C 1
78 Kortowo B 3
70 Kortrijk B 2
11 Korvala C 6
89 Koryčany B 5
91 Korytnica-Kúpele D 2
78 Korzeniste B 5
77 Korzeńsko B 5
69 Korzybie A 4
89 Koš C 6
151 Kosanica B 5
86 Kösching C 3
77 Kościan A 5
79 Kościelec, PL C 1
69 Kościerzyna A 5
154 Kosel A 2
68 Koserow A 1
88 Košetice B 3
91 Košice D 4
116 Kosjeric C 3
102 Koška C 2
22 Koskenkorva C 4
28 Koskenkyla C 3
28 Koskenniska B 4
27 Koskenpää A 8
27 Koski, Hämeen, SF B 8
27 Koski, Turun Ja Porin, SF C 6
22 Koskue C 4
14 Koskullskulle A 4
69 Köslin A 4
88 Kosmonosy A 2
22 Kosola B 4
152 Kosovska Mitrovica B 2
79 Kosów C 5
75 Koßdorf B 5
43 Kosta C 5
115 Kostajnica B 4
116 Kostajnik B 3
155 Kostakioí C 2
88 Kostalec n. Orlicé A 4
88 Kost'álov A 3
151 Kostanica C 5
114 Kostanjevica B 3
88 Kostelec n. Cernymi Lesy A 2
89 Kostelec na. Hané B 5
88 Kostice A 1
153 Kostinbrod B 5
69 Kostkowo A 6
116 Kostojeviči B 3
117 Kostolac B 5
77 Kostów B 7
77 Kostrzyn, Poznań, PL A 6
76 Kostrzyn, Zielona Góra, PL A 3
90 Kostuchna B 1
153 Kosturino C 4
25 Kosula C 5
69 Koszalin A 4
90 Koszarewa C 2
90 Koszecin B 1
101 Koszeg B 4
78 Koszwaly A 1
90 Koszyce B 3
91 Kótaj D 4
17 Kotajärvi C 9
11 Kotala, Lapin, SF B 9
23 Kotala, Vaasan, SF C 6
103 Kötegyán B 5
103 Kötelek A 4

153 Kotenovtsi A 5
74 Köthen B 3
28 Kotka C 4
69 Kotomierz B 6
151 Kotor C 4
115 Kotor Varoš C 5
101 Kotoriba C 4
116 Kotorsko B 2
116 Kotraža C 4
158 Kótronas C 3
99 Kötschach C 3
157 Kotserí C 2
21 Kottsjön B 5
87 Kötzting B 4
64 Koudum B 3
156 Koufós C 3
156 Koundouriótissa B 2
88 Kouřim A 2
87 Kout na Sumave B 5
159 Koutsopódhi B 3
28 Kouvola C 4
117 Kovačevac B 4
153 Kovachevtsi B 5
117 Kovačica A 4
101 Kovagoörs C 5
101 Kovarce A 6
11 Kovdor B 10
116 Kovilj A 4
117 Kovin B 4
21 Kovland C 6
152 Kovren A 1
79 Kowal C 2
78 Kowale Oleckie A 5
78 Kowalewo Pom. B 1
77 Kowary C 4
79 Kowiesy C 5
23 Köyhäjoki B 5
23 Koyhänpera B 7
27 Köyliö B 5
150 Kozanci B 2
154 Kozáni B 3
115 Kozarac C 4
91 Kozárd E 2
150 Kozica B 3
90 Kozieglowy B 2
79 Kozienice D 4
114 Kozina B 1
114 Kozje A 3
89 Kozle A 6
116 Kozluk B 3
77 Kozmin B 6
77 Koźminek B 7
87 Kozolupy B 5
77 Kożuchów B 4
116 Kožuhe B 2
32 Krackelbacken B 5
68 Krackow B 2
69 Krag A 4
45 Kragenæs C 4
35 Kragerø C 5
117 Kragujevac B 4
87 Kraiburg C 4
117 Krajišnik A 4
75 Krajková C 4
153 Krajkovac A 3
91 Krajná Pol'ana C 4
89 Krajné C 5
68 Krajnik Dolny B 2
4 Kråkberget B 3
4 Kråkmoen C 4
90 Kraków B 2
67 Krakow a. See B 5
89 Králiky A 4
114 Kraljevica B 2
117 Kraljevo C 4
101 Král'ov Brod A 5
91 Kral'ovany C 2
87 Kralovice B 5
88 Kralupy n. Vltavou A 2
21 Kramfors C 6
9 Krampenes B 10
98 Kramsach B 2
64 Kranenburg C 4
21 Krångede B 5
154 Kraniá, Grevená, GR C 3
156 Kraniá, Lárisa, GR C 1
155 Kraniá, Préveza, GR C 2
74 Kranichfeld C 3
159 Kranidhion B 4
114 Kranj A 2
114 Kranjska Gora A 1
150 Krapanj B 1
115 Krapina A 3
89 Krapkowice A 5
88 Kraselov B 1
114 Krašič B 3
78 Kraskowo A 4
75 Kraslice C 4
91 Krasna D 4
88 Krásná Hora n. Vltavou B 2
75 Krasná Lipa C 6
78 Krasne C 3
90 Krásno,CS C 1
114 Krasno,YU C 3
91 Krásnohorské-Podhradie D 3
78 Krasnosielc B 4
90 Krasocin B 3
153 Kratova B 4
100 Kraubath a. d. Mur B 2
75 Krausnick A 5
73 Krautheim D 3
88 Kravaře, Severočesky, CS A 2
89 Kravaře, Severomoravsky, CS B 5
117 Kravlje C 5
116 Krčedin A 4
71 Krefeld A 5
72 Kreiensen B 3
88 Křelovice B 3
66 Krembz B 4
154 Kremenica B 3
153 Kremikovtsi B 5
67 Kremmen C 6
116 Kremna C 3
91 Kremnica D 1
66 Krempe B 2
90 Krempna C 4
100 Krems a. d. Donau A 3
98 Kremsbrücke C 4
100 Kremsmünster A 2
88 Křemže C 2
79 Krepa D 1
117 Krepoljin B 5
69 Krepsko B 4
151 Kreševo B 4
153 Kresna C 5
97 Kreßbronn A 5
158 Kréstaina B 2
98 Kreuth B 2
71 Kreuzau B 5
100 Kreuzen A 2
97 Kreuzlingen A 5
71 Kreuztal B 6
67 Krewelin C 6
156 Kría Vrísi B 2
73 Kriegsfeld D 1
96 Kriens A 4
98 Krimml B 3
64 Krimpen a/d Ijssel C 2
97 Krimratshofen A 6
88 Křinec A 3
156 Krinidhes A 4
155 Krionérion D 3
43 Kristdala B 6
34 Kristiansand C 4
47 Kristianstad A 5
18 Kristiansund B 3
22 Kristiinankaupunki C 3
15 Kristineberg C 2
37 Kristinehamn B 6
22 Kristinestad C 3
156 Kristón B 2
150 Krito B 2
155 Kritsíni C 3
153 Kriva Feja B 4
153 Kriva Palanka B 4
91 Kriváň D 2
117 Krivi Vir C 5
153 Krivodol A 5
154 Krivogaštani A 3
153 Krivolak C 4
115 Križ B 4
88 Křižanov B 4
115 Križevci A 4
114 Krk B 2
153 Krklja B 4
117 Krnjača B 4
114 Krnjak B 3
117 Krnjevo B 5
89 Krnov A 5
77 Krobia B 5
35 Kroderen A 5
35 Krødsherad A 5
159 Krokeai C 3
39 Krokek D 3
13 Kroken B 6
31 Krøkhaug A 7
157 Krokíllion D 2
20 Krokom B 3
69 Krokowa A 6
35 Krokstadelva B 5
19 Krokstadøra B 5
36 Kroksund B 3
89 Kroměříž B 5
64 Krommenie B 2
91 Krompachy D 3
74 Kronach C 3
22 Kronoby B 5
66 Kronshagen A 3
29 Kronshtadt D 7
67 Kröpelin A 4
66 Kropp A 2
74 Kroppenstedt B 3
75 Kropstädt B 4
90 Krościenko C 3
79 Krośniewice C 2
90 Krosno C 4
76 Krosno Odrzańskie A 4
75 Krostitz B 4
77 Krotoszyn B 6
88 Krouna B 4
154 Kroustalopiví B 3
89 Krowiarki A 6
153 Krševica B 3
102 Krstur B 4
89 Křtiny B 4
71 Kruft B 6
70 Kruishoutem B 2
152 Krujë C 1
78 Kruklanki A 4
101 Krumbach,A B 4
86 Krumbach,D† C 2
98 Krun B 2
88 Krupá,CS A 1
115 Krupa,YU C 5
153 Krupac A 4
116 Krupanj B 3
91 Krupina D 2
153 Krupište C 4
88 Krupka A 1
153 Krupnik C 5
44 Kruså C 2
115 Kruščica, Bosna i Hercegovina, YU C 5
114 Kruščica, Hrvatska, YU C 3
117 Kruševac C 5
152 Krusevo C 3
69 Kruszwica C 6
79 Kruszyn, PL C 1
13 Krutå fellstue B 6
151 Krute C 5
22 Kruunupyy B 5
154 Kryevidh A 1
38 Krylbo B 3
90 Krynica C 3
78 Krynica Morska A 2
89 Krzanowice A 6
68 Krzecin B 3
90 Krzeczów C 2
77 Krzelów B 5
90 Krzepice B 1
77 Krzepielów B 5
90 Krzeszowice B 2
76 Krzeszyce A 4
78 Krzynowloga Mala B 3
76 Krzystkowice B 4
77 Krzywin B 5
69 Krzyż C 4
90 Ksiaz Wielkopolski, Krakow, PL B 3
77 Ksiaz Wielkopolski, Poznan, PL A 6
78 Ksiezy Lasek B 4
21 Kubbe B 7
97 Kublis B 5
154 Kuç B 1
153 Kučevište B 3
117 Kučevo B 5
77 Kuchary B 6
98 Kuchl B 4
79 Kucice C 3
79 Kuciny D 2
150 Kučišće C 3
152 Kućište B 2
102 Kucura C 3
78 Kuczbork B 3
89 Kudlov B 5
89 Kudowa Zdrój A 4
78 Kudypy B 3
98 Kufstein B 3
43 Kuggeboda C 5
86 Kühbach C 3
27 Kuhmalahti B 7
25 Kuhmo A 6
27 Kuhmoinen B 8
66 Kuhstedt B 1
64 Kuinre B 3
16 Kuivakangas A 2
16 Kuivaniemi B 4
28 Kuivanto C 4
22 Kuivasjärvi C 4
152 Kukës B 2
23 Kukko C 6
16 Kukkola B 3
78 Kuklin B 3
150 Kukljica A 1
116 Kukujevci A 3
154 Kukurecani A 3
117 Kula, BG C 6
117 Kula, Srbija, YU B 5
102 Kula, Vojvodina, YU C 3
153 Kulata C 5
115 Kulen Vakuf C 4
116 Kulina B 2
27 Kulju B 6
26 Kullaa B 5
42 Kulltorp B 3
87 Kulmain B 3
86 Kulmbach A 3
102 Kumane C 4
153 Kumanovo B 3
39 Kumla, Örebro, S C 2
38 Kumla, Västmanlands, S C 3
29 Kumpuranta B 7
26 Kumtinge C 3
103 Kunagota B 5
102 Kunbaja B 3
98 Kundl B 2
42 Kungälv B 1
38 Kungs-Husby C 4
38 Kungsåra C 3
42 Kungsäter B 2
42 Kungsbacka B 2
38 Kungsgården B 3
36 Kungshamn C 3
39 Kungsör C 3
103 Kunhegyes A 4
76 Kunice-Zarskie B 4
89 Kunín B 5
116 Kuninovo B 4
103 Kunmadaras A 4
89 Kunovice B 5
77 Kunowo B 6
39 Kunsangen C 4
89 Kunštát B 4
102 Kunszentmárton B 4
102 Kunszentmiklós A 3
88 Kunžak B 3
73 Künzelsau D 3
27 Kuohijoki B 7
23 Kuoho C 7
24 Kuopio C 4
25 Kuorevaara C 6
27 Kuorevesi B 7
23 Kuortane C 5
28 Kuortti B 4
11 Kuosku B 8
117 Kupci C 5
86 Kupferzell B 1
114 Kupjak B 2
85 Kuppenheim B 5
150 Kupres B 3
74 Küps C 3
152 Kurbnesh C 2
101 Kurd C 6
17 Kurenalus B 5
22 Kurikka C 4
153 Kurilo B 5
89 Kuřim B 4
78 Kurki B 3
24 Kurolanlahti B 4
79 Kurów D 5
79 Kurowice D 2
7 Kurravaara D 6
11 Kursu C 8
152 Kuršumlija A 3
10 Kurtakko B 4
71 Kürten A 6
17 Kurtti B 7
27 Kuru B 6
117 Kusadak B 4
71 Kusel C 6
66 Kusey C 4
15 Kusfors D 3
117 Kusići B 5
15 Kusmark D 4
97 Küsnacht A 4
152 Kušnin B 2
97 Küssnacht A 4
26 Kustavi C 4
24 Kutemajärvi C 3
66 Kutenholz B 2
115 Kutina B 4
115 Kutjevo B 5
88 Kutná Hora B 3
79 Kutnc C 2
10 Kuttainen A 2
96 Küttigen A 4
89 Kúty C 5
17 Kuusamo B 8
28 Kuusankoski C 4
25 Kuusjärvi C 5
27 Kuusjoki C 6
78 Kuzie B 4
91 Kuzmice D 4
116 Kuzmin A 3
89 Kuźnia Raciborska A 6
69 Kuznica Czarnkowska C 4
69 Kuźnica Żelichowska C 4
6 Kvænangen B 7
6 Kvænangsbotn B 8
44 Kværndrup B 3
4 Kvalnes B 2
6 Kvaløysletta B 4
8 Kvalsund B 3
18 Kvalsvik C 1
18 Kvalvåg B 3
19 Kvam, Nord Trøndelag, N A 7
31 Kvam, Oppland, N B 6
30 Kvamsøy B 3
30 Kvanndal C 3
18 Kvanne C 4
42 Kvänum A 3
33 Kvarnberg B 5
34 Kvarstein C 3
34 Kvås C 3
89 Kvasice B 5
22 Kvelax Koivulahti B 3
35 Kvelde B 5
12 Kvelia C 5
18 Kvenvær B 4
18 Kvernes B 3
42 Kvibille C 2
39 Kvicksund C 3
46 Kvidinge A 4
5 Kvikkjokk D 6
19 Kvikne, Hedmark, N C 6
31 Kvikne, Oppland, N B 6
87 Kvilda B 5
36 Kville C 3
43 Kvillsfors B 5
34 Kvinesdal C 2
34 Kvinlog C 2
40 Kvissel B 4
21 Kvissleby C 6
18 Kvisvik B 3
35 Kviteseid B 4
18 Kvitnes, More og Romsdal, N B 3
4 Kvitnes, Nordland, N B 4
69 Kwakowo A 5
78 Kwidzyn B 1
78 Kwietniewo B 2
77 Kwilcz A 5
88 Kyie A 2
89 Kyjov B 5
20 Kykrås B 3
25 Kylänlahti B 6
22 Kylänpää C 4
48 Kyle of Lochalsh D 3
48 Kyleakin D 3
48 Kylerhea D 3
48 Kylestrome C 3
71 Kyllburg B 5
27 Kylmäkoski B 6
16 Kylmälä C 5
28 Kymi C 4
23 Kymönkoski B 7
87 Kynšperk-nad Ohří A 4
67 Kyritz C 5
42 Kyrkesund A 1
37 Kyrkheden A 5
43 Kyrkhult C 4
30 Kyrkjebø B 2
18 Kyrksæterøra B 5
27 Kyrkslätt C 7
27 Kyrö C 5
27 Kyröskoski B 6
91 Kysuké Nové Mesto C 1
27 Kytäjä C 7
153 Kyustendil B 4
23 Kyyjärvi B 6

L

126 La Adrada B 1
130 La Alameda C 3
125 La Alberca C 3
131 La Alberca de Záncara B 4
129 La Albuera C 4
120 La Aldea de Portillo de Busto B 3
135 La Algaba B 4
125 La Aliseda de Tormes C 4
127 La Almarcha C 3
122 La Almolda C 2
127 La Almunia de Doña Godina A 4
122 La Ametlia de Mar D 3
122 La Ampolla D 3
119 La Arena A 4
135 La Aulaga B 4
108 La Balme-de-S. B 3
119 La Bañeza B 5
92 La Barre-de-Monts C 1
82 La Barre-en-Ouche C 2

87	Lalling	C	5
31	Lalm	B	6
87	Lam	B	5
143	Lama dei Peligni	B	5
112	Lama Mocogno	B	2
105	Lamagistère	C	3
84	Lamarche	B	2
95	Lamarche-sur-Saône	B	5
128	Lamarosa	B	2
104	Lamarque	B	2
124	Lamas	C	1
124	Lamas de Mouro	A	1
108	Lamastre	C	1
98	Lambach	A	4
80	Lamballe	B	4
62	Lamberhurst	B	4
109	Lambesc	D	2
158	Lámbia	B	2
62	Lambourn	B	2
124	Lamego	B	2
157	Lamía	D	2
50	Lamlash	B	2
43	Lammhult	B	4
27	Lammi	B	8
104	Lamothe-Cassel	C	4
93	Lamotte-Beuvron	B	6
80	Lampaul	B	1
24	Lamperila	C	4
73	Lampertheim	D	2
60	Lampeter	A	2
59	Lamport	C	3
98	Lamprechtshausen	B	3
75	Lamsfeld	B	6
72	Lamspringe	B	4
66	Lamstedt	B	2
108	Lamure-sur-A.	A	1
99	Lana	C	2
122	Lanaja	C	2
141	Lanamatrona	C	2
106	Lanarce	C	4
50	Lanark	B	4
56	Lancaster	B	4
51	Lanchester	C	6
144	Lanciano	A	3
81	Lancieux	B	4
87	Landau, Bayern, D†	C	4
72	Landau, Hessen, D†	B	3
85	Landau, Rheinland Pfalz, D†	A	5
97	Landeck	A	6
70	Landen	B	4
80	Landerneau	B	2
42	Landeryd	B	3
66	Landesbergen	C	2
132	Landete	B	1
80	Landévant	C	3
80	Landévennec	B	2
80	Landivisau	B	2
81	Landivy	B	5
100	Landl, Steiermark, A	B	2
98	Landl, Tirol, A	B	3
20	Landön	B	3
106	Landos	C	3
83	Landouzy	B	6
97	Landquart	B	5
83	Landrecies	A	5
84	Landreville	B	1
110	Landriano	B	4
86	Landsberg, D†	C	2
74	Landsberg, D*	B	4
68	Landsberg, PL	C	3
43	Landsbro	B	4
71	Landscheid	C	5
87	Landshut	C	4
46	Landskrona	B	3
64	Landsmeer	B	2
85	Landstuhl	A	4
80	Landudec	B	2
42	Landvetter	B	2
55	Lanesborough	A	4
80	Lanester	C	3
120	Lanestosa	A	3
44	Langå, DK	A	2
20	Långå, S	C	2
126	Langa de Duero	A	2
156	Langadhás	B	3
158	Langádhia	B	3
156	Langadhikia	B	3
35	Langangen	B	5
42	Längared	A	2
42	Långås	C	2
43	Långasjö	C	5
88	Langau	C	3
50	Langbank	B	3
106	Langeac	B	3
93	Langeais	B	4
27	Längelmäki	B	7
74	Langeln	B	2
72	Langelsheim	B	4
73	Langen, Hessen, D†	D	2
66	Langen, Niedersachsen, D†	B	1
86	Langenau	C	2
72	Langenberg, Nordrhein Westfalen, D†	B	2
71	Langenberg, Nordrhein Westfalen, D†	A	6
86	Langenburg	B	1
66	Langendamm	C	2
74	Langeneichstädt	B	3
101	Langenenzersdorf	A	4
4	Langenes	A	4
98	Längenfeld, A	B	1
71	Langenfeld, D†	A	5
66	Langenhagen	C	2
44	Langenhorn	C	1
100	Langenlois	A	3
71	Langenlonsheim	C	6
75	Langennaudorf	B	5
86	Langenneufnach	C	2
100	Langenrohr	A	4
85	Langensteinbach	B	5
96	Langenthal	A	3
100	Langenwang	B	3
86	Langenzenn	B	2
65	Langeoog	A	5
44	Langeskov	B	3
35	Langesund	B	5
18	Langevåg	C	2
74	Langewiesen	C	2
6	Langfjord	A	8
32	Långflon	B	3
65	Langförden	B	6
67	Langhagen	B	5
42	Länghem	B	3
112	Langhirano	B	2
51	Langholm	B	5
98	Langkampfen	B	3
43	Langlot	C	6
96	Langnau	B	3
45	Langø	C	4
106	Langogne	C	3
104	Langon	C	2
61	Langport	B	4
87	Langquaid	C	4
95	Langres	B	5
13	Långsele, Västerbottens, S	C	7
21	Långsele, Västernorrlands, S	B	6
36	Långserud	B	4
36	Langset	A	3
38	Långshyttan	B	3
49	Langskall	B	6
14	Långsund	B	6
15	Langtrask, Norbotten, S	C	5
15	Långträsk, Norrbotten, S	C	4
80	Languidic	C	3
21	Långviksmon	B	7
66	Langwarden	B	1
66	Langwedel	C	2
86	Langweid	C	2
97	Langwies	B	5
124	Lanheses	B	1
80	Lanildut	B	2
136	Lanjarón	C	3
71	Lank-Latum	A	5
27	Länkipohja	B	7
71	Lanklaar	A	4
10	Lankojärvi	C	4
80	Lanmeur	B	3
42	Lanna	B	3
37	Lannabruk	B	6
38	Lännaholm	C	4
80	Lannéanou	B	3
105	Lannemezan	D	3
84	Lanneuville-sur-Meuse	A	2
23	Lannevesi	C	7
80	Lannilis	B	2
80	Lannion	B	3
104	Lanouaille	B	4
107	Lansargues	D	4
27	Länsi-Teisko	B	6
10	Lansjärv	C	2
89	Lanškroun	B	4
108	Lanslebourg	B	3
107	Lanta	D	1
120	Lantadilla	B	2
104	Lanton	C	1
141	Lanusei	C	3
143	Lanuvio	C	3
80	Lanvollon	B	4
102	Lánycsók	B	2
118	Lanza	A	2
125	Lanzahita	C	5
89	Lanzhof	C	4
110	Lanzo Torinese	B	2
83	Laon	B	5
82	Laons	C	3
94	Lapalisse	C	3
107	Lapanouse	C	3
107	Lapanouse-de-Cernon	C	3
90	Lapczyna Wola	B	2
105	Lapeyrade	C	2
94	Lapeyrouse	C	2
108	Lapeyrouse-Mornay	B	1
28	Lapinjärvi	C	4
24	Lapinlahti	B	4
152	Laplje Selo	B	3
105	Laplume	C	3
85	Lapoutroie	B	4
117	Lapovo	B	5
23	Lappajärvi	B	5
29	Lappeenranta	B	6
22	Lappfjärd	C	3
26	Lappi	B	4
27	Lappila	C	8
8	Lappoluobbal	C	3
16	Lappträsk, S	A	2
28	Lappträsk, SF	C	4
22	Lappväärtti	C	3
22	Lapua	C	5
143	L'Aquila	B	4
118	Laracha	A	2
55	Laragh	A	5
109	Laragne	C	2
50	Larbert	A	4
108	l'Arbresle	B	1
39	Lärbro	C	5
105	Larceveau	D	1
109	Larche, Basses Alpes, F	C	3
104	Larche, Corrèze, F	B	4
34	Lårdål	B	4
120	Laredo	A	3
64	Laren	B	3
106	Largentière	C	4
108	l'Argentière	C	3
50	Largs	B	3
157	Lárimna	D	3
118	Lariño, E	B	1
144	Larino, I	B	3
157	Lárisa	C	2
50	Larkhall	B	4
35	Larkollen	B	6
80	Larmor-Plage	C	3
53	Larne	B	6
48	Laroch	E	3
71	Larochette	C	5
118	Laroco	B	3
105	Laroque	C	3
107	Laroque d'Olmes	E	1
106	Laroquebrou	C	2
94	Larouche	B	3
121	Larraga	B	5
105	Larrau	D	2
105	Larrazet	D	4
105	Laruns	E	2
136	Larva	B	3
35	Larvik	B	6
134	Las Antillas	B	3
126	Las Cabezadas	A	2
135	Las Cabezas de S. Juan	C	5
136	Las Correderas	A	3
132	Las Cuevas de Cañart	A	2
130	Las Herencias	B	2
131	Las Labores	B	3
123	Las Masucas	C	4
131	Las Mesas	B	4
136	Las Navas	B	2
135	Las Navas de la Concepción	B	5
126	Las Navas del Marqués	B	1
137	Las Negras	C	4
135	Las Pajanosas	B	4
131	Las Pedroñeras	B	4
123	Las Planas	B	5
120	Las Quintanillas	B	3
126	Las Rozas, Madrid, E	B	2
120	Las Rozas, Santander, E	B	2
125	Las Uces	B	3
125	Las Veguillas	C	4
126	Las Ventas con Peña Aguilera	C	1
130	Las Ventas de S. Julian	A	1
122	Las Vilas de Turbó	B	3
132	Las Villas de Benicasim	A	3
28	Läsäkoski	B	4
121	Lasarté	A	4
78	Lasin	B	2
79	Lask	D	2
79	Laskarzew	D	4
58	Laskill	A	2
114	Laško	A	3
79	Lasocin	C	2
122	Laspaules	B	3
155	Láspi	D	3
122	Laspuña	B	3
67	Lassan	B	6
81	Lassay	B	6
101	Lassee	A	4
83	Lassigny	B	4
26	Lassila	B	5
51	Lasswade	B	4
158	Lasteika	B	2
112	Lastra a Signa	C	3
126	Lastras de Cuéllar	A	1
119	Lastres	A	5
39	Lästringe	D	4
65	Lastrup	B	5
151	Lastva	C	4
121	Latasa	B	5
142	Látera	B	2
146	Laterza	B	2
65	Lather	B	5
49	Latheron	C	5
146	Latiano	B	3
13	Latikberg	C	9
143	Latina	C	3
99	Latisana	D	4
91	Látky	D	2
146	Latrónico	B	2
106	Latronquière	C	2
99	Latsch	C	1
96	Latterbach	B	3
73	Laubach	C	2
106	Laubert	C	3
75	Laubusch	B	6
74	Laucha	B	3
75	Lauchhammer	B	5
73	Lauda	D	3
34	Laudal	C	3
51	Lauder	B	5
72	Lauenau	A	3
66	Lauenburg	B	3
86	Lauf	B	3
73	Laufach	C	3
96	Laufelfingen	A	3
96	Laufen, CH	A	3
85	Laufen, Baden-Württemberg, D†	B	5
87	Laufen, Bayern, D†	D	4
96	Laufenburg	A	4
85	Lauffen	A	6
60	Laugharne	B	2
86	Lauingen	C	2
137	Laujar	C	4
14	Lauker	C	3
23	Laukkala	B	8
6	Lauksletta	A	6
4	Laukvik	C	3
60	Launceston	C	2
70	Launois	C	3
27	Launonen	C	7
96	Laupen	B	3
86	Laupheim	C	1
4	Laupstad	B	3
147	Laureana di Borrello	D	2
49	Laurencekirk	E	6
53	Laurencetown, GB	B	5
54	Laurencetown, IRL	A	3
146	Laurenzana	B	1
146	Lauria	B	1
104	Laurière	A	4
50	Laurieston, Kirkcudbright, GB	C	3
50	Laurieston, Stirling, GB	B	4
145	Laurino	C	4
96	Lausanne	B	2
74	Lauscha	C	3
100	Laussa	B	2
106	Laussonne	C	4
75	Lauta	B	6
27	Lautela	C	6
72	Lautenthal	B	4
97	Lauterach	A	5
85	Lauterbach, Baden-Württemberg, D†	B	5
73	Lauterbach, Hessen, D†	C	3
96	Lauterbrunnen	B	3
71	Lauterecken	C	6
86	Lauterhofen	B	3
16	Lautiosaari	B	3
86	Lautrach	D	2
107	Lautrec	D	2
12	Lauvsnes	C	2
34	Lauvvik	C	2
70	Lauwe	B	2
105	Lauzerte	C	4
104	Lauzun	C	3
111	Lavagna	C	4
84	Laval, Marne, F	A	1
81	Laval, Mayenne, F	B	6
100	Lavamund	C	2
4	Lavangen	B	6
160	Lavara	E	5
105	Lavardac	C	3
128	Lavaris	A	2
99	Lavarone	D	2
94	Lavau	B	2
107	Lavaur	D	1
107	Lavelanet	E	1
145	Lavello	B	4
66	Lavelsloh	C	1
59	Lavenham	C	4
110	Laveno	B	3
112	Lavezzola	B	3
27	Lavia	B	5
119	Laviana	A	5
145	Laviano	C	4
30	Lavik	B	2
106	Lavilledieu, Ardèche, F	C	4
105	Lavilledieu, Tarn et Garonne, F	C	4
99	Lavis	C	2
105	Lavit	D	3
157	Lávkos	C	3
95	Lavoncourt	B	5
5	Låvong	D	2
128	Lavos	A	2
128	Lavre	C	2
159	Lávrion	B	5
50	Lawers	A	3
78	Lawsk	B	5
76	Lawszowa	B	4
37	Laxå	C	6
13	Laxbäcken	C	8
56	Laxey	B	2
59	Laxfield	C	5
48	Laxford Brdige	C	3
20	Laxsjo	B	3
27	Läyliäinen	C	7
118	Laza	B	3
155	Lazaráta	D	2
116	Lazarevac	B	4
117	Lazarevo	A	4
99	Lazise	D	1
90	Laziska Graniczne	B	1
87	Lázně	A	4
88	Lázně Bělohrad	A	3
117	Laznica	B	5
56	Lazonby	B	4
90	Lazy	B	2
147	Lazzàro	E	1
107	Le Barcarès	E	3
104	Le Barp	C	2
106	Le Béage	C	4
109	Le Beausset	D	2
93	Le Blanc	C	5
106	Le Bleymard	C	3
123	Le Boulou	B	5
106	Le Bourg	C	1
108	Le Bourg-d'Oisans	B	3
108	Le Bourget-du-Lac	B	2
81	Le Bourgneuf-la-Forêt	B	6
107	le Bousquet	D	3
94	Le Breuil	C	3
82	Le Breuil-en-Auge	B	2
109	Le Brusquet	C	3
96	Le Bry	B	3
104	Le Bugue	C	3
109	Le Buis-les-Baronnies	C	2
105	Le Caloy	D	2
109	Le Cannet-des-Maures	D	3
107	Le Canourgue	B	3
83	le Cateau	A	5
107	Le Caylar	D	3
106	Le Cayrol	C	2
96	Le Châble	B	3
106	Le Chambon	B	4
106	Le Chambon-Feugerolles	B	4
104	Le Château	B	1
94	Le Châtelet	C	2
83	le Châtelet-en-Brie	C	4
109	Le Chêne	D	2
70	le Chesne	C	3
106	Le Cheylard	C	4
80	Le Conquet	B	2
95	Le Creusot	C	4
92	Le Croisic	B	1
63	le Crotoy	B	3
95	le Deschaux	C	5
108	le Desert	C	3
94	le Donjon	C	3
93	Le Dorat	C	5
80	Le Faou	B	2
80	Le Folgoët	B	2
105	Le Fossat	D	4
105	Le Fousseret	D	4
108	Le Freney	B	3
83	le Gault-la-Forêt	C	5
104	Le Gond	B	3

51 Lochgelly A 4
50 Lochgilphead A 2
50 Lochgoilhead A 3
48 Lochinver C 3
48 Lochlaggan Hotel E 4
51 Lochmaben B 4
48 Lochmaddy D 1
79 Lochów C 4
50 Lochranza B 2
50 Lochwinnoch B 3
117 Ločika C 5
101 Lockenhaus B 4
51 Lockerbie B 4
68 Löcknitz B 2
80 Locmaria C 3
80 Locmariaquer C 4
80 Locmine C 4
146 Locorotondo B 3
80 Locquirec B 3
147 Locri D 2
80 Locronan B 2
80 Loctudy C 2
126 Lodares de Osma A 3
46 Löddekopinge B 4
59 Loddon C 5
141 Lodè B 3
47 Löderup B 5
107 Lodève D 3
111 Lodi B 4
4 Lødingen B 4
121 Lodosa B 4
42 Lödöse A 2
90 Lodygowice C 2
79 Łódź D 2
126 Loeches B 2
30 Loen B 3
64 Loenen B 4
34 Løfallstrand A 2
98 Lofer B 3
96 Lofingen A 3
156 Lófos B 2
32 Lofsdalen A 4
43 Loftahammar B 6
30 Lofthus C 3
51 Loftus C 7
65 Loga, D† A 5
34 Loga, N C 2
114 Logatec B 2
21 Lögdeå B 8
57 Loggerheads D 4
111 Lograto B 5
121 Logroño B 4
130 Logrosan B 1
40 Løgstør C 3
44 Løgumkloster B 1
44 Lohals B 3
16 Lohijärvi A 3
29 Lohikoski B 6
10 Lohiniva B 5
27 Lohja C 7
72 Löhlbach B 2
75 Lohmen, Dresden, D* C 6
67 Lohmen, Schwerin, D* B 5
73 Löhnberg C 2
65 Löhne, Niedersachsen, D† B 6
65 Lohne, Nordrhein Westfalen, D† B 6
73 Lohr D 3
73 Lohra C 2
75 Lohsa B 6
23 Lohtaja A 5
112 Loiano B 3
27 Loimaa C 6
108 Loire B 1
141 Lóiri B 3
81 Loiron B 6
67 Loitz B 6
124 Loivos B 2
124 Loivos do Monte B 2
83 Loivre B 5
136 Loja B 2
27 Lojo C 7
39 Lojsta C 5
44 Løjt Kirkenby B 2
26 Lokalahti C 4
91 Lokca C 2
36 Løken B 3
70 Lokeren A 2
87 Loket A 4
11 Lokka B 7
40 Løkken B 3
19 Løkken Verk B 5
103 Lököháza B 5
117 Lokve A 5
73 Lollar C 2
100 Lölling C 2
160 Lom, BG D 3
88 Lom, Severočesky, CS A 1
91 Lom, Středoslovenský, CS D 2
31 Lom, N B 5
105 Lombez D 3
110 Lomello B 3
79 Lomianki C 3
46 Lomma B 4
75 Lommatzsch B 5
70 Lommel A 4
71 Lommerssum B 5
89 Lomnice B 4
88 Lomnice n. Lužnici B 2
88 Lomnice n. Popelkou A 3
21 Lomsjö A 5
78 Lomza B 5
43 Lönashult C 4
111 Lonato B 5
44 Lønbørg B 1
70 Londerzeel A 3
82 Londinières B 3
62 London B 3
53 Londonderry B 4
48 Londubh D 3
30 Lonevåg C 2
59 Long Bennington C 3
62 Long Crendon B 2
59 Long Eaton C 2
62 Long Hanborough B 2
59 Long Melford C 4
56 Long Preston B 4
59 Long Sutton C 4
158 Longá C 2
158 Longanikos B 3
99 Longare D 2
127 Longares A 4
99 Longarone C 3
113 Longastrino B 4
61 Longbridge Deverill B 4
84 Longchamp B 1
71 Longchamps B 4
95 Longchaumois C 5
95 Longeau B 5
95 Longecourt B 5
84 Longeville A 3
84 Longeville-en-Barrois B 2
55 Longford A 4
51 Longforgan A 4
51 Longhorsley B 6
51 Longhoughton B 6
149 Longi A 4
83 Longjumea C 4
70 Longlier C 4
82 Longny-au-Perche C 2
147 Longobucco C 2
104 Longre A 2
124 Longroiva C 2
49 Longside D 7
51 Longtown B 5
92 Longue B 3
83 Longueau B 4
84 Longuyon A 2
95 Longvic B 5
71 Longvilly B 4
84 Longwy A 2
99 Lonigo D 2
65 Löningen B 5
90 Loniów B 4
43 Lönneberga B 5
65 Lonneker B 4
95 Lons-le Saunier C 5
43 Lönsboda C 4
5 Lønsdal D 4
18 Lønset, More og Romsdal, N C 3
19 Lønset, Sør Trøndelag, N C 5
40 Lønstrup B 3
60 Looe C 2
64 Loon op Zand C 3
63 Loon-Plage A 4
100 Loosdorf A 3
114 Lopar C 2
116 Lopare B 2
154 Lopatica A 3
136 Lopera B 2
6 Loppa A 7
65 Loppersum, D† A 5
65 Loppersum, NL A 4
27 Loppi C 7
90 Lopuszno B 3
83 Lor B 6
31 Lora A 5
136 Lora de Estepa B 2
135 Lora del Rio B 5
127 Loranca del Campo B 3
20 Lorås B 4
133 Lorca D 1
71 Lorch B 6
36 Lørenfallet A 3
35 Lørenskog B 6
71 Lorentzweiler C 5
118 Lorenzana A 3
113 Loreo A 4
113 Loreto C 5
143 Loreto Aprutino B 5
108 Lorette B 1
109 Lorgues D 3
147 Lorica C 2
80 Lorient C 3
104 Lorignac B 2
91 Lorinci E 2
108 Loriol C 1
94 Lormes B 3
112 Loro Ciuffenna C 3
133 Lorqui C 1
85 Lörrach C 4
136 Lorreblascopedro B 3
94 Lorris B 2
65 Lorup B 5
79 Loś, PL D 3
33 Los, S B 6
133 Los Alcázares D 2
121 Los Arcos B 4
120 Los Ausines B 3
119 Los Barios de Luna B 5
135 Los Barrios C 5
135 Los Canos de Meca C 4
136 Los Carvajales B 2
137 Los Cerricos B 4
136 Los Corrales B 2
120 Los Corrales de Buelna A 2
133 Los Dolores D 2
132 Los Duques B 1
137 Los Gallardos B 5
131 Los Hinojosos B 4
132 Los Isidros B 1
129 Los Molinos, Badajóz, E C 4
126 Los Molinos, Madrid, E B 1
135 Los Morales B 5
126 Los Navalmorales C 1
126 Los Navalucillos C 1
133 Los Nietos D 2
118 Los Nogales B 3
135 Los Palacios y Villafranca B 5
118 Los Peares B 3
121 Los Rábanos C 4
125 Los Santos C 4
126 Los Santos de la Humosa B 2
129 Los Santos de Maimona C 4
120 Los Tojos A 2
136 Los Villares B 3
126 Los Yébenes C 2
125 Losacino B 3
129 Losar de la Vera A 5
100 Losenstein B 2
71 Losheim C 5
95 Losne B 5
44 Løsning B 2
85 Loßburg B 5
65 Losser B 5
49 Lossiemouth D 5
75 Lößnitz C 4
89 Loštice B 4
60 Lostwithiel C 2
43 Löt C 6
32 Løten C 2
93 Lothiers C 5
49 Lothmore C 5
39 Lotorp D 2
79 Lotowicz C 4
65 Lotte B 5
33 Lottefors B 7
43 Löttorp B 6
69 Lotyń B 4
141 Lotzorai C 3
80 Louargat B 3
106 Loubaresse C 3
80 Loudéac B 4
156 Loudhios B 2
93 Loudun B 4
82 Loué D 1
59 Loughborough C 2
53 Loughbrickland B 5
54 Loughrea A 3
95 Louhans C 5
52 Louisburgh C 2
158 Louká B 3
104 Loulay A 2
134 Loulé B 2
88 Louny A 1
105 Lourdes D 2
128 Loures C 1
105 Loures-Barousse D 3
128 Louriçal B 2
128 Lourinhã B 1
109 Lourmarin D 2
155 Loúron C 2
157 Lourtrá Aidhipsoú D 3
83 Loury D 4
128 Lousa, Coimbra, P A 2
128 Lousa, Lisboa, P C 1
118 Lousada, E B 3
124 Lousada, P B 1
158 Lousiká A 2
58 Louth B 3
159 Loutráki B 3
156 Loutrakion B 1
155 Loutrón D 3
157 Loutropiví C 2
156 Loutrós B 2
81 Louverne B 6
105 Louvie-Juzon D 2
82 Louviers B 3
81 Louvigné-du-Désert B 5
83 Louvres B 4
99 Lova D 3
15 Lövånger D 5
102 Lovasberény A 2
21 Lövåsen B 5
101 Lovászpatona B 5
20 Lövberga B 4
101 Lovčice A 5
16 Love A 4
160 Lovech D 4
70 Lovendegem A 2
37 Lovene C 5
71 Lövenich A 5
111 Lóvere B 5
47 Lövestad B 4
28 Loviisa C 4
91 Lovinobaña D 2
28 Lovisa C 4
114 Lovke B 2
101 Lövö B 4
88 Lovosice A 2
114 Lovran B 2
150 Lovrec B 2
103 Lovrin C 4
38 Lövstabruk B 4
12 Lovund A 4
67 Löwenberg C 6
85 Löwenstein A 6
59 Lowestoft C 5
79 Lowicz C 2
66 Loxstedt B 1
108 Lozanne B 1
116 Loznica B 3
101 Lozorno A 5
117 Lozovik B 5
126 Lozoya B 2
126 Lozoyuela B 2
99 Lozzo di Cadore C 3
23 Luakaa C 7
119 Luanco A 5
119 Luarca A 4
76 Lubań B 4
79 Lubanów D 2
74 Lübars A 4
69 Lubasz C 4
78 Lubawa B 2
77 Lubawka C 4
65 Lübbecke B 6
75 Lübben B 5
75 Lübbenau B 5
67 Lübbow C 4
48 Lubcroy D 4
68 Lubczyna B 2
66 Lübeck B 3
87 Lubenec A 5
104 Lubersac B 4
67 Lübesse B 4
127 Lubía A 3
119 Lubián B 4
68 Lubiatowo B 3
91 L'ubica C 3
69 Lubichowo B 6
78 Lubiel Nowy C 4
90 Lubień C 2
79 Lubień Kujawski C 2
79 Lubienia D 4
69 Lubieszewo B 3
77 Lubiń, Poznań, PL B 5
68 Lubin, Szczecin, PL B 2
77 Lubin, Wroclaw, PL B 5
76 Lubin, Zielona Góra, PL A 3
90 Lublin D 5
90 Lubliniec B 1
67 Lubmin A 6
117 Lubnica C 6
76 Lubniewice A 4
79 Lubochnia D 3
90 Lubomierz, Krakow, PL C 3
76 Lubomierz, Wroclaw, PL B 4
78 Lubomino A 3
77 Luboń A 5
78 Lubowidz B 2
69 Lubowo, Koszalin, PL B 4
77 Lubowo, Poznań, PL A 6
79 Lubraniec C 1
137 Lubrin B 4
89 Lubrza A 5
76 Lubsko B 3
66 Lübtheen B 4
69 Lubuczewo A 5
75 Luby C 4
67 Lübz B 5
106 Luc C 3
108 Luc-en-D. C 2
82 Luc-sur-Mer B 1
137 Lucainena de las Torres B 4
55 Lucan A 5
116 Lučani C 4
137 Lúcar B 4
93 Luçay-le-Mâle B 5
112 Lucca C 2
136 Lucena, Córdoba, E B 2
135 Lucena, Huelva, E B 4
132 Lucena del Cid A 2
94 Lucenay-lès-Aix C 3
95 Lucenay-l'Eveque B 4
91 Lučenec D 2
121 Luceni C 5
96 Lucens B 2
145 Lucera B 4
109 Luceram D 4
133 Luchente C 2
67 Lüchow C 4
130 Luciana C 2
112 Lucignano C 3
75 Lucka B 4
75 Luckau B 5
75 Luckenwalde A 5
21 Lucksta C 6
67 Lückstedt C 4
91 Lúčky C 2
143 Luco dei Marsi C 4
92 Luçon C 2
79 Lucynów C 4
101 Ludanice A 6
58 Ludborough B 3
115 Ludbreg A 4
71 Lüdenscheid A 6
67 Lüderitz C 4
83 Ludes B 6
58 Ludford Magna B 3
62 Ludgershall B 2
39 Ludgo D 4
65 Lüdinghausen C 5
57 Ludlow D 4
69 Ludomy C 4
46 Ludvigsborg B 4
38 Ludvika B 2
84 Ludweiler-Warndt A 3
85 Ludwigsburg B 6
67 Ludwigsfelde C 6
85 Ludwigshafen A 5
67 Ludwigslust B 4
74 Ludwigsstadt C 3
122 Luesia B 1
102 Lug C 2
111 Lugagnano Val d'Arda C 4
97 Lugano B 4
75 Lugau C 4
143 Lugnola B 3
21 Lugnvik C 6
95 Lugny C 4
118 Lugo, E A 3
113 Lugo, I B 3
103 Lugoj C 5
119 Lugones A 5
96 Lugrin B 2
136 Lugros B 3
61 Lugwardine A 4
89 Luhačovice B 5
27 Luhalahti B 6
28 Luhanka B 3
87 Luhe B 4
25 Luikonlahti C 5
110 Luino B 3
74 Luisenthal C 2
136 Lújar C 3
117 Luka B 6
88 Luka n. Jihlavou B 3
116 Lukavac B 2
88 Lukavec B 2
116 Lukavica B 2
24 Lukkarila B 4
78 Lukla B 3
160 Lukovit D 4
152 Lukovo, Makedonija, YU C 2
152 Lukovo, Srbija, YU A 3

117 Lukovo, Srbija, YU C 5
114 Lukovo Šugarje C 3
77 Lukowice C 6
35 Luksefjell B 5
141 Lula B 3
14 Luleå C 6
160 Lüleburgaz E 5
66 Lüllau B 2
150 Lumbarda C 3
121 Lumbier B 5
125 Lumbrales C 3
121 Lumbreras B 4
63 Lumbres B 4
16 Lumijoki C 4
70 Lummen B 4
26 Lumparland C 3
127 Lumpiaque A 4
38 Lumsheden B 3
122 Luna B 2
113 Lunano C 4
152 Lunar C 2
107 Lunas D 3
103 Lunca Cernii de Jos C 6
103 Luncani C 6
46 Lund B 4
44 Lunde, DK B 1
30 Lunde, Sogne Fjordane, N B 3
35 Lunde, Telemark, N B 5
21 Lunde, S C 6
66 Lunden A 2
36 Lunderseter A 4
44 Lunderskov B 2
66 Lüneburg B 3
107 Lunel D 4
107 Lunel-Viel D 4
71 Lünen A 6
84 Lunéville B 3
96 Lungern B 4
146 Lungro C 2
21 Lungsjön B 5
37 Lungsund B 6
31 Lunner C 7
64 Lunteren B 3
100 Lunz a. See B 3
141 Luogosanto A 3
22 Luopajärvi C 4
27 Luopioinen B 7
22 Luoto B 4
117 Lupac A 5
69 Lupawa A 5
136 Lupión A 3
75 Luppa B 4
136 Luque B 2
110 Lurago d'Erba B 4
141 Lúras B 3
94 Lurcy-Lévis C 2
95 Lure B 6
53 Lurgan B 5
5 Lurøy D 1
93 Lury-sur-Arnon B 6
115 Lušci Palanka C 4
110 Luserna San Giovanni C 2
99 Lusévera C 4
154 Lushnje B 1
28 Lusi B 4
93 Lusignan C 4
94 Lusigny C 3
83 Lusigny-sur-Barse C 6
124 Luso C 1
77 Lusówko A 5
14 Luspebryggan A 3
50 Luss A 3
104 Lussac, Gironde, F C 2
93 Lussac, Haute Vienne, F C 5
93 Lussac-les-Châteaux C 4
107 Lussan C 4
97 Lustenau A 5
88 Luštěnice A 2
30 Luster B 4
70 Lustin B 3
98 Lutago C 2
96 Lutern Bad A 3
66 Lütjenburg A 3
66 Lütjensee B 3
79 Lutomiersk D 2
62 Luton B 3
96 Lutry,CH B 2
78 Lutry,PL A 3
98 Luttach C 2
72 Lutter a. Barenberge B 4
85 Lutterbach C 4
59 Lutterworth C 2
77 Lututów B 7
74 Lützen B 4
67 Lützow B 4
29 Luumäki C 5
23 Luupuvesi B 8
11 Luusua C 7
26 Luvia B 4
71 Luxembourg C 5
95 Luxeuil B 6
105 Luxey C 2
105 Luz, F E 2
128 Luz, Évora, P C 3
134 Luz, Faro, P B 3
134 Luz, Faro, P B 2
83 Luzarches B 4
88 Luže B 4
105 Luzech C 4
96 Luzern A 4
101 Lužianky A 6
89 Lužice C 5
69 Luzino A 6
94 Luzy C 3
147 Luzzi C 2
77 Lwówek A 5
76 Lwówek Ślaski B 4
49 Lybster C 5
67 Lychen B 6
43 Lyckeby C 5
15 Lycksele D 2
62 Lydd C 4
62 Lydden B 5
57 Lydham D 4
61 Lydney B 4
31 Lykkja C 5
34 Lykling B 1
61 Lyme Regis C 4
62 Lymington C 2
62 Lympne B 5
60 Lympstone C 3
62 Lyndhurst C 2
61 Lyneham B 5
35 Lyngdal, Buskerud, N B 5
34 Lyngdal, Vest-Agder, N C 3
35 Lyngnør C 5
6 Lyngseidet B 6
4 Lyngvær B 3
60 Lynmouth B 3
60 Lynton B 3
108 Lyon B 1
82 Lyons-la Forêt B 3
37 Lyrestad C 6
89 Lysá B 6
88 Lysá n. Labem A 2
34 Lysebotn B 2
42 Lysekil A 1
89 Lysice B 4
6 Lysnes B 3
78 Lysomice B 1
96 Lyss A 3
44 Lystrup A 3
37 Lysvik A 5
56 Lytham St. Annes C 3

M

27 Maakeski B 8
22 Maalahti C 3
54 Maam Cross A 2
24 Maaninka B 4
17 Maaninkavaara A 7
25 Maanselka B 5
71 Maarheeze A 4
26 Maarianhamina C 2
64 Maarssen B 3
52 Maas B 3
71 Maaseik A 4
71 Maasniel A 5
64 Maassluis C 2
71 Maastricht B 4
23 Määttälä B 6
17 Määttälänvaara A 8
58 Mablethorpe B 4
94 Mably C 4
137 Macael B 4
128 Mação B 2
104 Macau B 2
97 Maccagno B 4
142 Maccarese C 3
144 Macchiagodena B 3
57 Macclesfield C 4
49 Macduff D 6
103 Macea B 5
118 Maceda B 3
124 Macedo de Cavaleiros B 3
124 Maceira, Guarda, P C 2
128 Maceira, Leiria, P B 2
113 Macerata C 5
113 Macerata Féltria C 4
83 Machault B 6
92 Machecoul C 2
90 Machowa B 4
50 Machrihanish B 2
57 Machynlleth D 3
124 Macieira B 1
79 Maciejowice D 4
153 Mačkatica B 4
74 Mackenrode B 2
101 Mačkovci C 4
141 Macomer B 2
70 Macon,B B 3
95 Macon,F C 4
53 Macosquin A 5
108 Macot B 3
125 Macotera C 4
54 Macroom C 3
110 Macugnaga B 2
91 Mád D 4
102 Madaras B 3
144 Maddaloni B 3
64 Made C 2
111 Maderno B 5
126 Maderuelo A 2
11 Madetkoski B 6
102 Madocsa B 2
99 Madonna di Campiglio C 1
126 Madrid B 2
131 Madridejos B 3
130 Madrigal de la Vera A 1
125 Madrigal de las Altas Torres B 4
129 Madrigalejo, Badajoz, E B 5
120 Madrigalejo, Burgos, E B 3
126 Madriguera A 2
131 Madrigueras B 5
129 Madroñera B 5
101 Madunice A 5
80 Maël-Carhaix B 3
122 Maella C 3
126 Maello B 1
19 Mære B 7
60 Maesteg B 3
121 Maestu B 4
128 Mafra C 1
129 Magacela C 5
121 Magallón C 5
126 Magán C 2
121 Magaña C 4
111 Magasa B 5
120 Magaz C 2
74 Magdeburg A 3
110 Magenta B 3
18 Magerholm C 2
105 Magescq D 1
53 Maghera B 5
53 Magherafelt B 5
56 Maghull C 4
79 Magierowa Wola D 4
113 Magione C 4
116 Maglaj B 2
47 Maglehem B 5
143 Magliano de Marsi B 4
142 Magliano in Toscana B 2
143 Magliano Sabina B 3
116 Maglić A 3
146 Máglie B 4
102 Maglód A 3
104 Magnac-Bourg B 4
93 Magnac Laval C 5
84 Magnières B 3
36 Magnor B 4
79 Magnuszew D 4
94 Magny-Cours C 3
82 Magny-en-Vexin B 3
101 Mágocs C 6
61 Magor B 4
128 Magoute C 1
129 Maguilla C 5
53 Maguiresbridge B 4
152 Magura B 3
103 Magyarbánhegyes B 4
103 Magyarcsanád B 4
103 Magyarhomorog A 5
101 Magyarkeszi C 6
102 Magyarszék B 2
151 Mahala C 5
119 Mahide C 4
23 Mahlu C 7
139 Mahón B 5
132 Mahora B 1
115 Mahovo B 4
87 Mähring B 4
124 Maia B 1
84 Maiche C 3
147 Maida D 2
61 Maiden Newton C 4
62 Maidenhead B 3
84 Maidières B 3
62 Maidstone B 4
97 Maienfeld B 5
83 Maignelay B 4
92 Maillezais C 3
83 Mailly-le-Camp C 6
94 Mailly-le-Château B 3
127 Mainar A 4
73 Mainbernheim D 4
87 Mainburg C 3
86 Mainhardt B 1
86 Mainleus A 3
82 Maintenon C 3
24 Mainua A 4
73 Mainz C 2
128 Maiorca A 2
135 Mairena del Alcor B 5
86 Maisach C 3
98 Maishofen B 3
70 Maison-Celle C 3
83 Maison-Rouge C 5
100 Maissau A 3
83 Maisse C 4
87 Maitenbeth C 4
84 Maizières-le-Vic B 3
84 Maizières-les-Moselles A 3
126 Majadahonda B 2
129 Majadas B 5
126 Majaelrayo A 2
12 Majavatn B 5
90 Majdan Królewski B 4
117 Majdanpek B 5
117 Majilovac B 5
102 Majs C 2
150 Makarska B 3
158 Makhairádhon B 1
9 Makkaur B 10
91 Makkoshotyka D 4
64 Makkum A 3
91 Maklár E 3
103 Makó B 4
77 Makoszyce C 6
89 Makov B 6
152 Makovac B 3
154 Makovo A 3
78 Maków Mazowiecki C 4
90 Maków Podhalanski C 2
69 Makowarsko B 5
157 Makrakómi D 2
156 Makrikhóri C 2
156 Makrikhorion B 2
157 Makrirrákhi C 2
156 Makríyialos B 2
154 Makrokhórion B 3
22 Maksamaa B 4
102 Mala Bosna B 3
115 Mala Bukovec A 4
150 Mala Cista B 1
117 Mala Krsna B 5
91 Malá Lehota D 1
102 Mala Pijace B 3
153 Mala Plana A 3
115 Mala Subotica A 4
101 Malacky A 5
136 Málaga C 2
130 Malagón B 3
126 Malaguilla B 2
55 Malahide A 5
155 Malakási C 3
112 Malalbergo B 3
157 Malandrínon D 2
6 Malangen B 4
77 Malanów B 7
15 Malåträsk C 2
109 Malaucène C 2
82 Malaunay B 3
22 Malax C 3
99 Malborghetto C 4
78 Malbork A 2
71 Malborn C 5
106 Malbouzon C 3
95 Malbuisson C 6
153 Malča A 4
99 Malcesine D 1
67 Malchin B 5
87 Malching C 5
67 Malchow B 5
135 Malcocinado A 5
77 Malczyce B 5
70 Maldegem A 2
62 Maldon B 4
99 Malè C 1
69 Malechowo A 4
104 Malemort B 4
66 Malente A 3
43 Målerås C 5
97 Malesco B 4
83 Malesherbes C 4
157 Malesína D 3
81 Malestroit C 4
149 Maletto B 4
123 Malgrat C 5
125 Malhadas B 3
102 Mali Iđos C 3
114 Mali Lošinj C 2
93 Malicorn-sur-Sarthe B 3
94 Maligny B 3
109 Malijai C 3
43 Målilla kyrkby B 5
43 Målilla station B 5
53 Malin A 4
52 Malin More B 3
91 Málinec D 2
38 Malingsbo C 2
106 Malingues B 3
77 Maliniec A 7
154 Maliq B 2
23 Maliskylä B 7
78 Malki B 2
78 Malkinia Graniczna C 5
48 Mallaig E 3
121 Mallén C 5
87 Mallersdorf C 4
97 Málles Venosta B 6
44 Malling A 3
98 Mallnitz B 4
54 Mallow B 3
28 Mallusjoki C 3
57 Mallwyd D 3
19 Malm A 7
43 Malmbäck B 4
14 Malmberget A 4
71 Malmedy B 5
61 Malmesbury B 4
39 Malmköping C 3
46 Malmö B 3
36 Malmon C 3
39 Malmslätt D 2
110 Malnate B 3
118 Malnica A 2
99 Malo D 2
153 Malo Konjari C 3
63 Malo-les-Bains A 4
97 Maloja B 5
76 Malomico B 4
153 Malošište A 3
30 Måloy B 2
129 Malpartida de Cáceres B 4
129 Malpartida de la Serena C 5
129 Malpartida de Plasencia B 4
122 Malpas,E B 3
57 Malpas,GB C 4
126 Malpica C 1
128 Malpico B 3
97 Mals B 6
85 Malsch B 5
6 Målselv B 4
88 Malšice B 2
6 Målsnes B 4
98 Malta C 4
94 Maltat C 3
58 Maltby B 2
96 Malters A 4
58 Malton A 3
32 Malung C 4
21 Malungen C 5
32 Malungsfors C 4
76 Maluszów A 4
90 Maluszyn B 2
125 Malva B 4
97 Malvaglia B 4
128 Malveira C 1
57 Malvern Wells D 4
19 Malvik B 6
78 Maly Plock B 5
91 Mályi D 3
124 Mamarrosa C 1
71 Mamer C 5
82 Mamers C 2
86 Mammendorf C 3
147 Mámmola D 2
141 Mamoiada B 3
152 Mamurras C 1
159 Mána B 3
139 Manacor B 4
17 Manamansalo C 6
125 Mancera de Abajo C 4
136 Mancha Real B 3
56 Manchester C 4
86 Manching C 3
129 Manchita C 4
142 Manciano B 2
105 Manciet D 3
84 Mancieulles A 2
34 Mandal C 3
42 Mandängsholm A 3
149 Mandanici B 5
141 Mándas C 3
147 Mandatoriccio C 2
127 Mandavona B 3
111 Mandello del Lario B 4
66 Mandelsloh C 2
71 Manderfeld B 5
71 Mandersheid B 5
157 Mandoúdhion D 3
159 Mándra A 4
146 Mandúria B 3
109 Mane, Basses Alpes, F D 2

105 Mane, Haute Garonne, F D 3
111 Manérbio B 5
121 Mañeru B 5
87 Manetin B 5
145 Manfredónia B 4
119 Manganeses de la Lampreana C 5
119 Manganeses de la Polvorosa B 5
30 Manger C 2
84 Manglennes A 2
61 Mangotsfield B 4
32 Mangsbodarna B 4
124 Mangualde C 2
99 Maniago C 3
135 Manilva C 5
90 Maniowy C 3
132 Manises B 2
100 Mank A 3
38 Månkarbo B 4
123 Manlleu B 5
140 Manne de Sisco B 2
97 Mannedorf A 4
101 Mannersdorf a. Leithageb B 4
85 Mannheim A 5
26 Mannila B 5
62 Manningtree B 5
105 Mano C 2
158 Manolás A 2
52 Manorhamilton B 3
109 Manosque D 2
69 Manowo A 4
123 Manresa C 4
123 Manresana C 4
42 Månsarp B 4
20 Månsåsen B 3
74 Mansfeld B 3
59 Mansfield B 2
59 Mansfield Woodhouse B 2
120 Mansilla de Burgos B 3
119 Mansilla de las Mulas B 5
36 Manskog B 4
104 Mansle B 3
140 Manso B 1
124 Manteigas C 2
87 Mantel B 4
82 Mantes-la-Jolie C 3
82 Mantes-la-Ville C 3
93 Manthelan B 4
39 Mantorp D 2
111 Mantova B 5
27 Mäntsälä C 8
27 Mänttä A 7
28 Mäntyharju B 4
17 Mäntyjärvi A 6
26 Mäntyluoto B 4
156 Mantzáridhes B 3
133 Manuel B 2
95 Manurolle B 6
119 Manzanal de Arriba B 4
131 Manzanares, Cuidad Real, E B 3
126 Manzanares, Madrid, E B 2
120 Manzaneda, Burgos, E B 3
119 Manzaneda, León, E B 4
118 Manzaneda, Orense, E B 3
126 Manzaneque C 2
132 Manzanera A 2
135 Manzanilla B 4
106 Manzat B 2
142 Manziana B 3
95 Manziat C 4
116 Maoča B 2
152 Maqellarë C 2
126 Maqueda B 1
124 Mar B 1
127 Mara A 4
136 Maracena B 3
120 Maraña A 1
127 Maranchón A 3
155 Marandokhóri D 2
112 Maranello B 2
144 Marano C 3
99 Marano Lagunare D 4
92 Marans C 3
146 Maratea C 1
128 Marateca C 2
159 Marathón A 4
60 Marazion C 1
85 Marbach, Baden-Württemberg, D† B 6
73 Marbach, Hessen, D† C 3
84 Marbache B 3
42 Marbäck B 3
136 Marbella C 2
95 Marboz C 5
34 Mårbu A 3
73 Marburg C 2
20 Marby B 3
101 Marcali C 5
114 Marčana C 1
112 Marcaria A 2
101 Marcelová B 6
106 Marcenat B 2
59 March C 4
126 Marchamalo B 2
95 Marchaux B 6
70 Marche-en-Famenne B 4
101 Marchegg A 4
135 Marchena B 5
93 Marchenoir B 5
104 Marcheprime C 2
70 Marchiennes-Ville B 2
105 Marciac D 3
142 Marciana Marina B 1
144 Marcianise B 3
94 Marcigny C 4
121 Marcilla B 5
106 Marcillac-la-Croisille B 2
94 Marcillat C 2
106 Marcilly B 4
83 Marcilly-le-Hayer C 5
83 Marcilly-sur-Seine C 5
69 Marcińkowice B 4
77 Marciszów C 5
63 Marck B 3
85 Marckolsheim B 4
124 Marco de Canevezes B 1
83 Marcoing A 5
20 Mårdsjön B 4
59 Mareham le Fen B 3
104 Marennes B 1
62 Maresfield C 4
63 Maresquel B 3
104 Mareuil B 3
94 Mareuil-sur-Arnon C 2
92 Mareuil-sur-Lay C 2
83 Mareuil-sur-Ourcq B 5
155 Margarítion C 2
62 Margate B 5
104 Margaux B 2
91 Margecany D 4
83 Margerie-Hancourt C 6
108 Margès B 2
145 Margherita di Savóia B 5
103 Marghita A 6
103 Mărgina C 6
117 Margita A 5
83 Margny B 4
110 Margone B 2
69 Margonin C 5
70 Margut C 4
137 Maria B 4
100 Maria Gail C 1
100 Maria Lankowitz B 3
101 Maria Lanzendorf A 4
100 Maria Neustift B 2
100 Maria Saal C 2
40 Mariager C 3
127 Mariana B 3
43 Mariannelund B 5
148 Marianópoli B 3
87 Mariánské Lázně B 4
98 Mariapfarr B 4
100 Mariazell B 3
45 Maribo C 4
100 Maribor C 3
39 Marieberg C 2
39 Mariedamm D 2
39 Mariefred C 4
26 Mariehamn C 2
46 Marieholm B 4
65 Marienbaum C 4
75 Marienberg C 5
70 Marienbourg B 3
71 Marienheide A 6
37 Mariestad C 5
144 Marigliano C 3
109 Marignane D 2
95 Marigny, Jura, F C 5
81 Marigny, Manche, F A 5
83 Marigny le Châtel C 5
115 Marija Bistrica A 4
153 Marikostinovo C 5
118 Marín B 2
150 Marina B 2
123 Marina de Cambrils C 4
142 Marina di Campo B 1
112 Marina di Carrara B 2
112 Marina di Cécina C 2
146 Marina di Ginosa B 2
147 Marina di Gioiosa Iónica D 2
142 Marina di Grosseto B 1
112 Marina di Massa B 2
146 Marina di Nováglie C 4
112 Marina di Pisa C 2
149 Marina di Ragusa C 4
113 Marina di Ravenna B 4
136 Marinaleda B 2
148 Marinella B 2
148 Marineo B 3
82 Marines B 3
71 Maring-Noviand C 5
128 Marinha das Ondas A 2
128 Marinha Grande B 2
124 Marinhas B 1
23 Marinkainen B 5
143 Marino C 3
126 Marjaliza C 2
75 Märk. Buchholz A 5
19 Markabygd B 7
46 Markaryd A 4
155 Markat C 2
91 Markaz E 3
97 Markdorf A 5
65 Markelo B 4
59 Market Bosworth C 2
59 Market Deeping C 3
57 Market Drayton D 4
59 Market Harborough C 3
58 Market Rasen B 3
58 Market Weighton B 3
53 Markethill B 5
59 Markfield C 3
65 Markhausen B 5
79 Marki C 4
51 Markinch A 4
14 Markitta A 5
10 Markkina A 2
75 Markkleeberg B 4
66 Marklohe C 2
64 Marknesse B 3
75 Markneukirchen C 4
72 Markoldendorf B 3
159 Markópoulon B 4
76 Markosice B 3
117 Markovac, Srbija, YU B 5
117 Markovac, Vojvodina, YU A 5
89 Markowice A 6
74 Markranstädt B 4
62 Marks Tey B 4
74 Marksuhl C 2
101 Markt Allhau B 4
86 Markt Erlbach B 2
86 Markt Indersdorf C 3
86 Markt Rettenbach D 2
87 Markt Schwaben C 3
100 Markt St. Florian A 2
73 Marktbreit D 4
73 Marktheidenfeld D 3
87 Marktl C 4
87 Marktleuthen A 3
97 Marktoberdorf A 6
87 Marktredwitz A 4
116 Markušica B 3
91 Markušovce D 3
71 Marl A 6
62 Marlborough B 2
83 Marle B 5
108 Marlens B 3
108 Marlhes B 1
108 Marlieux A 2
67 Marlow,D* A 5
62 Marlow,GB B 3
38 Marma B 4
105 Marmande B 3
155 Mármara C 2
159 Marmári A 5
33 Marmaverken B 7
134 Marmelete B 2
136 Marmolejo A 2
85 Marmoutier B 4
95 Marnay B 5
66 Marne B 2
5 Mårnes C 3
73 Marnheim D 2
61 Marnhull C 4
67 Marnitz B 4
136 Maro C 3
73 Maroldsweisach C 4
82 Marolles-les-Braults C 2
82 Maromme B 3
111 Marone B 5
103 Maroslele B 4
99 Maróstica D 2
113 Marotta C 5
121 Marquina A 4
70 Marquion B 2
63 Marquise B 3
112 Marradi B 3
10 Marrasjärvi C 5
10 Marraskoski C 5
64 Marrum A 3
130 Marrupe A 2
84 Mars A 2
107 Marsac D 2
106 Marsac-en-Livradois B 3
111 Marságlia C 4
148 Marsala B 2
142 Marsciano B 3
107 Marseillan D 3
109 Marseille D 2
82 Marseille-en-Beauvaisis B 3
145 Mársico Nuovo C 4
51 Marske by the Sea C 6
84 Marson B 1
84 Marspich A 3
38 Märsta C 4
44 Marstal C 3
42 Marstrand B 1
142 Marta B 2
146 Martano B 4
39 Martebo E 5
104 Martel C 4
71 Martelange C 4
132 Martés B 2
66 Martfeld C 2
102 Martfű A 4
104 Martha B 2
59 Martham C 5
104 Marthon B 3
158 Marthópolis B 2
125 Martiago C 3
92 Martigné-Briand B 3
81 Martigné-Ferchaud C 5
96 Martigny-Ville B 3
109 Martigues D 2
134 Martim-Longo B 3
91 Martin,CS C 1
59 Martin,GB B 3
126 Martin Muñoz de las Posadas A 1
97 Martina B 6
146 Martina Franca B 3
125 Martinamore C 4
84 Martincourt-sur-Meuse A 2
111 Martinengo B 4
128 Martingança B 2
16 Martinniemi B 4
157 Martínon D 3
100 Martinsberg A 3
85 Martinshöhe A 4
143 Martinsicuro B 4
97 Martinszel A 6
141 Mártis B 2
101 Martjanci C 4
61 Martock C 4
44 Martofte B 3
25 Martonvaara B 6
102 Martonvásár A 2
123 Martorell C 4
136 Martos B 3
101 Martovce B 6
105 Martres-Tolosane D 4
11 Martti B 8
27 Marttila C 5
117 Măru A 6
126 Marugán B 1
146 Marúggio B 3
128 Marvão B 3
106 Marvejols C 3
84 Marville A 2
78 Marwald B 2
76 Marxwalde A 3
49 Marykirk E 6
56 Maryport B 3
49 Marywell E 6
101 Marz B 4
112 Marzabotto B 3
75 Marzahna B 4
67 Marzahne C 5
149 Marzamemi C 5
113 Marzocca C 5
132 Mas de Barberáns A 3
122 Mas de la Matas D 2
120 Masa B 3
132 Masamagrell B 2
132 Masanasa B 2
149 Máscali B 5
126 Mascaraque C 2
124 Mascarenhas B 2
66 Maschen B 3
143 Mascioni B 4
127 Masegoso de Tajuña B 3
131 Masegoso Peñascosa C 4
96 Masera B 4
85 Masevaux C 4
30 Masfjorden C 2
58 Masham A 2
8 Masi C 3
118 Maside B 2
26 Masku C 5
105 Maslacq D 2
115 Maslovare C 5
123 Masnou C 5
110 Masone C 3
8 Måsøy A 5
112 Massa B 2
113 Massa Fiscáglia B 4
112 Massa Lombarda B 3
144 Massa Lubrense C 3
142 Massa Marittima A 1
143 Massa Martana B 3
146 Massafra B 3
123 Massanet de Cabrenys B 5
112 Massarosa C 2
105 Massat E 4
93 Massay B 5
73 Maßbach C 4
104 Masseret B 4
105 Masseube D 3
106 Massiac B 3
87 Massing C 4
20 Mässlingen C 1
39 Mästerby E 5
72 Mastholte B 2
141 Masúa C 2
125 Masueco B 3
10 Masugnsbyn B 2
152 Mašutište B 2
18 Måsvassbu C 3
76 Maszewo A 3
129 Mata de Alcántara B 4
121 Matalebreras C 4
119 Matallana B 5
127 Matamala A 3
120 Mataporquera B 2
126 Matapozuelos A 1
155 Mataránga, Aitolía-Akarnanía, GR D 3
157 Mataránga, Kardhitsa, GR C 2
123 Mataró C 5
136 Matarredonda B 2
151 Mataruge B 5
117 Mataruška Banja C 4
25 Mätäsvaara B 6
153 Matejče B 3
113 Matélica C 5
146 Matera B 2
132 Matet B 2
124 Mateus B 2
21 Matfors C 6
60 Mathry B 1
81 Matignon B 4
83 Matigny B 5
125 Matillo de los Caños del Rio C 4
152 Matka C 3
27 Matku C 6
59 Matlock B 2
124 Matosinhos B 1
95 Matour C 4
91 Mátraderecske E 3
91 Mátranovák D 2
91 Mátraverebély E 2
30 Matre C 2
98 Matrei am Brenner B 2
98 Matrei in Osttirol B 3
144 Matrice B 3
99 Mattarello C 2
101 Mattersburg B 4
98 Mattighofen A 4
145 Mattinata B 5
20 Mattmar B 2
128 Mattos B 2
98 Mattsee B 4
33 Mattsmyra B 6
114 Matulji B 2
87 Matzing D 4
83 Maubert-Fontaine B 6
70 Maubeuge B 2
105 Maubourguet D 3
50 Mauchline B 3
49 Maud D 6
101 Mauerbach A 4
98 Mauerkirchen A 4
87 Mauern C 3
107 Mauguio D 4
85 Maulbronn A 5
82 Maule C 3
92 Mauléon C 3
105 Mauléon-Barouse E 3
105 Mauléon-Soule D 2
92 Maulévrier B 3
98 Mauls C 2
54 Maum A 2
81 Maure-de-Bretagne C 5
107 Maureilhan D 3
117 Măureni A 5
106 Mauriac B 2
108 Maurin-Maljasset C 3
4 Maurnes B 4
81 Mauron B 4
106 Maurs-la-Jolie C 2

107	Maury	E	2
109	Maussane	D	1
18	Mausund	B	4
100	Mautern	A	3
100	Mautern i. Steiermark	B	2
98	Mauterndorf	B	4
100	Mauthausen	A	2
99	Mauthen	C	3
105	Mauvezin	D	3
96	Mauvoisin	B	3
92	Mauze-sur-le-Mignon	C	3
155	Mavréli	C	3
154	Mavrokhóri	B	3
158	Mavrommáti	B	2
156	Mavronér	B	2
156	Mavrothálassa	B	3
156	Mavroúdha	B	3
154	Mavrovë	B	1
152	Mavrovi Hanovi	C	2
152	Mavrovo	C	2
159	Mavrovoúnion	C	3
81	Maxent	C	4
84	Maxey-sur-Vaise	B	2
87	Maxhütte-Haidhof	B	4
128	Maxial	B	1
22	Maxmo	B	4
51	Maxwellheugh	B	5
121	Maya	A	5
125	Mayalde	B	4
122	Mayals	C	3
50	Maybole	B	3
71	Mayen	B	6
81	Mayenne	B	6
93	Mayet	B	4
59	Mayfield, Derby, GB	B	2
62	Mayfield, Sussex, GB	B	4
55	Maynooth	A	5
119	Mayorga	B	5
106	Mayres	C	4
98	Mayrhofen	B	2
23	Mäyry	C	5
135	Mazagón	B	4
122	Mazaleón	C	3
107	Mazamet	D	2
109	Mazan	C	2
158	Mazaráki	A	2
155	Mazarakiá	C	2
126	Mazarambroz	C	1
127	Mazarete	B	3
118	Mazaricos	B	2
148	Mazaro del Vallo	B	2
133	Mazarrón	D	1
106	Mazaye	B	2
107	Mazères	D	1
106	Mazet	B	4
92	Mazières-en-Gâtine	C	3
115	Mazin	C	3
120	Mazuelo	B	3
149	Mazzarino	B	4
149	Mazzarrà S. Andrea	A	5
97	Mazzo di Valtellina	B	6
78	Mchowo	B	3
78	Mdzewo	C	3
124	Mealhada	C	1
141	Meana Sardo	C	3
59	Measham	C	2
94	Meauine	C	2
83	Meaux	C	4
34	Mebo	C	3
120	Mecerreyes	B	3
70	Mechelen	A	3
71	Mechelen-aan-de-Maas	B	4
71	Mechernich	B	5
74	Mechterstädt	C	2
69	Mecikal	B	5
136	Mecina-Bombarón	C	3
97	Meckenbeuren	A	5
85	Meckenheim	A	5
85	Meckesheim	A	5
102	Mecseknádasd	B	2
110	Meda,I	B	4
124	Meda,P	C	2
114	Medak	C	3
110	Mede	B	3
72	Medebach	B	2
129	Medelim	A	3
129	Medellin	C	5
64	Medemblik	B	3
111	Medesano	C	5
39	Medevi	D	1
103	Medgyesbodzás	B	4
103	Medgyesegybáza	B	5
122	Mediano	B	3
160	Medias	B	4
112	Medicina	B	3
129	Medina de las Torres	C	4
120	Medina de Pomar	B	3
120	Medina de Rioseco	C	1
126	Medina del Campo	A	1
135	Medina-Sidonia	C	5
127	Medinaceli	A	3
125	Medinilla	C	4
15	Medle	D	4
20	Medstugan	B	1
114	Medulin	C	1
99	Meduno	C	3
153	Međveđa	B	3
117	Medveđa, Srbija, YU	B	5
117	Medveđa, Srbija, YU	C	5
115	Medvida	C	3
114	Medvode	A	2
91	Medzilaborce	C	4
154	Medžitlija	B	3
75	Meerane	C	4
70	Meerhout	A	4
70	Meerle	A	3
97	Meersburg	A	5
71	Meerssen	B	4
71	Meeuwen	A	4
6	Mefjordvær	B	3
155	Megála Kalívia	C	3
156	Megáli Panayiá	B	3
156	Megáli Stérna	A	2
158	Megalópolis	B	3
159	Mégara	B	4
5	Megården	C	4
155	Megárkhi	C	3
108	Megève	B	3
98	Meggenhofen	A	4
117	Mehadia	B	6
117	Mehadica	A	6
9	Mehamn	A	7
38	Mehedeby	B	4
74	Mehlis	C	2
94	Mehun-sur-Y.	B	2
51	Meigle	A	4
71	Meijel	A	4
97	Meilen	A	4
105	Meilhan	D	2
129	Meimóa	A	3
110	Meina	B	3
72	Meine	A	4
66	Meinersen	C	3
71	Meinerzhagen	A	6
74	Meiningen	C	2
118	Meira	A	3
96	Meiringen	B	4
75	Meißen	B	5
86	Meitingen	C	2
71	Meix-devant-Virton	C	4
25	Mekrijärvi	C	7
99	Mel	C	3
154	Melás	B	3
66	Melbeck	B	3
59	Melbourn	C	4
59	Melbourne	C	2
4	Melbu	B	3
89	Melč	B	5
19	Meldal	B	5
113	Méldola	B	4
66	Meldorf	A	2
111	Melegnano	B	4
103	Melenci	C	4
146	Melendugno	B	4
145	Melfi	B	4
124	Melgaço	A	1
120	Melgar de Arriba	B	1
120	Melgar de Fernamental	B	2
120	Melgar de Yuso	B	2
19	Melhus	B	6
132	Meliana	B	2
97	Melide	C	4
134	Melides	A	2
158	Meligalá	B	2
156	Melíki	B	2
149	Melilli	B	5
88	Mělinické Vtelno	A	2
95	Melisey	B	6
159	Melíssi	A	3
154	Melíti	B	3
147	Mélito di Porto Salvo	E	1
156	Melívoia	C	2
100	Melk	A	3
61	Melksham	B	4
21	Mellansel	B	7
70	Melle,B	A	2
65	Melle,D†	B	6
92	Melle,F	C	3
36	Mellerud	C	4
118	Mellid	B	2
27	Mellilä	C	5
66	Mellin	C	3
39	Mellösa	C	3
73	Mellrichstadt	C	4
56	Melmerby	B	4
117	Melnica	B	5
153	Melnik,BG	C	5
88	Mělník,CS	A	2
118	Melón	B	2
5	Meløy	D	2
51	Melrose	B	5
97	Mels	A	5
49	Melsetter	C	5
72	Melsungen	B	3
10	Meltaus	C	5
59	Melton	C	5
59	Melton Constable	C	5
59	Melton Mowbray	C	3
10	Meltosjärvi	C	4
83	Melun	C	4
48	Melvaig	D	3
49	Melvich	C	5
102	Mélykút	B	3
111	Melzo	B	4
154	Memaliaj	B	1
131	Membrilla	C	3
129	Membrío	B	3
107	Memer	C	1
86	Memmelsdorf	B	2
86	Memmingen	D	2
128	Memoria	B	2
97	Menággio	B	5
57	Menai Bridge	C	2
93	Menars	B	5
126	Menasalbas	C	1
94	Menat	C	2
121	Mendavia	B	4
121	Mendaza	B	4
106	Mende,F	C	3
102	Mende,H	A	3
71	Menden	A	6
128	Mendiga	B	2
97	Mendrisio	C	4
81	Ménéac	B	4
70	Menen	B	2
11	Menesjärvi	A	6
148	Menfi	B	2
101	Ménfocsanak	B	5
125	Mengamuñoz	C	5
85	Mengen	B	6
72	Mengeringhausen	B	2
114	Mengeš	A	2
136	Mengibar	B	3
87	Mengkofen	C	4
155	Menídi	C	3
103	Ménkerék	B	5
108	Mens	C	2
65	Menslage	B	5
143	Mentana	B	3
74	Menteroda	B	2
109	Menton	D	4
126	Méntrida	B	1
62	Meopham	B	4
109	Méounes-Les-Montrieux	D	2
65	Meppel	B	4
65	Meppen	B	5
122	Mequinenza	C	3
93	Mer	B	5
118	Mera, La Coruña, E	A	3
118	Mera, La Coruña, E	A	2
19	Meråker	B	7
99	Meran	C	2
99	Merano	C	2
111	Merate	B	4
70	Merbes-le-Château	B	3
139	Mercadal	B	5
113	Mercatale	C	4
113	Mercatino Conca	C	4
144	Mercáto San Severino	C	3
113	Mercato Saraceno	C	4
86	Merching	C	2
70	Merchtem	B	3
81	Merdignac	B	4
120	Meré,E	A	2
61	Mere,GB	B	4
70	Merelbeke	B	2
83	Meréville	C	4
65	Merfeld	C	5
129	Mérida	C	4
104	Merignac	C	2
16	Merijärvi	C	3
26	Merikarvia	B	4
88	Měřin	B	3
86	Mering	C	2
63	Merkem	B	4
86	Merkendorf	B	2
48	Merkland Lodge	C	4
87	Merklin	B	5
85	Merklingen	B	5
70	Merksem	A	3
70	Merksplas	A	3
71	Merkstein	B	5
84	Merlebach	A	3
45	Mern	B	5
158	Merópi	B	2
153	Merošina	A	3
82	Mers-les-Bains	A	3
71	Mersch	C	5
74	Merseburg	B	3
60	Merthyr Tydfil	B	3
86	Mertingen	C	2
134	Mertola	B	3
62	Merton	B	3
85	Mertzwiller	B	4
83	Méru	B	4
124	Merufe	A	1
95	Mervans	C	5
63	Merville	B	4
83	Méry-sur-Seine	C	5
71	Merzig	C	5
152	Mes	B	1
146	Mesagne	B	3
159	Mesagrós	B	4
124	Mesão Frio	B	2
130	Mesas de Ibor	B	1
72	Meschede	B	2
104	Meschers-sur-Gironde	B	2
154	Mešeišta	A	2
155	Mesenikólas	C	3
81	Meslay-du-Maine	C	6
31	Mesnalien	B	7
97	Mesocco	B	5
103	Mesöhegyes	B	4
155	Mesokhóra	C	3
154	Mesokhóri	B	3
113	Mésola	B	4
155	Mesolóngion	D	3
154	Mesopotamiá	B	3
147	Mesoraca	C	2
152	Mesqetë	C	1
81	Messac	C	5
71	Messancy	C	4
14	Messaure	B	4
67	Meßdorf	C	4
81	Messei	B	6
134	Messejana	B	2
149	Messina	A	5
58	Messingham	B	3
158	Messini	B	3
85	Meßkirch	C	6
85	Meßstetten	B	5
130	Mestanza	C	2
88	Městec Králové	A	3
67	Mestlin	B	4
89	Město-Albrechlice	A	5
89	Město Libavá	B	5
87	Město Touškov	B	5
99	Mestre	D	3
65	Mesum	B	5
144	Meta	C	3
156	Metallikón	A	2
156	Metamorfosis	A	2
156	Metaxás	B	1
65	Metelen	B	5
159	Méthana	B	4
59	Metheringham	B	3
51	Methil	A	5
49	Methlick	D	6
158	Methóni	C	2
50	Methven	A	4
59	Methwold	C	4
151	Metkovic	B	3
114	Metlika	B	3
100	Metnitz	C	2
158	Metókhi	A	2
117	Metovnica	C	6
17	Metsälä, Oulun, SF	B	6
22	Metsälä, Vaasan, SF	C	3
27	Metsämaa	C	6
64	Metslawier	A	4
155	Métsovan	C	3
87	Metten	C	4
71	Mettendorf	C	5
70	Mettet	B	3
65	Mettingen	B	5
71	Mettlach	C	5
96	Mettlen	B	3
71	Mettmann	A	5
84	Metz	A	3
84	Metzervisse	A	3
85	Metzingen	B	6
82	Meulan	C	3
70	Meulebeke	B	2
93	Meung-sur-Loire	B	5
95	Meursault	C	4
74	Meuselwitz	B	4
104	Meuzac	B	4
60	Mevagissey	C	2
58	Mexborough	B	2
108	Meximieux	B	2
49	Mey	C	5
66	Meyenburg,D†	B	1
67	Meyenburg,D*	B	5
106	Meymac	B	2
109	Meyrargues	D	2
109	Meyronnes	C	3
107	Meyrueis	C	3
106	Meyssac	B	1
108	Meysse	C	1
108	Meyzieux	B	1
107	Mèze	D	3
95	Mézériat	C	5
82	Mézidon	B	1
70	Mézières	C	3
93	Mézières-en-Brenne	C	5
104	Mézières-sur-Issoire	A	3
94	Mézilles	B	3
105	Mézin	C	3
103	Mezoberény	B	5
91	Mezocsát	E	3
101	Mezocsokonya	C	5
102	Mezofalva	B	2
103	Mezögyán	B	5
91	Mezokeresztes	E	3
101	Mezokomarom	C	6
103	Mezokovácsháza	B	4
91	Mezokövesd	E	3
101	Mezöörs	B	5
105	Mézos	C	1
101	Mezoszentgyörgy	C	6
102	Mezöszilas	B	2
91	Mezotárkány	E	3
103	Mezotúr	A	4
127	Mezquita de Jarque	B	5
113	Mezzano, Emilia Romagna, I	B	4
99	Mezzano, Trentino-Alto Adige, I	C	2
148	Mezzoiuso	B	3
97	Mezzoldo	B	5
99	Mezzolombardo	C	2
129	Miajadas	B	5
69	Mianowice	A	5
69	Miasteczko Krajeńskie	B	5
90	Miasteczko Śląsk	B	1
69	Miastko	A	4
78	Miastkowo	B	4
90	Micahowice	B	2
79	Michałów	D	4
74	Michelau, Bayern, D†	C	3
73	Michelau, Bayern, D†	D	4
86	Michelbach	B	2
100	Micheldorf	B	2
100	Michelhausen	A	3
87	Michelsneukirchen	B	4
73	Michelstadt	D	3
67	Michendorf	C	6
79	Michów	D	5
160	Michurin	D	5
62	Mickleton	A	2
49	Mid Yell	A	7
64	Middelburg	C	1
44	Middelfart	B	2
64	Middelharnis	C	2
63	Middelkerke	A	4
65	Middelstum	A	4
58	Middleham	A	2
61	Middlemarsh	C	4
51	Middlesbrough	C	6
59	Middleton, Norfolk, GB	C	4
48	Middleton, Tiree, GB	E	2
62	Middleton Cheney	A	2
56	Middleton in Teesdale	B	4
58	Middleton on the Wolds	B	3
53	Middletown	B	5
57	Middlewich	C	4
62	Midhurst	C	3
54	Midleton	C	3
66	Midlum	B	1
61	Midsomer Norton	B	4
30	Midtgulen	B	2
90	Miechów	B	3
127	Miedes	A	4
126	Miedes de Atienza	A	2
90	Miedzybodzie Bialskie	C	2
77	Miedzybórz	B	6
77	Miedzychód	A	4
89	Miedzygórze	A	4
89	Miedzylesie	A	4
76	Miedzyrzecz	A	4
68	Miedzywodzie	A	2
68	Miedzyzdroje	B	2
29	Miehikkälä	C	5
90	Miejsce Piastowe	C	4
77	Miejska Górka	B	5
68	Miekowo	B	2
105	Mielan	D	3
90	Mielec	B	4
68	Mielecin	B	2
69	Mielno	A	4
16	Mieluskylä	C	4
120	Miengo	A	3
123	Mieras	B	5
160	Miercurea Ciuc	B	4
103	Miersig	B	5
71	Miesau	C	6

34 Mosby C 3
124 Mosca B 3
114 Moščenicka Draga B 2
143 Mosciano S. Angelo B 4
77 Mościsko C 5
128 Moscovide C 1
74 Mosigkau B 4
77 Mosina A 5
12 Mosjøen B 5
157 Moskhokhórion D 2
30 Moskog B 3
90 Moskorzew B 2
14 Moskosel C 3
117 Mosna B 6
98 Moso C 2
101 Mosonmagyaróvár B 5
101 Mosonszentjános B 5
101 Mosonszentmiklós B 5
116 Mošorin A 4
91 Mošovce D 1
132 Mosqueruela A 2
35 Moss B 6
49 Mossat D 6
85 Mössingen B 6
34 Møsstrand B 4
151 Mostar B 3
34 Mosterhamn B 1
76 Mostki A 4
78 Mostkowo B 3
126 Móstoles B 2
101 Mostová A 5
69 Mostowo A 4
55 Mostrim A 4
89 Mosty,CS B 6
68 Mosty,PL B 2
57 Mostyn C 3
19 Mosvik B 6
89 Moszczenica B 6
131 Mota del Cuervo B 4
125 Mota del Marqués B 4
39 Motala D 2
50 Motherwell B 4
67 Möthlow C 5
132 Mótilla del Palancar B 1
96 Motôt B 3
114 Motovun B 1
121 Motrico A 4
136 Motril C 3
99 Motta D 2
99 Motta di Livenze D 3
145 Motta Montecorvino B 4
149 Motta San Anástasia B 4
110 Motta Visconti B 3
146 Móttola B 3
109 Mouans-Sartoux D 3
95 Mouchard C 5
96 Moudon B 2
109 Mougins D 3
27 Mouhijärvi B 6
92 Mouilleron-en-Pareds C 3
109 Moulinet D 4
94 Moulins C 3
94 Moulins-Engilbert C 3
82 Moulins-la-Marche C 2
93 Moulismes C 4
82 Moult B 1
54 Mount Bellew Bridge A 3
51 Mount Pleasant B 5
54 Mount Talbot A 3
60 Mountain Ash B 3
51 Mountbenger B 4
52 Mountcharles B 3
53 Mountfield B 4
55 Mountmellick A 4
55 Mountrath A 4
59 Mountsorrel C 2
134 Moura A 3
128 Mourão C 3
118 Mourelle B 3
105 Mourenx Ville-Nouvelle D 2
109 Mouriés,F D 1
156 Mouriés,GR A 2
83 Mourmelon-le-Grand B 6
128 Mouronho A 2
70 Mouscron B 2
107 Moussac D 4
84 Moussey B 3
80 Moustéru B 3
105 Moustey C 2
156 Mousthéni B 4
70 Moustier B 3
95 Mouthe C 6
95 Mouthier B 6
107 Mouthoumet E 2
96 Moutier A 3
108 Moutiers B 3
92 Moutiers-les-Mauxfaits C 2
94 Moux B 4
83 Mouy B 4
158 Mouzáki, Ilia, GR B 2
155 Mouzáki, Kardhitsa, GR C 3
84 Mouzay A 2
70 Mouzon C 4
40 Mov C 4
53 Moville A 4
49 Mowtie E 6
49 Moy, Inverness, GB D 4
48 Moy, Inverness, GB E 4
53 Moy, Tyrone, GB B 5
123 Moya C 5
52 Moyard C 1
54 Moycullen A 2
84 Moyenmoutier B 3
84 Moyenvic B 3
84 Moyeuvre A 3
54 Moylough A 3
119 Mózar C 5
114 Mozirja A 2
102 Mozs B 2
111 Mozzanica B 4
78 Mragowo B 4
117 Mramorak B 4
115 Mrazovac B 4
117 Mrčajevci C 4
115 Mrkonjić Grad C 5
114 Mrkopalj B 2
117 Mrmoš C 5
69 Mrocza B 5
77 Mroczen B 6
78 Mroczno B 2
79 Mrozy C 4
117 Mršinci C 4
68 Mrzezyno A 3
88 Mšec A 1
88 Mšeno A 2
90 Mstów B 2
90 Mszana Dolna C 3
79 Mszczonów D 3
150 Muč B 2
113 Muccia C 5
71 Much B 6
61 Much Marcle B 4
57 Much Wenlock D 4
74 Mücheln B 3
120 Mucientes C 2
54 Muckross B 2
91 Múcsony D 3
73 Mudau D 3
66 Müden C 3
71 Mudersbach B 6
127 Muel A 4
125 Muelas del Pan B 4
67 Mueß B 4
53 Muff A 4
118 Mugardos A 2
128 Muge B 2
75 Mügeln B 5
99 Múggia D 4
118 Mugía A 1
121 Mugica A 4
142 Mugnano A 3
105 Mugron D 2
85 Mühlacker B 5
98 Mühlbach am Hochkönig B 4
75 Mühlberg, Cottbus, D* B 5
74 Mühlberg, Erfurt, D* C 2
98 Mühldorf, Karnten, A C 4
100 Mühldorf, Steiermark, A C 3
87 Mühldorf, D† C 4
96 Mühleberg B 3
67 Mühlen,D* B 4
98 Mühlen,I C 2
67 Mühlenbeck C 6
73 Mühlhausen, Bayern, D† D 4
86 Mühlhausen, Bayern, D† B 3
74 Mühlhausen, D* B 2
85 Mühlheim B 5
74 Mühltroff C 3
23 Muhola B 7
16 Muhos C 4
98 Muhr B 4
64 Muiden B 3
55 Muine Bheag B 5
118 Muiños C 3
48 Muir of Ord D 4
51 Muirdrum A 5
50 Muirkirk B 3
160 Mukachevo A 3
133 Mula C 1
97 Mulegns B 5
98 Mules C 2
71 Mülheim, Nordrhein Westfalen, D† A 5
71 Mülheim, Rheinland-Pfalz, D† B 6
85 Mulhouse C 4
52 Mullaranny C 2
85 Müllheim C 4
37 Mullhyttan B 6
55 Mullinavat B 4
55 Mullingar A 4
60 Mullion C 1
75 Müllrose A 6
42 Mullsjö B 3
23 Multia C 6
21 Multrå B 6
125 Muñana C 4
119 Muñas A 4
74 Münchberg C 3
76 Müncheberg A 3
66 Münchehagen C 2
86 München C 3
73 Münchhausen C 2
121 Mundaca A 4
72 Münden B 3
98 Munderfing A 4
86 Munderkingen C 1
59 Mundesley C 5
59 Mundford C 4
131 Munera B 4
121 Munguia A 4
125 Muñico C 4
127 Muniesa A 5
46 Munka-Ljungby A 3
44 Munkebo B 3
36 Munkedal C 3
20 Munkflohögen B 3
37 Munkfors B 5
15 Munksund C 5
38 Munktorp C 3
73 Münnerstadt C 4
126 Muñopepe B 1
125 Muñotello C 4
22 Munsala B 4
86 Münsing D 3
96 Munsingen,CH B 3
85 Münsingen,D† B 6
39 Munsö C 4
96 Münster,CH B 4
85 Munster,F B 4
66 Munster, Niedersachsen, D† C 3
65 Münster, Nordrhein Westfalen, D† C 5
71 Münstereifel B 5
65 Muntendam A 4
100 Münzkirchen A 1
10 Muodoslompolo B 3
10 Muonio B 3
97 Muotathal B 4
106 Mur-de-Barrez C 2
80 Mur-de-Bretagne B 3
93 Mur-de-Sologne B 5
101 Murakeresztúr C 4
91 Muran D 3
99 Murano D 3
69 Muranowo C 4
118 Muras A 3
106 Murat B 2
107 Murat-sur-Vèbre D 2
100 Murau B 2
141 Muravera C 3
110 Murazzano C 3
124 Murça B 2
121 Murchante B 5
67 Murchin B 6
133 Murcia D 1
100 Mureck C 3
105 Muret D 4
106 Muret-le-Chateau C 2
97 Murg A 5
154 Murgaševo A 3
96 Murgenthal A 3
121 Murguia B 4
96 Muri A 4
119 Murias de Paredes B 4
126 Muriel Viejo A 3
152 Murigan B 1
121 Murillo de Rio Leza B 4
121 Murillo el Fruto B 5
152 Murino B 1
14 Murjek B 4
48 Murlaggan E 3
64 Murmerwoude A 3
98 Murnau B 2
139 Muro B 4
133 Muro del Alcoy C 2
145 Muro Lucano C 4
106 Murol B 2
27 Murole B 6
104 Muron A 2
118 Muros B 1
119 Muros de Nalón A 4
77 Murowana Goślina A 6
152 Murrë C 2
54 Murreagh B 1
96 Mürren B 3
86 Murrhardt C 1
101 Murska Sobata C 4
101 Mursko Središce C 4
136 Murtas C 3
128 Murteira B 1
96 Murten B 3
150 Murter B 1
51 Murton C 6
124 Murtosa C 1
17 Murtovaara B 8
107 Murviel D 3
100 Mürzsteg B 3
76 Murzynowo A 4
100 Mürzzuschlag B 3
105 Musculdy D 2
89 Mušov C 4
85 Mußbach a. d. Weinstrasse A 5
51 Musselburgh B 4
65 Musselkanaal B 5
104 Mussidan B 3
148 Mussomeli B 3
95 Mussy-sur-Seine B 4
22 Mustasaari B 3
27 Mustio C 6
78 Muszaki B 3
91 Muszyna C 3
100 Muta C 3
27 Mutala B 6
50 Muthill A 4
91 Mutné C 2
85 Mutterstadt A 5
85 Mutzig B 4
23 Muurame C 7
23 Muurasjärvi B 7
27 Muurla C 6
25 Muuruvesi B 5
81 Muzillac C 4
91 Mužla E 1
99 Muzzana del Turgnano D 4
49 Mybster C 5
21 Myckelgensjö B 6
15 Myckle D 4
94 Myennes B 2
89 Myjava C 5
31 Myking, Buskerud, N C 5
30 Myking, Hordaland, N C 2
35 Mykland C 4
74 Mylau C 4
28 Myllykoski C 4
23 Myllymäki C 6
26 Mynämäki C 4
35 Myra C 4
30 Myrdal C 4
4 Myre B 4
43 Myresjö B 4
15 Myrheden C 4
22 Myrkky C 3
28 Myrskylä C 3
36 Mysen B 3
77 Myslakowice C 4
90 Myślenice C 2
68 Myślibórz C 2
77 Myślinow B 5
90 Myslowice B 2
20 Myssjo C 3
31 Mysuseter B 6
90 Myszków B 5
78 Myszyniec B 4
91 Mýtna D 2
91 Mýtne Ludany D 1
91 Mýto, Středoslovenský, CS D 2
87 Mýto, Zapadočeský, CS B 5

N

64 Naaldwijk C 2
26 Naantali C 5
64 Naarden B 3
25 Naarva B 8
55 Naas A 5
124 Nabais C 2
87 Nabburg B 4
102 Nabybaracska B 2
88 Načeradec B 2
88 Nachod A 4
71 Nachrodt-Wiblingwerde A 6
69 Naclaw A 4
103 Nădab B 5
79 Nadarzyn C 3
103 Nadăs B 5
101 Nádasd C 4
103 Nădlac B 4
77 Nadolice B 6
103 Nădudvar A 5
34 Nærbø C 1
30 Nærøy, Fjordane Fylke, N C 3
12 Nærøy Nord-Trøndelay Flyde, N C 3
45 Næstved B 4
97 Näfels A 5
58 Nafferton A 3
87 Nagel B 3
64 Nagele B 3
21 Naggen C 4
38 Naglarby B 2
90 Naglowice B 3
85 Nagold B 5
78 Nagoszewo C 4
26 Nagu C 4
115 Nagyatad A 5
101 Nagybajom C 5
101 Nagybarat B 5
91 Nagybátony E 2
101 Nagyberény C 6
91 Nagybörzsöny E 1
101 Nagycenk B 4
102 Nagydorog B 2
102 Nagyfüged A 4
91 Nagyhalász D 4
102 Nagyharsany C 2
101 Nagyigmánd B 6
103 Nagyiván A 4
103 Nagykamaras B 5
101 Nagykanizsa C 5
102 Nagykáta A 3
103 Nagykereki A 5
101 Nagykonyi C 6
102 Nagykorós A 3
103 Nagykörü A 4
91 Nagylóc D 2
103 Nagymágocs B 4
101 Nagymányok C 6
91 Nagymaros E 1
91 Nagyoroszi D 2
103 Nagyrabe A 5
91 Nagyréde E 2
103 Nagyszénás B 4
101 Nagyszokoly C 6
101 Nagyvázsony C 5
102 Nagyvenyim B 2
127 Naharros B 3
66 Nahe B 3
117 Naidas B 5
74 Naila C 3
107 Nailloux D 1
61 Nailsea B 4
61 Nailsworth B 4
93 Naintré C 4
49 Nairn D 5
121 Nájera B 4
26 Nakkila B 4
35 Nakksjø B 5
69 Naklo A 5
69 Naklo nad Notecia B 5
103 Nakovo C 4
45 Nakskov C 4
121 Nalda B 4
20 Nälden B 3
79 Naleczów D 5
91 Nálepkovo D 3
92 Nalliers C 2
107 Nalzen E 1
87 Nalžovské Hory B 5
19 Namdalseid A 7
88 Náměšt n. Oslavou B 4
90 Námestovo C 2
32 Namnå C 3
12 Namsos C 3
12 Namsskogan, Nord-Trondelag, N C 4
12 Namsskogan, Nord-Trondelag, N C 5
70 Namur B 3
77 Namysłów B 6
94 Nançay B 2
121 Nanclares de la Oca B 4
84 Nancy B 3
83 Nangis C 4
107 Nant C 3
92 Nantes B 2
83 Nanteuil-le-Haudouin B 4
104 Nantiat A 4
108 Nantua A 2
57 Nantwich C 4
156 Náousa B 2
89 Napajedla B 5
78 Napiwoda B 3
144 Nápoli C 3
4 Napp B 2
119 Naraval A 4
60 Narberth B 2

107 Narbonne D 3
107 Narbonne Plage D 3
19 Narbuvollen C 7
146 Nardò B 4
141 Nareso C 2
16 Narkaus A 5
10 Narken C 2
143 Narni B 3
148 Naro B 3
22 Närpes C 3
22 Närpiö C 3
125 Narros del Castillo C 4
29 Närsäkkälä B 8
115 Narta B 4
22 Närvijoki C 3
4 Narvik B 6
110 Narzole C 2
39 Nas, Gotland, S E 5
33 Nås, Kopparbergs Län, S C 5
39 Näs, Östergötlands Län, S D 2
21 Näsäker B 5
106 Nasbinals C 3
59 Naseby C 2
42 Näset B 1
102 Nasice C 2
79 Nasielsk C 3
149 Naso A 4
71 Nassau B 6
86 Nassenfels C 3
67 Nassenheide C 6
98 Nassereith B 1
43 Nässjö B 4
13 Nästansjö C 8
71 Nastätten B 6
28 Nastola C 3
47 Näsum A 5
33 Näsviken B 7
117 Natalinci B 4
96 Naters B 4
70 Natoye B 4
14 Nattavaara B 4
14 Nattavaara by B 5
87 Natternberg C 4
98 Natters B 2
86 Nattheim C 2
43 Nättraby C 5
8 Nattvatnstua C 5
99 Naturno C 1
99 Naturns C 1
107 Naucelle C 2
97 Nauders B 6
67 Nauen C 5
55 Naul A 5
74 Naumburg B 3
75 Naundorf C 5
75 Naunhof B 4
30 Naustdal B 2
26 Nauvo C 4
119 Nava A 5
126 Nava de Arévalo B 1
126 Nava de la Asunción A 1
125 Nava del Rey B 4
125 Navacepeda C 4
126 Navacerrada B 1
129 Navaconcejo A 5
126 Navahermosa C 1
122 Naval B 3
125 Navalacruz C 5
130 Navalcán A 1
126 Navalcarnero B 1
121 Navaleno C 4
125 Navalguijo C 4
126 Navalmanzano A 1
126 Navalmoral B 1
130 Navalmoral de la Mata B 1
133 Navalón de Arriba C 2
126 Navalperal de Pinares B 1
130 Navalpino B 2
125 Navaltalgordo C 5
130 Navaltoril B 2
126 Navaluenga B 1
130 Navalvillar de Pela B 1
123 Navarclés C 4
158 Navarino C 2
125 Navarredonda de la Sierra C 4
105 Navarrenx D 2
133 Navarrés B 2
121 Navarrete B 4
126 Navarrevisca B 1
123 Navás C 4
126 Navas de Oro A 1
136 Navas de San Juan A 3
136 Navas del Cepillar B 2
126 Navas del Rey B 1
129 Navas Madroño B 4
122 Navascués B 1
124 Navasfrias C 3
111 Nave B 5
124 Nave de Haver C 3
39 Nävekvarn D 3
143 Navelli B 4
59 Navenby B 3
36 Naverstad C 3
123 Naves C 4
130 Navezuelas B 1
119 Navia A 4
119 Navia de Suarna B 4
126 Navillas C 1
95 Navilly C 5
155 Návpaktos D 3
159 Návplion B 3
78 Nawiady B 4
105 Nay D 2
62 Nayland B 4
128 Nazaré B 1
74 Nazza B 2
152 Ndrejaj B 1
152 Ndroq C 1
156 Néa Agathoúpolis B 2
157 Néa Ankhíalos C 2
156 Nea Apollonía B 3
159 Néa Artáki A 4
159 Néa Epidhavros B 4
155 Néa Filippiás C 2
156 Néa Fókaia B 3
156 Néa Kallikrátia B 3
156 Néa Kariá B 4
156 Néa Karváli B 4
156 Néa Khalkidhón B 2
159 Néa Kíos B 3
158 Néa Koróni C 2
155 Néa Kutsúfliani C 3
156 Néa Mádhitos B 3
159 Néa Mákri A 4
158 Néa Manolás A 2
156 Néa Mikhanióna B 2
156 Néa Moudhanié B 3
156 Néa Péramos B 4
156 Néa Pláyia B 3
156 Néa Potídhaia B 3
159 Néa Psará A 4
156 Néa Ródha B 3
156 Néa Sárda B 2
156 Néa Tríglia B 3
156 Néa Zíkhna A 3
157 Néai Kariaí C 4
154 Neápolis, Kozáni, GR B 3
159 Neápolis, Lakonía, GR C 4
60 Neath B 3
44 Nebel C 1
74 Nebra B 3
120 Nebreda C 3
88 Nechanice A 3
85 Neckar-Steinach A 5
85 Neckarelz A 6
85 Neckargemund A 5
85 Neckarsulm A 6
118 Neda A 2
19 Nedalshytta C 8
101 Neded A 5
115 Nedelišće A 4
64 Neder Hardinxveld C 2
70 Nederbrakel B 2
23 Nedervetil B 5
71 Nederweert A 4
89 Nedožery C 6
32 Nedreberg C 2
34 Nedstrand B 1
89 Nedvědice B 4
89 Nędza A 6
65 Neede B 4
59 Needham Market C 5
71 Neerkant A 4
65 Neermoor A 5
71 Neeroeteren A 4
70 Neerpelt A 4
72 Neesen A 2
66 Neetze B 3
57 Nefyn D 2
116 Negbina C 3
72 Negenborn B 3
156 Negorci A 2
117 Negotin B 6
153 Negotino C 4
99 Negrar D 1
126 Negredo A 3
118 Negreira B 2
107 Nègrepelisse C 1
119 Negueira A 4
71 Neheim A 6
9 Neiden C 9
73 Neider Ramstadt D 2
85 Neiderbronn-les-Bains B 4
121 Neila B 4
50 Neilston B 3
110 Néive C 3
75 Nejdek C 4
77 Nekla A 6
47 Neksø B 6
124 Nelas C 2
35 Nelaug C 4
107 Nelfiès D 3
9 Nellimö D 8
86 Nellingen C 1
56 Nelson C 4
91 Nemčiňany D 1
159 Neméa B 3
101 Nemesgörzsöny B 5
101 Nemeskér B 4
102 Nemesnádudvar B 3
101 Nemesszalók B 5
102 Németker B 2
83 Nemours C 4
89 Nemšová C 6
54 Nenagh B 3
97 Nendeln A 5
66 Nendorf C 1
91 Nenince D 2
67 Nennhausen C 5
97 Nenzing A 5
155 Neokhóri D 3
156 Neokhórion, Imathía, GR B 2
155 Neokhórion, Kardhitsa, GR C 3
156 Neokhórion, Khalkidhikí, GR B 3
159 Neokhórion, Voiotía, GR A 4
157 Néon Monastínon C 2
156 Néon Petritsi A 3
156 Neon Soúlion A 3
156 Néon Yinaikókaston B 2
156 Néos Marmarás B 3
156 Néos Milótopos B 2
156 Néos Skopós A 3
142 Nepi B 3
87 Nepomuk B 5
105 Nérac C 3
88 Neratovice A 2
75 Nerchau B 4
104 Néré B 2
86 Neresheim C 2
117 Neresnica B 5
143 Nereto B 4
114 Nerezine C 2
150 Nerezišća B 2
94 Néris-les-Bains C 2
136 Nerja C 3
158 Nerómilos B 2
94 Nérondes C 2
137 Nerpio A 4
135 Nerva B 4
99 Nervesa della Battáglia D 3
110 Nervi C 4
106 Nervieux B 4
31 Nes, Buskerud, N C 6
30 Nes, Fjordane Fylke, N B 4
31 Nes, Hedmark Fylke, N C 7
64 Nes, NL A 3
30 Nes, Sogne og Fjordane, N B 3
19 Nes, Sor Trøndelag Fylke, N B 5
31 Nesbyen C 6
75 Neschwitz B 6
160 Nesebut D 5
34 Nesflaten B 2
34 Nesland B 3
35 Neslandsvatn C 5
83 Nesle B 4
5 Nesna D 2
89 Nesovice B 5
9 Nesseby B 8
97 Nesselwang A 6
31 Nesset B 7
97 Nesslau A 5
65 Nessmersiel A 5
110 Nesso B 4
158 Nestáni B 3
100 Nestelbach B 3
57 Neston C 3
154 Nestórion B 3
30 Nesttun C 2
101 Nesvady B 6
50 Nether Howecleugh B 4
61 Nether Stowey B 3
34 Netlandsnes C 2
88 Netolice B 2
97 Netstal A 5
84 Nettancourt B 1
58 Nettlebarn B 3
72 Nettlingen A 4
143 Nettuno C 3
74 Netzschkau C 4
72 Neu Buddenstedt A 5
66 Neu Darchau B 3
73 Neu-Isenburg C 2
67 Neu Kaliß B 4
75 Neu Lübbenau A 5
75 Neu Petershain B 6
97 Neu-Ravensburg A 5
86 Neu-Ulm C 2
87 Neualbenreuth B 4
87 Neubau B 4
65 Neubeckum C 6
101 Neuberg B 4
67 Neubrandenburg B 6
66 Neubruchhausen C 1
67 Neubukow A 4
86 Neuburg C 3
96 Neuchâtel B 2
74 Neudietendorf C 2
89 Neudorf, A C 4
85 Neudorf, D† A 5
103 Neudorf, R B 5
101 Neudorfl B 4
85 Neuenbürg, Baden-Württemberg, D† B 5
65 Neuenburg, Niedersachsen, D† A 5
86 Neuendettelsau B 2
67 Neuendorf A 6
65 Neuenhaus B 4
96 Neuenkirch A 4
65 Neuenkirchen, Niedersachsen, D† B 6
66 Neuenkirchen, Niedersachsen, D† B 1
66 Neuenkirchen, Niedersachsen, D† B 2
65 Neuenkirchen, Nordrhein-Westfalen, D† B 5
71 Neuenrad A 6
86 Neuenstein B 1
66 Neuenwalde B 1
71 Neuerburg B 5
85 Neuf-Brisach B 4
87 Neufahrn, Bayern, D† C 4
86 Neufahrn, Bayern, D† C 3
70 Neufchâteau, B C 4
84 Neufchâteau, F B 2
83 Neufchâtel B 6
100 Neufelden A 2
85 Neuffen B 6
83 Neuflize B 6
74 Neugattersleben B 3
75 Neugersdorf C 6
86 Neuhaus, Bayern, D† B 3
87 Neuhaus, Bayern, D† C 5
72 Neuhaus, Niedersachsen, D† B 3
66 Neuhaus, Niedersachsen, D† B 2
66 Neuhaus, D* B 3
74 Neuhaus a Rennweg C 3
74 Neuhaus-Schierschnitz C 3
85 Neuhausen C 5
97 Neuhausen a. Rheinfall A 4
86 Neuhof B 2
100 Neuhofen A 2
93 Neuillé-Pont-Pierre B 4
83 Neuilly, Aisne, F B 5
94 Neuilly, Allier, F C 3
83 Neuilly-en-Thelic B 4
95 Neuilly-l'Eveque B 5
67 Neukalen B 5
98 Neukirchen, Oberösterreich, A B 4
98 Neukirchen, Oberösterreich, A A 4
44 Neukirchen, D† C 1
98 Neukirchen am Großvenediger B 3
87 Neukirchen beim Heiligen Blut B 4
71 Neukirchen-Vluyn A 5
67 Neukloster B 4
100 Neulengbach A 3
106 Neulise B 4
151 Neum C 3
71 Neumagen C 5
75 Neumark C 4
86 Neumarkt, D† B 3
99 Neumarkt, I C 2
98 Neumarkt am Wallersee B 4
100 Neumarkt i. Mühlkn. A 2
100 Neumarkt i. Steiermark B 2
87 Neumarkt St. Veit C 4
66 Neumünster A 2
87 Neunburg vorm Wald B 4
93 Neung-sur-Beuvron B 5
97 Neunkirch A 4
101 Neunkirchen, A B 4
73 Neunkirchen, Hessen, D† C 3
71 Neunkirchen, Rheinland-Westfalen, D† B 6
71 Neunkirchen, Saarland, D† C 6
87 Neuötting C 4
85 Neuret A 5
67 Neuruppin C 5
77 Neusalz B 4
101 Neusiedl A 4
101 Neusiedl am See B 4
71 Neuß A 5
106 Neussargues-Moissac B 3
85 Neustadt, Baden-Württemberg D† C 5
87 Neustadt, Bayern, D† B 4
87 Neustadt, Bayern, D† B 3
74 Neustadt, Bayern, D† C 3
86 Neustadt, Bayern, D† B 2
87 Neustadt, Bayern, D† C 3
73 Neustadt, Hessen, D† C 3
66 Neustadt, Schleswig-Holstein, D† A 3
75 Neustadt, Dresden, D* B 6
74 Neustadt, Gera, D* C 3
67 Neustadt, Potsdam, D* C 5
85 Neustadt a. d. Weinstrasse A 5
66 Neustadt am Rübenberge C 2
67 Neustadt-Glewe B 4
69 Neustettin B 4
98 Neustift im Stubaital B 2
67 Neustrelitz B 6
101 Neutal B 4
82 Neutchâtel-en-Bray B 3
76 Neutrebbin A 3
84 Neuves-Maisons B 3
104 Neuvic B 3
106 Neuvic-d'Ussel B 2
108 Neuville, Rhône, F B 1
82 Neuville, Seine Maritime, F B 3
83 Neuville-aux-Bois C 4
93 Neuville-de-Poitou C 4
95 Neuville-lès-Dames C 5
83 Neuvy-Santour C 5
93 Neuvy-St. Sépulcre C 5
94 Neuvy-sur-Barangeon B 2
71 Neuwied B 6
75 Neuzelle A 6
108 Névache B 3
88 Neveklov B 2
70 Nevele A 2
94 Nevers C 3
151 Nevesinje B 4
150 Nevest B 2
153 Nevestino B 4
80 Névez C 3
71 Neviges A 6
35 Nevlunghavn C 5
50 New Abbey C 4
49 New Aberdour D 6
62 New Alresford B 2
50 New Bridge B 4
53 New Buildings B 4
49 New Byth D 6
54 New Chapel Cross C 1
50 New Cumnock B 3
49 New Deer D 6
50 New Galloway B 3
58 New Holland B 3
55 New Inn A 4
54 New Kildimo B 3
57 New Mills C 5
61 New Milton C 5
49 New Pitsligo D 6
60 New Quay A 2
62 New Romney C 4
55 New Ross B 5
58 New Rossington B 2

136 Olias C 2
126 Olias del Rey C 2
141 Oliena B 3
122 Oliete D 2
110 Oligate Com. B 3
156 Olimbiás C 2
121 Olite B 5
133 Oliva C 2
129 Oliva de la Frontera C 4
129 Oliva de Mérida C 4
129 Oliva de Plasencia A 4
147 Olivadi D 2
128 Olival B 2
136 Olivar C 3
135 Olivares B 4
126 Olivares de Duero A 1
127 Olivares de Júcar C 3
124 Oliveira de Azemeis C 1
124 Oliveira de Frades C 1
124 Oliveira do Conde C 2
124 Oliveira do Hospital C 2
129 Olivenza C 3
93 Olivet B 5
97 Olivone B 4
90 Olkusz B 2
133 Olleria C 2
58 Ollerton B 3
44 Ollerup B 3
106 Olliergues B 3
109 Ollioules D 2
96 Ollon B 3
70 Olloy-sur-Viroin B 3
39 Ölmbrotorp C 2
37 Ölme B 5
127 Olmeda B 3
131 Olmedilla de Alarcón B 4
126 Olmedilla de Roa A 2
126 Olmedo,E A 1
141 Olmedo,I B 2
140 Olmeto C 1
119 Olmillos de Castro C 4
120 Olmos de Ojeda B 2
59 Olney C 3
132 Olocau del Rey A 2
43 Olofström C 4
126 Olombrada A 1
89 Olomouc B 5
92 Olonne-sur-Mer C 2
107 Olonzac D 2
105 Oloron-Sainte Marie D 2
123 Olost C 5
123 Olot B 5
116 Olovo B 2
71 Olpe A 6
89 Olšany B 5
72 Olsberg B 2
71 Olsbrücken C 6
70 Olsene B 2
37 Ölserud B 5
39 Olshammar D 1
75 Ölsig B 5
47 Olsker B 5
64 Olst B 4
90 Olsztyn, Katowice, PL B 2
78 Olsztyn, Olsztyn, PL B 3
78 Olsztynek B 3
76 Olszyna B 4
90 Olszyny C 4
34 Oltedal C 2
96 Olten A 3
160 Oltenita C 5
96 Oltringen A 3
34 Ølve B 1
74 Olvenstedt A 3
135 Olvera C 5
141 Olzai B 3
53 Omagh B 4
57 Ombersley D 4
110 Omegna B 3
145 Omignano Scalo C 4
114 Omišalj B 2
65 Ommen B 4
156 Omólion C 2
117 Omoljica B 4
22 Omossa C 3
157 Omvriakí C 2
70 On,B B 4
30 Øn,N B 2
120 Oña, E B 3
18 Ona, N C 2
142 Onano B 2
34 Onarheim B 1
121 Oñate A 4
56 Onchan B 2
132 Onda B 2
133 Ondará C 3
121 Ondárroa A 4
105 Onesse C 1
62 Ongar B 4
109 Ongles C 2
70 Onhaye B 3
133 Onil C 2
120 Onis A 2
25 Onkamo C 7
70 Onnain B 2
47 Onnestad A 5
91 Ónod D 3
5 Onøy D 1
42 Onsala B 2
44 Onsbjerg B 3
47 Onslunda B 5
65 Onstwedde A 5
133 Onteniente C 2
25 Ontojoki A 5
133 Ontur C 1
116 Onudovac B 2
93 Onzain B 5
119 Onzonilla B 5
64 Oost-en-West-Soubourg C 1
64 Oost-Vlieland A 3
70 Oostakker A 2
70 Oostburg A 2
70 Oostende A 1
64 Oosterbeek C 3
64 Oosterend A 3
64 Oosterhout C 2
65 Oosterwolde B 4
70 Oosterzele B 2
64 Oosthuizen B 3
70 Oostkamp A 2
70 Oostmalle A 3
70 Oostrozebeke B 2
63 Oostvleteren B 4
64 Oostvoorne C 2
65 Ootmarsum B 4
77 Opalenica A 5
88 Opařany B 2
117 Oparic C 5
114 Opatija B 2
90 Opatów, Katowice, PL B 1
90 Opatów, Kielce, PL B 4
77 Opatówek B 7
90 Opatowiec B 3
89 Opava B 5
20 Ope B 3
64 Opeinde A 4
71 Opglabbeerk A 4
70 Ophasselt B 2
99 Opicina D 4
71 Opladen A 6
64 Opmeer B 2
88 Opočno A 4
79 Opoczno D 3
77 Opole C 6
79 Opole Lubelskie D 4
79 Oporów C 2
117 Opovo A 4
75 Oppach B 6
19 Oppdal C 5
39 Oppeby D 3
35 Oppegård B 6
77 Oppeln C 6
85 Oppenau B 5
100 Oppenberg B 2
73 Oppenheim D 2
64 Oppenhuizen A 3
66 Oppenwehe C 1
85 Oppenweiler B 6
145 Oppido Lucano C 4
147 Óppido Mamertina D 1
100 Opponitz B 2
36 Oppstad A 3
32 Opsahedan C 4
151 Opuzen B 3
121 Oquendo A 3
99 Ora C 2
128 Orada C 3
103 Oradea A 5
104 Oradour-sur-Glane B 4
104 Oradour-sur-Vayres B 3
152 Orahovac B 2
115 Orahovica B 5
115 Orahovo B 5
109 Oraison D 2
10 Orajärvi C 4
109 Orange C 1
141 Orani B 3
75 Oranienbaum B 4
67 Oranienburg C 6
54 Oranmore A 3
117 Orašac, Srbija, YU B 4
153 Orašac, Srbija, YU A 4
116 Orašje, Bosna i Hercegovina, YU A 2
117 Orašje, Srbija, YU B 5
22 Oravainen B 4
22 Oravais B 4
25 Oravi C 5
24 Oravikoski C 4
117 Oraviţa A 5
91 Oravská Lesná C 2
90 Oravské Polhora C 2
90 Oravská Veselé C 2
91 Oravský-Podzámok C 2
133 Orba C 2
124 Orbacém B 1
44 Ørbæk B 3
83 Orbais C 5
110 Orbassano B 2
96 Orbe B 2
82 Orbec B 2
142 Orbetello B 2
142 Orbetello Scalo B 2
38 Örbyhus B 4
137 Orce B 4
137 Orcera A 4
95 Orchamps B 5
95 Orchamps-Vennes B 6
133 Orcheta C 2
70 Orchies B 2
77 Orchowo A 7
108 Orcières C 3
118 Ordenes A 2
49 Ordhead D 6
49 Ordie D 6
66 Ording A 1
123 Ordino B 4
121 Orduna B 4
33 Ore B 6
127 Orea B 4
150 Orebić C 3
39 Örebro C 2
102 Öregcsertö B 3
38 Öregrund B 5
45 Orehoved C 4
130 Orellana de la Sierra B 1
130 Orellana la Vieja B 1
118 Orense B 3
157 Oreoi D 3
122 Orés B 2
59 Orford C 5
123 Orgañá B 4
126 Orgaz C 2
95 Orgeiet C 5
31 Ørgenvika C 6
82 Orgères-en-Beauce C 3
105 Orgibet E 3
49 Orgill C 5
109 Orgnac-l'Aven C 1
109 Orgon D 2
141 Orgósolo B 3
137 Oria,E B 4
146 Oria,I B 3
83 Origny-Ste. Benoite B 5
133 Orihuela C 2
132 Orihuela del Tremedal A 1
154 Orik B 1
28 Orimattila C 3
156 Orini A 3
121 Orio A 4
128 Oriola C 3
146 Oriolo B 2
27 Oripää C 5
22 Orismala C 4
141 Oristano C 2
101 Oriszentpéter C 4
103 Oritişoara C 5
27 Orivesi B 7
27 Orivesi as B 7
153 Orizari C 4
18 Orjavik C 3
36 Ørje B 3
136 Orjiva C 3
19 Orkanger B 5
78 Orkartowo B 4
46 Orkelljunga A 4
102 Orkény A 3
74 Orlamünde C 3
153 Orlane B 3
152 Orlate B 2
79 Orle,PL C 1
79 Orle,PL C 1
93 Orléans B 5
89 Orlova B 6
117 Orlovat A 4
156 Órma B 1
43 Ormaryd B 4
110 Ormea C 2
35 Ormemyr B 5
156 Ormília B 3
115 Ormož A 4
59 Ormsby St. Margaret C 5
56 Ormskirk C 4
95 Ornan B 6
38 Ornäs B 2
5 Ørnes D 2
78 Orneta A 3
44 Ørnhøj A 1
21 Örnsköldsvik B 7
118 Orol A 3
116 Orolik A 2
102 Orom C 3
96 Oron-la-Ville B 2
79 Orońsko D 3
110 Oropa B 2
132 Oropesa, Castellon, E A 3
130 Oropesa, Toledo, E B 1
91 Oros E 4
141 Orosei B 3
103 Orosháza B 4
115 Oroslavje B 3
102 Oroszlány A 2
102 Oroszlo B 2
141 Orotelli B 3
121 Orozco A 4
49 Orphir C 5
34 Orre C 1
43 Orrefors C 5
38 Orresta C 3
20 Orrviken B 3
33 Orsa B 5
145 Orsara di Púglia B 4
83 Orsay C 4
71 Orscholz C 5
93 Orsennes C 5
43 Orserum A 4
96 Orsières B 3
43 Orsjö C 5
18 Ørskog C 2
45 Orslev B 4
143 Orsogna B 5
146 Orsomarso C 1
117 Orşova B 6
30 Ørstavik A 3
44 Ørsted A 3
38 Örsundsbro C 4
145 Orta Nova B 4
110 Orta san Giulio B 3
143 Orte B 3
87 Ortenburg C 5
101 Orth A 4
105 Orthez D 2
71 Ortho B 4
118 Ortigueira A 3
122 Ortilla B 2
99 Ortisei C 2
30 Ortnevik B 3
46 Ortofta B 4
56 Orton B 4
143 Ortona B 5
75 Ortrand B 5
15 Örträsk D 2
115 Orubica B 5
44 Ørum A 2
141 Orune B 3
126 Orusco B 2
128 Orvalho A 3
92 Orvault B 2
142 Orvieto B 3
15 Orviken D 5
143 Orvinio B 3
160 Oryakhovo D 3
89 Orzesze A 6
111 Orzinuovi B 4
111 Orzivécchi B 4
78 Orzysz B 4
19 Os C 7
103 Osanádpalota B 4
152 Osanonica A 2
43 Osbruk B 4
47 Osby A 4
90 Oščadnica C 1
75 Oschatz B 5
74 Oschersleben A 3
141 Oschiri B 3
78 Ościslowo C 3
66 Osdorf A 3
116 Osečina B 3
120 Oseja de Sajambre A 1
88 Osek A 1
19 Osen A 6
122 Osera C 2
101 Osi B 6
141 Osidda B 3
69 Osie B 6
79 Osieck D 4
77 Osieczna B 5
69 Osiek, Bydgoszcz, PL B 5
78 Osiek, Bydgoszcz, PL B 2
90 Osiek, Kielce, PL B 4
90 Osielec C 2
69 Osielsko B 6
102 Osijek C 2
141 Ósilo B 2
113 Ósimo C 5
115 Osinja C 5
117 Osipaonica B 5
79 Osjaków D 1
116 Osječani C 2
43 Oskarshamn B 6
42 Oskarström C 2
89 Oslany C 6
89 Oslavany B 4
35 Oslo B 6
39 Ösmo D 4
79 Osmolin C 2
65 Osnabrück B 6
26 Osnäs C 4
76 Ośno A 3
120 Osorno B 2
30 Osøyra C 2
110 Ospedaletti D 2
111 Ospitaletto B 5
64 Oss C 3
156 Ossa B 3
131 Ossa de Montiel C 4
141 Ossi B 2
31 Ossjøen C 5
105 Ossun D 2
47 Ostanå A 5
21 Östanbäck C 5
39 Östansjö C 1
33 Östanvik B 6
114 Oštarije B 3
20 Östavall C 4
65 Ostbevern B 5
32 Østby B 3
38 Östebybruk B 4
45 Osted B 4
113 Ostellato B 3
40 Øster Hornum C 3
40 Øster Hurup C 4
44 Öster Lindet B 2
47 Öster Marie B 6
40 Øster Tørslev C 4
40 Øster Vrå B 4
21 Österås B 6
67 Osterburg C 4
73 Osterburken D 3
41 Østerbyhavn B 5
43 Österbymo B 5
38 Österfärnebo B 3
74 Osterfeld B 3
21 Osterforse B 6
87 Osterhofen C 5
66 Osterholz-Scharmbeck B 1
43 Österkorsberga B 5
40 Østerlid B 2
38 Österlövsta B 4
98 Ostermiething A 3
72 Osterode B 4
66 Osterrönfeld A 2
20 Östersund B 3
27 Östersundom C 8
38 Östervåla B 4
36 Östervallskog B 3
65 Osterwick B 5
74 Osterwiek B 2
86 Osterzell D 2
101 Ostffyasszonyfa B 5
38 Östhammar B 5
85 Ostheim B 4
73 Ostheim v. d. Rhon C 4
73 Osthofen D 2
111 Ostiano B 5
112 Ostiglia A 3
121 Ostiz B 5
36 Östmark A 4
33 Östnor B 5
102 Ostojićevo C 4
113 Ostra C 5
37 Östra Amtervik B 5
39 Östra Husby D 3
46 Östra Ljungby A 4
39 Östra Ryd D 3
47 Ostraby B 4
85 Ostrach C 6
75 Ostrau B 5
89 Ostrava B 6
35 Østre Halsen B 6
152 Ostren i math C 2
65 Ostrhauderfehn A 5
85 Ostringen A 5
75 Ostritz B 6
89 Ostrob C 5
78 Ostróda B 2
78 Ostroleka B 4
69 Ostropole B 4
75 Ostrov C 4
88 Ostrov n. Oslavou B 3
78 Ostrów Mazowiecka C 4
77 Ostrów Wielkopolski B 6
79 Ostrówek D 1
69 Ostrowiec A 4
90 Ostrowiec Swietokrzyski B 4
77 Ostrowo A 7
79 Ostrowy C 2
151 Ostrožac, Bosna i Hercegovina, YU B 3
115 Ostrožac, Bosna i Hercegovina, YU C 3

126 Pastrana B 3
99 Pastrengo D 1
78 Pasym B 3
91 Pásztó E 2
101 Pata A 5
103 Păţal A 6
117 Pătas B 6
82 Patay C 3
58 Pateley Bridge A 2
16 Pateniemi B 4
132 Paterna B 2
135 Paterna de Rivera C 5
135 Paterna del Campo B 4
131 Paterna del Madera C 4
99 Paternion C 4
149 Paternò B 4
145 Paternópoli C 4
87 Patersdorf B 4
65 Paterswolde A 4
50 Patna B 3
77 Patnów A 7
9 Patoniva C 7
154 Patos B 1
158 Pátrai A 2
54 Patrickswell B 3
140 Patrimonio B 2
58 Patrington B 4
141 Pattada B 3
72 Pattensen, Niedersachsen, D† A 3
66 Pattensen, Niedersachsen, D† B 3
56 Patterdale B 4
149 Patti A 4
16 Pattijoki C 3
102 Páty A 2
105 Pau D 2
104 Pauillac B 2
24 Paukarlahti C 4
99 Paularo C 4
106 Paulhaguet B 3
107 Paulhan D 3
141 Paulilátino B 2
103 Păulis B 5
43 Pauliström B 5
111 Paullo B 4
74 Pausa C 3
13 Pauträsk C 9
110 Pavia, I B 4
128 Pavia, P C 2
132 Pavias B 2
82 Pavilly B 2
159 Pávlon A 4
112 Pavullo nel Frignano B 2
67 Päwesin C 5
90 Pawonków B 1
96 Payerne B 2
134 Paymoyo B 3
155 Páyoi C 1
104 Payrac C 4
160 Pazardzhik D 4
114 Pazin B 1
107 Paziols E 2
115 Pčelić B 5
90 Pcim C 2
153 Pčinja B 3
62 Peacehaven C 4
136 Peal de Becerro B 3
59 Peasenhall C 5
62 Peasmarsh C 4
152 Pec B 2
112 Péccioli C 2
102 Pécel A 3
153 Pečenjevce A 3
134 Pechão B 3
87 Pechbrunn B 4
9 Pechenga C 11
103 Pecica B 5
116 Pećinci B 3
103 Peciu Nou C 5
72 Peckelsheim B 3
91 Pečovská C 4
102 Pécs B 2
102 Pecsvárad B 2
151 Pečurice C 5
79 Peczniew D 1
113 Pedaso C 5
99 Pedavena C 2
121 Pedernales A 4
99 Pedérobba D 2
47 Pedersker B 5
99 Pedescala D 2
155 Pedhiní C 2
126 Pedrajas de S. Esteban A 1
132 Pedralba B 2
119 Pedralba de la Pradería B 4
126 Pedraza A 2
133 Pedreguer C 3
118 Pedreira A 2
136 Pedrera B 2
136 Pedro Abad B 2
125 Pedro Bernardo C 5
136 Pedro-Martinez B 3
131 Pedro Muñoz B 4
130 Pedroche C 2
134 Pedrogão, Beja, P A 3
129 Pedrogao, Castelo Branco, P A 3
128 Pedrógão, Leiria, P B 2
128 Pedrógao Grande B 2
121 Pedrola C 5
120 Pedrosa B 3
120 Pedrosa del Rey, León, E B 2
125 Pedrosa del Rey, Valladolid, E B 4
120 Pedrosa del Rio Urbel B 3
125 Pedrosilla B 4
125 Pedrosillo de los Aires C 4
69 Pedzewo B 6
51 Peebles B 4
56 Peel B 2
67 Peenemünde A 6
70 Peer A 4
157 Pefkíon C 3
124 Pega C 2
136 Pegalajar B 3
74 Pegau B 4
100 Peggau B 3
110 Pegli C 3
86 Pegnitz B 3
133 Pego C 2
128 Pegões-Estação C 2
128 Pegões Velhos C 2
51 Pegswood B 6
153 Pehčevo C 4
27 Pehula B 5
48 Peinchorran D 2
72 Peine A 4
99 Péio C 1
109 Peipan C 2
26 Peipohja B 5
108 Peisey-Nancroix B 3
98 Peißenberg B 2
98 Peiting B 1
75 Peitz B 6
116 Peka B 3
17 Pekkala A 5
126 Pelahustán B 1
157 Pelasyía D 2
68 Pelczyce B 3
155 Pélekas C 1
88 Pelhřimov B 3
109 Pélissanne D 2
11 Pelkosenniemi B 7
156 Pella B 2
108 Pellafol C 2
111 Pellegrino Parmense C 4
104 Pellegrue C 3
102 Pellérd B 2
113 Pellestrina A 4
93 Pellevoisin C 5
28 Pellinge C 3
99 Pellizano C 1
10 Pello C 4
130 Peloche B 1
10 Peltovuoma A 4
108 Pelussin B 1
102 Pély A 4
60 Pembrey B 2
60 Pembroke B 2
60 Pembroke Dock B 2
62 Pembury B 4
57 Pen-y-groes C 2
125 Peña de Cabra C 4
121 Peñacerrada B 4
128 Penacova A 2
126 Peñafiel, E A 1
124 Penafiel, P B 1
135 Peñaflor B 5
130 Peñalsordo C 1
124 Penalva do Castel C 2
129 Penamacor A 3
120 Penamellera Alta A 2
120 Peñamellera Baja A 2
125 Peñaparda C 3
125 Peñaranda de Bracamonte C 4
126 Peñaranda de Duero A 2
132 Peñarroya de Tastavins A 3
135 Peñarroya Pueblonuevo A 5
118 Peñarrubia, Lugo, E B 3
136 Peñarrubia, Málaga, E C 2
61 Penarth B 3
131 Peñas de San Pedro C 5
131 Peñascosa C 4
125 Peñausende B 4
91 Penc E 2
60 Pencoed B 3
154 Pendálofon B 3
155 Pendálofos D 3
60 Pendeen C 1
120 Pendueles A 2
124 Penedono C 2
128 Penela A 2
124 Penhas Juntas B 2
128 Peniche B 1
51 Penicuik B 4
75 Penig C 4
134 Penilhos B 3
132 Peñíscola A 3
58 Penistone B 2
153 Penkotsi B 4
57 Penkridge D 4
68 Penkun B 2
57 Penmaenmawr C 3
80 Penmarch C 2
113 Pennabilli C 4
105 Penne, F C 3
143 Penne, I B 4
98 Pennes C 2
50 Pennyghael A 2
57 Penrhyndeudraeth D 2
56 Penrith B 4
60 Penryn C 1
98 Pens C 2
57 Pentraeth C 2
60 Penzance C 1
98 Penzberg B 2
86 Penzing C 2
67 Penzlin B 6
109 Péone C 3
117 Pepeljevac C 5
78 Peplin B 1
154 Peqin A 1
101 Pér B 5
134 Pêra B 2
128 Pera Boa A 3
17 Perä-Posio A 6
124 Perafita B 1
156 Peraía, Pella, GR B 1
156 Peraía, Thessaloníki, GR B 2
159 Perakhóra A 3
158 Perakhórion A 1
130 Peraleda de la Mata B 1
130 Peraleda de S. Roman B 1
127 Peralejos B 4
127 Perales de Alfambra B 4
126 Perales de Tajuña B 4
121 Peralta B 5
122 Peralta de la Sal C 3
134 Peralva B 3
127 Peralveche B 3
159 Pérama B 4
17 Peranka B 8
22 Peräseinajöki C 5
120 Perbál A 2
101 Perchtoldsdorf A 4
81 Percy B 5
141 Perdasdefogu C 3
154 Perdhíka B 3
159 Pérdhika, Aîyina, GR B 4
155 Pérdhika, Thesprotia, GR C 2
122 Perdiguera C 2
124 Peredo B 3
134 Pereiro, Faro, P C 3
124 Pereiro, Guarda, P C 2
128 Pereiro, Santarém, P B 2
118 Pereiro de Aguiar B 3
123 Perelada B 6
129 Perelada de Zaucejo C 5
122 Perello D 3
125 Pereña B 3
125 Pereruela B 4
141 Pérfugas B 2
100 Perg A 2
99 Pérgine Valsugana C 2
113 Pérgola C 4
149 Pergusa B 4
23 Perho B 6
99 Peri D 1
103 Periam B 4
136 Periana C 2
81 Périers A 5
91 Perín D 4
111 Perino C 4
156 Peristéra B 3
156 Perithórion A 3
104 Périueux B 3
155 Perivóli C 2
102 Perkáta A 2
67 Perleberg B 4
117 Perlez A 4
78 Perly A 4
154 Përmet B 2
28 Pernå C 4
28 Pernaja C 4
87 Pernarec B 5
100 Pernegg a. d. Mur B 3
101 Pernek A 5
128 Pernes B 2
109 Pernes-les-Fontaines C 2
156 Pérni A 4
153 Pernik B 5
75 Pernink C 4
27 Perniö C 6
100 Pernitz B 3
128 Pero Pinheiro C 1
134 Peroguardia A 2
107 Pérols D 3
95 Peron C 5
83 Péronne B 4
70 Péronnes B 3
126 Perorrubio A 2
110 Perosa Argentina C 2
124 Perozinho B 1
123 Perpignan B 5
60 Perranporth C 1
95 Perrecy-lès-Forges C 4
110 Perrero C 2
106 Perrier B 3
96 Perrignier B 2
80 Perros-Guirec B 3
83 Persan B 4
37 Persberg B 6
100 Persenbeug A 3
57 Pershore D 4
38 Pershyttan C 2
43 Persnäs B 6
75 Perštejn C 5
46 Perstorp A 4
51 Perth A 4
98 Pertisau B 2
27 Pertteli C 6
109 Pertuis D 2
28 Pertunmaa B 4
116 Peručac C 3
113 Perúgia C 4
114 Perušic C 3
70 Péruwelz B 2
70 Perwez B 3
120 Pesadas de Burgos B 3
120 Pesaguero A 2
113 Pésaro C 4
99 Pescantina D 1
143 Pescara B 5
143 Pescasseroli C 4
99 Peschiera del Garda D 1
112 Péscia C 2
143 Pescina B 4
144 Pesco Sannita B 3
143 Pescocostanzo C 5
145 Pescopagano C 4
152 Peshk C 2
152 Peshkopi C 2
95 Pesmes B 5
126 Pesquera de Duero A 1
104 Pessac C 2
124 Pessegueiro C 1
154 Peštani A 2
155 Péta C 3
25 Petäiskylä B 6
17 Petäjäjärvi B 5
16 Petäjäskoski A 4
23 Petajävesi C 7
22 Petalax C 3
158 Petalídhion C 2
71 Pétange C 4
70 Petegem B 2
115 Peteranec A 4
59 Peterborough C 3
61 Peterchurch A 4
49 Peterculter D 6
49 Peterhead D 7
51 Peterlee C 6
62 Petersfield C 3
66 Petershagen, D† C 1
67 Petershagen, Frankfurt, D* C 6
76 Petershagen, Frankfurt, D* A 3
86 Petershausen C 3
87 Peterskirchen C 4
54 Peterswell A 3
91 Pétervására D 3
103 Petig B 6
147 Petília Policastro C 2
11 Petkula B 6
75 Petkus B 5
102 Petlovac C 2
116 Petlovača B 3
117 Petnic B 6
102 Petőfiszallás B 3
22 Petolahti C 3
139 Petra B 4
149 Petralia Sottana B 4
57 Petrefoelas C 3
133 Petrel C 2
152 Petrelë C 1
144 Petrella Tifernina B 3
140 Petreto-Bicchisano C 1
153 Petrich C 5
115 Petrijanec A 4
102 Petrijevci C 2
115 Petrinja B 4
89 Petřkovice B 6
133 Pétrola C 1
159 Petromagoúla A 3
147 Petronà C 2
101 Petronell A 4
160 Petroseni C 3
156 Petroúsa A 4
151 Petrovac, Crna Gora, YU C 4
117 Petrovac, Srbija, YU B 5
116 Petrovaradin A 3
89 Petrovice, Severomoravsky, CS B 6
87 Petrovice, Započesky, CS B 5
22 Petsmo B 3
100 Pettenbach B 2
51 Petterden A 5
52 Pettigoe B 4
87 Petting D 4
62 Petworth C 3
126 Peubla de Beleña B 2
119 Peubla de Sanabria B 4
98 Peuerbach A 4
119 Peunte de Domingo Flórez B 4
120 Peuntenansa A 2
62 Pevensey C 4
62 Pewsey B 2
65 Pewsum A 5
106 Peyrat-le-Château B 1
105 Peyrehorade D 1
107 Peyriac-Minervois D 2
108 Peyrins B 2
104 Peyrissac B 4
109 Peyruis C 2
83 Pežarches C 4
107 Pézenas D 3
101 Pezinok A 5
126 Pezuela de las Torres B 2
104 Pézuls C 3
86 Pfaffenhausen C 2
86 Pfaffenhofen, Bayern, D† C 2
86 Pfaffenhofen, Bayern, D† C 3
85 Pfaffenhoffen B 4
97 Pfäffikon A 4
64 Pfalzdorf C 4
87 Pfarrkirchen C 4
74 Pfarrweisach C 2
85 Pfedelbach A 6
87 Pfeffenhausen C 3
85 Pfetterhouse C 4
85 Pforzheim B 5
87 Pfreimd B 4
97 Pfronten A 6
85 Pfullendorf C 6
85 Pfullingen B 6
97 Pfunds B 6
97 Pfungen A 4
73 Pfungstadt D 2
97 Pfyn A 4
85 Phalsbourg B 4
70 Philippeville B 3
87 Philippsreut C 5
73 Philippsthal C 3
27 Phyäjärvi C 7
111 Piacenza B 4
112 Piacenza d'Adige A 3
111 Piádena B 5
140 Piana B 1
110 Piana Crixia C 3
148 Piana degli Albanesi B 3
144 Piana di Caiazzo B 3
142 Piancastagnáio B 2
112 Piandelagotti B 2
143 Pianella, Abruzzi, I B 5
112 Pianella, Toscan, I C 3
111 Pianello Val Tidone C 4
110 Piano C 3
112 Pianoro B 3
142 Pianosa B 1
97 Pians A 6
134 Pias A 3
79 Piaseczno C 4
68 Piasek C 2

69 Piasnica Wielka A 6
79 Piastów C 3
69 Piaszczyna A 5
79 Piatek C 2
90 Piatkowiec B 4
160 Piatra Neamt B 5
112 Piazza al Sérchio B 2
149 Piazza Armerina B 4
111 Piazza Brembana B 4
99 Piazzola sul Brenta D 2
132 Picasent B 2
113 Piccione C 4
145 Picerno C 4
100 Pichi b. Wels A 1
58 Pickering A 3
143 Pico C 4
130 Picón B 2
83 Picquigny B 4
61 Piddletrenthide C 4
109 Pie C 1
69 Piechcin C 6
78 Piecki B 4
69 Piecnik B 4
110 Piedicavallo B 2
140 Piedicroce B 2
144 Piedimonte d'Alife B 3
149 Piedimonte Etneo B 5
96 Piedimulera B 4
143 Piedipaterno sul Nera B 3
130 Piedra Escrita B 2
130 Piedrabuena B 2
119 Piedrafita, León, E A 5
119 Piedrafita, Lugo, E B 3
125 Piedrahita C 4
126 Piedralaves B 1
129 Piedras Albas B 4
142 Piegaro B 3
16 Piehinki C 3
90 Piekary Ślask B 1
24 Pieksamaki C 4
24 Pielavesi B 3
87 Pielenhofen B 3
77 Pielgrzymka B 4
78 Pieniezno A 3
84 Piennes A 2
76 Pieńsk B 4
142 Pienza A 2
123 Piera C 4
78 Pieranie C 1
127 Pieresteban C 3
49 Pierowall B 6
95 Pierre C 5
104 Pierre-Buffière B 4
108 Pierre-Châtel C 2
109 Pierrefeu D 3
106 Pierrefiche C 3
105 Pierrefitte-Nestalas E 2
84 Pierrefitte-sur-Aure B 2
83 Pierrefonds B 4
95 Pierrefontaine B 6
106 Pierrefort C 2
83 Pierrepont, Aisne, F B 5
84 Pierrepont, Meurthe, F A 2
98 Piesendorf B 3
101 Piest'any A 5
78 Pieszkow A 3
77 Pieszyce C 5
22 Pietarsaari B 4
86 Pietenfeld C 3
110 Pietra Ligure C 3
145 Pietragalla C 4
113 Pietralunga C 4
144 Pietramelara B 3
149 Pietraperzia B 4
112 Pietrasanta C 2
78 Pietrasze A 5
144 Pietravairano B 3
110 Pieve del Cairo B 3
111 Pieve di Bono B 5
99 Pieve di Cadore C 3
112 Pieve di Cento B 3
99 Pieve di Soligo D 3
110 Pieve di Teco C 2
113 Pieve Santo Stéfano C 4
143 Pieve Torina A 4
112 Pievepélago B 2
143 Piglio C 4
110 Pigna D 2
144 Pignataro Maggiore B 3
23 Pihlajavesi C 6
26 Pihlava B 4
23 Pihtipudas B 7
27 Piikkiö C 5
16 Piippola C 4
64 Pijnacker B 2
69 Pila B 5
156 Pilaía B 2
135 Pilas B 4
112 Pilastri B 3
77 Pilawa C 5
78 Pilawki B 2
89 Pilchowice, Katowice, PL A 6
77 Pilchowice, Wroclaw, PL C 4
20 Pilgrimstad C 4
155 Pili C 3
90 Pilica B 2
102 Pilis A 3
120 Piliscaba A 2
120 Pilisszántó A 2
102 Pilisvörösvár A 2
105 Pillelardit D 2
56 Pilling C 4
158 Pílos C 2
89 Pilszcz A 5
61 Pilton B 4
90 Pilzno C 4
122 Pina de Ebro C 2
136 Piñar B 3
105 Pinas D 3
102 Pincehely B 2
59 Pinchbeck C 3
103 Pincota B 5
90 Pińczów B 3
123 Pineda C 5
120 Pineda de la Sierra B 3
122 Pinell de Bray C 3
110 Pinerolo C 2
143 Pineto B 5
83 Piney C 6
101 Pinggau B 4
128 Pinhal-Novo C 2
124 Pinhão B 2
124 Pinheiro B 1
124 Pinheiro, Aveiro, P C 1
128 Pinheiro Grande B 2
124 Pinhel C 2
133 Pinilla C 1
125 Pinilla de Toro B 4
101 Pinkafeld B 4
66 Pinneberg B 2
101 Pinngsdorf B 4
75 Pinnow B 6
140 Pino B 2
120 Pino del Rio B 2
125 Pinofranqueado C 3
106 Pinols B 3
118 Piñor B 3
136 Pinos del Valle C 3
136 Pinos-Puente B 3
123 Pinosmar C 4
133 Pinoso C 1
17 Pintamo B 6
126 Pinto B 5
50 Pinwherry B 3
99 Pinzano al Tagliamento C 3
124 Pinzio C 2
99 Pinzolo C 1
113 Piòbbico C 4
109 Piolenc C 1
142 Piombino B 1
79 Pionki D 4
94 Pionsat C 2
113 Pióraca C 4
129 Piornal A 5
110 Piossasco C 2
79 Piotrków-Kujawski,PL C 1
79 Piotrków-Kujawski,PL C 1
79 Piotrków Trybunalski D 2
90 Piotrkowice B 3
79 Piotrowice C 4
89 Piotrowice Wielkie A 6
113 Piove di Sacco A 4
99 Piovene D 2
43 Piperskärr B 6
81 Pipriac C 5
154 Piqeras B 1
159 Piraiévs B 4
114 Piran B 1
152 Pirane B 2
81 Piré-sur-Seiche B 5
158 Pirgos B 2
158 Pirgos Dhiroú C 3
92 Piriac-sur-Mer B 1
27 Pirkkala B 6
85 Pirmasens A 4
75 Pirna C 5
153 Pirot A 4
150 Pirovac B 1
154 Pirsóyianni B 2
17 Pirttikoski A 6
22 Pirttikylä C 3
7 Pirttivuopio D 5
156 Piryetós C 2
154 Píryoi B 3
112 Pisa C 2
104 Pisany B 2
115 Pisarovina B 3
100 Pischelsdorf i. St. B 3
103 Pişchia C 5
145 Pisciotta C 4
103 Pişcolt A 6
111 Pisogne B 5
105 Pissos C 2
146 Pisticci B 2
112 Pistóia C 2
78 Pisz B 4
49 Pitcaple D 6
15 Piteå C 5
160 Piteşti C 4
156 Pithion B 2
83 Pithiviers C 4
142 Pitigliano B 2
27 Pitkäjärvi C 6
49 Pitlochry E 5
115 Pitomaca B 5
136 Pitres C 3
51 Pitscottie A 5
51 Pittenweem A 5
87 Pittersberg B 4
103 Pitvaros B 2
114 Pivka B 2
116 Pivnice A 3
151 Pivski Monastir B 4
90 Piwniczna C 3
77 Piwonice B 7
136 Pizarra C 2
99 Pizzano C 1
111 Pizzighettone B 4
147 Pizzo D 2
143 Pízzoli B 4
123 Plá de Monlleu C 4
123 Plá de Santa Maria C 4
80 Plabennec B 2
121 Placencia A 4
96 Plaffeien B 3
49 Plaidy D 6
105 Plaisance, Gers, F D 3
105 Plaisance, Haute Garonne, F D 4
107 Plaisance, Tarn, F D 2
122 Plan B 3
108 Plan-de-Baix C 2
109 Plan-d'Orgon D 1
109 Plan du Var D 4
87 Planá B 4
88 Planá n. Luznici B 2
88 Plaňany A 3
108 Planay B 3
94 Planchez B 4
81 Plancoët B 4
83 Plancy C 5
117 Plandište A 5
87 Plánice B 5
114 Planina B 2
117 Planinica C 6
85 Plankstadt A 5
129 Plasencia A 4
129 Plasenzuela B 4
114 Plaški B 3
32 Plassen B 3
91 Plášťovce D 2
87 Plasy B 5
159 Plataiai A 4
156 Platamón C 2
156 Plataniá,GR A 4
147 Platania,I C 2
158 Plátanos, Akhaïa, GR A 3
158 Plátanos, Ilía, GR B 2
156 Platí,GR B 2
147 Platì,I D 2
158 Platiána B 2
116 Platičevo B 3
157 Platíkambos C 2
87 Plattling C 4
67 Plau B 5
74 Plaue, Erfurt, D* C 2
67 Plaue, Potsdam, D* C 5
74 Plauen C 4
152 Plav B 1
91 Plaveč C 3
101 Plavecký Mikulás A 5
117 Plavişevița B 6
116 Plavna, Pokragina Vojvodina, YU A 3
117 Plavna, Srbija, YU B 6
91 Plavnica C 3
115 Plavno C 4
77 Plawce A 6
123 Playa de Aro C 6
106 Pleaux B 2
81 Pleine-Fougères B 5
86 Pleinfeld B 2
87 Pleinting C 5
81 Plélan-le-Grand C 4
80 Plémet-la-Pierre B 4
121 Plencia A 4
80 Pléneuf-Val-Andre B 4
80 Plerin B 4
91 Plešany D 4
91 Plešivec D 3
75 Plessa B 5
81 Plessé C 5
80 Plestin-les-Grèves B 3
77 Pleszew B 6
115 Pleternica B 5
71 Plettenberg A 6
153 Pletvar C 3
80 Pleubian B 3
93 Pleumartin C 4
80 Pleumeur-Bodou B 3
83 Pleurs C 5
160 Pleven D 4
89 Plevník-Drienové B 6
80 Pleyben B 3
80 Pleyber-Christ B 3
133 Pliego C 1
91 Pliešovce D 2
151 Pljevlja B 5
141 Ploaghe B 2
150 Ploče B 3
85 Plochingen B 6
79 Plock C 2
63 Ploegsteert B 4
80 Ploëmeur C 3
81 Ploërmel C 4
80 Plœuc-sur-Lie B 4
80 Plogastel St. Germain C 2
80 Plogoff B 2
160 Ploieşti C 5
95 Plombières-les-Bains B 6
95 Plombières-lès-Dijon B 4
114 Plomin B 2
66 Plön A 3
80 Plonéour-Lanvern C 2
79 Plońsk C 3
87 Ploßberg B 4
68 Ploty B 3
80 Plouagat B 3
80 Plouaret B 3
80 Plouay C 3
81 Ploubalay B 4
80 Ploubazlanec B 3
80 Ploudalmézeau B 2
80 Ploudiry B 2
80 Plouescat B 2
80 Plouézec B 4
80 Plougasnou B 3
80 Plougastel-Daoulas B 2
80 Plougonven B 3
80 Plougonver B 3
80 Plougrescant B 3
80 Plouguenast B 4
80 Plouguerneau B 2
80 Plouguernevel B 3
80 Plouha B 4
80 Plouhinec B 2
80 Plouigneau B 3
80 Ploumanc'h B 3
80 Plouray B 3
80 Plouzévédé B 2
160 Plovdiv D 4
80 Plozévet C 2
117 Plugova B 6
53 Plumbridge B 4
80 Pluméliau C 4
89 Plumlov B 5
78 Pluty A 3
80 Pluvigner C 4
151 Pluzine B 4
78 Pluznica B 1
60 Plymouth C 2
69 Plytnica B 4
87 Plzen B 5
79 Pniewo C 4
77 Pniewy A 5
121 Pobes B 4
87 Poběžovice B 4
77 Pobiedziska A 6
68 Pobierowo A 2
122 Pobla de Segur B 3
88 Počatky B 3
128 Poceirão C 2
100 Pöchlarn A 3
28 Pockar C 4
75 Pockau C 5
86 Pöcking D 3
87 Pocking, Bayern, D† C 5
58 Pocklington B 3
103 Pocsaj A 5
152 Poda B 1
153 Podareš C 4
91 Podbiel C 2
75 Podbořany C 5
91 Podbrezová D 2
79 Poddebice D 1
88 Poděbrady A 3
76 Podelzig A 3
124 Podence B 3
104 Podensac C 2
111 Podenzano C 4
101 Podersdorf a. See B 4
69 Podgaje B 4
150 Podgora B 3
116 Podgorac, Hrvatska, YU A 2
117 Podgorac, Srbija, YU C 5
154 Podgori B 2
114 Podgrad B 2
101 Podhájska A 6
156 Podhokhóri B 4
150 Podhum B 2
78 Podlejki B 3
91 Podlužany D 1
116 Podnovlje B 2
89 Podolie C 5
91 Podolínec C 3
115 Podravska Slatina B 5
116 Podromanija C 2
101 Podturen C 4
101 Podunajské Biskupice A 5
89 Podvin C 4
90 Podwilk C 2
70 Poelkapelle B 1
67 Poggendorf A 6
146 Poggiardo B 4
112 Poggibonsi C 3
112 Póggio a Caiano C 3
145 Poggio Imperiale B 4
143 Póggio Mirteto B 3
143 Póggio Moiano B 3
112 Póggio Renatico B 3
112 Póggio Rusco B 3
100 Poggstall A 3
154 Pogonianí B 2
77 Pogorzela B 6
69 Pogorzelice A 5
154 Pogradec B 2
78 Pogrodzie A 2
27 Pohja, Hämeen Lääni, SF B 7
27 Pohja, Uudenmaan Lääni, SF C 6
29 Pohjalankila B 6
22 Pohjanluoma C 4
23 Pohjaslahti C 6
27 Poho C 6
91 Pohorelá D 3
89 Pohorelice C 4
101 Pohranice A 6
91 Pohronská Polhora D 2
117 Poiana Mărului A 6
128 Poiares A 2
110 Poirino C 2
94 Poisson C 4
84 Poissons B 2
93 Poitiers C 4
82 Poix B 3
70 Poix-Terron C 3
154 Pojan B 2
103 Pojoga C 6
10 Pokka A 5
77 Pokój C 6
115 Pokupsko B 3
118 Pol A 3
119 Pola de Siero A 5
95 Polaincourt-et-Clairefontaine B 6
126 Polán C 1
89 Polanica Zdrój A 4
90 Polaniec B 4
69 Polanów A 4
152 Polatna A 3
71 Polch B 6
14 Polcirkeln B 5
69 Pólczno A 5
69 Polczyn-Zdrój B 4
62 Polegate C 4
122 Poleñino C 2
112 Polesella B 3
59 Polesworth C 2
100 Polfing-Brunn C 3
91 Polgár E 4
101 Polgárdi B 6
154 Poliçan B 2
68 Police B 2
89 Polička B 4
114 Poličnik C 3
146 Policoro B 2
79 Policzna D 4
156 Polidhéndron B 2
157 Polídhroson D 2
106 Polignac B 3
145 Polignano a Mare C 6
81 Poligné C 5
95 Poligny C 5
156 Polikárpi B 2
156 Polikastron B 2
154 Polipótamon B 3
147 Polistena D 2
159 Politiká A 4
156 Poliyíros B 3

149 Polizzi Generosa B 4
117 Poljana B 5
114 Poljčane A 3
116 Polje A 1
114 Poljica C 3
116 Poljice B 2
117 Poljna C 5
77 Polkowice B 5
48 Polla,GB C 4
145 Polla,I C 4
100 Pöllau B 3
74 Polleben B 3
6 Pollen B 6
86 Pollenfeld C 3
139 Pollensa B 4
30 Pollfoss B 4
66 Pollhagen C 2
95 Polliat C 5
145 Póllica C 4
125 Pollos B 4
54 Pollremon A 3
106 Polminhac C 2
88 Polná B 3
69 Polne B 4
91 Polomka D 2
60 Polperro C 2
100 Pöls B 2
68 Polßen B 1
91 Poltár D 2
25 Polvijärvi C 6
112 Pomarance C 2
134 Pomarão B 3
105 Pomarez D 2
146 Pomárico B 2
26 Pomarkku B 5
102 Pomáz A 3
128 Pombal B 2
143 Pomézia C 3
79 Pomiechówek C 3
160 Pomorie D 5
144 Pompei C 3
107 Pompignan D 3
113 Pomposa B 4
108 Poncin A 2
156 Pondokerasiá A 3
154 Pondokómi B 3
86 Pondorf C 3
70 Pondrôme B 4
119 Ponferrada B 4
120 Ponga A 1
79 Poniatowa D 5
77 Poniatowice B 6
77 Poniec B 5
78 Ponikiew Mala C 4
91 Poníky D 2
66 Pönitz A 3
123 Pons,E C 4
104 Pons,F B 2
112 Ponsacco C 2
70 Pont-á-Celles B 3
70 Pont-á-Marcq B 2
84 Pont-à-Mousson B 3
82 Pont-Audemer B 2
80 Pont-Aven C 3
110 Pont Canavese B 2
82 Pont Couronne B 3
80 Pont-Croix B 2
108 Pont-d'Ain A 2
123 Pont de Armentera C 4
108 Pont-de-Beauvoisin B 2
80 Pont-de-Buis B 2
108 Pont-de-Chéruy B 2
108 Pont-de-Claix B 2
106 Pont-de-Dore B 3
106 Pont-de-Labeaume C 4
82 Pont-de-l'Arche B 3
123 Pont de Molins B 5
84 Pont-de-Roide C 3
107 Pont-de-Salars C 2
122 Pont de Suert B 3
95 Pont-de-Vaux C 4
105 Pont-d'Espagne E 2
82 Pont d'Ouilly C 1
106 Pont-du-Château B 3
95 Pont-du-Navoy C 5
108 Pont-en-Royans B 2
81 Pont-Farcy B 5
83 Pont-Faverger B 6
80 Pont-l'Abbé C 2
82 Pont-l'Evêque B 2
63 Pont-Remy B 3
106 Pont-Salomon B 4
110 Pont-San-Martin B 2
80 Pont-Scorff C 3
109 Pont-St.-Esprit C 1
92 Pont-St. Martin B 2
84 Pont-St. Vincent B 3
83 Pont-Ste.-Maxence B 4
83 Pont-sur-Yonne C 5
105 Pontacq D 2
95 Pontailler-sur-Saône B 5
128 Pontão B 2
60 Pontardawe B 3
60 Pontardulais B 2
106 Pontarion B 1
95 Pontarlier C 6
112 Pontassieve C 3
81 Pontaubault B 5
106 Pontaumur B 2
108 Pontcharra B 3
108 Pontcharra-sur-T. B 1
81 Pontchâteau C 4
112 Ponte a Elsa C 2
112 Ponte a Moriano C 2
99 Ponte Arche C 1
97 Ponte Brolla B 4
111 Ponte Cáffaro B 5
111 Ponte d. Ólio C 4
124 Ponte de Barca B 1
124 Ponte de Lima B 1
128 Ponte de Sor B 2
99 Ponte di Barbarano D 2
99 Ponte di Legno C 1
110 Ponte di Nava C 2
99 Ponte di Piave D 3
113 Ponte Felcino C 4
99 Ponte Gardena C 2
140 Ponte Leccia B 2
99 Ponte nelle Alpi C 3
143 Ponte S. Giovanni A 3
111 Ponte San Pietro B 4
110 Ponte Tresa B 3
99 Pontebba C 4
144 Pontecagnano C 3
143 Pontecorvo C 4
110 Pontedássio D 3
110 Pontedécimo C 3
112 Pontedera C 2
58 Pontefract B 2
112 Ponteginori C 2
112 Pontelagoscuro B 3
51 Ponteland B 6
144 Pontelandolfo B 3
113 Pontelongo A 4
111 Pontenure C 4
105 Pontenx-les-Forges C 1
112 Pontepetri B 2
57 Ponterwyd D 3
57 Pontesbury D 4
118 Pontevedra B 2
111 Pontevico B 5
106 Pontgibaud B 2
112 Ponticino C 3
94 Pontigny B 3
93 Pontijou B 5
143 Pontínia C 4
110 Pontinvrea C 3
80 Pontivy B 4
93 Pontlevoy B 5
83 Pontoise B 4
137 Pontones A 4
105 Pontonx D 2
81 Pontorson B 5
112 Pontrémoli B 1
97 Pontresina B 5
57 Pontrhydfendigaid D 3
80 Pontrieux B 3
61 Pontrilas B 4
93 Pontvallain B 4
60 Pontyclun B 3
61 Pontypool B 3
60 Pontypridd B 3
120 Poo A 2
61 Poole C 4
63 Poperinge B 4
143 pópoli B 4
117 Popovac C 5
115 Popovaca B 4
69 Popowo Kościelne, Poznan, PL C 5
79 Popowo Kościelne, Warszawa, PL C 4
73 Poppenhausen, Bayern, D† C 4
73 Poppenhausen, Hessen, D† C 3
73 Poppenlauer C 4
112 Poppi C 3
91 Poprad C 3
116 Popučke B 3
124 Pópulo B 2
142 Populónia B 1
136 Porcuna B 2
99 Pordenone D 3
80 Pordic B 4
90 Poreba B 2
114 Poreč B 1
112 Poretta Terme B 2
26 Pori B 4
88 Poriči n. Sázavou B 2
14 Porjus B 3
27 Porkkala D 7
28 Porlammi C 4
97 Porlezza B 5
60 Porlock B 3
27 Pornainen C 8
86 Pörnbach C 3
92 Pornic B 1
92 Pornichet B 1
117 Porodin B 5
159 Póros B 4
103 Poroszló A 4
135 Porquera C 5
96 Porrentruy A 3
139 Porreras B 4
118 Porriño B 2
35 Porsgrunn B 5
80 Porspoder B 2
50 Port Askaig B 1
50 Port Bannatyne B 2
123 Port Bou B 6
109 Port-de-Bouc D 1
105 Port-de-Lanne D 1
104 Port-des-Barques B 1
57 Port Dinorwic C 2
50 Port Ellen B 1
81 Port-en-Bessin A 6
142 Port Ercole B 2
56 Port Erin B 2
49 Port Erroll D 7
60 Port Eynon B 2
50 Port Glasgow B 3
48 Port Henderson D 3
60 Port Isaac C 2
92 Port-Joinville C 1
107 Port-la-Nouvelle D 3
55 Port Laoise A 4
50 Port Logan C 3
80 Port-Louis C 3
80 Port Manech C 3
80 Port Navalo C 4
48 Port of Ness C 2
50 Port Sonachan A 2
109 Port-St.-Louis D 1
105 Port St. Marie C 3
56 Port St. Mary B 2
95 Port-sur-Saône B 6
60 Port Talbot B 3
123 Port Vendres B 6
50 Port William C 3
53 Portadown B 5
53 Portaferry B 6
129 Portaje B 4
128 Portalegre B 3
127 Portalrubio B 4
156 Portariá, Khalkidhikí, GR B 3
157 Portariá, Magnisía, GR C 2
55 Portarlington A 4
81 Portbail A 5
99 Portegrandi D 3
128 Portel C 3
128 Portela A 2
108 Portes C 1
105 Portet D 4
104 Portets C 2
129 Portezuelo B 4
53 Portglenone B 5
49 Portgower C 5
60 Porth B 3
60 Porthcawl B 3
60 Porthleven C 1
144 Portici C 3
112 Portico di Romagna B 3
120 Portilla de la Reina A 2
126 Portillo A 1
134 Portimão B 2
17 Portimo A 5
16 Portimojärvi A 2
128 Portinho da Anabida C 1
50 Portinnisherrich A 2
61 Portishead B 4
49 Portknockie D 6
57 Portmadoc D 2
49 Portmahomack D 5
133 Portman D 2
57 Portmeirion D 2
48 Portnacroish E 3
48 Portnaguiran C 2
50 Portnahaven B 1
140 Porto,F B 1
124 Porto,P B 1
128 Porto Alto C 2
142 Porto Azzurro B 1
97 Porto Ceresio C 4
139 Porto Colom B 4
134 Porto Covo B 2
139 Porto Cristo B 4
143 Porto d'Ascoli B 4
134 Porto de Lagos B 2
128 Porto de Mós B 2
128 Porto de Rei C 2
148 Porto Empédocle B 3
113 Porto Garibaldi B 4
159 Porto-Khéli B 4
110 Porto Maurízio D 3
139 Porto Petro B 4
113 Porto Potenza Picena C 5
113 Porto Recanati C 5
113 Porto San Giórgio C 5
142 Porto San Stefano B 2
113 Porto Sant'Elpidio C 5
113 Porto Tolle B 4
141 Porto Tórres B 2
140 Porto Vecchio C 2
144 Portocannone B 4
142 Portoferráio B 1
110 Portofino C 4
99 Portogruaro D 3
22 Pörtom C 3
112 Portomaggiore B 3
118 Portomouro B 2
118 Portonovo B 2
149 Portopalo C 5
35 Portør C 5
114 Portoroz B 1
141 Portoscuso C 2
112 Portovénere B 1
50 Portpatrick C 2
48 Portree D 2
53 Portrush A 5
80 Portsall B 2
100 Pörtschach C 2
49 Portskerra C 5
50 Portslogan C 2
62 Portsmouth C 2
49 Portsoy D 6
53 Portstewart A 5
121 Portugalete A 3
54 Portumna A 3
28 Porvoo C 3
130 Porzuna B 2
120 Posada, Oviedo, E A 2
119 Posada, Oviedo, E A 5
141 Posada, I B 3
120 Posada de Valdeón A 2
136 Posadas B 1
17 Posio A 7
153 Posjane B 3
97 Posohiavo B 6
99 Possagno D 2
74 Posseck C 4
75 Possendorf C 5
84 Possesse B 1
74 Poßneck C 3
143 Posta B 4
145 Posta Piana B 4
99 Postal C 2
86 Postbauer B 3
71 Posterholt A 5
99 Postioma D 3
150 Postira B 2
114 Postojna B 2
88 Postoloprty A 1
69 Postomino A 4
150 Posušje B 3
156 Potamiá B 4
69 Potegowo A 5
145 Potenza C 4
113 Potenza Picena C 5
120 Potes A 2
82 Potigny C 1
152 Potkrajci A 1
151 Potoci B 3
115 Potok B 4
154 Potom B 2
115 Potony B 5
133 Potries C 2
67 Potsdam C 6
89 Potštát B 5
89 Potštejn A 4
100 Pottenbrunn A 3
101 Pottendorf B 4
101 Pottenstein,A B 4
86 Pottenstein,D† B 3
62 Potters Bar B 3
86 Pöttmes C 3
59 Potton C 3
100 Pottschach B 3
101 Pöttsching B 4
79 Potworów D 3
81 Pouancé C 5
94 Pougues-les-Eaux B 3
95 Pouillenay B 4
95 Pouilly B 5
95 Pouilly-en-Auxois B 4
94 Pouilly-s/s-Ch. C 4
94 Pouilly-sur-Loire B 2
159 Poulithra B 3
80 Poullaouen B 3
56 Poulton le Fylde C 4
83 Pourcy B 5
157 Pournári C 2
94 Pourrain B 3
105 Pouy-de Touges D 4
105 Pouyastruc D 3
92 Pouzauges C 3
89 Považská Bystrica B 6
131 Povedilla C 4
129 Póvoa, Beja, P C 3
128 Póvoa, Santarem, P B 2
128 Póvoa da Galega C 1
124 Povoa de Lanhoso B 1
124 Póvoa de Varzim B 1
128 Póvoa e Meadas B 3
77 Powidz A 6
130 Poyales del Hoyo A 1
53 Poyntzpass B 5
126 Poyos B 3
89 Poysbrunn C 4
89 Poysdorf C 4
27 Pöytä C 5
120 Poza de la Sal B 3
126 Pozaldez A 1
122 Pozan de Vero B 3
153 Požaranje B 3
117 Požarevac B 5
116 Požega C 4
78 Pozezdrze A 4
83 Pozières A 4
77 Poznań A 5
137 Pozo Alcón B 4
133 Pozo Cañada C 1
131 Pozo de la Serna C 3
134 Pozo del Camino B 3
125 Pozoantiguo B 4
130 Pozoblanco C 2
131 Pozohondo C 5
132 Pozondón A 1
69 Pozrzadlo Wielkopolski B 3
127 Pozuel del Campo B 4
126 Pozuelo de Alarcón B 2
130 Pozuelo de Calatrava C 3
129 Pozuelo de Zarzón A 4
119 Pozuelo del Páramo B 5
130 Pozuelos de Calatrava C 2
149 Pozzallo C 4
141 Pozzomaggiore B 2
144 Pozzuoli C 3
113 Pozzuolo C 3
78 Prabuty B 2
88 Prachatice B 1
119 Prada B 3
108 Pradelle C 2
106 Pradelles C 3
122 Prades,E C 3
123 Prades,F B 5
90 Pradlla B 2
124 Prado B 1
135 Prado del Rey C 5
120 Pradoluengo B 3
45 Præstø B 5
87 Prag C 5
110 Pragelato B 1
114 Pragersko A 3
98 Prägraten B 3
88 Praha A 2
92 Prahecq C 3
117 Prahovo B 6
128 Praia B 1
146 Práia a Mare C 1
124 Praia da Granja B 1
134 Praia da Rocha B 2
128 Praia da Viera B 2
134 Praia da Zambugueira B 2
134 Praia de Carvœira B 2
124 Praia de Miramar B 1
111 Pralboino B 5
108 Pralognan B 3
116 Pranjani B 4
95 Praslay B 5
21 Prästmon B 6
79 Praszka D 1
122 Prat de Compte D 3
123 Prat de Llobregat C 5
99 Prata di Pordenone D 3
75 Pratau B 4
122 Pratdip C 3
144 Pratella B 3
112 Prato C 3
143 Prátola Peligna B 4
144 Pratola Serra C 3
123 Prats de Llusanes B 5
123 Prats-de-Mollo-la-Preste B 5
123 Prats del Rey C 4
96 Pratteln A 3
95 Prauthoy B 5
119 Pravia A 4
98 Praxmar B 2
105 Prayssac C 4
110 Prazzo C 2
82 Pré-en-Pail C 1

102 Rabe B 4
87 Rabi B 5
69 Rabino B 3
90 Rabka C 2
117 Rabrovo B 5
153 Raca, Srbija, YU A 3
117 Rača, Srbija, YU B 4
146 Rácale C 4
102 Rácalmás A 2
148 Racalmuto B 3
117 Răcăşdia B 5
110 Racconigi C 2
115 Rače A 3
84 Rachecourt B 2
78 Raciaz C 3
89 Racibórz A 6
89 Račice B 4
90 Raciechowice C 3
116 Račinovni B 2
37 Rackeby C 5
102 Ráckeve A 2
90 Raclawice, Krakow, PL B 3
89 Raclawice, Opole, PL A 5
77 Racot A 5
91 Racovec D 4
37 Råda A 5
116 Radalj B 3
160 Radauti B 4
101 Radava A 6
112 Radda in Chianti C 3
66 Raddingsdorf B 3
149 Raddusa B 4
75 Radeberg B 5
75 Radebeul B 5
75 Radeburg B 5
114 Radeče A 3
74 Radegast B 4
101 Radenci C 4
98 Radenthein C 4
71 Radevormwald A 6
153 Radičevo C 4
142 Radicófani B 2
112 Radicóndoli C 3
116 Radinci A 3
74 Radiumbad Brambach C 4
100 Radkersburg C 3
89 Radków A 4
89 Radlin A 6
100 Radlje C 3
90 Radlow B 3
100 Radmer a. d. Stube B 2
87 Radnice B 5
89 Radobica C 6
115 Radoboj A 3
103 Radojevo C 4
154 Radokal i Poshtem B 2
85 Radolfzell C 5
79 Radom D 4
78 Radomice C 2
78 Radomin B 2
153 Radomir B 4
79 Radomsko D 2
90 Radomyśl Wielki B 4
101 Radošina A 5
89 Radošovce C 5
78 Radostowo B 3
79 Radoszyce D 3
76 Radoszyn A 4
88 Radotin B 2
153 Radoviš C 4
114 Radovljica A 2
153 Radovnica B 4
154 Radožda A 2
98 Radstadt B 4
45 Radsted C 4
61 Radstock B 4
90 Radziechowy C 2
78 Radzieje A 4
79 Radziejów,PL C 1
79 Radziejów,PL C 1
79 Radziejowice C 3
90 Radzionków B 1
91 Radzovce D 2
79 Radzymin C 4
78 Radzyń Chelm. B 1
65 Raesfeld C 4
148 Raffadali B 3
8 Rafsbotn B 3
91 Ragály D 3
30 Raggsteinhytta C 4
61 Raglan B 4
75 Ragösen A 4
32 Rågsveden C 5
74 Raguhn B 4
21 Ragunda B 5
149 Ragusa C 4
66 Rahden C 1
36 Rahölt A 3
143 Raiano B 4
86 Rain C 2
100 Rainbach Mühlkreis A 2
128 Raio Pires C 1
22 Raippaluoto B 3
118 Rairiz de Veiga B 3
66 Raisdorf A 3
26 Raisio C 5
124 Raiva, Aveiro, P B 1
128 Raiva, Coimbra, P A 2
11 Raja-Jooseppi A 8
11 Rajala B 6
27 Rajamäki C 7
90 Rajbrot C 3
90 Rajcza C 2
89 Rajec B 6
89 Rájec-Jestrebi B 4
91 Rajecké Teplice C 1
89 Rajhrad B 4
115 Rajić B 5
101 Rajka B 5
91 Rakaca D 3
91 Rakamaz D 4
153 Rakevo A 5
157 Rákhes D 2
153 Rakita B 4
36 Rakkestad B 3
102 Rákóczifalva A 4
102 Rákócziújfalu A 4
77 Rakoniewice A 5
89 Raková B 6
117 Rakova Bara B 5
114 Rakovica B 3
88 Rakovnik A 1
67 Rakow, D† A 6
90 Raków, PL B 4
19 Råkvåg B 6
117 Ralja B 4
125 Ramacastañas C 4
149 Ramacca B 4
120 Ramales de la Victoria A 3
128 Ramalhais B 2
128 Ramalhal B 1
4 Ramberg B 2
84 Rambervillers B 3
82 Rambouillet C 3
84 Rambucourt B 2
43 Ramdala C 5
70 Ramet B 4
100 Ramingstein B 1
118 Ramiranes B 2
96 Ramiswil A 3
43 Ramkville B 4
44 Ramme A 1
37 Rämmen A 6
38 Ramnäs C 3
35 Ramnes B 6
160 Ramnicu Valcea C 4
84 Ramonchamp C 3
56 Rampside B 3
100 Ramsau,A A 3
98 Ramsau,D† B 3
72 Ramsbeck B 2
38 Ramsberg C 2
21 Ramsele B 5
59 Ramsey,GB C 3
56 Ramsey,GBM B 2
62 Ramsgate B 5
55 Ramsgrange B 5
20 Ramsjö C 4
71 Ramstein C 6
4 Ramsund B 5
21 Ramvik C 6
36 Rånåfoss A 3
98 Ranalt B 2
70 Rance B 3
113 Ranchio C 4
34 Randaberg B 1
30 Randabygd B 3
53 Randalstown B 5
106 Randan A 3
149 Randazzo B 4
32 Rånddalen A 4
100 Randegg A 2
44 Randers A 3
73 Randersacker D 3
118 Randín C 3
31 Randsverk B 6
14 Råneå C 6
82 Rânes C 1
50 Ranfurly B 3
42 Rångedala B 3
22 Rangsby C 3
67 Rangsdorf C 6
19 Ranheim B 6
74 Ranis C 3
97 Rankweil A 5
42 Rånnavåg B 3
73 Rannerod C 2
46 Ränneslöv A 4
48 Rannoch Station E 4
117 Ranovac B 5
37 Ransäter B 5
38 Ransta C 3
10 Rantajärvi C 3
29 Rantasalmi A 6
83 Rantigny B 4
16 Rantsila C 4
8 Ranttila C 5
44 Rantum C 1
17 Ranua B 5
40 Ranum C 3
75 Ranzig A 6
84 Raon-l'Étape B 3
99 Ráossi D 2
110 Rapallo C 4
109 Raphèle D 1
53 Raphoe B 4
49 Rapness B 6
112 Rapolano Terme C 3
145 Rapolla C 4
128 Raposa B 2
91 Rapovce D 2
97 Rapperswil A 4
156 Rapsáni C 2
122 Rasal B 2
38 Rasbo C 4
126 Rascafría B 2
73 Rasdorf C 3
53 Rasharkin B 5
120 Rasines A 3
25 Rasivaara C 6
152 Raška A 2
76 Raspenava C 4
122 Rasquera D 3
112 Rássina C 3
85 Rastatt B 5
65 Rastede A 6
74 Rastenberg B 3
25 Rastinjärvi B 6
116 Rastošnica B 2
125 Rasueros B 4
77 Raszków B 6
117 Rataje C 5
20 Ratansbyn C 3
100 Ratece C 1
114 Ratek B 2
66 Ratekau B 3
54 Rath Luirc B 3
55 Rathangan A 5
55 Rathcoole A 5
54 Rathcormack B 3
55 Rathdowney B 4
55 Rathdrum B 5
67 Rathebur B 6
49 Rathen D 7
67 Rathenow C 5
53 Rathfriland B 5
54 Rathkeale B 3
53 Rathmelton A 4
55 Rathmolyon A 5
54 Rathmore B 2
55 Rathnew B 5
55 Rathowen A 4
55 Rathvilly B 5
88 Ratibořské Hory B 2
71 Ratingen A 5
91 Rátka D 4
91 Ratková D 3
152 Ratkovac B 2
116 Ratkovo A 3
91 Ratkovské Bystré D 3
86 Rattelsdorf A 2
100 Ratten B 3
10 Rattosjärvi C 4
51 Rattray A 4
33 Rattvik C 6
66 Ratzeburg B 3
67 Rätzlingen C 4
70 Raucourt C 3
11 Raudanjoki B 6
23 Raudaskylä A 6
30 Raudeberg B 2
31 Raufoss C 7
29 Rauha B 6
10 Rauhala B 4
30 Rauhellern C 4
34 Rauland B 3
106 Raulhac C 2
26 Rauma B 4
30 Raundal C 3
59 Raunds C 3
98 Rauris B 4
24 Rautalampi C 3
7 Rautas D 5
25 Rautavaara B 5
23 Rautio A 6
104 Rauzan C 2
149 Ravanusa B 3
70 Ravels B 4
43 Rävemåla C 5
56 Ravenglass B 3
113 Ravenna B 4
67 Ravensbrück B 6
97 Ravensburg A 5
95 Ravières B 4
42 Rävlanda B 2
153 Ravna Banja B 3
153 Ravna Dubrava A 4
114 Ravna Gora B 2
117 Ravna Reka B 5
100 Ravne C 2
117 Ravnište C 5
116 Ravnje B 3
151 Ravno C 3
116 Ravno Selo A 3
79 Rawa Mazowiecka D 3
58 Rawcliffe B 3
56 Rawenstall C 4
77 Rawicz B 5
153 Rayko Daskalovo B 5
62 Rayleigh B 4
23 Räyrinki B 5
104 Razac-sur l'Isle B 3
114 Ražanac C 3
117 Ražanj C 5
115 Razboj B 5
153 Razdol C 5
104 Razes A 4
160 Razgrad D 5
153 Razlog C 5
153 Razlovci C 4
118 Razo A 2
62 Reading B 2
107 Réalmont D 2
49 Reay C 5
83 Rebais C 5
124 Rebordelo B 2
153 Rebrovo B 5
113 Recanati C 5
126 Recas,E B 2
103 Recas,R C 5
110 Recco C 4
54 Recess A 2
95 Recey-sur-Ource B 4
124 Recezinhos B 1
86 Rechberghausen C 1
101 Rechnitz B 4
114 Rečica B 3
151 Rečice B 3
65 Recke B 5
73 Reckendorf C 4
71 Recklinghausen A 6
99 Recoaro Terme D 2
70 Recogne C 4
91 Recsk E 3
68 Recz B 3
56 Red Dial B 3
48 Red Point D 3
69 Reda A 6
31 Redalen C 7
71 Redange C 4
62 Redbridge B 4
51 Redcar C 6
44 Redding B 2
57 Redditch D 5
67 Redefin B 4
101 Rédics C 4
49 Redland B 5
67 Redlin B 5
81 Redon C 4
118 Redondela B 2
128 Redondo C 3
133 Redován C 2
60 Redruth C 1
59 Reedham C 5
59 Reepham C 5
65 Rees C 4
58 Reeth A 2
67 Reetz B 4
4 Refsnes B 5
42 Reftele B 3
149 Regalbuto B 4
87 Regen C 5
87 Regensburg B 4
87 Regenstauf B 4
112 Reggello C 3
147 Réggio di Calabria D 1
112 Reggio nell'Emilia B 2
112 Reggiolo B 2
160 Reghin B 4
78 Regiele A 5
121 Régil A 4
75 Regis Breitingen B 4
106 Regny B 4
128 Rego da Leirosa A 2
101 Regöly C 6
124 Régua B 2
118 Regueiro B 2
128 Reguengo, Portalegre, P B 3
128 Reguengo, Santarém, P B 2
128 Reguengos C 3
74 Rehau C 4
66 Rehburg C 2
66 Rehden C 1
66 Rehna B 4
84 Rehon A 2
73 Reichelsheim D 2
86 Reichelshofen B 2
100 Reichenau, Karnten, A C 1
100 Reichenau, Nieder Österreich, A B 3
97 Reichenau, CH B 5
100 Reichenau i. Mühlkreis A 2
86 Reichenbach, Baden-Württemberg, D† C 1
87 Reichenbach, Bayern, D† B 4
75 Reichenbach, Dresden, D* B 6
74 Reichenbach, Karl Marx Stadt, D* C 4
77 Reichenbach, PL C 5
73 Reichenberg D 3
100 Reichenfels B 2
72 Reichensachsen B 4
86 Reichertshofen C 3
73 Reicholzheim D 3
85 Reichshoffen B 4
96 Reiden A 3
118 Reigada, Orense, E B 3
119 Reigada, Oviedo, E A 4
124 Reigada, P C 3
62 Reigate B 3
58 Reighton A 3
96 Reignier B 2
109 Reillanne D 2
83 Reims B 6
39 Reimyra D 2
96 Reinach, Argau, CH A 4
96 Reinach, Basel, CH A 3
66 Reinbek B 3
67 Reinberg A 6
4 Reine C 2
66 Reinfeld B 3
73 Reinheim D 2
31 Reinli C 6
120 Reinosa A 2
86 Reinstetten C 1
67 Reinstorf B 4
31 Reinsvoll C 7
99 Reisach C 4
87 Reisbach C 4
23 Reisjarvi B 6
49 Reiss C 5
98 Reit im Winkl B 3
19 Reitan C 7
24 Reittiö B 4
91 Rejdová D 3
117 Rekovac C 5
133 Relleu C 2
66 Rellingen B 2
102 Rém B 3
71 Remagen B 6
82 Remalard C 2
84 Rembercourt B 2
79 Rembertów C 4
128 Remedios B 1
65 Remels A 5
23 Remeskylä B 8
103 Remetea B 6
103 Remetea Mare C 5
103 Remeţi B 6
71 Remich C 5
84 Rémilly A 3
84 Remiremont B 3
72 Remlingen A 4
121 Remolinos C 5
109 Remoulins D 1
71 Remscheid A 6
32 Rena B 2
94 Renaison C 3
96 Renan A 2
81 Renazé C 5
85 Renchen B 5
108 Rencurel B 2
147 Rende C 2
157 Rendina C 1
66 Rendsburg A 2
126 Renedo A 1
120 Renedo de Valdetuéjar B 1
50 Renfrew B 3
33 Rengsjö B 7
160 Reni C 6
27 Renko C 7
28 Renkomäki C 3
64 Renkum C 3
19 Rennebu C 5
86 Rennertshofen C 3
81 Rennes B 5

Page	Name	Grid	
107	Rennes-les-Bains	E	2
98	Rennweg	B	4
44	Rens	C	2
121	Renteria	A	5
120	Reocin	A	2
101	Répcelak	B	5
22	Replot	B	3
26	Reposaari	B	4
8	Repvåg	B	5
132	Requena	B	1
107	Requista	C	2
67	Rerik	A	4
99	Resana	D	2
39	Resarö	C	5
97	Reschen	B	6
21	Resele	B	6
154	Resen	A	3
124	Resende	B	2
152	Rëshen	C	1
97	Résia	B	6
144	Resina	C	3
117	Reşiţa	A	5
68	Resko	B	3
117	Resnik	B	4
60	Resolven	B	3
83	Ressons	B	4
51	Reston	B	5
149	Resuttano	B	4
78	Reszel	A	4
129	Retamal	C	4
83	Rethel	B	6
66	Rethem	C	2
72	Rethen	A	3
70	Retie	A	4
81	Retiers	C	5
77	Retków	B	5
125	Retortillo	C	3
106	Retourrac	B	4
91	Rétság	E	2
100	Rettenegg	B	3
130	Retuerta de Bullaque	B	2
88	Retz	C	3
73	Retzbach	D	3
74	Reuden	A	4
123	Reus	C	4
70	Reusel	A	4
87	Reuth	B	4
85	Reutlingen	B	6
97	Reutte	A	6
71	Reuver	A	5
109	Revel, Basses Alpes, F	C	3
107	Revel, Haute Garonne, F	D	2
110	Revello	C	2
126	Revenga	B	1
112	Revere	A	3
109	Revest	C	2
84	Revigny	B	1
70	Revin	C	3
46	Revingeby	B	4
88	Řevnice	B	2
99	Revo	C	2
16	Revonlahti	C	3
30	Revsnes	B	4
20	Revsund	C	4
91	Revúca	D	3
69	Rewa	A	6
111	Rezzato	B	5
111	Rezzoáglio	C	4
117	Rgotina	B	6
71	Rhaunen	C	6
57	Rhayader	D	3
65	Rheda	C	6
65	Rhede, Niedersachsen, D†	A	5
65	Rhede, Nordrhein, Westfalen, D†	C	4
64	Rheden	B	4
71	Rheinbach	B	5
71	Rheinberg	A	5
65	Rheine	B	5
96	Rheinfelden,CH	A	3
85	Rheinfelden,D†	C	4
71	Rheinkamp	A	5
67	Rheinsberg	B	5
110	Rhemes-Notre-Dame	B	2
64	Rhenen	C	3
71	Rheydt	A	5
48	Rhiconich	C	4
67	Rhinow	C	5
110	Rho	B	4
60	Rhoose	B	3
57	Rhosllanerchrugog	C	3
57	Rhosneigr	C	2
60	Rhossili	B	2
50	Rhubodach	B	2
57	Rhyl	C	3
60	Rhymney	B	3
49	Rhynie	D	6
81	Riaillé	C	5
38	Riala	C	5
118	Rianjo	B	2
120	Riaño, E	B	1
143	Riano, I	B	3
109	Rians	D	2
126	Riaza	A	2
142	Riazze	B	2
120	Riba	A	3
127	Riba de Saelices	B	3
118	Ribadavia	B	2
120	Ribadedeva	A	2
118	Ribadeo	A	3
120	Ribadesella	A	1
121	Ribaflecha	B	4
121	Ribaforada	C	5
117	Ribare, Srbija, YU	C	5
117	Ribare, Srbija, YU	B	5
152	Ribariće	B	2
132	Ribarroja	B	2
122	Ribarroja de Ebro	C	3
123	Ribas de Freser	B	5
118	Ribas de Sil	B	3
44	Ribe	B	1
85	Ribeauville	B	4
124	Ribeira da Pena	B	2
83	Ribemont	B	5
148	Ribera	B	3
123	Ribera de Cardos	B	4
129	Ribera del Fresno	C	4
104	Ribérac	B	3
132	Ribesalbes	A	2
109	Ribiers	C	2
116	Ribnica, Bosna i Hercegovina, YU	B	2
114	Ribnica, Slovenija, YU	B	2
100	Ribnica, Slovenija, YU	C	3
117	Ribnica, Srbija, YU	C	4
67	Ribnitz-Damgarten	A	5
142	Ribolla	B	2
119	Ricabo	A	5
89	Říčany, Jihomoravsky, CS	B	4
88	Říčany, Středočeský, CS	B	2
58	Riccall	B	2
144	Riccia	B	3
113	Riccione	B	4
112	Riccò del Golfo	B	1
84	Richebourg	B	2
93	Richelieau	B	4
97	Richisau	A	4
62	Richmond, London, GB	B	3
58	Richmond, Yorks., GB	A	2
56	Richmond Hill	B	2
67	Richtenberg	A	5
97	Richterswil	A	4
66	Rickling	A	3
62	Rickmansworth	B	3
127	Ricla	A	4
38	Riddarhyttan	C	2
64	Ridderkerk	C	2
96	Riddes	B	3
57	Ridley Green	C	4
51	Ridsdale	B	5
80	Riec-sur-Bélon	C	3
97	Ried i. Oberinntal	A	6
98	Ried im Innkreis	A	4
98	Riedau	A	4
87	Riedenburg	C	3
86	Riedlingen	C	1
100	Riegersburg	B	3
119	Riego de la Vega	B	5
119	Riego del Camino	C	5
119	Riello	B	5
73	Rieneck	C	3
70	Rienne	C	3
65	Riepe	A	5
120	Riera	A	1
75	Riesa	B	5
99	Riese Pio X	D	2
65	Riesenbeck	B	5
149	Riesi	B	4
74	Riestedt	B	3
72	Rietberg	B	2
143	Rieti	B	3
75	Rietschen	B	6
105	Rieumes	D	4
107	Rieupeyroux	C	2
107	Rieux, Ande, F	D	2
105	Rieux, Haute Garonne, F	D	4
109	Riez	D	3
96	Riggisberg	B	3
107	Rignac	C	2
145	Rignano Gargánico	B	4
94	Rigny-sur-A.	C	4
99	Rigolato	C	3
50	Rigside	B	4
112	Rigutino	C	3
88	Rihořov	B	3
27	Riihikoski	C	5
25	Riihilahti	A	7
27	Riihimäki	C	7
28	Riihiniemi	B	4
11	Riipi	B	6
22	Riispyy	D	3
25	Riistavesi	C	5
27	Riitiala	B	5
114	Rijeka	B	2
151	Rijeka Crnojev	C	5
64	Rijen	C	2
70	Rijkevorsel	A	3
64	Rijnsburg	B	2
65	Rijssen	B	4
64	Rijswijk	B	2
4	Riksgränsen	B	7
153	Rila	B	5
148	Rilievo	B	2
108	Rillieux	B	1
58	Rillington	A	3
127	Rillo de Gallo	B	4
91	Rimavská Baňa	D	2
91	Rimavská Seč	D	3
91	Rimavská Sobota	D	3
91	Rimavské Janovce	D	3
38	Rimbo	C	5
106	Rimeize	C	3
43	Rimforsa	A	5
113	Rimini	B	4
17	Rimmi	C	8
160	Rîmnicu Sărat	C	5
70	Rimogne	C	3
73	Rimpar	D	3
136	Rincón de la Victoria	C	2
121	Rincón de Soto	B	5
18	Rindal	B	5
30	Rinde	B	3
43	Ringarum	A	6
44	Ringe	B	3
31	Ringebu	B	7
50	Ringford	C	3
44	Ringkøbing	A	1
155	Ringladhes	C	2
31	Ringsaker	C	7
45	Ringsted	B	4
61	Ringwood	C	5
47	Rinkaby	B	5
43	Rinkabyholm	C	6
118	Rinlo	A	3
98	Rinn	B	2
4	Rinøyvåg	B	4
72	Rinteln	A	3
118	Rio	B	3
128	Rio do Coures	B	2
124	Río Douro	B	2
128	Rio Frio	C	2
126	Rio Frio de Riaza	A	2
128	Rio Maior	B	2
142	Rio Marina	B	1
118	Riobo	B	2
132	Riodeva	A	1
120	Riofavar	A	1
126	Riofrio, Avila, E	B	1
119	Riofrío, Zamora, E	C	4
136	Riogordo	C	2
137	Rioja	C	4
112	Riola	B	3
141	Riola Sardo	C	2
129	Riolobos	B	4
107	Riols	D	2
106	Riom	B	3
106	Riom-ès-Montagnes	B	2
112	Riomaggiore	B	1
158	Rion	A	2
105	Rion-des-Landes	D	2
119	Ríonegro del Puente	B	4
145	Rionero in Vúlture	C	4
131	Riopar	C	4
106	Riorges	A	4
118	Ríos	C	3
119	Riosa	A	5
119	Ríoseco de Tapia	B	5
108	Riotord	B	1
118	Riotorto	A	3
95	Rioz	B	6
103	Ripa	B	5
115	Ripač	C	3
145	Ripacándida	C	4
117	Ripanj	B	4
113	Ripatransone	C	5
59	Ripley	B	2
123	Ripoll	B	5
58	Ripon	A	2
149	Riposto	B	5
83	Ris-Orangis	C	4
151	Risan	C	4
13	Risbäck	C	7
61	Risca	B	3
72	Rischenau	B	3
105	Riscle	D	2
15	Risliden	D	3
101	Rišnovce	A	5
16	Risögrund	B	2
35	Risør	C	5
4	Risøyhamn	B	4
20	Rissna	B	4
28	Ristiina	B	5
17	Ristijärvi	C	7
16	Risudden	A	2
156	Ritíni	B	2
66	Ritterhude	B	1
111	Riva	B	5
82	Riva-Bella	B	1
110	Rivanazzano	C	4
110	Rivarolo Canavese	B	2
112	Rivarolo Mantovano	A	2
103	Rive-de-Gier	B	1
92	Rivedoux-Plage	C	2
146	Rivello	B	1
111	Rivergaro	C	4
107	Rivesaltes	E	2
107	Rivière	C	3
99	Rivignano	D	4
110	Rivoli	B	2
111	Rivolta d'Adda	B	4
85	Rixheim	C	4
36	Rixo	C	3
155	Rízoma	C	3
156	Rizómata	B	2
155	Rizovoúni, Kardhitsa, GR	C	3
155	Rizovoúni, Préveza, GR	C	2
30	Rj	A	2
35	Rjukan	B	4
47	Rø,DK	B	5
38	Rö,S	C	5
126	Roa,E	A	2
31	Roa,N	C	7
59	Road Weedon	C	2
59	Roade	C	3
51	Roadhead	B	5
44	Roager	B	1
19	Roan	A	6
106	Roanne	A	4
9	Roavvegiedde	C	7
110	Róbbio	B	3
67	Röbel	B	5
62	Robertsbridge	C	4
15	Robertsfors	D	4
38	Robertsholm	B	3
71	Robertville	B	3
58	Robin Hood's Bay	A	3
125	Robleda	C	3
129	Robledillo de Trujillo	B	5
131	Robledo, Albacete, E	C	4
119	Robledo, León, E	B	4
126	Robledo de Chavela	B	1
126	Robledo del Buey	C	1
130	Robledo del Mazo	B	2
130	Robledollano	B	1
74	Röblingen	B	3
125	Robliza de Cojos	C	4
122	Robres	C	2
121	Robres del Castillo	B	4
123	Rocafort de Queralt	C	4
123	Rocallaura	C	4
104	Rocamadour	C	4
143	Rocca di Mezzo	B	4
143	Rocca di Papa	C	3
146	Rocca Imperiale	B	2
113	Rocca Priora	C	5
112	Rocca San Casciano	B	3
143	Rocca Sinibalda	B	3
147	Roccabernarda	C	2
111	Roccabianca	B	5
145	Roccadáspide	C	4
142	Roccafederighi	A	2
143	Roccafluvione	B	4
143	Roccagorga	C	4
142	Roccalbegna	B	2
149	Roccalumera	B	5
148	Roccamena	B	3
144	Roccamonfina	B	2
146	Roccanova	B	2
148	Roccapalumba	B	3
143	Roccapassa	B	4
143	Roccaraso	C	5
143	Roccasecca	C	4
142	Roccastrada	A	2
147	Roccella Iónica	D	2
145	Rocchetta S. António	B	4
59	Rocester	C	2
56	Rochdale	C	4
95	Roche-les-Beaupré	B	6
104	Rochechouart	B	3
70	Rochefort,B	B	4
104	Rochefort,F	B	2
81	Rochefort-en-Terre	C	4
106	Rochefort-Montagne	B	2
95	Rochefort-sur-Nenon	B	5
108	Rochemaure	C	1
106	Rocher	C	4
71	Rocherath	B	5
92	Rocheservière	C	2
62	Rochester, Kent, GB	B	4
51	Rochester, Northumberland, GB	B	5
62	Rochford	B	4
55	Rochfortbridge	A	4
75	Rochlitz	B	4
135	Rociana del Condado	B	4
71	Rockenhausen	C	6
38	Rockhammar	C	2
54	Rockhill	B	3
43	Rockneby	C	6
71	Rocourt	B	4
123	Roda de Bara	C	4
123	Roda de Ter	C	5
74	Rodach	C	2
85	Rodalben	A	4
31	Rødberg	C	5
45	Rødby	C	4
40	Rødding	C	2
70	Rode	B	3
43	Rödeby	C	5
118	Rodeiro	B	3
44	Rødekro	B	2
48	Rodel	D	2
65	Roden	A	4
127	Ródenas	B	4
72	Rodenberg	A	3
66	Rodenkirchen	B	1
75	Rodewisch	C	4
107	Rodez	C	2
73	Rodheim Bieber	C	2
156	Rodhiá	C	2
158	Rodhodháfni	A	3
156	Rodhópolis	A	3
145	Rodi Gargánico	B	4
119	Rodiezmo	B	5
87	Roding	B	4
44	Rødkærsbro	A	2
156	Rodolívos	B	3
20	Rödön	B	3
123	Rodoñá	C	4
5	Rødøy	D	2
6	Rødsand	B	3
18	Rødven	C	3
45	Rødvig	B	5
45	Rødy Havn	C	4
78	Rodzanów	C	3
71	Roermond	A	4
63	Roesbrugge-Haringe	B	4
85	Roeschwoog	B	5
70	Roeselare	B	2
49	Roesound	A	7
71	Roetgen	B	5
70	Rœulx	B	3
106	Roffiac	B	3
37	Röfors	C	6
145	Rofrano	C	4
153	Rogacica, Kosovo, YU	B	3
116	Rogačica, Srbija, YU	B	3
77	Rogalin	A	5
67	Rogäsen	C	5
115	Rogatec	A	3
116	Rogatica	C	3
74	Rogätz	A	3
66	Roggendorf	B	4
146	Roggiano Gravina	C	2
147	Rogliano	C	2
109	Rognac	D	2
5	Rognan	C	4
31	Rogne	B	6
109	Rognes	D	2
94	Rogny	B	2
69	Rogowo	C	5
78	Rogóz	A	3
77	Rogoznica, PL	B	5
150	Rogoznica, YU	B	1
69	Rogozno	C	4
33	Rogsta	B	8
79	Roguszyn	C	4
80	Rohan	B	4
89	Rohatec	C	5
86	Röhlingen	C	2
101	Rohožnik	A	5
74	Rohr	C	2
100	Rohr i Gebirge	B	3
100	Rohrbach,A	A	1
85	Rohrbach,F	A	4
66	Rohrberg	C	4
100	Rohrendorf	A	3
86	Rohrenfels	C	3
87	Röhrnbach	C	5
83	Roiglise	B	4

83 Roisel B 5
70 Roiselaar B 3
74 Roitzsch B 4
133 Rojales C 2
33 Röjeråsen C 5
31 Røkenvik C 7
79 Rokiciny D 2
77 Rokietnica A 5
77 Rokitki B 4
18 Rokkum C 4
15 Roknäs C 5
77 Rokoszyce B 5
87 Rokycany B 5
89 Rokytnice Orlickych A 4
95 Rolampont B 5
40 Rold C 3
34 Røldal B 2
65 Rolde B 4
16 Rolfs B 2
35 Rollag A 5
125 Rollán C 4
96 Rolle B 2
34 Rom C 3
143 Roma,I C 3
39 Roma,S E 5
110 Romagnano Sésia B 3
81 Romagné B 5
39 Romakloster C 5
160 Roman B 5
141 Romana B 2
111 Romano di Lombardia B 4
153 Romanovce B 3
108 Romans-sur-Isère B 2
97 Romanshorn A 5
84 Rombas A 3
118 Romeán B 3
95 Romenay C 5
126 Romeral C 2
18 Romfo C 4
74 Romhild C 2
83 Romilly C 5
38 Romme B 2
96 Romont B 2
93 Romorantin B 5
25 Romppala C 6
73 Romrod C 3
62 Romsey C 2
36 Rømskog B 3
40 Ronbjerg C 2
122 Roncal B 2
104 Ronce-les-Bains B 1
121 Roncesvalles A 5
84 Ronchamp C 3
99 Ronchi dei Legionari D 4
142 Ronciglione B 3
110 Ronco Canavese B 2
110 Ronco Scrivia C 3
135 Ronda C 5
31 Rondablikk B 6
44 Rønde A 3
39 Rone E 5
70 Rongy B 2
42 Rönnäng B 1
47 Rønne B 5
74 Ronneburg C 4
43 Ronneby C 5
39 Rönneshytta D 2
39 Rönninge C 4
20 Rönnöfors B 2
88 Ronov n. Doubravou B 3
86 Ronsberg D 2
70 Ronse B 2
58 Roos B 3
70 Roosbeek B 3
64 Roosendaal C 2
52 Roosky C 4
90 Ropa C 4
90 Ropczyce B 4
153 Ropotovo C 3
84 Roppe C 3
119 Ropuerelos del Páramo B 5
109 Roqueb-Ilière C 4
107 Roquebrun D 3
109 Roquebrune D 3
107 Roquecourbe D 2
105 Roquefort C 2
109 Roquemaure C 1
109 Roquesteron D 3
122 Roquetas D 3
137 Roquetas de Mar C 4
109 Roquevaire D 2
19 Røra B 7
32 Rörbäcksnäs B 3
42 Rörö B 1
19 Røros C 7
12 Rørøy B 4
97 Rorschach A 5
5 Rørstad C 4
12 Rørvik,N C 3
43 Rörvik,S B 4
99 Rosà D 2
134 Rosal de la Frontera B 3
134 Rosário B 2
147 Rosarno D 1
123 Rosas B 6
71 Rosbach B 6
55 Rosbercon B 5
103 Roşcani C 6
66 Rosche C 3
77 Rościslawice B 5
78 Rościszewo C 2
80 Roscoff B 3
54 Roscommon A 3
55 Roscrea B 4
147 Rose C 2
100 Rosegg C 2
55 Rosegreen B 4
49 Rosehearty D 6
132 Rosell A 3
122 Roselló C 3
49 Rosemarkie D 4
63 Rosendaël A 4
85 Rosenfeld B 5
43 Rosenfors B 5
98 Rosenheim B 3
67 Rosenow B 6
38 Rosersberg C 4
143 Roseto degli Abruzzi B 5
145 Roseto Valfortore B 4
85 Rosheim B 4
112 Rosia,I C 3
103 Roşia,R B 6
89 Rosice B 4
106 Rosières B 3
112 Rosignano Marittimo C 2
112 Rosignano Solvay C 2
75 Rositz B 4
48 Roskhill D 2
45 Roskilde B 5
154 Roskovec B 1
38 Roslags-Bro C 5
38 Roslags-Kulla C 5
40 Røslev C 2
64 Rosmalen C 3
129 Rosmaninhal B 3
44 Røsnæs B 3
50 Rosneath A 3
149 Rosolini C 4
153 Rosoman C 3
77 Rososzyca B 7
80 Rosporden C 3
128 Rosquete B 2
71 Rösrath B 6
54 Ross Carbery C 2
61 Ross-on-Wye B 4
97 Rossa B 5
146 Rossano C 2
124 Rossas, Aveiro, P C 1
124 Rossas, Braga, P B 1
74 Roßbach B 3
54 Rosscahill A 2
74 Roßdorf C 2
6 Rossfjord B 4
97 Roßhaupten A 6
110 Rossiglione C 3
71 Rossignol C 4
74 Roßla B 3
55 Rosslare B 5
55 Rosslare Harbour B 5
74 Roßlau B 4
74 Roßleben B 3
21 Rosson B 5
79 Rossoszyca D 1
67 Rossow B 6
64 Rossum C 3
13 Røssvassbukt B 6
75 Roßwein B 5
51 Rossyth A 4
46 Röstånga A 4
67 Rostock A 5
160 Rostorii-de-Vede C 4
80 Rostrenen B 3
53 Rostrevor B 5
152 Rostuša C 2
15 Rosvik C 5
102 Röszke B 4
32 Rot B 5
86 Rot am See B 2
135 Rota C 4
147 Rota Greca C 2
33 Roteberg B 6
143 Rotella B 4
71 Rotem A 4
72 Rotenburg, Hessen, D† C 3
66 Rotenburg, Niedersachsen, D† B 2
86 Roth, Bayern, D† B 3
71 Roth, Rheinland Westfalen, D† B 6
75 Rötha B 4
51 Rothbury B 6
67 Rothemühl B 6
86 Röthenbach B 3
75 Rothenburg B 6
86 Rothenburg ob der Tauber B 2
81 Rothéneuf B 5
68 Rothenklempenow B 2
87 Rothenstadt B 4
86 Rothenstein C 3
58 Rotherham B 2
49 Rothes D 5
50 Rothesay B 2
58 Rothwell, Northants., GB B 2
59 Rothwell, Yorkshire, GB C 3
146 Rotonda C 2
146 Rotondella B 2
133 Rótova C 2
86 Rott D 2
98 Rottach-Egern B 2
49 Rottal E 5
86 Röttenbach B 3
98 Rottenbuch B 1
85 Rottenburg, Baden-Württemberg, D† B 5
87 Rottenburg, Bayern, D† C 4
100 Rottenmann B 2
64 Rotterdam C 2
87 Rotthalmünster C 5
73 Röttingen D 3
43 Rottne B 4
37 Rottneros B 5
111 Rottofreno B 4
85 Rottweil B 5
87 Rötz B 4
70 Roubaix B 2
88 Roudnice n. Labem A 2
89 Roudno B 5
80 Roudovallec B 3
82 Rouen B 3
85 Rouffach C 4
81 Rougé C 5
95 Rougemont B 6
104 Rouillac B 2
93 Rouillé C 4
107 Roujan D 3
95 Roulans B 6
55 Roundwood A 5
89 Rousinov B 4
104 Roussac A 4
107 Rousses C 3
108 Roussilion B 1
84 Roussy-le-Village A 3
83 Rouvroy-sur-Audry B 6
94 Rouy B 3
16 Rovaniemi A 4
16 Rovastinaho B 5
111 Rovato B 4
88 Rovensko p. Troskami A 3
99 Roverbella D 1
99 Rovereto D 2
67 Rövershagen A 5
36 Roverud A 4
157 Roviaí D 3
112 Rovigo A 3
114 Rovinj B 1
115 Rovišće B 4
68 Rów C 2
51 Rowanburn B 5
69 Rowy A 5
65 Roxel C 5
104 Royan B 1
106 Royat B 3
108 Roybon B 2
48 Roybridge E 4
83 Roye B 4
18 Röymoen C 4
137 Royos B 4
12 Røyrvik C 5
59 Royston C 3
119 Rozadas A 4
152 Rožaj B 2
126 Rozalén del Monte C 3
78 Rózan C 4
68 Różańsko C 2
116 Rožanstvo C 3
126 Rozas B 1
83 Rozay-en-Brie C 4
88 Rožďalovice A 3
90 Rozdziele C 4
78 Rozental B 2
69 Rozewie A 6
153 Rozhen C 5
88 Rožmital p. Třemšinem B 1
91 Rožňava D 3
89 Rožnov p. Radhoštěm B 6
78 Rozogi B 4
83 Rozoy-sur-Seine B 6
89 Rozstáni B 4
88 Roztoky A 2
87 Rozvadov B 4
154 Rrogozhinë A 1
153 Rsovci A 4
57 Ruabon D 3
129 Ruanes B 5
34 Rubbestadneset B 1
57 Rubery D 5
123 Rubi C 5
120 Rubiacedo de Abajo B 3
119 Rubiana B 4
131 Rubielos Bajos B 4
132 Rubielos de Mora A 2
112 Rubiera B 2
152 Rubik C 1
120 Rucandio B 3
78 Ruciane-Nida B 4
35 Rud A 6
43 Ruda B 6
79 Ruda Maleniecka D 3
79 Ruda Pilczycka D 3
90 Ruda Śląsk B 1
91 Rudabánya D 3
100 Ruden C 2
86 Rudersberg C 1
101 Rudersdorf,A B 4
67 Rüdersdorf,D* C 6
87 Ruderting C 5
71 Rüdesheim C 6
44 Rudkøbing C 3
100 Rudmanns A 3
88 Rudná,CS A 2
77 Rudna,PL B 5
117 Rudna Glavna B 6
152 Rudnik, Kosovo, YU B 2
117 Rudnik, Srbija, YU B 4
90 Rudniki, Kalowice, PL B 2
79 Rudniki, Lodź, PL D 1
78 Rudno, Gdańsk, PL B 1
77 Rudno, Wroclaw, PL B 5
116 Rudo C 3
74 Rudolstadt C 3
76 Rudowica B 4
45 Ruds Vedby B 4
37 Rudskoga B 6
58 Rudston A 3
89 Rudy A 6
63 Rue B 3
125 Rueda B 5
127 Rueda de Jalón A 4
96 Ruegsauschachen B 3
104 Ruelle B 3
120 Ruerrero B 3
122 Ruesta B 1
146 Ruffano C 4
104 Ruffec A 3
95 Ruffey B 5
56 Rufford C 4
112 Rufina C 3
59 Rugby C 2
57 Rugeley D 4
74 Rugendorf C 3
117 Rugi A 6
82 Rugles C 2
30 Rugsund B 2
66 Rühen C 3
74 Ruhla C 2
75 Ruhland B 5
65 Ruhle B 5
65 Rühlertwist B 5
87 Ruhmannsfelden C 4
98 Ruhpolding B 3
87 Ruhstorf C 5
131 Ruidera C 4
65 Ruinen B 4
70 Ruiselede A 2
17 Rukajärvi A 8
71 Rulles C 4
95 Rully C 4
85 Rülzheim A 5
101 Rum B 4
116 Ruma A 3
151 Rumboci B 3
75 Rumburk C 6
116 Rumenka A 3
69 Rumia A 6
83 Rumigny B 6
108 Rumilly B 2
84 Rumont B 2
128 Runa B 1
57 Runcorn C 4
71 Runderoth B 6
6 Rundhaug B 4
21 Rundvik B 8
33 Runemo B 7
45 Rungsted B 5
38 Runhällen B 3
24 Runni B 3
78 Runowo A 3
43 Runsten C 6
10 Ruokojärvi B 4
29 Ruokolahti B 6
106 Ruoms C 4
26 Ruosniemi B 4
145 Ruoti C 4
28 Ruotsinpyhtää C 4
27 Ruovesi B 7
114 Rupa B 2
71 Ruppichteroth B 6
84 Rupt-sur-Moselle C 3
136 Rus A 3
117 Rusca A 6
103 Rusca Montană C 6
160 Ruse,BG D 5
100 Ruše,YU C 3
15 Rusele D 2
116 Ruševo A 1
55 Rush A 5
59 Rushden C 3
103 Rushiţa C 6
79 Rusiec D 1
69 Rusinowo B 4
102 Ruski Krstur C 3
59 Ruskington B 3
103 Rusko Selo C 4
91 Ruskov D 4
15 Rusksele D 2
101 Rusovce A 5
73 Russelsheim D 2
8 Russenes B 5
113 Russi B 4
101 Rust B 4
9 Rustefjelbma B 8
109 Rustrel D 2
79 Ruszki C 3
28 Rutalahti B 3
136 Rute B 2
72 Rüthen B 2
50 Rutherglen B 3
57 Ruthin C 3
51 Ruthwells C 4
97 Rüti A 4
145 Rutigliano B 6
30 Rutledal B 2
116 Rutoši C 3
64 Rutten B 3
16 Ruukki C 4
65 Ruurlo B 4
27 Ruutana B 7
145 Ruvo del Monte C 4
145 Ruvo di Púglia B 5
71 Ruwer C 5
91 Ružomberok C 2
44 Ry A 2
89 Rybany C 6
78 Rybina A 2
89 Rybnik A 6
78 Rychliki B 2
79 Rychlocice D 1
89 Rychnov n. Kneznou A 4
78 Rychnowo B 3
77 Rychtal B 6
89 Rychvald B 6
77 Rychwal A 7
79 Ryczywól, Kielce, PL D 4
69 Ryczywól, Poznań, PL C 4
43 Ryd C 4
43 Rydaholm C 4
42 Rydal B 2
42 Rydboholm B 2
62 Ryde C 2
42 Rydöbruk C 3
46 Rydsgård B 4
43 Rydsnäs B 5
89 Rydultowy A 6
77 Rydzyna B 5
62 Rye C 4
35 Rygene C 4
35 Rygge B 6
90 Ryglice C 4
29 Ryhälä B 6
78 Ryiewo B 1
79 Ryki D 4
68 Rymań B 3
90 Rymanów C 4
89 Rýmařov B 5
26 Rymättylä C 4
78 Ryn B 4
69 Rynarzewo B 5
44 Ryomgård A 3
78 Rypin B 2
33 Ryssa C 5
42 Ryssby C 4
69 Rytel B 5
23 Rytky B 8
90 Rytro C 3
27 Ryttylä C 7
78 Rzaśnik C 4
69 Rzeczenica B 5

79 Rzeczniów D 4
79 Rzeczyca D 3
79 Rzejowice D 2
76 Rzepin A 3
79 Rzgów D 2

S

64 's Gravendeel C 2
64 's Gravenhage B 2
64 's Gravenpolder C 1
64 's Gravenzande B 2
64 's-Hertogenbosch C 3
23 Sääksjärvi B 5
27 Sääksmäki B 7
73 Saal, Bayern, D† C 4
87 Saal, Bayern, D† C 3
98 Saalbach B 3
74 Saalburg C 3
85 Saales B 4
74 Saalfeld C 3
98 Saalfelden B 3
29 Sääminki B 6
96 Saanen B 3
85 Saarbrücken A 4
71 Saarburg C 5
29 Saari B 7
23 Saarijärvi C 7
17 Saarivaara C 8
71 Saarlouis C 5
96 Saas-Fee B 3
116 Šabac B 3
123 Sabadell C 5
143 Sabáudia C 4
112 Sabbioneta B 2
120 Sabero B 1
122 Sabiñánigo B 2
137 Sabinar A 4
91 Sabinov C 4
136 Sabiote A 3
81 Sablé-sur-Sarthe C 6
81 Sables-d'Or-les-Pins B 4
134 Sabóia B 2
114 Saborsko B 3
105 Sabres C 2
124 Sabrosa B 2
124 Sabugal C 2
91 Šaca D 4
127 Sacecorgo B 3
127 Saceda del Rio B 3
127 Sacedón B 3
130 Saceruela C 2
98 Sachsenburg C 4
99 Sacile D 3
85 Säckingen C 4
103 Sacoşu Turcesc C 5
126 Sacramenia A 2
103 Sacu C 6
103 Săcueni A 6
91 Saćurov D 4
118 Sada A 2
121 Sádaba B 5
50 Saddell B 2
123 Sadernas B 5
69 Sadki B 5
81 Sadkowice D 3
76 Sadów A 3
88 Sadská A 2
5 Sädvaluspen D 5
30 Sæbø A 3
34 Sæbøvik B 1
40 Sæby B 4
126 Saelices C 3
120 Saelices de Mayorga B 1
65 Saerbeck B 5
44 Særslev B 3
4 Sætran B 6
35 Sætre B 6
30 Sævareid C 2
134 Safara A 3
91 Šafárikovo D 3
37 Säffle B 4
62 Saffron Walden A 4
37 Safsnäs A 6
03 Sag C 5
67 Sagard A 6
60 Sageston B 2
33 Sågmyra C 6
40 Sagone B 1
34 Sagres B 2
03 Sagu B 5
91 Ságújfalu C 3
32 Sagunto B 2
01 Ságvár D 2
95 Sagy C 5
20 Sahagún B 1
27 Sahalahti B 7
23 Sahrajärvi C 7
91 Šahy D 1
96 Saignelegier A 2
11 Saija B 8

106 Sail B 3
123 Saillagouse B 5
108 Sain-Bel B 1
83 Sains-Richaumont B 4
51 St. Abb's B 5
43 St. Åby A 4
100 St. Aegyd a Neuwalde B 3
107 St. Affrique D 2
108 St. Agnan, Drôme, F C 2
94 St. Agnan, Saône-et-Loire, F C 3
104 St. Agnant B 2
60 St. Agnes C 1
106 St. Agrève B 4
93 St. Aigan B 5
81 St. Aignan-sur-Roë C 5
106 St. Alban-sur-Limagnole C 3
62 St. Albans B 3
94 St. Amand-en-Puisaye B 3
70 St. Amand-les-Eaux B 2
93 St. Amand-Longpre B 5
94 St. Amand-Mont-Rond C 2
106 St. Amans B 3
107 St. Amans-Soult D 2
106 St. Amant-Roche-Savine B 3
85 St. Amarin C 4
107 St.-Ambroix C 4
95 St. Amour C 5
101 St. Andra B 4
109 St. André-de-Alpes D 3
108 St.-André-de-Corcy B 1
104 St. André-de-Cubzac C 2
82 St. André-de-l'Eure C 3
107 St. André-de-Sangonis D 3
107 St. Andre-de-Valborgne C 3
72 St. Andreasberg B 4
51 St. Andrews A 5
100 St. Andria A 2
70 St. Andries A 2
106 St. Angel B 2
39 St. Anna D 3
100 St. Anna A. Aig C 3
64 St. Annaland C 2
64 St. Annaparochie A 3
82 St. Anne C 2
106 St. Anthême B 3
64 St. Anthonis C 3
105 St. Antoine C 2
97 St. Anton a. Arlberg A 6
100 St. Anton a. d. Jeßnitz B 3
97 St. Antönien B 5
107 St. Antonin-Noble-Val C 1
106 St. Armand B 3
82 St. Arnoult C 3
57 St. Asaph B 3
104 St. Astier B 3
60 St. Athan B 3
96 St.-Aubin,CH B 2
95 St. Aubin,F B 3
81 St. Aubin-d'Aubigné B 5
81 St. Aubin-du-Cormier B 5
95 St. Aubin-en-Ch. C 3
84 St. Aubin-sur-Aire B 2
82 St. Aubin-sur-Mer B 1
104 St. Aulaye B 2
60 St. Austell C 2
93 St. Avertin B 4
106 St. Avit B 2
84 St. Avold A 3
109 St. Aygulf D 3
107 St. Bauzille-du-Putois D 3
105 St. Béat E 3
56 St. Bees B 3
94 St. Benin-d'Azy C 3
93 St. Benoît-du-Sault C 5
84 St. Benoit-en-W. B 2
96 St.-Blaise,CH A 2
85 St. Blaise,F B 3
85 St. Blasien C 5
60 St. Blazey C 2
84 St. Blin B 2
108 St. Bonnet, Hautes Alpes, F C 3
106 St. Bonnet, Lozère, F C 3
95 St. Bonnet-de-Joux C 4
106 St. Bonnet-le-Château B 4
108 St. Bonnet-le-F. B 1
92 St. Brévin-les-Pins B 1
81 St. Briac B 5
61 St. Briavels B 5
81 St. Brice-en-Coglès B 5
80 St. Brieuc B 4
94 St. Bris-les Vineux B 5
81 St. Broladre B 5

60 St. Buryan C 1
93 St. Calais B 4
109 St. Cannat D 2
81 St. Cast B 4
106 St. Céré B 2
96 St. Cergue B 2
96 St. Cergues B 2
107 St. Cernin D 2
106 St. Chamant B 1
109 St.-Chamas D 2
108 St. Chamond B 1
106 St. Chély d'Apcher C 3
106 St. Chely-d'Aubrac C 2
107 St. Chinian D 2
107 St. Christol C 4
104 St. Christoly-Médoc B 2
92 St. Christophe-du-Ligneron C 2
95 St. Christophe-en-B. C 4
108 St. Christophe-en-Oisans C 3
104 St. Ciers-sur-Gironde B 2
106 St. Cirgues B 3
82 St. Clair-sur-Epte C 2
105 St. Clar D 3
104 St. Claud B 3
95 St. Claude C 5
60 St. Clears C 1
95 St. Colombe-sur-Seine B 4
60 St. Columb Major C 2
49 St. Combs D 7
106 St. Côme-d'Olt B 3
82 St. Cosme-de-Vair C 2
104 St. Cyprien C 4
83 St. Cyr C 5
95 St.-Cyr, Ain, F C 4
109 St.-Cyr, Var, F D 2
49 St. Cyrus E 6
109 St. Dalmas-de-T. C 4
45 St. Damme C 5
60 St. David's B 1
83 St. Denis C 4
94 St. Denis-de-l'H. B 2
104 St. Denis-d'Oléron A 1
81 St. Denis-d'Orques B 6
108 St. Denis-en-Bugey B 2
95 St. Didier C 4
106 St. Didier-en-V. B 4
84 St. Dié B 3
84 St. Dizier B 1
106 St. Dizier-Leyrenne A 1
108 St.-Egrève B 2
94 St. Eloy-les-Mines C 2
104 St. Emilion C 2
105 St. Esteben D 1
104 St. Estèphe B 2
106 St. Etienne B 1
108 St. Étienne-de-Cuines B 3
104 St. Etienne-de-Fursac A 4
92 St. Etienne-de-Montluc B 2
108 St. Étienne-de-St. G. B 2
109 St. Étienne-de-Tinée C 3
95 St. Étienne-du-Bois C 5
109 St. Etienne-les-Orgues C 4
94 St. Fargeau B 3
108 St. Félicien B* 1
107 St. Félix D 1
49 St. Fergus D 7
50 St. Fillans A 5
108 St. Firmin, Hautes Alpes, F C 3
95 St. Firmin, Saône et Loire, F C 4
140 St. Florent B 2
81 St. Florent-le-Vieil C 5
94 St.-Florent-sur-Cher C 2
83 St. Florentin D 5
106 St. Flour B 2
93 St. Flovier C 5
108 St. Fons B 1
104 St. Fort-sur-le-Né B 2
108 St. Fortunat C 1
92 St. Fulgent C 1
100 St. Gallen,F B 3
97 St. Gallen,CH A 5
97 St. Gallenkirch A 5
105 St. Gaudens D 3
93 St. Gaultier C 5
107 St. Gély-du-Fesc D 3
92 Ste. Gemme-la-Plaine C 2
70 St. Genesius B 2
106 St. Genest-Malifaux B 4
95 St. Gengoux-le-National B 4
107 St. Genies D 3
109 St. Geniez D 2
106 St. Geniez-d'Olt C 2
104 St. Genis-de-Saintonge B 2
95 St. Genis-Pouilly C 6

108 St. Genix-sur-Guiers B 2
85 St. Georgen B 5
100 St. Georgen a. d. Gusen A 2
100 St. Georgen a. d. Stiefing C 3
100 St. Georgen a. Reith B 2
98 St. Georgen im Attergau B 4
100 St. Georgen o. Judenburg B 2
100 St. Georgen o. Murau B 2
70 St. Georges, B B 4
104 St. Georges, Charente Maritime, F B 1
106 St. Georges, Puy de Dôme, F B 2
81 St. Georges-Buttavent B 6
106 St. Georges-d'Aurac B 3
108 St. Georges-de-C. B 2
104 St. Georges-de-Didonne B 2
107 St. Georges-de Luzençon C 2
108 St. Georges-de-R. A 1
105 St.-Georges-en-C. B 3
93 St. Georges-lès-Baillargeaux C 4
81 St. Georges-sur-Loire C 6
105 St. Geours-de-Marenne D 1
94 St. Gérand C 3
94 St. Gérand-de-Vaux C 3
70 St. Gérard B 3
107 St. Germain, Aveyron, F C 3
95 St. Germain, Haute Saône, F B 6
83 St. Germain, Yvelines, F C 4
94 St. Germain-Chassenay C 3
104 St. Germain-de-Confolens A 3
95 St. Germain-de-Joux C 5
94 St. Germain-des-Fossés C 3
95 St. Germain-du-Bois C 5
95 St. Germain-du-Plain C 4
94 St. Germain-du-Puy B 2
106 St. Germain-Laval B 4
94 St. Germain-l'E. C 3
106 St. Germain-Lembron B 2
104 St. Germain-les-Belles B 4
106 St. Germain-l'Herm B 3
108 St. Gervais, Haute Savoie, F B 3
106 St. Gervais, Puy de Dôme, F A 2
107 St. Gervais-sur-Mare D 3
80 St. Gildas-de-Rhuys C 4
81 St. Gildas-des-Bois C 4
98 St. Gilgen B 4
109 St. Gilles, Gard, F D 1
81 St. Gilles, Ille-et-Vilaine, F B 5
92 St. Gilles-sur-Vie C 2
70 St. Gillis A 3
96 St. Gingolph B 2
105 St. Girons, Ariège, F E 4
105 St. Girons, Landes, F D 1
105 St. Girons-Plage D 1
71 St. Goar B 6
71 St. Goarshausen B 6
83 St. Gobain B 5
80 St. Guénolé B 3
56 St. Helens C 4
81 St. Helier A 4
92 Ste. Hermine C 2
47 St. Herrestad B 4
94 St. Hilaire C 3
107 St. Hilaire-de-l'Aude D 2
92 St. Hilaire-des-Loges C 3
81 St. Hilaire-du-Harcouët B 5
92 St. Hilaire-du-Riez C 2
108 St. Hilaire-du-Rosier B 2
104 St. Hiliare-de Villefranche C 2
106 St. Hippolyte, Aveyron, F B 2
84 St. Hippolyte, Doubs, F C 3
107 St. Hippolyte-du-Fort D 3
94 St. Honoré C 3
106 St. Hostein B 3
70 St. Hubert B 4
96 St. Imier A 3
85 St. Ingbert A 4

63 St. Inglevert B 3
60 St. Ives, Cornwall, GB C 1
59 St. Ives, Hunts., GB C 3
107 St. Izaire D 2
100 St. Jacob C 2
64 St. Jacobiparochie A 3
81 St. Jacques-de-la-Lande B 5
81 St. Jacut B 4
98 St. Jakob C 2
100 St. Jakob i. Walde B 3
98 St. Jakob in Defereggen C 3
81 St. James B 5
95 St. Jean, Côte d'Or, F B 5
83 St. Jean, Seine-et-Marne, F C 5
80 St. Jean-Brévelay C 4
104 St. Jean-d'Angély B 2
108 St. Jean-d'Ardières A 1
94 St. Jean-de-B., Loiret, F C 3
108 St. Jean-de-B., Savoie, F B 3
108 St.-Jean-de-Bournay B 2
107 St. Jean-de-Brue C 3
104 St. Jean-de Côle B 3
81 St. Jean-de-Daye A 5
107 St. Jean-de-Fos B 3
105 St. Jean-de-Luz D 1
108 St. Jean-de-M.,F B 1
108 St.-Jean-de-M.,F B 3
92 St. Jean-de-Monts C 1
107 St. Jean-de-Védas D 3
104 St. Jean-d'Illac C 2
108 St.-Jean-en-R. B 2
109 St. Jean-la-Riviere D 4
93 St. Jean-le-B. B 5
105 St. Jean-Pied-de-Port D 1
105 St. Jean-Poutge D 3
84 St. Jean-Rohrbach A 3
109 St. Jeannet D 4
96 St. Jeoire B 3
92 St. Joachim B 1
100 St. Johann a. Tauern B 2
98 St. Johann am Walde A 4
100 St. Johann i. Saggautal C 3
98 St. Johann im Pongau B 4
98 St. Johann in Tirol B 3
56 St. John's B 2
53 St. Johnstown B 4
108 St. Jorioz B 3
70 St. Joris Winge B 3
105 St. Jory D 4
93 St. Jouin-de-Marnes C 3
107 St. Juéry D 2
123 St. Juliá de Loria B 4
96 St.-Julien, Haute Savoie, F B 2
106 St.-Julien, Loire, F B 3
81 St. Julien, Loire Atlantique, F C 5
106 St. Julien-C. B 4
92 St. Julien-de-Concelles B 2
109 St. Julien-de-Verdon D 3
83 St. Julien-du-Sault C 3
105 St. Julien-en-Born C 1
93 St. Julien-l'Ars C 4
108 St. Julien-M. M. B 1
108 St. Julien-Mont-Denis B 3
95 St. Julien-sur-R. C 5
104 St. Junien B 3
109 St. Just,F C 1
60 St. Just,GB C 1
83 St. Just-en-Chaussée B 3
106 St. Just-en-Chevalet B 3
105 St. Justin D 2
100 St. Katharein a. d. Laming B 3
100 St. Kathrein a. Hauenstein B 3
100 St. Kathrein a. Offenegg B 3
60 St. Keverne C 1
70 St. Kruis A 2
93 St. Lambert-des-Levées C 3
100 St. Lambrecht B 2
70 St. Lambrechts-Herk B 3
122 St. Lary B 3
109 St.-Laurent, Alpes Maritimes, F D 4
81 St. Laurent, Calvados, F A 6
107 St. Laurent-d'Aigouze D 4

58 Saltfleet B 4
58 Saltfleetby St. Clement B 4
124 Salto B 2
39 Saltsjöbaden C 5
43 Saltvik,S B 6
26 Saltvik,SF C 3
113 Saludécio C 4
99 Salurn C 2
110 Salussola B 3
110 Saluzzo C 2
132 Salvacañete A 1
134 Salvada B 3
107 Salvagnac D 1
129 Salvaleón C 4
128 Salvaterra de Magos B 2
129 Salvaterra do Extremo B 4
121 Salvatierra, Álava, E B 4
129 Salvatierra, Badajóz, E C 4
129 Salvatierra de Santiago B 4
104 Salviac C 4
65 Salzbergen B 5
98 Salzburg B 4
72 Salzgitter A 4
72 Salzgitter-Bad A 4
66 Salzhausen B 3
72 Salzkotten B 2
74 Salzmünde B 3
67 Salzwedel C 4
119 Sama A 5
105 Samadet D 2
141 Samassi C 2
105 Samatan D 3
147 Sambiase D 2
78 Samborowo B 2
90 Samborzec B 4
148 Sambuca di Sicília B 3
97 Samedan B 5
63 Samer B 3
158 Sámi A 1
27 Sammaljoki B 6
27 Sammatti C 6
145 Sammichele di Bari C 5
115 Samobor B 3
84 Samogneux A 2
101 Samorín A 5
118 Samos B 3
123 Sampedor C 4
122 Samper de Calanda C 2
110 Sampéyre C 2
149 Sampieri C 4
84 Sampigny B 2
78 Samplawa B 2
56 Sampool Bridge B 4
142 Samprugnano B 2
155 Sampsoús C 2
67 Samtens A 6
6 Samuelsberg B 6
141 Samugheo C 2
78 Samulewo A 4
121 San Adrián B 5
123 San Agaró C 6
144 San Ágata de Goti B 3
146 San Agata di Ésaro C 1
145 San Agata di Púglia B 4
118 San Amaro B 2
144 San Anastasia C 3
141 San Andrea Frius C 3
119 San Andrés de Rabanedo B 5
145 San Ángelo dei Lombardi C 4
144 San Antimo C 3
141 San Antioco C 2
119 San Antolin A 4
141 San Antónia B 3
138 San Antonio Abad C 2
123 San Antonio de Calonge C 6
146 San Arcángelo B 2
121 San Asensio B 4
126 San Augustín B 2
123 San Augustin de Llusanés B 5
134 San Bartolomé de la Torre B 3
126 San Bartolomé de las Abiertas C 1
126 San Bartolomé de Pinares B 1
144 San Bartolomeo in Gáldo B 4
123 San Baudillo C 5
143 San Benedetto del Tronto B 4
112 San Benedetto in Alpe C 3
112 San Benedetto Po A 2
130 San Benito C 2
129 San Benito Contienda C 3
148 San Biágio Plátani B 3
143 San Biágio Saracinisco C 4
99 San Bonifácio D 2
135 San Calixto B 5
98 San Cándido C 3
97 San Carlo,CH B 4
148 San Carlo,I B 3
138 San Carlos B 2
132 San Carlos de la Rápita A 3
131 San Carlos del Valle C 3
142 San Casciano d. Bagni B 2
112 San Casciano in Val di Pesa C 3
146 San Cataldo, Puglia, I B 4
149 San Cataldo, Sicilia, I B 3
142 San Caterina B 2
119 San Cebrián C 5
123 San Celoni C 5
146 San Cesárea Terme B 4
146 San Cesário di Lecce B 4
146 San Chirico Raparo B 2
148 San Cipirello B 3
118 San Ciprián de Viñas B 3
131 San Clemente, Cuenca, E B 4
119 San Clemente, León, E B 4
139 San Clemente, Menorca, E B 5
111 San Colombano al Lambro B 4
113 San Costanzo C 5
118 San Cristóbal C 3
119 San Cristóbal de Entreviñas B 5
119 San Cristóbal de la Polantera B 5
126 San Cristobal de la Vega A 1
123 San Cugat del Vallés C 5
110 San Damiano d'Asti C 3
110 San Damiano Macra C 2
99 San Daniele del Friuli C 4
146 San Demétrio Corone C 2
143 San Demetrio ne Vestini B 4
146 San Domenica Talao C 1
99 San Donà di Piave D 3
146 San Dónaci B 3
143 San Donato Val di Comino C 4
143 San Egídio alla Vibrata B 4
144 San Elia a Pianisi B 3
143 San Elia Fiumerapido C 4
119 San Emiliano B 5
119 San Esteban A 4
126 San Esteban de Gormaz A 2
125 San Esteban de la Sierra C 4
122 San Esteban de Litera C 3
119 San Esteban de Valdueza B 4
119 San Esteban del Molar C 5
125 San Esteban del Valle C 5
147 San Eufémia d'Aspromonte D 1
145 San Fele C 4
143 San Felice Circeo C 4
112 San Felice sul Panaro B 3
120 San Felices B 3
125 San Felices de los Gallegos C 3
123 San Felio C 5
123 San Feliu de Codinas C 5
123 San Feliu de Guixols C 6
123 San Feliu Saserra C 5
119 San Feliz de las Lavanderas B 5
145 San Ferdinando di Púglia B 5
135 San Fernando, Cádiz, E C 4
138 San Fernando, Formentera, E C 2
126 San Fernando de Henares B 2
147 San Filo C 2
142 San Fiora B 2
146 San Foca B 4
141 San Francesco d'Aglientu A 3
138 San Francisco C 2
138 San Francisco Javier C 2
149 San Fratello A 4
141 San Gavino Monreale C 2
110 San Germano Vercellese B 3
143 San Germini B 3
98 San Giácomo, Trentino-Alto Adige, I C 2
143 San Giácomo, Umbria, I B 3
112 San Gimignano C 3
113 San Ginésio C 5
143 San Giórgio a Liri C 4
144 San Giórgio del Sannio B 3
99 San Giórgio della Richinvelda C 3
110 San Giórgio di Lomellina B 3
99 San Giórgio di Nogaro D 4
112 San Giorgio di Piano B 3
146 San Giórgio Iónico B 3
145 San Giovanni a Piro C 4
111 San Giovanni Bianco B 4
111 San Giovanni in Croce B 5
147 San Giovanni in Fiore C 2
112 San Giovanni in Persiceto B 3
143 San Giovanni Reatino B 3
145 San Giovanni Rotondo B 4
141 San Giovanni Suérgiu C 2
112 San Giovanni Valdarno C 3
141 San Giusta C 2
113 San Giustino C 4
112 San Godenzo C 3
145 San Gregòrio Magno C 4
112 San Guiliano Terme C 2
123 San Hilario Sacalm C 5
123 San Hipólito de Voltregá B 5
123 San Jaime dels Domenys C 4
133 San Javier D 2
128 San Jorge B 2
137 San José, Almería, E C 4
138 San José, Ibiza, E C 2
138 San Juan Bautista B 2
133 San Juan de Alicante C 2
135 San Juan de Aznalfarache B 4
126 San Juan de la Nava B 1
123 San Juan de las Abadesas B 5
123 San Juan de Vilasar C 5
135 San Juan del Puerto B 4
119 San Justo de la Vega B 4
112 San Lazzaro di Sávena B 3
113 San Leo C 4
121 San Leonardo C 3
98 San Leonardo in Passiria C 2
142 San Lorenzo a Merse A 2
110 San Lorenzo al Mare D 2
146 San Lorenzo Bellizzi C 2
130 San Lorenzo de Calatrava C 3
139 San Lorenzo de Descardazar B 4
127 San Lorenzo de la Parilla C 3
123 San Lorenzo de Morunys B 4
126 San Lorenzo del Escorial B 1
98 San Lorenzo di Sebato C 2
113 San Lorenzo in Campo C 4
142 San Lorenzo Nuovo B 2
123 San Lorenzo Savall C 5
147 San Luca D 2
147 San Lúcido C 2
139 San Luis B 5
135 San Luis de Sabinillas C 5
113 San Marcello C 5
112 San Marcello Pistoiese B 2
125 San Marcial B 4
147 San Marco Argentano C 2
144 San Marco dei Cavoti B 3
145 San Marco in Lamis B 4
144 San Maria Cápua Vétere B 3
143 San Maria d'Angeli A 3
149 San Maria di Licodia B 4
142 San Marinella B 2
113 San Marino C 4
135 San Martin C 5
119 San Martin de Castañeda B 4
118 San Martin de Covas A 2
125 San Martin de la Vega, Avila, E C 4
126 San Martin de la Vega, Madrid, E B 2
123 San Martin de Llemaná B 5
119 San Martin de Luiña A 4
123 San Martin de Maldá C 4
126 San Martín de Montalbán C 1
119 San Martin de Oscos A 4
126 San Martín de Pusa C 1
123 San Martin de Tous C 4
121 San Martin de Unx B 5
126 San Martín de Valdeiglesias B 1
123 San Martin Sarroca C 4
128 San Martinho C 2
128 San Martinho do Porto B 1
99 San Martino di Campagna C 3
99 San Martino di Castrozza C 2
144 San Martino in Pénsilis B 4
132 San Mateo A 3
122 San Mateo de Gállego C 2
146 San Máuro Forte B 2
99 San Michele all'Adige C 2
149 San Michele di Ganzaria B 4
110 San Michele Mondovi C 2
138 San Miguel B 2
120 San Miguel Aguayo A 3
126 San Miguel de Arroyo A 1
126 San Miguel de Bernuy A 2
133 San Miguel de Salinas D 2
120 San Millán B 3
121 San Millán de la Congolla B 4
112 San Miniato C 2
125 San Muñoz C 3
135 San Nicholás del Puerto B 5
147 San Nicola da Crissa D 2
147 San Nicola del'Alto C 2
112 San Nicolo B 3
141 San Nicoló Gerrei C 3
143 San Oreste B 3
126 San Pablo C 1
123 San Pablo de Seguries B 5
146 San Pancrazio Salentino B 3
141 San Pantaleo A 3
145 San Paolo di Civitate B 4
131 San Pedro, Albacete, E C 4
119 San Pedro, Oviedo, E A 4
128 San Pedro da Cadeira B 1
136 San Pedro de Alcántara C 2
126 San Pedro de Arroyo B 1
119 San Pedro de Ceque B 4
119 San Pedro de Latarce C 5
128 San Pedro de Muel B 1
123 San Pedro de Riudevitlles C 4
120 San Pedro de Valderaduey B 2
133 San Pedro del Pinatar D 2
119 San Pedro del Puerto A 4
120 San Pedro del Romeral A 3
121 San Pedro Manrique B 4
123 San Pedro Pescador B 6
111 San Pellegrino Terme B 4
112 San Piero a Sieve C 3
113 San Piero in Bagno C 3
149 San Piero Patti A 4
149 San Pietro B 4
112 San Pietro in Casale B 3
99 San Pietro in Gu D 2
112 San Pietro in Palazzi C 2
99 San Pietro in Volta D 3
111 San Pietro Vara C 4
146 San Pietro Vernótico B 3
123 San Pol de Mar C 5
112 San Polo d'Enza B 2
141 San Príamo C 3
123 San Quirico de Besora B 5
142 San Quirico d'Orcia A 2
126 San Rafael, Ávila, E B 1
138 San Rafael, Ibiza, E C 2
126 San Román B 1
121 San Román de Cameros B 4
125 San Roman de Hornija B 4
120 San Román de la Cuba B 2
135 San Roque C 5
120 San Roque de Riomera A 3
145 San Rufo C 4
110 San Salvatore Monferrato C 3
144 San Salvo A 3
121 San Sebastián A 5
136 San Sebastián de los Ballesteros B 2
126 San Sebastián de los Reyes B 2
110 San Sebastiano Curone C 4
111 San Secondo Parmense C 5
142 San Severa B 2
147 San Severina C 2
146 San Severino Lucano B 2
113 San Severino Marche C 5
145 San Severo B 4
134 San Silvestre de Guzmán B 3
146 San Sosti C 2
145 San Spirito B 3
123 San Sudurni de Noya C 4
135 San Telmo, Huelva, E B 4
138 San Telmo, Mallorca, E B 3
141 San Teresa Gallura A 3
118 San Tirso de Abres A 3
142 San Venanzo B 3
129 San Vicente de Alcántara B 3
121 San Vicente de Arana B 4
123 San Vicente de Castellet C 4
120 San Vicente de la Barquera A 2
118 San Vicente de Rábade A 3
133 San Vicente del Raspeig C 2
119 San Vietro C 4
99 San Vigilio C 2
142 San Vincenzo A 1
141 San Vito C 3
99 San Vito al Tagliamento D 3
144 San Vito Chietino A 3
146 San Vito de Normanni B 3
99 San Vito di Cadore C 3
148 San Vito lo Capo A 2
143 San Vito Romano C 4
143 San Vittoria in Matenano A 4
50 Sanaigmore B 1
109 Sanary D 2
139 Sancellas B 3
94 Sancergues B 2
94 Sancerre B 2
84 Sancey-le-Grand C 3
126 Sanchidrián B 1
126 Sanchonuño A 1
94 Sancoins C 2
125 Sancti-Spiritus C 3
34 Sand B 2
43 Sanda C 5
30 Sandane B 3
153 Sandanski C 5
42 Sandared B 2
33 Sandarne B 8
67 Sandau C 5
87 Sandbach, Bayern, D† C 5
73 Sandbach, Hessen, D† D 3
57 Sandbach, GB C 4
43 Sandbäckshult B 6
50 Sandbank B 3
6 Sandbukt B 7
45 Sandby C 4
65 Sande, D† A 6
30 Sande, Fjordane Fylke, N B 2
30 Sande, More Og Romsdal Fylke, N A 2

35 Sande, Vestfold Fylke, N B 6
35 Sandefjord B 6
34 Sandeid B 1
74 Sandersdorf B 4
74 Sandersleben B 3
31 Sanderstølen C 6
66 Sandesneben B 3
49 Sandgarth B 6
34 Sandhaug A 3
50 Sandhead C 3
42 Sandhem B 3
65 Sandhorst A 5
43 Sandhultsbrunn B 4
118 Sandianes B 3
94 Sandillon B 2
100 Sandl A 2
4 Sandnes, Langøya, N B 3
34 Sandnes, Rogaland Fylke, N C 1
34 Sandnes, Vestagder Fylke, N C 3
49 Sandness A 7
12 Sandnessjøen A 4
125 Sando C 3
90 Sandomierz B 4
102 Sándorfalva B 4
62 Sandown C 2
18 Sandøy C 2
35 Sandøysund B 6
103 Sandra C 4
99 Sandrigo D 2
43 Sandsbro C 4
4 Sandset B 3
43 Sandsjöfors B 4
21 Sandslån B 6
18 Sandstad B 5
14 Sandträsk B 5
47 Sandvig B 5
6 Sandvik B 4
31 Sandvika, N C 8
20 Sandvika, S B 1
38 Sandviken, Gälveborgs Län, S B 3
21 Sandviken, Västernorrlands Län, S B 7
62 Sandwich B 5
49 Sandwick A 7
59 Sandy C 3
120 Sanfelices A 3
158 Sånga,GR B 3
21 Sånga,S B 6
63 Sangatte B 3
118 Sangenjo B 2
74 Sangerhausen B 3
16 Sanginjoki C 5
17 Sanginkylä C 5
16 Sangis B 2
133 Sangonera D 1
121 Sanguesa B 5
105 Sanguinet C 1
97 Saninaun B 6
67 Sanitz A 5
24 Sänkimäki B 4
47 Sankt Olof B 5
135 Sanlúcar de Barrameda C 4
134 Sanlúcar de Guadiana B 3
135 Sanlúcar la Mayor B 4
141 Sanluri C 2
33 Sanna B 8
110 Sannazzaro de' Burgondi B 3
67 Sanne C 4
145 Sannicandro di Bari C 5
145 Sannicandro Gargánico B 4
35 Sannidal C 5
79 Sanniki C 2
50 Sanquhar B 4
110 Sanremo D 2
113 Sansepolcro C 4
115 Sanski Most C 4
134 Sant-Ana de Cambas B 3
139 Sant Cristófol B 5
135 Sant Olalla del Cala B 4
129 Santa Amalia B 4
129 Santa Ana B 5
134 Santa Ana da Serra B 2
126 Santa Ana de Pusa C 1
132 Santa Bárbara A 3
134 Santa Bárbara de Casa B 3
134 Santa Bárbara de Padrões B 3
134 Santa Catarina B 3
149 Santa Caterina Villarmosa B 4
134 Santa Clara-a-Nova B 2
134 Santa Clara-a-Velha B 2
134 Santa Clara de Louredo B 3
123 Santa Coloma de Farnés C 5
123 Santa Coloma de Queralt C 4
119 Santa Colomba de Curueño B 5
119 Santa Colomba de Somoza B 4
118 Santa Comba A 2
124 Santa Comba Dão C 1
124 Santa Comba de Rossas B 3
111 Santa Cristina B 4
119 Santa Cristina de la Polvorosa B 5
149 Santa Croce Camerina C 4
144 Santa Croce di Magliano B 3
118 Santa Cruz, E A 2
128 Santa Cruz, P B 1
136 Santa Cruz de Alhama B 3
121 Santa Cruz de Campezo B 4
127 Santa Cruz de Grio A 4
126 Santa Cruz de la Salceda A 2
129 Santa Cruz de la Sierra B 5
126 Santa Cruz de la Zarza C 2
132 Santa Cruz de Moya B 1
131 Santa Cruz de Mudela C 3
129 Santa Cruz de Paniagua A 4
126 Santa Cruz de Retamar B 1
125 Santa Cruz del Valle C 4
149 Santa Doménica Vittória B 4
136 Santa Elena A 3
119 Santa Elena de Jamuz B 5
130 Santa Eufemia C 2
118 Santa Eugenia B 2
132 Santa Eulalia, E A 1
129 Santa Eulália, P C 3
119 Santa Eulalia de Oscos A 3
138 Santa Eulalia del Rió C 2
136 Santa Fe de los Boliches C 2
138 Santa Inés, Ibiza, E B 2
136 Santa Inés, Málaga, E C 2
134 Santa Iria B 3
122 Santa Isabel C 2
124 Santa Leocadia B 1
112 Santa Luce C 2
113 Santa Lucia C 4
149 Santa Lucia del Mela A 5
134 Santa Luzia B 2
98 Santa Maddalena Vallalta C 3
132 Santa Magdalena de Pulpis A 3
128 Santa Margarida B 2
134 Santa Margarida do Sado A 2
139 Santa Margarita B 4
148 Santa Margherita di Belice B 3
110 Santa Margherita Ligure C 4
97 Santa Maria, CH B 6
122 Santa Maria, Huesca, E B 2
139 Santa Maria, Mallorca, E B 3
131 Santa Maria De Campo Rus B 4
120 Santa Maria de Cayón A 3
123 Santa Maria de Corco B 5
127 Santa Maria de Huerta A 3
126 Santa María de la Alameda B 1
126 Santa Maria de las Hoyas A 2
123 Santa Maria de Miralles C 4
137 Santa Maria de Nieva B 5
136 Santa Maria de Trassierra B 2
120 Santa Maria del Camp B 3
119 Santa María del Páramo B 5
111 Santa Maria del Taro C 4
111 Santa Maria della Vérsa C 4
126 Santa Maria la Real de Nieva A 1
120 Santa Maria Ribarredonda B 3
119 Santa Marina del Rey B 5
131 Santa Marta, Albacete, E B 4
129 Santa Marta, Badajóz, E C 4
129 Santa Marta de Magasca B 4
124 Santa Marta de Penaguião B 2
148 Santa Ninfa B 2
126 Santa Olalla B 1
123 Santa Pau B 5
133 Santa Pola C 2
140 Santa Severa B 2
113 Santa Sofia C 3
128 Santa Suzana, Évora, P C 3
128 Santa Suzana, Setúbal, P C 2
149 Santa Teresa di Riva B 5
141 Santadi C 2
136 Santaella B 2
136 Santafé B 3
149 Sant'Ágata di Militello A 4
113 Sant'Agata Féltria C 4
113 Sant'Alberto B 4
128 Sant'Ana,P C 2
128 Santana,P C 1
128 Santana do Mato C 2
120 Santander A 3
113 Sant'Angelo in Vado C 4
111 Sant'Angelo Lodigiano B 4
99 Sant'Anna D'Alfaedo D 1
139 Santany B 4
113 Sant'Arcángelo di Romagna B 4
128 Santarém B 2
119 Santas Martas B 5
103 Santău A 6
127 Santed A 4
113 Sant'Elpidio a Mare C 5
145 Santéramo in Colle C 5
120 Santervas de la Vega B 2
121 Santesteban A 5
110 Santhià B 3
129 Santiago de Alcántara B 3
136 Santiago de Calatrava B 2
118 Santiago de Compostela B 2
137 Santiago de la Espade A 4
125 Santiago de la Puebla C 4
133 Santiago de la Ribera D 2
129 Santiago del Campo B 4
134 Santiago do Cacém B 2
128 Santiago do Escoural C 2
128 Santiago Maior C 3
125 Santibáñez de Béjar C 4
120 Santibañez de la Peña B 2
119 Santibáñez de Murias A 5
119 Santibáñez de Vidriales B 4
129 Santibáñez el Alto A 4
129 Santibáñez el Bajo A 4
119 Santielle A 4
112 Sant.Ilário d'Enza B 2
120 Santillana A 2
135 Santiponce B 4
136 Santisteban del Puerto A 3
126 Santiuste de Pedraza A 2
126 Santiuste de S. J. Bautista A 1
125 Santiz B 4
134 Santo Aleixo A 3
134 Santo Amador A 3
128 Santo Amaro C 3
134 Santo André A 2
128 Santo Antonio da Charneca C 1
129 Santo Domingo C 3
121 Santo Domingo de la Calzada B 4
120 Santo Domingo de Silos C 3
134 Santo Estêvão B 3
128 Santo Estévão, Santarém, P C 2
140 Santo-Pietro-di-Tenda B 2
110 Santo Stéfano Belbo C 3
111 Santo Stefano d'Aveto C 4
99 Santo Stéfano di Cadore C 3
149 Santo Stéfano di Camastra A 4
112 Santo Stéfano di Magra B 1
148 Santo Stéfano Quisquina B 3
99 Santo Stino di Livenza D 3
124 Santo Tirso B 1
136 Santo Tomé A 3
133 Santomera C 1
120 Santoña A 3
101 Sántos C 5
120 Santotis A 2
120 Santovenia, Burgos, E B 3
119 Santovenía, Zamora, E C 5
141 Santu Lussúrgiu B 2
121 Santurce A 3
95 Sanvignes-les-Mines C 4
146 Sanza B 1
134 São, Faro, P Miguel do Pinheiro B 3
134 São Barnabé B 2
134 São Bartolomé de Serra A 2
134 São Bartolomeu de Messines B 2
124 São Bento B 1
134 São Braz de Alportel B 3
128 São Braz do Reguedoura C 2
128 São Cristóvão C 2
134 São Domingos B 2
128 São Geraldo C 2
124 São João da Madeira C 1
124 São João da Pesqueira B 2
128 São João da Ribeira B 2
124 São João da Serra C 1
134 São João da Venda B 3
134 São João dos Caldeiréiros B 3
129 São Julião B 3
134 São Lourenco A 2
134 São Luiz B 2
128 São Marcos C 3
134 São Marcos da Ataboeira B 3
134 São Marcos da Serra B 2
128 São Marcos de Campo C 3
134 São Martinho das Amoreiras B 2
128 São Martino A 2
134 São Matias, Beja, P A 3
128 São Matias, Evora, P C 2
128 São Miguel d'Acha A 3
128 São Miguel de Machede C 3
124 São Pedro da Torre B 1
134 São Pedro de Solis B 3
124 São Pedro do Sul C 1
128 São Romao, Evora, P C 2
134 São Romão, Faro, P B 3
129 São Romão, Portalegre, P C 3
134 São Sebastião B 3
134 São Teotónio B 2
128 São Tiago de Litem B 2
124 São Torcato B 1
153 Saparevo B 5
128 Sapataria C 1
23 Sapeli C 8
124 Sapiãos B 2
63 Sapignies B 4
99 Sappada C 3
65 Sappemeer A 4
146 Sapri B 1
17 Säräisniemi C 5
17 Sarajärvi B 6
116 Sarajevo C 2
105 Saramon D 3
103 Sáránd A 5
156 Sarandáporon B 2
155 Sarandë C 2
117 Saranovo B 4
117 Saraorci B 5
160 Saray E 5
69 Sarbinowo, Koszalin, PL A 3
76 Sarbinowo, Szczecin, PL A 3
102 Sárbogárd B 2
83 Sarcelles C 4
99 Sarche di Calavino C 1
123 Sardanyola C 5
141 Sárdara C 2
155 Sardhínina D 3
128 Sardoal B 2
126 Sardón de Duero A 1
116 Šarengrad A 3
99 Sarentino C 2
111 Sarezzo B 5
97 Sargans A 5
102 Sári A 3
119 Sariego A 5
128 Sarilhos Grandes C 2
122 Sariñena C 2
91 Sárisáp E 1
103 Sarkad B 5
103 Sarkadkeresztúr B 5
101 Sárkeresztes B 6
28 Särkilahti B 3
29 Särkisalmi B 7
27 Särkisalo C 5
104 Sarlat C 4
104 Sarliac-sur-l'Isle B 3
101 Sármellék C 5
32 Särna B 4
32 Särnaheden B 3
113 Sarnano C 5
96 Sarnen B 4
111 Sárnico B 4
144 Sarno C 3
99 Sarnónico C 2
67 Sarnow, D* B 6
90 Sarnów, PL B 4
77 Sarnowa B 5
99 Sarnthein C 2
42 Säro B 1
110 Saronno B 4
102 Sárosd A 2
91 Sárospatak D 4
91 Šarovce D 1
36 Sarpsborg B 3
120 Sarracin B 3
85 Sarralbe A 4
105 Sarrancolin E 3
108 Sarras B 1
118 Sarraus B 3
85 Sarre-Union B 4
123 Sarreal C 4
85 Sarrebourg B 4
85 Sarreguemines A 4
103 Sárrétudvari A 5
118 Sarria B 3
123 Sarria de Ter B 5
109 Sarrians C 1
132 Sarrión A 2
122 Sarroca C 3
105 Sarron D 2
83 Sarry C 6
113 Sársina C 4
72 Sarstedt A 3
101 Sárszentmihály B 6
102 Sárszentmiklós B 2
71 Sart B 4
142 Sarteano B 2
140 Sartène C 1
156 Sárti B 3
81 Sartilly B 5
110 Sartirana Lomellina B 3
103 Sarud A 4
101 Sárvát B 4
22 Sarvela C 4
22 Sarvijöki C 3
112 Sarzana B 1
80 Sarzeau C 4
128 Sarzedas B 3
70 Sas van Gent A 2
153 Sasa B 4
120 Sasamón B 2
117 Sasca Montană B 5
101 Sásd C 6
27 Sasi B 6
69 Sasino A 5
141 Sássari B 2
110 Sassello C 3
65 Sassenberg C 6
64 Sassenheim B 2
142 Sassetta A 1
67 Sassnitz A 6
142 Sasso d'Ombrone B 2
112 Sasso Marconi B 3
113 Sassocorvaro C 4
113 Sassoferrato C 4
112 Sassoleone B 3
112 Sassuolo B 2
122 Sástago C 2
101 Saštinske Stráže A 5
91 Sáta D 3

19 Såtåhaugvoll C 6
124 Satão C 2
103 Satchinez C 5
36 Såtenäs C 3
38 Säter B 2
39 Säterbo C 2
42 Sätila B 2
108 Satillieu B 1
116 Satnica Đakovačka A 2
91 Satoraljaújhely D 4
117 Satornja B 4
67 Satow B 4
89 Satre Město B 4
44 Satrup C 2
11 Sattanen B 6
97 Satteins A 5
97 Sattel A 4
100 Sattledt A 2
160 Satu Mare B 3
142 Saturnia B 2
104 Saucats C 2
124 Saucelle B 3
34 Sauda B 2
34 Saudasjøen B 2
84 Saudrupt B 2
101 Sauerbrunn B 4
86 Sauerlach D 3
106 Saugues C 3
35 Sauherad B 5
104 Saujon B 2
27 Saukkola C 6
35 Sauland B 4
108 Saulces C 1
70 Saulces Monclin C 3
86 Saulgau C 1
98 Saulgrub B 2
95 Saulieu B 4
95 Saulon-la-Chapelle B 5
109 Sault C 2
108 Sault-Brénaz B 2
105 Sault-de-Navailles D 2
95 Saulx B 6
84 Saulxures-sur-Moselotte C 3
94 Saulzier-le-Potier C 2
104 Saumos C 2
93 Saumur B 3
25 Saunajärvi B 6
11 Saunavaara B 7
60 Saundersfoot B 2
107 Saurat E 1
99 Sáuris C 3
12 Saus B 4
109 Sausset-les-Pins D 2
107 Sauteyrargues D 3
106 Sauvagnat B 2
107 Sauvas C 4
107 Sauve D 3
105 Sauveterre D 2
104 Sauveterre-de-Guyenne C 2
104 Sauviat-sur-Vige B 4
27 Sauvo C 5
106 Sauxillanges B 3
104 Sauzé-Vaussais A 3
108 Sauzét, Drôme, F C 1
105 Sauzet, Lot, F C 4
80 Sauzon C 3
146 Sava B 3
19 Savalen C 6
136 Savalonga C 3
15 Sävar E 4
14 Sävast C 5
42 Säve B 1
147 Savelli C 2
81 Savenay C 5
105 Saverdun D 4
85 Saverne B 4
23 Sävia B 8
83 Savières C 5
110 Savigliano C 2
104 Savignac-les-Eglises B 3
145 Savignano di Púglia B 4
113 Savignano sul Rubicone B 4
95 Savigny-en Revermont C 5
95 Savigny-lès Beaune B 4
93 Savigny-sur-Braye B 4
25 Savijärvi B 6
25 Savikyla B 5
108 Savines C 3
102 Savino Selo C 3
113 Savio B 4
103 Săvirşin B 6
29 Savitaipale B 5
151 Šavnik C 5
97 Savognin B 5
110 Savona C 3
23 Savonkylä B 5
29 Savonlinna B 6
25 Savronranta C 6
43 Sävsjö B 4
43 Sävsjöström B 5
11 Savukoski B 8
158 Savvália B 2
62 Sawbridgeworth B 4
59 Sawston C 4
59 Sawtry C 3
133 Sax C 2
37 Saxdalen A 6
58 Saxilby B 3
59 Saxmundham C 5
13 Saxnäs C 7
59 Saxthorpe C 5
126 Sayatón B 3
75 Sayda C 5
155 Sayiádha C 2
23 Saynätsalo C 7
25 Säyneinen B 5
88 Sazava, Jihomoravsky, CS B 3
88 Sázava, Stredočesky, CS B 2
80 Scaër B 3
143 Scafa B 5
144 Scafati C 3
50 Scalasaig A 1
58 Scalby A 3
146 Scalea C 1
149 Scaletta Zanclea A 5
49 Scalloway A 7
58 Scamblesby B 3
147 Scandale C 2
112 Scandiano B 2
111 Scandolara Ravara B 5
143 Scanno C 4
142 Scansano B 2
146 Scanzano B 2
48 Scarastavore D 1
58 Scarborough A 3
113 Scardovari B 4
54 Scariff B 3
48 Scarinish E 2
59 Scarning C 4
112 Scarperia C 3
95 Scey-sur-Saône-et-St. Aubin B 5
73 Schaafheim D 3
97 Schaan A 5
101 Schachendorf B 4
66 Schacht-Audorf A 2
97 Schaffhausen A 4
74 Schafstädt B 3
66 Schafstedt A 2
86 Schäftlarn D 3
64 Schagen B 2
98 Schalchen A 4
74 Schalkau C 3
87 Schalldorf D 4
96 Schangnau B 3
85 Schapbach B 5
87 Schärding,A C 5
87 Schärding,D† C 5
98 Scharnitz B 2
65 Scharrel A 5
101 Schattendorf B 4
66 Scheeßel B 2
113 Schéggia C 4
100 Scheibbs A 3
75 Scheibenberg C 4
97 Scheidegg A 5
100 Scheifling B 2
73 Scheinfeld D 4
86 Schelklingen C 1
66 Schenefeld, Hamburg, D† B 2
66 Schenefeld, Schleswig-Holstein, D† A 2
73 Schenklengsfeld C 3
65 Schepsdorf-Lohne B 5
72 Scherfede B 3
65 Schermbeck C 4
64 Schermerhorn B 2
70 Scherpenheuvel B 3
64 Scherpenzeel B 3
86 Scheßlitz B 3
64 Schiedam C 2
87 Schierling C 4
64 Schiermonnikoog A 4
97 Schiers B 5
85 Schifferstadt A 5
64 Schijndel C 3
75 Schildau B 4
65 Schildwolde A 4
71 Schillingen C 5
86 Schillingsfürst B 2
97 Schilpário B 6
85 Schiltach B 5
99 Schio D 2
85 Schirmeck B 4
87 Schirnding A 4
85 Schirrheim B 4
74 Schkeuditz B 4
74 Schkölen B 3
75 Schlabendorf B 5
72 Schladen A 4
98 Schladming B 4
98 Schlaiten C 3
99 Schlanders C 1
72 Schlangen B 2
71 Schleiden B 5
85 Schleithal B 5
74 Schleiz C 3
66 Schleswig A 2
74 Schleusingen C 2
75 Schlieben B 5
85 Schliengen C 4
98 Schliersee B 2
73 Schlitz C 3
72 Schloß Neuhaus B 2
74 Schloßvippach B 3
74 Schlotheim B 2
85 Schluchsee C 5
73 Schlüchtern C 3
99 Schluderbach C 3
99 Schluderns C 1
74 Schmalkalden C 2
72 Schmallenberg B 2
71 Schmelz C 5
87 Schmidham C 5
87 Schmidmühlen B 3
75 Schmiedeberg C 5
74 Schmiedefeld C 2
98 Schmirn B 2
75 Schmölln, Leipzig, D* C 4
68 Schmölln, Neubrandenburg, D* B 2
87 Schnaitsee C 4
86 Schnaittach B 3
87 Schnaittenbach B 4
75 Schneeberg C 4
69 Schneidemühl B 5
74 Schneidlingen B 3
98 Schneizireuth B 3
66 Schneverdingen B 2
100 Schöder B 2
71 Schoenberg B 5
67 Schollene C 5
73 Schöllkrippen C 3
85 Schömberg B 5
85 Schonach B 5
87 Schönach, Bayern, D† C 4
85 Schönau, Baden-Württemberg, D† C 4
87 Schönau, Bayern, D† C 4
67 Schönbeck B 6
87 Schönberg, Bayern, D† C 5
66 Schönberg, Schleswig-Holstein, D† A 3
66 Schönberg, D* B 3
74 Schönebeck A 3
75 Schoneck C 4
71 Schönecken-Wetteldorf B 5
67 Schönermark B 6
75 Schönewalde B 5
98 Schongau B 1
101 Schöngrabern A 4
72 Schönhagen B 3
87 Schönhaid B 4
67 Schönhausen C 5
72 Schönholthausen B 2
72 Schöningen A 4
65 Schöninghsdorf B 5
66 Schönkirchen A 3
87 Schönsee B 4
87 Schönthal B 4
73 Schonungen C 4
97 Schonwies A 6
70 Schoondijke A 2
65 Schoonebeek B 4
64 Schoonhoven C 2
85 Schopfheim C 4
86 Schopfloch B 2
85 Schopp A 4
72 Schöppenstedt A 4
98 Schörfling B 4
86 Schorndorf C 1
65 Schorten A 5
70 Schoten A 3
72 Schötmar A 2
73 Schotten C 3
85 Schramberg B 5
89 Schrattenbg. C 4
73 Schrecksbach C 3
88 Schrems C 3
100 Schrems b. Frohnleiten B 3
101 Schrick A 4
85 Schriesheim A 5
86 Schrobenhausen C 3
97 Schröcken A 6
73 Schrozberg D 3
97 Schruns A 5
54 Schull C 2
96 Schüpfheim B 4
86 Schussenried D 1
85 Schutterwald B 4
65 Schüttorf B 5
101 Schützen a. Gebirge B 4
67 Schwaan B 5
86 Schwabach B 3
86 Schwabhausen C 3
86 Schwäbisch Gmünd C 1
86 Schwäbisch Hall B 1
86 Schwabmünchen C 2
101 Schwadorf A 4
65 Schwagstorf, Niedersachsen, D† B 5
65 Schwagstorf, Niedersachsen, D† B 6
85 Schwaigern A 6
100 Schwanberg C 3
97 Schwanden B 5
87 Schwandorf B 4
74 Schwanebeck B 3
98 Schwanenstadt A 4
66 Schwanewede B 1
73 Schwanfeld D 4
97 Schwangau A 6
67 Schwante C 6
66 Schwarmstedt C 2
74 Schwarza, Gera, D* C 3
74 Schwarza, Suhl, D* C 2
98 Schwarzach im Pongau B 4
101 Schwarzau a. Steinfelde B 4
100 Schwarzau i. Gebirge B 3
88 Schwarzenau C 3
74 Schwarzenbach C 3
74 Schwarzenbach a. W. C 3
66 Schwarzenbek B 3
75 Schwarzenberg C 4
96 Schwarzenburg B 3
87 Schwarzenfeld B 4
75 Schwarzheide B 5
98 Schwaz B 2
101 Schwechat A 4
68 Schwedt B 2
65 Schwei A 6
71 Schweich C 5
77 Schweidnitz C 5
85 Schweighausen B 4
85 Schweighouse B 4
73 Schweinfurt C 4
75 Schweinitz B 5
67 Schweinrich B 5
71 Schwelm A 6
75 Schwemsal B 4
98 Schwendt B 3
85 Schwenningen B 5
75 Schwepnitz B 5
67 Schwerin B 4
71 Schwerte A 6
85 Schwetzingen A 5
97 Schwyz A 4
148 Sciacca B 3
149 Scicli C 4
68 Ściechów C 3
96 Sciez B 2
147 Scigliano C 2
147 Scilla D 1
77 Ścinawa B 5
108 Scionzier A 3
149 Scoglitti C 4
59 Scole C 5
110 Scopello B 3
149 Scórdia B 4
99 Scorze D 3
58 Scotch Corner A 2
48 Scourie C 3
49 Scousburgh B 7
49 Scrabster C 5
52 Scramoge C 3
54 Screeb A 2
55 Screggan A 4
113 Scritto C 4
58 Scunthorpe B 3
97 Scuol-Schuls B 6
143 Scurcola Marsic B 4
62 Seaford C 4
51 Seaham C 6
51 Seahouses B 6
58 Seamer A 3
56 Seascale B 3
61 Seaton C 3
51 Seaton Delaval B 6
106 Seauve-sur-S. B 4
107 Sebazac-Concourès C 2
152 Sebecevo A 2
56 Sebergham B 4
100 Sebersdorf B 3
160 Sebes C 3
103 Sebiş B 6
75 Sebnitz C 6
83 Seboncourt B 5
88 Seč, Vychodočeský, CS B 3
87 Seč, Zapadočeský, CS B 5
117 Sečanj A 4
117 Secăşeni A 5
90 Secemin B 2
85 Seckach A 6
100 Seckau B 2
63 Seclin B 5
92 Secondigny C 3
91 Sečovce D 4
91 Sečovská Polianka D 4
128 Sêda B 3
70 Sedan C 3
56 Sedbergh B 4
136 Sedella C 2
109 Sédéron C 2
51 Sedgefield C 6
88 Sedičany B 2
99 Sédico C 3
141 Sedilo B 2
141 Sédini B 2
115 Sedlarica B 5
88 Sedlec-Prčice B 2
88 Sedlice B 1
79 Sedziejowice D 2
90 Sedziszów Malopolski B 4
98 Seeboden C 4
66 Seefeld,D† B 1
67 Seefeld,D* C 6
98 Seefeld in Tirol B 2
67 Seehausen C 4
98 Seekirchen Markt B 4
85 Seelbach B 4
76 Seelow A 3
72 Seelze A 3
87 Seeon D 4
75 Seerhausen B 5
82 Sées C 2
72 Seesen B 4
98 Seeshaupt B 2
98 Seewaichen B 4
117 Sefkerin A 4
31 Segalstad bru B 7
31 Segård C 7
33 Segersta B 7
101 Segesd C 5
37 Segmon B 5
104 Segonzac B 2
132 Segorbe B 2
126 Segovia B 1
81 Segré C 6
106 Ségur-les-Villas B 2
129 Segura B 3
135 Segura de León A 4
127 Segura de los Baños B 5
130 Segurrilla A 2
72 Sehnde A 3
124 Seia C 2
81 Seiches-sur-le-Loire C 6
9 Seida B 8
100 Seiersberg B 3
75 Seifhennersdorf C 6
94 Seignelay B 3
118 Seijo C 2
106 Seilhac B 1
70 Seilles B 4
30 Seim C 2
22 Seinäjoki C 4
105 Seissan D 3
100 Seitenstetten Markt A 2
14 Seitevare B 2
128 Seixal C 1
100 Seizthal B 2
155 Sékliza C 3
90 Sekowa C 4
101 Sekule A 5
31 Sel B 6
21 Selånger C 6
28 Selänpää B 4
23 Seläntaus B 7
141 Selárgius C 3
74 Selb C 4
74 Selbitz C 3
19 Selbu B 7
19 Selbustrand B 6
58 Selby B 2
150 Selca B 2
152 Selcë, AL B 1
91 Selce, CS D 2
89 Selec C 5

No.	Name	G1	G2	No.	Name	G1	G2	No.	Name	G1	G2	No.	Name	G1	G2	No.	Name	G1	G2
116	Selenča	A	3	114	Sentvid	A	2	135	Setenil	C	5	147	Siderno	D	2	123	Sils	C	5
154	Selenicë	B	1	123	Seo de Urgel	B	4	19	Seter	B	5	156	Sidhirókastron	A	3	6	Silsand	B	3
85	Sélestat	B	4	118	Seoane de Caurel	B	3	4	Setermoen	B	7	61	Sidmouth	C	3	58	Silsden	C	4
103	Seleuş,R	B	5	96	Seon	A	4	117	Setonje	B	5	90	Sidzina	C	2	28	Siltakyla	C	4
117	Seleuš,YU	A	4	144	Sepino	B	3	36	Setskog	B	3	101	Siebenbrunn	A	4	97	Silvaplana	B	5
117	Selevac	B	4	69	Sepólne Krajenskie	B	5	71	Setterich	B	5	75	Siebenlehn	B	5	128	Silvares	A	3
122	Selgua	C	3	78	Sepopol	A	3	110	Settimo Torinese	B	2	79	Siedlce	C	5	43	Silverdalen	B	5
101	Selice	A	5	65	Seppenrade	C	5	56	Settle	B	4	72	Siedlinghausen	C	4	59	Silverstone	C	2
73	Seligenstadt	C	2	103	Šepreus	B	5	128	Setúbal	B	3	69	Siedlisko	C	4	134	Silves	B	2
74	Seligenthal	C	2	109	Septèmes	D	2	86	Seubersdorf	B	3	71	Siegburg	B	6	143	Silvi	B	5
33	Selja	B	5	82	Septeuil	C	3	141	Seui	C	3	73	Siegen	C	2	65	Silvolde	C	4
30	Selje	A	2	95	Septmoncel	C	5	141	Seúlo	C	3	87	Siegenburg	C	3	98	Silz	B	1
6	Seljelvnes	B	5	126	Sepúlveda	A	2	95	Seurre	C	5	101	Sieggraben	B	4	95	Simandre	C	4
35	Seljord	B	4	99	Sequals	C	3	154	Sevaster	B	1	100	Sieghartskirchen	A	4	116	Šimanovci	B	4
11	Selkalä	C	9	125	Sequeros	C	3	44	Sevel	A	1	71	Sieglar	B	6	103	Simanti	B	5
51	Selkirk	B	5	71	Seraing	B	4	60	Seven Sisters	B	3	98	Siegsdorf	B	3	95	Simard	C	5
49	Sellafirth	A	7	83	Seraucourt-le-Grand	B	5	62	Sevenoaks	B	4	68	Siekierki	C	2	133	Simat de Valldigna	B	2
143	Sellano	B	3	112	Seravezza	C	2	124	Sever do Vouga	C	1	75	Sielow	B	6	141	Simáxis	C	2
93	Selles-sur-Cher	B	5	123	Serchs	B	4	107	Séverac-le-Château	C	3	79	Sielpia	D	3	87	Simbach	C	5
95	Sellières	C	5	101	Sered'	A	5	110	Séveso	B	4	78	Sieluń	C	4	147	Simbário	D	2
67	Sellin	A	6	102	Seregélyes	A	2	88	Ševětín	B	2	78	Siemiany	B	2	103	Simbâta	B	6
115	Sellye	B	5	110	Seregno	B	4	83	Sévigny-Waleppe	B	6	90	Siemiechow	C	3	103	Simbáteni	B	5
65	Selm	C	5	81	Sérent	C	4	135	Sevilla	B	5	112	Siena	C	3	117	Simićevo	B	5
19	Selnes	B	5	97	Serfaus	A	6	126	Sevilla la Nueva	B	1	75	Sieniawka	C	6	153	Simitli	B	5
100	Selnica	C	3	111	Seriate	B	4	130	Sevilleja de la Jara	B	2	79	Siennica	A	2	42	Simlångsdalen	C	3
95	Selongey	B	5	82	Sérifontaine	B	3	114	Sevnica	A	3	10	Sieppijärvi	B	3	86	Simmelsdorf	B	3
109	Selonnet	C	3	159	Sérifos	B	5	108	Sevrier	B	3	79	Sieradz	D	1	71	Simmerath	B	5
67	Selow	B	4	107	Sérignan	D	3	64	Sexbierum	A	3	77	Sieraków	A	5	97	Simmerberg	A	5
12	Seløy	A	4	111	Serina	B	4	42	Sexdrega	B	3	69	Sierakowice	A	5	71	Simmern	C	6
62	Selsey	C	3	40	Serjerslev	C	2	99	Sexten	C	3	77	Sierakowo	A	7	73	Simmringen	D	3
66	Selsingen	B	2	83	Sermaises	C	4	104	Seyches	C	3	85	Sierentz	C	2	152	Simnica	C	2
123	Selsona	C	4	84	Sermaize-les-Bains	B	1	75	Seyda	B	4	84	Sierk-les-Bains	A	3	16	Simo ås	B	4
71	Selters	B	6	84	Sermamagny	C	3	109	Seyne	C	3	100	Sierning	A	2	29	Simola	C	6
85	Seltz	B	5	112	Sérmide	A	3	107	Seynes	C	4	90	Sieroty	B	1	91	Šimonovce	D	3
139	Selva,E	B	3	143	Sermoneta	C	3	108	Seyssel	B	2	78	Sierpc	C	2	60	Simonsbath	B	3
19	Selva,N	B	5	128	Sernache de Bonjardim	B	2	114	Sežana	B	1	129	Sierra de Fuentes	B	4	39	Simonstorp	D	3
123	Selva de Mar	B	6	124	Sernancelhe	C	2	83	Sézanne	C	5	122	Sierra de Luna	B	2	102	Simontornya	B	2
99	Selva di Cadore	C	3	79	Serock	C	4	88	Sezemice	A	3	118	Sierra de Outes	B	2	158	Simópoulon	B	2
99	Selva di Val Gardena	C	2	79	Seroczyn	C	4	88	Sezimovo-Ústi	B	2	136	Sierra de Yeguas	B	2	29	Simpele	B	7
30	Selvik, Sogn Fjordane Fylke, N	B	2	137	Serón	B	4	124	Sezulfe	B	2	96	Sierre	B	3	96	Simplon	B	4
35	Selvik, Vestfold Fylke, N	B	6	127	Serón de Nájima	A	3	143	Sezze	C	3	79	Siestrzeń	C	3	47	Simrishamn	C	4
111	Selvino	B	4	64	Serooskerke	C	1	113	Sforzacosta	C	5	122	Sietamo	B	2	160	Sinaia	C	4
35	Sem	B	6	122	Serós	C	3	61	Shaftesbury	B	4	23	Sievi	B	6	112	Sinalunga	C	3
116	Semeljci	A	2	134	Serpa	B	2	60	Shaldon	C	3	90	Siewierz	B	2	154	Sinanaj	B	1
84	Semide,F	A	1	147	Serra San Bruno	D	2	54	Shanagolden	B	2	35	Sigdal	A	5	155	Sinarádhes	C	1
128	Semide,P	A	2	113	Serra San Quirico	C	5	62	Shanklin	C	2	117	Sige	B	5	132	Sinarcas	B	1
88	Semily	A	3	145	Serracapriola	B	4	56	Shap	B	4	107	Sigean	D	2	40	Sindal	B	4
147	Seminara	D	1	126	Serrada	A	1	48	Shawbost	C	2	4	Sigerfjord	B	4	85	Sindelfingen	B	6
117	Semlacu	A	5	148	Serradifalco	B	3	57	Shawbury	D	4	160	Sighet	B	3	156	Síndhos	B	2
83	Semoine	C	6	129	Serradilla	B	4	62	Sheerness	B	4	160	Sighişoara	B	4	141	Sindia	B	2
115	Šemovci	A	5	125	Serradilla del Arroyo	C	3	58	Sheffield	B	2	113	Sigillo	C	4	103	Sinersig	C	5
114	Sempeter	A	2	156	Serrai	A	3	62	Shefford	A	3	85	Siglingen	A	6	134	Sines	B	2
100	Semriach	B	3	141	Serramanna	C	2	152	Shëmëri	B	2	85	Sigmaringen	B	2	10	Sinettä	C	5
95	Semur-en-Auxois	B	4	112	Serramazzoni	B	2	152	Shëngjin	C	1	109	Signes	D	2	139	Sineu	B	4
122	Sena	C	2	126	Serranillos	B	1	154	Shepër	B	2	88	Signumdsherberg	C	3	85	Singen	C	5
119	Sena de Luna	B	5	113	Serrapetrona	C	5	59	Shepshed	C	2	83	Signy-l'Abbaye	B	6	62	Singleton	C	3
94	Senan	B	3	147	Serrastretta	C	2	61	Shepton Mallet	B	4	83	Signy-le-Pet	B	6	19	Singsås	C	6
82	Sénarpont	B	3	143	Serravalle,I	B	4	61	Sherborne	C	4	104	Sigogne	B	2	141	Siniscóla	B	3
109	Sénas	D	2	113	Serravalle,RSM	C	4	58	Sherburn	A	3	38	Sigtuna	B	2	150	Sinj	C	2
114	Šenčur	A	2	143	Serravalle di Chienti	A	3	58	Sherburn in Elmet	B	2	118	Sigueiro	B	2	125	Sinlabajos	B	5
86	Senden	C	2	110	Serravalle Scrivia	C	3	53	Shercock	C	5	127	Sigüenza	A	3	73	Sinn	C	2
65	Sendenhorst	C	5	110	Serraville	B	3	59	Sheringham	C	5	122	Sigues	B	1	141	Sínnai	C	3
125	Sendim	B	3	145	Serre	C	4	61	Sherston	B	4	26	Siikainen	B	4	34	Sinnes	B	2
101	Senec	A	5	129	Serrejón	B	5	48	Shieldaig	D	3	16	Siikajoki	C	3	103	Sinnicolau Mare	A	4
70	Seneffe	B	3	141	Serrenti	C	2	57	Shifnal	D	4	24	Siilinjärvi	C	3	97	Sins	A	4
141	Séneghe	B	2	109	Serres	B	5	152	Shijak	C	1	22	Siippy	C	3	85	Sinsheim	B	5
137	Senés	B	4	108	Serrières	B	1	51	Shilbottle	B	6	20	Sikås	B	4	103	Sintana	A	4
109	Senez	D	3	95	Serrigny	B	4	51	Shildon	C	6	159	Sikéa	C	3	103	Sintea Marea	B	5
75	Senftenberg	B	6	147	Sersale	B	2	55	Shillelagh	B	5	91	Sikenica	D	1	128	Sintra	C	1
65	Sengwarden	A	6	128	Serta	B	2	61	Shillingstone	C	4	14	Sikfors, Norrbottens Län, S	C	5	85	Sinzheim	B	5
89	Senica	C	5	97	Sertig Dörfli	B	5	48	Shinness	C	4	37	Sikfors, Örebro Län, S	B	6	71	Sinzig	B	6
89	Senice na Hané	B	5	84	Servance	C	3	59	Shipdham	C	4	156	Sikiá	B	3	101	Siófok	C	6
113	Senigállia	C	5	106	Serverette	C	3	58	Shipley	B	2	31	Sikilsdalsseter	B	6	96	Sion	B	3
141	Sénis	C	2	156	Sérvia	B	1	62	Shipston on Stour	A	2	102	Siklós	B	5	53	Sion Mills	B	4
146	Senise	B	2	107	Servian	D	3	152	Shkodër	B	1	14	Siknas	C	6	92	Sion-sur-l'Océan	C	2
117	Seniski Rudnik	C	5	107	Serviers	C	4	62	Shoreham-by-sea	C	3	79	Sikórz	C	2	104	Siorac-en-Périgord	C	3
114	Senj	C	5	113	Servigliano	C	5	62	Shotley Gate	B	5	156	Sikoúrion	C	1	115	Šipovo	C	5
117	Senje	C	5	116	Servojno	C	3	50	Shotts	B	4	99	Silandro	C	1	85	Sipplingen	C	5
6	Senjehopen	B	3	139	Ses Salines	B	4	57	Shrewsbury	D	4	141	Silanus	B	2	28	Sippola	C	5
83	Senlis	B	4	126	Seseña	B	2	61	Shrewton	B	5	116	Šilbaš	A	3	34	Sira	B	2
42	Sennan	C	2	128	Sesimbra	C	1	62	Shrivenham	B	2	66	Silberstedt	A	2	149	Siracusa	B	5
72	Senne I	B	2	53	Seskanore	B	4	69	Sianów	A	4	97	Silbertal	A	6	103	Sirbi	C	6
72	Senne II	B	2	16	Seskarö	B	4	154	Siátista	B	3	59	Sileby	C	2	160	Siret	B	5
95	Sennecy-le-Grand	C	4	121	Sesma	B	4	106	Siauges	B	3	137	Siles	A	4	34	Sirevåg	C	1
60	Sennen	C	1	128	Sesmo	B	3	47	Sibbhult	A	5	124	Silgueiros	C	2	116	Sirig	A	3
141	Sennori	B	2	144	Sessa Aurunca	B	2	150	Šibenik	B	1	108	Silhac	C	1	153	Sirishtnik	B	5
97	Sennwald	A	5	111	Sesta Godáno	C	4	115	Sibinj	B	5	141	Silíqua	C	2	10	Sirkka	B	5
60	Sennybridge	B	3	121	Sestao	A	4	160	Sibiu	C	4	35	Siljan	B	5	9	Sirma	B	7
82	Senoches	C	3	113	Sestino	C	4	62	Sible Hedingham	B	4	33	Siljansnäs	C	5	111	Sirmione	B	5
88	Senohraby	B	2	99	Sesto	C	3	117	Sibnica	B	4	15	Silkeå	D	4	17	Siriniö	E	3
91	Senohrad	D	2	110	Sesto Calende	B	3	33	Sibo	B	7	44	Silkeborg	A	2	91	Sirok	B	5
85	Senones	B	3	144	Sesto Campano	B	3	71	Sibret	C	4	132	Silla	B	2	91	Široké	C	3
141	Senorbi	C	3	112	Sesto Fiorentino	C	3	59	Sibsey	B	5	82	Sillé-le-Guillaume	C	1	113	Sirolo	C	5
114	Senožeče	B	2	112	Séstola	B	2	153	Sićevo	A	4	118	Silleda	A	5	130	Siruela	C	1
83	Sens	C	5	111	Sestri Levante	C	3	103	Şicláu	B	5	65	Sillenstede	A	3	115	Sisak	B	3
81	Sens-de-Bretagne	B	5	110	Sestriere	C	1	103	Şicula	A	4	36	Sillerud	A	3	131	Sisante	B	3
102	Senta	C	4	29	Sestroretsk	C	7	148	Siculiana	B	3	98	Sillian	C	3	115	Šišljavić	B	3
122	Senterada	B	3	141	Sesto	C	3	116	Šid	A	4	56	Silloth	B	3	96	Sissach	B	5
100	Sentilj	C	3	115	Sesvete	B	4	65	Siddeburen	A	3	69	Silno	B	5	83	Sissonne	B	5
				107	Sète	D	3	22	Sideby	C	3					124	Sistelo	B	1
								21	Sidensjö	B	7					109	Sisteron	C	2

225

120 Solórzano A 3
96 Solothurn A 3
45 Solrød B 5
12 Solsem B 3
18 Sølsnes C 3
30 Solsvik C 1
102 Solt B 3
66 Soltau C 2
102 Soltszentimre B 3
102 Soltvadkert B 3
131 Soluélamos B 4
12 Solum C 3
35 Solumsmo B 5
30 Solund B 1
60 Solva B 1
38 Solvarbo B 2
47 Sölvesborg A 5
30 Solvorn B 4
102 Solymar A 2
32 Somådal A 2
70 Somain B 2
102 Somberek B 2
95 Sombernon B 4
102 Sombor C 3
70 Sombreffe B 3
71 Someren A 4
27 Somerniemi C 6
27 Somero C 6
59 Somersham C 4
61 Somerton B 4
119 Somiedo A 4
69 Sominy A 5
110 Somma Lombardo B 3
110 Sommariva del Bosco C 2
5 Sommarset C 4
149 Sommatino B 4
84 Sommedieue A 2
64 Sommelsdijk C 2
43 Sommen A 4
84 Sommepy A 1
74 Sömmerda B 3
67 Sommerfeld C 6
68 Sommersdorf B 2
44 Sommersted B 2
83 Sommesous C 6
107 Sommières D 4
93 Sommières-du-Clain C 4
12 Sømna B 4
120 Somo A 3
101 Somogyfajsz C 5
101 Somogyjád C 5
101 Somogysámson C 5
101 Somogysárd C 5
101 Somogyszil C 6
101 Somogyszob C 5
115 Somogyudvarhely A 5
101 Somogyvár C 5
137 Somontin B 4
126 Somosierra A 2
91 Somoskoújfalu D 2
79 Sompolno,PL C 1
79 Sompolno,PL C 1
83 Sompuis C 6
35 Son,N B 6
64 Son,NL C 3
139 Son Severa B 4
96 Sonceboz A 3
120 Soncillo B 3
111 Soncino B 4
35 Søndeled C 5
44 Sønder Broby B 3
44 Sønder Felding B 1
44 Sønder Hygum B 1
40 Sønder Kongerslev C 4
44 Sønder Lem A 1
44 Sønder Omme B 1
44 Sønderborg C 2
44 Sønderho B 1
74 Sondershausen B 2
44 Søndersø B 3
36 Søndre Enningdal Kappel C 3
32 Søndre Osen B 2
97 Sóndrio B 5
30 Songdalfjøra B 4
35 Songe C 5
82 Songeons B 3
24 Sonkajärvi B 4
47 Sönnarslöv B 5
74 Sonneburg C 3
74 Sonnefeld C 3
75 Sonnewald B 5
143 Sonnino C 4
97 Sonogno B 4
71 Sonsbeck A 5
126 Sonseca C 2
32 Sønsterud C 3
39 Sonstorp D 2
102 Sonta C 3
86 Sontheim C 2
97 Sonthofen A 6
72 Sontra B 3
105 Soorts D 1
121 Sopelana A 4
115 Sopje B 5
69 Sopot A 6
154 Sopotnica A 3
117 Sopotu Nou B 5
101 Sopron B 4
116 Šor B 3
18 Sør Aukra C 2
143 Sora C 4
111 Soragna C 5
21 Söråker C 6
142 Sorano B 2
5 Sørarnøy C 2
76 Sorau B 4
112 Sorbara B 3
137 Sorbas B 4
21 Sörberge C 6
50 Sorbie C 3
94 Sorbier C 3
112 Sórbolo B 2
21 Sörbygden C 5
49 Sordale C 5
105 Sore C 2
96 Sörenberg B 4
111 Soresina B 4
107 Sorèze D 2
5 Sørfjorden D 2
5 Sørfold C 4
15 Sörfors E 4
33 Sörforsa B 7
4 Sørgard B 7
104 Sorges B 3
141 Sórgono B 3
109 Sorgues C 1
121 Soria C 4
147 Soriano Cálabro D 2
142 Soriano nel Cimino B 3
27 Sorila B 6
137 Sorinhuela del Guadalimar A 3
48 Sorisdale E 2
6 Sørkjosen B 6
78 Sorkwity B 4
101 Sormás C 4
50 Sorn B 3
45 Sorø B 4
6 Sørreisa B 4
144 Sorrento C 3
24 Sorsakoski C 4
13 Sorsele B 9
32 Sörsjön B 4
5 Sørsjona D 2
141 Sorso B 2
6 Sørstraumen B 7
123 Sort B 4
29 Sortavala B 8
149 Sortino B 5
4 Sortland B 4
31 Sørum C 7
36 Sørumsand B 3
39 Sorunda C 4
44 Sörup C 2
8 Sørvær B 2
4 Sørvågen C 2
32 Sörvattnet A 3
19 Sørvika C 7
105 Sos C 3
121 Sos del Rey Católico B 5
156 Sosándra B 2
47 Sösdala A 4
114 Sošice B 3
90 Sosnowiec B 2
109 Sospel D 4
114 Šoštanj A 3
30 Sotaseter B 4
118 Sotelo de Montes B 2
126 Sotillo de Adrada B 1
126 Sotillo de la Ribera A 2
116 Sotin A 3
25 Sotkamo A 5
119 Soto de los Infantes A 4
119 Soto del Barco A 4
120 Soto la Marina A 3
120 Sotobañado y Priorato B 2
101 Sótony B 4
125 Sotoserrano C 3
120 Sotresgudo B 2
140 Sotta C 2
12 Søttaren B 4
82 Sotteville B 3
113 Sottomarina A 4
66 Sottrum B 2
26 Sottunga C 3
84 Souain A 1
107 Soual D 2
83 Soucy C 5
83 Soudron C 6
85 Soufflenheim B 4
104 Souillac C 4
84 Souilly A 2
104 Soulac-sur-Mer B 1
84 Soulaines-Dhuys B 1
159 Soúli B 3
85 Soultz, Bas Rhin, F B 4
85 Soultz, Haut Rhin, F C 4
71 Soumagne B 4
105 Soumoulou D 2
83 Souppes C 4
105 Souprosse D 2
105 Souquet D 1
81 Sourdeval B 6
128 Soure A 2
123 Sournia B 5
124 Souro Pires C 2
157 Soúrpi C 2
82 Sours C 3
106 Sousceyrac C 2
128 Sousel C 3
94 Sousmes B 2
105 Soustons D 1
62 South Benfleet B 4
60 South Brent C 3
58 South Cave B 3
48 South Dell C 2
50 South Feorline B 2
62 South Godstone B 3
62 South Hayling C 3
58 South Kirkby B 2
60 South Molton B 3
51 South Shields C 6
62 South Woodham Ferrers B 4
59 Southam C 2
62 Southampton C 2
62 Southborough B 4
51 Southdean B 5
50 Southend B 2
62 Southend-on-Sea B 4
59 Southery C 4
62 Southminster B 4
56 Southport C 3
59 Southwell B 3
62 Southwick C 3
59 Southwold C 5
128 Souto A 3
128 Souto da Carpalhosa B 2
51 Soutra Mains B 5
118 Soutuchao C 3
94 Souvigny C 3
147 Soverato D 2
147 Soveria Mannelli C 2
47 Sövestad B 4
150 Soviči B 3
18 Søvik C 2
58 Sowerby A 2
108 Soyons C 1
160 Sozopol D 5
71 Spa B 4
101 Špačince A 5
149 Spadafora A 5
85 Spaichingen B 5
64 Spakenburg B 3
59 Spalding C 3
87 Spálené Poriči B 5
86 Spalt B 2
152 Spance A 3
72 Spangenberg B 3
34 Spangereid C 3
39 Spångsholm D 2
144 Sparanise B 2
19 Sparbu B 7
44 Sparkær A 2
61 Sparkford B 4
39 Sparreholm C 3
149 Spartà A 5
158 Spárti B 3
155 Spartokhóri D 2
159 Spáta B 4
48 Spean Bridge E 4
35 Spedalen C 4
71 Speicher C 5
32 Spekedalssetra A 2
143 Spello A 3
65 Spenge B 6
51 Spennymoor C 6
75 Sperenberg A 5
157 Sperkhiás D 2
149 Sperlinga B 4
143 Sperlonga C 4
159 Spétasi B 4
49 Spey Bridge D 4
85 Speyer A 5
80 Spézet B 3
146 Spezzano Albanese C 2
147 Spezzano della Sila C 2
54 Spiddle A 2
65 Spiekeroog A 5
73 Spielbach D 4
96 Spiez B 3
110 Spigno Monferrato C 3
65 Spijk A 4
64 Spijkenisse C 2
112 Spilamberto B 3
158 Spiliá B 2
99 Spilimbergo C 3
58 Spilsby B 4
145 Spinazzola C 5
84 Spincourt A 2
34 Spind C 2
88 Spindleruv-Mlýn A 3
110 Spinetta C 2
146 Spinoso B 1
115 Spišić Bukovica B 5
91 Spišská-Belá C 3
91 Spišská Nova Ves D 3
91 Spišská Stará Ves C 3
91 Spišské Bystré D 3
91 Spišské-Hanušovce C 3
91 Spišské-Podhradie C 3
91 Spišské Vlachy D 3
91 Spišský-Štvrtok C 3
100 Spital a. Semmering B 3
98 Spittal C 4
49 Spittal of Glenshee E 5
100 Spitz A 3
35 Spjærøy B 6
44 Spjald A 1
18 Spjelkavik C 2
43 Spjutsbygd C 5
150 Split B 2
97 Splügen B 5
44 Spodsbjerg C 3
58 Spofforth B 2
155 Spoláïta D 3
143 Spoleto B 3
143 Spoltore B 5
99 Spondigna C 1
99 Spondinig C 1
36 Sponvika B 3
67 Spornitz B 4
110 Spotorno C 3
86 Spraitbach C 1
66 Sprakensehl C 3
21 Sprängsviken C 6
78 Sprecowo B 3
75 Spremberg B 6
73 Sprendlingen, Hessen, D† C 2
73 Sprendlingen, Rheinland-Pfalz, D† D 1
99 Spresiano D 3
71 Sprimont B 4
72 Springe A 3
151 Spuž C 5
78 Spychowo B 4
36 Spydeberg B 3
90 Spytkowice C 2
147 Squillace D 2
146 Squinzano B 4
115 Sračinec A 4
115 Srbac B 5
152 Srbica B 2
102 Srbobran C 3
116 Srebrenica B 3
116 Srebrnik B 2
115 Središče A 4
152 Sredska B 2
77 Śrem A 6
103 Şria B 5
120 Srkereszfúr A 2
87 Srní B 5
116 Srnice B 2
79 Śrock D 2
77 Środa Śląska B 5
77 Środa Wielkopolski A 6
78 Srokowo A 4
103 Srpska Cinja C 4
103 Srpski Itebej C 4
102 Srpski Miletic C 3
89 Staatz C 4
70 Stabroek A 3
87 Stachy B 5
33 Stackmora B 5
66 Stade B 2
70 Staden B 2
100 Stadl a. d. Mur B 1
98 Stadl-Paura A 4
19 Stadsbygd B 6
65 Stadskanaal B 4
73 Stadt-Allendorf C 3
72 Stadthagen A 3
74 Stadtilm C 3
71 Stadtkyll B 5
73 Stadtlauringen C 4
74 Stadtlengsfeld C 2
65 Stadtlohn C 4
72 Stadtoldendorf B 3
74 Stadtroda C 3
74 Stadtsteinach C 3
97 Stäfa A 4
46 Staffanstorp B 4
86 Staffelstein A 2
57 Stafford D 4
100 Stainach B 2
51 Staindrop C 6
62 Staines B 3
84 Stainville B 2
100 Stainz C 3
147 Staiti D 2
153 Stajevac B 4
117 Stalać C 5
96 Stalden B 3
59 Stalham C 5
30 Stalheim C 3
154 Stalin B 1
39 Stallarholmen C 4
37 Ställberg B 6
37 Ställdalen B 6
100 Stallhofen B 3
87 Stallwang B 4
5 Staloluokta C 5
59 Stamford C 3
58 Stamford Bridge B 3
85 Stammheim B 5
155 Stamná D 3
30 Stamnes C 2
98 Stams B 1
20 Stamsele B 4
87 Stamsried B 4
4 Stamsund B 2
56 Standish C 4
62 Standon B 4
39 Stånga C 5
32 Stange C 2
112 Stanghella A 3
6 Stangnes B 3
18 Stangvik C 4
51 Stanhope C 6
79 Stanin D 5
102 Stanišić C 3
79 Stanislawów C 4
153 Stanke Dimitrov B 5
87 Staňkov B 5
150 Stankovci B 1
51 Stanley C 6
51 Stannington B 6
155 Stános, Aitolía Kai Akarnanía, GR D 3
156 Stanós, Khalkidhikí, GR B 3
96 Stans B 4
62 Stansted Mountfitchet B 4
59 Stanton C 4
90 Stany B 4
100 Stanz i. Murztal B 3
97 Stanzach A 6
102 Stapar C 3
65 Staphorst B 4
59 Stapleford C 2
62 Staplehurst B 4
79 Staporków D 3
88 Stará Boleslav A 2
77 Stara Kamienica C 4
91 Stará-L'ubovňa C 3
102 Stara Moravica C 3
116 Stara-Pazova B 4
75 Stará Role C 4
68 Stara Rudnica C 2
89 Stara Turá C 5
76 Stara Woda B 4
160 Stara Zagora D 4
79 Starachowiçe D 4
154 Staravina A 3
117 Starčevo B 4
60 Starcross C 3
89 Staré Hamry B 6
91 Staré Hory D 2
78 Stare Jablonki B 3
89 Staré Město B 5
78 Stare Pole A 2
88 Stare Sedlo B 2
68 Stargard Szczeciński B 3
30 Stårheim B 2
117 Stari Banovci B 4
151 Stari Bar C 5
156 Stari Dojran A 2
115 Stari Gradac B 5
116 Stari Jankovci A 2
152 Stari Kačanik B 3
115 Stari Majdan C 4
116 Stari Mikanovci A 2
152 Stari Raušić B 2
150 Starigrad B 2
114 Starigrad Paklenice C 3
75 Staritz B 5
86 Starnberg C 3
153 Staro Nagoričane B 3
115 Staro Petrovo Selo B 5
117 Staro Selo B 5
68 Starogard B 3

69 Starogard Gdański B 6
77 Starościn C 6
78 Stary Dzierzgoń B 2
89 Stary Hrozenkov C 5
69 Stary Jaroslaw A 4
87 Stary Plzenec B 5
90 Stary Sacz C 3
91 Starý-Smokovec C 3
89 Staškov B 6
74 Staßfurt B 3
90 Staszów B 4
35 Stathelle B 5
85 Staufen C 4
59 Staughton Highway C 3
61 Staunton B 4
18 Staurset B 4
152 Štavalj A 2
34 Stavanger C 1
58 Staveley B 2
71 Stavelot B 4
67 Stavenhagen B 5
64 Stavenisse C 2
64 Staveren B 3
35 Stavern C 6
36 Stavnäs B 4
20 Stavre C 4
21 Stavreviken C 6
156 Stavros B 2
158 Stavrós, Itháki, GR A 1
157 Stavrós, Lárisa, GR C 2
156 Stavroúpolis, Thessaloníki, GR B 2
156 Stavroúpolis, Xánthi, GR A 4
31 Stavseng B 6
31 Stavsjø C 7
78 Stawiski B 5
77 Stawiszyn B 7
35 Steane B 4
96 Stechelberg B 3
88 Štechovice B 2
67 Stechow C 5
97 Steckborn A 5
97 Steeg A 6
64 Steenbergen C 2
63 Steenvoorde B 4
64 Steenwijk B 4
157 Stefanavíkion C 2
148 Stéfano Quisquina B 3
96 Steffisburg B 3
73 Stegaurach D 4
45 Stege C 5
67 Stegelitz B 6
101 Stegersbach B 4
4 Steigen C 3
66 Steimbke C 2
96 Stein, CH A 3
48 Stein, GB D 2
97 Stein a. Rheinfall A 4
98 Steinach, A B 2
85 Steinach, Baden-Württemberg, D† B 5
73 Steinach, Bayern, D† C 4
74 Steinach, D* C 3
73 Steinau, Hessen, D† C 3
66 Steinau, Niedersachsen, D† B 1
74 Steinbach-Hallenberg C 2
76 Steinbeck A 2
98 Steinberg am Rofan B 2
100 Steindorf C 2
85 Steinen C 4
98 Steinerkirchen a. d. Traun A 4
98 Steinfeld, A C 4
65 Steinfeld, D† B 6
71 Steinfort C 4
98 Steingaden B 1
8 Steingammen B 5
65 Steinhagen B 6
100 Steinhaus A 2
74 Steinheid C 3
86 Steinheim, Baden-Württemberg, D† C 2
72 Steinheim, Nordrhein-Westfalen, D† B 3
76 Steinhöfel A 3
66 Steinhorst C 3
75 Steinigtwolmsdorf B 6
19 Steinkjer A 7
64 Steins A 3
75 Steinsdorf A 6
18 Steinshamn C 2
35 Steinsholt B 5
32 Steinvik B 2
70 Stekene A 3
66 Stelle B 3
64 Stellendam C 2
18 Stemshaug B 4
43 Stenåsa C 6
84 Stenay A 2
43 Stenberga B 5
67 Stendal C 4
70 Stene A 1
159 Steni Dhirfios A 4
154 Stenje B 2
49 Stenness A 7
158 Stenón B 3
38 Stensätra B 3
13 Stensele B 9
21 Stensjö B 5
42 Stenstorp A 3
44 Stenstrup B 3
5 Stenudden D 6
42 Stenungsund A 1
152 Steoci B 2
89 Štěpánov B 5
117 Stepejevac B 4
98 Stephanskirchen B 3
68 Stepnica B 2
73 Sterbfritz C 3
72 Sterderdorf A 4
79 Sterdyń C 5
78 Sterlawki Wielkie A 4
67 Sternberg B 4
89 Šternberk B 5
44 Sterup C 2
73 Sterzhausen C 2
98 Sterzing C 2
77 Steszew A 5
88 Štěti A 2
85 Stetten am kalten Markt B 6
68 Stettin B 2
62 Stevenage B 3
50 Stevenston B 3
50 Stewarton B 3
53 Stewartstown B 5
62 Stewkley B 3
66 Steyerburg C 2
62 Steyning C 3
100 Steyr A 2
69 Stezyca A 5
111 Stezzano B 4
112 Stia C 3
142 Sticciano Scalo B 2
46 Stidsvig A 4
44 Stige B 3
36 Stigen C 4
146 Stigliano B 2
39 Stigtomta D 3
115 Stijena C 4
19 Stiklestad B 7
157 Stilís D 2
58 Stillington A 2
147 Stilo D 2
159 Stimánga B 3
152 Štimlje B 3
103 Stina de Vale B 6
141 Stintino B 2
145 Stio C 4
153 Štip C 4
159 Stira A 5
50 Stirling A 4
91 Štítnik D 3
89 Stity B 4
39 Stjärnhov C 4
38 Stjärnsund B 3
19 Stjern A 6
19 Stjørdalshalsen B 6
19 Stjørna B 5
69 Stobno B 4
33 Stocka B 8
85 Stockach C 6
96 Stockalp B 4
43 Stockaryd B 4
62 Stockbridge B 2
39 Stockby C 4
66 Stockelsdorf B 3
101 Stockerau A 4
39 Stockholm C 5
57 Stockport C 4
57 Stocksbridge B 2
51 Stockton on Tees C 6
21 Stockvik C 6
79 Stoczek C 4
79 Stoczek Lukowski D 4
19 Stod A 7
21 Stöde C 5
5 Stødi D 4
44 Stoholm A 2
59 Stoke Ferry C 4
57 Stoke-on-Trent C 4
60 Stokenham C 3
51 Stokesley C 6
35 Stokke B 6
45 Stokkemarke C 4
35 Stokken C 4
19 Stokksund A 6
5 Stokkvåg D 2
4 Stokmarknes B 3
88 Štoky B 3
151 Stolac B 3
71 Stolberg, D† B 5
74 Stolberg, D* B 2
75 Stollberg C 4
32 Stöllet C 4
66 Stollhamm B 1
78 Stolno B 1
69 Stolp A 5
75 Stolpen B 6
66 Stolzenau C 2
71 Stommeln A 5
151 Ston C 3
88 Stonařov B 3
62 Stone, Bucks., GB B 3
57 Stone, Staffs., GB D 4
59 Stone Street C 5
49 Stonehaven E 6
61 Stonehouse, Gloucester., GB B 4
50 Stonehouse, Lanark., GB B 4
6 Stonglandet B 3
30 Stonndalen C 4
62 Stony Stratford A 3
87 Stoó B 5
101 Stoob B 4
117 Stopanja C 5
90 Stopnica B 3
32 Stor-Elvdal B 2
38 Storå C 2
20 Storåbranna B 3
19 Storbudal C 6
26 Storby C 2
19 Stordal, Nord-Trøndelag Fylke, N B 7
18 Stordal, Romsdal Fylke, N C 3
45 Store Heddinge B 5
9 Store Molvik B 8
43 Storebro B 5
8 Storekorsnes B 3
19 Støren B 6
31 Storfjellseter B 7
6 Storfjord B 5
8 Storfjordbotn B 6
30 Storfjorden A 3
37 Storfors B 6
5 Storforshei D 3
8 Storfosen C 5
31 Storhøliseter B 6
5 Storjord D 3
76 Storkow, Frankfurt, D* A 2
68 Storkow, Neubrandenburg, D* B 2
18 Storli C 5
20 Storlien B 1
6 Stormoen B 3
145 Stornara B 4
48 Stornoway C 2
111 Storo B 5
18 Storoddan B 5
16 Storön B 2
62 Storrington C 3
20 Storsjö C 2
6 Storsteinnes B 5
14 Storsund C 4
13 Storuman B 9
5 Storvik, N D 2
38 Storvik, S B 3
38 Storvreta C 4
91 Štos D 3
74 Stößen B 3
66 Stotel B 1
62 Stotfold A 3
97 Stötten A 6
74 Stotternheim B 3
57 Stourbridge D 4
57 Stourport on Severn D 4
40 Støvring C 3
51 Stow B 5
62 Stow-on-the-Water B 2
59 Stowmarket C 4
78 Stozne A 5
75 Straach B 4
53 Strabane B 4
49 Strachan D 6
79 Strachówka C 4
50 Strachur A 2
153 Stracin B 4
65 Strackholt A 5
59 Stradboroke C 5
111 Stradella B 4
153 Stradlovo B 4
53 Stradone C 4
78 Straduny B 5
71 Straelen A 5
117 Stragari B 4
88 Strakonice B 1
141 Stralaus B 3
100 Strallegg B 3
43 Strålsnäs A 5
67 Stralsund A 6
71 Stramproij A 4
32 Strand, Hedmark Fylke, N B 2
4 Strand, Hinnøya, N B 4
34 Stranda, Rogaland Fylke, N B 1
18 Stranda, Romsdal Fylke, N C 2
40 Strandby B 4
30 Strandebarm C 2
32 Strandlykkja C 2
30 Strandvik C 2
53 Strangford B 6
39 Strängnäs C 4
39 Strångsjö D 3
89 Stráni C 5
52 Stranorlar B 4
50 Stranraer C 2
148 Strasatti B 2
85 Strasbourg B 4
67 Strasburg B 6
88 Strašice B 1
100 Straß A 3
100 Straß i. Steiermark C 3
38 Stråssa C 2
100 Straßburg C 2
59 Stratford-upon-Avon C 2
50 Strathaven B 3
48 Strathkanaird D 3
51 Strathmiglo A 4
48 Strathpeffer D 4
50 Strathyre A 3
115 Stratinska C 4
156 Stratoniki B 3
156 Stratónion B 3
60 Stratton C 2
61 Stratton on the Fosse B 4
67 Straubing C 4
4 Straumen, Hinnøya, N B 5
19 Straumen, Nord-Trøndelag Fylke, N B 7
5 Straumen, Nordland Fylke, N C 3
18 Straumen, Smøla, N B 4
4 Straumsjøen B 3
4 Straumsnes, Langøya, N B 3
5 Straumsnes, Nordland Fylke, N C 4
6 Straumsnes, Senja, N B 3
75 Straupitz B 6
76 Strausberg A 2
74 Straußfurt B 2
156 Stravrós B 3
88 Stráž n. Nezárkov B 2
117 Straža B 5
89 Strážnice C 5
87 Stražný C 5
91 Strážske D 4
91 Štrba C 3
91 Štrbské Pleso C 3
62 Streatley B 2
91 Strečno C 1
70 Strée B 3
61 Street B 4
75 Strehla B 5
101 Strekov B 6
89 Strelice B 4
91 Strelníky D 2
101 Strem B 4
116 Stremska Mitrovica B 3
116 Stremska-Rača B 3
116 Stremski Karlovci A 3
100 Strengberg A 2
4 Strengelvåg B 4
58 Strensall A 2
110 Stresa B 3
74 Streuldorf C 2
153 Strezimirovci B 4
153 Strezovce B 3
44 Strib B 2
37 Striberg B 6
87 Stříbro B 4
49 Strichen D 6
99 Strigno C 2
101 Štrigova C 4
64 Strijen C 2
156 Strimonikón A 3
116 Strizivojna A 2
115 Strmica C 4
88 Strmilov B 3
117 Strmosten B 5
66 Ströhen C 1
153 Strojkovce B 3
52 Strokestown C 3
33 Strömbacka B 7
72 Stromberg, Nordrhein Westfalen, D† B 2
71 Stromberg, Rheinland-Pfalz, D† C 6
48 Stromeferry D 3
48 Stromemore D 3
15 Strömfors, S D 4
28 Stromfors, SF C 4
35 Strømmen B 6
13 Strömnäs C 8
49 Stromness C 5
38 Strömsberg B 4
33 Strömsbruk B 8
39 Strömsfors D 3
42 Strömsnasbruk C 3
36 Strömstad C 3
20 Strömsund, Jämtland, S B 4
13 Strömsund, Västerbotten, S B 8
37 Strömtorp B 6
50 Stronachlachar A 3
50 Strone, Argyll, GB B 3
50 Strone, Argyll, GB A 3
30 Strongfjorden B 2
155 Strongilí C 1
147 Stróngoli C 3
89 Stronie A 4
48 Strontian E 3
91 Stropkov C 4
110 Stroppiana B 3
61 Stroud B 4
90 Stróźa C 2
152 Štrpce B 3
65 Strücklingen A 5
44 Struer A 1
154 Struga A 2
86 Strullendorf B 2
153 Strumica C 4
90 Strumień C 1
48 Struy D 4
79 Stryków D 2
30 Stryn B 3
44 Strynø C 3
78 Strzegawo C 3
79 Strzegocin C 3
77 Strzegom C 5
79 Strzelce C 2
68 Strzelce-Krajeńskie C 3
89 Strzelce Opolskie A 6
77 Strzelin C 6
69 Strzelno C 6
90 Strzemierzyce Wielkie B 2
69 Strzepcz A 6
90 Strzybnica B 1
78 Strzygi B 2
79 Strzyze C 4
90 Strzyżów C 4
153 Stubal, Srbija, YU B 4
117 Stubal, Srbija, YU C 4
45 Stubbekøbing C 5
6 Stubbeng B 5
44 Stubberup B 3
97 Stuben A 6
100 Stubenberg B 3
115 Stubičke Toplice B 3
117 Štubik B 6
116 Stubline B 4
153 Studena, BG B 5
88 Studená, CS B 3
153 Studena, YU B 4
152 Studencăne B 2
150 Studenci B 3
117 Studenica C 4
67 Stüdenitz C 5
89 Studénka B 6
100 Studenzen B 3
101 Studienka A 5
61 Studland C 5
59 Studley C 2
21 Studsviken B 7
69 Studzienice A 5
67 Stuer B 5
19 Stugudal C 7
20 Stugun B 4
72 Stukenbrock B 2
87 Stulln B 4
75 Stülpe A 5
101 Stupava A 5
153 Stupnica A 4
61 Sturminster Newton C 4
91 Štúrovo E 1
62 Sturry B 5
85 Stuttgart B 6
74 Stützerbach C 2
87 Štvolny A 5
101 Štvrtok A 5
36 Styri A 3

21 Styrnäs B 6
42 Styrsö B 1
120 Suances A 2
87 Suben C 5
143 Subiaco C 4
121 Subijana B 4
94 Subligny B 2
102 Subotica B 3
91 Sučany C 1
160 Suceava B 5
90 Sucha Beskidzkaj C 2
91 Suchá Hora C 2
68 Suchan B 3
88 Suchdol n. Luznici C 2
79 Suchedniów D 3
69 Suchorze A 5
79 Suchozebry C 5
71 Süchteln A 5
133 Sucina D 2
150 Sucuraj B 3
59 Sudbury, Derby, GB C 2
62 Sudbury, Suffolk, GB A 4
66 Süderbrarup A 2
44 Süderlügum C 1
88 Sudoměřice u. Bechyné B 2
132 Sueca B 2
141 Suelli C 3
73 Sugenheim D 4
106 Sugères B 3
70 Sugny C 3
74 Suhl C 2
66 Suhlendorf C 3
152 Suhodoll C 2
115 Suhopolje, Hrvatska, YU B 5
116 Suhopolje, Bosna i Hercegovina, YU B 3
84 Suippes A 1
154 Sukë B 2
24 Sukeva B 4
153 Sukhostrel C 4
151 Sukobin C 5
150 Sukošan A 1
102 Süksöd B 2
153 Sukovo A 4
90 Suków B 3
91 Šul'a, CS D 2
18 Sula, N B 4
56 Sulby B 2
34 Suldal B 2
40 Suldrup C 3
76 Sulechów A 4
76 Sulecin A 4
78 Sulecin-Szlachecki C 4
79 Sulejów D 2
79 Sulejówek C 4
97 Sulgen A 5
68 Sulibórz B 3
66 Sulingen C 1
68 Suliszewo B 3
5 Sulitjelma C 5
29 Sulkava B 6
23 Sulkavanjärvi B 8
90 Sulkowice C 2
94 Sully B 2
79 Sulmierzyce, Lódź, PL D 2
77 Sulmierzyce, Poznań, PL B 6
143 Sulmona B 4
90 Suloszowa B 2
77 Sulów B 6
22 Sulva B 3
85 Sulz B 5
86 Sulzbach C 1
87 Sulzbach-Rozenberg B 3
66 Sülze C 3
85 Sulzfeld A 5
150 Sumartin B 2
121 Sumbilla A 5
101 Sümeg C 5
23 Sumiainen C 8
96 Sumiswald A 3
28 Summa C 5
58 Summer Bridge A 2
55 Summerhill A 5
88 Šumná C 3
89 Šumperk B 4
117 Sumrakovac C 6
17 Sumsa C 8
89 Šumvald B 5
62 Sunbury B 3
87 Sünching C 4
5 Sund, N C 3
26 Sund, SF C 3
38 Sundborn B 2
21 Sundbron B 7
40 Sundby C 2
34 Sunde, Hordaland Fylke, N B 1
18 Sunde, Trøndelag Fylke, N B 5
35 Sundebru C 5
51 Sunderland C 6
71 Sundern A 6
36 Sundet A 3
21 Sundhamn C 7
39 Sundre F 5
44 Sunds A 2
18 Sundsbø C 2
20 Sundsjö C 4
34 Sundstøyl C 4
21 Sundsvall C 6
141 Suni B 2
115 Sunja B 4
19 Sunnan A 7
37 Sunnansjö A 6
30 Sunndal B 2
18 Sunndalsøra C 4
20 Sunne, Jämtlands Län, S B 3
37 Sunne, Värmlands Län, S B 5
37 Sunnemo B 5
38 Sunnersta C 4
27 Suodenniemi B 5
23 Suolahti C 7
8 Suolovuobme C 3
28 Suomenniemi B 5
27 Suomusjärvi C 6
17 Suomussalmi C 8
24 Suonenjoki C 4
109 Super-Sauze C 3
150 Supetar B 2
143 Supino C 4
72 Supplingen A 4
9 Supru C 8
103 Supuru de Sus A 6
101 Súr B 6
38 Surahammar C 3
101 Surany A 6
116 Surčin B 4
153 Surdulica B 4
104 Surgères A 2
87 Surheim D 4
64 Surhuisterveen A 4
123 Suria C 4
104 Surin A 3
153 Šurlane B 3
18 Surnadalsøra C 4
78 Surowe B 4
96 Sursee A 4
42 Surte B 2
65 Surwold B 5
106 Sury B 4
110 Susa B 2
114 Susak C 2
117 Šušara B 5
97 Susch B 6
99 Susegana D 3
66 Süsel A 3
87 Sušice B 5
120 Susilla B 2
86 Sußen C 1
71 Susteren A 4
78 Susz B 2
117 Sutjeska A 4
151 Sutomore C 5
142 Sutri B 3
59 Sutterton C 3
62 Sutton B 3
59 Sutton Bridge C 4
59 Sutton Coldfied C 2
59 Sutton in Ashfield B 2
58 Sutton-on-Sea B 4
62 Sutton Scotney B 2
29 Suur-Miehikkälä C 5
152 Suva Reka B 2
142 Suvereto A 1
109 Suze-la-Rousse C 1
112 Suzzara B 2
33 Svabensverk B 6
46 Svalöv B 4
21 Svanavattnet A 5
36 Svaneholm B 4
47 Svaneke B 6
43 Svängsta C 4
10 Svanstein C 3
9 Svanvik C 10
7 Svappavaara D 7
38 Svärdsjö B 2
35 Svarstad B 5
27 Svarta C 6
37 Svarta, Örebro, S B 6
39 Svärta, Södermanlands, S D 4
14 Svartbyn, Norrbottens Län, S C 5
16 Svartbyn, Norrbottens Län, S A 1
47 Svarte B 4
30 Svartemyr B 2
39 Svartinge D 3
38 Svartnäs B 3
9 Svartnes B 11
21 Svartvik C 6
31 Svatsum B 6
46 Svedala B 4
33 Sveg A 5
34 Sveio B 1
44 Svejbæk A 2
30 Svelgen B 2
18 Svellingen B 4
35 Svelvik B 6
44 Svendborg B 3
35 Svene B 5
42 Svenljunga B 3
39 Svennevad C 2
12 Svenningdal B 5
6 Svensby B 5
15 Svensbyn C 5
42 Svenshögen A 1
27 Svenskby C 6
20 Svensta B 2
20 Svenstavik C 3
40 Svenstrup C 3
102 Sveremle B 2
88 Švermov A 2
91 Švermovo D 3
151 Sveti Nikola D 5
153 Sveti Nikole C 3
151 Sveti Stefan C 4
88 Světiá n. Sázavou B 3
102 Svetozar C 3
117 Svetozarevo C 5
9 Svettijärvi C 8
91 Svidník C 4
87 Švihov B 5
116 Svilaj A 2
117 Svilajnac B 5
160 Svilengrad E 5
36 Svindal B 3
117 Svinita B 6
45 Svinninge B 4
160 Svistov D 4
91 Svit C 3
89 Svitavy B 4
91 Svodín E 1
153 Svoge B 5
4 Svolvær B 3
19 Svorkmo B 5
88 Svratka B 4
89 Svrčinovec B 6
153 Svrljig A 4
32 Svukurist A 3
36 Svulrya A 4
59 Swadlincote C 2
59 Swaffham C 4
71 Swalmen A 5
61 Swanage C 5
62 Swanley B 4
53 Swanlinbar B 4
60 Swansea B 3
77 Swarzedz A 6
53 Swatragh B 5
61 Sway C 5
78 Swiatki B 3
77 Świdnica, Wroclaw, PL C 5
76 Świdnica, Zielona Góra, PL B 4
78 Świdry B 5
69 Świdwin B 3
77 Świebodzice C 5
76 Świebodzin A 4
90 Świecany C 4
69 Świecie B 6
78 Świedziebnia B 2
76 Świeradów Zdrój C 4
89 Świerki A 4
77 Świerzawa C 4
68 Świerzno B 2
90 Świeta Anna B 2
78 Świetajno B 4
69 Świetlino B 4
77 Świetno A 5
78 Świetoslaw B 1
89 Świętów A 5
64 Swifterbant B 3
62 Swindon B 2
59 Swineshead C 3
52 Swinford C 3
79 Świnice C 1
C 1
68 Świnoujście B 2
51 Swinton B 5
68 Swobnica B 2
55 Swords A 5
90 Swoszowice C 2
69 Sycewice A 4
77 Syców B 6
76 Sycowice A 4
4 Sydalen B 3
30 Syfteland C 2
23 Sykäräinen B 6
66 Syke C 1
35 Sylling B 6
18 Sylte C 3
50 Symington B 4
60 Synod Inn A 2
69 Sypniewo, Bydgoszcz, PL B 5
69 Sypniewo, Koszalin, PL B 4
78 Sypniewo, Warszawa, PL B 4
49 Syre C 4
28 Sysmä B 3
32 Syssleback C 3
59 Syston C 2
10 Syväjärvi B 5
24 Syvänniemi C 4
30 Syvde A 2
101 Szabadbattyán B 6
120 Szabadegyhaza A 2
102 Szabadszállás B 3
79 Szadek D 1
90 Szaflary C 3
102 Szakály B 2
101 Szakcs C 6
102 Szakmár B 3
102 Szalánta C 2
102 Szaljol A 4
102 Szalkszentmárton B 3
91 Szalonna D 3
69 Szamocin B 5
77 Szamotuly A 5
101 Szany B 5
103 Szarvas B 4
91 Szarvasko E 3
101 Szászvár C 6
103 Szbadkigyós B 5
90 Szczawa C 3
90 Szczawnica C 3
77 Szczawno Zdrój C 5
78 Szczechy Wielkie B 4
68 Szczecin B 2
69 Szczecinek B 4
90 Szczekociny B 2
79 Szczerców D 2
90 Szczucin B 4
69 Szczuczarz B 4
78 Szczuczyn B 5
78 Szczuki C 3
90 Szczurowa B 3
90 Szczyrk C 2
78 Szczytno B 3
90 Szebnie C 4
91 Szécsény D 2
102 Szedres B 2
102 Szeged B 4
103 Szeghalom A 5
102 Szegvár B 4
101 Székesfehérvár B 6
102 Szekszárd B 2
78 Szelków C 4
69 Szemud A 6
91 Szendehely E 2
91 Szendro D 3
101 Szentantalfa C 5
91 Szentdomonkos D 3
102 Szentendre A 3
102 Szentes B 4
101 Szentgál B 5
101 Szentgotthárd C 4
91 Szentistván E 3
115 Szentlörinc A 5
102 Szentmártonkáta A 3
101 Szenyér C 5
101 Szepetnek C 4
91 Szerencs D 4
103 Szerep A 5
90 Szerzyny C 4
78 Szestno B 4
102 Szigetszentmiklós A 3
120 Szigetújfalu A 2
115 Szigetvár A 5
91 Szihalom E 3
91 Szikszó D 3
101 Szil B 5
91 Szilvásvárad D 3
91 Szirmabesenyo D 3
76 Szklarska Poreba C 4
77 Szlichtyngowa B 5
91 Szob E 1
91 Szokolya E 1
102 Szolnok A 4
101 Szombathely B 4
101 Szony B 6
102 Szöreg B 4
101 Szorosad C 6
79 Szpetal Graniczny C 2
77 Szprotawa B 4
78 Szreńsk B 3
78 Sztum B 2
78 Sztutowo A 2
69 Szubin B 5
91 Szucsi E 2
115 Szulok A 5
91 Szurdokpüspöki E 2
69 Szwecja B 4
89 Szybowice A 5
90 Szydlów, Kielce, PL B 4
79 Szydlów, Lodz, PL D 2
79 Szydlowiec D 3
69 Szydlowo, PL B 4
78 Szydlowo, PL B 3
79 Szymanów C 3
90 Szymbark C 4
90 Szynwald C 4
78 Szyrokoye A 3

T

27 Taalintendas C 5
29 Taavetti C 5
101 Tab C 6
120 Tabanera de Valdavia B 2
126 Tabanera la Luenga A 1
153 Tabanovce B 3
119 Tábara C 5
74 Tabarz C 2
120 Tabenera de Cerrato B 2
42 Taberg B 4
137 Tabernas B 4
133 Tabernes de Valldigna B 2
123 Tabescán B 4
111 Tabiano Terme C 5
118 Taboada B 3
118 Taboadela B 3
88 Tábor B 2
102 Táborfalva A 3
115 Taborište B 4
124 Tábua C 1
124 Tabuaço B 2
127 Tabuenca A 4
119 Tabuyo del Monte B 4
39 Täby C 5
101 Tác B 6
87 Tachov B 4
58 Tadcaster B 2
62 Tadley B 2
121 Tafalla B 5
18 Tafjord C 3
15 Täfteå E 4
46 Tågarp B 3
110 Tággia D 2
143 Tagliacozzo B 4
113 Táglio di Po A 4
83 Tagnon B 6
137 Tahal B 4
91 Tahitótfalu E 2
123 Tahús B 4
85 Tailfingen B 6
81 Taillis B 5
49 Tain D 4
108 Tain-l'H. B 1
29 Taipalsaari B 6
17 Taivalkoski B 7
26 Taivassalo C 4
117 Takovo B 4
102 Taksony A 3
91 Taktaharkány D 4
118 Tal B 2
113 Talamello C 4
142 Talamone B 2
130 Talarrubias B 1
129 Talaván B 4
126 Talavera de la Reina C 1
129 Talavera la Real C 4
130 Talavera la Vieja B 1
129 Talayuela B 5
132 Talayuelas B 1
34 Talgje B 1
124 Talhadas C 1
129 Taliga C 3
106 Talizat B 3
112 Talla Subbiano C 3
48 Talladale D 3
55 Tallaght A 5
109 Tallard C 3
33 Tallåsen B 7
33 Tällberg C 5
39 Tallboda D 2
55 Tallow B 3
55 Tallowbridge B 3
15 Tallsjö D 2
24 Talluskyla B 4
121 Talmantes C 5
95 Talmay B 5
104 Talmont, Charente Maritime, F B 2
92 Talmont, Vendée, F C 2
146 Talsano B 3

146 Talsarno B 3
15 Tålsmark D 4
8 Talvik B 2
57 Talybont D 3
126 Tamajón B 2
125 Tamame B 4
125 Tamames C 3
123 Tamarit C 4
122 Tamarite de Litera C 3
101 Tamási C 6
74 Tambach-Dietharz C 2
119 Tameza A 4
70 Tamines B 3
27 Tammela C 6
27 Tammisaari D 6
117 Tamnit B 6
27 Tampere B 6
98 Tamsweg B 4
130 Tamurejo C 2
123 Tamuriu C 6
59 Tamworth C 2
60 Tan-y-groes A 2
9 Tana B 8
120 Tañabueyes B 3
159 Tanágra A 4
101 Tanakajd B 4
141 Tanaunella B 3
82 Tancarville B 2
53 Tandragee B 5
20 Tandsbyn B 3
33 Tandsjöborg B 5
44 Tandslet C 2
55 Tang A 4
46 Tånga A 3
32 Tangen C 2
67 Tangerhütte C 4
67 Tangermünde C 4
11 Tanhau B 7
96 Taninges B 2
11 Tankapirtti A 7
73 Tann C 4
74 Tanna C 3
42 Tannåker C 3
20 Tännäs C 1
70 Tannay, Ardennes, F C 3
94 Tannay, Nièvre, F B 3
20 Tänndalen C 1
74 Tanne B 2
75 Tannenbergsthal C 4
87 Tännesberg B 4
97 Tannheim A 6
16 Tannila B 4
68 Tanowo B 2
36 Tanum C 3
36 Tanumshede C 3
107 Tanus C 2
88 Tanvald A 3
149 Taormina B 5
128 Tapada C 2
102 Tápe B 4
86 Tapfheim C 2
119 Tapia de Casariego A 4
102 Tápiógyörgye A 3
102 Tápioság A 3
102 Tápiósáp A 3
102 Tápiósüly A 3
102 Tápiószecso A 3
102 Tápioszele A 3
102 Tápiószentmárton A 3
101 Tapolca C 5
101 Tapolcafö B 5
11 Tappionniemi C 7
39 Tappstrom C 4
91 Tar E 2
123 Taradell C 5
14 Tårajaur B 3
118 Taramundi A 3
126 Tarancón B 2
146 Táranto B 3
115 Tarany A 5
108 Tarare B 1
109 Tarascon D 1
107 Tarascon-sur-Ariège E 1
121 Tarazona C 5
131 Tarazona de la Mancha B 5
133 Tárbena C 2
50 Tarbert, Argyll, GB B 2
48 Tarbert, Lewis, GB D 2
54 Tarbert, IRL B 2
105 Tarbes D 3
50 Tarbet A 3
50 Tarbolton B 3
91 Tarcal D 4
103 Tarcea A 6
99 Tarcento C 4
151 Tarčin B 4
79 Tarczyn D 3
127 Tardelcuende A 3
105 Tardets D 2
122 Tardienta C 2
10 Tärendö B 2
104 Targon C 2
160 Târgoviste C 4
160 Târgu Mures B 4
160 Targu Ocno B 5
135 Tarifa C 5
134 Tariquejo B 3
120 Tarján A 2
101 Tárkány B 6
49 Tarland D 6
56 Tarleton C 4
90 Tarlów A 4
44 Tarm B 1
66 Tarmstedt B 2
13 Tärnaby B 7
102 Tarnaörs A 4
103 Tarnaszentmiklós A 4
9 Tårnet C 10
90 Tarnobrzeg B 4
105 Tarnos D 1
91 Tarnov C 4
90 Tarnów B 3
90 Tarnowskie Góry B 1
38 Tärnsjö B 3
124 Tarouca B 2
44 Tarp C 2
57 Tarporley C 4
142 Tarquínia B 2
123 Tarragona C 4
61 Tarrant Hinton C 4
123 Tarrasa C 4
123 Tárrega C 4
98 Tarrenz B 1
40 Tårs B 4
105 Tartas D 2
27 Tarvasjoki C 5
49 Tarves D 6
57 Tarvin C 4
99 Tarvisio C 4
21 Tåsjö A 4
103 Tăşnad A 6
88 Tasov B 4
151 Tasovčići B 3
102 Tass A 3
108 Tassin-la-Demi-Luna B 1
45 Tåstrup B 5
101 Taszár C 5
91 Tát E 1
102 Tata A 2
102 Tatabánya A 2
102 Tatárszentgyörgy A 3
91 Tatranská Kotlina C 3
91 Tatranská-Lomnica C 3
34 Tau B 1
73 Tauberbischofsheim D 3
75 Taucha B 4
98 Taufers C 2
87 Taufkirchen C 4
80 Taulé B 3
109 Taulignan C 1
44 Taulov B 2
61 Taunton B 3
147 Taurianova D 2
146 Taurisano C 4
121 Tauste C 5
103 Taut B 5
106 Tauves B 2
102 Tavankut B 3
96 Tavannes A 3
28 Tavastila C 4
95 Tavaux B 5
15 Tavelsjo D 4
147 Taverna C 2
97 Taverne B 4
142 Tavernelle A 3
112 Tavernelle Val di Pesa C 3
111 Tavernola Bergamasca B 5
83 Taverny B 4
146 Taviano C 4
134 Tavira B 3
60 Tavistock C 2
117 Tavnik C 4
52 Tawnyinah C 3
156 Taxiárkhis B 3
50 Taychreggan A 2
50 Taynuilt A 2
51 Tayport A 5
119 Tazones A 5
78 Tczew A 1
48 Teangue D 3
144 Teano B 3
152 Tearce B 3
136 Teba C 2
56 Tebay B 4
99 Techendorf C 4
65 Tecklenburg B 5
46 Teckomatorp B 4
160 Tecuci C 5
23 Teerijärvi B 5
51 Teesside C 6
71 Tegelen A 5
38 Tegelsmora B 4
98 Tegernsee B 2
145 Teggiano C 4
91 Téglás E 4
112 Tegoleto C 3
74 Teichel C 3
60 Teignmouth C 3
118 Teijeiro A 2
27 Teijo C 5
81 Teillay C 5
98 Teisendorf B 3
27 Teisko B 6
74 Teistungen B 2
129 Tejada de Tiétar A 5
127 Tejado A 3
125 Tejares C 4
119 Tejera A 4
47 Tejn B 5
117 Tekija B 6
160 Tekirdag E 5
91 Tekovské-Lužany D 1
88 Telč B 3
57 Telford D 4
98 Telfs B 2
65 Telgte C 5
66 Tellingstedt A 2
141 Telti B 3
67 Teltow C 6
126 Tembleque C 2
88 Temelin B 2
158 Teméni A 3
116 Temerin A 3
120 Temiño B 3
16 Temmes C 4
141 Témpio Pausánia B 3
56 Temple Sowerby B 4
55 Templemore B 4
54 Templenoe C 2
70 Templeuve B 2
67 Templin B 6
53 Tempo B 4
70 Temse A 3
153 Temska A 4
65 Ten Boer A 4
27 Tenala C 6
108 Tenay B 2
57 Tenbury Wells D 4
60 Tenby B 2
106 Tence B 4
109 Tende C 4
4 Tengelfjord B 4
87 Tengling D 4
27 Tenhola C 6
43 Tenhult B 4
102 Tenja C 2
71 Tenneville B 4
4 Tennevol B 6
38 Tensta B 4
62 Tenterden B 4
118 Teo B 2
145 Teora C 4
10 Tepasto B 4
154 Tepelenë B 2
87 Teplá B 4
88 Teplice A 1
88 Teplice n. Metuji A 4
91 Teplička C 1
12 Teplingan C 4
65 Ter Apel B 5
121 Tera C 4
143 Téramo B 4
65 Terborg C 4
91 Terchová C 2
117 Teregova A 6
103 Teremia Mare C 4
128 Terena C 3
133 Teresa de Cofrentes B 1
87 Terešov B 5
132 Tereul A 1
115 Terezino Polje B 5
83 Tergnier B 5
23 Terjärv B 5
99 Terlan C 2
99 Terlano C 2
145 Terlizzi B 5
129 Termas de Monfortinho A 4
142 Terme di Roselle B 2
144 Terme di Súio B 2
110 Terme di Valdieri C 2
122 Termens C 3
106 Termes C 3
148 Términi Imerese B 3
143 Terminillo B 3
144 Termoli A 4
53 Termonfeckin C 5
104 Ternasson B 4
100 Ternberg B 2
40 Terndrup C 4
70 Terneuzen A 2
143 Terni B 3
100 Ternitz B 4
75 Terpe B 6
91 Terpes E 3
156 Térpillos A 2
156 Terpni B 3
157 Terpsithéa C 2
143 Terracina C 4
12 Terråk B 4
141 Terralba C 2
146 Terranova da Sibari C 2
146 Terranova di Pollino C 2
124 Terras do Bouro B 1
148 Terrasini A 3
120 Terrazos B 3
132 Terriente A 1
59 Terrington St. Clement C 4
128 Terrugem C 3
141 Tertenia C 3
22 Tervajoki C 4
27 Tervakoski C 7
24 Tervo C 3
16 Tervola A 3
70 Tervuren B 3
127 Terzaga B 4
116 Tešanj B 1
101 Tesárske-Mlyňany A 6
115 Teslič C 5
70 Tessenderlo A 4
67 Tessin A 5
81 Tessy-sur-Vire B 5
101 Tét B 5
61 Tetbury B 4
84 Téterchen A 3
67 Teterow B 5
115 Tetovo, Bosna i Hercegovina, YU C 5
152 Tetovo, Makedonija, YU B 2
74 Tettau C 3
97 Tettnang A 5
87 Teublitz B 4
74 Teuchern B 4
133 Teulada,E C 3
141 Teulada,I D 1
10 Teurajärvi C 2
74 Teutschenthal B 3
22 Teuva C 3
102 Tevel B 2
51 Teviothead B 5
61 Tewkesbury B 4
74 Thale B 3
71 Thalfang C 5
98 Thalgau B 4
75 Thalheim C 4
97 Thalkirch B 5
97 Thalkirchdorf A 6
86 Thalmässing B 3
97 Thalwil A 4
62 Thame B 3
85 Thann C 4
86 Thannhausen C 2
84 Thaon-les-Vosges B 3
75 Tharandt C 5
134 Tharsis B 3
156 Thásos B 4
62 Thatcham B 2
62 Thaxted B 4
97 Thayngen A 4
55 The Downs A 4
62 Theale B 2
66 Thedinghausen C 2
74 Theeßen A 4
74 Themar C 2
93 Thénezay C 3
104 Thenon B 4
156 Theológos B 4
155 Theópetra C 3
109 Théoule D 3
156 Thérmi B 3
155 Thérmon D 3
63 Thérouanne B 4
105 These D 2
159 Thespiai A 4
155 Thesprotikón C 2
156 Thessaloniki B 2
59 Thetford C 4
152 Theth B 1
71 Theux B 4
107 Thézan D 2
84 Thiaucourt B 2
82 Thiberville B 2
83 Thibie C 6
84 Thiéblemont-Farémont B 1
94 Thiel C 3
75 Thiendorf B 5
99 Thiene D 2
86 Thierhaupten C 2
96 Thierrens B 2
106 Thiers B 3
87 Thiersheim A 4
87 Thierstein A 4
141 Thiesi B 2
67 Thießow A 6
106 Thiezac B 2
84 Thil A 2
84 Thionville A 3
56 Thirlspot B 3
82 Thiron C 3
58 Thirsk A 2
40 Thisted C 2
159 Thívai A 4
82 Thivars C 3
104 Thiviers B 3
106 Thizy A 4
64 Tholen C 2
54 Thomas Street A 3
55 Thomastown B 4
108 Thônes B 3
84 Thonnance-les-Joinville B 2
96 Thonon B 2
109 Thorame-Bse. C 3
109 Thorame-Hte. C 3
108 Thorens-Glières B 3
83 Thorigny-sur-Oreuse C 5
100 Thörl B 3
51 Thornaby on Tees C 6
58 Thorne B 3
59 Thorney C 3
50 Thornhill, Dumfries, GB B 4
50 Thornhill, Perth., GB A 3
56 Thornthwaite B 3
56 Thornton Cleveleys C 3
58 Thornton-le-Dale A 3
62 Thorpe-le-Soken B 5
92 Thouarcé B 3
92 Thouars C 3
158 Thouria B 3
83 Thourotte B 4
59 Thrapston C 3
56 Threlkeld B 3
88 Thrová Kamenice B 3
49 Thrumster C 5
106 Thueyts C 4
70 Thuin B 3
123 Thuir B 5
86 Thumau A 3
96 Thun B 3
73 Thüngen D 3
106 Thuret B 3
95 Thurey C 5
97 Thuringen A 5
108 Thurins B 1
67 Thürkow B 5
55 Thurles B 4
44 Thurø B 3
56 Thursby B 3
49 Thurso C 5
81 Thury-Harcourt B 6
97 Thusis B 5
40 Thyborøn C 2
44 Thyregod B 2
128 Tiamagal B 2
133 Tibi C 2
37 Tibro C 6
62 Ticehurst B 4
58 Tickhill B 2
42 Tidaholm A 3
37 Tidan C 6
43 Tidersrum B 5
125 Tiedra B 4
87 Tiefenbach B 4
97 Tiefencastel B 5
74 Tiefenort C 2
76 Tiefensee A 2
64 Tiel C 3
126 Tielmes B 2
70 Tielt B 2
70 Tienen B 3
85 Tiengen C 5
81 Tiercé C 6
127 Tierga A 4
122 Tiermas B 1
38 Tierp, Uppsala Län, S B 4
38 Tierp, Uppsala Län, S B 4
50 Tighnabruaich B 2
94 Tigy B 2
101 Tihany C 5
23 Tiistenjoki C 5
150 Tijesno B 1
64 Tijnje A 3
137 Tijola B 4
23 Tikkakoski C 7
23 Tikkala C 7
64 Tilburg C 3
62 Tilbury B 4

95 Tilchâtel B 5
103 Tileagd A 6
105 Tilh D 2
105 Tillac D 3
38 Tillberga C 3
83 Tillé B 4
50 Tillicoultry A 4
62 Tillingham B 4
84 Tilloy-et-Bellay A 1
81 Tilly-sur-Seulles A 6
19 Tiltrem B 5
99 Timau C 4
98 Timelkam A 4
155 Timfristós D 3
103 Timişoara C 5
42 Timmele B 3
66 Timmendorfer Strand B 3
43 Timmernabben C 6
37 Timmersdala C 5
54 Timoleague C 3
55 Timolin B 5
46 Timsfors A 4
44 Tin Stby. A 1
55 Tinahely B 5
128 Tinalhas B 3
103 Tinca B 5
81 Tinchebray B 6
63 Tincque B 4
4 Tind C 2
119 Tineo A 4
62 Tingewick B 2
44 Tinglev C 2
43 Tingsryd C 4
39 Tingstäde E 5
18 Tingvoll C 4
35 Tinnoset B 5
60 Tintagel C 2
81 Tinténiac B 5
61 Tintern Parva B 4
71 Tintigny C 4
99 Tione di Trente C 1
54 Tipperary B 3
62 Tiptree B 4
152 Tiranë C 1
97 Tirano B 6
160 Tiraspol B 6
160 Tîrgu Jiu C 3
131 Tiriez C 4
132 Tirig A 3
147 Tiriolo D 2
156 Tírnavos C 2
103 Tirnova B 5
159 Tirós B 3
112 Tirrénia C 2
87 Tirschenreuth B 4
44 Tirstrup A 3
130 Tirteafuera C 2
89 Tišnov B 4
91 Tisovec D 2
36 Tistedal B 3
44 Tistrup B 1
45 Tisvildeleje A 5
103 Tiszabö A 4
103 Tiszacsege A 5
91 Tiszadada D 4
103 Tiszaderzs A 4
91 Tiszadob D 4
103 Tiszadorogma A 4
91 Tiszaeszlár D 4
102 Tiszaföldvár B 4
103 Tiszafüred A 4
91 Tiszagyulaháza E 4
103 Tiszaigar A 4
91 Tiszakarád D 4
102 Tiszakécske B 4
91 Tiszakeszi E 3
102 Tiszakürt B 4
91 Tiszalök D 4
91 Tiszalúc D 4
103 Tiszána A 4
91 Tiszanagyfalu D 4
103 Tiszaörs A 4
91 Tiszapalkonya E 4
102 Tiszapüspöki A 4
103 Tiszaroff A 4
103 Tiszasüly A 4
103 Tiszaszentimre A 4
102 Tiszasziget B 4
103 Tiszaszölös A 4
103 Tiszatenyö A 4
91 Tiszavasvári E 4
132 Titaguas B 1
117 Titel A 4
157 Tithoréa D 2
85 Titisee C 5
145 Tito C 4
151 Titograd C 5
153 Titov Veles C 3
115 Titova Korenica C 3
116 Titovo Užice C 3
18 Titran B 4
87 Tittling C 5
87 Tittmoning C 4
71 Titz A 5
22 Tiukka C 3
151 Tivat C 4
37 Tived C 6
60 Tiverton C 3
122 Tivisa C 3
143 Tivoli C 3
44 Tjæreborg B 1
39 Tjällmo D 2
14 Tjåmotis B 2
36 Tjärno C 3
4 Tjeldnes B 5
22 Tjöck C 3
5 Tjongsfjord D 2
35 Tjønnefoss C 4
46 Tjörnarp A 4
12 Tjøtta B 4
78 Tluchowo C 2
89 Tlumačov B 5
79 Tluszcz C 4
102 Toalmás A 3
112 Toano B 2
74 Toba B 2
133 Tobarra C 1
53 Tobermore B 5
48 Tobermory E 2
98 Toblach C 3
38 Tobo B 4
104 Tocane-St. Apre B 3
128 Tocha A 2
135 Tocino B 5
36 Töcksfors B 3
18 Todal C 4
143 Todi B 3
56 Todmorden C 4
85 Todtnau C 4
118 Toén B 3
12 Toft B 4
39 Tofta, Gotlands Län, S E 5
37 Tofta, Skaraborgs Län, S C 5
35 Töfte B 6
36 Toftedal C 3
44 Toftlund B 2
25 Tohmajärvi C 7
23 Toholampi B 6
27 Toijala B 6
23 Toivakka C 8
116 Tojšići B 2
91 Tokajhegy D 4
79 Tokary D 1
91 Tokod E 1
102 Tököl A 2
25 Tokrajärvi C 7
160 Tolbukhin D 5
91 Tolcsva D 4
126 Toledo C 1
113 Tolentino C 5
142 Tolfa B 2
38 Tolfta B 4
43 Tolg B 4
19 Tolga C 7
28 Tolkis C 3
28 Tolkkinen C 3
78 Tolkmicko A 2
47 Tollarp B 4
42 Tollered B 2
62 Tollesbury B 4
62 Tolleshunt D'Arcy B 4
45 Tølløse B 4
99 Tolmezzo C 4
114 Tolmin A 1
102 Tolna B 2
101 Tolnanémedi C 6
159 Tolón B 3
121 Tolosa, E A 4
128 Tolosa, P B 3
136 Tolox C 2
122 Tolva, E B 3
17 Tolva, SF A 7
145 Tolve C 5
128 Tomar B 2
117 Tomaševac A 4
115 Tomašica C 4
101 Tomášikovo A 5
79 Tomaszów Mazowiecki D 3
49 Tomatin D 5
143 Tomba di Nerone C 3
105 Tombeboeuf C 3
48 Tomdoun D 3
47 Tomelilla B 4
126 Tomellosa B 3
131 Tomelloso B 3
49 Tomintoul D 5
77 Tomislawice A 7
44 Tommerup B 3
18 Tömmervåg B 3
49 Tomnavoulin D 5
18 Tomra C 2
35 Tomter B 6
123 Tona C 5
141 Tonara B 3
62 Tonbridge B 4
124 Tondela C 1
44 Tønder C 1
70 Tongeren B 4
48 Tongue C 4
30 Tønjum B 4
11 Tonkopuro C 8
104 Tonnay-Boutonne B 2
104 Tonnay-Charente B 2
105 Tonneins C 3
94 Tonnerre B 3
66 Tönning A 1
31 Tonsåsen C 6
35 Tonsberg B 6
34 Tonstad C 2
6 Tønsvik B 5
53 Toome B 5
55 Toomyvara B 3
54 Toormore C 2
137 Topares B 4
125 Topas B 4
27 Topeno C 7
117 Toplet B 6
153 Topli Dol A 4
117 Topola B 4
154 Topolčani A 3
101 Topol'cany A 6
101 Topol'čianky A 6
159 Topóliá A 4
101 Topol'níky B 5
103 Topolovǎtu Mare C 5
117 Topolovnik B 5
101 Toponár C 5
76 Toporów A 4
60 Topsham C 3
115 Topusko B 3
118 Toques B 3
143 Tor Vaiánica C 3
123 Torá C 4
119 Toral B 4
119 Toral de los Guzmanes B 5
60 Torbay C 3
32 Tørberget B 3
42 Torbjörntorp A 3
111 Torbole B 5
146 Torchiarolo B 4
82 Torcy-le-Petit B 3
103 Torda C 4
35 Tørdal B 4
119 Tordehumos C 5
125 Tordesilla B 4
127 Tordesilos B 4
14 Töre C 6
37 Töreboda C 6
45 Toreby C 4
46 Torekov A 3
145 Torella dei Lombardi C 4
123 Torelló B 5
119 Toreno B 4
75 Torgau B 4
68 Torgelow B 2
48 Torgyle Bridge D 4
43 Torhamn C 5
9 Torhop B 8
70 Torhout A 2
110 Toriglia C 4
81 Torigni-sur-Vire A 6
126 Torija B 2
132 Toril A 1
110 Torino B 2
145 Toritto C 5
122 Torla B 2
103 Tormac C 5
11 Törmänen A 7
17 Törmänmäki C 6
47 Tormestorp A 4
111 Törmini B 5
128 Tornada B 1
125 Tornavacas C 4
66 Tornesch B 2
49 Torness D 4
142 Torniella A 2
143 Tornimparte B 4
16 Tornio B 3
102 Tornjoš C 3
127 Tornos B 4
125 Toro B 4
102 Törökbalint A 2
103 Törökszentmiklós A 4
101 Torony B 4
141 Torpè B 3
49 Torphins D 6
31 Torpo C 5
60 Torpoint C 2
43 Torpsbruk B 4
21 Torpshammar C 5
60 Torquay C 3
120 Torquemada B 2
141 Torralba B 2
126 Torralba de Burgo A 3
130 Torralba de Calatrava B 3
128 Torrão C 2
144 Torre Annunziata C 3
136 Torre-Cardela B 3
128 Torre das Vargens B 3
122 Torre de Capdella B 3
128 Torre de Coelheiros C 3
124 Torre de D. Chama B 2
131 Torre de Juan Abad C 3
135 Torre de la Higuera B 4
129 Torre de Miguel Sesmero C 4
124 Torre de Moncorvo B 2
129 Torre de Sta. Maria B 4
119 Torre del Bierzo B 4
126 Torre del Burgo B 2
136 Torre del Campo B 3
122 Torre del Español C 3
144 Torre del Greco C 3
112 Torre del Lago Puccini C 2
136 Torre del Mar C 2
149 Torre di Faro A 5
124 Torre do Terranho C 2
132 Torre Embesora A 2
127 Torre los Negros B 4
145 Torre Orsáia C 4
133 Torre-Pacheco D 2
110 Torre Péllice C 2
146 Torre S. Susanna B 3
126 Torreblacos A 3
132 Torreblanca A 3
127 Torrebuceit C 3
126 Torrecaballeros A 1
130 Torrecampo C 2
127 Torrecilla B 3
130 Torrecilla de la Jara B 2
125 Torrecilla de la Orden B 4
126 Torrecilla del Pinar A 1
121 Torrecilla en Cameros B 4
129 Torrecillas de la Tiesa B 5
123 Torredembarra C 4
136 Torredonjimeno B 3
122 Torregrosa C 3
124 Torreira C 1
126 Torrejón de Ardoz B 2
126 Torrejón de Velasco B 2
126 Torrejón del Rey B 2
129 Torrejón el Rubio B 4
129 Torrejoncillo B 4
126 Torrelaguna B 2
127 Torrelapaja A 4
120 Torrelavega A 2
125 Torrelobatón B 4
126 Torrelodones B 2
145 Torremaggiore B 4
133 Torremanzanas C 2
129 Torremegia C 4
129 Torremocha B 4
136 Torremolinos C 2
142 Torrenieri A 2
132 Torrenostra A 3
143 Torrenova C 3
132 Torrente B 2
131 Torrenueva, Ciudad Real, E C 3
136 Torrenueva, Granada, E C 3
129 Torreorgaz B 4
136 Torreperogil A 3
136 Torres B 3
136 Torres-Cabrera B 2
126 Torres de la Alameda B 2
128 Torres Novas B 2
128 Torres Vedras B 1
120 Torresandino C 3
44 Tørresø B 3
133 Torrevieja D 2
99 Torri del Benaco D 1
40 Torriby B 3
146 Torricella B 3
48 Torridon D 3
126 Torrijos C 1
49 Torrish C 5
112 Torrita di Siena C 3
128 Torroal C 2
49 Torroboll C 4
123 Torroella de Montgri B 6
136 Torrox C 3
36 Torrskog B 4
38 Torsåker B 3
43 Torsås C 5
37 Torsby A 4
39 Torshälla C 3
6 Torsken B 3
43 Torskors C 5
42 Torslanda B 1
40 Torslev B 3
44 Torsminde A 1
6 Torsvåg A 5
102 Törtel A 3
50 Torthorwald B 4
125 Tórtoles C 4
120 Tórtoles del Esgueva C 2
141 Tortoli C 3
110 Tortona C 3
146 Tórtora C 1
143 Tortoreto Lido B 4
149 Tortorici A 4
122 Tortosa D 3
128 Tortosendo A 3
127 Tortuera B 4
126 Tortuero B 2
78 Toruń B 1
40 Torup, DK B 3
42 Torup, S C 3
56 Torver B 3
18 Torvikbukt C 3
11 Torvinen B 6
136 Torviscón C 3
13 Torvsjö C 9
91 Torysa C 3
76 Torzym A 4
12 Tosbotn B 4
111 Toscolano B 5
12 Tosen B 4
123 Tossa de Mar C 5
20 Tossåsen C 2
105 Tosse, F D 1
36 Tosse, S C 4
143 Tossícia B 4
66 Tostedt B 2
102 Tószeg A 4
89 Toszek A 6
136 Totalán C 2
133 Totana D 1
43 Totebo B 6
82 Tôtes B 3
103 Tótkomlós B 4
62 Totland, GB C 2
30 Totland, N B 2
34 Tøtlandsvik B 2
60 Totnes C 3
101 Totszerdahely C 4
12 Tøttdal C 3
27 Tottijärvi B 6
62 Totton C 2
124 Touça B 2
94 Toucy B 3
109 Touët D 4
84 Toul B 2
94 Toulon, Allier, F C 3
109 Toulon, Var, F D 2
94 Toulon-sur-Arroux C 4
105 Toulouse D 4
70 Tourcoing B 2
81 Tourlaville A 5
155 Tourlís D 3
70 Tournai B 2
83 Tournan-en-Brie C 4
105 Tournay D 3
70 Tournes C 3
108 Tournon B 1
105 Tournon-d'Agenais C 3
93 Tournon-St. Martin C 4
95 Tournus C 4
118 Touro, E B 2
124 Touro, P C 2
82 Tourouvre C 2
104 Tourriers B 3
93 Tours B 4
83 Tours-sur-Marne B 6
109 Tourves D 2
82 Toury C 3
107 Toutens D 1
124 Touvedo B 1
92 Touvois C 2
87 Toužim A 4
89 Tovačov B 5
116 Tovariševo A 3
116 Tovarnik A 3
34 Tovdal C 4
18 Toven C 4
18 Tovik, Møre Og Romsdal Fylke, N C 3
4 Tovik, Troms Fylke, N B 5
153 Tovrljane A 3
51 Tow Law C 6
59 Towcester C 2
51 Town Yetholm B 5
57 Towyn D 2
156 Toxótai A 4
23 Töysä C 5
118 Trabada A 3
119 Trabadelo B 4
125 Trabanca B 3

119 Trabazo C 4
77 Trabczyn A 6
71 Traben-Trarbach C 6
148 Trabia B 3
100 Traboch B 2
153 Trabotivište C 4
83 Tracy-le-Mont B 4
110 Tradate B 3
42 Trädet B 3
128 Trafaria C 1
127 Tragacete B 4
157 Tragána D 3
134 Traganheira B 2
158 Traganón B 2
154 Tragjas B 1
100 Tragwein A 2
103 Traian Vuia C 6
132 Traiguera A 3
83 Trainel C 5
100 Traisen A 3
101 Traiskirchen A 4
100 Traismauer A 3
87 Traitsching B 4
39 Träkvista C 4
54 Tralee B 2
122 Tramacastilla B 2
141 Tramaríglio B 2
141 Tramatza B 2
96 Tramelan A 3
99 Tramonti di sopra C 3
55 Tramore B 4
110 Trana B 2
43 Tranås, Jönköpings Län, S A 4
47 Tranås, Kristianstads Län, S B 5
124 Trancoso C 2
44 Tranebjerg B 3
44 Tranekær C 3
42 Tranemo B 3
51 Tranent B 5
42 Trånghalla B 4
32 Trängslet B 4
20 Trångsviken B 3
145 Trani B 5
36 Trankil B 3
154 Tranóvalton B 3
4 Tranøy B 4
109 Trans-en-Provence D 3
32 Transtrand B 4
148 Trapani A 2
82 Trappes C 3
42 Traryd C 3
143 Trasacco C 4
129 Trasierra C 4
28 Träskby C 3
42 Träslövsläge B 2
118 Trasmiras B 3
126 Traspinedo A 1
97 Trauchgau A 6
100 Traun A 2
87 Traunreut D 4
87 Traunstein D 4
42 Tråvad A 3
66 Travemünde B 3
112 Traversétolo B 2
118 Traviesa A 2
115 Travnik C 5
111 Travo C 4
57 Trawfynydd D 3
114 Trbovlje A 3
117 Trbušani C 4
94 Tréban C 3
89 Třebařov B 4
75 Trebbin A 5
67 Trebel C 4
88 Třebenice A 1
154 Trebenište A 2
80 Trébeurden B 3
88 Třebíč B 3
151 Trebinje C 4
146 Trebisacce C 2
91 Trebišov D 4
75 Trebitz B 4
79 Treblinka C 5
114 Trebnje B 2
88 Třeboň B 2
89 Třebovice B 4
75 Trebsen B 4
135 Trebujena C 4
149 Trecastagni B 5
110 Trecate B 3
112 Trecenta A 3
61 Tredegar B 3
112 Tredózio B 3
99 Treffen C 4
95 Treffort C 5
74 Treffurt B 2
57 Trefriw C 3
57 Tregaron D 3
80 Trégastel B 3
99 Tregnago D 2
80 Tréguier B 3
80 Trégunc C 3
60 Treherbert B 3
21 Trehörningsjö B 7
113 Tréia C 5
106 Treigna B 1
94 Treignat C 2
71 Treis B 6
43 Trekanten C 6
153 Treklyano B 4
81 Trélazé C 6
60 Trelech B 2
104 Trélissac B 3
46 Trelleborg B 4
83 Trélon A 6
83 Tréloup B 5
82 Tremblay C 3
153 Tremelkovo B 4
128 Tremês B 2
97 Tremezzo C 5
87 Třemošná B 5
122 Tremp B 3
89 Trenčianska Turná C 6
89 Trenčianske Mitlice C 6
89 Trenčianske Teplá C 6
89 Trenčianske Teplice C 6
89 Trenčin C 6
72 Trendelburg B 3
30 Trengereid C 2
105 Trensacq C 2
67 Trent A 6
99 Trento C 2
60 Treorchy B 3
152 Trepča B 2
146 Trepuzzi B 4
111 Trescore Balneàrio B 4
97 Tresenda B 6
18 Tresfjord C 3
112 Tresigallo B 3
102 Trešnjevac C 3
117 Trešnjevica C 5
141 Tresnurágnes B 2
120 Trespaderne B 3
88 Třešt B 3
113 Tréstina C 4
61 Tretower B 3
109 Trets D 2
31 Tretten B 7
86 Treuchtlingen C 2
74 Treuen C 4
75 Treuenbrietzen A 4
35 Treungen B 4
136 Trevelez C 3
143 Trevi B 3
143 Trevi nel Lázi C 4
121 Treviana B 3
111 Treviglio B 4
142 Trevignano Romano B 3
99 Treviso D 3
108 Trévoux B 1
73 Treysa C 3
94 Trézelles C 3
111 Trezzo B 4
153 Trgovište B 4
88 Trhové Sviny C 2
91 Trhovište D 4
118 Triacastela B 3
92 Triaize C 2
84 Triaucourt B 2
85 Triberg B 5
67 Tribsees A 5
150 Tribunj B 1
145 Tricárico C 5
146 Tricase C 4
99 Tricésimo C 4
105 Trie D 3
97 Trieb B 4
100 Trieben B 2
74 Triebes C 4
67 Triepkendorf B 6
71 Trier C 5
99 Trieste D 4
84 Trieux A 2
155 Trífos D 3
145 Triggiano B 5
159 Triglia A 4
67 Triglitz B 5
92 Trignac B 1
135 Trigueros B 4
120 Trigueros del Valle C 2
152 Trijebine A 1
157 Tríkeri C 3
155 Tríkkala C 3
158 Trikkala, Korinthia, GR B 3
156 Trikkala, Thessaloníki, GR B 2
150 Trilj B 2
53 Trillick B 4
156 Trilofon B 2
83 Trilport C 4
55 Trim A 5
51 Trimdon C 6
62 Trimley B 5
49 Trinafour E 4
134 Trindade, Beja, P B 3
124 Trindade, Bragança, P B 2
89 Třinec B 6
62 Tring B 3
141 Trinita d'Agultu B 2
145 Trinitápoli B 5
110 Trino B 3
124 Trinta C 2
110 Triora D 2
158 Tripi B 3
158 Trípolis B 3
143 Triponzo B 3
74 Triptis C 3
66 Trittau B 3
144 Trivento B 3
110 Trivero B 3
145 Trivigno C 4
101 Trnava,CS A 5
116 Trnava,YU A 2
117 Trnjane C 5
101 Trnovec A 5
151 Trnovo B 4
82 Troarn B 1
85 Trochelfingen B 6
38 Trödje B 4
44 Trœnse B 3
124 Trofa B 1
100 Trofaiach B 3
12 Trofors B 5
150 Trogir B 2
36 Trøgstad B 3
145 Tróia B 4
149 Troina B 4
71 Troisdorf B 6
83 Troissy B 5
71 Troisvierges B 5
79 Trojanów D 4
44 Troldhede B 1
42 Trollhätan A 2
110 Tromello B 3
35 Tromøy C 4
6 Tromsdalen B 5
6 Tromsø B 4
124 Tronco B 2
19 Trondheim B 6
94 Tronget C 3
42 Tronninge, Halland, S C 2
42 Trönninge, Halland, S B 2
33 Tröno B 7
84 Tronville-en-Barrois B 2
110 Tronzano-Vercellese B 3
93 Trôo B 4
50 Troon B 3
158 Trópaia B 2
147 Tropea D 1
152 Tropojë B 2
78 Tropy B 2
39 Trosa D 4
83 Trosly B 4
73 Trossenfurt D 4
85 Trossingen B 5
87 Trostberg C 4
78 Troszyn B 4
82 Trouville B 2
61 Trowbridge B 4
83 Troyes C 6
150 Trpanj B 3
152 Trpezi B 2
116 Trpinja A 2
89 Třsice B 5
91 Trstená C 2
115 Trstenci B 5
152 Trstenik, Kosovo, YU B 2
117 Trstenik, Srbija, YU C 5
151 Trsteno C 3
101 Trstice A 5
101 Trstin A 5
119 Trubia A 5
119 Truchas B 4
129 Trujillanos C 4
129 Trujillo B 5
48 Trumpan D 2
153 Trŭn, BG B 4
97 Trun, CH B 4
82 Trun, F C 2
60 Truro C 1
74 Trusetal C 2
44 Trustrup A 3
88 Trutnov A 3
43 Tryserum A 6
32 Trysil B 3
21 Trysunda B 7
69 Tryszczyn B 5
115 Tržac C 3
90 Trzciana B 4
69 Trzcianka, Poznań, PL B 4
79 Trzcianka, Warszawa, PL C 4
77 Trzciel A 4
68 Trzebiatów A 3
69 Trzebielino A 5
77 Trzebień B 4
68 Trzebiez B 2
90 Trzebinia-Siersza B 2
77 Trzebnica B 6
77 Trzebnice B 5
69 Trzeciewiec B 6
77 Trzemeszno A 6
76 Trzemeszno Lubuskie A 4
90 Trzetrzewina C 3
114 Tržič A 2
114 Trzin A 2
68 Trzińsko Zdroj C 2
157 Tsangarádha C 3
156 Tsaritsaňi C 2
97 Tschagguns A 5
75 Tschernitz B 6
156 Tsináforon B 2
157 Tsiótion C 2
154 Tsotílion B 3
157 Tsoúka D 2
153 Tsŭrkva B 5
153 Tsurvaritsa B 4
90 Ttzemesnia C 3
124 Tua B 2
54 Tuam A 3
54 Tuamgraney B 3
52 Tubbercurry B 3
65 Tubbergen B 4
120 Tubilla C 3
85 Tübingen B 6
70 Tubize B 3
88 Tučapy B 2
150 Tučepi B 3
107 Tuchan E 2
67 Tucheim C 5
67 Tüchen B 5
88 Tuchlovice A 1
69 Tuchola B 5
69 Tuchomie A 5
90 Tuchów C 4
22 Tuckur B 4
69 Tuczno B 4
35 Tuddal B 4
121 Tudela B 5
126 Tudela de Duero A 1
57 Tudweiliog D 2
82 Tuffé C 2
8 Tufjord A 3
32 Tufsingdalen A 2
88 Tuhaň A 2
91 Tuhár D 2
48 Tuirnaig D 3
153 Tulare B 3
103 Tulca B 5
160 Tulcea C 6
91 Tulčik C 4
109 Tulette C 1
77 Tuliszków A 7
54 Tulla B 3
55 Tullamore A 4
106 Tulle B 1
6 Tulleng B 4
39 Tullinge C 4
108 Tullins B 2
101 Tulln A 4
55 Tullow B 5
53 Tullyhogue B 5
77 Tulowice C 6
52 Tulsk C 3
39 Tumba C 4
49 Tummel Bridge E 5
36 Tun C 4
43 Tuna, Kalmar Län, S B 6
38 Tuna, Uppsala Län, S B 5
38 Tuna Hästberg B 2
21 Tunadal C 6
62 Tunbridge Wells B 4
134 Tunes B 2
30 Tungaseter A 4
39 Tungelsta C 5
43 Tunnerstad A 4
31 Tunnhovd C 5
12 Tunnsjø C 5
28 Tuohikotti B 5
7 Tuolluvaara D 6
113 Tuoro sul Trasimeno C 4
69 Tupadly C 6
153 Tupale B 3
116 Tupanari B 2
76 Tuplice B 3
102 Tura A 3
91 Turany C 2
115 Turbe C 5
97 Turbenthal A 4
119 Turcía B 5
128 Turcifal B 1
85 Turckheim B 4
160 Turda B 3
126 Turégano A 2
79 Turek C 1
27 Turenki C 7
160 Tŭrgovishté D 5
145 Turi C 6
115 Turija C 3
132 Turis B 2
101 Türje C 5
103 Túrkeve A 4
86 Turkheim C 2
26 Turku C 5
91 Turna D 3
100 Turnau B 3
50 Turnberry B 3
70 Turnhout A 3
71 Türnich B 5
100 Türnitz B 3
88 Turnov A 3
160 Turnovo D 4
103 Turnu B 5
160 Turnu Mâgurele D 4
160 Turnu Severin C 3
137 Turón C 3
78 Turośl, Bialystok, PL B 4
78 Turośl, Olsztyn, PL B 4
75 Turoszów C 6
128 Turquel B 1
141 Turri C 2
49 Turriff D 6
137 Turrilla A 4
146 Tursi B 2
96 Turtmann B 3
10 Turtola C 3
89 Turzovka B 6
149 Tusa B 4
142 Tuscánia B 2
79 Tuszyn D 2
59 Tutbury C 2
152 Tutin B 2
25 Tutjunniemi C 6
116 Tutnjevac B 2
67 Tutow B 6
85 Tuttlingen C 5
86 Tutzing D 3
28 Tuukkala B 4
27 Tuulos B 7
25 Tuupovarra C 7
25 Tuusniemi C 5
58 Tuxford B 3
118 Tuy B 2
116 Tuzla B 2
42 Tvååker B 2
15 Tvärålund D 3
101 Tvdošovce A 6
35 Tvedestrand C 4
6 Tverrelvmo C 5
40 Tversted B 4
36 Tveta B 4
43 Tving C 5
89 Twardawa A 6
77 Twardogóra B 6
49 Twatt B 5
50 Tweedshaws B 4
65 Tweelbäke A 6
64 Twello B 4
59 Twenty C 3
66 Twistringen C 1
60 Two Bridges C 3
90 Tworóg B 1
62 Twyford B 2
61 Twyning A 4
69 Tychówko B 4
69 Tychowo B 4
90 Tychy B 1
19 Tydal B 7
59 Tydd St. Giles C 4
37 Tyfors A 6
46 Tygelsjö B 4
90 Tylawa C 4
90 Tylicz C 4
31 Tylldal A 7
40 Tylstrup B 3
90 Tymbark C 3
90 Tymowa C 3
88 Týn n. Vitavou B 2
50 Tyndrum A 3
88 Tynec n. Labem A 3
51 Tynemouth B 6
37 Tyngsjö kapell A 5
88 Tyniste n. Orlici A 4
16 Tynkä C 3
31 Tynset A 7
35 Tynstrand A 6
55 Tyrellspass A 4
46 Tyringe A 4

16 Tyrnävä C 4
27 Tyrväntö B 7
34 Tysnes A 1
30 Tysse, Hordaland Fylke, N C 2
30 Tysse, Osterøya, N C 2
34 Tyssedal A 2
39 Tystberga D 4
34 Tysvær B 1
60 Tywardreath C 2
64 Tzummarum A 3

U

116 Ub B 4
109 Ubaye C 3
64 Ubbergen C 3
45 Ubby B 4
136 Ubeda A 3
100 Übelbach B 3
85 Uberlingen C 6
121 Ubidea A 4
135 Ubrique C 5
126 Ucero A 2
107 Uchaud D 4
95 Uchizy C 4
66 Uchte C 1
84 Uckange A 3
71 Uckerath B 6
62 Uckfield C 4
126 Uclés C 3
149 Ucría A 4
115 Udbina C 3
42 Uddebo B 3
64 Uddel B 3
37 Uddenholm A 5
36 Uddevalla C 3
37 Uddheden B 4
64 Uden C 3
74 Uder B 2
89 Udiča B 6
99 Udine C 4
153 Udovo C 4
102 Udvar C 2
85 Ueberach B 4
68 Ueckermünde B 2
86 Uehlfeld B 2
65 Uelsen B 4
66 Uelzen C 3
66 Uetze C 3
86 Uffenheim B 2
146 Uggiano la Chiesa B 4
137 Ugijar C 3
108 Ugine B 3
116 Uglejevik B 3
114 Ugljan C 3
150 Ugljane B 2
101 Ugod B 5
116 Ugrinovci B 4
89 Uherské Hradiště B 5
89 Uherský Brod B 5
88 Uhlířské-Janovice B 3
88 Uhříněves A 2
75 Uhyst B 6
48 Uig, Lewis, GB C 1
48 Uig, Skye, GB D 2
25 Uimaharju C 7
91 Uinica D 2
64 Uitgeest B 2
64 Uithoorn B 2
65 Uithuizen A 4
65 Uithuizermeeden A 4
70 Uitkerke A 2
79 Ujazd, Lódź, PL D 2
89 Ujazd, Opole, PL A 6
89 Újezd B 5
91 Újfehértó E 4
102 Újhartyán A 3
103 Újkígyós B 5
102 Újpetre C 2
69 Ujście B 5
102 Ujsolt B 3
102 Újszász A 4
91 Újszentmargita E 4
121 Ujué B 5
43 Ukna A 6
49 Ulbster C 5
58 Ulceby Cross B 4
151 Ulcinj D 5
44 Uldum B 2
35 Ulefoss B 5
137 Uleila del Campo B 4
44 Ulfborg A 1
65 Ulft C 4
117 Uljma A 5
21 Ullånger B 7
48 Ullapool D 3
42 Ullared B 2
14 Ullatti A 5
34 Ullatun B 2
23 Ullava B 5
132 Ulldecona A 3
122 Ulldemolins C 3
30 Ullensvang C 3
44 Ullerslev B 3
44 Ullerup C 2
37 Ullervad C 5
102 Üllo A 3
6 Ullsfjord B 5
33 Ullvi, Kopparbergs Län, S C 6
38 Ullvi, Västmanlands Län, S C 3
86 Ulm C 1
128 Ulme B 2
71 Ulmen-Meiserich B 5
31 Ulnes C 6
151 Ulog B 4
42 Ulricehamn B 3
87 Ulrichsberg C 5
101 Ulrichskirchen A 4
73 Ulrichstein C 3
43 Ulrika A 5
20 Ulriksfors B 4
65 Ulrum A 4
19 Ulsberg C 6
49 Ulsta A 7
40 Ulsted B 4
18 Ulsteinvik C 1
44 Ulstrup A 2
64 Ulvenhout C 2
56 Ulverston B 3
30 Ulvik C 3
26 Ulvila B 4
33 Ulvkälla A 5
21 Ulvöhamn B 7
4 Ulvsvåg B 4
66 Ulzburg B 2
108 Ulzio B 3
114 Umag B 1
113 Umbértide C 4
147 Umbriático C 2
13 Umbukta fjellstue A 6
117 Umčari B 4
15 Umeå E 4
13 Umfors B 7
98 Umhausen B 1
117 Umka B 4
65 Ummelm C 6
13 Umnäs B 8
26 Unaja B 4
48 Unapool C 3
10 Unari B 5
122 Uncastillo B 1
37 Undenås C 6
20 Undersåker B 2
33 Undersvik B 7
30 Undredal C 4
87 Úněšov B 5
98 Ungenach A 4
160 Ungeny B 5
88 Unhošt A 2
89 Uničev B 5
69 Unichowo A 5
79 Uniejów C 5
69 Uniescie A 4
69 Unislaw B 6
71 Unkel B 6
98 Unken B 3
71 Unna A 6
120 Unquera A 2
86 Unsernherrn C 3
32 Unset B 2
86 Unt.-Schwarzach D 1
26 Untamala, Turin Ja Porin Lääni, SF C 4
22 Untamala, Vaasan Lääni, SF B 4
85 Unter Reichenbach B 5
73 Unter-Schönmattenwag D 2
73 Unter-Steinbach D 4
98 Unterach B 4
97 Unterageri A 4
86 Unterbaar C 2
86 Unterhaching C 3
97 Unteriberg A 4
86 Unterkochen C 2
66 Unterlüß C 3
86 Untermünkheim B 1
85 Untermunstertal C 4
97 Unterschachen B 4
86 Unterschwaningen B 2
74 Untersiemau C 2
100 Unterweißenbach A 2
87 Unterzell B 4
62 Upavon B 2
50 Uphall B 4
88 Upice A 4
53 Upper Ballinderry B 5
60 Upper Chapel A 3
57 Upper Tean D 5
55 Upperchurch B 3
42 Upphärad A 2
59 Uppingham C 3
38 Upplands-Väsby C 4
38 Uppsala C 4
57 Upton, Cheshire, GB C 4
61 Upton, Dorset, GB C 4
57 Upton upon Severn D 4
85 Urach B 6
141 Uras C 2
77 Uraz B 5
113 Urbánia C 4
73 Urberach D 2
113 Urbino C 4
94 Urçay C 2
130 Urda B 3
121 Urdax A 5
118 Urdilde B 2
105 Urdos E 2
152 Ur'e Shtrenjte B 1
154 Urë Vajgurorë B 1
146 Urgento C 4
27 Urjala B 6
64 Urk B 3
101 Úrkut B 5
79 Urle C 4
55 Urlingford B 4
56 Urmston C 4
97 Urnäsch A 5
30 Urnes B 4
152 Uroševac B 3
117 Urovica B 6
137 Urracal B 4
122 Urries B 1
121 Urroz B 5
121 Urrugne A 5
87 Ursensollen B 3
43 Ursholt C 4
114 Uršna Sela B 3
73 Urspringen D 3
79 Ursus C 3
78 Urszulewo C 2
83 Ury C 4
160 Urziceni C 5
141 Urzulei B 3
129 Usagre C 4
117 Ušće C 4
90 Uście-Gorlickie C 4
68 Usedom B 1
71 Useldange C 4
141 Usellus C 2
78 Usiek B 1
141 Usini B 2
61 Usk B 4
34 Uskedal B 1
160 Usküdar E 6
72 Uslar B 3
65 Usquert A 4
141 Ussássai C 3
107 Ussat-les-Bains E 1
93 Ussé B 4
110 Usséglio B 2
106 Ussel B 2
72 Usseln B 2
93 Usson-du-Poitou C 4
106 Usson-en-F. B 3
107 Usson-les-Bains E 2
31 Ustaoset C 5
105 Ustaritz D 1
88 Úštěk A 2
97 Uster A 4
71 Usterath A 5
89 Ústi B 5
88 Ústí n. Labem A 2
89 Usti n. Orlici B 4
116 Ustibar C 3
116 Ustikolina C 2
116 Ustipraca C 3
69 Ustka A 4
90 Ustroń C 1
68 Ustronie Morskie A 3
121 Usurbil A 4
102 Uszód B 2
17 Utajärvi C 5
34 Utåker B 1
21 Utansjö C 6
34 Utbjoa B 1
122 Utebo C 2
87 Utery B 4
132 Utiel B 1
30 Utne C 3
64 Utrecht B 3
135 Utrera B 5
127 Utrillas B 5
34 Utstein kloster B 1
98 Uttendorf B 3
86 Uttenweiler C 1
45 Utterslev C 4
28 Utti C 4
86 Utting C 3
59 Uttoxeter C 2
34 Utvik, Rogaland Fylke, N B 1
30 Utvik, Sogn og Fjordane Fylke, N B 3
12 Utvorda C 2
29 Uukuniemi B 7
98 Uunterwössen B 3
23 Uurainen C 7
25 Uusi-Värtsilä C 7
22 Uusikaarlepyy B 4
26 Uusikaupunki C 4
28 Uusikylä C 4
88 Uvaly A 2
31 Uvdal C 5
117 Uzdin A 4
78 Uzdowo B 3
80 Uzel B 4
104 Uzerche B 4
109 Uzès C 1
160 Uzhgorod A 3
97 Uznach A 5
154 Uznovë B 1
160 Uzunköprü E 5

V

47 Vä B 5
23 Vaajakoski C 7
24 Vaajasalmi C 3
28 Vääksy B 3
17 Vaala C 5
11 Vaalajärvi B 6
66 Vaale B 2
29 Vaalimaa C 5
17 Vaaranniva B 7
23 Vaaraslahti B 8
22 Vaasa B 3
64 Vaassen B 3
23 Väätäiskylä C 6
10 Vaattojärvi B 4
107 Vabre D 2
91 Vác E 2
74 Vacha C 2
91 Váchartyán E 2
43 Väckelsång C 4
38 Vad B 2
112 Vada C 2
38 Väddö C 5
39 Väderstad D 1
30 Vadheim B 2
125 Vadillo de la Sierra C 4
127 Vadillos B 3
34 Vadla B 2
112 Vado B 3
110 Vado Ligure C 3
39 Vadsbro D 3
9 Vadsø B 9
39 Vadstena D 1
103 Vadu Crişului B 6
40 Vadum B 3
97 Vaduz A 5
45 Væggerløse C 4
156 Vafiokhóri A 2
35 Vafos C 5
101 Vág B 5
5 Vågaholmen D 2
155 Vagalat C 2
31 Vågåmo B 6
5 Vågan C 3
42 Vaggeryd B 4
112 Váglia C 3
145 Váglio Basilicata C 4
84 Vagney B 3
39 Vagnhärad D 4
18 Vågos,N B 4
124 Vagos,P C 1
18 Vågstranda C 3
26 Vahto C 5
112 Vaiano C 3
81 Vaiges B 6
85 Vaihingen B 5
95 Vaillant B 5
83 Vailly B 5
94 Vailly-sur-Sauldre B 2
29 Vainikkala C 6
144 Vairano Scalo B 3
109 Vaison-la-Romaine C 2
95 Vaite B 5
21 Väja C 6
36 Väjern C 3
102 Vajszló C 2
13 Våjtjajaure kapell B 7
160 Vakarel D 3
30 Vaksdal C 2
153 Vaksevo B 4
118 Val B 2
119 Val de S. Lorenzo B 4
128 Val de Santarém B 2
126 Val de Sto. Domingo B 1
109 Val d'Esquières D 3
108 Val-d'Isère B 3
95 Val Suzon B 4
128 Valada B 2
20 Vålådalen B 1
124 Valadares B 1
128 Valado B 1
117 Valakonje C 5
104 Valance B 3
153 Valandovo C 4
156 Valanídha C 2
31 Vålåsjø A 6
91 Valaska D 2
89 Valaská Belá C 6
91 Valaská Dubová C 2
89 Valašská-Polanka B 5
89 Valašské Klobouky B 6
89 Valašské Meziříčí B 5
4 Valberg,N B 2
37 Vålberg,S B 5
38 Valbo B 4
124 Valbom B 1
97 Valbondione B 6
108 Valbonnais C 2
126 Valbuena de Duero A 1
91 Valča C 1
103 Válcani C 4
121 Valcarlos A 5
99 Valdagno D 2
32 Valdalen A 3
126 Valdaracete B 2
122 Valdealgorfa D 2
130 Valdecaballeros B 1
127 Valdecabras B 3
125 Valdecarros C 4
126 Valdeconcha B 3
135 Valdeflores B 4
119 Valdefresno B 5
132 Valdeganga B 1
125 Valdelacasa C 4
130 Valdelacasa de Tajo B 1
135 Valdelarco B 4
125 Valdelosa B 4
122 Valdeltormo D 3
130 Valdemanco de Esteras C 2
43 Valdemarsvik A 6
126 Valdemorillo B 1
126 Valdemoro B 2
127 Valdemoro-Sierra B 4
129 Valdeobispo A 4
127 Valdeolivas B 3
131 Valdepeñas C 3
136 Valdepeñas de Jaén B 3
119 Valdepiélago B 5
120 Valdepolo B 1
119 Valderas B 5
148 Valdérice A 2
122 Valderrobres D 3
120 Valderrueda B 2
126 Valdestillas A 1
119 Valdeteja B 5
126 Valdetorres de Jarama B 2
130 Valdeverdeja B 1
119 Valdevimbre B 5
110 Valdieri C 2
126 Valdilecha B 2
99 Valdobbiádene D 3
126 Valdocondes A 2
118 Valdoviño A 2
134 Vale de Açol B 3
128 Vale de Açor B 3
134 Vale de Agua B 2
124 Vale de Cambra C 1
128 Vale de Prazeres A 3
128 Vale de Reis C 2
134 Vale de Rosa B 3
134 Vale de Vargo B 3
128 Vale do Peso B 3
117 Valea Bistrei A 6
117 Valea Boului A 6
103 Valea lui Mihai A 6
124 Valega C 1
99 Valéggio sul Mincio D 1
128 Valeiro C 2
124 Valença do Minho A 1
93 Valençay B 5
108 Valence, Drôme, F C 1
105 Valence, Tarn-et-Garonne, F C 3
107 Valence-d'Albigeois C 2
105 Valence-sur-Baise D 3
132 Valencia B 2
129 Valencia de Alcántara B 3
119 Valencia de Don Juan B 5
129 Valencia de las Torres C 4
129 Valencia de Mombuey C 3
129 Valencia del Ventoso C 4
70 Valenciennes B 2

119 Villamayor de Campos C 5
126 Villamayor de Santiago C 3
119 Villamejil B 4
129 Villamesias B 5
126 Villaminaya C 2
120 Villamóndar B 3
125 Villamor de los Escuderos B 4
120 Villamoronta B 2
126 Villamuelas C 2
120 Villamuriel de Cerrato C 2
105 Villandraut C 2
146 Villanova B 3
145 Villanova d. Battista B 4
110 Villanova d'Asti C 2
110 Villanova Mondovi C 2
141 Villanova Monteleone B 2
120 Villante B 3
111 Villantério B 4
126 Villanubla A 1
126 Villanueva de Alcardete C 2
127 Villanueva de Alcorón B 3
136 Villanueva de Algaidas B 2
120 Villanueva de Argano B 3
118 Villanueva de Arosa B 2
126 Villanueva de Bogas C 2
133 Villanueva de Castellón B 2
136 Villanueva de Cauche C 2
136 Villanueva de Córdoba A 2
122 Villanueva de Gállego C 2
136 Villanueva de la Concepción C 2
131 Villanueva de la Fuente C 4
131 Villanueva de la Jara B 5
136 Villanueva de la Reina A 3
129 Villanueva de la Serena C 5
129 Villanueva de la Sierra A 4
130 Villanueva de la Vera A 1
119 Villanueva de las Peras C 5
137 Villanueva de las Torres B 3
134 Villanueva de los Castillejos B 3
131 Villanueva de los Infantes C 3
136 Villanueva de Mesia B 3
119 Villanueva de Oscos A 4
130 Villanueva de San Carlos C 3
135 Villanueva de San Juan B 5
136 Villanueva de Tapia B 2
125 Villanueva del Aceral B 5
137 Villanueva del Arzobispo A 4
119 Villanueva del Campo C 5
130 Villanueva del Duque C 1
129 Villanueva del Fresno C 3
127 Villanueva del Huerva A 4
135 Villanueva del Rey A 5
135 Villanueva del Rio B 5
136 Villanueva del Rosario C 2
136 Villanueva del Trabuco B 2
123 Villanueva y Geltru C 4
102 Villány C 2
118 Villaodrid A 3
119 Villaornate B 5
118 Villapedre A 3
141 Villaputzu C 3
119 Villaquejida B 5
119 Villaquilambre B 5
108 Villar d'Arène B 3
118 Villar de Barrio B 3
127 Villar de Cañas C 3
132 Villar de Canes A 2
133 Villar de Chinchilla C 1
124 Villar de Ciervo C 3
127 Villar de Domingo Garcia B 3
127 Villar de los Navarros A 4
129 Villar de Rena B 5
118 Villar de Santos B 3
132 Villar del Arzobispo B 2
125 Villar del Buey B 3
132 Villar del Cobo A 1
127 Villar del Humo C 4
130 Villar del Pedroso B 1
129 Villar del Rey B 4
121 Villar del Rio B 4
127 Villar del Saz B 3
110 Villar Perosa C 2
130 Villaralto C 2
120 Villarcayo B 3
108 Villard-Bonnot B 2
108 Villard-de-Lans B 2
108 Villard-sur-D. B 3
119 Villardeciervos C 4
119 Villardefrades C 5
118 Villardevós C 3
132 Villareal B 2
129 Villareal de S. Carlos B 4
126 Villarejo A 2
127 Villarejo de Fuentes C 3
119 Villarejo de Orbigo B 5
126 Villarejo de Salvanés B 2
127 Villares del Saz C 3
110 Villaretto B 2
132 Villargordo del Cabriel B 1
125 Villarino B 3
118 Villarino de Conso B 3
132 Villarluengo A 2
120 Villarobe B 3
149 Villarosa B 4
120 Villarramiel B 2
135 Villarrasa B 4
121 Villarreal de Alava B 4
119 Villarrin de Campos C 5
131 Villarrobledo B 4
132 Villarroya de los Pinares A 2
131 Villarrubia de los Ojos B 3
126 Villarrubia de Santiago C 2
126 Villarrubio C 3
108 Villars-les-Dombes B 2
132 Villarta B 1
130 Villarta de los Montes B 2
131 Villarta de San Juan B 3
120 Villasandino B 2
120 Villasante A 3
120 Villasarracino B 2
127 Villasayas A 3
125 Villasdardo B 3
119 Villaseca B 4
126 Villaseca de Henares B 3
126 Villaseca de la Sagra C 2
125 Villaseco B 3
125 Villaseco de los Reyes B 3
126 Villasequilla de Yepes C 2
141 Villasimíus C 3
149 Villasmundo B 5
141 Villasor C 2
110 Villastellone C 2
126 Villatobas C 2
125 Villatoro C 4
119 Villaturiel B 5
141 Villaurbana C 2
121 Villava B 5
132 Villavaliente B 1
121 Villavelayo B 4
137 Villaverde de Guadalimar A 4
135 Villaverde del Rio B 5
119 Villaviciosa A 5
135 Villaviciosa de Córdoba A 5
126 Villaviciosa de Odón B 2
132 Villavieja, Castellon, E B 2
119 Villavieja, Orense, E B 3
125 Villavieja de Yeltes C 3
119 Villayón A 4
108 Villaz B 3
85 Villé B 4
84 Ville-sous-la-Ferté B 1
84 Ville-sur-Illon B 3
84 Ville-sur-Tourbe A 1
104 Villebois-Lavalette B 3
106 Villecomtal C 2
81 Villedieu-les-Poëles B 5
93 Villedieu-sur-Indre C 5
104 Villefagnan A 3
107 Villefort C 3
94 Villefranche, Allier, F C 2
109 Villefranche, Alpes Maritime, F D 4
108 Villefranche, Rhône, F B 1
94 Villefranche, Yonne, F B 3
107 Villefranche-d'Albigeois D 2
107 Villefranche-de-Lauragais D 1
104 Villefranche-de-Lonchat C 3
107 Villefranche-de-Panat C 2
107 Villefranche-de-Rouergue C 2
104 Villefranche-du-Périgord C 4
93 Villefranche-sur-Cher B 5
94 Villegenon B 2
104 Villegrains C 2
83 Villejuif C 4
132 Villel A 1
83 Villemaur-sur-Vanne C 5
105 Villemur D 4
133 Villena C 2
83 Villenauxe C 5
104 Villenave-d'Ornon C 2
96 Villeneuve, CH B 2
109 Villeneuve, Alpes Maritime, F D 4
107 Villeneuve, Aude, F E 2
106 Villeneuve, Haute-Loire, F B 3
105 Villeneuve, Haute Garonne, F D 3
83 Villeneuve, Seine-et-Marne, F B 4
110 Villeneuve, I B 2
106 Villeneuve-d'Aveyron C 2
108 Villeneuve-de-Berg C 1
105 Villeneuve-de-Marsan D 2
83 Villeneuve-la Guyard C 5
83 Villeneuve-l'Archevêque C 5
83 Villeneuve-le-Comte C 4
109 Villeneuve-les-Avignon D 1
83 Villeneuve St. Georges C 4
94 Villeneuve-sur-Allier C 3
105 Villeneuve-sur-Lot C 3
83 Villeneuve-sur-Yonne C 5
83 Villeparisis C 4
104 Villeréal C 3
120 Villerias C 2
93 Villeromain B 5
81 Villers-Bocage, Calvados, F A 6
83 Villers Bocage, Somme, F B 4
83 Villers-Bretonneux B 4
83 Villers Carbonnel B 4
83 Villers Cotterets B 5
95 Villers-Farlay C 5
70 Villers-le-Gambon B 3
82 Villers-sur-Mer B 2
95 Villersexel B 6
84 Villerupt A 2
82 Villerville B 2
83 Villeseneux C 6
105 Villeséque C 4
93 Villetrun B 5
143 Villetta Barrea C 4
107 Villeveyrac D 3
108 Villevocance B 1
159 Villia A 4
83 Villiers C 5
94 Villiers-St. Benoît B 3
83 Villiers-St. Georges C 5
85 Villingen B 5
73 Villmar C 2
120 Villoldo B 2
125 Villoría C 4
99 Villotta D 3
27 Vilppula A 7
40 Vils C 2
87 Vilsbiburg C 4
87 Vilshofen C 5
43 Vilshult C 4
151 Vilusi C 4
125 Vilvestre B 3
70 Vilvoorde B 3
128 Vimeiro B 1
111 Vimercate B 4
118 Vimianzo A 1
128 Vimieiro C 3
125 Vimioso B 3
43 Vimmerby B 5
82 Vimoutiers C 2
23 Vimpeli B 5
87 Vimperk B 5
63 Vimy B 4
97 Vinadi B 6
110 Vinadio C 2
122 Vinaixa C 3
132 Vinaroz A 3
33 Vinäs C 5
108 Vinay B 2
42 Vinberg C 2
123 Vinca, F B 5
117 Vinča, YU B 4
144 Vinchiaturo B 3
112 Vinci C 2
44 Vindeby B 3
15 Vindelgransele C 2
15 Vindeln D 3
44 Vinderup A 1
34 Vindsvik B 2
83 Vinets C 6
103 Vinga B 5
39 Vingåker C 2
19 Vingelen C 6
31 Vingnes B 7
107 Vingrau E 2
124 Vinhais B 3
115 Vinica, Hrvatska, YU A 4
153 Vinica, Makedonija, YU C 4
153 Viničani C 3
152 Vinicka B 1
121 Viniegra de Arriba B 4
30 Vinje, Hordaland Fylke, N C 3
34 Vinje, Telemark Fylke, N B 3
18 Vinjeøra B 4
26 Vinkkilä C 4
116 Vinkovci A 2
15 Vinliden D 1
37 Vinninga C 5
109 Vinon D 2
47 Vinslöv A 4
18 Vinsternes B 4
31 Vinstra B 6
38 Vintjärn B 3
98 Vintl C 2
39 Vintrosa C 1
130 Viñuela, Ciudad Real, E C 2
136 Viñuela, Málaga, E C 2
125 Viñuela de Sayago B 4
126 Viñuelas B 2
121 Vinuesa C 4
67 Vinzelberg C 4
66 Viöl A 2
110 Viola C 2
108 Violay B 1
98 Vipiteno C 2
150 Vir, Bosna i Hercegovina, YU B 3
114 Vir, Hrvatska, YU C 3
97 Vira B 4
103 Virciorog B 6
81 Vire B 6
43 Vireda B 4
70 Vireux B 3
103 Virfurile B 6
98 Virgen B 3
136 Virgen de la Cabeza A 2
53 Virginia C 4
95 Viriat C 5
108 Virieu-le-Grd. B 2
115 Virje A 5
27 Virkby C 6
27 Virkkala C 6
44 Virklund A 2
29 Virmutjoki B 6
29 Virojoki C 5
29 Virolahti C 5
115 Virovitica B 5
151 Virpazar C 5
23 Virrat C 5
38 Virsbo bruk C 3
9 Virtaniemi D 8
24 Virtasalmi C 4
71 Virton C 4
96 Viry B 2
150 Vis B 2
103 Visag C 5
109 Visan C 1
154 Vísani C 2
65 Visbek B 6
44 Visby,DK B 1
39 Visby,S C 5
103 Visca B 6
71 Visé B 4
116 Višegrad C 3
43 Viserum B 5
124 Viseu C 2
160 Viseu de Sus B 4
127 Visiedo B 4
42 Viskafors B 2
43 Vislanda C 4
34 Visnes B 1
114 Višnja Gora B 2
88 Višňové C 4
37 Visnum B 6
90 Višný Mirošov C 4
151 Visoko B 4
110 Visone C 3
96 Visp B 3
43 Vissefjärda C 5
66 Visselhövede C 2
44 Vissenbjerg B 3
154 Vissiniá B 3
143 Visso B 4
132 Vistabella del Maestrazgo A 2
18 Vistdal C 3
14 Vistheden C 4
23 Visuvesi C 5
148 Vita B 2
117 Vitanovac C 4
142 Viterbo B 3
154 Vithkuq B 2
125 Vitigudino B 3
158 Vitina, GR B 3
150 Vitina, Bosna i Hercegovina, YU B 3
153 Vitina, Kosovo, YU B 3
88 Vitis C 3
89 Vítkov B 5
117 Vitkovac C 4
154 Vitolište A 3
88 Vitonice C 4
121 Vitoria B 4
81 Vitré B 5
95 Vitrey B 5
109 Vitrolles D 2
152 Vitromirica B 2
63 Vitry-en-Artois B 5
84 Vitry-le-François B 1
37 Vitsand A 4
7 Vittangi D 7
42 Vittaryd C 3
95 Vitteaux B 4
84 Vittel B 2
38 Vittinge C 4
14 Vittjärv C 5
149 Vittória C 4
99 Vittório Veneto D 3
47 Vittsjö A 4
47 Vittskövle B 5
16 Vitvattnet A 2
110 Viù B 2
44 Viuf B 2
35 Viul A 6
25 Viuruniemi C 5
140 Vivano B 2
127 Vivel del Río Martín B 5
30 Viveli C 4
132 Viver B 2
118 Vivero A 3
106 Viverols B 3
131 Viveros C 4
109 Viviers C 1
70 Viviers-au-Court C 3
106 Viviez C 2
93 Vivonne C 4
21 Vivsta C 6
93 Vivy B 3
108 Vizille B 2
89 Vizovice B 5
140 Vizzavona B 2
149 Vizzini B 4
64 Vlaardingen C 2
89 Vlachovice B 5
91 Vlachovo D 3
88 Vláchovo Březi B 1
153 Vladičin Han B 4
116 Vladimirci B 3
88 Vladislav B 3
65 Vlagtwedde A 5
117 Vlajkovac A 5
158 Vlakháta A 1
158 Vlakhérna B 3
159 Vlakhióti C 3
158 Vlakhokerasia B 3
158 Vlakhópoulon B 2
156 Vlakhoyiánni C 2
63 Vlamertinge B 4
116 Vlasenica B 2
88 Vlašim B 2
153 Vlasina B 4
153 Vlasotince B 4
154 Vlásti B 3
65 Vledder B 4
64 Vlijmen C 3
64 Vlissingen C 1
157 Vlokhós C 2
154 Vlorë B 1
72 Vlotho A 2
111 Vobarno B 5
108 Vocance B 1
115 Voćin B 5
98 Vöcklabruck A 4
98 Vöcklamarkt A 4
117 Vodanj B 4
101 Voderady A 5
150 Vodice B 1
88 Vodňany B 2
114 Vodnjan C 1
40 Vodskov B 4
49 Voe A 7
71 Voerde A 5

154 Vogatsikón B 3
110 Voghera C 4
96 Vogogna B 4
116 Vogošća C 2
106 Vogué C 4
86 Vohburg C 3
87 Vohenstrauß B 4
85 Vöhrenbach B 5
86 Vöhringen C 2
84 Void B 2
28 Voikkaa C 4
28 Voikoski B 4
108 Voiren B 2
82 Voise C 3
95 Voisey B 5
117 Voiteg A 5
95 Voiteur C 5
100 Voitsberg B 3
103 Voivozi A 6
44 Vojens B 2
116 Vojka B 4
117 Vojlovica B 4
115 Vojnic B 3
101 Vojnice B 6
114 Vojnik A 3
103 Vojvoda Stepa C 4
113 Volano B 4
99 Volargne D 1
88 Volary C 1
156 Volax A 3
30 Volda A 3
64 Volendam B 3
158 Volímais B 1
73 Volkach D 4
100 Völkermarkt C 2
84 Völklingen A 3
72 Volkmarode A 4
72 Volkmarsen B 3
18 Voll C 3
106 Vollore-Montagne B 3
108 Vollouise C 3
47 Vollsjö B 4
65 Volmerdingsen B 6
157 Vólos C 2
110 Volpiano B 2
111 Volta B 5
110 Voltággio C 3
112 Volterra C 2
110 Voltri C 3
22 Voltti B 4
145 Volturara Appula B 4
144 Volturara Irpina C 3
109 Volx D 2
106 Volyio B 3
88 Volyné B 1
155 Vónítsa D 2
101 Vönöck B 5
44 Vonsild B 2
64 Voorburg B 2
64 Voorschoten B 2
64 Voorthuizen B 3
22 Vörå B 4
100 Vorau B 3
44 Vorbasse B 2
100 Vorchdorf A 1
100 Vordemberg B 2
65 Vorden B 4
100 Vorderweißenbach A 2
45 Vordingborg B 4
152 Vorë C 1
108 Voreppe B 2
106 Vorey B 3
44 Vorgod A 1
36 Vormsund A 3
86 Vorra B 3
40 Vorså B 4
66 Vorsfelde C 3
71 Vorst A 5
40 Vorupør C 2
154 Voskopojë B 2
30 Voss C 3
70 Vosselaar A 3
88 Votice B 2
120 Voto A 3
83 Voué C 6
93 Vouillé C 4
84 Voujeaucourt C 3
159 Voúla B 4
159 Vouliagméni B 4
155 Voúlista Panayiá C 2
83 Voulx C 4
158 Voúnargon B 2
157 Vounikhóra D 2
108 Vourey B 2
94 Voussac C 3
158 Voutiánoi B 3
93 Vouvray B 4
96 Vouvry B 2
124 Vouzela C 1
157 Voúzi C 2
84 Vouziers A 1
82 Voves C 3
33 Voxna B 6
49 Voy B 5
17 Voynitsa B 9
22 Vöyri B 4
40 Vrå B 3
101 Vráble A 6
117 Vračev Gaj B 5
89 Vracov C 5
35 Vrådal B 4
158 Vrakhnéika A 2
34 Vraliosen B 4
115 Vranduk C 5
42 Vrångo B 1
117 Vranić B 4
116 Vranići C 2
153 Vranje B 3
153 Vranjska Banja B 3
88 Vranov, Jihomoravský, CS C 3
91 Vranov, Vychodoslovenský, CS D 4
89 Vranovice C 4
114 Vransko A 2
151 Vrapčići B 3
152 Vrapčište C 2
156 Vrasná B 3
156 Vrastá B 3
117 Vratarnica C 6
89 Vratimov B 6
88 Vratislavice A 3
152 Vratnica B 3
115 Vratno A 4
160 Vratsa D 3
117 Vražogrnac C 6
116 Vrbanja B 2
102 Vrbas C 3
115 Vrbaška B 5
152 Vrbica B 2
115 Vrbljani C 4
150 Vrbnik, Hrvatska, YU A 2
114 Vrbnik, Krk, YU B 2
89 Vrbno p. Pradedern A 5
91 Vrbov C 3
89 Vrbovcé C 5
101 Vrbove A 5
115 Vrbovec B 4
114 Vrbovsko B 3
88 Vrchlabí A 3
117 Vrčin B 4
88 Vrdy B 3
65 Vreden B 4
40 Vrejlev B 4
39 Vrena D 3
117 Vreoci B 4
37 Vretstorp B 6
115 Vrgin Most B 3
150 Vrgorac B 3
114 Vrhnika B 2
115 Vrhpolje, Bosna i Hercegovina, YU C 4
116 Vrhpolje, Srbija, YU B 3
65 Vriezenveen B 4
70 Vrigne-aux-Bois C 3
43 Vrigstad B 4
150 Vrlika B 2
117 Vrmbaje C 4
117 Vrnjačka Banja C 4
114 Vrnovine C 3
63 Vron B 3
159 Vrondamás C 3
156 Vrondoú B 2
65 Vroomshoop B 4
75 Vroutek C 5
116 Vrpolje A 2
152 Vrrië C 2
117 Vršac A 5
115 Vrtoče C 4
115 Vručica C 5
91 Vrútky C 1
152 Vrutok C 2
87 Všeruby B 4
88 Všestary A 3
88 Všetaty A 2
89 Vsetín B 5
152 Vuča B 2
152 Vučitrn B 2
153 Vucje B 3
117 Vučkovica C 4
64 Vught C 3
95 Vuillafans B 6
153 Vukan B 4
116 Vukovar A 3
19 Vuku B 7
5 Vuoggatjålme D 5
28 Vuohijärvi B 4
11 Vuojärvi B 6
25 Vuokatti A 5
25 Vuokko B 6
29 Vuoksenniska B 6
28 Vuolenkoski B 4
17 Vuolijoki C 6
14 Vuollerim B 4
25 Vuonislahti B 6
29 Vuoriniemi B 7
11 Vuotso A 7
14 Vuottas B 5
153 Vŭrba B 4
153 Vŭrshets A 5
95 Vy-lès-Lure B 6
29 Vyborg C 6
88 Vyčapy B 3
91 Východná C 2
101 Vydrany A 5
91 Vyhne D 1
89 Vyškov B 5
91 Vyšná Radvaň C 4
91 Vyšné-Raslavice C 4
89 Vysoká B 6
88 Vysoké Mýto B 4
88 Vyšši Brod C 2

W

66 Waabs A 2
98 Waakirchen B 2
64 Waalwijk C 3
70 Waarschoot A 2
72 Wabern B 3
78 Wabrzezno B 1
78 Wach B 4
70 Wachtebeke A 2
73 Wächtersbach C 3
87 Wackersdorf B 4
62 Waddesdon B 3
59 Waddington B 3
64 Waddinxveen B 2
60 Wadebridge C 2
75 Wadelsdorf B 6
97 Wädenswil A 4
71 Wadern C 5
62 Wadhurst B 4
79 Wadlew D 2
90 Wadowice C 2
57 Waenfawr C 2
66 Wagenfeld-Haßlingen C 1
64 Wageningen C 3
87 Waging D 4
98 Wagrain B 4
69 Wagrowiec C 5
71 Wahlscheid B 6
75 Wahlsdorf B 5
66 Wahlstedt B 3
66 Wahrenholz C 3
85 Waiblingen B 6
99 Waidbruck C 2
87 Waidhaus B 4
88 Waidhofen a. d. Thaya C 3
100 Waidhofen a. d. Ybbs B 2
71 Waimes B 5
59 Wainfleet All Saints B 4
86 Waischenfeld B 3
100 Waisenburg C 2
98 Waizenkirchen A 4
58 Wakefiedl B 2
71 Walbeck A 5
77 Walbrzych C 5
98 Walchen B 2
98 Walchensee B 2
98 Walchsee B 3
65 Walchum B 5
69 Walcz B 4
97 Wald A 4
73 Wald-Michelbach D 2
73 Waldaschaff D 3
71 Waldböckelheim C 6
71 Waldbröl B 6
72 Waldeck B 3
101 Waldegg B 4
85 Waldenbuch B 6
75 Waldenburg, D* C 4
77 Waldenburg, PL C 5
85 Waldfischbach A 4
100 Waldhausen i. Strudengau A 2
75 Waldheim B 5
72 Waldkappel B 3
85 Waldkirch B 4
87 Waldkirchen C 5
100 Waldkirchen a. Wesen A 1
87 Waldkraiburg C 4
71 Waldmohr C 6
85 Waldmössingen B 5
87 Waldmünchen B 4
71 Waldrach C 5
98 Waldring B 3
87 Waldsassen A 4
85 Waldshut C 5
97 Waldstatt A 5
87 Waldthurn B 4
84 Waldwisse A 3
97 Walenstadt A 5
77 Walichnowy B 7
83 Walincourt A 5
72 Walkenried B 4
62 Walkern B 3
56 Wallasey C 3
73 Wallau C 2
73 Walldürn D 3
74 Wallenfells C 3
101 Wallern i. Burgenland B 4
70 Wallers B 2
87 Wallersdorf C 4
86 Wallerstein C 2
74 Wallhausen B 3
62 Wallingford B 2
97 Wallisellen A 4
67 Wallitz B 5
49 Walls A 7
44 Wallsbüll C 2
57 Walsall D 4
74 Walschleben B 2
70 Walshoutem B 4
66 Walstrode C 2
71 Walsum A 5
97 Waltenhofen A 6
74 Waltershausen C 2
58 Waltham B 3
62 Waltham Forest B 3
59 Waltham on the Wolds C 3
62 Walton B 3
56 Walton le Dale C 4
62 Walton-on-the-Naze B 5
71 Waltrop A 6
126 Wamba A 1
72 Wanfried B 4
66 Wangels A 3
97 Wangen A 5
65 Wangerooge A 5
66 Wangersen B 2
97 Wangi A 4
71 Wanne-Eickel A 6
59 Wansford C 3
62 Wantage B 2
74 Wanzleben A 3
68 Wapnica B 3
69 Wapno C 5
59 Warboys C 3
72 Warburg B 3
55 Ward A 5
65 Wardenburg A 6
62 Ware B 3
70 Waregem B 2
61 Wareham C 4
70 Waremme B 4
67 Waren B 5
65 Warendorf C 5
51 Warenford B 6
65 Warffum A 4
64 Warga A 3
67 Warin B 4
51 Wark B 5
79 Warka D 4
51 Warkworth B 6
57 Warley D 4
62 Warlingham B 3
78 Warlubie B 1
83 Warmeriville B 6
61 Warminster B 4
73 Warneck D 4
67 Warnemünde A 5
65 Warnsveld B 4
53 Warrenpoint B 5
57 Warrington C 4
65 Warsingsfehn A 5
58 Warsop B 2
67 Warsow B 4
66 Warstade B 2
72 Warstein B 2
79 Warszawa C 3
79 Warta D 1
100 Wartberg i. Mürztal B 3
97 Warth A 6
59 Warwick C 2
74 Warza C 2
49 Wasbister B 5
70 Wasmes B 2
78 Wasosz, Bialystok, PL B 5
77 Wasosz, Wroclaw, PL B 5
85 Wasselonne B 4
97 Wassen B 4
64 Wassenaar B 2
86 Wasseralfingen C 2
97 Wasserauen A 5
71 Wasserbillig C 5
87 Wasserburg C 4
86 Wassertrüdingen B 2
84 Wassy B 1
74 Wasungen C 2
60 Watchet B 3
72 Watenstedt A 4
59 Waterbeach C 4
55 Waterford B 4
54 Watergrasshill B 3
49 Wateringhouse C 5
70 Waterloo B 3
54 Waterville C 1
62 Watford B 3
66 Wathlingen C 3
59 Watlington C 4
63 Watten, F B 4
49 Watten, GB C 5
98 Wattens B 2
59 Watton C 4
97 Wattwil A 5
71 Waubach B 5
70 Wavre B 3
79 Wawolnica D 5
59 Waxham C 5
56 Wearhead B 4
57 Weaverham C 4
90 Wechadłów B 3
66 Wedel B 2
61 Wedmore B 4
70 Weelde A 3
72 Weende B 3
65 Weener A 5
71 Weert A 4
64 Weesp B 3
71 Weeze A 5
74 Weferlingen A 3
71 Wegberg A 5
74 Wegeleben B 3
97 Weggis A 4
77 Wegierki A 6
76 Wegliniec B 4
78 Wegorzewo A 4
68 Wegorzyno B 3
69 Wegrów C 5
87 Wegscheid C 5
66 Wehdel B 1
85 Wehr C 4
73 Weibersbrunn D 3
86 Weichering C 3
74 Weida C 4
87 Weiden B 4
73 Weidenau C 2
75 Weidenhain B 4
86 Weidenstetten C 1
71 Weierbach C 6
101 Weigelsdorf B 4
73 Weikersheim D 3
86 Weil C 2
85 Weil d. Stadt B 5
73 Weilburg C 2
71 Weilerswist B 5
86 Weilheim, Baden-Württemberg, D† C 1
98 Weilheim, Bayern, D† B 2
72 Weimar, D† B 3
74 Weimar, D* C 3
86 Weinberg B 2
97 Weinfelden A 5
86 Weingarten, Baden-Württemberg, D† D 1
85 Weingarten, Baden-Württemberg, D† A 5
73 Weinheim D 2
73 Weisbaden C 2
74 Weischlitz C 4
86 Weisendorf B 2
86 Weisensteig C 1
86 Weismain A 3
99 Weißbriach C 4
100 Weißenbach, Nieder Österreich, A B 4
97 Weißenbach, Tirol, A A 6
100 Weißenbach a. d. Enns B 2
75 Weißenberg B 6
74 Weißenbrunn C 3
86 Weißenburg B 2
74 Weissenfels B 3
86 Weißenhorn C 2
100 Weißenkirchen i. d. Wachau A 3
74 Weißensee B 3
100 Weißkirchen i. Steiermark B 2
97 Weisstannen B 5
75 Weißwasser B 6
67 Weitendorf B 5
73 Weiterode C 3
88 Weitersfeld C 3
100 Weitersfelden A 2
97 Weitnau A 6
88 Weitra C 2
100 Weiz B 3
69 Wejherowo A 6

We-Wr

51 Weldon Bridge B 6
71 Welkenraedt B 4
75 Wellaune B 4
86 Wellheim C 3
70 Wellin B 4
59 Wellingborough C 3
57 Wellington, Shropshire, GB D 4
61 Wellington, Somerset, GB C 3
55 Wellingtonbridge B 5
73 Wellmünster C 2
61 Wells B 4
59 Wells next the Sea C 4
65 Welplage B 6
100 Wels A 2
98 Welsberg C 3
96 Welschenrohr A 3
99 Welschnofen C 2
57 Welshpool D 3
74 Welsleben A 3
100 Weltensfeld C 2
71 Welver A 6
62 Welwyn B 3
62 Welwyn Garden City B 3
86 Welzheim C 1
75 Welzow B 6
57 Wem D 4
86 Wemding C 2
50 Wemyss Bay B 3
72 Wenden, Niedersachsen, D† A 4
71 Wenden, Nordrhein Westfalen, D† B 6
75 Wendisch-Rietz A 5
86 Wendlingen C 1
62 Wendover B 3
69 Wenecja C 5
98 Weng, Ober Österreich, A A 4
100 Weng, Steiermark, A B 2
100 Wenigzell B 3
72 Wennigsen A 3
98 Wenns B 1
60 Wenvoe B 3
70 Wépion B 3
75 Werben, Cottbus, D* B 6
67 Werben, Magdeburg, D* C 4
75 Werbig B 5
70 Werchter B 3
75 Werdau C 4
67 Werder C 5
71 Werdohl A 6
98 Werfen B 4
64 Werkendam C 2
71 Werl A 6
65 Werlte B 5
71 Wermelskirchen A 6
75 Wermsdorf B 4
87 Wernberg B 4
71 Werne A 6
67 Werneuchen C 6
74 Wernigerode B 2
87 Wernstein,A C 5
87 Wernstein,D† C 5
97 Wertach A 6
73 Wertheim D 3
86 Wertingen C 2
70 Wervik B 2
61 Wesbury B 4
65 Weseke C 4
71 Wesel A 5
67 Wesenberg B 5
66 Wesendorf C 3
79 Wesola C 4
66 Wesselburen A 1
71 Wesseling B 5
86 Wessobrunn D 3
51 West Auckland C 6
59 West Bridgford C 2
57 West Bromwich D 4
50 West Calder B 4
59 West Haddon C 2
50 West Kilbride B 3
57 West Kirby C 3
51 West Linton B 4
61 West Lulworth C 4
62 West Meon B 2
62 West Mersea B 4
64 West Terschelling A 3
62 West Wittering C 3
65 Westbevern B 5
61 Westbury on Severn B 4
98 Westendorf B 3
65 Westerbork B 4
71 Westerburg B 6
65 Westerhaar B 4
62 Westerham B 4
65 Westerholt A 5
65 Westerkappeln B 5
44 Westerland C 1
70 Westerlo A 3
65 Westerstede A 5
86 Westheim, Baden-Württemberg, D† B 1
72 Westheim, Nordrhein Westfalen, D† B 2
86 Westhelm B 2
73 Westhofen D 2
70 Westkapelle A 2
65 Westkirchen C 6
59 Weston C 3
61 Weston-super-Mare B 4
57 Weston upon Trent D 4
50 Westport,GB B 2
52 Westport,IRL C 2
65 Westrhauderfehn A 5
51 Westruther B 5
60 Westward Ho! B 2
56 Wetheral B 4
58 Wetherby B 2
73 Wetter, Hessen, D† C 2
71 Wetter, Nordrhein, D† A 6
70 Wetteren A 2
74 Wettin B 3
96 Wettingen A 4
65 Wettringen B 5
97 Wetzikon A 4
73 Wetzlar C 2
70 Wevegem B 2
72 Wewer B 2
55 Wexford B 5
100 Weyer B 2
71 Weyerbusch B 6
85 Weyersheim B 4
61 Weymouth C 4
98 Weyregg B 4
70 Wezemaal B 3
64 Wezep B 4
76 Wezyska A 3
57 Whaley Bridge C 5
56 Whalley C 4
51 Whalton B 6
50 Whauphill C 3
51 Wheatley Hill C 6
60 Wheddon Cross B 3
60 Whiddon Down C 3
50 Whitburn B 4
58 Whitby A 3
62 Whitchurch, Bucks., GB B 3
62 Whitchurch, Hants., GB B 2
61 Whitchurch, Hereford, GB B 4
57 Whitchurch, Shropshire, GB D 4
48 Whitebridge D 4
54 Whitegate B 3
49 Whitehall,GB B 6
55 Whitehall,IRL B 4
56 Whitehaven B 3
53 Whitehead B 6
51 Whitekirk A 5
50 Whithorn C 3
60 Whitland B 2
51 Whitley Bay B 6
62 Whitstable B 5
57 Whittington D 4
59 Whittlesey C 3
58 Whitwell B 2
77 Wiazów C 6
79 Wiazowna C 4
49 Wick C 5
71 Wickede A 6
62 Wickford B 4
62 Wickham C 2
59 Wickham Market C 5
55 Wicklow B 5
69 Wicko A 5
71 Wickrath A 5
79 Widawa D 1
51 Widdrington B 6
57 Widnes C 4
68 Widuchowo B 2
71 Wiebelskirchen C 6
69 Wiecbork B 5
72 Wiedenbrück B 2
65 Wiefelstede A 6
74 Wiegersdorf B 2
74 Wiehe B 3
71 Wiehl B 6
67 Wiek A 6
78 Wielbark B 3
69 Wiele B 5
69 Wieleń C 4
77 Wielichowo A 5
90 Wieliczka C 3
78 Wielka Laka B 1
90 Wielopole-Skrzyńskie C 4
90 Wielowies B 1
79 Wieluń D 1
101 Wien A 4
101 Wiener Neustadt B 4
67 Wiepke C 4
65 Wierden B 4
66 Wieren C 3
77 Wieruszów B 7
79 Wierzbica, Kielce, PL D 4
79 Wierzbica, Warszawa, PL C 4
68 Wierzbiecin B 3
68 Wierzbno B 2
69 Wierzchowo B 4
79 Wierzchy D 1
100 Wies C 3
87 Wiesau B 4
100 Wieselburg A 3
97 Wiesen B 5
75 Wiesenburg A 4
87 Wiesenfelden B 4
87 Wiesent B 4
85 Wiesental A 5
73 Wiesentheid D 4
85 Wiesloch A 5
101 Wiesmath B 4
65 Wiesmoor A 5
65 Wietmarschen B 5
66 Wietze C 2
56 Wigan C 4
96 Wiggen B 3
59 Wigston C 2
56 Wigton B 3
50 Wigtown C 3
64 Wijchen C 3
64 Wijhe B 4
64 Wijk bij Duurstede C 3
70 Wijnegem A 3
97 Wil A 5
90 Wilamowice C 2
78 Wilczeta A 2
79 Wilczkowice C 2
100 Wildalpen B 2
85 Wildbad B 5
67 Wildberg C 5
89 Wilden-dürnbach C 4
86 Wildenroth C 3
65 Wildervank A 4
66 Wildeshausen C 1
100 Wildon C 3
97 Wildpoldsried A 6
85 Wilferdingen B 5
79 Wilga D 4
85 Wilgartswiesen A 4
75 Wilhelm-Pieck-Stadt B 6
100 Wilhelmsburg,A A 3
67 Wilhelmsburg,D* B 6
86 Wilhelmsdorf D 1
65 Wilhelmshaven A 6
100 Wilhering A 2
86 Wilhermsdorf B 2
78 Wilkasy A 4
75 Wilkau-Haßlau C 4
79 Wilków, Lublin, PL D 4
77 Wilków, Wroclaw, PL B 4
90 Wilkowice C 2
78 Wilkowo A 4
72 Willebadessen B 3
70 Willebroek A 3
57 Willersley D 3
54 Williamstown A 3
71 Willich A 5
72 Willingen B 2
51 Willington C 6
96 Willisau A 4
60 Williton B 3
57 Wilmslow C 4
70 Wilrijk A 3
75 Wilsdruff B 5
59 Wilshamstead C 3
66 Wilster B 2
65 Wilsum B 4
61 Wilton B 5
71 Wiltz C 4
59 Wimblington C 4
61 Wimborne Minster C 5
63 Wimereux B 3
63 Wimille B 3
85 Wimmenau B 4
96 Wimmis B 3
83 Wimy B 5
61 Wincanton B 4
61 Winchcombe B 5
62 Winchelsea C 4
62 Winchester B 2
101 Winden am See B 4
56 Windermere B 4
87 Windischeschenbach B 4
100 Windischgarsten B 2
87 Windorf C 5
86 Windsbach B 2
62 Windsor B 3
51 Windygates A 4
62 Wing B 3
70 Wingene A 2
62 Wingham B 5
66 Wingst B 2
87 Winhöring C 4
87 Winklarn B 4
98 Winklern C 3
86 Winnenden C 1
72 Winnigstedt A 4
73 Winnweiler D 1
65 Winschoten A 5
66 Winsen, Niedersachsen, D† B 3
66 Winsen, Niedersachsen, D† C 2
57 Winsford C 4
61 Winsham C 4
77 Wińsko B 5
62 Winslade B 2
62 Winslow B 3
64 Winsum, Friesland, NL A 3
65 Winsum, Groningen, NL A 4
71 Winterbach C 6
72 Winterberg B 2
61 Winterbourne Abbas C 4
67 Winterfeld C 4
85 Winterlingen B 6
65 Winterswijk C 4
97 Winterthur A 4
58 Winterton B 3
59 Winterton-on-Sea C 5
85 Wintzenheim B 4
87 Winzer C 5
100 Wipasssing B 3
74 Wipperdorf B 2
71 Wipperfürth A 6
74 Wippra B 3
59 Wirksworth B 2
59 Wisbech C 4
62 Wisborough Green B 3
66 Wischhafen B 2
50 Wishaw B 4
90 Wisla C 1
90 Wisla Wielka C 1
90 Wiślica B 3
67 Wismar B 4
79 Wiśniew C 5
78 Wiśniewo B 3
90 Wiśniowa, Krakow, PL C 3
90 Wiśniowa, Rzeszow, PL C 4
90 Wiśniówka B 3
63 Wissant B 3
85 Wissembourg A 4
71 Wissen B 6
73 Wißmar C 2
90 Witanowice C 2
62 Witham B 4
60 Witheridge C 3
58 Withern Tothill B 4
58 Witherness B 4
77 Witkowo A 6
64 Witmarsum A 3
62 Witney B 2
76 Witnica A 3
79 Witonia C 2
71 Witry C 4
83 Witry-lès-Reims B 6
85 Wittelshiem C 4
71 Witten A 6
75 Wittenberg B 4
67 Wittenberge C 4
66 Wittenburg B 4
85 Wittenheim C 4
75 Wittichenau B 6
66 Wittingen C 3
86 Wittislingen C 2
71 Wittlich C 5
100 Wittmannsdorf C 3
65 Wittmund A 5
66 Wittorf B 2
67 Wittstock B 5
72 Witzenhausen B 3
60 Wivelscombe B 3
62 Wivenhoe B 4
63 Wizernes B 4
78 Wizna B 5
69 Wladyslawowo A 6
77 Wleń B 4
79 Wloclawek C 2
89 Wlodzienin A 5
90 Wlostów B 4
90 Wloszczowa B 2
67 Wöbbelin B 4
62 Woburn Sands B 3
90 Wodzislaw B 3
89 Wodzislaw Śl. A 6
64 Woerden B 2
85 Woerth B 4
96 Wohlen A 4
84 Woippy A 3
78 Wojciechy A 3
77 Wojcieszów C 4
90 Wojkowice Kościelne B 2
90 Wojnicz C 3
62 Woking B 3
62 Wokingham B 3
90 Wola Jachowa B 3
79 Wola Niechcicka D 2
65 Wolbeck C 5
79 Wolbórz D 2
90 Wolbrom B 2
77 Wolczyn B 7
67 Woldegk B 6
85 Wolfach B 5
101 Wolfau B 4
86 Wolfegg D 1
74 Wolfen B 4
72 Wolfenbüttel A 4
73 Wölfersheim C 2
86 Wolfertschwenden D 2
72 Wolfhagen B 3
86 Wolfratshausen D 3
100 Wolfsbach A 2
100 Wolfsberg C 2
66 Wolfsburg C 3
67 Wolfshagen B 6
71 Wolfstein C 6
97 Wolfurt A 5
67 Wolgast A 6
96 Wolhusen A 4
68 Wolin B 2
90 Wólka A 3
75 Wolkenstein,D* C 5
99 Wolkenstein,I C 2
101 Wolkersdorf A 4
75 Wölkisch B 5
74 Wolkramshausen B 2
59 Wollaston C 3
101 Wöllersdorf B 4
75 Wollin A 4
74 Wolmirsleben B 3
74 Wolmirstedt A 3
86 Wolnzach C 3
79 Wolomin C 4
77 Wolów B 5
51 Wolsingham C 6
77 Wolsztyn A 5
67 Woltersdorf C 6
72 Woltorf A 4
64 Wolvega B 3
57 Wolverhampton D 4
59 Wolverton C 3
59 Wolvey C 2
51 Wolviston C 6
64 Wommels A 3
59 Woodbridge C 5
55 Woodenbridge B 5
59 Woodhall Spa B 3
62 Woodstock B 2
61 Wool C 4
60 Woolacombe B 2
51 Wooler B 5
57 Woore D 4
61 Wootton Bassett B 5
78 Woplewo B 3
96 Worb B 3
74 Worbis B 2
57 Worcester D 4
98 Wörgl B 3
56 Workington B 3
58 Worksop B 2
64 Workum B 3
75 Wörlitz B 4
64 Wormerveer B 2
63 Wormhoudt B 4
51 Wormit A 5
73 Worms D 2
66 Worphausen B 1
66 Worpswede B 1
100 Wörschach B 2
73 Worth, Bayern, D† D 3
87 Wörth, Bayern, D† B 4
85 Wörth, Rheinlandpfalz, D† A 5
62 Worthing C 3
61 Wotton-under-Edge B 4
70 Woumen A 1
90 Wożniki, Katowice, PL B 2
79 Wozniki, Łódź, PL D 1
58 Wragby B 3
59 Wrangle B 4

90 Wreczyca Wielka B 1
67 Wredenhagen B 5
66 Wremen B 1
59 Wrentham C 5
57 Wrexham C 4
66 Wriedel B 3
76 Wriezen A 3
66 Wrist B 2
62 Writtle B 4
78 Wrocki B 2
77 Wroclaw B 6
77 Wronki A 5
62 Wrotham B 4
79 Wrotnów C 5
62 Wroughton B 2
59 Wroxham C 5
77 Września A 6
69 Wrzosowo A 3
77 Wschowa B 5
65 Wulfen,D† C 5
74 Wulfen,D* B 3
101 Wulkaprodersdorf B 4
67 Wulkau C 5
67 Wulkow C 5
72 Wünnenberg B 2
75 Wünsdorf A 5
87 Wunsiedel A 4
66 Wunstorf C 2
71 Wuppertal A 6
87 Wurmannsquick C 4
85 Wurmlingen B 4
71 Würselen B 5
74 Wurzbach C 3
73 Würzburg D 3
75 Wurzen B 4
67 Wust, Magdeburg, D* C 5
67 Wust, Potsdam, D* C 5
73 Wüstensachsen C 3
67 Wusterhausen C 5
67 Wustermark C 5
67 Wustrow A 5
70 Wuustwezel A 3
78 Wydminy B 5
90 Wygoda B 2
44 Wyk C 1
76 Wymiarki B 4
59 Wymondham C 5
69 Wyrzysk B 5
79 Wyśmierzyce D 3
69 Wysoka, Bydgoszcz, PL B 5
77 Wysoka, Wroclaw, PL B 4
78 Wysokie Maz. C 5
90 Wysowa C 4
79 Wyszków C 4
79 Wyszogród C 3
77 Wyszonowice C 6

X
71 Xanten A 5
156 Xánthi A 4
84 Xertigny B 3
156 Xifónia B 2
159 Xilókastron A 3
156 Xilópolis B 3
157 Xinía C 2
154 Xinón Nerón B 3
158 Xirokámbi C 3

Y
160 Yablanitsa D 4
153 Yakovo C 5
160 Yambol D 5
51 Yarm C 6
62 Yarmouth C 2
61 Yate B 4
61 Yatton B 4
59 Yaxley C 3
100 Ybbs a. d. Donau A 3
100 Ybbsitz B 2
40 Ydby C 2
60 Yealmpton C 3
126 Yebra B 3
122 Yebra de Basa B 2
133 Yecla C 1
125 Yecla de Yeltes C 3
156 Yéfira B 2
157 Yefiri C 2
60 Yelverton C 4
108 Yenne B 2
61 Yeovil C 4
126 Yepes C 2
156 Yerakaroú B 3
159 Yeráki C 3
154 Yérmas C 3
158 Yerolimin C 3
156 Yeroplátanon B 3
64 Yerseke C 2
82 Yerville B 2

137 Yeste A 4
80 Yffiniac B 4
105 Ygos-St. Saturnin D 2
94 Ygrande C 2
157 Yiáltra D 2
155 Yiannádhes C 1
156 Yiannitsá B 2
157 Yiannitsoú D 2
156 Yimna B 2
159 Yimnón A 4
114 Yipava B 1
159 Yíthion C 3
22 Ykspihlaja B 5
29 Ylämaa C 5
27 Yläne C 5
23 Yli-Iesti B 6
16 Yli-Kärppä B 4
16 Yli-Ii B 4
10 Yli-Muonio A 3
17 Yli-Näljänka B 7
16 Yli-Paakkola A 3
22 Ylihärmä B 4
16 Ylikiiminki B 5
22 Ylimarkhu C 4
22 Ylistaro C 4
16 Ylitornio A 2
23 Ylivieska A 6
27 Ylöjärvi B 6
82 Ymonville C 3
47 Yngsjö B 5
57 Ynys D 3
58 York B 2
55 Youghal C 4
58 Youlgreave B 2
59 Yoxford C 5
27 Ypäjä C 6
82 Yport B 2
16 Yppäri C 3
106 Yssingeaux B 4
47 Ystad B 4
60 Ystalyfera B 3
34 Ystebøhamn B 1
60 Ystrad B 3
60 Ystradgynlais B 3
30 Ytre Arna C 2
35 Ytre Flåbygd B 4
18 Ytre Fræna C 3
6 Ytre Laksvatn B 5
32 Ytre Rendal B 2
20 Ytteran B 3
42 Ytterby B 1
16 Ytterbyn B 4
33 Ytterhogdal A 5
32 Yttermalung C 4
20 Ytterolden B 2
126 Yuncos B 2
136 Yunguera C 2
126 Yunquera de Heras B 2
121 Yurre A 4
96 Yverdon B 2
82 Yvetot B 2
81 Yvignac B 4
70 Yvoir B 2
96 Yvonand B 2
82 Yvré l'Eveque C 2
37 Yxsjöberg A 6
94 Yzeure C 3

Z
70 Zaamslag A 2
64 Zaandam B 2
116 Zabalj A 4
103 Zábałt C 5
91 Zabar D 3
117 Žabari B 5
154 Zaberzan B 2
78 Zabiele B 4
90 Zabierzów B 2
78 Zabikowo B 2
79 Zabki C 4
90 Zabkowice B 2
89 Zabkowice Ślaskie A 4
117 Zablaće C 4
151 Žabljak B 5
90 Žabno,PL B 2
115 Žabno,YU B 4
115 Zabok A 3
79 Zabokliki C 5
89 Žabokreky C 6
103 Zábrani B 5
89 Zábřeh B 2
78 Zabrowo B 2
90 Zabrze B 1
90 Zaczernie B 2
114 Zadar C 3
79 Zadzim D 1
136 Zafarraya C 3
149 Zafferana Etneo B 5
129 Zafra C 4

117 Zagajica B 5
76 Zagań B 4
116 Zaglavak C 3
156 Zaglivérion B 3
90 Zagnansk B 3
157 Zagorá C 3
114 Zagorje A 3
77 Zagórów A 6
90 Zagórzany C 4
117 Zagrađe B 4
115 Zagreb B 3
136 Zagrilla B 2
117 Žagubica B 5
150 Zagvozo B 3
77 Zagwizdzie C 6
102 Zagyvarékas B 4
91 Zagyvaróna D 2
135 Zahara B 2
135 Zahara de los Atunes C 5
129 Zahinos C 4
75 Zahna B 4
88 Záhoří B 2
88 Záhrádka B 3
66 Zahrensdorf B 3
122 Zaidin C 3
86 Zainingen C 1
152 Zajas C 2
117 Zaječar C 6
91 Zákamenné C 2
101 Zakany C 4
158 Zákha B 2
158 Zakháro B 2
158 Zakhloroú A 3
158 Zákinthos B 1
90 Zakliczyn C 3
91 Zakopane C 2
79 Zakroczym C 3
79 Zakrzów D 4
88 Zákupy A 2
101 Zalaapáti C 5
101 Zalabaksa C 4
101 Zalaegerszeg C 4
101 Zalakoppány C 5
101 Zalalovó C 4
129 Zalamea de la Serena C 5
135 Zalamea la Real B 4
101 Zalaszentgrót C 5
101 Zalaszentiván C 4
101 Zalaszentmihály C 4
160 Zalău B 3
101 Zalavár C 5
121 Zaldibar A 4
114 Žalec A 3
78 Zalewo B 2
120 Zalla A 3
103 Zalnoc A 6
64 Zaltbommel C 3
103 Zam B 6
101 Zamárdi C 5
69 Zamarte B 5
89 Zamberk A 4
136 Zambra B 3
78 Zambrów C 5
153 Zamfirovo A 5
120 Zámoly B 3
125 Zamora B 2
78 Zamość B 4
97 Zams A 6
91 Zámutov D 4
88 Žandov A 2
64 Zandvoort B 2
127 Zaorejas B 3
86 Zapfend A 2
79 Zapole D 1
9 Zapolyarnyy C 10
157 Zappion C 2
145 Zapponeta B 4
122 Zaragoza C 2
103 Zărand B 5
121 Zarauz A 4
137 Zarcilla de Ramos B 5
78 Zareby B 4
159 Zárka A 5
90 Zarki B 2
157 Zárkon C 2
91 Žarnovica D 1
79 Zarnów D 3
69 Zarnowiec A 6
77 Zarów C 5
70 Zarren A 1
66 Zarrentin B 4
76 Žary B 4
130 Zarza-Capilla C 1
129 Zarza de Alange B 4
129 Zarza de Granadilla A 4
126 Zarza de Tajo B 3
129 Zarza la Mayor A 4
133 Zarzadilla de Totana D 1
126 Zarzalejo B 1
126 Zarzuela del Monte B 1
126 Zarzuela del Pinar B 1

118 Zas A 2
116 Zasavica B 3
76 Zasieki B 3
88 Zásmuky B 3
75 Žatec C 5
76 Zatonie B 4
90 Zator B 2
75 Zauchwitz A 5
110 Zavattarello C 4
91 Závažná Poruba C 2
116 Zavidovići B 2
116 Zavlaka B 3
78 Zawady B 4
90 Zawadzkie B 1
90 Zawichost B 4
76 Zawidów B 4
78 Zawidz C 2
90 Zawiercie B 2
90 Zawoja C 2
77 Zawonia B 6
91 Zázrivá C 2
77 Zbaszyń A 4
77 Zbaszynek A 4
101 Zbehy A 6
77 Zbiersk B 7
87 Zbiroh B 5
91 Zborov C 4
69 Zbrachlin B 6
88 Zbraslav C 2
88 Zbraslavice B 3
90 Zbyszyce C 3
115 Zdala A 5
91 Žďaňa D 4
89 Žďánice B 5
88 Žďár n. Sázavou B 3
115 Zdenci B 5
91 Žďiar C 3
88 Zdiby A 2
88 Zdice B 1
114 Zdihovo B 3
88 Zdirec n. Doubravou B 3
89 Zdounky B 5
117 Zdravinje C 5
152 Zdunje C 3
79 Zduńska Wola D 1
79 Zduny, Lódź, PL C 2
77 Zduny, Poznań, PL B 6
79 Zdzary D 3
89 Zdziszowice A 6
88 Žebrák B 1
129 Zebreira B 3
76 Zebrzydowa B 3
67 Zechlin B 5
98 Zederhaus B 4
102 Žednik C 3
70 Zeebrugge A 2
153 Zegra B 3
79 Zegrze B 2
79 Zegrzynek C 4
67 Zehdenick C 6
75 Zehren A 5
73 Zeil C 4
101 Zeiselmauer A 4
64 Zeist B 3
75 Zeithain B 5
87 Zeitlarn B 4
74 Zeitz B 2
88 Želatava B 3
69 Zelazno A 5
70 Zele A 3
89 Zelechovice n. Drev B 5
79 Zelechów C 4
153 Zelen Dol B 5
88 Železnice A 3
117 Zeleznik B 4
114 Železniki A 2
88 Železny Brod A 3
65 Zelhem B 4
91 Želiezovce D 1
115 Zelina B 4
152 Zelino C 3
157 Zélion D 2
78 Zelki A 5
69 Zelkowo A 5
96 Zell, CH A 3
85 Zell, Baden-Württemberg, D† B 5
85 Zell, Baden-Württemberg, D† C 4
73 Zell, Bayern, D† D 3
71 Zell, Rheinland Pfalz, D† B 6
98 Zell am Zee B 3
98 Zell am Ziller B 3
100 Zell b. Zellhof A 3
88 Zellerndorf A 4
73 Zellingen B 3
91 Želovce D 2
79 Zelów B 2
74 Zelta D 6

100 Zeltweg B 2
70 Zelzate A 2
91 Žemberovce D 1
90 Zembrzyce C 2
153 Zemen,BG B 4
117 Zemen,YU C 6
89 Zemianske-Kostol'any C 6
89 Zemianske Podhradie C 5
101 Zemné B 6
70 Zemst B 3
114 Zemunik C 3
115 Zenica C 5
116 Žepče B 2
142 Zepponami B 3
115 Zeprešic B 3
89 Žeravice B 5
74 Zerbst B 4
71 Zerf C 5
103 Zerind B 5
77 Zerków A 6
96 Zermatt B 3
97 Zernez B 6
67 Zerpenschleuse C 6
65 Zetel A 5
74 Zeulenroda C 3
66 Zeven B 2
64 Zevenaar C 4
64 Zevenbergen C 2
159 Zevgolatión B 3
99 Zévio D 2
79 Zgierz D 2
76 Zgorzelec B 4
116 Zgošča B 2
152 Zgozdh C 2
103 Zgribeşti C 6
153 Zheleznitsa B 5
78 Zheleznodorozhnyy A 4
153 Zhivovtsi A 4
154 Ziákas B 3
91 Žiar D 1
140 Zicavo C 2
67 Zickhusen B 4
67 Ziddorf B 4
89 Zidlochovice A 4
89 Ziębice A 5
67 Ziegendorf B 4
73 Ziegenhain C 3
74 Ziegenrück C 3
89 Zieleniec A 4
68 Zieleniewo A 3
76 Zielona Gòra B 4
79 Zielonka C 4
78 Zielonka Paslecka B 2
78 Zieluń C 2
86 Ziemetshausen C 2
64 Zierikzee C 1
100 Ziersdorf A 3
67 Zierzow B 4
74 Ziesar A 4
67 Ziesendorf B 4
68 Ziethen C 1
156 Zigos A 4
87 Žihle B 5
89 Žilina B 6
101 Zillingdorf A 4
85 Zillisheim C 4
75 Ziltendorf A 6
103 Zimandu Nou B 3
78 Zimna Woda B 3
160 Zimnicea D 4
96 Zinal B 3
110 Zinasco B 4
67 Zingst A 5
39 Zinkgruvan D 2
68 Zinnowitz A 1
101 Zirc B 5
114 Ziri A 2
158 Ziria A 2
98 Zirl B 2
86 Zirndorf B 2
152 Žirovnica, Makedonia, YU C 2
117 Zirovnica, Srbija, YU B 5
88 Žirovnice B 3
101 Zistersdorf A 4
117 Zitište C 4
117 Žitkovac C 5
153 Zitna Potok A 3
153 Zitorađa C 2
155 Zitsa C 2
75 Zittau B 3
115 Živaja B 4
116 Živince B 2
152 Zjum A 4
115 Zlatar A 4
115 Zlatar Bistrica A 4
89 Zlate Hory A 5
101 Zlaté Klasy A 5
101 Zlaté Moravce A 5
101 Zlatná n. Ostrove B 6
160 Zlatni Pyassatsi D 6

PRINTED IN GREAT BRITAIN BY GEORGE PHILIP PRINTERS LIMITED, LONDON.

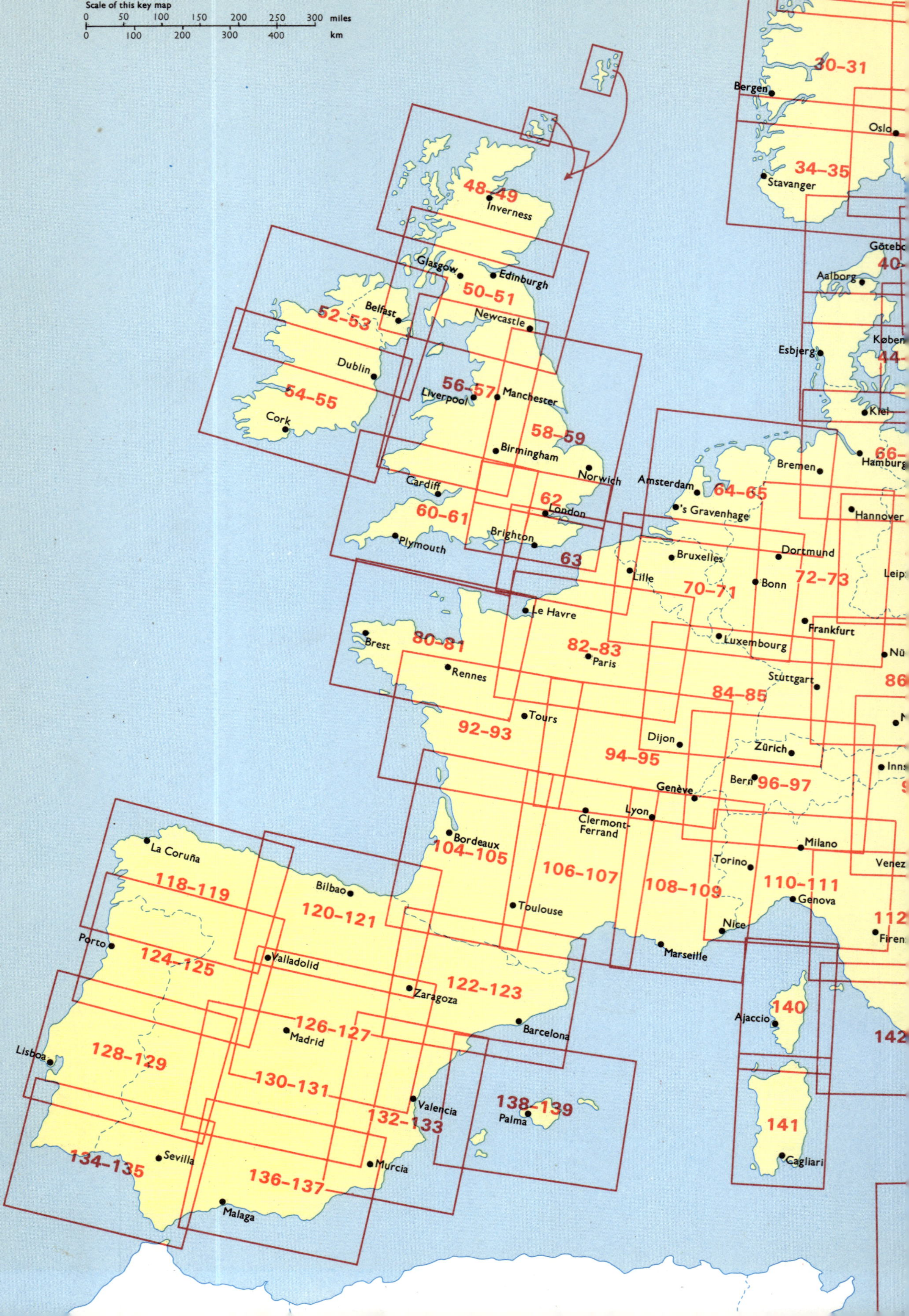

18-19

30-31

Bergen

34-35

Oslo

Stavanger

Götebo

Aalborg

40-

48-49
Inverness

Glasgow
Edinburgh

50-51

Belfast
Newcastle

52-53

Esbjerg

Køben

44-

Dublin

54-55

56-57
Liverpool   Manchester

Kiel

Cork

58-59

Birmingham

Norwich   Amsterdam

Bremen

Hamburg

66-

Cardiff

62
London

's Gravenhage

64-65

Hannover

60-61

Brighton

Plymouth

63

Bruxelles

Lille

Dortmund

Bonn

72-73

Leip

Le Havre

70-71

Frankfurt

Brest

80-81

82-83
Paris

Luxembourg

Nü

Rennes

84-85

Stuttgart

86

92-93

Tours

94-95

Dijon

Zürich

Bern

96-97

Inns

Genève

9

Lyon

La Coruña

Clermont-
Ferrand

Bordeaux

Milano

110-111

Venez

118-119

Bilbao

104-105

106-107

108-109

Torino

Genova

112

Porto

120-121

Toulouse

Nice

Firen

124-125

Valladolid

Marseille

Zaragoza

122-123

Lisboa

126-127
Madrid

Barcelona

Ajaccio

140

142

128-129

130-131

Valencia

138-139

141

132-133
Palma

134-135

Sevilla

Murcia

136-137

Cagliari

Malaga